TIMBER AND MEN

Ralph W. Hidy, Frank Ernest Hill
Allan Nevins

TIMBER

AND The Weyerhaeuser Story

MEN

RESEARCH ASSOCIATES:

Vincent P. Carosso, Frederick W. Kohlmeyer

Norman F. Thomas, Mira Wilkins

THE MACMILLAN COMPANY, NEW YORK
COLLIER-MACMILLAN LIMITED, LONDON

First Printing

The Macmillan Company, New York
Collier-Macmillan Canada Limited, Toronto, Ontario
Divisions of The Crowell-Collier Publishing Company

Printed in the United States of America

Library of Congress catalog card number: 63–7450

Designed by Andor Braun

Table of Contents

Illustrations

Frederick Weyerhaeuser

Frederick Carl August Denkmann

Northern Wisconsin logging camp in 1860's

An early loggers' bunkhouse

Log jam on St. Croix River

Weyerhaeuser & Denkmann Rock Island mill

Frederick Weyerhaeuser family's first home

William Harris Laird

James Laird Norton

Matthew George Norton

Chancy Lamb

W. J. Young

Thomas Irvine

Edward Rutledge

O. H. Ingram

The steamboat C. J. Caffrey

Frederick Weyerhaeuser in Wisconsin woods

Loggers' cookhouse on Chippewa River

Wood Indian and Little Falls Dam

J. P. Weyerhaeuser

R. L. McCormick

John A. Humbird, Sr.

William Irvine

C. A. Weyerhaeuser

R. Drew Musser

R. M. Weyerhaeuser

F. E. Weyerhaeuser

Cloquet Lumber Company mill

Johnson-Wentworth Company mill

Peter M. Musser

A. W. Laird, Frederick Weyerhaeuser, and P. M. Musser

Introduction

When Captain John Smith and William Bradford watched log cabins and stockades rise on our Atlantic Coast, practically the whole of the present-day United States east of the Mississippi was covered by dense woods of variegated character. The pioneer had to learn to conquer and use a bewildering variety of trees. He could shape masts and building timbers, and make boxes of the Eastern white pine; vehicles of tough white ash; polished furniture of walnut, black cherry, or curly maple; fenceposts of honey locust; farm implements and chairs of hickory; canoes of birch, barrels of elm, light utensils of basswood, and long-enduring planks and beams of oak and chestnut. From the forest came food—maple sugar, berries, and nuts; from it came a multitude of indispensable articles, ranging from cradles at the beginning of life to coffins at the end; from it came shelter, warmth, and such invaluable special products as potash, resins, and turpentine. Ally and enemy, aid and hindrance, according to circumstance, the forest did much to shape all American life until the tides of settlement rolled out on the wide plains beyond the Missouri.

Yet the history of the role it played, of its reckless use and still more reckless abuse, and of its final incorporation into a fairly well balanced pattern of American life, has been unjustly neglected. The enterprise of the men who hewed out farms, who trapped for furs, who sank mines for iron, copper, and gold, who built railroads and created the wide cattle-ranching industry, has been celebrated more thoroughly and colorfully than that of the lumbermen. Too few people comprehend the manysided character of the story of our timber resources and their development; the variety of regional scenes, business undertakings, skills, and sciences involved in the narrative.

This book is the history of a set of lumbering enterprises begun on the banks of the Mississippi before the Civil War under the leadership of Frederick Weyerhaeuser and a few associates. It deals with the use of a single great natural resource. It treats the activities of one closely knit group of rugged men, the Weyerhaeusers, Denkmanns, Nortons, Lairds, Mussers, Ingrams, and others, who called in a gradually widening body of aides. Yet the story touches diverse phases of American life, and mirrors a striking sequence of changes in the practical demands of the people and their attitude toward labor, conservation, and the role of government in industry.

The initial scene of action in this book lies in the wild woodlands of Wisconsin and Minnesota, where perhaps the finest stands of white pine on the globe had to be felled and converted into lumber for the thickening farm and town population of the Middle West. The log rafts floating down the Chippewa and upper Mississippi, the logging camps, booms, dams, and perilous logjams, and the clashes of lumbermen representing rival companies, give adventure and color to this scene. Then the center of activities rapidly shifts from the St. Croix to the Columbia and other Far Western waters and to Idaho; the staple of the mills changes to the ponderosa pine, Western white pine, Engelmann spruce, Douglas fir, and other gigantic trees. The forests of the South, too, with their longleaf, shortleaf, and loblolly pines, soon enter the narrative. Each region has presented its own complex problems in the construction of mills, the improvement of equipment, and the provision of road, rail, river, and ocean transportation.

Technological advances, as this volume shows, became increasingly numerous and important. The application of power in lifting enormous tree trunks, like jackstraws, from precipitous tangled slopes; the use of "cats" in building roads and of powerful trucks in hauling; the invention of ever more efficient bandsaws and gangsaws; the swift removal of bark from huge trunks by hydraulic jets—this is a large story in itself. Twenty scientific uses of wood and wood pulp were found where one had previously existed. Ideas of efficiency management came into a once rough-and-ready industry. As they did, a decent concern for the health, safety, and comfort of millhands and lumberjacks began to replace the old callous attitudes toward labor—the activities of legislators and union organizers assisting.

Most interesting of all the strands in this varicolored narrative is the gradual development of a sound body of ideas upon forest conservation, and the story of their slow acceptance by public and private interests. In the 1880's no sight in America was sadder than a cutover area in Michigan or Wisconsin, a wasteland littered with refuse, choked with worthless brush, exposed to fire, and losing its topsoil by erosion. To achieve conservation, tariffs had to be modified, taxation reformed, the greed of many lumbermen checked, and a smooth working alliance established among the national Bureau of Forestry (after 1905 the Forest Service), the states, the schools of forestry, and private holders of woodland. Over great areas the nation, the state, and the private corporations held forests in an elaboratedly intermeshed pattern. To save the nation's timber, experts had to make careful plans to fight fire, combat insect pests, battle tree diseases, build roads, and conduct reforestation. The group whose history is here traced gained an honorable primacy in the union of tree cutting with systematic tree planting and tree seeding, in order to reach a sustained-yield basis.

This book had its origin in conversations which Frederick K. Weyerhaeuser and John Musser held with Allan Nevins, as a result of which Columbia University agreed to undertake general oversight of the effort to produce a scholarly and objective history of the enterprises of the Weyerhaeuser group. Mr. Hidy, Mr. Hill, and Mr. Nevins have shared equally in the planning and writing of the volume; not a single sentence fails to represent the thought and effort of all three. Their work, done on ordinary academic salaries, has been carried out under conditions of absolute independence. For whatever merits it may possess Columbia University is to be credited; for its shortcomings the authors alone are responsible.

Acknowledgments

In more than the usual sense this book is a cooperative product. Not only have the three authors worked together for a number of years, but, as the entries on the title page indicate, several research associates have labored long and hard to give it both depth and breadth. Outstanding contributions were made by Vincent P. Carosso, now Professor of History at New York University, Fred W. Kohlmeyer, Assistant Professor of Economics at the University of Illinois and Editor of *Agricultural History,* Norman F. Thomas, now Dean of the Undergraduate School and Associate Professor of History at the University of Puget Sound and Mira Wilkins, Project Director of a History of American Business Abroad, Graduate School of Business, Columbia University. Without diligent research and preliminary writing by those associates, the three authors would have found it impossible to hew a path through the overwhelmingly voluminous and widely scattered sources of information.

Associates in research and authors alike experienced nothing but the most enthusiastic cooperation on the part of officers of companies and custodians of records at every location where research was conducted. Individuals too numerous to mention in Rock Island, Muscatine, Eau Claire, Cloquet, and St. Paul in the Upper Mississippi Valley as well as in Boise, Coeur d'Alene, Lewiston, Potlatch, Everett, Tacoma, Longview, Springfield, Snoqualmie Falls, and Klamath Falls in the Pacific Northwest took time to help locate records and arrange interviews. Their aid has been gratefully received and will never be forgotten.

Among family and company representatives three persons gave more assistance than any others. Norton Clapp, now president of Weyerhaeuser Company, and other representatives of the Laird and Norton families, opened private records in Winona, thus providing a significant addition to the information now available to scholars in the Laird, Norton Papers at the Minnesota Historical Society in St. Paul. John M. Musser enthusiastically supported all efforts to locate documents of all companies with which his family was connected and also opened private archives of his family.

Important as the contributions of the foregoing individuals were, Frederick K. Weyerhaeuser, more than any other person, made this history possible. Not only was he among those that took the lead in initiating the project, he was unstinting in his efforts to make available the papers of his grandfather, father, and uncles as well as his own. His requests quickly opened doors from Rock Island and St. Paul to Lewiston and Tacoma. He has even extended his efforts to reading of page proof! His geniality and kindliness have lightened our labors.

Such a study as *Timber and Men,* being the first of its kind in the forest products industry, not only had to rely heavily on collections of private papers but also had to be based upon extensive use of books, periodicals, government books and other documents, and sources of information in numerous public repositories. Only in such sources could supplementary details and data on the forest products industry be found. The authors gratefully acknowledge assistance of librarians and curators of manuscripts in libraries at Eau Claire, Wisconsin, Duluth (St. Louis County Historical Society), and Winona (Winona County Historical Society) in Minnesota as well as those of the Wisconsin Historical Society, University of Minnesota, Columbia University, Harvard University, and elsewhere. Standing out above all others in contributions, however, was the Minnesota Historical Society, St. Paul. A cursory examination of the list of references cited will show that we owe a deep debt to Miss Lucile Kane and others at that institution, a debt which we cheerfully recognize that we can never adequately repay.

Much valuable information for this study also came from interviews with more than 50 individuals associated with a wide range of companies. We are indebted to the interviewees for their cooperation and to the Oral History Office at Columbia University for aiding us at the start of the project and for depositing many typed interviews in Special Collections at the Butler Library there. We also wish to thank the Forest History Society in St. Paul for making available two recorded interviews to us.

Throughout this study shines faith in the forest on the part of four generations of several families who have worked together since 1870. Policies and practices of scores of their firms over the years reflect almost daily adjustment to changing economic and political environments, coupled with continuous efforts to create new, more favorable environments for profitable operations. Leaders of the families and firm have steadily moved toward identification of public and private interest in the wise use of a valuable natural resource and in turning out an almost complete range of forest products for consumers in this nation and elsewhere. That it is a story of errors in judgment as well as sound decisions, with the successes outweighing the mistakes, makes it a representative, if not typical, example of the American historical achievement in business. From the decisions of men like Frederick Weyerhaeuser, his associates, and their descendants has evolved the unprecedented productive and distributive mechanism that constitutes the economy of the United States today.

New York, January 1963   R.W.H.
                                                                            F.E.H.
                                                                            A.N.

TIMBER AND MEN

The Partners

W HEN THE FLOW of settlement carried a large population out upon the half treeless prairies of the Middle West, the massive pine forests of the Great Lakes region took on a new significance. States hungry for lumber, from Indiana to Kansas, looked eagerly to those wide timber belts. To a thousand communities still distant in 1850 from railroads, it was a happy fact that the Upper Mississippi and its northern tributaries threaded these forests. Steamboats and rafts could bring them the superabundant wood.

The river town of Rock Island in Illinois stood in a strategic position between forest and prairie. Here the Mississippi, dropping down from Minnesota and Wisconsin, makes a sharp bend toward the plains region. Near the point where it alters its course, the smoke of three cities mingles in one industrial agglomeration: Rock Island, Moline, and Davenport, the first two on the level Illinois shore, the third and largest on the Iowa bluffs. Each early gained note for its special industries—Davenport for its flour mills, Moline for the implement works that began when John Deere built his plow factory in 1848, and Rock Island for the national arsenal on the limestone island that gives the place its name. All, but especially Rock Island, were at one time concerned with lumber.

During the 1840's a new element of immigration brought this area hope of rapid growth. "Our German fellow citizens began to come to Davenport in large numbers," recalled a pioneer resident, "and many of them possessed a good deal of money, which the country sadly needed. They entered large tracts of land, which they immediately improved." Rock Island similarly received many Germans. In those years the three towns formed the only river center of note between Galena on the north

and Quincy on the south. Rock Island, the foremost, had been created
in 1841 by the union of two villages, but though it was a county seat it
did not have a daily newspaper, the *Argus,* until 1854, or a school system
until 1856. As late as 1860 the census reported a population of only
5,130. A considerable part of this was of German extraction. An Evan-
gelical Lutheran Church was erected in 1856; a German Methodist
Church came into existence two years later; and in 1857 a Bavarian
physician founded the first German newspaper, the *Beobachter am Mis-
sissippiam.*[1]

Incoming settlers realized that they lived in a river world. Steamboat
traffic reached its apogee in the picturesque years between the Mexican
and Civil War; and although the river Mark Twain described was south
of Hannibal and St. Louis, the northern half carried an equally important
commerce. Down it floated huge rafts of logs, mainly white pine from
Wisconsin, together with a smaller but increasing number of lumber rafts.
A few of these contained what would become more than a million feet of
lumber, and the average content of a raft ran well above ten thousand feet.
Guided by powerful rudders fore and aft, carrying crews of hard-muscled,
hard-drinking, hard-fighting Mike Finks, and struggling with eddies and
snags, they sometimes traveled forty miles a day. Because the Keokuk
rapids were an impediment to further passage, many of the rafts halted
at the upriver ports of Lyons, Dubuque, Rock Island, and Davenport.
Others continued down the river. Lumber traffic for the new farms, villages, and cities had superseded the once heavy traffic in furs, and St.
Louis was the largest distributing center for the new trade.

The Tri-Cities were well-adapted, by good transportation facilities, a
little waterpower at the Rock Island rapids, and a growing labor supply,
for primary manufactures. A railroad from Chicago to Rock Island, destined later to grow into the Chicago, Rock Island & Pacific, was completed
to the river in 1854. Everyone familiar with Lincoln's life recalls that in
1856 the collision of a steamboat, the *Effie Afton,* with a pier of the newly
completed Rock Island bridge, gave rise to a famous litigation in which
the railroad employed Lincoln as counsel. As rails spread through Illinois
and Iowa, and as settlements thickened, the towns did an increasing business in supplying the region with staples. Pork-packing plants, gristmills,
and flour mills arose. Blacksmith shops grew into new farm-implement
factories.

Rock Island became particularly interested in lumber manufacture.
"The woodlands of this section," wrote a county historian in 1876, "oc-
cupy about one-sixth of the entire surface, consisting of different varieties
of oak, black and white walnut, yellow poplar, wild cherry, linden, yellow
birch."[2] But if the first sawmills used local timber, Wisconsin pine very
soon became the principal wood. Every farm required its frame house,

barn, sheds, and fences. Significantly, a saw factory, the Rock Island Saw Works, was established in 1857 to make and distribute mill saws throughout the region.

To Rock Island in March, 1856, came a sturdy, alert, transparently upright German of twenty-one, a day laborer who had been in the United States for only four years. Frederick Weyerhaeuser first found brief employment in helping build the Rock Island Railroad, carrying chain for the surveyors, and doing other odd jobs. Later he went to work for a German brewer, but as he had observed in the East how often such men drank to excess, he looked about for a more congenial place. He found it in the primitive Mead, Smith & Marsh sawmill, owned by two Yankees and an Irishman. "Look, Weyerhaeuser," we may imagine one of the partners saying, "You can have a job as a night fireman." He began in this fashion; but he was soon put to keeping tally on logs and production and sorting the stock into four simple grades.

2

This young German was a native of the upper Rhine basin, born on November 21, 1834, in the village of Niedersaulheim in the wine country fourteen miles southwest of Mainz. Though he came of a relatively prosperous family, for his father had owned fifteen acres of farmland and three acres of grapes and was much in demand for his skill in setting out new vineyards, he was not well educated in the academic sense. He had attended a Lutheran parochial school until he was thirteen or fourteen. Unfortunately, the death of his father in 1846 made it necessary for him to quit his studies as soon as he became large enough to help carry on the farm.

Thus he always knew hard work and responsibility. In his teens he did a man's work growing crops, cultivating the vineyard, and tending the three or four cows. As the family was large, for his father had two children by a first wife and eleven by Frederick's mother, he had to help look after his younger brothers and sisters. He was taught thrift and given careful religious instruction, devoting every Wednesday and Saturday afternoon in his school years to the Bible and the catechism. In the crowded home circle he developed kindliness, honesty, and a keen sense of equity.

But despite the hard work, he enjoyed his boyhood life in Germany. The district was full of history, with the Mainz of Gutenberg and Worms of Martin Luther close by, and it possessed scenic beauty. An uncle had been a veteran of Napoleon's Grand Army, and, wrote Weyerhaeuser later, "delighted to tell about the campaign in Russia, where he saw whole regiments standing lifeless, frozen stiff by the frosts of that terrible winter."[3]

Some brief memoirs he wrote late in life made it clear that he early developed the strong feeling for family solidarity that he always cherished and that was to mark his descendants. His widowed mother, managing the farm with his aid and that of hired men, did so well that the acres not only supported them all but yielded a surplus. Had the family stood alone, Frederick might well have remained in Germany. But when a brother-in-law named Koch lost his money keeping a grocery store, the Weyerhaeusers had to help support him and his four children, "a heavy tax upon our resources."

The whole circle began to look toward America for a new start. Frederick's uncle of Napoleonic memories and his wife, with another aunt, were the first to emigrate, about the year 1849. While Frederick later wrote that they were attracted simply by cheap land, it is possible that the revolutionary troubles of 1848 may also have furnished a motive. From Erie, Pennsylvania, seat of a German settlement—with at least one family that had come earlier from Niedersaulheim and from which Frederick was to select his wife—they sent back encouraging reports of the country.

In 1852 those left behind decided to follow. The migration to America, as Frederick later recorded, was "a great event." To go boldly overseas, to leave the troubles and fetters of Europe behind, to make a home in a half-empty land bright with opportunity: this was a tremendous adventure.

The farm was divided among the heirs, and the portions of the older children were sold, but as Frederick was a minor his share was reserved until he should come of age. The available proceeds more than paid for the voyage. Frederick gives so graphic a picture of the trip that we wish it were longer:

For the voyage we had to provide our own food. No one would be received on board ship who did not have supplies for fifty days. We baked a lot of bread, baking it twice (Zweibach), and laid in a store of flour, ham, beans, rice, sugar, molasses, and a few potatoes. We took a few household articles, and Koch took his nail-making tools. This latter proved a mistake, for better and cheaper tools were to be had in the United States.

We started about the middle of May and journeyed by boat down the Rhine to Rotterdam. There we waited a few days and got a boat to London. After another delay of a few days we took a sailing ship from London to New York. Our fellow passengers were chiefly Welsh, Irish, and English and some Germans. The voyage occupied about six weeks, and was somewhat rough at times; but I enjoyed every hour of it, and the harder the wind blew the happier was I.

We landed in New York early in July, and went on at once to North East, Pa., about fifteen miles from Erie. . . . Mr. Koch and his family went on to Erie, where he secured work in a foundry at seventy-five cents a day.[4]

In this corner of Pennsylvania the youth found employment first in a small brewery established by one of his brothers-in-law and then, after two years, with a farmer named Pickett who paid him $13 a month. While thus busy near North East, he became friendly with the John Philip Bloedel family (later anglicized as Bladel) from Niedersaulheim; Bloedel was a skilled blacksmith who had a small shop where he made axes, hatchets, and other edged tools. Frederick was especially attracted by Bloedel's Sarah Elizabeth, about five years younger than himself.*

At twenty-one he received the money due him from the sale of the German property, and restlessly decided to start west. A paternal cousin who had bought a farm eighteen miles south of Rock Island had expatiated in his letters on the wonderful richness of the prairie soil. Frederick also might have taken a farm, but Rock Island plainly offered larger opportunities.

He was gaining self-reliance, and when he joined the sawmill crew he soon proved his abilities. Once, when his employer Marsh was at dinner, some Germans came to buy lumber. Though Weyerhaeuser had no authority to sell, he disposed of material for $60 in gold, and found that the firm was delighted. "Marsh took a liking to me," he writes; "and it was not long before I had charge of the yard and the sales and presently was looking after all the business. My wages were raised from time to time." He said his steady rise "lay simply in my readiness to work. I never counted the hours, or stopped until I had finished what I had in hand."

East of Rock Island on the railroad lay the town of Coal Valley where bituminous mines supplied fuel for the area and where local merchants sold goods to a rich farming country. Late in 1857 the firm sent Weyerhaeuser there to take charge of a lumberyard. This was its last enterprising act. The panic of 1857 had reached the West. Mead, Smith & Marsh might have weathered it but for the dishonesty of a supplier, who sold them a raft or two of logs, took their note in payment and discounted it at a bank, and then, instead of delivering the cargoes, sold them for cash in Clinton, Iowa, a town upstream. The firm, its resources always limited, was ruined. For a time the profits of the yard Weyerhaeuser was managing kept it afloat, but late in 1858 the sheriff took possession.

Weyerhaeuser was not alone when this blow fell. Early in 1857 young Elizabeth Bloedel had come to Rock Island, partly to help her older sister, Mrs. F. C. A. Denkmann, through a childbirth, and partly because she was now eighteen and wished to earn her own living. She was a girl of independent spirit. After a courtship of six months, she and Frederick were married. He had built a small two-story frame house at a cost of

* According to F. E. Weyerhaeuser, his grandmother's name was Elizabeth Blödel. However, her husband called her "Sarah" or "Setta." She later signed her name "E. S. Weyerhaeuser."

$1,200 or $1,300, including the lot, and they moved into it. "To pay for it was a close squeeze," he later wrote, "but I had succeeded and here we had built our home." When he went to Coal Valley, his firm erected a similar house for him there. Though family tradition states that his sister-in-law opposed the marriage, no reason is given; perhaps she thought Sarah Elizabeth too young.

The failure of Mead, Smith & Marsh gave Weyerhaeuser his first business opportunity. A relative of the senior partner who had lent the firm money suggested that Weyerhaeuser purchase the Coal Valley assets and take over the debt. He followed this advice. "I bought largely," writes Weyerhaeuser, who was able to get credit and wished to take advantage of the prevailing low prices. The Rock Island sawmill was stopped, but he kept on retailing lumber, even though the panic had driven ready cash out of circulation. "I went round among the farmers exchanging lumber for horses, oxen, hogs, eggs, anything they had," he explains. "This country produce I traded to the raftsmen for logs or to the merchants for stoves, tinware, and logging kits." While carrying on his business by this complicated process of barter, he also purchased wheat on commission for a Rock Island firm.

Seeing the Rock Island mill standing idle, he decided to lease and run it. "I bought a raft of logs then lying in the eddy at Davenport for $5 a thousand," he later recalled, "getting ten percent discount for cash payment in gold. I hired John Potter to saw them for me, paying him $2 a thousand for sawing (including the rent of the mill) and $1 for freight to Coal Valley." Simultaneously he set up as contractor, building houses for farmers, schoolhouses, county buildings, and miscellaneous structures. To his astonishment, he closed his first nine months as an independent businessman with a profit of $3,000 and his second year with one of $5,000.

Frederick Weyerhaeuser always credited much of his early success to his good fortune in buying when prices were lowest and when every month of recovery from the depression increased the value of his assets. Other men, such as his future associates William H. Laird and the Norton brothers (James L. and Matthew G.), had precisely the opposite experience; they went into debt when prices were highest, were almost wiped out by the panic of 1857, and struggled for years to recover.[5] But it is clear that much besides good luck entered into Weyerhaeuser's success.

He toiled early and late, often rising at two in the morning to drive to Port Byron on the Mississippi for lime or other supplies and getting back to Coal Valley to put in a ten-hour day at his yard. Physically so strong that he easily carried a two-bushel sack of wheat, 120 pounds, up a plank into a boxcar, he maintained his health, he used to say, by drinking a quart of buttermilk daily, taking reasonable exercise in the fresh air and sunshine, and above all, refusing to worry. He scrupulously kept the Sabbath and attended church. In time, he joined the Odd Fellows and

Masons in Coal Valley and found companionship in these fraternal bodies. As a hobby he took up beekeeping; and it is recorded that once a helper shook down from a tree a swarm that landed squarely on Weyerhaeuser's head, and he had to spend five days in bed while Elizabeth poulticed his stings.

Working hard, keeping serenely good-natured, quoting aphorisms from *Poor Richard's Almanac* with a twinkle in his blue eyes, he won the liking and esteem of nearly everybody he met. He had an effective way of illustrating ideas by relating anecdotes in his soft voice of quaint German accent. Meanwhile, no one in the region grasped a business problem more incisively or displayed greater resourcefulness in meeting it.[6]

He had a capable helpmate in Elizabeth, a tall, graceful woman of wiry strength. Out of his early profits, on February 14, 1859, he bought the little house the defunct firm had built for him in Coal Valley. Children came in steady succession: the eldest, John Philip, on November 4, 1858.[7] How the tiny rooms held them all is a marvel. John Philip always remembered the trundle bed in which he slept, pushed by day under the larger beds. Elizabeth helped her husband with clerical work. She was unstintingly hospitable to family connections and to her husband's business acquaintances. Before long her father came to live with them. We can well believe the son who writes: "Mother's household resembled an accordion in its power of expansion. She was an excellent manager."

These Coal Valley years, in spite of the almost terrifying hard work of Weyerhaeuser and his wife, had an idyllic quality. The Weyerhaeusers owned enough land to provide poultry (in Niedersaulheim fashion they paid special attention to geese), eggs, milk, cream, vegetables, and fruit for themselves and their guests. Elizabeth filled spacious shelves in the cellar with preserves and jellies; they heaped neighboring bins with apples and potatoes. "Father dearly loved to entertain people," states his son, "and was never happier than when he could break bread with them at his own table." Whenever the Lutheran pastor called, homemade wine was served with a lavish repast. Every Saturday evening boots were shined for the church service next day. Weyerhaeuser used to say with pride that although he thought more of his credit than of his clothes, he always, even when poorest, had a special suit for Sunday. As each child grew old enough, he or she shared in the household work, from dishwashing to wood splitting to quartering apples for apple butter.[8]

Weyerhaeuser became known in the whole Rock Island area as a shrewd trader, so honest that immigrant farmers unable to read or write paid his lumber bills without question. Though he made his business mistakes, he learned from them. By 1860 he had taken a partner, was employing a number of men, and looked to larger activities in both manufacturing and selling lumber.[9]

3

"Uncle Denkmann" was the partner: Frederick C. A. Denkmann, the husband of Elizabeth Weyerhaeuser's older sister. Weyerhaeuser brought about the alliance because he wanted a helper in buying and operating the old sawmill of Mead, Smith & Marsh and because Denkmann had special reason to consider new employment. Now nearly forty, Denkmann had been trying with scant success to make a living out of a small grocery and his trade of machinist. Restless by nature, he had decided to join the settlers who had created Auraria (Denver) in the new gold diggings of Colorado and sell groceries in that needy land. As he acquired a wagon and began to stock it, no doubt his family took an anxious view of the future.

The sawmill, which Weyerhaeuser had thus far leased, was now for sale with eighteen or nineteen town lots in Rock Island and Coal Valley. It represented an opportunity. Already, according to one unsubstantiated story, Rock Island millowners were making such difficulties in supplying him with proper assortments of lumber at fair prices that his retail business was endangered. He knew that Denkmann was an excellent mechanic who would quickly learn all about sawing and planing. He knew also that they could buy the mill at a low figure; although it had once been valued at $17,000, it had gone through four changes of management in ten years and was now to be auctioned off at a sheriff's foreclosure sale.

"We formed an equal partnership," wrote Weyerhaeuser later. But while they were to share equally in the profits, Weyerhaeuser made the larger investment and took the greater risk. Under date of May 1, 1860, he agreed to deliver as his contribution $4,616.51—proof that he had done well in his independent business. Of this, $3,212.80 was in cash, and the remainder a strange conglomeration of assets—buggy, wagon, two horses, two cows, seven hogs, and even "one brass collar." Denkmann engaged to deliver $1,607.03, of which $810 was his stock of groceries and $400 was cash. He itemized "one sckiff" at $15, doubtless a boat for river fishing and picknicking. To equalize the investment, Denkmann gave Weyerhaeuser his note for $1,504.74 at 10 percent interest, a fair going rate.

Already the principal creditors of the defunct firm had agreed to transfer their interest in the mill to the new partnership. The cost of buying them out came to $5,100, of which $2,100 was paid in cash. When all obligations were settled, the mill would be theirs.[10]

If a certain pathos attached to the agreements and inventories made out by the two struggling immigrants in quaintly illiterate English, they themselves did not feel it. We may be sure that Weyerhaeuser looked to the future with exuberant confidence and Denkmann with relieved hope.

Apart from their houses and household effects, they had put in absolutely everything they possessed in the world, down to "three sets harness," "one corn sheller," and "sundries." But they knew the West was growing, and had faith that it would rise from the depression and that its appetite for lumber would be keen.[11] "We could manufacture about three million feet of lumber per year," Weyerhaeuser wrote later; "and the height of our ambition, attained a few years later, was to manufacture ten million. In two years we made enough money to pay off all our indebtedness." He quoted *Poor Richard's Almanac* on thrift with good reason.

The partners, beginning an association of families in business enterprise that was to continue and broaden, had the advantage of complementary aptitudes and skills. Weyerhaeuser was becoming a master at judging men and opportunities, bargaining, and making contracts. He already knew something of the rafting trade and freight charges on river and railroad. Denkmann not only learned the intricacies of mill operation, but gained skill in handling subordinates in both manufacturing and marketing. He was an intense, nervous, dynamic man, his dark eyes and the mobile features of his round face, fringed with a beard in the style of Oom Paul Kruger, mirroring his impatient energy. His outbursts of temper, quick recoveries to geniality, and snapping commands stirred his millworkers to more strenuous effort: "He was up and a-coming and everybody else had to come, too." Like Weyerhaeuser, outside business he was quiet and retiring; he devoted himself to his family, spending his evenings reading with his wife and children, and to his church, for he was a devout Lutheran. He shunned public notice, and though in later years the greater attention given Weyerhaeuser irked him, he was glad to remain obscure.[12]

The mill that Weyerhaeuser & Denkmann acquired stood in what was then the west end of Rock Island. The original equipment had included a sash saw, a small circular saw, lath-making machinery, and a device for splitting shingles, but no planers. By the time of the purchase the sash saw had given way to a muley saw, the antecedent of the modern gang saw, and perhaps other smaller improvements had been made.[13]

Nevertheless, the mill was badly designed, crowded, and by modern standards dangerous. The headlong Denkmann, a fearless man completely preoccupied with his work, several times came near losing his life. Once as he intently watched the muley saw, a slab swung round and struck him a fearful blow in the face, leaving it raw; once when a raft of loose logs escaped from the boom near the mill and started downstream, he ran out to save it and disappeared under the logs, whence he was rescued with difficulty; and once he let his hand get caught in the planer knives, losing some fingers—but came back to work the next day.[14]

The partners began operations in what was a gloomy economic year; Midwest lumber prices dropped to distressingly low levels in 1860. They had put all their resources into the new firm and had to pay off a mortgage before they could fully possess their mill. But the falling market did not daunt them. Like other enterprising young men of the time—Collis P. Huntington, Philip D. Armour, J. P. Morgan, and John D. Rockefeller— they relied upon their own energy, insight, and resourcefulness, and upon the inevitable development of the country.

N O T E S

1. Burrows in J. W. Spencer and J. M. D. Burrow (Quaife, ed.), *The Early Days of Rock Island and Davenport,* 196.

2. *Past and Present of Rock Island County,* 151.

3. Frederick E. Weyerhaeuser, a son, completed in 1939 a long, thorough, and well-written manuscript of 807 pages, entitled "A Record of the Life and Business Activities of Frederick Weyerhaeuser, 1834–1914," marked by exhaustive research and general objectivity of temper. The first chapter contains a fascinating ten-page autobiographical sketch by the senior Weyerhaeuser covering the years 1834–1869. This MS will hereafter be cited as FEW Record.

4. FEW Record, 15.

5. *Ibid.,* 19.

6. *Ibid.,* 27–44. Weyerhaeuser was never able to pronounce the diphthong "th," and throughout life was wont to refer to Thursday, with a chuckle, as "the day following Wednesday."

7. John Philip was named after an uncle in the Bloedel family.

8. FEW Record, 54. In their reminiscences some of the children show a tendency to confuse the Coal Valley years with the Rock Island years just following; this is unimportant.

9. *Ibid.,* 39.

10. See Hauberg, *Weyerhaeuser & Denkmann,* 17–38; "Two Men of Vision Became Leaders in Timber Industry," Rock Island *Argus,* 75th Anniversary edition, 1935; Weymouth, "Frederick Weyerhaeuser Made a Millionaire by Luck," Chicago *Sunday Tribune,* Oct. 20, 1907; and FEW Record, 20–22, 31 ff.

11. For the slow Western recovery see Merk, *Economic History of Wisconsin,* 61.

12. Hauberg, *op. cit.,* 50–54, 59; FEW Record, 86 ff.

13. The sash saw was so called because it was fixed in a frame or sash. The muley saw was a stiff long perpendicular saw, moving up and down as it slashed through the timbers with an oscillating motion; Denkmann called it the "osculating saw."

14. FEW Record, 90; Hauberg, *op. cit.,* 56–57.

II

A Heritage and an Industry

WEYERHAEUSER and Denkmann had chosen an ancient and fascinating occupation. In mid-century America, where almost every building, bridge, fence, road vehicle, ship, and steamboat was made of wood, lumbering was one of the dominant industries. When the two partners began their labors, they were town dwellers with little feeling for "the murmuring pines and the hemlocks," for the great forest that still overspread much of the continent. Weyerhaeuser, however, soon came to love the pinewoods of the Lake States, and both men faced the difficulties of their business with the exhilaration of a new adventure.

Though the forest by 1855 had yielded much ground to the lumberman and farmer, it still covered great areas of the United States with a virgin stand. "You have only to travel for a few days into the interior and back parts even of many of the old States," Thoreau had written a few years earlier, "to come to that very America which the Northmen, and Cabot, and Gosnold, and Smith, and Raleigh visited." New York had a huge Adirondack forest so wild that an Indian was still necessary to guide scientists into the area. Sixty miles above Bangor in Maine, "the country is virtually unmapped and unexplored, and there still waves the virgin forest of the New World."[1] The geologist Charles Lyell, traversing the pine barrens of the South, scarcely touched except for turpentine, thought that they constituted "one of the marked features in the geography of the globe, like the pampas of South America;" and Fredrika Bremer in the early 1850's was awed by the primeval forests of Wisconsin and Minnesota—though she also noted the "vast timber-floats" of loggers waging a war of attrition on these areas. In the Far Northwest axes had hardly stirred an echo among the gigantic Douglas firs and western white pines.

Nearly everywhere on the Atlantic Coast the forest originally came down to the sea, so that the first white men who sailed into the bays and rivers saw endless vistas of magnificent trees. As Fenimore Cooper put it, "a bird's-eye view of the whole region east of the Mississippi must then have offered one vast expanse of woods"—while an eagle soaring over the West would have seen the Black Hills clothed in verdure, the lower slopes and valleys of the Rockies and Sierras densely wooded, and wide expanses of the Pacific slope bearing trees, a few of which had been contemporary with the pharaohs and many with Charlemagne or Alfred.[2]

With exploration and settlement, a number of distinctive forest concentrations came to be recognized. Upper New England had valuable timberlands of white pine, birch, maple, and spruce. A great part of the East and Middle West was covered with mixed stands of birch, beech, maple, hemlock, oak, chestnut, and hickory. Longleaf pine forests in the coastal and Piedmont areas of the South had special commercial value; and so did the white pine and red pine stands of Michigan, Wisconsin, and Minnesota. The river bottoms of the South, including much of the lower valley of the Mississippi, offered, in addition to the yellow pine, unique stretches of cypress, tupelo, and sweet gum.

Proceeding westward, the pioneer encountered a broad zone of treeless country, but beyond this expanse were additional woodlands of distinctive nature. In the upper Rockies stood forests of western white pine and white fir, with some Douglas fir, ponderosa pine, red cedar, larch, and spruce; to the south ponderosa, Douglas fir, and white fir, in that order, dominated, with some Engelman spruce and larch. In the upper Pacific Coast areas Douglas fir was outstanding, with hemlock also important, but there was a scattering of white fir, Pacific silver fir, red cedar, and spruce; farther south, in what is now southern Oregon, ponderosa pine was king, with Douglas fir, white fir, sugar pine, and a miscellany of incense cedar, red fir, and western white pine as the lesser species. Still farther to the south, in the California coastal mountains, stood the redwood forests, the most impressive of all.

Many estimates have been made of the volume of the timber that once mantled the continent from the Chesapeake to Puget Sound and from the Sierra Madre to the Yukon. The geographer J. Russell Smith conjectures that the original virgin forest area in eastern United States covered 681,000,000 acres and that in the western region 140,800,000 acres. One estimate puts the commercial lumber contained in these areas at 5,200,-000,000,000 board feet. But the significant fact is that the first comers found the magnitude of the forest overwhelming.[3]

These early settlers regarded the forest as both friend and foe, asset and encumbrance. William Bradford's Pilgrims at Plymouth and Captain John Smith's adventurers in Virginia used it to build their dwellings, and sent shiploads of clapboard back to England. But the forest harbored the panther, the wolf and the Indian lurking for an opportunity to slay, while its shaded pools bred malaria. The traveler without a compass could lose himself in the dense woods as completely as if he had sunk in the ocean. Not until the forest was practically gone would many pioneer families feel free to venture any considerable distance alone. Men happily laid their axes to the woods.

The clearing of the land was of course also essential to agriculture. For a rough kind of tillage, trees could be killed by girdling and crops sown among the dead trunks; but to make a really satisfactory farm, the woods had to be cut down and the stumps grubbed out. The anonymous author of the first important work on New World farming, *American Husbandry* (1775), describes this process as almost universal along the advancing frontier, and states that the planks, shingles, staves, fenceposts, and potash often nearly paid the expense of the work.[4] So much was the conquest and utilization of the forest a part of the pioneer farmer's work, when he came to the open prairies of the West he at first clung to wooded streams.

Farmers and forest fires together destroyed far more of the timber east of the Missouri than the lumbermen ever cut. The antagonism of countless settlers toward the wilderness was so irrational that in hewing out farms many would not even preserve a woodlot. Joseph C. G. Kennedy, superintendent of the United States Census, wrote in 1850:

It is lamentable, in view of present ruthlessness and the demands of posterity, to observe the utter disregard manifested by the American people . . . for valuable trees, the destruction of which is not necessary to good cultivation, and the existence whereof would not only add greatly to the value of their property, but contribute vastly to health, the fertility of their farms, and the comfort of their livestock. We have seen thousands of farms rendered less productive and of much less intrinsic value by the destruction of timber, especially on their north and west boundaries, where they protect from the colds of winter.[5]

This was also the complaint of the author of *American Husbandry,* who accused the settlers of "ravaging rather than cutting down the woods," and of so wantonly destroying forests that along the coast even firewood had become expensive and was imported from the Kennebec.[6] The vastness of the woodlands led most people to assume that, like the passenger pigeons and buffalo, they were inexhaustible. When timber was cleared from one district, it could be found in another; moreover, unlike the coal beds and iron deposits, when once exhausted it might be regrown.

Although woodworking machinery had a slow evolution in America, it was fairly well developed when Weyerhaeuser bought his Rock Island sawmill. The early settlers had done good work with the ax, adze, rasp,

handsaw, pitsaw, and whipsaw, but had been slow to erect sawmills. This
was partly because British sawyers long resisted mechanization. Edward
H. Knight, writing the chapter on American mechanical progress in *The
First Century of the Republic* (1876), remarked: "The writer distinctly
recollects when logs and tree trunks were habitually sawed from end to
end, to work them into dimension stuff, by two sawyers, one standing on
the log and the other in a pit beneath with a veil over his eyes to keep out
the sawdust. And what a hard working, sad, drunken set these sawyers
were, and how the top-sawyer bossed the wretch in the hole, who pulled
down while he above, with shoulders like an Atlas, swung his weight upon
the handles above!"[7] Generally speaking, however, by the nineteenth century sawmills, driven by horsepower, steampower, or waterpower, had
become ubiquitous, and every large city had shops where rough lumber
was converted into planed boards, dimension lumber, scaleboard, and
veneers.

The circular saw had been introduced in England in 1790 and was
gradually adopted in the United States. The most renowned of all the inventors of the woodworking industry, Sir Samuel Bentham, patented in
1793 the bench, slit, parallel guide, and the sliding bevel glide. He also
invented the first good planing knife in 1791, and the British engineer
Joseph Bramah improved upon this in 1802 with the traverse planer. He
also built a self-acting mortising machine in 1793 which used a rotating
cutter, and devised a pivoted table for oblique mortising and a forked
chisel for making narrow parallel mortises. Other inventors, British and
American, lent their aid. By the time Weyerhaeuser entered the industry,
some eastern sawmills had attained a fairly advanced stage.[8]

In the Middle West the mills were only beginning to adopt improvements, and the typical frontier logging operation in Weyerhaeuser's early
days was still primitive. The "State of Maine" lumber camp that spread
through the Great Lakes region usually consisted of one log-built structure, perhaps fifty feet long and thirty wide, with a roof of shakes sloping
from the central ridgepole down to low side walls. Clay served for chink-
ing, while pine boughs were sometimes spread over the roofshakes. A
central fire built on a large stone platform supplied heat, the better camps
having a mud-and-stick chimney, the ruder ones a mere smoke hole in
the roof. The camp was illuminated only by the fire and by dim lanterns,
for windows were luxuries seldom provided. On one side of the blaze was
the long "deacon's seat" where the men, basking at night in the heat, relaxed, swapped jokes and stories, and played cards. A great bunk platform
stretching the full length of the building provided a crowded sleeping
space, all too often verminous. Spruce or hemlock boughs took the place
of mattresses, a folded mackinaw made a pillow, and thick blankets or
quilts, with an occasional buffalo robe, covered the sleepers.[9]

The camp cook had a domain of his own, sometimes in a separate building, sometimes in a projection of the main structure. Here he ruled over a cookstove, barrels of flour, beans, and salt pork, and the rude wooden tables where meals were eaten. This same room or building usually doubled as repair shop, with a grindstone, extra ax helves, files for saws, and other tools; and it contained the wash sink, handbasins, and water barrel, with other odd items.

Sometimes the food was unpalatable, although with increasing settlement it improved. Isaac Stephenson, a former state-of-Maine man, relates that one early Wisconsin camp afforded almost no vegetables. "We were rarely able to obtain any at all. For five and a half months one winter we did not see a vegetable and were given fresh meat only once. Camp fare consisted of the inevitable pork and beans, bread, and tea which we sweetened with Porto Rico rum instead of sugar." Tea was not served at noon—merely water. "Sometimes when I was detained, . . . I found the water which had been poured into my tin cup frozen and had to break the ice to drink. Tea seemed so much of a luxury that I promised myself that, if I ever had a home of my own . . . I would have tea three times a day." But as to the food in general he added, "We made the most of our unvarying fare and ate with a keen zest that comes of long days of work in the open, the keen, crisp air of the winter and the tang of the pine forests."

Roused long before dawn, the hardworking gangs remained in the woods until daylight failed, and cut tremendous quantities of timber. Martin Page, another Wisconsin pioneer, writes that in the 1850's his crew of fifteen, with two oxen, cut a million feet of logs each winter and drove them downstream in spring.[10] It was such lumber camps and logging outfits that Weyerhaeuser saw when he first visited the northern woods.

2

Throughout the northern part of the United States, most people by the 1850's had acquired with good reason a marked preference for white pine lumber. The logs are light and float easily in water. The wood is soft yet durable and effectively resists warping, shrinking, splintering, and decay. It holds paints and glues well and is the cabinetmaker's and woodworker's delight, for it can be quickly fashioned into almost any desired form. Nails not only penetrate white pine easily but can be removed and replaced firmly in the same hole. When fresh from the planing mill the boards are as smooth as velvet and have a beautiful pearly sheen. No other wood had an equal appeal to farmers and builders as long as the supply was plentiful and the price reasonable.

In fact, lumber users were committed to a virtual white pine economy when Weyerhaeuser and Denkmann began their sawmill enterprise. In

1869 this one wood accounted for 62.7 percent of the softwood lumber produced in the United States and for 45.4 percent of all lumber sawed. Oak might appeal to the well-to-do for flooring and furniture, and walnut for interior decoration, but for general utility pine had no peer. The problem for lumbermen was to satisfy the demand.

One obstacle to lumbering, the Indians' title to the land, had been largely eliminated by treaties between 1825 and 1855. Meanwhile, the federal government was presenting lumbermen with a bewildering variety of avenues for acquiring timberland. In 1860 Weyerhaeuser and Denkmann could buy standing timber ("stumpage") or land from those who had already acquired title or they could bid for it at public land sales. If lumbermen wished to act as squatters, they could buy tracts at minimum prices under the Pre-emption Act. They could acquire swampland at low cost or patent tracts by presenting military scrip originally given to soldiers and later purchased by speculators. Each state also had school lands for sale. In 1862 Congress passed the Homestead Act, while the Morrill Act in the same year gave large grants to state agricultural and mechanical colleges, and the Pacific Railroad Act made the first extensive gift of land for transcontinental railroad construction.

This confusing mixture of land-disposal laws was the response to a wide range of pressures from agrarian, business, and educational groups for use of the public domain at a time when capital was scarce and costly. The mélange really constituted the forest policy of the United States, for, beyond legislation protecting timber reserves for naval purposes, no provision was made for a planned management of the magnificent forest heritage.

The hodgepodge opened opportunities for investors large and small, honest and dishonest. Thousands of men with little capital used one law or another to get holdings. Men of substantial capital acquired extensive tracts of timberland at public land sales or by use of scrip. Many purchasers of large acreages, notably those who bought railroad lands, received alternate sections and had to "block up" their holdings. This was often done by the employment of dummy entrymen. Unlawful cutting of trees on the public domain was inevitable as long as the lands had not been opened to purchase. The practice was so widespread, particularly in the Lake States, 1850–1870, that the General Land Office, instead of instituting criminal action, permitted offenders to pay for the stumpage and the costs of collection. Actually, there was no legal way for lumbermen to acquire timber on public lands prior to auction sales. Wiser national policies were possible but not practically feasible.[11]

To many ambitious men anxious to buy land and timber cheaply, the unhappiest result of the laws was the concentration of large acreages in the hands of a few owners. Cornell and other universities held immense tracts given them by the federal government; so did the railroads. These properties had, of course, been intended for early sale in order to aid education and stimulate the growth of a transportation system. However, such men as Philetus Sawyer and James Jenkins of Oshkosh, Francis Palms of Detroit, Dorilus Morrison and T. B. Walker of Minneapolis, and Isaac Stephenson of Stillwater, while logging extensive areas, acquired and held huge tracts in the hope of making speculative profits. Forced to stay out of the stumpage and timberland market for lack of capital during the 1860's,[12] most lumbermen on the Middle Mississippi later found that they had to pay higher prices than these early purchasers.

For the small sawmiller on the Mississippi the disadvantage in price was offset by the willingness of Cornell University, railroads, and most speculative investors to extend credit. They sold their timber and land for a down payment in cash and annual installments as the timber was cut.[13] Without such long-term financing many a small lumber firm on the Middle Mississippi, like Weyerhaeuser & Denkmann, might never have been able to purchase timberland. Late buyers also enjoyed the advantage of getting a clear title with a minimum of friction, for original purchasers had to patent the land, make certain they had a right to transfer it, and later meet the accusation of abusing the land laws.

Lumbermen in the Lake States had also been presented by nature with a cheap and extensive water transportation system. By the 1850's logs and lumber were moving in quantity down numerous Michigan streams, destined for markets in Milwaukee and Chicago. In eastern and northern Wisconsin, as well as northern Minnesota, creeks and rivers flowed into Lakes Michigan and Superior. West and south of these regions lay the Upper Mississippi and its tributaries. Streams originating far north in Wisconsin and Minnesota meandered southward toward the Great River. For more than a generation, agile crews on the Black, Chippewa, St. Croix, Wisconsin, and lesser streams delivered logs and lumber to mill and market.

As Weyerhaeuser and Denkmann soon discovered, lumbermen in the Upper Mississippi Valley selected widely different types of locations for their plants. Some started mills on the Middle Mississippi near potential markets, assuming that they could acquire their raw materials upstream; others built at or near the source of raw material. By the 1860's, however, sawmillers were tending to concentrate their plants in a few towns. A group of mills flourished at the Falls of St. Anthony—a waterpower site as well as head of navigation on the Mississippi. On the St. Croix, Stillwater had become the chief sawmill town. On the Chippewa, mills were most numerous at Chippewa Falls and Eau Claire. On the Black River, La Crosse lumbermen had taken leadership, utilizing logs sorted at the boom near Onalaska, the birthplace of Hamlin Garland.

Concentration of plants was much less evident on the Wisconsin and Middle Mississippi. Clusters of relatively small mills had been erected at numerous points on the Wisconsin. On the Mississippi practically every town from St. Paul to St. Louis had a sawmill, usually small. Only during the sixties did a few firms emerge as leaders.

The growth of the lumber industry in the Middle West was stimulated by a fast-expanding demand. In the relatively treeless area west of the Mississippi, population increased very rapidly during the 1860's—Missouri, 46 percent; Iowa, 77; Minnesota, 156; Kansas, 240; Nebraska, 326; and the Dakotas, 213.[14]

Railroad extension, demanding lumber for ties, trestles, bridges, and buildings, brought in settlers and was the most dynamic factor in the growth of the region. Though little new track was laid west of the Mississippi during the war, after Appomattox a number of railroads raced to connect with the Union Pacific at Council Bluffs. The Chicago & North Western system reached the goal in 1867, the Rock Island two years later, and both the Illinois Central and Burlington in 1870. Lumber dealers followed them. The Southern Minnesota line, shortly to be a part of the Milwaukee Road, had by 1870 extended the market of La Crosse sawmillers 168 miles west to Winnebago, and the Winona & St. Peter railroad, begun in 1862 and operated as part of the Chicago & North Western lines after 1867, had enabled Winona lumbermen to sell as far west as Janesville.

Until the late sixties the position of railroads largely determined the pattern of competition west of the Mississippi. Rail lines ran westward in roughly parallel fashion from lumber centers at river crossings. Along the railroad, wholesalers of any given town normally competed not only with other wholesalers but also with local sawmillers, and some Chicago wholesalers usually entered the market if a Mississippi River town had railroad connections both east and west, as did Burlington, Clinton, Hannibal, and Rock Island. But in many towns a few firms dominated the market, maintaining prices at profitable margins. Not until after 1870 did the rapid addition of north-south railways to the east-west lines throw the markets into competitive confusion.

While restricted competition had its attractions, ease of entry into the industry was probably still more appealing to lumbermen. Weyerhaeuser and Denkmann started with about $3,600 in actual cash, and the average capital investment in an American sawmill in 1860 was $3,123. Most lumbermen put their savings into a single phase of the industry—stumpage or timberland or logging or a sawmill or a planing mill or wholesaling or retailing—though many combined two or more of these undertakings as soon as finances permitted.[15]

3

The Lake States lumber industry attracted men of diverse backgrounds. Of 131 leading lumbermen of the area, more than four-fifths were born in the northeastern states or eastern Canada. Weyerhaeuser and Denkmann were atypical; only four of the group originated in Germany. More than half started life on farms, and almost 60 percent ended their formal education with the common schools. These men had accumulated their initial capital from savings or from families and friends. They sometimes expanded their enterprises with funds from the East, but chiefly by short-term loans or by reinvesting their profits.[16] Entrepreneur and worker alike found the forests and the transport system of the Lake States so similar to those in the East that they could transfer their tools and techniques with little change.[17]

Experienced woodsmen from the Middle Atlantic States, New England, and eastern Canada formed the nucleus of the labor force. Some were brought west by their migrating employers. Isaac M. Stephenson persuaded an all but invaluable sawmill man to come with him from the east. "I could build a batteau," Stephenson recalled, "make all the tools used for river driving, ox yokes and sleighs, shoe oxen and horses and exercise generally the functions of a blacksmith, carpenter, or millwright —all of which stood me in very good stead." But he needed an expert in the mill. Others were enticed by state agencies, companies, friends, relatives, or advertisements. The imminent exhaustion of eastern white pine influenced them, together with the excitement of new opportunities.

Logging operations, as in the East, were conducted by owners of timberland, purchasers of stumpage (the timber and not the land), and contractors. They sent their crews of six to twenty men into the woods with the first winter weather; swampy areas were then frozen solid and heavy snow soon buried stones, providing smooth passage for the ox-drawn sleds. The men began by cutting the timber nearest the streams. One young lumberman on his way westward met an older man who was returning east. "Go back home," the latter told him, "the lumbering days are over in this country." He meant that there were no more stands on the shores of rivers or lakes—to him the only timber worth taking.

For falling, saw bosses selected only the best white pine, free from rot and insect damage. In the 1850's logs were marketable only if eighteen inches or more in diameter at the smallest end and completely sound, comparable figures for the late 1860's being sixteen inches and 90 percent. White pine comprised no more than 5 percent of the stand in many southern Wisconsin tracts and seldom exceeded 60 percent anywhere in the Great Lakes region. But the other trees—hemlock, birch, spruce, and maple—were left for later cutting by lumbermen or clearing off by farmers. The process was highly wasteful.

"Choppers," the artists of logging (later to be known as "fallers"), felled the large white pines with axes or two-man crosscut saws, the combination of both saw and ax becoming more common in the late sixties. "Barkers" next trimmed off branches and some bark to expedite dragging the log over the snow. Scalers then estimated the amount of lumber in the log, usually employing Scribner's Straight and Sound rule, one of thirteen possible methods.[18] Meanwhile, "swampers" cleared paths to the riverbank or tote road. Utilizing "go-devils" and bobsleds, teamsters guided ox teams as these slid or carried the stripped trunks to the bank. There sawyers "bucked" them with crosscut saws into twelve-, fourteen-, and sixteen-foot lengths, and put bark and stamp marks on them. With canthooks, peaveys (patented in 1858), and inclined poles (block and tackle at a later date) the men piled the logs on "rollways" or "landings," ready for release into the stream when the spring thaw came.

Loggers rose at four o'clock in the morning and labored at a steady, unhurried pace through the daylight hours. They normally ate three large meals, which increasingly included some vegetables, often grown locally by the logging operator, who also raised hay for his oxen. After supper the men sat around the box stove, talking, or turned in. Sometimes a whole crew slept in one long bunk. "A blanket was spread from one end of the row of bodies to the other," records a participant. "It was a laughable sight to see so many heads 'all in a row,' presenting all colors of hair and whiskers, with as many different kinds of noses." The blanket was as wide as the men were tall and "as long as may be necessary."[19]

Storage, driving, and sorting techniques also followed eastern patterns. The men built dams of brush, logs, and stones for storage reservoirs. Floating logs were confined by booms—long lines of logs bound together with rope or chain—which were owned and operated by corporations at key points along the Mississippi and its tributaries. Foremen of the drives recruited men from logging crews and supervised the shepherding of the logs from far up the tributaries to the mainstream and beyond it. Wearing calked boots, "the river-men scurried from log to log. They were cowboys on wooden horses, wonders of practical acrobatics who made it seem as easy to stay on a log as a novice found it to fall off." Sometimes they moved in small boats or along the banks, nudging into the main current with peavies such logs as had stranded or were caught by sandbars or rocks. A man who slipped into the icy water could usually dry out on shore or in the "wanigan," as they called the floating office and cookhouse.

The loss in logs was much higher than in men, however. Driving crews congratulated themselves if their "shrinkage" amounted to no more than 10 percent of what they started with.

To deliver logs on the Middle Mississippi, men assembled them into rafts, either at mill booms or at specially constructed sorting works on tributary streams. Crews collected logs bearing the mark of each owner, arranged them side by side, laid poles crosswise on the logs, then placed a rope over the pole and through twin holes bored in each of the two outside logs. Wooden plugs driven into the holes alongside the ends of the rope bound the mass firmly in a "string," usually about sixteen feet in width. Several strings made up a raft. In the early sixties crews rode these cumbersome craft down the Mississippi, adding speed and giving direction to them with large sweeplike oars. The hazards were floods, sandbars, mudflats, rapids, sloughs, and piers of bridges.

During the 1860's steamboats replaced the hardworking raftsmen. Frederick Weyerhaeuser knew of steamboat towing by line astern on lakes Pepin and St. Croix. He had also seen the operation on the river at Rock Island. Raftsmen found that frustrating breakups and costly delays required a special vessel for their purpose—one that could not only push the unwieldy logs but would also be equipped with a workable capstan for manipulating guide lines to the stern corners of the raft. It must also have a crew trained to operate both boat and capstan efficiently. A powerful sternwheeler, built by J. W. Van Sant and his son of Le Claire, Iowa, met such requirements. In 1868 and 1869 Weyerhaeuser had hired steamboats for towing logs from the St. Croix and Chippewa, and in 1870 he rode down the river on the maiden voyage of Van Sant's pride with a raft for his Rock Island mill.[20]

Weyerhaeuser and Denkmann not only saw the steamboat replace the raftsman but lived through a comparable revolution in sawmill technology. During the fifties and sixties such Milwaukee suppliers of sawmill equipment as E. P. Allis & Company and Filer, Stowell & Company presented mill operators with a galaxy of new machines: for example, varieties of "bull" chains to drag logs to the deck near the headsaw, mechanical log turners or steam "niggers," invented in 1868, and friction-feed and steam-feed carriages to move logs back and forth past the saw.

Faster log flow to the headsaw came when the muley saw of 5,000 to 6,000 board feet capacity per day was superseded by the circular saw, which could cut 20,000 to 25,000 feet daily. In the sixties one sawmiller after another adopted the more modern circular, although it cut a half-inch kerf, wobbled excessively, and turned out a product that often "more nearly resembled washboards than lumber."

The desire to expand output led to adoption of the gang, a series of saws set equidistant (normally one inch) from each other in a heavy frame. Though these were designed to cut an even board, more than one sawmiller found boards produced by his first gang too crooked to put through a planing mill. To handle the gang's output, suppliers soon pro-

vided double edgers to manufacture boards of uniform widths, trimming
saws to eliminate defective spots and to turn out lumber of standard
lengths, and live rolls to convey lumber from the saws.[21]

While sawmillers modernized their equipment, many aspects of mill
operation remained unchanged. The typical building continued to be a
barnlike structure, cluttered with a maze of beams, belts, and saws. Sawdust drifted everywhere. By 1870 practically every mill had a refuse
burner and a towering stack to carry off the smoke from the boilers. On
the "green chain" each mill employed a few skilled men to mark and sort
the lumber into grades; at Rock Island in 1860, Weyerhaeuser & Denkmann milled four grades: clear, common, No. 2, and sheeting.[22] Other
workers transferred the lumber by wagon to the yard for stacking and
drying in the open air. When the firm began operations, most midwestern
sawmills produced only rough lumber, planing being done on a custom
basis by planing mills or by wholesalers with their own finishing facilities.

Local sawmill operators like Weyerhaeuser and Denkmann competed in a market crowded with lumber from all the Lake States. Chicago
wholesalers, drawing their stocks from Michigan and eastern Wisconsin,
shipped them as far west as was profitable. Some local wholesalers on the
Mississippi purchased their lumber from drifting rafts, a few got supplies on order, others relied on partners upstream, and still others assured
their supply by annual contracts for future delivery. Millmen on the
Black, Chippewa, Wisconsin, St. Croix, and Upper Mississippi piled their
rough lumber into cribs, usually 16 feet long and 12 feet wide, of twelve
to twenty layers held together by crosspieces at top and bottom tightly
fixed by wooden grub pins through holes at the end of the crosspieces.
One partner usually had charge of the selling, and normally set an overall price for lumber in a raft, exclusive of lath and shingles. The whole-
saler-buyers pulled the wet, muddy, often damaged lumber from the river;
dried, planed, sorted, and seasoned it; and sold the product to retailers in
the vicinity or along radiating rail lines.[23]

Marketing techniques were simple. Sawmillers and wholesalers displayed their wares in lumberyards, sometimes operating a retail section
for local customers. Competition of such firms as Weyerhaeuser & Denkmann with local wholesalers forced sawmill owners to sort and classify
their lumber more carefully than did the upriver millmen who rafted their
product downstream for sale. Both wholesalers and sawmill owners compiled price lists based on prevailing rates in their communities and on
Chicago quotations. Orders were solicited almost entirely by mail, though
one partner often acted as traveling bill collector and salesman.

4

Since the lumber industry was so fixed in pattern and so favored by
circumstances, it might be assumed that Weyerhaeuser & Denkmann had

only to learn the simple techniques and watch the money roll into their tills. Nothing could be further from the truth. Profitable operation demanded great astuteness, and the failure rate was high.[24] At times survival seemed almost a matter of luck.

Hazards beset every phase of the industry. They began with the buying of logs—the all-important raw material. Purchasers in the markets at Onalaska, Stillwater, and Eau Claire had to judge the quality of the logs accurately, buy at the best price possible, and time their purchases shrewdly. More than one lumberman failed because he bought logs unwisely.

Equally hazardous was the purchase of timberlands. An amateur could easily err in the selection of a tract. Careful estimates of volume and quality could be made only by expert and honest cruisers. The buyer also had to consider the distance the timber must be transported and its proximity to other land he might own. Above all, the wise investor had to allow for a possible drop in the market.

Even when he had taken all possible precautions, the buyer often lost his entire investment as a result of appallingly frequent fires. Every year witnessed many small blazes, and Wisconsin experienced serious fires in 1863, 1864, and 1868. In 1871 Weyerhaeuser and Denkmann read of a holocaust in the Great Lakes forests, the Peshtigo fire, which took at least a thousand lives while running wild through more than a million acres of valuable timber.[25]

After cutting all the merchantable pine on a tract, lumbermen had to dispose of the land fairly soon, or find it a liability. New settlers in these areas had two immediate needs—roads and schools. To pay for them, county governments levied taxes on all landowners, and usually made no distinction between logged and unlogged land, a fact that prompted timberland owners to sell their cutovers quickly or relinquish them for taxes.[26] Moreover, the timberland owner wanted to get his money out of the land so that he could invest it in new tracts farther north.

Transporting logs, Weyerhaeuser and Denkmann soon discovered, was an obstacle race. Some winters brought so little snow that logging operations were impossible. In others, the loggers had to suspend cutting because it was too deep. Subnormal rainfall in the spring could cripple the driving of logs or completely forbid it, and the logs would be left in the woods for the season, prey to fire, insect attack, and sapstain.

One drought had a devastating impact on Mississippi Valley sawmills. In 1861 boom companies on the Black and St. Croix rivers, the only two streams sending logs downstream in any quantity, processed 150,000,000 board feet of logs, many of which went to Middle Mississippi mills. Then came the dry years, and the figure dropped in 1862 to a miserable 32,000,000, rose only to 35,000,000 the next year, and reached a mere 46,000,000 in 1864.[27] Lumbermen long remembered the

lean, dry years, and had a compelling reason for looking beyond the Black
and St. Croix for their logs.

Too much rain was nearly as bad as too little rain. Plunging, whirl-
ing waters sent logs down the river too fast for catchment facilities to hold
them. Booms were broken and logs sent hurtling past the mills. In extremely high water, logs drifted out beyond the channel to be left, when
the streams subsided, high and dry and far from the water. At times logs
piled up, causing gigantic jams.

Weyerhaeuser first experienced a serious jam in 1869, when logs
cluttered the Chippewa River for fifteen miles above Chippewa Falls.
They were piled from the bottom of the river more than twenty feet above
the waterline. Scores of men labored weeks to get the timber to the mills,
and *Harper's Weekly* sent a man from New York to report the calamity.
Owners anxiously awaited the hour when their property would be free.
As Lieutenant-Governor Thaddeus C. Pound rode along the banks, he
pointed out to his companion, William Irvine (later one of Weyerhaeuser's associates), a weary figure trudging above Chippewa Falls toward
the jam: "There goes Weyerhaeuser looking for his logs."[28]

Even after Weyerhaeuser got his logs, he had to bring them to Rock
Island. In the early days rafts often tied up on lakes Pepin and St. Croix
because of too little or too much wind. When steamboats were engaged to
do the towing, it required all the skill the captains possessed to navigate
valuable cargoes down a hazardous waterway. Snags and sandbars,
sloughs and mudflats, low water and floods, and finally the rapids above
Rock Island offered a challenge to every steamboat captain. Man-made
obstacles—the bridges on the river—multiplied the difficulties. Abraham
Lincoln learned in the *Effie Afton* case that rivermen considered the spans
an "invention of Satan and the Rock Island Railroad." By 1868 the Rock
Island Bridge was but one of six, and by 1874 of ten.[29]

Milling the logs raised a series of problems during the 1860's. Only
by adopting the new improvements offered by sawmill suppliers could ill-
equipped establishments like Weyerhaeuser & Denkmann keep pace with
leaders in the industry, for some plants were expanding production from
a high mark of 50,000 feet of lumber daily in 1860 to more than 200,000
feet ten years later.[30] But each improvement led to another. Introduction
of the circular headsaw, for example, required new devices to speed logs
to and from the saws. Millmen were thus forced to invest more money in
machinery. Expanded operations called for more workers, and more
money went into wages.

The growth in the size of mills and their stocks of unsold lumber increased the fire risk and insurance costs. Because they lacked sprinkler
systems, plants relied on bucket brigades for fighting fires, which were almost as prevalent and dangerous as in petroleum refineries. It was esti-

mated that 350 sawmills burned during 1889 in Wisconsin alone.[31] As fires sent insurance rates up, many millowners elected to operate without financial protection. Weyerhaeuser and Denkmann never had a disastrous fire in their first Rock Island mill, but were less fortunate in several other plants, and gladly joined fellow lumbermen in seeking means to reduce insurance costs.

The two Germans also found many uncertainties in the market. The purchasing power of the farmers, the chief consumers of lumber in the Upper Mississippi Valley, depended upon the weather, other crop conditions, and the markets. Even the better farmers operated on financial shoestrings. "Complete stagnation in the lumber trade" in 1860, the year Weyerhaeuser & Denkmann began operations so confidently, was attributed to the near failure of the wheat, oat, and hay crops in Illinois and Missouri.[32]

Through 1856 good years had outnumbered bad. Though lumber sold for as high as $20 per thousand feet before the panic of 1857, shortly thereafter it dropped as low as $6, and the price rose little prior to the Civil War.[33]

Prices in the Chicago wholesale market mirrored the variations of the sixties. Lumber sold for $12 a thousand in October, 1850. By May, 1861, it was down to $6.75 and moved upward slowly for more than two years. With the Civil War came less railroad building, and fewer settlers moved west of the Mississippi. These changes temporarily reduced calls for lumber, and mill output far exceeded the demand. Then, partly because of the drought-induced short supply of logs and partly because of wartime inflation, lumber prices rose sharply in the fall of 1863, reaching $23 per thousand in 1864. Floods and a return of peace sent them down to $10 in 1865. This drop was speedily countered by new railroad construction and a heightened movement of settlers westward. But production increased so rapidly that the market became glutted: prices began falling in 1867, and for three years continued downward.[34]

Along with the cyclical variations in price, lumbermen on the Middle Mississippi encountered marked seasonal fluctuations. Every spring upriver sellers raced their lumber rafts to downriver points to skim the cream off the market. One observer in June, 1860, noted that the river was lined with rafts, that the first sales had been made at $10 per thousand board feet, that the asking price was then $8, and that some salesmen expected to dispose of their inventories at no more than $7.[35] Mississippi River lumbermen were almost as much slaves of the market as the farmers who had to dispose of their wheat as soon as it was harvested.

In the circumstances it was not surprising that capital was scarce and costly in lumbering as in other budding industries on the western frontier. The state of Wisconsin realistically made any percentage up to 12 a legal rate of interest.[36] In view of limited funds, the numerous risks, and high interest rates, most sawmill owners on the Middle Mississippi stayed out of the timber market during the 1860's. They had only enough capital to expand the output of lumber at their mills.[37]

By the time Weyerhaeuser and Denkmann formed their partnership, the first fumbling days of midwestern lumbering were over. Many firms had already failed. Newcomers could profit by learning lessons from their predecessors' errors, and they could also profit through the low capitalization of business erected on purchased bankrupt property. The partners took full advantage of both opportunities.

NOTES

1. Thoreau's essays "Ktaadn" and "Chesuncook" record observations on journeys into Maine in 1846 and 1853.
2. One much photographed sequoia log has a center dating from A.D. 923 and was a very large tree at the time of Magna Charta. However, the largest of living sequoias are estimated to be as old as 4,000 years. *Trees: The Yearbook of Agriculture, 1949, passim.*
3. *Ibid.,* 109–14; Smith, *North America,* 630; *Timber Depletion,* Report on Senate Resolution 311, 66th Cong., 3rd Sess., p. 32. As to the forests of the Pacific Northwest, the description given above is based on a detailed report of species logged in various areas made by the Weyerhaeuser Timber Company to the authors, July 11, 1958.
4. Carman, ed., *American Husbandry,* 74–91.
5. *Eighth Census,* 1864, clxix, ff.
6. Carman, 61, 62.
7. Knight was one of a group of American authors writing a volume of careful monographs for the Harper & Brothers Centennial Series, *The First Century of the Republic.*
8. *Ibid.,* 80.
9. See the illustration of such a camp in *Harper's Weekly,* May 7, 1870; also, Everett Dick, *Vanguards of the Frontier,* 390–409.
10. Stephenson, *Recollections,* 86–88; Martin Page, "The Camp in the 50's," Eau Claire *Daily Telegram,* Feb. 24, 1916.
11. Gregory, ed., *West Central Wisconsin History,* I, 109–12.
12. Norton, *Mississippi River Logging Company,* 92.
13. For examples, Gates, *The Wisconsin Pine Lands of Cornell University,* 215 and *passim.*
14. Bureau of the Census, *Statistical Abstract of the United States.*
15. Bureau of the Census, Census of Manufactures: 1905, *Lumber and Timber Products,* 7; Current, *Pine Logs and Politics,* 194; Larson, *White Pine Industry,* 48–50, 105.
16. F. W. Kohlmeyer, "Northern Pine Lumbermen: A Study in Origins and Migrations," *The Journal of Economic History* XVI, No. 4 (Dec., 1956), pp. 529–538; Reynolds, *The Daniel Shaw Lumber Company,* 129–139.
17. Comparisons of tools and techniques used in the East with those in the Middle West are based on data from Wood, *Lumbering in Maine, 1820–1861;* Engberg, "Lumber Industry, 1830–1930"; Fries, *Empire in Pine;* Larson, *White Pine Industry;* Rector,

Log Transportation in Lake States; Reynolds, *The Daniel Shaw Lumber Company;* Stephenson, 82.

18. Rector, 63. See U.S.D.A., Farmer Bulletin No. 1210, *Measuring and Marketing Farm Timber.* As more and more stands away from banks of streams were logged, "bucking" in the woods became a common practice.

19. Rector, 71, quoting McClung, *Minnesota As It Is in 1870,* 145, and Lillard, *The Great Forest,* 92 (quoting Wabasha County *Herald,* April 30, 1862).

20. FW Papers, Notebook, July 20, 24, 1868; FEW Record, 119; Larson, 95; Rector, 154–161.

21. Hotchkiss, *Lumber and Forest Industry in the Northwest,* 614, 654; Gilman, "History of the Development of Sawmilling and Woodworking Machinery," *Miss. Valley Lbrmn.,* XXVI, Feb. 1, 1895, pp. 59–69; Merk, *Economic History of Wisconsin,* 71–72; Disston, *The Saw in History;* Von Tassel, *et al., Mechanization in the Lumber Industry.*

22. FEW Record, 17, 98.

23. Pierce, *History of Chicago,* II, 38, 67, 77, 103–105, 496; Hotchkiss, 437–443, 450–465; Merk, 80–81; *Nwn. Lbrmn.,* XI, Jan. 26, 1878, p. 5; Bartlett Papers, D. C. Clark to Daniel Shaw, June 18, 1865; O. H. Ingram Papers, Ingram & Kennedy receipts to R. R. Cable, Davenport, and to D. F. Robinson, Rock Island, March 24, 1874; Ingram, Kennedy & Co. receipts to Horton & Hamilton, Winona, April 27, 1874; Reynolds, 106–139.

24. See Hotchkiss, Chaps. 29, 32–33, 35–37, 39–40, *passim.*

25. John D. Guthrie, "The History of Great Forest Fires of America," *Crow's Pacific Coast Lumber Digest,* Oct. 31, 1936, p. 15; Merk, 101–104; Fries, 105; Larson, 344–345.

26. Gates, 137–176.

27. Larson, 25; Rector, 308.

28. Gregory, II, 824; FEW Record, 163.

29. Larson, 12; Russell, *A-rafting on the Mississippi,* 73; Rector, 159.

30. Merk, 71–72.

31. *Marinette Eagle,* Feb. 28, Dec. 5, 1891, and Jan. 9, 1892, cited in Kleven, "Wisconsin Lumber Industry," 254.

32. Isaac Crowe Papers, P. C. Ransom to Crowe, June 20, 1860.

33. Hotchkiss, 613.

34. Merk, 61–63; Chicago Board of Trade, *Annual Reports,* cited in Johnson and Reynolds, "Distribution and Marketing." Reynolds, 119–120, says that Daniel Shaw of Eau Claire disposed of lumber along the Mississippi for $7.50 per thousand in 1861, for $20.00 in 1865, for $15.00 in 1867, and $14.00 in February 1868.

35. Isaac Crowe Papers, P. C. Ransom to Crowe, June 22, 1860.

36. Fries, 14.

37. Norton, 92–93.

III

Growth in the Sixties

O N JANUARY 1, 1860, Weyerhaeuser and Denkmann bid in the mill property at the sheriff's sale for $3,859.72 and $6.85 in costs. Their cash outlay for title to the property thus was $2,-466.57—$500 for the mortgage, $1,600 for quit claims, and an additional payment of $366.57 at the sale. The partners invested about $1,-500 in repairs and logs at the start of operations in 1860. Thus, as already noted, the firm began with less than $4,000 expenditure in cash and used only $3,000 in credit, the deferred payment on the mortgage.

The Weyerhaeuser & Denkmann mill carried equipment typical of many small lumber establishments in the Middle West. Powered by steam, the basic units were a muley saw, which squared the logs on the downstroke, and a circular saw for cutting the cants into boards. Shingles and lath were made with hand machines. Estimated capacity ranged from 6,000 to 10,000 board feet per day, though actual production probably did not exceed 1,000,000 feet during the first trying year of operation.[1]

Revenues could come from three primary sources. The Coal Valley yard was the major retail outlet, though sales were also made at the mill to local buyers and to westward-moving settlers. Unless the partners made additional investments, the only other income would be derived from the mill store.

Within ten years the gamble had wholly paid off. Not only had the partners acquired clear title to the mill property on May 15, 1862, but profits also had enabled them to retire the last promissory note held by a creditor. On January 29, 1866, Denkmann had repaid Weyerhaeuser his loan of $1,504.74, plus an equal amount borrowed at the end of the first three years, and then had proceeded to build a new house. Three years later, temporarily driven out of Coal Valley by a scarlet-fever epidemic, Weyerhaeuser had decided to settle permanently in Rock Island with his wife and children. For $11,000 he had purchased a large brick house with twenty acres of orchard, vineyard, ravine, and pasture land. By 1869 the partners were thus out of debt and had clear title to a profitable property, not to mention good credit and substantial homes.[2]

2

Weyerhaeuser & Denkmann's problems and policies were quite characteristic of successful small lumber enterprises on the Mississippi in the sixties. Throughout the early years of the enterprise the firm was definitely a family affair. At first Denkmann bought the logs, either in rafts at Rock Island or on the Black River at Onalaska. He also recruited and trained a mill crew, familiarized himself with the plant machinery, kept it running six days per week during the sawing season, and mastered the intricacies of manufacturing lumber for the current market. Though Weyerhaeuser did the selling, in three or four years he became increasingly absorbed in the problem of procuring logs. For a time Michael Koch, a brother-in-law of Weyerhaeuser, acted as bookkeeper, yard salesman, timekeeper, and paymaster. Michael's eldest son John was the first engineer of the Weyerhaeuser & Denkmann mill, and other relatives of the partners and their wives also worked in the plant or at the Coal Valley yard.[3]

The slight information available on relations with millworkers indicates that the partners followed the prevailing pattern in the industry of the country at the time. Denkmann insisted on "being the boss." He set a furious pace, and expected the men in the mill to follow his lead. On one occasion the workers wanted a holiday on Labor Day. Denkmann refused. Enough men left of their own volition to cause him to shut down the mill. The following morning no whistle blew, and the mill remained closed until the men begged him to open. "Nun habt ihr euer Labor Day," he was heard to say. Though the floor of the building was crowded with machinery unprotected by shields, few accidents were serious enough for report in the local newspapers. On the other hand, Weyerhaeuser and Denkmann, unlike many other employers at the time, "never failed to pay their men in full," usually in cash. Apparently they did not take advantage of the mill store to pay in time checks or in merchandise.

Between 1858, a depression year, and 1865, one characterized by inflation and scarcity of labor, Weyerhaeuser & Denkmann doubled the wages paid. The head sawyers, the most skilled men in any mill, received $1.50 per day in 1858 and $3.00 seven years later. The lowest wage, that of unskilled workers and boys, rose from $0.40 to $0.75 for a twelve-hour day, with an hour off for lunch on some days. "It took my breath to get so much," one man recalled. In 1858 the most common daily wage, received by thirteen workers, was $0.75. In 1865 the amount had risen to $1.75, received by ten in 1865. Meanwhile the total number of laborers had grown only from twenty-six to thirty-one, the new men being employed in the shingle mill. In other words, the sawmill proper employed the same number of men in both years, though the total daily payroll for the twenty-six rose from $23.65 to $43.74, plus the payment for a part-time employee and a bookkeeper-timekeeper.[4]

By refusing to increase his work force, applying his mechanical ingenuity, and making some judicious investments, Denkmann gradually expanded the production of the mill and presumably lowered unit costs. He speeded up the machinery, installed an oscillating muley saw, and by 1862 raised capacity to 20,000 board feet daily, or to about 3,000,000 annually. As funds became available, he added such mechanical equipment as edgers, trimmers, automatic shingle machines, and lath saws. Early in the 1860's he also found a place in the crowded plant for a planing machine, which enabled the firm to finish its lumber as the market required. By the winter of 1867–1868 the partners were able to build an extension at one end of the mill and put in new machinery, almost doubling capacity. "Heretofore," the *Rock Island Daily Union* waggishly reported of Weyerhaeuser & Denkmann, "50 feet was as long a log as they could handle. They are now putting an addition to their mill which will enable them to saw timber long enough, wide enough, and strong enough for a Republican platform."[5]

Eighteen months later, the same newspaper noted that by reinvesting profits and adding to the capacity of the mill year by year, Weyerhaeuser & Denkmann had "one of the best lumbering establishments on the river." The firm counted sixty employees and a mill that was a "perfect wilderness of saws," which had cut, the preceding week, 200,000 feet of lumber, 72,000 lath, and 85,000 shingles. Among the customers was the Union Pacific Railway Company, one of whose orders had been for 950,000 feet of bridge lumber. Anticipating additional demand as soon as a new railroad to Rockford was completed, the partners were planning soon to put in two additional engines of 40 horsepower each, which would in turn require further expansion of the mill. The extensions were expected to raise capacity to at least 8,000,000 feet of lumber a season.

Weyerhaeuser & Denkmann had continued to operate an expanding business throughout the Civil War. As that conflict became more grim, Frederick Weyerhaeuser was prepared to shoulder arms in defense of his new country. "Father fully expected to go along with the others," said his son later; he had indeed been drafted. But his employees urged that he stay so that "the payrolls could be continued as fully as possible," and he hired a substitute, a common practice in the Civil War.

As early as December 1, 1862, the production of the mill had grown until the Coal Valley yard could not handle it, and Weyerhaeuser & Denkmann took out its first wholesaler's license. Through price lists and correspondence, if they followed the practice of the industry, the partners solicited sales throughout western Illinois as far from Rock Island as they could compete with Chicago prices and as far west as Council Bluffs.[6]

3

Until the late 1860's at least, the partners relied on the open market for their supply of logs. They purchased them from raftsmen at Rock Island or from original owners at booms on the Black, the Chippewa, and the St. Croix, the rafts at first being floated downstream to the main river and later towed on contract to Rock Island by steamboats. Though Frederick Weyerhaeuser apparently acquired stumpage (timber but not the land) as early as 1868, the first documented transaction is dated December 14, 1870.

By the middle sixties Weyerhaeuser had already begun to buy logs from dealers and even loggers on the Minnesota and Wisconsin tributaries. His youngest son later believed that he, and possibly Denkmann, went to the Black River to contract with loggers or rafters, and Frederick Weyerhaeuser was "in the woods" in December, 1866, when his mother-in-law died. William Irvine, for years an employee and close associate, remembered that his friend appeared on the Chippewa in 1868, and said that previously Weyerhaeuser & Denkmann had obtained its logs from the Black River and the St. Croix. Fragmentary office records support this assertion. It was a significant experience for him. He was following the logs to their source, working his way up the larger timbered streams by boat or sleigh or afoot, meeting the loggers and the picturesque rivermen, sleeping in river shacks or forest camps, and seeing at firsthand how wooded areas were cruised, how logs were scaled, how trees were felled, and what were the hazards of driving logs down the rivers.

Such knowledge was to have immense practical value. From Weyerhaeuser's expanding acquaintance with these processes, and with buying and selling, he could understand the causes for the alternating gluts and shortages that plagued the millowners farther down the Mississippi. Undoubtedly he considered buying stumpage,[7] noting the risks and the potential high profits. Though he was still a local manufacturer, he was acquiring the facts and experience necessary for operating on a regional scale—an activity he and Denkmann would undertake sooner than they expected.

But of almost equal importance was the effect of the forest on the man. With Weyerhaeuser, it was love at first sight. The noble stands of pine, the rushing rivers, the packed snows of the winter roads, the pure air, the very hardships were a delight. Samuel R. Van Sant once asked Weyerhaeuser why he undertook the grueling activities of the winter, and received the reply, "Captain, I like the woods life."

Not until 1872 did the first entry recording the purchase of timberland appear in one of Weyerhaeuser's notebooks. The partners may well have felt that during the sixties they lacked money for such purchases. However, an even more important consideration may have been that they lacked the information and experience for making sound investments in stumpage.[8]

With the late sixties, the money for such purchases had become available. This fact is reflected in the partners' acquisition of a half-interest in a second sawmill on July 6, 1869, the Rock Island mill of Gray, Cropper & Anawalt. The new lumber plant was capitalized at $16,200, and was called Anawalt, Denkmann & Company. It owned and operated not only a sawmill but also a sash, door, and molding works, which included a planing mill. It sold its products locally but also extended its operations westward, and ultimately delivered lumber in Kansas to the west and Texas to the south. Its gross income for 1870 amounted to $104,350.34, of which $64,636.33 came from lumber sales, and the net earnings for the year were $12,659.30.[9] The expansion of the first mill and the purchase of a half-interest in the second were largely financed by plowing back an unknown percentage of the profits.

Every effort had been made to curtail expenses and increase gains. There had been no structural enlargement of the first mill until 1868, although each year had seen new machinery installed; and even after the size of the building was increased, the workers had little elbow room. Neither partner spent much on clothes or furnishing, and practically nothing for frivolous pleasure. Even their new houses were unostentatious. Debts were collected conscientiously, though on occasion, if family tradition is accurate, insistence on payment was tempered with generosity. The partners kept their eyes focused on the business by means of year-end accounts, as stipulated in their original agreement. Perhaps an element in their success was another provision of the partnership contract that neither partner was to endorse a note of a third person without consent of the other. That clause tended to make investments in outside enterprises a matter for joint action.

As a matter of fact, the record of Weyerhaeuser & Denkmann in ventures outside the lumber business was distinctly spotty during the first ten years of their association. With two partners, Weyerhaeuser made a profit in buying and selling coal lands at Coal Valley, but he and Denkmann, with others, invested and lost $18,000 in a flour mill there. The mill started up on October 1, 1867, just as the local farmers were turning to corn production, and when the grinding of wheat purchased upstream proved unprofitable, the plant was closed. Not quite so unsatisfactory was the investment of $35,000 by Weyerhaeuser & Denkmann and three partners in a woolen mill in Rock Island. Convinced that the managing partner was not able, Weyerhaeuser soon agreed to take some goods and a mortgage for $30,000 on nine houses as payment for his firm's share in the woolen venture. Obviously, the partners were not infallible in judging either business projects or the abilities of the men who conducted them.[10]

4

As the firm had grown, so had the Weyerhaeuser and Denkmann families.

The Weyerhaeusers first resided in the small two-story house in Coal Valley, with a ground area about 16 by 32 feet, which had been built for Frederick by Mead, Smith & Marsh when the firm asked him to move from Rock Island to the smaller town. He still retained the Rock Island house, similar in size, and in 1859 bought the Coal Valley residence for $151. In the first years of the partnership the couple, as already noted, lived there, and Eliza (Elise), Frederick's sister, soon joined them to help with the housework and the babies, now arriving at frequent intervals.

John C. Hill, a friend of the lumberman for many years, gives a vivid picture of the young couple as they sat in the Coal Valley lumberyard office at night. "With the doors all open he and his wife could be seen, she with her sewing, and he with his books and money, covering the day's transactions, entirely oblivious of his inviting robbery or trouble, until some friend advised him to be more careful."

Six Weyerhaeuser children were born in Coal Valley: John Philip, November 4, 1858; Elise, July 15, 1860; Margaret, July 18, 1862; Apollonia, February 14, 1864; Charles, April 2, 1866; and Rudolph, March 11, 1868. The little house was bursting at the seams. Its capacity was further taxed by the guests, employees or business friends, whom Weyerhaeuser casually brought to meals and often to stay overnight. However, by a division of labor that allotted the cooking to Eliza and the housework to Elizabeth, the establishment ran with surprising efficiency.

"Mother" had all but infinite patience, and a winning smile for everyone. Only once, in March, 1868, when Rudolph was a few days old, was she disturbed. A log raft broke away from the booms at Rock Island, and Frederick Weyerhaeuser dashed off to rescue the valuable timbers. His son records that his mother never understood "how Father had the heart to leave her and the newborn baby for a raft of logs." No such episode occurred on November 4, 1872, when their last child, Frederick E., was born in their Rock Island home.

The now prosperous lumberman was proud of his new house and land. About the residence spread broad lawns, from three to four acres

of Concord grapes, and fifteen acres of woodland and farmland which, as
a son recalled later, "fairly duplicated" his father's farm at Niedersaulheim. The family raised vegetables, gathered fruit from the orchard trees,
and kept livestock. From the Concords, wine was also made. To quote the
son again, "Most of the food for the family came from the little farm, but
no effort was made to sell any of the products although the boys were
privileged to sell all the grapes they picked. . . . There were horses,
cows, chickens, pigs, pigeons, and all the other animals common to a small
farm. All kinds of vegetables were raised and corn in quantities sufficient
for the livestock. Once a year the butcher came to kill some of the hogs.
. . . Back of the kitchen was a smoke house for preserving the hams and
there were ample cellars for keeping fruit and vegetables during the
winter."

The Denkmanns had been in Rock Island since the 1850's, and their
family too had expanded. When the partnership began, F. C. A. Denkmann already had two daughters and a son (Marie, Apollonia, and Frederick Carl), the latter about John Weyerhaeuser's age. Later, four more
girls and another son were born (Jacob Edward Philip), not including
children who died in infancy. Edward Denkmann (Jacob Edward Philip)
attended Phillips Andover with Charles Weyerhaeuser, who was a year
older than he. There were fifteen cousins, and they exchanged visits frequently, one favorite spot for play being a deep ravine on the Weyerhaeuser farm where sugar maples, oaks, elms, walnuts, and butternuts
grew, and where the boys dammed the stream for wading and swimming.

Altogether the partners had six sons who might later join them in
their business enterprises. The growth of the families thus meant a potential growth of the business, and as young men these cousins were later
to be associated in work as in play.[11]

5

The firm of Weyerhaeuser & Denkmann was one of a number of
lumber businesses scattered along the Mississippi from southern Minnesota to St. Louis. Most of them carried on comparable activities, serving
their own communities intensively and extending their operations as far
afield as they found practicable. The larger ones had common problems:
the financing of business expansion, fluctuating prices, the meeting of competition from Chicago and St. Louis wholesalers, and the procuring of an
adequate supply of logs.

In the early 1860's each firm went its own way, often competing
vigorously, even bitterly, with one or more of its local fellows. Then they
were alerted to the need for meeting their problems together, particularly
the procurement of logs for their mills.

One of Weyerhaeuser & Denkmann's most enterprising allies was to be Laird, Norton & Co., located at Winona in the southeastern corner of Minnesota. John C. Laird had come to the town in the early 1850's and soon started a lumber business with his brothers, William H. and Matthew J. The firm had been reorganized in 1856 to include two cousins, James Laird Norton and Matthew G. Norton. All five partners had come from the vicinity of Lewisburg, Pennsylvania, and none had any earlier experience in lumbering, although they had engaged in various mechanical and business pursuits. During the 1860's John C. and Matthew J. Laird left the partnership. The three who remained were all relatively young, James Laird Norton having been born in 1825, Matthew G. in 1831, and William Harris Laird in 1833. All were deeply religious, the Lairds Congregationalists and the Nortons Methodists. To a steamboat captain Matthew G. Norton later wrote a sharp rebuke for working on a Sunday. "We regard that day as given us for other purposes, and that six days in the week are all sufficient for work and business; if we cannot get along on that basis, we prefer not to go at all."

The Laird, Norton firm began under handicaps and grew slowly. Geographically, its situation was excellent, for immediately to the west lay the rapidly populating region of Minnesota, while the best log sources were close at hand—the St. Croix River and the chief tributaries of the Mississippi in Wisconsin. Laird and the Nortons could also ship lumber cheaply downriver. However, they bought a large log supply at high prices early in 1857 and during the panic almost went bankrupt. Escaping this economic hazard, they ultimately prospered. Judicious in the shaping of long-term policies, frugal but prepared to try bold experiments, they developed an enterprising, dependable business. Their sawmill, built in 1857, was enlarged, then supplemented in 1868 by a planing mill. By 1870 they had a capacity of 12,000,000 board feet a year and were buying pinelands; they had established the first of a chain of retail branch yards in 1864.

In Winona, E. S. and A. B. Youmans had also founded a flourishing firm, which competed briskly with Laird, Norton & Co. By the early 1870's their plant produced 9,000,000 feet a year, operating with two circular saws, a gang, an edger, a slab saw, and a shingle and lath mill.[12]

Lyons, Iowa, lay some 180 miles south of Winona, and might be termed the northern limit of the Iowa-Illinois region where lay most of the establishments on the Middle Mississippi. Travelers on a lumber raft descending the river, with Iowa to the west, Illinois to the east, would come first to Lyons, then a few miles south to Clinton, Iowa, then thirty miles farther on to Moline, Illinois. Not ten miles to the southwest the raft would pass Rock Island on the Illinois shore and Davenport exactly opposite in Iowa. Another thirty miles in the same direction it would reach Muscatine, Iowa, where lay the last of the plants here considered.

In Lyons, David Joyce, originally from Massachusetts, had leased a sawmill in 1861. With S. I. Smith (Joyce & Smith was the firm name) he had developed the mill to a daily capacity of 50,000 board feet and was later to extend his lumber investments into the South and to the Far West.[13]

In Clinton, Chancy Lamb and his son Artemus had established the firm of C. Lamb & Son, later to become "Sons" when the younger Lafayette ("Lafe") Lamb joined it. The older Lamb was a man of unusual skill and vigor. He had been a wagonmaker and millwright and had built and operated sawmills in New York, Pennsylvania, and Illinois. By the middle sixties he had erected two mills of his own in Clinton and had acquired a three-quarter interest in a third—Lamb, Byng & Company. His was a keen mechanical mind; he was credited with having invented an edger with movable saws, a machine for trimming logs to any desired length, and a friction log turner ("nigger") which, however, he soon learned had been patented by another. Lamb was among the first to use a bull chain for pulling logs out of water, and one of the pioneers in assembling a fleet of steamboats to bring rafts of logs down the river. But his business acumen matched his mechanical ingenuity, making him a director of five banks and later a responsible leader among the mill-owners. Both his sons were able and popular men, Artemus in particular showing a vision, resourcefulness, and judgment that endeared him to Frederick Weyerhaeuser.[14]

The Lambs, for all their abilities, found in W. J. Young, also of Clinton, a formidable competitor. A strong-minded, vividly articulate Ulster Irishman, born in 1827, he was capable of holding his own against any rival. He had come to the United States when nineteen and chosen Clinton as a suitable site for a mill that he transported from La Crosse, Wisconsin. He made it pay from its establishment in 1859 and soon bought out his early partners, but later took in John McGraw of Ithaca, New York, who was a member of a timber-investment firm. W. J. Young & Company grew steadily. Young rebuilt the first mill in 1860 and six years later erected a second, "the largest mill in the world." With a muley, a large circular, and six gang saws, this plant alone could produce 50,000,000 feet of lumber annually, 20,000,000 shingles, and 15,000,000 lath.

Young had prodigious physical strength and a fiery independence of spirit. Once in a fit of rage he threw one of his sons down a stairway and almost killed him. As an individualist he was a twin to Chancy Lamb, who told Frederick Weyerhaeuser apropos of a plan to introduce common practices in manufacturing and selling: "Mr. Weyerhaeuser, do you propose to come into my mill and tell me how to make lumber, and into my office and tell me how to sell it? You might just as well know right now that hell will freeze over first." But both Lamb and Young were usually delightful associates, and both were to work with other millowners for the common good of the group.[15]

At Moline, Illinois, the mill of Dimock, Gould & Company gave Weyerhaeuser & Denkmann plants active competition along rail lines east and west. John M. Gould, born in New Hampshire, had formed a partnership with D. C. Dimock; then in 1868 Gould had joined Charles R. Ainsworth, a Vermonter, in organizing a $150,000 corporation.[16]

Weyerhaeuser & Denkmann also met competition from another Rock Islander, New York–born Jerome S. Keator and his partner W. J. H. Wilson. Keator had eastern financial backing that enabled him to buy stumpage on the Black River at bargain prices. He thus became one of the first manufacturers on the Middle Mississippi to invest in standing timber, and his example could not have been without influence on Weyerhaeuser & Denkmann. He owned two mills, one in Moline and another in Rock Island.[17]

Across the river from Rock Island, in Davenport, a number of substantial lumber firms were located, that most immediately important being Schricker & Mueller, a partnership founded in 1868. Schricker for a brief period was to be the nominal leader of the Middle Mississippi group.[18]

Preeminent among the firms in Muscatine was the wholesale-retail house of Richard Musser & Company, previously known as Hoch & Musser. Emigrants from Lancaster County, Pennsylvania, Peter (born 1826) and Richard Musser (born 1819) were partners until 1864, when Peter M. Musser (born 1841) a nephew, entered the firm. Richard managed the Muscatine yard of the company, and Peter and Peter M. successively a second one established at Iowa City in 1856. Of mingled English, Scottish, German, and Swiss ancestry, the Mussers were Methodists, and active in community affairs. Stern circumstances in their younger days made them extremely thrifty; they "always had a bone buried in the back yard." That habit, together with shrewd planning and carefully weighed decisions, undoubtedly enabled them to finance the building of their first sawmill in the winter of 1870–1871.[19] They were to be close collaborators and friends of Frederick Weyerhaeuser, and descendants have continued the association to the present day.

A second important firm in Muscatine was that of Benjamin Hershey, who had migrated from Pennsylvania in 1851, rented a mill, which he later bought, and in 1857 on the same site had built a new one costing $70,000. Hershey had "remarkable force of character, sagacity, and foresight." Reportedly the first sawmiller on the Mississippi to speed production by the use of gang saws, he experienced the usual difficulties of the innovator in turning out a satisfactory product.[20]

Thus the firms on the Middle Mississippi were captained by men of varied background—from New England, the Middle Atlantic States, Ireland, Germany. They showed differing abilities, whether in mechanical fields, in merchandising, or in planning. All had steadily increased the capacities of their mills and were enlarging their areas of operation. But as they grew in strength and competed increasingly with each other, they faced a common problem: a dependable supply of logs. The chief source of supply was rapidly becoming the Chippewa River region in Wisconsin, and during the late 1860's various incidents were interfering with steady deliveries from that stream. As a result, the millowners on the Middle Mississippi were forced to consider joint action.

NOTES

1. Hotchkiss, *Lumber and Forest Industry,* 607; FEW Record, 89, 98; Hauberg, *Weyerhaeuser & Denkmann,* 35, 52; *Amer. Lbrmn.,* Feb. 24, 1900; *American Lumbermen,* II, 100; FEW Record. FEW states that the capacity of the mill was 8,000 to 10,000 ft. daily, while Hotchkiss and the *Amer. Lbrmn.* agreed on 6,000 ft. as the figure. The book, *American Lumbermen,* and the FEW Record set the annual output as 3,000,000 ft., a figure dating from 1862.

2. Hauberg, *op. cit.,* 36, 48; FEW Record, 22, 37, 43, 56–57. Weyerhaeuser's new home was at 3052 Lee Street, later renamed Tenth Avenue on a hill in Rock Island.

3. Hauberg, *op. cit.,* 50, 58–59; FEW Record, 87–89. Michael Koch and the two partners came to a parting of the ways shortly after Koch was elected an alderman of Rock Island. At a meeting of that board he voted that fire engines should have freedom of access to the river, even though lumber of Weyerhaeuser & Denkmann would have to be cleared away. As the story goes, Weyerhaeuser thought Koch should have thought first of his employers' business.

4. Hauberg, *op. cit.,* 51–53; FEW Record, 87–89; FW Papers, FW time book, 1858–1865. The titles of the various jobs were not given.

5. FEW Record, 98; Hauberg, *op. cit.,* 52, 58; *Rock Island Daily Union,* Jan. 16, 1868.

6. *Rock Island Daily Union,* Aug. 12, 1869, in Hauberg, *op. cit.,* 53, 64; FEW Record, 39–40, 43.

7. Charles A. Weyerhaeuser, the original Frederick's son, stated that his father was first advised to buy timberland instead of logs by L. E. Torinus, a lumberman in Stillwater, Minn. (letter of F. K. Weyerhaeuser to the authors, June 11, 1958).

8. Hotchkiss, 607; Lillard, *Great Forest,* 198; FW Notebooks; FEW Record, 117–126, 145–146, 163, 157; *American Lumbermen,* II, 103. Lillard gives the Upper Chippewa as the area of Weyerhaeuser's first purchase of timber, and says that he began by buying "standing timber" in 1864, but there is no documentation for the statement. Hotchkiss gives the same date. *American Lumbermen* sets the initial purchases in 1868. Weyerhaeuser & Denkmann did not own a steamboat until 1874.

9. Hauberg, *op. cit.,* 69–72; *Rock Island Daily Union,* Half Century Edition; *Rock Island Argus,* April 29, 1941; FEW Papers, 1870 statement labeled, "This seems to be Anawalt, Denkmann Co."; and J. H. Hauberg to FEW, Feb. 15, 1934.

10. FEW Record, 21–22, 45, 98; Hauberg, *Weyerhaeuser & Denkmann,* 42–44, 67–68. One episode sheds an amusing light on the way in which creditors were handled. "What's the cow doing here?" Denkmann asked one day as he noticed the animal tied to a hitching post in front of the main office. "That's the only way we can get anything on that bill," replied the collector. "Well, take her back," said Denkmann. "We won't go that far." As to the nine houses, these were retained by Weyerhaeuser & Denkmann and its successor corporation until 1918, when they were donated to the local YWCA, which tore them down when repair bills became exorbitantly high.

11. FEW Record, 41–43, 51, 55–56; Weyerhaeuser Papers, "Denkmann Family Tree."

12. Hotchkiss, 464–469; Davis and Davis, *Timber Roots* (dealing with Laird, Norton in play form); *American Lumbermen,* II, 13–20; LN Papers, Laird, Norton to D. Shaw, Jan. 14, June 20, 1869, and memo dated Feb. 10, 1869.

13. Hotchkiss, 594, 605; *American Lumbermen,* III, 165–168.

14. *American Lumbermen,* I, 21–28; 53–56; *Miss. Val. Lbrmn.,* XXVIII, July 16, 1897; Hotchkiss, 590–593, FEW Record, 209, 211. O. H. Ingram of Eau Claire (*Autobiography,* 36) states that he invented an edger, apparently in 1853, which seems to have been similar to, and perhaps earlier than, that devised by Lamb.

15. Hotchkiss, 588–590; FEW Record, 155–156; G. W. Sieber, "Sawmilling on the Mississippi: The W. J. Young Lumber Company," unpublished dissertation, University of Iowa, Chap. 1.

16. Hotchkiss, 611–613; Wickstrom and Ainsworth, *Always Lumber.*

17. *American Lumbermen,* I, 231–234; Hotchkiss, 608, 613.

18. Hotchkiss, 600–605; *Miss. Val. Lbrmn.,* XXXI, Sept. 14, 1900, p. 1; *American Lumbermen,* II, 65–68.

19. RDM Papers, "Extracts from Recollections of J. P. Walton, published by Muscatine *Saturday Mail,* and . . . in book form in 1899"; "A few Facts Selected From the Life Work of Mr. Peter Musser, completed Feb. 22, 1906, when 80 years old"; extracts from *History of Muscatine County, Iowa* (1911); obituary pamphlet on Peter Musser; *Miss. Val. Lbrmn.,* XXXI, July 6, 1900; Interview with J. C. Patience; Hotchkiss, 617–619. Peter M. Musser bought out Peter Musser's interest in the partnership in 1864, but Peter returned to the firm in 1870.

20. Hotchkiss, 614, 619–620.

IV

Conflict on the Chippewa

THE FIRST YEARS following the Civil War saw a rapid expansion of settlement and industry throughout the Middle West, with soldiers returning from the war and immigrants from Europe pushing westward across the plains. Lumber prices soared even above the peak of the most profitable war years. "Never had the ax and saw found such busy and profitable employment," writes a chronicler of the industry. The effect upon both the forest areas of the Lake States and the millowners on the Mississippi who depended upon them was dramatic. To understand it, a brief glance at the chief pine-bearing areas to the north is essential.

The Mississippi winds down from its source in central Minnesota across that state to its southeastern corner. The upper reaches of that river tapped numerous pine forests, but they did not feel the woodman's ax extensively until the last two decades of the century. In the middle 1860's the first timbered valley intensively logged was that of the Rum River, which flows down from the north to join the Mississippi a little above the Falls of St. Anthony (Minneapolis). Farther downstream the St. Croix empties into the great river. It drained a rich white pine country rapidly being logged after 1870. A raft floating southward from that point would pass in succession the mouths of three more rivers notable for their pine-dark basins—the Chippewa, the Black, and the Wisconsin. It was from the St. Croix and these last three streams that the millowners of Illinois and Iowa had chiefly drawn their logs.

The prosperous postwar period marked the growth on all these rivers not only of logging activity but of manufacturing. Mills had been built on them since the 1840's and had steadily grown in number and size. By 1866 every log that came down the Upper Mississippi (for some logging was done there) or the Rum was taken by the thirteen plants near the Falls of St. Anthony. At or near Stillwater on the St. Croix nine commercial mills were making lumber; on the Chippewa and its chief tributary the Menomonie, seventeen; on the Black, at least eight; on the Wisconsin, approximately twenty.

The output of these units on the Mississippi and its tributaries, swelling year by year, mounted to an impressive volume by the late sixties. The grand total without question exceeded 600,000,000 board feet annually. A part of this amount went to communities in southern and western Minnesota or was consumed locally, but many rafts went down the Mississippi to help meet the strong demand for lumber in the flourishing central Middle West. This upriver lumber thus came increasingly into competition with the product of the Illinois and Iowa mills. Several firms on the St. Croix and the Chippewa had also special contractual relationship with or had acquired part interests in wholesale-retail yards in towns like Quincy, Hannibal, Burlington, and Dubuque.

What was of greater importance, most of these mills in the pine areas owned extensive stumpage near the rivers on which they operated. Large stands of white pine on the St. Croix were held by Stillwater firms; the Wisconsin River timberlands had been almost entirely acquired by plants on that river; and a similar situation was developing on the Black. Mill-owners on the Menomonie had acquired considerable stumpage, and those on the Chippewa, although their holdings were smaller, also possessed extensive timberland. Many operators on the chief white pine rivers partially owned or controlled wholesale-retail yards and had built up timber reserves, thus functioning on three levels where most of the Mississippi lumbermen were active on only two—milling and wholesaling.[1]

While the mills on such rivers were thus becoming vigorous competitors in the markets of the Central States, the Mississippi plants south of Minnesota faced an even sharper challenge from Chicago wholesalers. Their shipments of lumber had risen steadily, and by 1870 would reach 583,491,000 feet, much of which went to consignees west of the Mississippi. As if they had opened so many gates into the rapidly growing Middle West, the railroads were providing transportation for the Chicago dealers into hundreds of communities where the mills of Rock Island, Davenport, and Muscatine had previously fought chiefly with one another.[2]

The double competition was keenly felt by members of the Middle Mississippi group, especially when prices began to fall after 1867. But their chief concern was their supply of logs, the veritable lifeblood of sawmilling. Without an adequate supply of logs they would lose much of the expanding market to their rivals by default. Moreover, as noted, all had been enlarging their existing plants or building or acquiring new

ones, and to ensure economy of operation the log supply must not only
be maintained but increased. Logs were still obtainable on the Black and
the St. Croix, and some shipments had come down from the Chippewa.
But what of the future? The answer lay in long-term arrangements with
logging contractors in the pine regions and, most important, in the acquisition of stumpage. Yet while the individual Mississippi firms were ready
to pursue such measures, on the very streams where they must seek their
raw material, logs and standing timber were both being snapped up by the
local mills. In other words, their competitors were taking from them the
means of meeting competition!

Frederick Weyerhaeuser was on the St. Croix in 1866 and 1867, and
in at least one of these two years visited the Black. On both he perceived
the discouraging outlook for the future. Indeed, writes his son, "At an
early date he was told . . . that the supply of timber on the Black would
soon be exhausted and that he would better go on to the Chippewa for a
permanent supply." As for the Wisconsin River, its stumpage was staked
out; moreover, as F. E. Weyerhaeuser writes, "It was a difficult river to
drive, and did not contribute greatly to the log supply of the lower
[Mississippi] river operators."

Others among the Mississippi millmen perceived the dismal prospect;
for example, Laird and the Nortons were thoroughly familiar with conditions on the St. Croix and Chippewa. Still, the idea of taking common
action for their needs grew slowly in the group. Some were long-standing
competitors—W. J. Young with the Lambs, for example, Benjamin Her-
sey with the Mussers, Keator & Wilson with Weyerhaeuser & Denkmann.
"Many members of the Mississippi valley group were ready to fight one
another upon the slightest pretext," wrote Frederick Weyerhaeuser's son.
"There was little if any spirit of cooperation." Nonetheless they had a
common need and, although they did not yet know it, in Frederick Weyerhaeuser a man of resolute energy who was convinced of its importance.
He had been told to go to the Chippewa, and in 1868 he did so, with
Lorenzo Schricker of Davenport, Iowa.[3]

2

The Chippewa is a rapid river of picturesque beauty, deep enough
in its lower reaches for steamboats but interrupted some sixty miles above
its mouth by cascades that give the city of Chippewa Falls its name, and
at two points constricted by rock cliffs into a narrow channel, the upper
and lower Dells. At Eau Claire, where a tributary of that name joins it,
the main stream broadens to make, as the first lumbermen to arrive in the
valley perceived, an admirable site for sawmill activities.

With its tributaries—the Menomonie, the Eau Claire, the Jump, the

Flambeau, and the Court Oreilles—the Chippewa covers a broad basin of gentle slopes, with numerous small lakes. Along its shores and those of the streams feeding into it towered lordly stands of white pine, in many places interspersed with Norway (or red) pine and with birch and hemlock. In the 1860's the rushing waters and thickly forested slopes, with their deer, bear, porcupines, and wolverines gave the country an air of wildness. Its great natural resources had been recognized in the 1840's, when a few sawmills were erected on its shores. Twenty years later townships had been surveyed, the little settlements of Eau Claire and Chippewa Falls established, and logging operations had bitten into the wilderness both on the Chippewa and on the Menomonie.

Frozen in winter, with spring the river often rose in destructive floods. Despite these catastrophes, the falls, the winter ice, and other channel obstructions, it offered as many advantages for logging as any stream in the Lake States region. "The Chippewa valley might be called a logger's paradise," says F. E. Weyerhaeuser, "a very large part of its area being heavily forested with the finest quality of white pine timber, while rivers, streams, and lakes offered a network of excellent transportation facilities."

Actually, the Chippewa was the largest of all the pine-bearing tributaries of the Mississippi. According to one expert estimate, the river drained 34.1 percent of northern Wisconsin, the timber area of the state. The Wisconsin River drained 21 percent of the same region, the St. Croix 13.7 percent, and the Black only 6.8 percent. In addition, the Chippewa's original timber stands far exceeded those of these other rivers—an estimated 46.6 billion board feet. Although the Wisconsin had once carried 30 billion, by 1868 a larger portion of this had been cut. The St. Croix (originally 12.5 billion) and the Black (9 billion) had also lost a large proportion of their pine.[4]

For Weyerhaeuser and Schricker in 1868–1869, the Chippewa offered another important advantage: relatively little of the stumpage in its basin was under the control of millowners. It was held either by the federal government, which was still selling sections and quarter-sections to anyone making locations, or by institutions, railroads, or individuals. For example, by 1867 Cornell University had acquired a domain of 499,126 acres, and investors like Francis Palms of Detroit, Moses M. Davis of Appleton, and James Jenkins of Oshkosh also possessed immense tracts. Although some of the Cornell lands had already been resold, most large owners had been in no hurry to dispose of their timberlands. Like strategically situated plots in a growing city, they were almost sure to increase greatly in value.[5]

Frederick Weyerhaeuser and Lorenzo Schricker must have spent only a short time on the Chippewa before realizing that they had struck a bonanza. The extent and quality of the basin's timber could not have failed to surpass their most fantastic hopes. At the same time they were quickly made aware that they might face formidable difficulties in acquiring stumpage and bringing out logs. For while the local millowners possessed only modest amounts of pineland, they nevertheless expected to log and manufacture the greater part of the vast forest lying around them.

Nor did the Chippewa men lack resources to justify such ambitions. On the Menomonie, the firm of Knapp, Stout maintained three mills that were producing double the volume of the plants of W. J. Young & Company, largest of the Mississippi River firms. At Eau Claire, the Eau Claire Lumber Company was a well-organized and powerful establishment, while Ingram, Kennedy & Company and the Daniel Shaw Lumber Company were prosperous firms. At Chippewa Falls, from its organization in 1869, the Union Lumber Company with its "Big Mill" was the dominant concern, owning timberlands, dams, and logging outfits in addition to its impressive manufacturing facilities.

Some years earlier this group of mills, with other Wisconsin plants, had been strong enough to check federal prosecutions for the illegal cutting of timber on government lands and to force the dismissal of John W. Wilson, the Commissioner of the General Land Office, who had taken measures to protect the nation's property. When Cornell University and the various investors previously noted had purchased their extensive holdings, the Chippewa millmen had screamed at "absentee capitalists seeking to wrest control of the government pine lands from them." Now, on the first appearance of the Mississippi River lumbermen, they muttered ominously of "invaders," and asserted that Chippewa logs should be converted into lumber in the valley where they were cut, and not "stolen" by "aliens" to provide jobs in Illinois and Iowa that would otherwise be available to Wisconsin workers.

But fortunately for Weyerhaeuser and the firms soon to be associated with him, the loggers and large timber owners on the Chippewa, who had already sent some of their cuts downstream to consignees on the Mississippi, were prepared to welcome outsiders who would bid for their products and lands. The conflict of interest between them and the mills had already sharpened before Weyerhaeuser and Schricker appeared. The loggers, who often had stumpage to cut and certainly services to sell, and the owners of great tracts of pine, who wanted to sell at a good price, both vehemently rejected the idea that the local mills should be their only customers. For, as T. E. Randall, a partisan of the plants, was later to write, "while the mills on the Chippewa were the only purchasers of logs, they [the loggers and owner] saw themselves completely at the mercy of a dozen or twenty monopolists."[6]

Actually, the Chippewa millowners were not seeking a monopoly.

They simply felt, with sound business instinct, that too many outsiders bidding for logs might push the price up; or, on the other hand, that a continuous sale in volume to the Mississippi River mills might produce competition and lower the price of lumber. Either or both could squeeze their profits uncomfortably. In addition, more logs on the Chippewa meant more work in sorting for every mill along the river.

Naturally, the timber owners and loggers hardly sympathized with such considerations: they merely wanted a better market for their logs. The owners had greater resources than the loggers for taking some action that would keep the basin open to outside customers. They had been considering such action before Weyerhaeuser and Schricker arrived. The timber owners needed a site on the river for collecting logs and rafting them for delivery to mills on the Mississippi, and such a site existed near the mouth of the Chippewa in a body of water called Beef Slough.

3

"When I first came on the Mississippi River," writes an oldtime raftsman, "Beef Slough was the main channel of the river, and the Beef Slough bar was for many years a noted obstacle to boats and rafts. The way this place got its name [is as follows]: a government boat loaded with beef cattle for the soldiers at Fort Snelling, Minnesota, could not get over the bar. The cattle were unloaded, and the boat went on. The incident gave this place the name of Beef Slough."

Actually, the slough was not a part of the Mississippi, but a branch of the Chippewa—a second outlet for that river. Some dozen miles above the point where it reached the Mississippi, the Chippewa split, the main stream flowing almost due south but a minor portion of it edging southeastward to form a body of water, with no visible current, eventually meandering into the great river.

The slough was ideal as a site for collecting and processing logs. It could be prepared for use with relatively little effort and expense. As the seasoned river pilot Walter A. Blair later wrote, "By dredging and digging at its head, and removing obstacles in its course, the diversion [of water from the Chippewa] was much increased into this slough, and then a long, heavy sheer boom placed diagonally across the Chippewa, not only turned all the logs into Beef Slough but greatly accelerated the current and gave good water to work on." The increased current would also take log rafts out of the slough at the farther end into the Mississippi when this was desired. Of course, booms and sorting works would have to be constructed, but the builders could make a service charge that would ensure a profitable operation.

The Chippewa millmen were aware of the strategic value of the slough, and before their opponents acted, they moved to block any attempt to use the channel against their interests. By mid-April 1866 the partners of the Knapp, Stout firm had acquired title to key plots of land at the entrance to the slough. Meanwhile J. G. Thorp, Thaddeus Pound, and other Wisconsin millowners pushed acts through the Wisconsin legislature empowering certain individuals to erect booms and dams for converting the slough into a sorting and rafting area and giving the Chippewa River Improvement Company, a corporation controlled by them, a franchise to clear the river of snags and sandbars and construct dams "for the better driving of logs, the running of lumber and the better navigation" of the stream.

In effect, the Chippewa millowners had locked the door to the slough and pocketed the key. If the place were ever to be used as a collecting and sorting area, they would control it, sending down whatever logs of their own they might desire to sell and dictating the terms on which loggers and timber owners might send any of theirs. Apparently they never intended to use the slough at all.[7]

Meanwhile an event of strategic benefit to the timber owners occurred. The legislative act which had established the slough as a possible sorting and rafting area had designated one James H. Bacon of Ypsilanti, Michigan, as among those empowered to improve it; and Bacon, a partner of Francis Palms, quickly ranged himself with the timberland owners. Late in 1866, with Elijah Swift and Timothy Crane, he made a survey of the slough and reported to Palms and the others that the area was entirely suitable for their sorting and rafting project.

Palms and his associates obviously felt that through Bacon they could claim a legal right to develop the slough and that with this done they could win a charter for driving logs on the river. The Chippewa River Improvement Company, the dummy firm set up by the lumbermen, showed no signs of exercising the rights it had won, and the legislature might be persuaded to cancel its franchise and grant one to Palms and his associates.

At any rate, on April 27, 1867, the latter groups formed the Beef Slough Manufacturing, Booming, Log Driving & Transportation Company, a Wisconsin corporation located at Alma, just below the outlet of the slough. Bacon, Davis, Jenkins, Palms, Crane, and Swift were the incorporators, together with four businessmen of the slough area. The company was capitalized at $100,000 and was empowered to manufacture wood products as well as to collect and sort logs. It was authorized to employs boats and barges on both the Chippewa and the Mississippi.[8]

The new firm's stockholders moved at once. They appointed Crane superintendent and directed him to begin improving the slough. At the same time, they sought from the legislature a franchise to use it. Moses M. Davis, a state senator, seems to have been confident of success. But the millowners, represented in the legislature by Thorp and Pound, blocked him both in 1867 and 1868. However, in the later year, by "a sly maneuver," he at least established Bacon's authority to improve the slough. By inserting a rider in a routine power-company bill, he wrote into the state law a provision that whenever rights or privileges had been accorded *to a group of separately enumerated persons,* they could be exercised by *any of the individuals so designated.*

Thus fully empowered to act, Bacon transferred his rights to the Beef Slough Company. At once the millowners sealed the entrance to the slough with a raft of slabs and logs. The Beef Slough Company applied for an injunction against such obstructions, and meanwhile tore the raft out. During the winter it had contracted for 50,000,000 board feet of logs to be cut on the Upper Chippewa, and now began to drive these downstream with a crew of 125 men, led by Big John and Black Dan McDonald, two of the best drivers on the river.[9]

It will be recalled that during the winter the loggers "banked" their logs at the edge of a convenient lake or stream and in spring got them into the rising water. Each bore a mark indicating ownership by some mill or contractor farther down the river. Often one company had the responsibility for driving and sorting all logs on a river, and it then policed all consignments of logs. On the Chippewa no firm took this role, a fact which explains why, with its first big installment of logs, the Beef Slough Company sent a crew of experienced rivermen.

Each mill in theory caught its own logs and diverted them behind its boom or booms. If it found other logs with them, these were culled out and sent downstream. Usually, in order to get its own consignments, a mill caught all the logs approaching it and "sorted" them at a works behind its booms. This took time, and the more mills on a stream, the more delay there might be for those at the far end of a drive, while a sudden glut of logs and a jam might hold everything up for days or even weeks.

In order to catch downcoming logs, a boom was extended into the river, broad enough for a man to walk on and so placed as to let through boats and logs. At some mills fins or rudders could be manipulated to use the force of the current to swing the boom to one side, though most booms were stationary.[10]

As the Beef Slough Company's crew of 125 men took its logs downstream in the spring of 1868, they were met at Jim Falls by another crew acting for the Chippewa Falls millowners, who proposed to stop the drive and sort the logs. After some brawling had resulted in numerous injuries, the two McDonalds got their logs past, but at Eau Claire faced two hundred men who again proposed to hold them. Open battle was averted, the

Beef Slough men cut some of the booms, and many of the logs went on down to the slough. On the Menomonie, the Beef Slough men collided with the employees of Knapp, Stout. The manager of that organization was thrown into the river by Palms's drivers, but a parley ensued, and by employing extra sorting crews, the company sped the logs on their way. After this episode there was never any significant trouble in connection with drives on this stream. However, only 12,000,000 board feet of logs out of 50,000,000 contracted for came down to the slough in 1868.[11]

By this time the Beef Slough Company had established a working relationship with the Illinois and Iowa mills. Its officials dealt with individual firms; separate sales were made to the Lambs and the Mussers. Weyerhaeuser and Schricker also bought logs for their respective firms, and in 1869 were acting together. Beef Slough Company correspondence with Weyerhaeuser & Denkmann for that year shows that the Alma company delivered 3,278,783 feet of logs to "your pilot."

The Mississippi River firms, encouraged by the deliveries they obtained, also began buying timberland. Laird, Norton acquired its first pine lands on the Chippewa in 1868 and continued from time to time to buy additional timber. W. J. Young & Company, through John McGraw, a silent partner, participated with Philetus Sawyer of Oshkosh, Knapp, Stout & Company, and others in the purchase of 247,680 acres on the Chippewa originally allotted to railroads. Weyerhaeuser and Schricker also bought logs in 1868.[12]

Thus the Mississippi River firms were being drawn into the conflict on the Chippewa, hitherto wholly local. They were able to buy logs on the Black and the St. Croix as well as on the Chippewa, and had met their expanding needs. But clearly they must consolidate their position on the Chippewa, and Weyerhaeuser must have realized that unless the Beef Slough Company could get its logs down the river, they could not count on deliveries. He may have been encouraged when in 1869, despite a notable logjam, the footage of logs processed at the slough rose to 26,000,000.

Meanwhile, the Beef Slough Company, struggling still to acquire its franchise for operations on the river, found the prospect favorable. The Chippewa Falls and Eau Claire mill groups were at odds over the construction of a dam at the Dells. Finally, Eau Claire men threw their support behind the bill for the Beef Slough Company's franchise, and this was won in March, 1870. A new statute, repealing all previous conflicting laws, authorized the development of the slough, with proper safeguards against undue diversion of the river water and obstruction to navigation, and granted the right, and fixed charges, to drive logs on the Chippewa, to boom, sort, and raft them in the slough, and deliver them to customers at the far end.[13] It is probable that the Eau Claire group did not realize the scale of the undertaking that would now be launched, for they soon renewed their opposition to the idea of sending millions of logs to the Mississippi River firms.

But unfortunately the long struggle for a legal status and the expense of operations on the river had strained the resources of Palms and his associates. Now nature dealt them a final blow. Scarcely had the coveted franchise been obtained when the Chippewa rose in the most disastrous flood in the memory of lumbermen, swept away the boom of the Union Lumber Company at Chippewa Falls, and piled a confused mass of logs into those of the Eau Claire mills. Sorting proceeded with painful slowness, and of 54,000,000 feet of logs launched for downriver sale, only 10,000,000 came down to the slough to be processed for sale to the Mississippi River firms. In three years the Beef Slough Company had received only 48,000,000 feet of logs on which it could levy the tolls and fees so essential to its existence.

As a result, the company was bankrupt in fact if not in name. Palms was quoted to the effect that he had sunk in the company $20,000 for shares and $100,000 for loans, and intended to invest no more. His associates were quite as unwilling to send good money after bad. They had recently felt obliged to dismiss their superintendent for mismanagement, and were soon to file a suit against him in the Circuit Court.[14]

For the Mississippi River firms the situation had its desperate aspects. They had been prospering, had expanded their plants, and the Chippewa basin seemed to hold the key to greater expansion and prosperity. Economically, the Middle West was flourishing. In 1850 the North Central States had supported only 5,500,000 people; they now counted 13,000,-000. The supply of lumber had kept pace with the population, the 5,300,000,000 board feet produced in 1849 rising to 13,000,000,000 in 1869. Weyerhaeuser and his associates were bound to ride the crest of increasing demand to further prosperity if they could be sure of raw materials they required. On the other hand, the collapse of the Beef Slough Company would shut them from their most promising supply of logs. "It was apparent," wrote Matthew G. Norton in recounting the situation, "that even a fair proportion of them [the logs] could not be got through the boom for several years; and for a millman to have his capital tied up for that length of time meant certain ruin and disaster."

But Frederick Weyerhaeuser had different ideas. "Mr. Weyerhaeuser," says Norton, "was not inclined to give up an undertaking which seemed to him to have great merit and with great foresight and determination decided on a new course; so that when the Beef Slough partners were inclined to abandon the enterprise, he with Mr. Schricker and Mr. Elijah Swift leased the boom . . . to see whether they could put new life into the project."

The lease was taken on November 1, 1870, for five years. It was not the best of leases, for under it the profits of the company were to be devoted to paying off the creditors—Palms, Jenkins, and others—until these were satisfied, and a limit of $5,000 was put upon improvements at the slough. However, Weyerhaeuser and Schricker were prepared to go ahead with what they would get. They jointly purchased 840 acres of stumpage in Chippewa County from Jenkins on December 14, 1870, an expression of their confidence in the new venture.[15]

Obviously the two men would not have taken this important step for themselves alone. They must have been assured of support from the Mississippi River firms as well as from the timberland owners. Clear documentation is lacking, but F. E. Weyerhaeuser states that the former were "then in process of organization," and jottings in his father's notebook—a list of plants on whose support he apparently felt he could count—indicate that plans for a union were being made by the fall of 1870. Norton also speaks of continued conferences with lumbermen "between Beef Slough and St. Louis," saying that "nearly all the most substantial manufacturers in the long stretch of territory were brought in." He indicates that this occurred after the lease was taken, but the time span for such work would then have been very brief, and it is more probable that taking the lease was an act calculated to force a decision by many firms already considering cooperative action.

A union of the Mississippi firms was effected at a conference held in Chicago on December 28 and 29, 1870, less than two months after the signing of the Beef Slough lease. It was of course the merest common sense and self-interest. Weyerhaeuser compared it to what happened in Neidersaulheim in his youth, where a dozen farmers hired one boy to drive their cows to pasture instead of each providing a herdsman for his own. But on the Chippewa the need for cooperation was far greater: there was not only a common job to be done but a conflict to be waged, and unity of action was mandatory.

The union took the form of a corporation, the Mississippi River Logging Company. It comprised seventeen firms, and its authorized capital of $1,000,000 was represented by shares of $1,000 each. No capital was paid in, but each firm pledged itself to take a certain footage of logs, each million board feet representing six shares. It was thus "a service corporation, not organized primarily for profit to itself." Its twenty-year Iowa charter was granted on January 2, 1871. Four St. Louis firms made pledges, but the other members were Minnesota, Iowa, or Illinois establishments, and included Laird, Norton and the Youmans, the Lambs and W. J. Young, Schricker & Mueller, Dimock, Gould, Keator & Wilson, Benjamin Hershey, and Weyerhaeuser & Denkmann. The Mussers, the

Clinton Lumber Company, and Joyce & Smith were not represented. Altogether, $222,000 in log pledges were made. Lorenzo Schricker was elected president, W. H. Laird secretary, and W. J. Young vice-president. Frederick Weyerhaeuser appeared only as a member of the executive committee.[16]

4

The conflict on the Chippewa was now no longer local. With the timber owners and the independent loggers the Mississippi River Logging Company had firmly allied itself against the mills at Eau Claire and Chippewa Falls and the Knapp, Stout interests on the Menomonie. The mills in turn had staunch allies in the operators of the steamboat line who ran their boats back and forth from Chippewa Falls to the Mississippi.

The new company began its work in the spring of 1871 with the purchase of 34,000,000 feet of logs. The future seemed to smile upon it, but by July the directors were deeply disheartened to learn that less than a third of the logs put in upstream had actually arrived at Beef Slough.

They appointed a committee to examine the river from Chippewa Falls to its mouth, and its members, among whom was Matthew G. Norton, covered the entire stretch in "small batteaux." "It was not cheering," Norton recalled later, "to see so many logs scattered along in the various bays and on the banks of the rivers instead of being in their own booms." The fault clearly lay with the Chippewa millmen who made no effort to expedite logs bound for the slough.

The Mississippi River Logging Company now made overtures to the Chippewa plants, proposing cooperation in sorting and driving, a practice long established on the Black, but the local manufacturers were not interested. In fact, they soon attempted to convince the legislature that the Beef Slough Company was a menace to "free navigation" and that its franchise should be canceled because it had ignored those provisions in the instrument that forbade it to obstruct shipping on the stream. In this effort the steamboat interests joined. Obviously, if the Beef Slough Company were killed the Mississippi River Logging Company could procure no logs, would have no excuse for existence, and full control of the entire basin would rest with the local mills.

The Mississippi River men countered with an aggressive campaign of their own. They decided, writes Norton, that their most effective strategy for the coming season "was to put in so many logs that they [the Chippewa millowners] could not detain them all without filling their own booms with logs that did not belong to them, thus interfering with their own supply for the season." At the same time Weyerhaeuser and Schricker, the first in November, 1871, and the second three months later, transferred their shares in the Beef Slough lease to the Logging Company, thus investing it with full power to manage booming and rafting operations.[17]

Happily, the Wisconsin legislature was not responsive to the mill-owners' effort to get the franchise of the sorting company cancelled. In vain the act's opponents argued that the boom at the entrance of the slough diverted too much water from the main river and impaired its navigability. In vain they pushed a boat of shallow draft through the channel to prove that the slough was navigable and should therefore not be clogged with logs, rafts, booms, and sorting works. The legislators took the position that loose logs had as much right in the Chippewa River as steamboats and that "free navigation" could not be invoked by the latter in order to exclude the former. They went further and passed a bill that repealed "all laws requiring that a passage be kept open in sloughs when there was a navigable channel open in the main part of the stream." In other words, so long as the main river was navigable, the slough could be used as a storage and rafting area even if that meant closing it to vessels.

Meanwhile the crash strategy of overwhelming the Chippewa mills with logs proved successful. The crews at Beef Slough during the season of 1872 processed 54,873,000 feet of logs for the downriver mills, a 450 percent increase over the 12,000,000 feet of 1871.

The directors of the Logging Company, greatly encouraged, desired to expand the booming and rafting facilities, a move that had been blocked in 1872. But they hesitated to spend money with no more title to the sorting works than a lease that now had less than four years to run, and the $5,000 limit on expenditures stood in the way of extensive improvements. Accordingly, they opened negotiations for the purchase of 502 shares of the Beef Slough Company, enough to give them majority control. For $27,000 the sale was made on September 4, 1872.

The transfer of certain lands about the slough to the Mississippi River Logging Company and a settlement of the claims of former stockholders who had advanced money to the original Beef Slough Company were features of the transaction. Two days later Elijah Swift conveyed his lease-hold rights in that firm to the Mississippi River Logging Company for $5,364, and the latter had the control it desired. Both Schricker and Swift had been paid bonuses in connection with the surrender of their leasehold rights. This later rankled somewhat with Frederick Weyerhaeuser. In his notebook for 1885 appears an entry: "Trades—Beef Slough—Swift $3,000 bonus. Schricker $1,000 bonus and two years rafting. F. W. done the work for nothing."[18]

5

By 1872 it had become apparent that Schricker was not a good president. He had been tactless in handling his sixteen partners; there were charges that he had shaved time checks for his own profit; and the company's books were in confusion. Still worse, he drank to excess.

When the stockholders gathered on September 5, 1872, W. G. Clark of Hill, Lemmon & Company made a motion to unseat him. He particularly stressed Schricker's overindulgence in liquor. The president was indignant. He had a habit when excited of striking his index finger against his nose. Now, according to report, he rose to his feet, violently made this gesture, and shouted, "Schricker drunk, knows more as Clark sober!"

The stockholders did not agree. They passed Clark's motion and proceeded to elect as president the man who had been most active in opening up the Chippewa basin and in creating the Logging Company: Frederick Weyerhaeuser. For the post of secretary they chose, apparently at Weyerhaeuser's request, Thomas Irvine of the Benjamin Hershey Company. Schricker & Mueller, with some of the weaker firms, soon withdrew from the organization, but several strong companies meanwhile joined it: Joyce & Smith of Lyons, the Clinton Lumber Company of Clinton, and Musser & Company of Muscatine in 1871, Pelan & Randall of Dubuque in 1872. At the beginning of 1873 the associates numbered fifteen, the roster for four years.

The company combined cooperation with pungent individualism. No firm surrendered an iota of control over its manufacturing or sales. Yet with a common objective, and under the leadership of Frederick Weyerhaeuser, they became an effective team for buying, driving, and sorting logs.

Despite numerous conflicts of interest, many of the group came to be warm personal friends. Weyerhaeuser soon counted among his advisers and business associates both the Lambs and W. J. Young, W. H. Laird and Matthew G. Norton, Peter M. Musser, and David Joyce. A spirit of comradeship gradually infected the others, although friendships were closest among men not in direct competition with each other. Later Norton was to write that "the members of this Company were more like brothers in their intercourse with one another than would be found in most organizations for profit and the promotion of business. A very kindly feeling and brotherly affection grew up among them, and it was a joy to them when they could from time to time meet one another and, laying aside even for a brief hour the cares of business, enjoy a season of social intercourse."[19]

This idyllic atmosphere, at best incipient in 1873, must have grown from the moment Weyerhaeuser and Irvine took charge. They also pushed improvements at the slough, these and the reorganization of driving operations requiring expenditures of $98,150 by 1874. Both were calculated to increase the deliveries of logs. "It was evident," wrote F. E. Weyerhaeuser later of his father's concern, "that he must solve this phase of the

problem promptly before his associates lost their courage and before
their ability to meet drafts had disappeared."

The new president and secretary were successful. The volume of logs
that passed through the slough in 1874 reached a total more than ten
times that of 1871, or 129,000,000 feet. This achievement was repeated
in 1875.[20]

But although the Chippewa mills had temporarily been foiled, they
were only stirred to renewed efforts by the success of the "invaders." Soon
they attacked again on two fronts: on the river and in the courts.

On the river they planned a dam and sorting works above Chippewa
Falls. On September 30, 1872, the Eagle Rapids Flood, Dam & Boom
Company was formed, its stockholders representing both Chippewa Falls
and Eau Claire. The millowners of the latter city still hoped to improve
the river in their vicinity but had become reconciled to the Eagle Rapids
project. The Mississippi River Logging Company was opposed to both
developments, fearing that they would obstruct the driving of logs and add
charges for sorting. However, the construction of the dam proceeded and
was completed early in 1873, only to be washed out by freshets that same
spring. It was soon rebuilt.

Meanwhile, the Chippewa millowners and the Mississippi River men
were carrying their war to the courtrooms, for in 1873 Levi Pond and the
Eau Claire Lumber Company had sued the Beef Slough and the Mississippi River Logging Companies for using, without royalties, a fin boom
at Round Hill, near the entrance to Beef Slough, to guide downcoming
logs into the channel for sorting and rafting. On this particular type of
boom Pond and the Eau Claire Company had received in 1868 a patent
which their opponents considered invalid because fin booms had been used
at Eau Claire in earlier years. Were its use forbidden, the result might be
to cripple the entire activity at the slough and destroy the Mississippi
River Logging Company in its infancy. But before the plaintiffs won the
case, as they did in October, 1875, they had agreed to permit the defendants to use the boom during the life of the patent for a fee of $15,000.

The determining element in the settlement appears to have been a
patent for a sheer boom obtained by Thomas Irvine on February 2, 1875
(No. 159,328) providing a new method of operating the fins. (The sheer
boom itself was not patentable, and only the method of manipulation was
in question.) "The patent," writes F. E. Weyerhaeuser, "seems to have
had the effect of bringing about a reasonable settlement with the owners
of the original fin boom patent." Irvine's device was never manufactured
or used, and during the suit the Mississippi River Logging Company had
continued to use the fin boom. The litigation was as ineffectual in stopping the flow of logs to the slough as had been the ill-starred Eagle Rapids
dam.[21]

6

Meanwhile, all the Mississippi River lumbermen were feeling the effect of economic changes that took place in the Middle West from 1868 to 1875. These all but compelled them to expand operations on the Chippewa.

In the early years of this period prices had dropped sharply; a marked upturn had followed in 1871 and 1872. The drop in the late sixties had followed the rapid railroad expansion already mentioned in this chapter. This had made possible the direct shipping of lumber to hundreds of small communities, some now being reached for the first time by the rails and some springing up with the extension of lines to connect with the first transcontinental line, the Union Pacific. Lumbermen scrambled to serve the new markets, with an intensification of competition at such Missouri River points as Kansas City and Omaha.[22]

Even after the panic of 1873 the increased demand for lumber persisted. Where credit could be arranged or where produce could be taken in exchange, as was widely possible, the marketing of lumber continued briskly.

The depression naturally made itself felt. Inventories piled up with retailers, prices sagged, profit margins narrowed; and yet by skillful adaptation to conditions most lumbermen could operate at a profit. Firms like Laird, Norton and Knapp, Stout increased their shipments in 1874 and 1875 and with complete vertical integration (stumpage, manufacturing, marketing) and careful management, maintained a steady if modest prosperity. Other millmen also cut their margin of profit and, to compensate for this, increased their output. Weyerhaeuser & Denkmann steadily built up their production, which rose from 8,000,000 board feet in 1869 to 17,000,000 six years later. So did the Mussers, W. J. Young, and C. Lamb & Son. It was actually a period of overproduction, the result of expanding rail facilities, the scramble for orders, and the need for greater volume to counterbalance the smaller profits.[23]

As raw materials for their rapid increase in production to 1875, all the Mississippi River firms depended on a mounting volume of logs from the Chippewa. The St. Croix and the Black together were still maintaining a steady output: the production from the boom on the Black actually rose from 1872 to 1874 (125,766,000 board feet to 188,907,000), while that of the St. Croix fell by about the same amount (180,000,000 to 120,000,-000). However, from these sources the Minnesota, Illinois, and Iowa firms could count on only a limited supply; their source for growth was the Chippewa, which in 1874 yielded entirely to them the 129,000,000 board feet that passed through Beef Slough. The maintenance of this supply, if not its increase, was vital.

Many firms had expanded operations, adding new equipment and new mills and enlarging their yards, and finally entering on the purchase of steamboats. Weyerhaeuser & Denkmann bought their first, the *C. J. Caffrey,* in 1874. Aside from the need to produce more because of small profit margins, all these new facilities had to be paid for and could only be paid for by use. Decreased production, in fact, could have meant loss or even bankruptcy.

Another important reason for increasing production sprang from the acquisition of timberlands. Many of the Mississippi River Logging Company members had been making purchases. Laird, Norton had acquired 7,800 acres at $10 an acre from Philetus Sawyer in 1873; a year earlier Weyerhaeuser had recorded in his notebook the buying of 8,120 acres on the Jump River, a Chippewa tributary, from Francis Palms at $8 an acre. Such purchases—and others of the associates had made them—had represented an effort to provide stumpage that would ensure the continuance of expansion. The purchases had been made possible by the liberal terms offered: Laird, Norton had been required to make a down payment of only $8,000 and had seven years in which to work off its full obligation. Weyerhaeuser had been granted thirteen! But interest at 10 percent made a formidable charge that could be met only by increasing the manufacture of lumber, which meant logging the timber as rapidly as possible. Needless to say, these acquisitions were not the only ones made by the two firms during these years.[24]

As Weyerhaeuser swung into his work as president of the Logging Company, the importance of enlarging the Chippewa activities dominated his thinking and planning. A series of activities clamored for his attention. Driving must be better organized, the works at the slough still further enlarged and improved. As the partners pushed from the Chippewa up to its tributaries for new sources of timber, improvements on those streams must be made. Above all, the position of the Mississippi River Logging Company must be vigorously defended from new attacks certain to be made by the Chippewa lumbermen.

NOTES

1. Larson, *White Pine Industry,* 34, 36–37, 148; Blair, *A Raft Pilot's Log,* 37. Since the only mills on the Mississippi River other than those in the group we have discussed were those in the vicinity of Minneapolis, the "Miss. River firms" or "Miss. lumbermen" will be used to indicate the Winona, Minn., manufacturers and those in Iowa and Illinois.

2. Merk, *Economic History of Wisconsin,* 63; Hotchkiss, *History of the Lumber and Forest Industry of the Northwest,* 444–445, 474–483, 501–505; Fries, *Empire in Pine,* 65; Larson, 14–23; *Nwn. Lbrmn.,* XI, Jan. 26, 1878, p. 5.

3. Merk, 63; Hotchkiss and Fries, *op. cit.;* FEW Record, 116, 123, 127, 154.

4. FEW Record, 127, 169; Roth, *Forestry Conditions of Northern Wisconsin,* 6–16. The estimates of area and original stumpage are Roth's; he was detached from the U.S. Forest Service to make a survey for the state of Wisconsin.

5. Gates, *Wisconsin Pine Lands of Cornell University,* 106, 124.

6. *Ibid.,* 73–74; Randall, *History of Chippewa Valley,* 142–143; Blair, 33–34; Reynolds, *Daniel Shaw Lumber Company,* 19; Hotchkiss, 482, 486, 497–499, 625, and elsewhere; Rector, *Log Transportation,* 33–34. The *Amer. Lbrmn.,* the St. Paul *Pioneer Press,* and the *Miss. Val. Lbrmn.* give information on the Chippewa firms, as do the books cited.

7. Blair, 47; Kleven, "Wisconsin Lumber Industry" (quoted on name of Beef Slough), 168; Fries, 142–143; Burlington (Iowa) *Post,* Nov. 8, 1930; *Miss. Val. Lbrmn.* IV, Sept. 26, 1879, p. 2.

8. BSMBLD&T Co., Record Bk.; *Nwn. Lbrmn.,* V, Jan., 1875; Hotchkiss, 449; Fries, 142–143. Palms subscribed for 323 shares, Jenkins 236, Bacon 150, Davis and Crane 118. The four local men took only 55 shares all told.

9. Fries, 143–144; Gregory, *West Central Wisconsin,* II, 827–828.

10. Fries, 50–53; R. K. Boyd, "Up and Down the Chippewa River," *Wis. Mag. of Hist.,* XIV, March, 1931, pp. 243 ff.

11. Fries, 144 (citing local newspapers); Randall, 143; Gregory, II, 828; BSMBLD&T Co. Record Bk., July 15, 1867; Blair, 53.

12. FEW Record, 120, 154; LN Papers, Laird, Norton to D. Shaw, Jan. 14, 1869, and memo of Feb. 10, 1869.

13. Private and Local Laws, 1869, Chaps. 86 and 299 (in Union Lbr. Co. Minute Book); General Laws, 1869, Chap. 15, Sec. 112 (cited in Fries, 145 n.); *Miss. Val. Lbrmn.,* Aug. 24, 1876.

14. Blair, 53; Randall, 144; BSMBLD&T Co. Record Bk., June 1, 8, 1870.

15. Norton, 13–14; FW Notebook; BSMBLD&T Co. Record Bk., copy of lease and entries of Dec. 17, 1870, and Dec. 29, 1874.

16. FEW Record, 123–124, 128, 157–159; FW Notebook; Norton, 14, 34 ff.; LN Papers, copy of MRLC articles of incorporation; Fries, "The Miss. R. Logging Co.," 435. The original stockholders, by city, with their pledges in millions of bd. ft. were as follows: Winona, Minn., Laird, Norton & Co. (3), and Youmans Bros. (3); Lansing, Iowa, Hemmenway, Wood & Co. (1); McGregor, Iowa, W. & J. Fleming & Co. (2); Clinton, Iowa, Chancy Lamb & Son (3) and W. J. Young & Co. (3); Davenport, John L. Davies (3) and Schricker & Mueller (3); Moline, Dimock, Gould & Co. (3); Rock Island, Keator & Wilson (2); and Weyerhaeuser & Denkmann (3); Muscatine, Benjamin Hershey (2); Keokuk, Taber & Co. (2); and St. Louis, A. Boeckler & Co. (2½); Hill, Lemmon & Co. (1½); H. S. Parker (½); and Jacob Tamm & Co. (½). The total pledges thus amounted to 37,000,000 bd. ft., or 6 times 37 shares, or $222,000.

17. MRLC Min. Bk., entries for July, 1871; Norton, 15–16, 36; *Dunn County News,* Oct. 14, 1871; Wabasha *Herald,* Aug. 31, 1871; *Burlington Post,* Nov. 22, 1930.

18. Fries, 148–149, and newspapers cited in Note 16; MRLC Min. Bk., Sept. 4, 6, 1872, and Jan. 24, 1873; LN Papers, correspondence on claims, 1872–1873; FEW Record, 306, 309.

19. FEW Record, 130; MRLC Min. Bk., Sept. 5, 1872 and *passim;* LN Papers,

Statistical Report on Deliveries of
Logs, 1871–1876; Norton, 46.

20. BSMBLD&T Co. Record Bk., May
27, 1874; FEW Record, 162. For
records of logs assorted, by year, see
Appendix I. The withdrawing firms
were Hemmenway, Wood & Co., W.
& J. Fleming, Parker & Co., Jacob
Tamm & Co., and Atlee & Son (in
1871–1872 season only), besides
Shricker & Mueller.

21. *Nwn. Lbrmn.*, V., Jan., 1875, p. 19;
Miss. Val. Lmbrmn., XXXI, March
16, 1900, p. 1; FEW Papers, Capt.
C. H. Henry to FEW, March 11,
1934; MRLC Min. Bk., Jan. 22,

Sept. 18, 1873; Sept. 23, 1874; R.
K. Boyd, "Up and Down the Chip-
pewa River," *Wis. Mag. of Hist.*,
XIV, March, 1931, p. 256; FEW
Record, 33–34.

22. Larson, 107.

23. LN Papers, Record Bk., Winona;
Reynolds, 158; Fries, 111, 126; *Nwn.
Lbrmn.*, XI, Jan. 26, 1878, p. 4, and
Sept. 28, 1878, p. 1; Hotchkiss, 587–
589.

24. LN Papers, Ltr. Bk., MHS; Fries,
111, 126; Rector, 308; Larson, 25;
FEW Record, 121–122, 145–147;
F. W. Notebooks, 1872–1874.

V

Drive for Victory

As president of the Mississippi River Logging Company, Frederick Weyerhaeuser had shown competence and vision. While he promptly made himself familiar with the business problems of the organization, he divested himself of time-taking detail by making Thomas Irvine company secretary. More important, since getting logs on the Chippewa was a Wisconsin activity, he planted both Irvine and himself in Wisconsin—Irvine for the entire year and Weyerhaeuser for the greater part of it.

Canadian-born, originally a schoolteacher, Irvine on coming to the Middle West had worked for Benjamin Hershey in Muscatine, demonstrating unusual talent for accounting and other office work and finally taking over the routine management of the Hershey interests. Weyerhaeuser, recognizing his ability, had asked for his services. "Mr. Hershey was unwilling to let Mr. Irvine leave Muscatine," says F. E. Weyerhaeuser, "but finally in the interest of the group consented to his taking an active part in the management of the Mississippi River Logging Company." Irvine was soon not only keeping its accounts but also directing operations at Beef Slough, making his summer home there.

As for Weyerhaeuser, he devoted himself to field activities, primarily the procurement and scaling of logs and their dispatch downstream to the slough, though these functions had a relationship also to larger matters. Among these were the just apportionment of shipments to the various partners, the financing of such shipments, a close attention to hostile moves against the company by the millmen and steamboat owners on the Chippewa, and, a subtle but highly important matter, the relationship of the Mississippi River Logging Company to owners of standing timber, townsfolk, farmers, and logging contractors on the watershed of the river.

Getting the logs was the most important task, and logging was primarily a winter occupation. The new president gave almost his entire time during this season to the Wisconsin woods. "Father spent whole winters in the pineries," said his son, "returning to his home in Rock Island only for a short period during the holidays." To spend so much time away from home was a sacrifice for him and an even greater one for his wife.

The Chippewa basin covered an area approximately seventy miles in breadth on an air line and one hundred and sixty miles in length. For Weyerhaeuser's purposes there were few railroads, and since the river was not navigable above Chippewa Falls, little transportation by steamboat. Travel was by horse-drawn wagons or sleighs, by foot, or by raft and bateau. Since wide areas had to be covered to make arrangements with timber owners, loggers, and river crews, there was no escape from a perpetual, physically taxing round of journeys in weather often below zero— a routine few men would have attempted and fewer could have endured.

Frederick Weyerhaeuser at this time was exceptionally well fitted for such an ordeal. Forty years of age in 1874, he was above medium height, of unusual strength and ruggedness, modest but unremitting in energy, and ready to sleep, if necessary, in a logging-camp bunkhouse or the loft of a stable. Patient, shrewdly humorous, optimistic, he edged into the "woods life" as if born to it.[1]

But if the period was one of varied hardships and difficulties for Weyerhaeuser, it was also a happy one. His duties took him through a country of singular beauty. Much of the watershed was still untouched. Weyerhaeuser's blue eyes must have kindled to the stands of lordly white pine rising straight up for a hundred and fifty feet or more. He must have enjoyed the winter silence of the woods, only emphasized by the stroke of a distant ax, the occasional leap of a deer, or the rustle of a disappearing wolverine. The sheer extent of the forest presented a kind of imperial arrogance, as if disdainful of man, but Weyerhaeuser recognized it as a tremendous economic resource. He later entered the virgin woodlands in Minnesota, Louisiana, Idaho, and western Washington, but on the Chippewa he first encountered a relatively untouched forest, and it must have given him a thrill never quite repeated.

The scenes that marked the forests' passing were ruggedly picturesque —the woods camps with their log buildings and curling smoke; the gangs of lusty fallers, trimmers, and drivers; the log decks by lake or river shore; the drives on the rivers with their shouting, red-and-blue-shirted crews; the jams that filled streams for miles and rose from twenty to seventy feet above water level.

Weyerhaeuser was familiarizing himself with facts, methods, and the habits of men essential to a mastery of the lumber business. He won a sense of the relationships among loggers, timber agents, millowners, and rivermen. He soon perceived that far more could be gained if all the persons and labor involved in the basin could be united in a common purpose; rivalries were impediments to the task of harvesting timber and could be as destructive as drought, floods, or forest fire. Almost from the beginning Weyerhaeuser labored to harmonize the undertakings of the entire area.

By the early 1870's Weyerhaeuser knew the Chippewa region better than most of those who lived in it. In 1872 T. J. Cunningham, a reporter for the Madison *Democrat,* met him at the home of Edward Rutledge and asked him for information about the area, which he wanted to describe for his paper. "Mr. Weyerhaeuser, who knew the country, furnished me the material for my article, which was copied all over in other newspapers and gave Chippewa Falls its first boom as the greatest white pine section in the west." By this time Weyerhaeuser had established a reputation that enabled him to conduct any enterprise with the full confidence of other people. "Mr. Weyerhaeuser," says Cunningham, "was one of the few men not required to put up collateral when he wanted money."[2]

He became acquainted with a number of influential persons throughout the basin. The most outstanding was Edward Rutledge, an Irish-born woodsman who had come to Wisconsin by way of Canada and had a farm on the east bank of the Chippewa about three miles below the point where the Flambeau joined it. Rutledge was a slight, blue-eyed, wiry man "who could travel through the woods like a jackrabbit," and knew the Chippewa basins timber better than anyone there. The Rock Islander may have bought stumpage through Rutledge as early as 1868. Quite as important were Rutledge's advice on men and conditions and his aid in introducing Weyerhaeuser to timber owners, loggers, and expert woodsmen.

By 1875 both the Mississippi River lumbermen and the many groups in the Chippewa basin recognized that Weyerhaeuser was a leader. He was not yet "the master spirit of the Mississippi Valley so far as logs and lumber are concerned," as the *Northwestern Lumberman* was later to call him, but he was equipping himself to assume that role.[3]

2

For Frederick Weyerhaeuser the major problem facing the company was its long-term supply of logs. He recognized that he and his partners were putting into the Chippewa from 40,000,000 to 50,000,000 board feet of logs a year, that the amount would increase, and that the local mills were manufacturing as much or more. Soon the desirability of large tracts of stumpage for future use would be apparent to everyone. He felt, as Matthew Norton wrote later, that "pine land would have to be purchased so far as means were available to us." This conviction, as Norton notes, "brought to the Company its final success."

Ample stumpage was still available. The Chippewa mills had of course acquired some timberlands; so had many of the individual firms of the Mississippi River Logging Company. But most of the large tracts held by speculative investors or railroads farther back from the stream or on the tributaries were still unsold. They were beginning to be offered, and the easy terms available made it possible to undertake large transactions without strain.

An excellent opportunity to provide for the future soon presented itself when H. C. Putnam and John McGraw offered the company 50,000 acres of Chippewa pinelands purchased from Cornell University. The asking price was $10 per acre, payment could be made over a ten-year span with interest at 7 percent, and Weyerhaeuser found strong support among his associates for the investment. Artemus Lamb and W. J. Young joined him in recommending action; David Joyce made the motion for acceptance; and this first joint purchase was authorized on October 20, 1875.[4]

The act was important. The company could now log its own lands when piecemeal buying from small owners and loggers did not supply its needs. The anticipated board footage exceeded 500,000,000. More significant, the Mississippi millmen had now committed themselves to a policy of joint acquisition and ownership of timber, and possessed a large property in common. Weyerhaeuser could discount any fears of secession and devote himself to getting the timber cut and improving the processes for bringing it down the river. The Chippewa River mills were at the same time alerted to a greater need for opposing the "invaders."

This first purchase was not unique for the area, but it was large enough to make the associates extremely cautious. When a proposal was soon made that they buy from Cornell 50,000 additional acres for $2.50 an acre, they drew back as if from an abyss. "This was a great mistake on the part of . . . the Company," writes Norton, "because these 'rejected' lands really carried nearly as good a quality of pine and about as much to the acre as that which was bought for $10 an acre; and some years later the Company bought this same land, paying over $18 an acre for what it had declined to take at $2.50."

However, smaller purchases were made by the company later, and Weyerhaeuser & Denkmann bought additional stumpage from Captain Charles H. Henry (acting for Chipman, Hosmer & Gilmore of Washington, D.C.) and others. Rutledge found a great deal of stumpage for the Rock Islanders. In 1877 T. J. Cunningham heard Rutledge report to Weyerhaeuser that he had located "one hundred forties" (4,000 acres), and could provide more if Weyerhaeuser could raise the money. The latter replied: "Don't worry about that, Ed. I will find the money, you find the timber."

Meanwhile other members of the Mississippi group were buying individually, W. J. Young taking 25,000 acres in 1876. By December, 1879, Mississippi River Logging and its individual members controlled 300,000 acres of pine, which represented something between 3,000,000,000 and 5,000,000,000 board feet.[5]

3

In October, 1875, the Eagle Rapids Dam and Boom Company, which had been rebuilding its washed-out dam, made a proposal to the Mississippi River firms. It would sort 10,000,000 feet of logs daily in floodtime for eight consecutive days and pass on all the logs destined for Beef Slough, charging only 12½ cents per thousand feet as compared with the 35 cents it charged the Chippewa Falls plants.

The Mississippi River Logging Company rejected the offer. It had no desire to pay a fee on logs when it had been sending them down the river free for some years. Apparently the Eagle Rapids Company could collect for its services only if they were acceptable to those who paid for them. Nevertheless, the Chippewa group, and particularly the Union Lumber stockholders, resented the refusal of Weyerhaeuser and his associates, and the bitterness it had already felt toward them was intensified.[6]

On their part, the Mississippi River firms decided to put their organization in a stronger position to meet any new attacks. On September 27, 1876, they altered the Mississippi River Logging Company from an association based on subscriptions in logs to a company with stock valued at $25,000 a share. Forty-three shares were issued, representing a value of $1,075,000. Half the amount subscribed was paid in. The number of firms participating was reduced to thirteen. The chief firms maintained their membership, the Lambs and W. J. Young with six shares each, Benjamin Hershey with five, Weyerhaeuser & Denkmann, the Laird, Nortons and the Youmans brothers with four each.

The charter gave the corporation great freedom of action. It could engage in rafting and booming and hold stock in other companies. While its headquarters were in Clinton, Iowa, its stockholders and officers could transact business "at any place they may see proper to meet, whether within or without the state of Iowa."

At the same time, plans were made to buy all outstanding shares of the Beef Slough Manufacturing, Booming, Log Driving & Transportation Company, and these were acquired between 1877 and 1881. Thus possible obstruction by minority stockholders was eliminated. The second half of the subscriptions for stock to the reorganized Mississippi River Logging Company was declared fully paid up as of September 17, 1879, presumably by the application of earnings. The paid-in money was applied to timberland and log purchases, to improvements on the Chippewa and at the slough, and to the acquisition of stock in subsidiary companies.[7]

Weyerhaeuser and Thomas Irvine had completely regularized the financing of the enterprise. For their varied activities they drew (made calls) on the stockholders at designated intervals. Two Rock Island banks, the Rock Island National and the People's National, financed all transactions and often discounted the calls made on individual firms when these found it inconvenient to furnish cash.

Both the paid-in capital and "calls" were needed, for Weyerhaeuser was constantly increasing his log purchases and arranging to cut some of the Logging Company's own lands. In 1876 the stockholders authorized their officers "to purchase and put in during the coming winter 100 percent more logs than the amount of the subscription" (up to now 43,000,000 board feet). Roughly one-half of the new total was to be cut from the company's own timberlands—50,000,000 feet. At first Weyerhaeuser established and operated some camps to log such stumpage but soon let out the work on contract.[8]

The position of the company, as the largest single customer in the Chippewa basin, was favorable for driving close bargains. But Weyerhaeuser wanted the goodwill of the contractors, and paid fair rates for their services—$2.75 to $3.00 per thousand feet. His average price for logs banked by contractors ran as high as $5.75, but in 1875–1876, while the effect of the depression was still widely felt, he paid only $4.65 for 11,400,000 feet. This was a period in which one lumber journal declared that "no money was made in 1876, either by loggers or manufacturers."

Weyerhaeuser also bought logs from dealers who brought them to the slough, paying higher prices there. In 1875 he bought 10,655,000 feet at the slough for $6.65 and in 1876 took 7,658,000 feet at $6.40.[9]

Meanwhile, to expedite the increasing volume of Chippewa logs, Weyerhaeuser, Chancy Lamb, William J. Young, and Earl S. Youmans had organized (February 1, 1876) the Chippewa River Improvement & Log Driving Company, a Wisconsin corporation with headquarters at Nelson, a village on the slough. Eau Claire opponents prepared to bring suit to set aside the company's franchise. O. H. Ingram of Ingram, Kennedy & Company led this fight, although he was vigorously supported by Thad Pound and others associated with the Union Lumber Company at Chippewa Falls. But short of legal action these millowners could do nothing to stop the new driving company when it should become active.

If activities on the river itself required a new organization, a new effort was needed at the slough. In 1876 a total of 154,141,000 board feet of logs was rafted there, and the facilities were not adequate for such an output, let alone the larger volume expected in the future. It was decided to provide two rafting works. The lower one, already in existence, was to be improved and used for the logs of nonmembers of the company and for special consignments of individual members in excess of their regular quotas. An expanded upper rafting works was to serve the company only. Here a building 36 by 80 feet was erected to accommodate the eighty men employed. A bridge 1,800 feet long was also built over the soggy bottom of the slough to be used for hauling in supplies from the mainland, and additional rafting facilities were constructed on the east side of the slough near the residence of the superintendent.

The storage capacity of the entire works was increased, and more than four miles of chain boom built. The sorting and rafting potential was now raised to 3,500,000 feet a day, with storage capacity for upward of 100,000,000 feet of logs. These improvements cost about $300,000, which would be soon paid for by increased deliveries to the slough.[10]

Irvine was now at the slough for most of the open season and often in the winter months. He had married in 1875 and established a residence near the rafting works, where on January 12, 1878, his son, Horace Hills Irvine, later to be associated with the expanding Weyerhaeuser enterprises, was born.

Frederick Weyerhaeuser occasionally brought his wife to the Chippewa, but in general spent his time there alone. He was still caught in a round of perpetual travel, often of rugged difficulty.

His eldest son John had begun to take an active part in Weyerhaeuser & Denkmann affairs. He wrote to his father on April 27, 1876, about a trip by steamboat from Rock Island up the Mississippi, apparently to get some logs from the slough. "We had a great time picking up logs, which you know is very hard work. When we got to Fountain City [about ten miles south of Alma on the Minnesota shore] we had to wait for the ice to run out of the Chippewa. I am afraid you will have a hard time getting the logs together, a great many ran into the woods and will be lost. We did not loose [sic] any logs in our raft." He also reported that the Weyerhaeuser & Denkmann mill was cutting 95,000 feet of lumber a day and expected soon to do 120,000 easily.[11]

Although up to and through 1876 the delivery of logs to the slough had proceeded briskly, Frederick Weyerhaeuser from his knowledge of the Chippewa basin was aware of the difficulties that might arise in seasons of drought. In later years, reading family letters during this period, F. E. Weyerhaeuser realized that his father "must have been constantly fearful of a failure of the spring drives." The danger was compounded by logging operations, now being pushed well up the tributaries. On each stream contractors needed a good head of water to take their logs down to the main river and enough there to speed them on to the slough.

Weyerhaeuser and others had early perceived the desirability of constructing dams on the tributaries, and a number were built. The spring of 1877 provided a dramatic demonstration of the need for more dams in general, and particularly for one on the main river. A freshet washed out

the Eagle Rapids installations for a second and final time, and there was
no way of holding the water anywhere. The winter had been short of snow
and long on mud, and contractors had with great difficulty got their logs
"to the landings where they waited in vain for floods to carry them to the
mills." Shrinkage rose far above the 35 percent often expected on the
first drive of a season's cut, and summer rainfall was below normal.

As a result, logs rafted at Beef Slough dropped from 154,141,000 in
1876 to 82,658,000 in 1877, and the Mississippi firms found their funds
tied up in timber and rafting facilities, with interest running from 8 to 10
percent annually. In May, 1877, they authorized Weyerhaeuser to build
such dams as he thought essential. They also assigned the driving of logs
above Eagle Rapids and on the tributaries to the newly created Chippewa
River Improvement & Log Driving Company and below that point to the
Logging Company. Five dams were ultimately built or purchased for
$130,000, including the cost of a large dam on the Chippewa itself.[12]

Another dry year, 1878, which saw only 91,873,000 feet of logs
rafted at the slough, hastened the completion of this main structure, the
Little Falls dam. Located about thirty miles above Chippewa Falls, some
six miles below the junction of the Chippewa and the Flambeau and also
below the mouth of the Jump, it could impound the waters from the upper
main river and all the upper branches. Built by Elijah Swift of Eau Claire
and Joseph Viles of Chippewa Falls, it rose from foundations 63 feet wide,
with abutments having a width of 100 feet. Icebreakers above the dam, a
jam boom, 9 miles of chain boom, and a 270-foot wing dam below the
main one featured the overall installation. Thirty-two floodgates, which
could be operated singly or together, were provided. The water could be
raised to a depth of 16 feet and, when high, created a reservoir extending
ten miles upriver. When the floodgates were opened the water at Beef
Slough, 100 miles away, was raised by 3 feet. With the gates closed, the
river level below the dam fell sharply, sometimes stranding steamboats.[13]

The network of dams, steadily expanded, offered insurance against
light rainfall and low water. It had a profound effect on logging and lumbering during the next few years.

4

Weyerhaeuser and his associates had acted wisely in consolidating
their position on the Chippewa. They were now to face a series of attacks
that would call for all their vigilance, energy, and resources.

As previously noted, the Eau Claire millowners had long sought the
right to develop a dam and sorting facilities that would utilize the natural
advantages provided by the Dells and Half Moon Lake. In 1875 they had
won a charter in the form of an amendment to that of the municipality of
Eau Claire. In November, 1876, the State Supreme Court declared the

enacted law constitutional, and the millmen at Eau Claire immediately organized the Dells Improvement Company, capitalized at $200,000, and let a contract for the construction of the dam.

Members of the Mississippi River Logging Company had always regarded a Dells dam and its supplementary improvements as a dangerous nuisance, probably because of a proposed toll of 35 cents per thousand feet on all logs processed for the slough. They actively resisted the passage of the original bill and made futile efforts to halt the work by litigation.[14]

Meanwhile Union Lumber at Chippewa Falls had attempted to better its precarious financial position by issuing two types of securities—one a series of first-mortgage bonds bearing 8 percent interest to the sum of $350,000, maturing July 1, 1882, and the other, $650,000 worth of 7 percent bonds payable November 1, 1880. In 1876, the outlook still remaining dark, the company's officers in extreme desperation attempted to sell their entire property to the Mississippi River Logging Company, which refused because some members were "not sufficiently advised as to the advantages" of such an acquisition.

Union Lumber Company owners fully understood the attitude of their opponents but saw a possibility of changing it. If they could initiate successive legal and legislative actions that would show the high nuisance value of their position, Weyerhaeuser and his friends, they believed, would soon conclude that it would be cheaper to buy them out, even at an inflated price, than to carry on expensive battles year after year in the courts and at the state capital.[15]

The Chippewa Falls group quickly adopted this policy. The Wisconsin courts had steadfastly refused to nullify riparian rights granted by the state, but in 1874 Army engineers had made a report on increasing the navigability of the Chippewa, and in 1876 Congress had appropriated $10,000 for improvements at its mouth. Assuming that federal authority over the river had now been indicated, in 1877 the lawyers of the Union Lumber Company once more invoked the doctrine of free navigation and asked Attorney General Charles Devens for an injunction against loose logs and obstructive river installations. They alleged that the Weyerhaeuser group had shown "a reckless disregard" of both private rights and the public interest.

The Mississippi River firms counterattacked at once. When the formal bill of complaint against them was filed on June 27, 1877, they promptly entered a stout demurrer containing depositions by numerous informed persons, including Captain E. E. Heerman and J. W. Carlysle, co-owners of the steamboat *Monitor,* operating on the river. These two stated that they had "never made any complaint of or concerning the running of loose logs in the Chippewa River, nor have they authorized anyone to complain or object to such running of loose logs."[16]

Weyerhaeuser's own deposition clearly stated the position of his group. Loose logs, he pointed out, had always been floated down rivers to sawmills located on their banks. The Chippewa sawmill owners themselves had used the river for driving logs, which had never interfered with steamboat navigation. "Boats on the said river made their regular trips day and night during the time the said logs were floating most thickly." The piers at Round Hill, Weyerhaeuser asserted, were not "an obstruction or hindrance to the navigation" on the river. "The lessening of commerce by steamboats on said river is owing solely and only to the building of railroads during the last ten years." The demurrer was eventually sustained.

While Weyerhaeuser and his associates were able to block a number of nuisance moves by their opponents at Madison and in Washington,[17] Pound and his associates succeeded in instituting a second federal suit in 1878. In August that year, in a period of low water caused by the closing of the gates of the Little Falls Dam, one of Heerman's steamers struck a sunken log, while later in the fall the river was too low to navigate for several days. Wrathful, Heerman shifted his allegiance. On January 31, 1879, Thomas Irvine was roused from his bed at midnight to accept a summons in the suit of Heerman *v.* Beef Slough . . . Company *et al.* The steamboat owner had applied for an injunction restraining the Weyerhaeuser corporations from running loose logs on the Chippewa, and asked for a court order for the removal of all the booms, dams, and piers of the Weyerhaeuser group.

In December, 1879, the court ruled that the alleged obstructions were not "to be abated by a court of equity, even if the plaintiff had shown that he was especially damaged by them, which he has not." The court pointed out that the interests of those using the river for transporting their logs were "very large" and that the alleged interference with navigation had been "acquiesced in for a long time." The three judges were unanimous in their decision, and Laird, Norton sent copies of it to newspapers in Winona, Chippewa Falls, Muscatine, and Madison, and to the leading lumber journals of the region. The issue of "free navigation" seemed to be settled once for all.[18]

By 1879 the Chippewa basin was divided by a feud so bitter that the entire history of lumbering could hardly show its like. The resentment of the local millmen against the "invaders" who were manufacturing Wisconsin timber into lumber in alien states had steadily mounted with the successive victories of the Weyerhaeuser group. The multitudes of logs annually dumped into the river had made assorting along its banks all but impossible. "We were helpless to stop our logs," recalled the stubborn Eau Claire fighter O. H. Ingram. At Chippewa Falls the Mississippi River Logging Company was blamed by the officials of the Union Lumber Company for their inability to salvage their investment.

On the other side, Weyerhaeuser and his associates could look back on a series of interferences, losses, legislative battles, and hazardous lawsuits, all attributable to the Eau Claire and Chippewa Falls firms. Psychologically the two groups glared at each other across an abyss as wide as the Grand Canyon.

Fortunately there was one resident of the basin who had won the confidence of men in both the opposing groups. Roujet D. Marshall, a young attorney of Chippewa Falls, had acted for the Logging Company as early as 1876, when Thomas Irvine employed him to collect a debt which Lorenzo Schricker owed the Beef Slough Company. Failing in a direct approach, Marshall had quietly taken the necessary legal steps, then seized a quantity of Schricker's logs. This crisp action convinced Frederick Weyerhaeuser that here was a young attorney who would produce results.

Marshall had meanwhile appraised the situation on the river in much the same manner as had Weyerhaeuser. "I had not long been engaged in business at Chippewa Falls," he wrote later, "before it became plain that the hostile feeling between the lumbermen of Chippewa Falls and those of Eau Claire and those of the two places and the mill owners on the Mississippi River had been, in general, destructive; . . . and that their mutual interests and the general good could be best sub-served by a permanent treaty of peace; and that he who could accomplish that would be entitled to be regarded as a great public benefactor." Marshall determined to earn that designation, and soon events operated to give him an opportunity.[19]

One occurrence was a change in the status of the Union Lumber Company. That corporation had finally collapsed in 1878, and at a trustees' sale was bought up by Senator William A. Wallace of Clearfield, Pennsylvania. He leased the mill, whose production had fallen from 32,-000,000 board feet in 1877 to a pathetic 3,500,000 in 1878, to Peck & Barnard. The firm resumed operations in May, 1879, and Barnard's announcement that he meant to saw at least 1,000,000 feet of lumber a week was joyously greeted by the 6,000 inhabitants of Chippewa Falls. But the important fact about the new situation was that the ownership was now in the hands of an Easterner seemingly unidentified with any local group and inclined to sell his property if he could do so advantageously. Also important was his selection of Marshall to act for him in legal matters.[20]

With the spring of 1879 certain other developments lifted Marshall's hope for peace. As the time came for the ice to break, every contractor, driver, and millowner on the river, along with the Mississippi River firms, waited for the floods that might carry the accumulated logs to their destinations. Finally, in late May enough rain fell to raise the river by fifteen inches. At once the dams on the tributaries and the big dam on the Chippewa were opened. The rivermen leaped to their tasks, the streams were soon dark with moving logs, and in five days 100,000,000 feet of them were sluiced over the Little Falls Dam.

Already the value of the dams constructed and controlled by the Chippewa River Improvement & Log Driving Company had been demonstrated, for they had helped to maintain the essential volume of water, but they were now to render additional and highly strategic services. The Dells Improvement Company could sort only 10,000,000 feet of logs a day, and the managers of the four leading Eau Claire plants asked Weyerhaeuser if he could and would feed through no more than that amount each twenty-four hours. He agreed. Again in June, when the Chippewa fell so low that a jam formed at the Dells, he released enough water to break it. Finally, in early July, when heavy rains disabled one of the Eau Claire booms, he directed that water should be held at Little Falls until the boom could be repaired. The *Chippewa Herald* noted these occurrences, observing that "a spirit of accommodation pervaded the entire operations of the managers of the Little Falls dam."[21]

This spirit of cooperation was extended when the Chippewa River Improvement & Log Driving Company joined with the Chippewa River Manufacturers' Driving Company, headed by Ingram and Eugene Shaw, to conduct a drive. By the last weeks in August the remaining logs readied for that season were being swept down the river by waters released from a score of dams on the tributaries. In April the Eau Claire press had tended to condemn the Little Falls Development as a menace to their town, but now the local correspondent of the *Northwestern Lumberman* undoubtedly voiced local opinion when he reported that the dam, "in the building of which many prominent men and loggers turned a deaf ear to solicitation for assistance, has proved itself to be an indispensable institution on the Chippewa." Toward the end of the year Ingram, Kennedy & Company willingly sold its flowage rights at the Little Falls Dam to the Improvement & Log Driving Company.[22]

Meanwhile Marshall had not been idle. He was in frequent touch with both Weyerhaeuser and Wallace during this period. "On every proper occasion," he relates, "I promoted, on the one side, acquirement of the particular property [the Union Lumber Company] by the Weyerhaeuser combination, and on the other, the idea of Senator Wallace and his associates selling out to the former." Weyerhaeuser was "an easy convert" to the idea but for some time could not see how the two parties "could even meet to negotiate." But, writes Marshall, in time "he came to see that I afforded the necessary bridge to span the chasm and to encourage me to proceed in my own way to bring about the much desired result."

This was not quickly achieved. Late in 1879 Weyerhaeuser laid before his associates an offer from Union to sell all its properties for

$1,260,000. He stressed the importance of the dams, booms, and riparian rights included, and personally vouched for the stumpage. But his associates, on this ground, declined the offer, although appointing a committee to continue negotiations.

On December 19th Wallace, Barnard, Peck, and Fletcher Coleman organized a new corporation, the Chippewa Lumber & Boom Company, to take over the properties and charter rights of the Union Lumber Company. They set a value of $850,000 on the holdings and capitalized the new unit at $1,230,000, of which only $220,000 was issued in stock. Wallace held $90,000 worth of this and mortgages for $630,000. During the winter session of the legislature his group maneuvered for various obstructive ends but were blocked by the Mississippi firms. Old animosities were thus kept alive, and in the spring of 1880 the two factions faced each other with no diminution of their long-standing hostility.[23]

Weyerhaeuser and his associates had now consolidated their position on the Chippewa, and organized efficiently all the agencies through which they operated. During the season of 1879 they processed 249,194,000 feet of logs at the slough, and reduced the original charge for rafting these from 75 cents to 50 cents.

The works at the slough were impressive. The sorting area, wrote one observer, "contains piles, piers, and booms until you can't rest." Miles of plank catwalk connected its various sections. As logs came into either of the two chief pockets, they were checked on entrance by the scalers, who called out the board footage in each log to the talleymen, who in turn entered the figures on their sheets. From the full record thus prepared any purchaser of logs could quickly get full data on his consignments.

To expedite the formation of rafts, in 1875 W. J. Young had devised the "brail" to replace the "string." Rafts had formerly been composed of ten or more strings (each 16 x 400 feet) but were now made up of six brails, each a mass of logs roughly 45′ x 400′ to 600′ enclosed in a boom. The new system required fewer holes and boom plugs, provided a tighter raft, and the larger units increased the total footage from about 800,000 feet to more than 1,000,000. Brails involved less labor and waste than strings, and by 1879 the new method of rafting had completely superseded the old. Coincidentally with the invention of brailing, Chancy Lamb perfected the capstan, and Mississippi River millmen entered extensively into steamboat operations.[24]

The acquisition of stumpage, as already indicated, had steadily continued, both for the Logging Company and for individual members. During the 1870's the General Land Office in Washington had charged the company with two cases of timber trespass, one involving the buying of logs cut on government lands and the other the cutting of such timber by the company's agents. In both cases Irvine had conceded involuntary error (the second involving 45,000 feet of logs instead of the 2,000,000 originally alleged), and made settlement.

Weyerhaeuser during this period often presented to his company opportunities for purchasing small amounts of timber, and these were often accepted. But, as his son recalls, on occasion a majority of his associates opposed large investments. Sometimes the Rock Islander would already have acquired the stumpage, in which case he would propose to keep it. But if it were still for sale he would remark: "Well, gentlemen, Weyerhaeuser & Denkmann will buy. If you wish the property later you can have it at cost." In both cases, on second thought, his associates would usually take the timber, adding to their reserves. With time, they were as ready to invest as he.[25]

Thus the "invaders" occupied in 1879 a position far superior to that they had known in 1870 or even in 1875. They had large reserves of pine; two out of every three logs that came down the river were now theirs; their network of dams and their river-driving crews were the chief factors in the transportation of logs to the mills; and their works at the slough were efficiently processing ample materials for the members' mills on the Mississippi. Yet they were still engaged in a war that had been both difficult and expensive, and Weyerhaeuser's dream of a union of all interests on the Chippewa seemed as far from realization as ever.

6

Paradoxically, that union was to be promoted by a calamity. Early in June, 1880, after a week of heavy rains, the Chippewa was rising to a record height. On June 12th it reached a level twenty-four feet above its low-water mark and now poured down in a titanic flood described as "the greatest disaster that ever visited this valley." Sweeping along the logs already put in and others banked for driving, it made a shambles of the installations at Paint Creek above Chippewa Falls and roared down with 150,000,000 feet of logs "in a solid body over the Falls, grinding, tearing, and crushing their way through all the booms, piers, and sorting works, carrying out the two bridges at Chippewa Falls and numerous houses, barns and fences which lined the shores on the bottom lands."

Reaching Eau Claire by evening, the mass beat for a few hours at the booms and jam piers above the Dells dam. Then in the early morning it plunged over the dam, crashed into the bridge below, battering through it, and charged on toward the slough, bearing houses, barns, shops, and one entire sawmill on its crest. A reported 180,000,000 feet of logs were now riding the flood, 110,000,000 feet of which belonged to the mills at Chippewa Falls and Eau Claire. Less than 50,000,000 feet of this destructive cargo finally went into the slough. The remainder was tossed up along the river for 125 miles, often strewn, after the flood had subsided, from one to three miles from the banks of the river.

For the Chippewa River mills the prospect was grim. With time and labor the logs could be hauled or skidded back to the river; none of them could profitably be transported upstream. They would have to be manufactured at points below the Dells—in other words, by the Mississippi River firms. A log-exchange agreement was possible. But the Chippewa millowners knew that Weyerhaeuser and his associates had often charged them with holding and sawing Logging Company logs. Now the Mississippi group could exact retribution. Wallace, Barnard, Ingram, and Shaw feared that they would.

Finally they deputed Marshall to approach Weyerhaeuser and if possible negotiate an exchange agreement. The Logging Company president had wasted no time in facing up to the emergency. Even before the river began to fall he had dispatched three steamboats and sixty men to pick up logs and had called a meeting of all log owners concerned to evolve a comprehensive plan for salvage. "Now was the time," wrote Marshall later, "for making a treaty without prejudice to the downriver [MRLC] men, which would make those who had long been bitterly hostile their warm friends."

At any rate, Weyerhaeuser included in a meeting of log owners representatives of all the Chippewa River plants except the Chippewa Lumber & Boom Company, whose officers "kept aloof." He suggested to Marshall that he draw up an agreement by which, first, a plan for the recovery of the stranded logs would be provided and, second, another by which the Mississippi River Logging Company would take all logs washed down by the flood, credit them to their proper owners, and give in exchange a like board-foot volume of their own logs from upriver. O. H. Ingram and Weyerhaeuser were chosen to administer the two plans. "The up-river people," says Marshall, "were surprised by the utter absence, on the part of the down-river parties, of any disposition to selfishly use their position of advantage to drive a hard bargain. . . . They . . . resolved that, if the arrangement which had been made should be administered, throughout, with the same spirit of fairness . . . that they would do all in their power to make an agreement of a permanent character which would render a recurrence of the situation that formerly existed improbable if not impossible."[26]

The agreements were fairly administered, and the upriver mills, with logs supplied under the exchange provisions, were soon back in operation. The total board footage processed that season, 260,785,000, exceeded the 206,932,000 board feet manufactured in 1879. With prices of lumber excellent, the "ruined" firms were soon in better condition financially than if the flood had never occurred.[27]

The happy outcome of the disaster promoted the idea of a permanent arrangement in which all those active on the river could share. On November 22–24, 1880, at the Grand Pacific Hotel in Chicago, the two groups drew up a provisional agreement "for the purpose of uniting in one interest the purchasing, owning, driving, scaling, grading and distributing the several amounts of logs to each of the parties who shall subscribe and pay for them, in the best and cheapest manner." The division of stock in the company formed to implement the agreement was to be "in proportion to the quantity of logs so subscribed for, which as now understood and agreed will give about 2/5 to the parties on the Chippewa." The same division of interest was "to cover and govern in the ownership of such timberlands, improvements and franchises" as might thereafter be purchased "for the use and benefit of such united interests." Weyerhaeuser was authorized to purchase desirable properties on such terms as he himself approved.[28] The agreement became the basis for the Chippewa Logging Company.

The Chippewa Lumber & Boom properties were still to be acquired, and because of the persistently antagonistic attitude of their owners they were essential to the complete harmonization of interests in the basin. Negotiations proved to be difficult. Tempers flared. The Chippewa Falls millmen had offered all their properties, including an estimated 450,000,-000 feet of stumpage, for $1,500,000. Most of Weyerhaeuser's associates thought this price too high.

Weyerhaeuser and Marshall now advanced a proposal that the property should be acquired jointly by the Mississippi River firms and six lumber companies below Chippewa Falls. This arrangement would leave the ownership partly in local hands. The Wallace-Barnard group was suspicious and hostile. Finally, on March 1, 1881, the sale was consummated. It involved a payment of $275,000 in cash and $1,000,000 in bonds of the Chippewa Lumber & Boom Company, these being guaranteed individually by the stockholders of the Mississippi River Logging Company. In return, the Logging Company and its allies received the 12,300 shares of stock which Wallace, Barnard, and others had held, the Logging Company acquiring 7,380 of these.[29]

The transaction terminated "the most memorable struggle" on the Chippewa. It was widely reported in lumber journals and the regional press. Unquestionably it had been a victory for Weyerhaeuser and the Mississippi River mills. They emerged in control of the basin, with the Eau Claire manufacturers holding a substantial but minority interest. But the full significance of their new status, as it was revealed in the next few years, represents another stage in the Chippewa story.

NOTES

1. FEW Record, 117, 220, 272, 316, 320.

2. Letter to A. A. McDonnell, St. Paul, Jan. 10, 1935, as quoted in FEW Record, 325. Cunningham, after his experiences as a reporter, became a publisher and a local historian of reputation.

3. FEW Record, 324–336; *Nwn. Lbrmn.*, April 19, 1884. Rutledge sometimes claimed Ireland as a birthplace, sometimes Canada, but the former seems the more likely.

4. Norton, *Mississippi River Logging Co.*, 42–43; Gates, *Wisconsin Pine Lands*, 213–217; MRLC Min. Bk., Oct. 20, 1875.

5. Norton, 42–43; Gates, 112, 231; *MVL&M*, I, Aug. 24, 1876, p. 1; FEW Record, 326. Other individual purchases in the basin had run as high as 75,000 acres, and the total acreage of pine in the area exceeded 4,000,000.

6. Hotchkiss, 478, 486, 614, 624; Union Lbr. Co., Min. Bks., 1869–1878; *Nwn. Lbrmn.*, XI, Jan. 26, 1878, p. 4; Fries, 123; MRLC Min. Bk., Oct. 21, 1875.

7. FEW Record, 164–167; MRLC Min. Bk., Sept. 27, 1876. The remaining subscribers were the Clinton Lumber Co. (2), Dimock, Gould & Co. (2), A. Boeckler & Co. (2), John L. Davies & Son (surrendered) (2), P. M. Musser & Co. (2), David Joyce (1), J. S. Keator (2), Pelan & Randall (1), Hill Lemmon & Co. (never issued) (2).

8. FEW Record, 166 (quoting Peetz, letter to FEW of Feb. 16, 1939); MRLC Min. Bk., Oct. 20, 1875; Sept. 27, 1876; Sept. 18, 1878; Sept. 17, 1879.

9. FEW Papers, Rutledge to FW, Sept. 25, 1877; FW Notebook, 1874–1875; LN Papers; MRLC Statements, 1875–1876; *MVL&M*, I, Nov. 3, 1876, p. 8, and Nov. 17, 1876, p. 4.

10. FEW Record, 163; CRI&LD Co. Papers; Ingram, *Autobiography*, 53; *MVL&M*, I, March 23, 1877; BSMBLD&T Co., Rec. Bk., May 24, 1877; May 22, 1878.

11. FEW Record, 69–72, 320.

12. FEW Record, 175; *Nwn. Lbrmn.*, XI, Jan. 26, 1878, p. 23; LN Papers, 8, Log statement, 1874–1878; MRLC Min. Bk., May 23, 1877; Sept. 18, 1878; BSMBLD&T Co. Record Bk., May 24, 1877. The Little Falls dam accounted for $90,400 of the $130,-000.

13. FEW Papers, C. H. Henry to FEW, Dec. 4, 1933; *MVL&M*, III, Feb. 14, 1879; Capt. Fred A. Bill, *Burlington Post*, Nov. 22, 1930.

14. Hotchkiss, 482; Gregory, *West Central Wisconsin History*, II, 832–833; *MVL&M* I, Jan. 12, 1877, p. 2 and IV, Dec. 26, 1879, p. 1; LN Papers, LN to FW, Feb. 22, 1878. The completed project cost about $400,000, of which $128,000 was spent on the dam. Included in the installations were a canal from above the dam to Half Moon Lake, a log sluiceway, a raft slide, piers, booms, and sorting works. The lake was used as a storage reservoir for many of the mills.

15. Fries, *Empire in Pine*, 150–153; Bill, *Burlington Post*, July 12–Nov. 30, 1930; *Nwn. Lbrmn.*, XIV, Dec. 30, 1879, pp. 4–5.

16. *Chippewa Herald*, Jan. 26, 1877; *MVL&M*, I, May 4, 1877, p. 7; FEW Papers, Windom to FW, April 11, 1877; LN Papers, depositions of May, June, 1877; BSMBLD&T Co. Papers, Information & Bill of Complaint . . . United States *v.* BSMBLD&T Co., MRL Co., and CRI&LD Co.

17. LN Papers, copy deposition of FW, June 14, 1877, and correspondence, 1878–1879; U.S. *v.* Beef Slough . . . Co., *et al.*, *Fed.* 1064 (1879); Current, *Pine Logs and Politics*, 122–125.

18. Bill, *Burlington Post*, Aug. 9, 16, 1930; LN Papers, corresp., 1879;

Heerman *v.* Beef Slough . . . Co., *et al., Fed. Reporter,* 145–146 (1880); *Nwn. Lbrmn.,* XIV, Dec. 20, 1879, pp. 4–5; Winona *Daily Republican,* Dec. 10, 1879.

19. Marshall, *Autobiography,* I, 260–264; FEW Record, 192.

20. Fries, *Empire in Pine,* 150–153; Bill, *Burlington Post,* July 12–Nov. 30, 1930; *Nwn. Lbrmn.* XIV, Oct. 20, 1879.

21. *MVL&M,* III, May 30, 1879, p. 4, and July 18, 1879, p. 5; *Nwn. Lbrmn.,* XIII, May 31, 1879, p. 2.

22. *Ibid.,* XIV, Sept. 6, 1879, p. 2; *MVL&M,* III, April 4, 1879, p. 1; CRI&LD Papers, Agreement of Dec. 29, 1879.

23. Marshall, *op. cit.;* MRLC Min. Bk., Dec. 18, 1879; FEW Record, 217 ff.; CL&B Co. Min. Bk., Dec. 20, 1879, and other papers, including articles of association.

24. Appendix I (for logs processed); *Laws of Wisconsin,* 1870, Chap. 299, Sec. 3; BSMBLD&T Co., Rec. B. and statements, 1875–1879 (costs); *MVL&M,* IV, Sept. 26, 1879, p. 2; LN Papers, LN to W. E. Law, April 15, 1880; Hotchkiss, 588; Blair, *A Raft Pilot's Log,* 47; information from Thomas Irvine; Rector, 151–152. On steamboats, see Chapter X.

25. General Land Office Records, Timber Division, National Archives (infractions); FEW Record, 189. In the first instance mentioned, the MRLC had unknowingly bought 179,241 bd. ft. of logs from a trespassing contractor. It acknowledged making the purchase, and settled with the government.

26. *MVL&M,* IV, June 17, 1880, p. 4; *Nwm. Lbrmn.,* June 2, 1880, p. 3; Marshall, 280; O. H. Ingram Papers, Corresp., June–July, 1880.

27. *MVL&M,* V, Jan. 28, 1881 (statistics).

28. LN Papers, Copy of Resolution.

29. The full holdings at the end of 1881 were Miss. River Logging Co., 7,380 shares; Empire Lumber Co., 1,260 shares; Carson & Rand, 730; Eau Claire Lumber Co., 730; Northwestern Lumber Co., 730; Daniel Shaw Lumber Co., 630; Badger State Lumber Co., 520; Roujet D. Marshall, 270; William H. Phipps, 50.

VI

Peace in Wisconsin

WITH THE PURCHASE of the Chippewa Lumber & Boom Company the forces favoring a full coordination of all activities on the river finally possessed the power to realize their objective. On June 28, 1881, they put a plan for harmonious operation into effect.

On that day O. H. Ingram, W. A. Rust, and D. R. Moon formally organized the Chippewa Logging Company, a Wisconsin corporation. All were Eau Claire millowners, and that fact undoubtedly reflected Weyerhaeuser's desire that Chippewa as well as Mississippi River lumbermen should take a share in the enterprise. The new company was empowered to provide "saw logs, timber, fence posts, railroad ties, telegraph and telephone poles for and to its stockholders." It could also make loans and acquire stocks in or purchase other corporations; and its by-laws provided for assessments, subscriptions for logs, the purchase, pricing, marking, and scaling of logs, and for accounting procedures. The unit was owned 65 percent by the Mississippi River Logging Company and 35 percent by the Eau Claire manufacturers.

The Chippewa Logging Company was the controlling agency for the cutting, driving, and apportioning of logs for all the participating firms. To some extent it displaced the Mississippi River Logging Company, which had previously coordinated the activities of Weyerhaeuser and his associates. Acting for the chief interests of the region, Chippewa Logging was called the "pool," and all agencies were related to it.

If timberlands were to be purchased for the use of the entire group, the Chippewa Logging Company now bought most of them. It arranged for the logging of its own lands and exercised general supervision over all other logging. It conducted the driving of logs on the tributaries and the upper river. Finally, it allocated them among the various firms.

But all the previously created corporations continued to exist and to perform certain functions. The Mississippi River Logging Company retained possession of all stumpage previously acquired, added more occasionally, contracted for its logging, and drove all logs on the river below Eau Claire. It conducted the sorting, rafting, and allocation of logs to sawmillers on the Middle Mississippi. The Beef Slough Manufacturing, Booming, Log Driving & Transportation Company owned the facilities at Beef Slough and shared the costs of maintaining the Little Falls Dam. The Chippewa River Improvement & Log Driving Company (owned 60 percent by Mississippi River Logging and 40 percent by the Eau Claire firms) leased various essential dams to the Chippewa Logging Company and confined its work to building, buying, and maintaining a major portion of the (at least) 148 dams in the Chippewa basin that came under the management of the associated groups.

The recently acquired Chippewa Lumber & Boom Company was not in the "pool," but owned timberlands, logged them, operated the Big Mill at Chippewa Falls, marketed the lumber, and held riparian rights and dams vital to the success of the common effort on the Chippewa. Since it was owned 60 percent by Mississippi River Logging and 40 percent by the Eau Claire firms, it conducted its activities in harmony with those of its stockholders.[1]

The six Eau Claire firms that had finally cast their lot in with the "invaders" were the Empire Lumber Company, the Valley Lumber Company, the Eau Claire Lumber Company, the Northwestern Lumber Company, the Daniel Shaw Lumber Company, and the Badger State Lumber Company.

Of the executives of these organizations, some were to have only a passing relationship with Weyerhaeuser; others were to become close fellow workers and friends. Among the latter were O. H. Ingram of Empire, William Carson of Valley, William A. Rust of the Eau Claire, Delos R. Moon and Sumner T. McKnight of Northwestern, and Samuel Chinn of Badger State. Several officials of the Eau Claire and the former Chippewa Falls firms, not owners, were to take important roles in the new regime.[2]

Not a little nonsense has been written about the "pool." Almost at once it was referred to as a monopoly, and later Weyerhaeuser's feat in uniting the Chippewa and Middle Mississippi interests was compared with Rockefeller's unification of refining and pipeline interests in the oil industry.

As to the Standard Oil, that company dealt with the facilities of an entire industry and for a time achieved control of more than 80 percent of all refining and fully as extensive a control of pipeline operations in the United States. In contrast, through the pool Weyerhaeuser and his associates coordinated logging and driving activities on a single river, the Chippewa. The pool did not control operations on the upper Mississippi, the St. Croix, the Black, or the Wisconsin, or in northern Minnesota, northern Wisconsin, Michigan, or any of the eastern states. Important as was the output of the Chippewa basin in 1881, it was actually only about 1.66 percent of the total estimated production of lumber for all the United States.[3]

As for monopoly, it is true that the pool had superior facilities for driving and sorting logs, with important riparian rights. On the other hand, as F. E. Weyerhaeuser pointed out, the union of interests "was consummated not through the ruthless use of power . . . but solely because of the leadership of Frederick Weyerhaeuser." To be sure, the Chippewa River millowners would have preferred to dominate activities in the basin themselves and came into the pool because otherwise, as O. H. Ingram later stated, "neither Chippewa Falls nor Eau Claire would have amounted to very much." Yet although a minority group, they helped make and implement decisions and competed actively in manufacturing and marketing except in operations of the Big Mill.

Nor were contractors and millowners outside the pool treated unfairly. "They made use of the facilities provided by the pool and the Mississippi River Logging Company," says F. E. Weyerhaeuser, "on exactly the same terms as those given the associates in the pool." William G. Rector in his *Log Transportation in the Lake States* confirms this statement when he remarks that even lumbermen who were not members benefited from the pool's activities.[4]

Thus the coordination of activity on the Chippewa was a limited operation affecting one area, represented a voluntary union of varied interests on equal terms, and operated in a liberal manner. How happily the plan would work could be proved only as it was carried into practice.

2

If the millowners in Eau Claire were concerned chiefly about the effective operation of the pool, the inhabitants of Chippewa Falls were particularly anxious about the fate of the Big Mill of the Chippewa Lumber & Boom Company. William Irvine, then the secretary and office manager of this company, noted years later that during the negotiations for its purchase (1880–1881) the prediction was freely made: "If Weyerhaeuser gets the property the mill will be immediately shut down, the timber cut and the logs sent to the river mills, and grass will grow in the streets of Chippewa Falls." The prophecy affected the entire community, for the mill employed several hundred men, and with it the little town would flourish or wither.

As Irvine said, "Mr. Weyerhaeuser was always a builder, never a wrecker." He was president of Chippewa Lumber & Boom, as he was of Mississippi River Logging and Chippewa Logging. He quickly showed that he would work as hard to serve the first of these companies as he would the other two. He ordered an enlargement and improvement of the Big Mill and saw that contracts were let to log its extensive stumpage. The mill was soon producing in greater volume than ever, employing 300 men, and before it finally shut down in 1911 it was to turn out 1,500 million feet of lumber.[5]

But the major challenge facing Weyerhaeuser and his associates was the Chippewa Logging Company. Fortunately, men of ability were available for key posts. Under Weyerhaeuser himself as president, D. R. Moon served as vice-president, while O. H. Ingram, as director and member of the executive committee (Weyerhaeuser and W. J. Young completed this body), took an energetic role in the new firm. Ingram was also vice-president of Chippewa Lumber & Boom, and as a resident of Eau Claire could deal promptly with any local problem.

Samuel W. Chinn of the Badger State Lumber Company became secretary and general manager of Chippewa Logging, serving capably until his death in 1896. As his field representative, Charles Harmon Henry supervised logging, scaling, and driving. A Civil War veteran who had won a captaincy in the 25th Wisconsin Infantry at sixteen, he had been known as the "young fighting devil," and attacked the problems he met in woods and on river with the same incisiveness he had shown in war. As already noted, he had acted for a time as an agent for absentee timber owners in the basin, then in 1879–1880 had taken charge of Ingram, Kennedy & Company's (later merged into the Empire) woods and river operations.

A word should be said here as to the management of Chippewa Lumber & Boom, which, while outside the pool, was closely associated with it. When that corporation changed hands in 1881, E. W. Culver was directing its operations. He was aggressive and able but soon became involved in "a serious misunderstanding" with Frederick Weyerhaeuser, supposed to have revolved around a demand for a much larger salary. At any rate, Weyerhaeuser, dissatisfied with Culver, one day met William Irvine on the streets of Chippewa Falls. He had watched his work, and now asked him: "William, do you think *you* could manage the business of the Chippewa Lumber & Boom Company?" Although stunned by the prospect dangled before him, Irvine managed to reply that he could and was promptly installed in Culver's place.

William Irvine was a neatly dressed, alert man of medium height, quick in movement, with a "terrific temper usually well controlled," and great force of character. He had an excellent memory, perceived the

significance of facts for both the present and the future, and was method-
ical and prompt. Approachable and companionable, he was at the same
time wholly devoted to his work. He was to guide more than one firm
through critical situations for the next forty years, becoming an esteemed
and loyal associate of Frederick Weyerhaeuser and his chief partners.[6]

To return to the pool, its allocating functions can be explained
simply. When its agents collected logs from the landings, they recorded
their board footage and quality and gave credit for the amount of logs
collected from each firm. The logs then became the property of the pool,
and were intermingled, but later allotments were made to the respective
companies up to the amount of their credits. Each allotment was of comparable quality. This process avoided the almost impossible task of keeping separate the logs of every pool member and independent owner, but
of course would be satisfactory only if each company received the equivalent of what it had contributed in the first place.

The entire routine therefore had to be exact. It began with logging.
As already indicated, some of this was directly contracted for by Chippewa
Logging, some by Mississippi River Logging. It was also undertaken by
most of the individual firms, among them Weyerhaeuser & Denkmann,
Laird, Norton; Empire, Valley, and the Daniel Shaw Company. Chippewa
Lumber & Boom, which had maintained fifty-one camps in 1879–1880,
continued such activity after 1881.

Naturally, logging practices had to be uniform and agreeable to all
companies and contractors. The Chippewa Logging Company began preparing standard contracts for common use. These, usually negotiated with
the loggers in August or September, set the approximate acreage to be
cut and, where the contracts ran for several years, the amount to be logged
annually. All logs were bark-marked to show the logger, year, and place,
and stamped to identify the owner. Each consignment was scaled.

Under the bylaws of Chippewa Logging, logs had to be scaled again
at the major dams. To supervise the two operations, the company appointed as chief scaler Henry Morford, who directed twelve inspectors
(soon called "Morford's twelve apostles"), each covering a specified area
or district. They visited each landing at ten-day intervals during the
logging season to examine the work of the scalers employed by the individual camps. They also supervised scaling at the major dams if these
were in their districts. They in turn operated under the general supervision
of the official state scaling inspector. No camp scaler could serve any one
contractor for more than two successive years.

Weyerhaeuser and Captain Henry, Chinn's deputy, watched the
processes of scaling and grading with meticulous care. The board footage
of the logs and their classification as No. 1 or No. 2 quality were both
important in determining the credit which a company received (No. 1

logs might range from $7.00 to $7.25 per thousand in price when second-grade logs were worth only from $4.00 to $4.50). Careless or venal scalers were summarily dealt with. One was shown to have overpaid his contractor; when Henry suggested that he be transferred to river work, Weyerhaeuser refused. The man, he asserted, could not work for the company in any capacity, "not even to clean spittoons," and he sternly forbade his deputies to employ anybody "that steals from us." F. E. Weyerhaeuser believed that Morford and his twelve were "undoubtedly the master log scalers of all time, for nowhere else in the world ever existed such absolute necessity of having a perfectly uniform scale of such vast quantities of logs."[7]

Difficulties developed with respect to grading standards, which differed considerably from landing to landing. Many companies loudly protested that they had been given insufficient credit. Weyerhaeuser, Ingram, and Henry attempted to set and enforce standards. A classification of No. 1, No. 2, and culls (commercially worthless) was adopted and enforced. In practice the average landing showed 50 percent No. 1, 35 percent No. 2, and 15 percent culls. No credit was given for the latter. Specifications became very precise by late 1883.

Thus with time and practice, scaling and grading proceeded smoothly and were accepted by the member firms and the independents. By common consent the chief credit was given to Frederick Weyerhaeuser. Undoubtedly the vision, energy, and persistence that had pushed the pool to success were chiefly his, but he was also fortunate in the men who worked immediately with him—Chinn, Ingram, Henry, and William Irvine, the routine managers.[8]

3

The success of the Chippewa Logging and Mississippi River Logging companies owed much to the facilities both commanded for the transportation and handling of logs. The mammoth installations at Beef Slough, Eau Claire Dells, Chippewa Falls, Paint Creek, and Little Falls, as well as lesser improvements on the main river and its ganglia of tributaries, entailed a large outlay of capital, but they paid rich dividends. They eliminated costly delays, assured regularity of log supplies, and swelled the volume of logs bound for the mills. In ninety-three days during the spring and summer of 1885 the Beef Slough boom passed through approximately 500,000,000 feet of logs, or more than 5,000,000 feet daily. In the spring of 1886 a journalist reported that "the perfect system of dams" on the Chippewa would enable driving crews "to get out with the logs, but it is questionable on all other streams."[9]

Captain Henry had charge of all river operations for the pool, and his judgment or authority was rarely questioned. He attacked his task with the zest of a field commander. It was comparable with the manipulation of a brigade, for he directed some 1,800 men during the season, and in addition to the drives, supervised scores of minor improvement projects. New dams were promptly built when required, and repairs were quickly made when installations were damaged. Captain Henry and his agents spent much time and money buying "flowage rights," which permitted the flooding of lands along the streams by waters backed up by the dams and allowing river crews to cross the properties affected, remove logs, and carry out other duties.[10] Driving activities required a synchronization of numerous tasks and much advance preparation. Camping equipment and food for an impressive force of men had to be provided, and equipment of all types, from wanigans to dynamite, had to be assembled. Possible mishaps, ranging from a logjam to the capsizing of a bateau and the injury of a man, had to be anticipated and prepared for.

Labor relations presented no serious problem. Chippewa Logging never started its river crews before dawn or permitted them to work after dark, though elsewhere both practices were followed. Captain Henry writes that his men "would charge upon the logs all day, and when they would reach the camp at night supper would be ready for them; the cooks would yell, take it boys; and the men would . . . move over to where the food, tea, and coffee were, and the campmaking crew were lined up to wait upon them by putting food upon their plates and tea in cups. Then the best class of fighting lumberjacks in the world would gather closely around the fires."

The only strike of record occurred on the South Fork of the Flambeau in the spring of 1889. The rear crew reached a point three miles below Pike Lake dam where a jam had built up. Persuaded by some dissident elements, the men struck for an additional fifty cents a day. They knew that the company wanted to finish the drive and felt that they were in a favorable position. However, Captain Henry had learned that contractors on another tributary had just completed their drives and released their crews. He discharged the strikers, hired the available men, and finished his drive ahead of schedule.[11]

Breaking the rollways, that is, getting the logs at the landings into the water for their journey downstream, was the responsibility of the logging contractor in the 1870's, but eventually in most cases Chippewa Logging supplied specialists for the task. It was better practice, for the break could be coordinated with other driving activities. Some firms, however, continued to insist on starting their own consignments, often at a cost higher than the charge made by Chippewa Logging for breaking a landing or releasing dam waters.

As logging operations were pushed back from the streams, the prob-

lem of banking logs became increasingly difficult. Up to a point it could
be solved by the improvement of roads and skidways. By watering ruts
in the snow, which quickly iced and formed smooth grooves in which the
runners of sleds were firmly held, astonishingly heavy loads could be
hauled for considerable distances with speed and safety. However, a more
basic remedy was required when timber supplies came to stand more than
six miles from the streams.[12]

In 1882 the Chippewa Logging Company constructed ten and a half
miles of railroad from timberlands acquired from Cornell University to
a point on the Soo line. Near the terminus the town of Weyerhaeuser was
laid out. In 1883 the line was vested in the Chippewa River & Menomonie
Railway Company with an authorized capital of $1,500,000, subscribed
by Chippewa Logging and furnished as required. However, such roads
represented a limited activity in the state; in 1885 all of them covered
but 55 miles as against 520 miles in Michigan.[13]

Getting the logs to river or railhead, scaling and grading them, and
driving them to Eau Claire and Beef Slough—this was the operational
essence of the pool. It converted what had previously been a fumbling
activity, confused by numerous conflicting interests, into a smooth, organic
operation. Everyone on the Chippewa strove to relate his activities to one
common effort, and everyone profited.

If integrated operation was essential to the pool, so was an enduring
supply of timber. From 1881 forward, Weyerhaeuser had standing orders
to buy at least as much timber each year as was cut from lands owned
by Chippewa Logging and Mississippi River Logging. This directive was
practicable in the 1880's; it became more difficult in the ensuing decade,
for the supply of stumpage was steadily dwindling and was increasingly
held by firms that wanted to mill it themselves. Weyerhaeuser steadily
made purchases, sometimes in the name of allied companies, sometimes,
when a transaction seemed doubtful, on his own responsibility.

Though many acquisitions were piecemeal, Weyerhaeuser preferred
to buy in large blocks. In 1881–1882 he acquired 100,200,000 feet of
timber from fourteen different owners for a total cost of $153,854. But
his greatest single purchase was made in 1882, when he acquired 109,601
acres from Cornell University for $1,841,746. By estimate this acquisition
comprised 597,931,000 board feet of pine, priced at $3.00 per thousand
and $0.50 an acre for land. As a result of this large transaction, some
50,000 additional acres were bought to "block up" the original purchase,
many smaller lots being intermingled with the Cornell tracts, or adjoining
them.

Weyerhaeuser sometimes bought sawmill properties in order to acquire timber. The first case of this type had been Chippewa Lumber &
Boom, which when acquired in 1881 owned 80,000 acres of pineland,

46,000 uncut. The estimated footage was 457,511,000. In 1887 Mississippi River Logging purchased three mills of the Eau Claire Lumber Company with an estimated 680,000,000 feet of stumpage, paying $1,020,000. After this purchase had been approved, Weyerhaeuser presented a proposal from Eau Claire Lumber to sell its Meridean mill for $200,000. When acceptance was moved, Weyerhaeuser revealed that he had already made the purchase![14] It was unanimously ratified, but such advance moves sometimes annoyed Weyerhaeuser's associates, as did other purchases soon to be related.

As accessible timber grew scarcer, Weyerhaeuser purchased some lands lying far to the north. There was violent argument about some of these tracts. In one case the company invested $1,025,886 to buy and make accessible an estimated volume of stumpage exceeding 204,000,000 feet. It paid taxes and interest for ten years and finally built a logging railroad. Then, a total of $831,155 was realized from timber cut on the land, which was then sold for $1,500,000! In numerous instances negotiations broke down, in others the investments showed little profit. Actual losing ventures were few, though on a purchase of 27,588 acres in 1887 Chippewa Logging lost well over $200,000. By the mid-nineties almost all the remaining merchantable timber in the valley, except the extensive Knapp, Stout holdings on the Menomonie, was owned by individuals or firms associated with Frederick Weyerhaeuser. Reflecting the dwindling supply, stumpage costs rose steadily from approximately $2.00 per thousand feet in 1880 to $10.00 by 1902.[15]

Though by 1884 all the routine procedures on the Chippewa had been set, a few events interrupted their smooth application. In 1885, for one thing, Weyerhaeuser's leadership was seriously challenged. In January of that year he arranged for Chippewa Logging to buy from the North Wisconsin Lumber Company 36,040 acres of land, with an estimated 200,000,000 feet of pine, at $4.00 per thousand feet. Soon after this sale W. J. Young offered 30,000 acres of pineland to Chippewa Logging on the same terms as those made with North Wisconsin. Since the holdings were scattered through forty-five townships, Weyerhaeuser declined the offer as not in the best interests of the company. Apparently feeling that Weyerhaeuser had bought his own land while refusing to buy a comparable tract from an associate, Young then challenged the North Wisconsin purchase as a "very remarkable transaction" made without his knowledge (He had seconded the motion approving it!). He demanded a complete audit by outside experts of the books of the Chippewa Logging Company and of the collective enterprises from the beginning of operations.

Actually, E. S. Youmans had requested such an audit for the Mississippi River Logging Company in 1883, a wholly proper procedure. Then, as later, Weyerhaeuser had felt that since it was not customary to call in outside auditors, the proposal indicated a lack of confidence in the officers, and in him particularly. Youmans ultimately withdrew his request, but, on a motion by Ingram, an audit of Chippewa Logging and its subsidiaries had begun in 1884.

Doubtless as a matter of sound business practice, Ingram now seconded Young's demand. Weyerhaeuser was cut to the quick. He acted promptly to bring the entire question into the open, calling a special stockholders' meeting for March 18, 1885. Jottings in his notebook show his deep feeling and indicate the tenor of the remarks he planned to make:

Get the land back. 2. History of land trades. 3. Talk to the MRL Company. 4. Beef Slough Co. 5. Same salary as Schricker. Resign. 6. Read letter—not give name. Leave you hope God may bless you all and never feel as I have felt for the last five weeks.

When the meeting convened, Weyerhaeuser called Ingram to the chair, then explained the purpose of the meeting. W. J. Young moved that a committee be appointed to investigate the transaction, but apparently the stockholders were aware of Weyerhaeuser's feelings, for the motion was not adopted. Rust then moved that the purchase in question be "reratified and approved." This motion was carried. Weyerhaeuser now tendered his resignation, but J. M. Gould moved that it not be accepted and that "all his acts have been with a view to the best interests of this company and that we heartily endorse them." This motion won unanimous approval.

Later Young's central grievance was met. In October, 1888, the Mississippi River Logging Company paid him $4.00 per thousand board feet for stumpage and a small land fee for 26,869 acres of the pineland he had previously offered—a total of $450,000 for an estimated yield of 107,476,000 feet of pine. Somewhat later Young sold the company an additional 70,738 acres for $980,000. By 1904, when all the timber had been cut, the company had fully recovered the cost of the two purchases and had made a profit of $800,000.[16]

Another untoward event was the destruction, on September 6, 1886, of the Big Mill of Chippewa Lumber & Boom. It was struck by lightning and entirely consumed by fire. Many local citizens whispered, "It's the end of manufacturing at Chippewa Falls."

A meeting called on September 23rd completely refuted the rumors. Weyerhaeuser moved that the company immediately build a large mill capable of making lumber "the best and most economical way." The motion was passed, and construction began at once on two plants; one began operations on June 18, 1887, the second on August 1st. Daily output rose from the 235,835 board feet daily average of 1885, for the old mill, to 311,070 in 1889, and 336,354 in 1905 for the new. Almost all

costs of production were reduced through the use of more efficient machinery and better organization of the labor force.[17]

Work at the Big Mill was interrupted by only two strikes. One occurred in 1886 for a ten-hour instead of an eleven-hour day, a demand
supported by several lumber journals. The men did not win the shorter
work span, but the daily wage for common labor was increased from $1.25
to $1.37½. The second strike, twelve years later, was initiated by an affili-
ate of the American Federation of Labor, and completely closed the mill.
William Irvine wired to Frederick Weyerhaeuser for advice, and received
the reply: "If you are sure that your men's wages are fair, urge them to
go back to work. If they will not, open the booms and let the logs go down
the Chippewa." Confronted with this threat, the men gave in.[18]

Compared with the Big Mill, other operations of the associates were
unimportant. The Sherman mill, the three mills of the Eau Claire Lumber
Company, and the Meridean mill were all closed by 1892, with records
of small profits. A hardwood mill which the Chippewa Logging Company
established in 1895 at Apollonia proved to be a losing venture and was
sold in 1902.[19]

Some charter members of the pool withdrew from the corporation, or
sold their properties. The Daniel Shaw Company ceased to be a participating firm in 1886, although it continued to make use of pool facilities.
As noted, Mississippi River Logging bought out Eau Claire Lumber in
1887. To be sure, such new adherents as the Winona Lumber Company,
the Hannibal Saw Mill Company, and the Standard Lumber Company
were accepted, but others withdrew. Ultimately the percentage of pool
logs taken by Mississippi River Logging rose from an original 65 to
76.6 percent.

Providing this firm with logs finally led to the associates' biggest
headache. By 1888 the accumulation of silt, sand, and sawdust below
Round Hill, at the juncture of the Chippewa and Beef Slough, was seriously
interfering with the diversion of logs into the sorting and rafting area.
Officials considered using powerful sand pumps to clear the channel but
decided that this method and others would not be practicable. During the
dry summer of 1888 some 100,000,000 feet of logs were unable to pass
the obstructions, and an effort to get a congressional appropriation to clear
the passage failed when opposed by local politicians. What was more
discouraging, the company was even denied permission by local Army
engineers to undertake the task at its own expense.[20]

Fortunately, during the 1880's a supplemental storage area had been
developed by the associates at West Newton Slough, on the west bank of
the Mississippi eight miles south of Beef Slough. In 1889, when efforts to
improve the existing sorting area had failed, Weyerhaeuser proposed that

all logs now be sent down the Chippewa to the Mississippi and across that river to West Newton for sorting and rafting.

Investigations showed that the transfer of the works was practicable, although expensive. Accordingly, work was begun immediately on the improvement of the West Newton area, and a boom was soon ready to receive and handle the logs. While the transfer meant that the Beef Slough works had to be abandoned, the new installations and storage space proved to be superior to the old. The Minnesota Boom Company, incorporated on April 16, 1889, under Minnesota Law, owned the new works and conducted the sorting and rafting activities. It was capitalized at $100,000 and entirely owned by the Mississippi River Logging Company and a few of its individual members.[21]

Contrary to expectations, the new departure provoked an extensive and varied opposition. In Wisconsin the shift from Beef Slough to another state revived the old clamor against the exportation of natural wealth, while a group in Eau Claire, angered in 1882 when Weyerhaeuser removed pool headquarters to Chippewa Falls to avoid a local tax levied on logs, now seized the opportunity to attack him. Meanwhile, when the first large consignment of logs was sent to West Newton, a foreman of the driving crew found that access to the area was partially blocked by an old government dam. On his own responsibility, he blew up a portion of the structure, and the Army, the attorney general, and even Congress were alerted.

The course of these disputes cannot be followed in detail. While there was much talk of prohibiting loose logs on the Mississippi and reopening the old debate about "freedom of navigation," steamboats were now almost an anachronism, while logs from the Chippewa represented an annual value of $5,000,000 and provided jobs for thousands of workmen at the mills. Mississippi River Logging offered to pay for the damage to the dam, estimated at from $1,500 to $2,000, and threats of punitive action evaporated. In spite of the refusal of the War Department to permit the erection of a sheer boom on the Mississippi, the work was successfully carried on without it.

Opponents in Wisconsin had at first looked toward federal action, but when this failed to develop they filed numerous suits for damages alleged to have been caused by the pool's installations on the Chippewa. Begun in 1890, actions referred back to the floods of 1884. A number of payments were made in settlement of these claims.

Eventually the associates also had their difficulties in Minnesota, when J. H. Mullen, surveyor general of the district in which West Newton lay, insisted on scaling all logs entering the sorting area and charging for this unwanted service. The situation involved a lawsuit and the seizure and sale of logs by Mullen's deputies. He won some popularity as the champion of the public against a wealthy corporation allegedly trying to evade its just obligations. Knute Nelson, the governor of Minnesota, who had made his early reputation by attacking James J. Hill and the Great Northern, helped to publicize the case and was reported to have remarked of Weyerhaeuser, "I'll show that French dude where to get off!"[22]

Undoubtedly an important cause for the troubles arising in connection with the West Newton Slough had been the growing hostility of the American public to large corporations. "Monopoly" was a hated word, and journalists from Henry Demarest Lloyd to Ida M. Tarbell and Charles Edward Russell leaped to attack it, while Nelson in Minnesota, in denouncing corporate power, merely did in a state what Bryan and others in 1896 and 1900 essayed on a national scale. "The pool" had a sinister connotation, and when the term "Weyerhaeuser syndicate" became current, the union of interests on the Chippewa was widely assumed to have the characteristics of an oppressive combine.

Early statements by the *Mississippi Valley Lumberman* had vigorously defended the pool companies and Weyerhaeuser. "He has a passion for the management of vast interests," it conceded, but noted his unselfish service. "There is nothing," it asserted, "to the suppositional corner of Wisconsin lumber." The companies had saved money for their members by "methods more economical than those which were previously in force in handling timber from the stump to the mill—and that is all." Their success had been attained "without the oppression of the logger, or extorting unjust or excessive tribute from the consumer."[23] Such views were either ignored or forgotten.

The rash of damage suits and the dispute as to the scaling of logs at West Newton became disastrous publicity for Weyerhaeuser and his associates. Millions of Americans heard of them, never ascertained the truth, and assumed that they indicated grave abuses instead of the relatively trivial litigations, often lacking substance, which they actually were. Later the muckraking journalists were to inflate these occurrences, using them to color absurd charges that are discussed in detail later.

5

This journalistic evaluation was based not only on Weyerhaeuser operations in the Chippewa basin but on others in the St. Croix River Valley and northern Wisconsin. There the pattern of activity, much influenced by railroads, became quite different from that in west central Wisconsin. Participation in partnerships became extraordinarily mixed; timber was acquired for new mills built near at hand as well as for the old mills on the Middle Mississippi. Even cooperation in log driving took a different form from that on the Chippewa.

A new railroad company provided the first of the sawmilling opportunities. By 1880 a crisscross of railroad lines was penetrating the northern reaches of Wisconsin: the Wisconsin Central, the Chicago & North Western, the West Wisconsin, and the North Wisconsin companies. Coming from the south, the West Wisconsin had reached Eau Claire in 1870 and pushed on to St. Paul the following year. The North Wisconsin had thrust up from Hudson, a little south of Stillwater on the St. Croix, to a point beyond Shell Lake on the way to Duluth. From this point a branch had been built to the northeast to the Lake Superior port of Ashland. Endowed with land grants totaling 1,228,000 acres, the two lines merged in May, 1880, into the new Chicago, St. Paul, Minneapolis & Omaha.

By mid-1880 the Omaha line, needing money for an ambitious construction program, was eager to sell its timberlands in the northwestern sector of Wisconsin at prices ranging from $1.73 to $5.91 per acre. Its tracks made logs and lumber produced along them accessible to existing markets. Forward-looking lumbermen whose sources of logs on streams like the Chippewa were approaching exhaustion saw a new empire opened to them, and trooped into it.[24]

Among the newcomers was Anthony J. Hayward, timber cruiser and former associate of the veteran lumberman Senator Philetus Sawyer. In 1880 Hayward visited the Namakagon River at a place almost a hundred miles directly north of Eau Claire and about fifty south of Lake Superior. Noting the tracks being pushed northward, he acquired considerable timber, ample frontage on the river, and an unfinished small mill, and named for himself the town he envisaged growing there.

Offering a site on a drivable river and rail connections with Great Lakes ports to the north and St. Paul to the southwest, with immense unpurchased timberlands "tributary" to the project, Hayward quickly enlisted Laird, Norton interest. On November 11th, to process the timber, the North Wisconsin Lumber Company was incorporated with an authorized capital of $60,000. Hayward owned one-third, Laird, Norton another third, and Robert Laird McCormick the remainder.[25]

McCormick became the manager of the new enterprise, a logical choice but one which in practice did not work out happily at first. William H. Laird's nephew, he had been given a responsible part in the offices of Laird, Norton at Winona in 1868, at age twenty-one. Later he had bought and operated a lumberyard as Waseca, Minnesota, while continuing to serve the company. Having only one year of schooling beyond the grammar grades, McCormick was a personable, articulate young man who had served as mayor of Waseca and was still serving in St. Paul as a state senator. It was he who had brought Hayward to Laird, Norton. McCormick had invested in the new venture and was eager to make it a success. But he had never lived in the woods, had never built a mill or a town, bought timberlands, or managed a large group of men. His talents were actually for accounting, selling, and public relations rather than for construction work on the lumbering frontier.[26]

McCormick and his associates were soon smothered with problems typical of such ventures. Laird, Norton had no experience in starting a new operation deep in the woods, and Hayward, who was scheduled to assist in the enterprise, was busy locating new timberlands. The original incomplete small mill did not begin operations until August 18, 1882, forty-five days behind schedule, and then limped along with mechanical breakdowns and insufficient water power.[27]

Meanwhile, to finance the company's acquisition of more timberland and to erect the large mill, the stockholders in June, 1882, had voted to increase capitalization from the original $60,000 to $450,000. McCormick and Hayward took but one-sixth instead of their former one-third of the stock, Laird and the Nortons subscribing the remainder. However, Hayward soon found himself unable to meet the assessments due, and Frederick Weyerhaeuser agreed to advance the necessary funds, Hayward to repay him later. Weyerhaeuser, who had earlier purchased almost 70,000 acres for North Wisconsin from the Omaha, also took over the stock of William H. Laird in 1884. Contrary to the Rock Islander's expectations, his partner Denkmann refused to share in the North Wisconsin investment, and Frederick Weyerhaeuser temporarily had difficulty in finding money.[28]

McCormick floundered in a morass of detail and finally had to be given assistance. Laird, Norton took over designing and arranging for construction of the enlarged manufacturing facilities, which included a planing mill and a shingle and lath mill. Even a second dam did not provide enough water power, so further improvements had to be made, even after the big mill swung into operation on June 11, 1883. Meanwhile, workers were complaining constantly about the meals and a succession of poor cooks. Laird, Norton finally hired a store manager as well as a highly proficient mill superintendent, Captain Clayton E. Rogers. At his insistence, responsibilities were clearly divided, with Hayward supervising woods operations, Rogers himself taking charge of the mill and the yard, and McCormick handling purchases, finances, and sales.[29]

Almost all the lumber manufactured in the nineteen years of the company's operations was shipped by way of the Omaha line. By battling constantly for lower rates and for rebates (which were granted in these days according to the shipper's bargaining skill), McCormick seems to have kept his freight costs reasonable. He sold some lumber to the Laird, Norton Co. but also won customers throughout southern Minnesota, Dakota, Iowa, and other middle western states. His chief competition came from southern yellow pine and neighboring white pine mills. To some extent he met this challenge by developing a market in the East, especially during the depression years of 1893–1897.

North Wisconsin's profits were more than acceptable. It paid its first dividend in 1891 and continued them regularly until 1902, when the remaining productive properties were sold to the Edward Hines Lumber Company. Eventually the cutover lands went to the American Immigration Company. According to W. L. McCormick's (son of R. L.) recollection, North Wisconsin stockholders received 1,000 percent on their original investment of $450,000.[30]

At the same time that Hayward was scouting for North Wisconsin's timber, two neighboring families, the Joyces of Lyons and the Lambs of Clinton, were joining Delos R. Moon and William A. Rust of Eau Claire in negotiating for stumpage. Apparently the flood on the Chippewa River in 1880 induced them to seek an alternative investment in the northwestern Wisconsin timberlands.

Joyce and his associates soon acquired extensive tracts to the southwest of Hayward. Probably still in 1880, they purchased or built a mill at Barronett on the Omaha Railroad and organized a lumber company bearing that name with an authorized capital of $150,000. A year later essentially the same group formed the Shell Lake Lumber Company, with a plant at Shell Lake about nine miles to the south of Barronett.

The Lambs and Joyces dominated both companies. Lafayette Lamb, the younger son of Chancy, became the first president of Barronett and his brother Artemus of Shell Lake. David Joyce acted as secretary-treasurer of both and in 1893 became president. Weyerhaeuser & Denkmann early became stockholders in both enterprises, acquiring approximately a third of the Barronett stock and eventually two-fifths of the Shell Lake shares. In Minneapolis the two companies soon established a joint sales office, operated by William T. Joyce, David's able son, and officials induced the Omaha to accord the new firms the same rates as on shipments of lumber from Eau Claire—but no rebates.

Both enterprises had prospered up to 1894, when the noted Hinckley fire swept over an extensive district along the upper St. Croix and its tributaries. On September 1st Captain W. R. Bourne, the "outspoken, testy" manager at Barronett, was in the Minneapolis office assuring a group of lumbermen that his mill was in no danger because all the timber within three-quarters of a mile of it had been cleared. While he was still talking, word came that Barronett was on fire. Flames driven by a violent southwest wind had whipped across the protective area and were destroying the town and the mill. Actually, refugees from Barronett had already poured into Shell Lake, where they joined in fighting fires that menaced that settlement. Happily, although fifty-three dwellings were burned, most of the town, including the Shell Lake mill, was saved.

The Barronett and Shell Lake operations were now consolidated, with Bourne as general manager of the larger Shell Lake Lumber Company, with an authorized capital of $500,000. He enlarged its plant and acquired additional stumpage. Up to 1894 Barronett Lumber Company had distributed dividends of $750,000 on the $90,000 actually paid in by stockholders. From 1888 to the end of operations in 1902 the Shell Lake company declared dividends of $3,000,000, profits represented in large part by appreciation in timber values toward the end of the century; book charges rose from $2.00 per thousand for stumpage in 1881 to $5.00 in 1899.[31]

The fires that had destroyed Barronett and seared Shell Lake had swept northward and reached the little town of Mason, Wisconsin, where another venture had been under way since 1882. In that year John A. Humbird, a rugged railroader and lumberman who had operated a mill at Clayton a hundred miles to the south, procured extensive timberlands from the Omaha line and organized the White River Lumber Company. Frederick Weyerhaeuser soon owned an eighth interest. David Joyce was also an investor and company officer, but Humbird, the president, treasurer, and general manager of the new organization, was the initiator and person primarily responsible for the early success of the enterprise.

Having helped to organize a company in which $460,000 was invested, he set up a middle-sized mill with two gangs and two circulars. It was located on a small stream that Humbird improved, but driving at times was almost impossible, and he built a logging railroad to assist bringing in the logs. The season was shorter than at Hayward, temperatures going as low as 54 degrees below zero, but production went on.

In 1888 J. A. Humbird moved to St. Paul, and his son, Thomas J., took over the management. He was in charge when the fire of 1894 destroyed the mill and the entire season's output of lumber. He built a more modern plant and continued the enterprise until he left Wisconsin six years later to take charge of the Humbird Lumber Company at Sandpoint, Idaho. Frederick Weyerhaeuser counseled him in St. Paul: "You will make many mistakes, but try not to make the same mistake twice." He then started him at a generous salary, saying, "I will treat you just like one of my own sons," which, said Humbird later, he always did.

In the twenty-three years up to 1905, White River Lumber paid $2,025,000 in dividends on an initial investment of $460,000. It still held 400,000,000 feet of stumpage when it was sold to Edward Hines for $2,620,000. Despite inferior timber, it brought its stockholders an even better return than did the neighboring North Wisconsin Lumber Company.[32]

One St. Croix enterprise, and one only, resulted in the manufacture of lumber by the associates. Weyerhaeuser and Rutledge had acquired

stumpage permits on the Minnesota side of the St. Croix along the line
of the St. Paul & Duluth Railroad, mostly from this road. The Rutledge
Lumber & Manufacturing Company owned this venture, with Weyer-
haeuser & Denkmann, Rutledge, and Sauntry subscribing for 1,050 shares
each and Edward Douglas taking 400 and James D. McCormick 80.
Douglas, former superintendent at Beef Slough, ran the mill, Sauntry and
Rutledge took care of the logging, while McCormick served as secretary
and general manager. The plant was appropriately located at Rutledge,
Minnesota, about a hundred miles north of St. Paul, on the St. Paul &
Duluth Railroad, as well as on the Kettle River.

The company, launched just before the panic of 1893, was hit hard
by the depression. Rutledge soon reported that he and his associates were
"financially busted as they don't sell any lumber or collect any money
on what they have sold." John P. Weyerhaeuser advanced funds to maintain operations as the mill lost money steadily year after year. But by
1897 earnings were $51,162, with many of the company assets written off.
Profits then rose gradually until timber was exhausted in 1906. Approximately 200,000,000 feet of lumber had been sawed in fifteen years, and
$1,250,000 had been distributed to the stockholders.[33]

As early as 1891 Weyerhaeuser and Rutledge had purchased stumpage about Lake Nebagamon, a wild area bordering on Lake Superior to
the north and to the south touching headwaters of small streams tributary
to the St. Croix. Their largest acquisition, again from the Omaha, cost
$580,000, and others almost doubled their holdings, which ran to above
an estimated half-billion board feet.

Not until 1898, however, with the depression of the nineties past,
did the two veteran partners organize a corporation to process the timber
—the Nebagamon Lumber Company. Having an authorized capital of
$100,000, it was launched with Rutledge as president, Frederick Weyer-
haeuser as vice-president, and E. L. Ainsworth as secretary-treasurer.
Except for two shares held by the latter, Rutledge, Frederick Weyerhaeuser, and John Philip Weyerhaeuser each owned approximately a third
of the stock.

Frederick Weyerhaeuser assigned the managership of the new enterprise to his eldest son, who had become discouraged with the routine and
competitive difficulties of running the diminishing business at the mills in
Rock Island. Advised by his father and Rutledge, John Philip laid out the
mill site, supervised the construction of 7½ miles of railroad to connect
with the Omaha, platted the town, and built the mill, office, stables, boarding and rooming houses, a most necessary store, and other facilities. He
visited mills in Minneapolis to inspect machinery, and decided to install
two bands and a resaw, later acquiring a secondhand gang from the North
Wisconsin Lumber Company and some surplus items from Rock Island.

To this makeshift town in the wilderness, remote from school and hospitals, he brought his wife and three children in September, 1899.

By this time the venture was off to an excellent start. Lumber prices were good: at $12 per thousand board feet in Milwaukee and Chicago the net profit was an estimated clean $2. And the timber supply seemed adequate: by March, 1900, Frederick Weyerhaeuser and Rutledge had advanced a total of $1,089,160, chiefly for purchasing pinelands.

Despite the personal tragedy of losing his wife in 1900, John Philip easily guided his firm to prosperity. In its brief span of activity (1898–1907) it made profits of $3,516,000. Much of this was stumpage appreciation ($1,995,000) and money realized from the sales of such properties as the railroad and the company store.[34]

Frederick Weyerhaeuser's final milling venture in Wisconsin began in 1907, just after the Nebagamon venture closed. George H. Atwood, who had just shut down his own mill at Willow River, Minnesota, in the St. Croix watershed, persuaded the Rock Islander to acquire large tracts of hemlock timber, which also contained tamarack, balsam, birch, and maple, in north central Wisconsin. Altogether, 53,807 acres were purchased, about 70 percent from the Wisconsin Central Railroad, for $243,000. On June 11, 1907, the Atwood Lumber & Manufacturing Company was incorporated at Park Falls, Wisconsin, with an authorized capital of $200,000.

The venture did not succeed. The timber proved to be inferior, logging costs were high, a severe fire destroyed part of the stumpage, and the market for products of the mill was consistently poor. Even at the end of the first year Weyerhaeuser looked for a purchaser and could find none. On February 19, 1913, he finally disposed of the entire property to Edward Hines for $700,000. Hines, who was rapidly taking over all the northern timberlands he could buy at good prices, also paid Mississippi River Logging, Chippewa Logging, and the American Immigration Company $1,000,000 for additional birch and hemlock stumpage. The owners considered themselves fortunate to get rid of the unprofitable venture.[35]

6

While buying timber and building mills on railroads in northern Wisconsin, Weyerhaeuser and his friends had also been using the St. Croix as a source of logs for mills on the Middle Mississippi. The area of the upper St. Croix straddles the borderline between Wisconsin and Minnesota. Unlike the territory in which such projects as Hayward, Barronett, Shell Lake, White River, and Nebagamon operated, it was not effectively opened up by the coming of the railroads, for such tributaries of the St. Croix as the Moose, Totogatic, Clam, Kettle, and Ann, along with the

Upper St. Croix itself, afforded driving possibilities for taking logs down to Stillwater and beyond.

Up to 1880 the area had seen only sporadic logging activity, because of available timber farther down the St. Croix and the intensive activity on the Chippewa. But with the impending exhaustion of these and other sources and the increasing usability of logging railroads to reach remoter districts, the whole Upper St. Croix began to interest lumbermen as a source of logs.

The first Upper St. Croix timber in which Frederick Weyerhaeuser became interested lay on the Moose River, in Douglas County, Wisconsin. Here William Sauntry and Albert Tozer, two young loggers, had taken an option on the holdings of Isaac Staples, a pioneer lumberman of Stillwater. Sauntry, soon to be closely associated with Weyerhaeuser in various enterprises, was rough in speech and manner and inclined to be impetuous and overbearing. Yet he had great natural ability and drive, and was skilled in cruising and the buying of timberlands as well as in logging and river driving. The Mussers were interested in the Staples property and were willing to join Weyerhaeuser & Denkmann in buying it. Eventually the purchase was made on November 30, 1883.

With additional lands bought from the Omaha Railroad, the cost of 10,625 acres amounted to $262,819. Eventually 93,821,000 board feet of logs were cut. Weyerhaeuser & Denkmann held a third interest in the undertaking, the Mussers a third, and Sauntry and Tozer the remainder, although their share was financed by the others. Sauntry took complete charge of logging, driving, and rafting. Harrison McKusick of his office handled the routine aspects of the enterprise, including the sale of logs, which were driven down the Moose to the St. Croix and on to Lake St. Croix just south of Stillwater, where they were rafted and delivered to purchasers.[36]

The undertaking was unquestionably profitable and supplied logs to a number of Mississippi River firms besides Weyerhaeuser & Denkmann and the Mussers.

Satisfaction with the "Moose Deal" and the continuing need for logs led to another venture. On July 10 in 1886 the Musser-Sauntry Land, Logging, & Manufacturing Company, an Iowa firm, was incorporated with a capital stock of $1,000,000, of which $420,000 was issued. In this organization Weyerhaeuser & Denkmann, the Mussers, and Dimock, Gould & Company each held two-sevenths of the stock, with Sauntry & Tozer holding one-seventh financed at 8 percent interest by the others. The basis for the firm was a large purchase from the Omaha line and smaller ones from Staples and John A. Humbird. Logging these pinelands and others acquired later from time to time, the company procured 796,320,000 board feet of logs from 1888 to 1907.

In general, despite some unprofitable transactions, the corporation was of great value to its stockholders and to other Mississippi River lumbermen. The St. Croix, indeed, through such activities as this one, became for a time a major source of supply for the firms from Winona to Muscatine. In 1892, of 52,427,570 board feet of logs sawed by the three Weyerhaeuser & Denkmann mills at Rock Island, 47 percent originated along the St. Croix, while 43 percent came from the Chippewa "pool" and 10 percent from Mississippi River Logging.[37]

Certain other ventures in the St. Croix area can be dismissed with only brief comment. In the so-called "Superior Deal" of 1886, Weyerhaeuser & Denkmann engaged with the Mussers, Lambs, Sauntry, and others in an investment which yielded few logs for the Mississippi River plants (85 percent of the 193,089,000 cut going to Duluth sawmills) and became an investment in timber. Edward Hines bought the remaining unlogged lands the group had acquired along and near the westernmost Superior shore, paying $1,800,000 for them in 1902. Other joint ventures, such as investments in timber on the Ann, Clam, and Totogatic rivers, and Mille Lacs in Minnesota, swelled the number of logs going to mills on the Middle Mississippi. Almost always Laird, Norton, the Lambs, and Mussers joined Weyerhaeuser & Denkmann in such enterprises.[38]

When a lumber manufacturing enterprise is dependent on river transportation, the possession of substantial stumpage does not in itself assure a steady supply of logs. The Chippewa experience had shown the vital importance of controlling the river as well. Weyerhaeuser and his associates by the late eighties were active in half a dozen areas on the upper St. Croix and wanted to organize on a cooperative basis the St. Croix Boom, which processed every log coming down the river.

This boom was comparably famed with the Tittabawasee (Michigan) and the Beef Slough booms and was to outlast both. Situated just above Stillwater where the river widens into Lake St. Croix, it had an admirable location for the sorting, storing, and rafting of logs. The St. Croix Boom Corporation had been chartered by the Minnesota territorial legislature on February 27, 1856.[39]

In the 1880's Martin Mowrer won a controlling interest in the company. Negotiations by Weyerhaeuser and his associates to purchase his stock proved futile, but on April 2, 1889, he finally agreed to lease the boom for twenty years at an annual rental of $12 a share.

Among the Stillwater lumbermen there was no small amount of jealousy of the "outsiders" who were also their competitors and who were pushing in to acquire stumpage upriver and now to reorganize the operation of the boom. The local press referred to the "octopus" and the "scourge of locusts" emerging from nether regions to devour the pine timber of Minnesota. Only one editor pointed out that "Eau Claire is just

finding out that Mr. Weyerhaeuser is not the monster he has been painted.
. . . The lumber interest on the St. Croix has undoubtedly suffered for
years from the lack of some such organization of interests as Mr. Weyerhaeuser has the faculty for accomplishing."[40]

The loggers involved agreed with the editor. They joined Frederick
Weyerhaeuser in organizing the St. Croix Dam & Boom Company to deal
with Mowrer and administer the boom. They chose Sauntry as their president, Jacob Bean vice-president, and Samuel McClure secretary-treasurer.
On Weyerhaeuser's recommendation, the group constructed a dam comparable with that at Little Falls on the Chippewa, eleven miles north of
St. Croix Falls (some fifty miles north of Stillwater). This prevented log
jams, controlled the level of water for driving, and ensured a steady run
of logs to the boom. A large expenditure for the improvement of boom
facilities was made. The Nevers Dam, as it was called, was completed in
1889 and stood until 1952, when most of it was swept away by spring
floods. To operate the river facilities a separate corporation, the St. Croix
Lumbermen's Dam & Boom Company, was organized with a capitalization of $120,000.

After large expenditures for the franchises, dam, and other improvements in the early years, outlays naturally diminished and the revenue
rose. Fees were charged for booming, rafting, and scaling. Soon the
management was able to pay its stockholders dividends after the annual
settlement with Mowrer. For the twenty-year lease period the corporations
returned dividends of $428 a share, a pleasant bonus additional to the
chief benefit accruing: the orderly processing of logs for the firms concerned. The boom, incidentally, continued to function for a few years
after the expiration of the lease, the last log being allocated on the afternoon of August 12, 1914, fifty-eight years after the first charter rights
had been granted.[41]

7

The share of Weyerhaeuser and his associates in the regional lumber
output and the extent of their timber holdings in northern Wisconsin and
on the St. Croix can be fixed only approximately. In some areas they were
the major owners; in others they held little. In the winter of 1898, when
Frederick Weyerhaeuser and Edward Douglas journeyed through the
forests above the headwaters of the Chippewa, they discovered that virtually all the uncut pine was already owned by one or more of their numerous associates. But by that date the pine was almost gone!

This increasing scarcity, along with a steady demand for lumber,
brought a sharp increase after 1897 in the value of white pine stumpage
and many inferior logs for the first time became salable. As a result,

loggers removed smaller trees and defective timber; after 1897 the Mississippi River Logging policy was to cut logs down to six inches in diameter at the small end and to take windfalls ten inches thick, "even if wormy." The activities of the Weyerhaeuser groups, like those of others in the North Wisconsin, Chippewa, and St. Croix regions, was part of a gigantic mopping-up operation. The possibility of holding cutover lands for their potential harvest of hemlock, birch, and second-growth pine was considered, but the expense of fire protection, high state taxes, and the lure of more attractive opportunities elsewhere all forbade such action. Instead, the cutover lands were sold as rapidly as possible.[42]

With minor exceptions, the operations in northern Wisconsin and on the St. Croix had been richly remunerative. They had brought Weyerhaeuser many new associates, some to join him in operations elsewhere. They were, however, the final activities that supplied logs to the firms on the Middle Mississippi, and as the flow of logs from the north ceased, so did the operations of the firms comprising the Mississippi River Logging Company.

W. J. Young & Company's operations tapered off in 1893 and ceased entirely after Young's death in 1896. The Clinton Lumber Company closed in 1893. Laird, Norton terminated its mill operations in 1905, as did Weyerhaeuser & Denkmann, which had not rebuilt its Renwick, Shaw & Crossett mill after it burned in 1901. Similarly, the Chippewa mills, which had taken no small amount of logs from the north Wisconsin enterprises, shut down at various dates from the middle nineties to 1912, when the Daniel Shaw Lumber Company, the last, went out of business. The last log was sawed at the Big Mill of Chippewa Lumber & Boom on August 2, 1911.

Chippewa Logging had reached the apex of its activity in 1884, when 741,837,000 board feet of logs were banked, but production had continued high for the next dozen years. For the first two decades of its existence the pool had distributed 6,493,811,000 board feet of logs, an average of 324 million a year, and for the longer period to 1906 the Beef Slough and West Newton works had processed a grand total of 7,864,047,000 feet.

The two chief associations, Mississippi River Logging and Chippewa Logging, had not been designed for profit but for service—to get the logs to the mills. Yet eventually both paid cash dividends, largely out of earnings on timber holdings. Mississippi River Logging declared its first in 1900, when $396,000 was divided among eight member firms. By the time the firm was dissolved in 1929, it had distributed $7,623,734 to shareholders. The Beef Slough and Chippewa Logging companies paid only $600,000 (to 1889) and $611,325 (to 1903), respectively. Chippewa Logging had really finished its work by 1899, when its directors voted to dissolve it. The most profitable of all the corporations had been Chippewa Lumber & Boom, which sawed 1,507,103,439 board feet of lumber and paid its stockholders $11,228,020 between 1903 and 1920; nine years later, at dissolution, it still showed undivided profits of $1,228,791.[43] The dividends for all companies were increased by the disposal of their lands, many of which, although cut over, contained stands of hemlock and hardwood. Other revenues came from sale of their equipment and buildings, and their dams and riparian rights to electric-light and power corporations.

For many firms and individuals these events marked the end of long lumber activity; for all they wrote off a dramatic, prosperous era. But in the case of Weyerhaeuser and many of his associates, the end was also a beginning. They had long since invested Wisconsin profits in other regions, to continue in the Far West, in the South, and most immediately in Minnesota their roles in the saga of American lumbering and in the economic development of the United States.

NOTES

1. MRLC Min. Bk. and its annual statements; Chip. Log. Co. (hereafter cited as CLC) Min. Bk.; CL&B Stock Ledger. The MRLC really represented a supplementary pool, operated for the benefit of its members, but since it worked within the larger framework represented by Chippewa Logging, it will not be referred to here as a pool. By 1886 upward of $600,000 had been invested in dams and improvements on the Chippewa. F. W. Kohlmeyer compiled a list of 148 dams. See *Nwn. Lbrmn.*, June 7, 1884, and CRI&LD Co. Papers, April 30, 1886.
2. Reynolds, *Daniel Shaw Lumber Co.*, 19; Hotchkiss, *Lumber and Forest Industry of the Northwest*, 482–631; Rector, *Log Transportation*, 33–34; *MVL&M*, I, Oct. 5, 1876, p. 12; *Amer. Lbrmn.*, I, 319–322; FEW Record File (clippings).
3. Rector, 305–310; Steer, *Lumber Production in the United States*, 10. Rector estimates the board footage of logs driven down the Chippewa in 1881 at 300,000,000 feet; Steer sets the national production of all lumber in 1879 (closest date given) at more than 18,000,000,000 feet.
4. Ingram, *Autobiography*, 54; FEW Record, 278; Rector, 267.
5. FEW Record, 221; CL&B Co. Min. Bk., *passim*.
6. Comment by FKW, July 17, 1959 (Irvine); FEW Record File, obit. newspr. clips. (Culver); *ibid.*, Henry to FEW, Dec. 8, 1933 (Irvine); FEW Record, 215 (personnel CLC), 225 (Culver-Irvine), and 272–273 (Henry). Thomas and William Irvine were not related.
7. FEW Record File, Henry and FW Notebks., 1885–1886, 1889–1890; FEW Record, 249.
8. FEW Record File, Ingram to Henry, March 31, 1883; *ibid.*, Scaling Instructions; *Nwn. Lbrmn.*, April 19, 1884. All No. 1 logs had to be smooth, straight, scaling not less than two-thirds round and not less than 12 inches in diameter at the small end for white pine and 18 for Norway, with the latter having to be 24 feet or longer and the former 16 feet.

9. MVL&M, X, Aug. 21, 1885, p. 10, and March 26, 1886, p. 8.

10. FEW Record, 229, quoting letter of Aug. 8, 1925, from Colin McMillian to George F. Lindsay; CLC and CRI&LD Co. Papers (showing innumerable flowage right agreements). Considerable tracts were bought outright so that they could be flooded; at Little Falls 2,951 acres were so purchased and at Paint Creek another 2,336. If the owner made claims for exceptional damages which the companies questioned, arbitrators were appointed to settle the dispute and fix a payment if one was to be awarded.

11. FEW Record File, Henry to FEW, Sept. 3 and Oct. 30, 1934.

12. FEW Record File, Henry letters; FEW Record, 170.

13. CLC Min. Bk., Sept. 13, 1882 (articles of incorporation for the road); CR&M Rwy. Papers, MHS; Rector, 196, 221–222; Nwn. Lbrmn., XXV, Feb. 14, 1885, pp. 14–15.

14. CLC and MRLC Min. Bks., 1883, 1885; FW Notebk., 1885 (policy and practice); LN Papers, Statement (purchases, 1882); Norton, Mississippi River Logging Co., 94–95; Gates, Wisconsin Pinelands, 229; MRLC annual statements.

15. CLC Papers, corresp., 1887–1905, and Min. Bk., 1887; MRLC annual statements.

16. LN Papers, corresp., 1882 and 1885; FW Notebk., 1885; CLC Min. Bk., March 18, 1885; FW Papers, FW to WJY, July 25, 1892 (Young's lands); MRLC annual statements. Young did not own personally all the acreage he sold, some being held jointly with Dwight & McGraw and with D. P. Simons.

17. CL&B Co. Min. Bk., Sept. 23, 1886; CRI&LD Papers, MHS: LN Papers, W. Irvine to FW, Sept. 16, 1887; FEW Record File, Irvine to FEW, Dec. 19, 1910; CL&B Co. annual reports.

18. FEW Record, 243; LN Papers, MHS; CL&B Papers, MHS. Total cost of the new mill was $126,540.

19. LN Papers, Winona, MRLC Balance Sheets and Statements; CLC annual statements; Hotchkiss, 438; MVL&M VI, No. 43 (May 26, 1882), p. 4.

20. FW Papers and JPW Papers, corresp. 1889, 1895, 1899 (percentage of logs taken by MRLC); FEW Record, 140; MGN Papers, Winona, Norton to R. L. McCormick, 1893 (on silting); MVL, Feb. 27, 1891, p. 5, open letter by Thomas Irvine.

21. FEW Record, 140; Minn. Boom Co., Arts. of Incorpn., Min. Bk. The MRLC took $96,500 of the stock, with various individual firms holding small amounts. Frederick Weyerhaeuser was president and treasurer, Thomas Irvine secretary.

22. Fifty-second Congress, 1st Sess., House Exec. Doc. 178 and 183 (W. Newton dam and general situation); FEW Record File, clippings from Eau Claire newspapers; CLC annual statements and those of allied companies, MGN Papers, March–May, 1893 (scaling); FEW Record, 142 (litigation and Nelson).

23. MVL, XXX, No. 9 (Oct. 7, 1887), p. 2.

24. The Railway and Locomotive Historical Society, Inc., The Railroads of Wisconsin, 33, 36; FEW Record, 332–333.

25. LN Papers, MHS, corresp., 1881; FEW Record, 349–351.

26. MVL, XXIV, March 23, 1894, p. 5; Amer. Lbrmn., 1905, pp. 1, 295; Winona Republican Herald, Feb. 6, 1911.

27. LN Papers, MHS, corresp., 1881–1882.

28. Ibid., corresp., 1882–1883; FEW Record, 349, 352–353. Weyerhaeuser could not procure a loan from his regular bankers but got one from another Rock Islander banker. FEW states that Denkmann had intended to invest in the North Wisconsin venture but that his son, F. C. Denkmann, objected. Frederick Weyerhaeuser was "shocked." Eventually Hayward forfeited his stock, and it was taken over in October, 1896, by T. J. and J. F. Robinson, who had originally ad-

vanced Weyerhaeuser the money he needed in 1882.

29. LN Papers, corresp., 1882–1883.
30. FEW Record, 351, copy of W. L. McCormick to FEW, Nov. 23, 1933.
31. FEW Record, 345–357; FEW Record File, W. R. Bourne to JPW, Sept. 16, 1894; LN Papers, MHS, LN to No. Wis. Lbr. Co., July 30, 1884; LN Papers, Winona, Sept., 1894; FW Papers, corresp. 1894; Weyerhaeuser Documents, St. Paul, Shell Lake Lbr. Co. annual reports; *MVL*, XXIII, Nov. 24, 1893, p. 7; Hotchkiss, 595; Holbrook, *Burning an Empire*, 77–86.
32. FEW Record, 359–361; MS, "White River Lumber Co.," compiled by John A. Humbird, West Vancouver, B.C.; FEW Papers, WRLC annual reports.
33. Musser-Sauntry Land, Logging & Manufacturing Co. (MSLI&MC) Papers, MHS (timber purchases); JPW Papers, corresp., 1891–1897; Weyerhaeuser Documents, Rut. Lbr. & Mfg. Co., annual reports.
34. Nebagamon Lbr. Co. Papers, MHS, Min. Bk., agreements, deeds, and other documents; FW Papers, 1891 (stumpage); JPW Papers, corresp., 1898–1899, and financial statements and auditor's reports, 1898–1907; FEW Record, 365–366, 403, 408, 799.
35. FEW Record, 388–389; FEW Papers, deeds, agreements, correspondence, 1907–1913.
36. FEW Record, 367–368 (quoting letter from McKusick); MSL&MC Papers, MHS, agreements of 1883 and 1884.
37. FEW Record, 369–370; LN Papers, Winona, corresp., 1897–1903 (Bean); FW Papers, F. C. Denkmann to FW, Jan. 13, 1893. An expenditure of $220,000 for land held by Jacob Bean yielded logs at excessively high cost.

38. P. & P. M. Musser Papers, MHS, and FEW Record, 372–376 (Superior Deal); LN Papers, MHS, and CRI&LD Papers, MHS, corresp., 1893–1898 (Clam River); FW Papers, MRLC Min. Bk., and LN Papers, Winona (Ann River); FW Papers, corresp., 188–192 (Totogatic); LN Papers, MHS and FW Papers, corresp., 1889–1892 (Mille-Lacs). The Mille Lacs venture was called "the Sabin Deal," from Dwight W. Sabin, a promoter and politician who paid Soldiers Additional Homestead scrip for most of the land involved. The Superior Timber Company, organized in 1901, disposed of cutover lands from the "Superior Deal," relinquishing the last for tax delinquency in the 1930's.
39. Laws of Minnesota, 1856, an Act to Organize the St. Croix Boom Corporation.
40. *Miss Val. Lmbrmn.*, XII, Sept. 9, 1887, p. 2; Sept. 30, 1887, p. 2; XIII, March 2, 1888; LN Papers, Winona, and Ann River Land Co. Papers, MHS, Leasehold Agreement, April 2, 1889; *Minneapolis Tribune*, April 4, 1889.
41. FEW Record, 381–382; LN Papers, Winona, St. Croix Dam & Boom Co., Statement of June 1, 1891, and annual reports; St. Croix Lbrmn's Dam & Boom Co., charter, etc. (LN Papers, Winona). The lease of facilities from the Boom Company by the Dam Company was arranged on May 15, 1890.
42. LN Papers, Winona, F. S. Bell to D. N. Connors, Dec. 23, 1899 (MRLC practices); *Miss. Val. Lmbrmn.*, XII, Oct. 28, 1887, p. 2 (ownership of lands); JPW Papers, FW to JPW, Feb. 6, 1898 (the same).
43. Records, Min. Bks., and annual statements of the corporations concerned.

VII

Beginnings in Minnesota

A<small>T THE ANNUAL MEETING</small> of the Mississippi River Logging Company in September, 1888, David Joyce suggested that the directors take an interest in the St. Paul Boom Company and its pinelands on the upper Mississippi. As a result, a committee was appointed to probe the question. But it did nothing, and at the next annual meeting in Clinton, Iowa, on November 18, 1889, Frederick Weyerhaeuser brought Minnesota properties again before the directors, reporting "a proposition from Mr. E. C. Whitney of Minneapolis to sell this company 330 million feet of pine timber principally on Pine River, a tributary of the Mississippi, not to exceed 30 percent Norway, together with a controlling interest in the Mississippi & Rum River Boom and a one-half interest in the St. Paul Boom for $1,300,000."

The offer was dramatic and important. If accepted, it would meet the need of the Mississippi River Logging stockholders for a supply of logs to supplement the dwindling Wisconsin output; and it would establish Weyerhaeuser and his associates in a new region, with most of the strategic advantages that had taken years of struggle to win on the Chippewa. Edwin C. Whitney was acting for a group which in the middle eighties had organized the St. Anthony Lumber Company, whose properties comprised not only an impressive stumpage but also a logging railroad and the control of boom companies.

However, the offer was *not* accepted. A resolution was passed that same day to the effect that "the Mississippi River Logging Company now declines to entertain the purchase of any pine that has to be manufactured above the Falls of St. Anthony."[1] As the Falls of St. Anthony are at Minneapolis, the resolution rejected all activity on the upper Mississippi.

Reasons for this rejection can only be surmised. Chief among them was probably the fact that a number of stockholders had engaged in lumbering for years, had amassed fortunes, were aging, and now wanted to close out their enterprises, and retire. Others may have shrunk from the uncertainties of the venture. To bring the inferior Minnesota logs down from remote streams, risk possible obstruction by Minneapolis lumbermen, and then convey them farther downriver must have seemed speculative indeed.

At any rate, the negative decision was unequivocal, with important consequences. It was as if in the early eighties the leaders of the Standard Oil group had decided to undertake no activity west of the Alleghenies, and John D. Rockefeller and a few others had been forced to start anew. Actually, Frederick Weyerhaeuser was never again to unite for common action so many able and wealthy associates as he had on the Chippewa.

2

He decided that something should be done in Minnesota, and he was not without supporters. To understand his and their attitudes, it should be pointed out that Weyerhaeuser was not a stranger to the state. He had engaged in several ventures in its northeastern counties and had been busy with his associates along the St. Croix. Laird, Norton Co. had of course drawn logs from the St. Croix watershed for years.

Minnesota held one of the great timber reserves of the northern Middle West. Four-fifths of the state was originally woodland. Only in two relatively narrow strips, one along the southern and the other along the western border (the Red River Valley), did it shelve into the prairie regions. The "big forest," chiefly oak, elm, butternut, and black walnut, comprised 5,000 square miles just north and east of the prairie lands. The remainder of the state's woodland was pine, mostly white, with some Norway, although in numerous swampy areas the only trees were spruce, cedar and tamarack. Most of the pine lay east of the Mississippi and to the north, where forests swept to the Canadian border. The whole area was a tenth larger than the Michigan pinelands and almost a third larger than Wisconsin's, although in quality most of it was inferior. The soil in central and northern Minnesota was less favorable to forest growth than the richer soils of the other two states.

By 1890 much of the St. Croix and the Rum River stands had been cut. Already Rum River logs had helped to establish Minneapolis as an important lumber center, which manufactured 343,574,000 board feet in that year. But the central and northern forests, while tapped by small logging projects, still stood relatively intact.

Various factors had combined to delay the openings of these regions. First of all, Minnesota, more remote from the older settled areas of the

United States than Michigan and Wisconsin, had been touched later by the tide of westward migration.

The French penetrated Minnesota in the 1670's. They found a land of gentle slopes (the state's highest point is 2,230 feet, the lowest 602) with dark forests thinning into prairies at the south and drained by many rivers. Carved by glacial action, much of the terrain held water in rock-floored pockets, and thousands of blue lakes broke the woodlands.

But while the land dazzled its white discoverers with wild beauty, its remoteness permitted only a few missions and trading posts. Even when the United States Army moved in after the War of 1812, settlement was barred for more than a generation by Indian tribes, particularly the aggressive Chippewa and Sioux. Minnesota was known to Americans chiefly through the reports of explorers like Pike, Schoolcraft, Long, and Catlin. However, after 1837 various treaties opened the land. The Sioux were pushed across the Missouri, the Chippewa and other tribes confined to reservations.

By 1855 general settlement became possible and went forward rapidly after the coming of the railroads in 1862. By 1890 the trunk lines of both the Northern Pacific and the Great Northern crossed the state, while in the southern areas numerous other roads had been built. The forest had melted to ax and flame as the settlers cleared the land for farms, and the prairie filled rapidly. The market for lumber grew comparably, extending westward as the Dakotas were peopled. By the late eighties railroads were supplementing rivers in providing transportation for logs, but large-scale cutting in most forest areas had not been undertaken. When extensive tracts of white and red pine were sold by the government in the seventies and eighties, rich men like John S. Pillsbury and Thomas B. Walker increased their already notable holdings.

Weyerhaeuser and his associates were not then bidders, but by the late eighties they could no longer ignore Minnesota. Various boom companies and railroads had made its forests more accessible, and it was part of the general domain in which the associates had been working.[2] In 1890 it supported 1,310,283 inhabitants, and St. Paul, where Frederick Weyerhaeuser was soon to make his home, was a city of 164,000. There too resided William H. Phipps of the Omaha Railroad, from whom he had bought timber on the Chippewa, and James J. Hill, whose lines would later provide access to some of the more westward and northern timberlands.[3]

By 1890 the Mussers, Laird-Nortons, Weyerhaeusers, and Denkmanns all were ready to operate in farther Minnesota. True, they might have picked up the Whitney option when it was rejected by the Mississippi River Logging Company. Perhaps they could not then find enough investors for such a project. W. J. Young seems at that time to have contemplated retirement, and Artemus Lamb was unreceptive. But in January, 1890, Weyerhaeuser and the others took up an offer from the Northern Pacific Railroad to buy large tracts of timberland on the Upper Mississippi that comprised portions of a government grant made in 1864 —all told 212,722 acres in eight counties.

The Pine Tree Lumber Company was formed on June 24, 1890, under Iowa law, to acquire the property for $452,330. Capitalized at $1,000,000, its stock was chiefly held by the Mussers, Laird-Nortons, and Weyerhaeuser & Denkmann, with a small amount reserved for company officers and for the sons of Peter Musser and Frederick Weyerhaeuser— R. Drew Musser and Charles A. Weyerhaeuser.[4]

The entrance of Weyerhaeuser and his associates into central Minnesota was hailed by its inhabitants with as much enthusiasm as a new trunk railroad. The *Mississippi Valley Lumberman* reported that a hundred citizens of Brainerd were "hard at work in anticipation of a visit by the Weyerhauser [sic] syndicate." Two other towns on the river, Little Falls, and St. Cloud, also offered sites for the mill which the newcomers were known to have planned. Finally Little Falls was selected, primarily because of its facilities for boom and storage space, but partly because a small sawmill on the east side of the river could be purchased. This was soon bought, but a new, modern, much larger mill was also planned.[5]

3

At six o'clock on Monday morning, May 18, 1891, the whir of machinery in the existing mill announced the beginning of work by the Pine Tree Lumber Company. Two young men doubtless smiled as they heard the clatter of belts and the drone of the saw. Charles Weyerhaeuser and Drew Musser, managers of the new enterprise, had long known each other because of the friendship and business relationships of their fathers. As Musser years later wrote to F. E. Weyerhaeuser, "The thought that your father and my father had in mind was to make an investment in timber with which your brother Charlie and I would be connected."

The young men made a startling contrast. Drew Musser was slight, cautious, and economical; Charles was tall, powerful, and bursting with vitality. The athlete among the four sons of Frederick Weyerhaeuser, he alone had a touch of the flamboyant. Where Drew counted pennies, Charles pondered new projects; where Drew was silent, Charles talked with abandon; if young Musser loved his ledgers, young Weyerhaeuser exulted in the plunging logs on the river, and the clatter of the mill.

But each respected the other. Drew, secretary of the young company, presided over the office and sales, Charles over logging, sorting, and milling. Drew was willing to consider Charles's proposals and adopt the sounder ones. Charles in turn recognized the importance of Drew's cool economy and was much more the merchant than he appeared at first sight. "Charlie loved to dicker and trade," said his younger brother of boyhood days, "just as father did when a boy," and his shrewd handling of men was to further the young company's success. Both had some years of experience, Drew with his father, Charles in the Weyerhaeuser & Denkmann yards at Rock Island and at its Davenport, Iowa, mill, which he managed for a time under the watchful eye of his older brother John.[6] "We are young and inexperienced," wrote Charles to Matthew G. Norton, "and would like to have you give our men and ourselves such good advice as you give us when you are here." There were plenty of advisers. Frederick Weyerhaeuser and Peter Musser, the president of Pine Tree, dropped in frequently, and the former, after watching the circular saw, ordered a band saw to "conserve timber" and a "steam nigger" to handle the logs more effectively. Quite as important in the new undertaking was the Laird, Norton Co., with whose leaders Drew and Charles carried on an intensive correspondence covering everything from the sorting of logs to insurance.

Even more directly of aid was William Sauntry. He had supervised the cruising of the Northern Pacific purchase and had acted as general manager for Pine Tree until the spring of 1891. With the opening of the mill he directed the construction of the boom and the sorting works. Edward Rutledge also appeared at the mill to supplement Sauntry's counsel about logging.[7]

By the fall of 1891 much had been accomplished. The boom and sorting facilities had been completed; the little sawmill, now running day and night, was sawing from 90,000 to 100,000 board feet daily; a site for the new mill had been selected, and Frank McDonough, an expert builder and millman, was supervising its construction. But already orders for lumber had been filled, a price list prepared, and a survey of sales possibilities begun.[8]

Meanwhile the partners were negotiating for a second large purchase of timberlands, comprising 45,000 acres owned or controlled by A. W. Wright and Charles H. Davis, of Saginaw, Michigan. The asking price for the property was high, and the $1,200,000 eventually paid was almost triple the cost of Pine Tree's first acquisition. But the stumpage was estimated as greater, with excellent stands on the Swan River and on the Mesabi Range.

A disagreement arose with respect to title. The Weyerhaeuser group insisted on fee simple for all lands bought; but the timber cruiser for Wright & Davis reported difficulty in fixing section lines because of the erratic behavior of his compass. Davis became convinced that this indicated the presence of iron ore, and at the final meeting of June 24, 1892, he refused to sell more than the timber rights, unless given an additional $100,000. Weyerhaeuser wanted to pay it, but his associates were contemptuous of the mineral prospects and finally took timber rights only. They were to regret this decision when the Mahoning and other mines proved that Davis's hopes had been sound. Some years later, Weyerhaeuser watched a Great Northern train coming from the very mines he had lost, laden with ore; and after counting 52 cars, turned to his companion, who happened to be C. H. Davis, Jr., and remarked with a whimsical smile, "And to think we could have had all that land for $100,000!"

With other purchases, Pine Tree by the close of 1892 owned or held timber rights on 274,292 acres, mostly in Cass, Aitkin, St. Louis, and Itasca counties. The young company was well endowed with stumpage—the lifeblood for its future activities.[9]

4

Even while the Wright & Davis purchase was being negotiated, the associates had cast an acquisitive eye upon the timberlands of the St. Anthony Lumber Company. M. G. Norton remarked in February, 1892, that if Pine Tree could get 250,000,000 additional feet from that source "it would put us in very good shape for pine." Whitney made a formal offer to sell on August 8, 1892, putting up timberlands, a large interest in the Mississippi & Rum River Boom Company, a half-interest in the St. Paul Boom Company, and all the stock of the Cross Lake Logging Company and the Northern Mississippi Railroad Company for $1,840,-526. This was $500,000 more than he had asked in 1889, but more properties seem to have been included.

Early in 1892 Pine Tree was envisaged as an agency for dealing with all purchases in central Minnesota, but several factors now worked against this assumption. One was that the Mussers wanted to make no further investments. Another was that both W. J. Young and the Lambs were now eager to put some money into Minnesota timber, and R. L. McCormick, nephew to William H. Laird, and William Sauntry wanted an interest in any corporation formed to buy the St. Anthony properties.

A purchase agreement was drawn up for the St. Anthony properties on January 28, 1893, with a price of $1,810,901. On February 3, a $3,000,000 corporation, to be chartered in Iowa, was projected, with a view to the establishment of a manufacturing center even more imposing than Pine Tree's.

But in the financial panic and general depression which began in the spring of 1893, failure led to failure, and by June the New York banks were resorting to clearinghouse certificates. As a result, when the stockholders of the new Mississippi River Lumber Company met on September 20th, the capitalization was scaled down to $1,500,000, with the Lambs and Youngs taking $300,000 each in stock, Weyerhaeuser & Denkmann and Laird, Norton $375,000 each, McCormick $125,000, and Sauntry $25,000. In the same proportion these investors had already advanced the sum of $444,178, and the $1,944,178 total permitted the new corporation to cover the original purchase price plus payments for some additional lands.[10]

Meanwhile, sales and prices of lumber reflected the grim economic situation of the country. Hence some opportunities for expansion were rejected. One was an offer from the Pillsbury interests of the Northern Mill Company properties, with 600,000,000 feet of pine, and sawmills in Brainerd and Minneapolis. Another was a proposal by Thomas B. Walker to sell his timberlands and manufacturing plants. The mood of most stockholders was crisply phrased by M. G. Norton in a July letter to McCormick:

> In ordinary times we should say that this was a splendid opportunity to make a good investment . . . but just as things are now we deem it prudent to forego the possibility of making some money, rather than get ourselves into the shape in which Mr. Walker seems to be at present. He evidently has more land and pine than he has money. . . .

Accordingly, Mississippi River Lumber took no steps to acquire milling facilities. It merely prepared to operate the boom companies and to cut a certain amount of timber to sell as logs. At first, Whitney acted as manager, but Richard H. Chute was soon brought from Meridean, Wisconsin, where he had been supervising a Chippewa Logging plant. He gradually assumed control of the Mississippi River Lumber units, although not confirmed as manager until 1895. A gentleman of the old Boston tradition, son of a Congregational minister and a devout churchgoer, he was a diligent, charming, and able executive, although never fully at ease with the rough lumbermen with whom he had to deal.

To the credit of those who pooled their talent in the venture, it soon fought its way to a limited success against considerable odds. Operating to an extent through its own subsidiary, the Cross Lake Logging Company, but for the most part on contract to outside loggers like the Swan River Logging Company, it cut 50,574,000 feet in 1893, and 62,428,000 the following year, and was able to show profits of $153,402 and $178,484 respectively. These returns in part represented the dividends from the boom companies, but in the main came from the sale of logs. An early project was the improvement of boom facilities, for which additional river frontage and some small islands opposite St. Paul were acquired.[11]

Meanwhile, the new company was encountering no small amount of suspicion. Many Minneapolis millmen, including some of its customers, owned timberlands up the river and received logs from them or by purchase from loggers there. The Weyerhaeuser name was associated with the

Mississippi River Logging Company pool, and while no evidence existed of unfair practices on the Chippewa, some feared that the boom companies which Weyerhaeuser and his associates now controlled might function to the detriment of others.

Bringing down logs from the tributaries of the Upper Mississippi was no simple process. The Northern Boom Company (only partly owned by Mississippi Lumber at first) brought all logs from far upriver to the Brainerd dam for various rates: the Mississippi & Rum River Boom Company charged $0.30 for the long drive from Brainerd to St. Anthony Falls, and St. Paul Boom collected $0.75 for sorting and rafting logs below the falls. But these charges were well established, and the mill-owners were chiefly concerned about the role of the Pine Tree Lumber Company at Little Falls. There, in order to get its own logs, Pine Tree, like the Big Mill on the Chippewa, had to hold and sort everything coming down the river. As a result, logjams built up, which stranded many logs and increased the number of "sinkers." If low water compounded the delay caused by sorting, the Minneapolis mills might even be forced to close.

Rarely was there a year in which the millowners could not find grounds for dissatisfaction. Represented on the "Log Committee" which served as an advisory board to the Mississippi & Rum River Boom Company, they complained forcibly about jams, delays, shortages in logs delivered, and other aspects of transportation that often neither the boom companies nor Pine Tree officials could control.

One instance illustrates the complexity of the problem. In June, 1895, H. C. Akeley appealed directly to Weyerhaeuser, protesting that logs belonging to him and others were being held unnecessarily at Little Falls. Weyerhaeuser in reply pointed out that (1) it had been proposed to send a large number of logs down the preceding fall, which would have lessened the congestion, but that the log owners refused and that (2) during the spring the water had been low and winds slowed the drive. Conditions had now altered for the better, and, he ended, "I think we are passing the logs much faster than you have any idea of." That very year the Minneapolis millmen presented Chute with a plan for an Upper Mississippi log pool, but it came to nothing.[12]

Business conditions improved slightly in 1895 and 1896, and by careful management Chute was able to show modest profits. By reducing its cut, the organization swung smoothly into the better times marking the last years of the century.[13]

Throughout this period the Mississippi River Lumber Company and its affiliates were targets for damage suits by farmers and timber owners. A rash of log piracy—thefts by various individuals or gangs who carried off stranded or floating timber to use or sell—also caused the company

considerable loss and even more annoyance; eventually half a dozen employees regularly policed the riverbanks. Even near St. Paul losses by
theft were feared. "We are doing the best we can to protect the logs until
the rafting crew arrives," wrote Chute to Norton in August, 1894. But
he added, "I've no doubt the pirates will get some of them."

Almost as annoying as the thefts were recurrent charges that the
company, together with Pine Tree, was using its powers to injure others
and was leaving valuable timber to rot in the woods. The correspondence
for the period amply refutes both allegations. The Weyerhaeuser associates were as much injured by jams as any others and sought persistently
to prevent or clear them. As to leaving good timber, the constant instructions were, "Bring in all merchantable logs." In fact, Charles on one
occasion explained to a friend that losses had been incurred by bringing
in partly rotten logs, "but the consolation we receive is the feeling that
if we did not take quite a number of worthless logs we surely would leave
something in the woods that we ought to take." Yet as late as 1907 the
Seattle *Daily Times* in attacking the "Weyerhaeuser monopoly" cited the
case of the Mississippi & Rum River Boom Company and repeated the old,
groundless allegations.

In these discouraging years Frederick Weyerhaeuser stood forth like
a sturdy prophet of a golden future, offering resolutions for the continuous buying of timber. Purchases were made in 1896 and 1898. At the
request of "nearly all persons interested in logs handled and manufactured
in Minneapolis," the company in 1897 bought out the minority stockholders in the Northern Boom Company for $35,000, thus extending
control of timber drives above Brainerd. By 1899 it was ready to increase
its logging activities again and to adopt an aggressive policy in timberland
purchases marked by the acquisition of 60,000,000 feet from the C. A.
Smith Lumber Company (J. S. Pillsbury) for $300,000.[14]

5

While Weyerhaeuser and his associates were negotiating with Wright
& Davis in 1892, Frank McDonough, under the eyes of the young Pine
Tree Company managers, was completing that firm's new mill. It stood
on a sixty-acre tract of level, rather boggy land on the west bank of the
Mississippi. On the eastern side rose the new office building of the company, a few hundred yards upriver from the town of Little Falls. Its inhabitants were soon constantly aware of the Pine Tree mill which quickly
doubled the population of the community and dominated its life. All year
long they would look across the water at its monumental smokestack, its
buildings and yards, and for eight months could hear the hum of its
machinery and the blasts of its whistle as it summoned men to work
or released them.[15]

Frederick E. Weyerhaeuser was later to say with the wisdom of hindsight that while the mill was a good one for its day, it had three defects traceable to the company's three chief groups of stockholders. Weyerhaeuser & Denkmann insisted on the 127-foot-high brick smokestack which rose at the southeast end of the main mill, the Mussers on two flue boilers, and Laird, Norton on a slide valve engine. "All three were serious blunders." At the time no one was conscious of them.

Just after the plant began first operations in April 1892, Frederick Weyerhaeuser expressed his satisfaction, and two weeks later Sauntry, Rutledge, Peter Musser, and Fred Denkmann echoed his opinion. Ira L. Warren, later superintendent of the plant, first saw it in October and wrote Laird, Norton that "it certainly is one of the finest constructed plants I ever saw." Finally, a writer for the *Mississippi Valley Lumberman* who made a tour of the works in July, 1893, stated that except for a few mills in Minneapolis still under construction "there is not a sawmill in the northwest that has the modern and complete equipment that this mill has." He praised its location, its two McDonough band saws and the Wicks 38-saw gang, the devices for grading the automatically sorted sawed lumber, and the automatic loader that put lumber in trucks for stacking in the yards.

The plant had four chief buildings in addition to sheds and engine rooms—the main mill, the shingle and lath mill, the planing mill, and the blacksmith and machine shops. A modern feature was the installation of electric lights, then a novelty, for the night shift. An enormous refuse burner eventually took care of the residues that could not be used as fuel or sold for firewood to the townfolk.

The yard of the mill was planned by McDonough after a study of other yards and the requirements of insurance companies. Ample space was left between the buildings and the stacks of lumber, which in turn were separated by twenty-foot alleys. Water mains with hydrants were strategically located. Facilities for handling and storing lumber were superb; a former teamster in the Pine Tree yards boasted that men "could haul lumber all day and never touch a board."

Almost as important for Pine Tree as the new mill were the facilities for catching, sorting, and holding the logs that came downriver. Sauntry had supervised the construction of these facilities, and he arranged a lease of riparian rights from the Mississippi & Rum River Boom Company that he made over to a subsidiary, the Little Falls Improvement & Navigation Company, incorporated March 30, 1891. It took over entirely the work of catching, sorting, and storing. The unit, financed by Pine Tree, employed a crew averaging forty men. Sorting, as indicated, was vital to both Pine Tree and the Minneapolis lumbermen. The year 1892 occasioned no particular trouble, partly because Pine Tree operations were just beginning and partly because low water limited the amount of logs that could be driven. But with 1893 were to come exasperating waits during periods of low water and adverse winds, followed by sudden floods which brought miles of logs down on the boom works at once.

By mid-April of 1892 both mills were running briskly on single shifts. Full crews had been assembled. Business was good. Even Drew, never inclined to overlook the smallest cloud on the horizon, wrote on September 10th, "Our trade is all we could ask." Inquiries about lumber were coming daily, the planing mill of the new plant had been started, and plans had been made for going to two shifts in 1893. The cut for 1892 was 71,708,210 feet.[16] Constant attention had been given during this first season to making suitable water connections and providing devices for fighting fires, soon used to aid the town.

The spring of 1893 opened with no indication of the panic that was soon to strike. The first sign of trouble appeared in June, when the failure of a South Dakota grain elevator company lost Drew a large order. "Our trade and collections have fallen off greatly this week," wrote Charles to Laird, Norton on July 3. On August 12th, the company reduced wages slightly, and on the 23rd Drew reported that the Little Falls banks had been unable to supply currency for the payroll, which he and Charles had to procure themselves. On October 2nd he observed to Norton "that we are cutting over three times as much as we are selling." Actually, their sales were 500,000 feet less than those for the same period in 1892. They increased their sales force and worked harder, but the grip of the depression still tightened on the country and the lumber industry.

Meanwhile, a series of crises occurred in the handling of logs. Several jams built up, and the Pine Tree and boom company crews worked furiously to keep the river clear.[17] Actually, the lumbermen were facing a new situation in central Minnesota, for these years marked the apex of lumbering activities there. The boom company had never dealt with such a volume of logs, and the sorting at Little Falls was also a new and impeding factor. The Hinckley fire of 1894 forced the logging of extensive areas despite the poor market for lumber. A final factor was the accumulation of logs on the banks. Fifteen thousand men had logged the woods in the winter of 1893–1894, and, what was worse, because of recurrent low water they had not put in the full amount of their cut the preceding year. In the spring of 1894, conditions were favorable, and with one impulse the various operators dumped their accumulated cuts into the streams.

The spate of logs was beyond the capacity of the boom company and Little Falls crews to deal with. A jam developed that old-timers later remembered as a waking nightmare. It extended from the Northern Pacific bridge above the plant for seven miles upriver, and was often half a mile wide and fifty feet high; photographs show the boom workers walking like pygmies on its crest. Working with one hundred and fifty men, five

horses, and a steam engine, the crews finally broke the jam. One witness
stated that "all the men working on it jumped and ran to safety for the
pressure and power was so great that some of the smaller logs were broken
to pieces and crumbled up like tissue paper and some . . . were shoved
up the banks some distance by this great force." Though no comparable
jam developed in 1895, there was sufficient delay that year, as noted, to
bring protests from Minneapolis millowners and send Frederick Weyerhaeuser to Little Falls.[18]

From 1893 to 1896 Pine Tree had sought to curtail the amount
of timber cut by the contractors. The firm's president, Peter Musser, remarked early in July that "if money matters continue this way, we shall
not want any logs next season." For their part, the loggers had contracts,
had made preparations for work, and were reluctant to scale down their
activities, particularly as men were plentiful and wages low. But the logs
were a drug on the market, and in 1893 and 1894 the loggers agreed to
considerable reductions. They were less tractable in 1895, as shown by
the lively correspondence with Swan River Logging in that year. Only
after hard things were said on both sides did Frederick Weyerhaeuser
enter the dispute. He deftly harmonized the interests of the two parties
and smoothed the Swan plumage, ruffled grievously by the younger and
older Mussers.[19]

From the beginning the company had faced a situation in which obligations and expenditures were bound for several years to exceed profits.
The paid-in capitalization of $1,000,000 was offset by the payment of
$452,330 for Northern Pacific lands and $1,200,000 Wright & Davis timber. While the first obligation was met from capital funds, the second was
partly covered by loans from the stockholders in proportion to their holdings. Further outlays were imperative from 1891 to 1894 for the mills
and boom works, for which total expenditures had reached $287,724.
Normally profits from the sale of lumber would have absorbed the costs
of construction and soon begun the retiring of loans made by the stockholders. Profits were indeed made in 1892 and 1893, $145,851 and
$82,844, but by 1894 the depression was visible in a loss of $94,748, and
small earnings in 1895 and 1897 were more than offset by a $34,668
loss in 1896 and a greater one of $77,690 for 1898, this amount being
on an authorized capitalization of $2,000,000 established a year earlier.[20]

In addition to their concern over the larger aspects of company
welfare, Drew and Charles were perplexed and exasperated by various
routine problems such as insurance, and a rash of lawsuits, mostly brought
by farmers who alleged damage to their properties from the operations of
the logging companies. "Unjust" taxes furnished another major annoyance. On both damage suits and taxes the legal adviser of the company
was Charles A. Lindbergh, father of the renowned flyer, and a representa-

tive from his district in Congress. The damage suits were dealt with on the common-sense basis of ascertaining the facts, paying when a settlement was warranted, and fighting each unreasonable claim.

The tax problem was more difficult. Lindbergh termed the tax level on land and timber in northern Minnesota confiscatory. "The more you pay without objection, the more the officers . . . will try to get out of you. . . . In these northern counties the treasury is usually without funds. . . . The counties scheme all sorts of ways to get a little money, and any one company that pays a large sum into the treasury each year is watched with close interest and every scheme used to increase this." He advised getting acquainted with officials on the town, county, and state levels, constantly presenting the company's case, and persistently remonstrating against injustices. In the end, it was better to withhold the payment of excessive taxes and even propose to let the land revert to the state. The counties, rather than get nothing, "will remit all the penalties and part of the original taxes provided the owners agree to pay the tax." Pine Tree at once developed a firmer attitude and won a number of skirmishes with the assessors.[21]

The young managers complemented each other and developed an able leadership for their company. Drew was resourceful in selling. Charles, according to those who knew him, "possessed the happy faculty of giving orders to his associates and to men working for the Company without the slightest of offense or superiority." The two friends roomed in attic quarters above the office. Both followed a Spartan regimen, Drew living on his income even when it was only $750 a year and Charles attempting the feat but breaking down under a generous impulse or a fancied necessity. It was a happy time for both when, after a bad year in 1898, they marched to success in 1899 with a profit of $201,916. By that time both had married, but they continued their close relationship, building homes side by side on a tract overlooking the river just south of Little Falls.[22]

6

In the history of lumbering, the pine forests of Minnesota can be thought of as falling into four groups, each determined by one or more rivers. The first to be cut lay on the western bank of the St. Croix, the heaviest stands of timber being found along the Snake and Kettle rivers. The second was the drainage basin of the Upper Mississippi, including such tributaries as the Long Prairie, the Rum, and the Swan. The third area of forested lands lay generally in the watershed of the St. Louis River, which empties into Lake Superior at Duluth. Still farther north, in areas long considered inaccessible, stood more widely scattered timber, along streams flowing westward into the Red River and northward into the Rainy.

In the St. Croix region, as already noted, Weyerhaeuser had taken some interest. Through Pine Tree and the Mississippi River Lumber Company he and his associates had logged on the Upper Mississippi. He was now to broaden his operations in the third region, which, although the St. Louis was its chief river, came in time to be known as the name of a tributary, the Cloquet. This was also the name of the town where the expanding Weyerhaeuser enterprises were soon centered. Since 1883 Weyerhaeuser had been a stockholder in the firm that later became the Cloquet Lumber Company, and he had acquired an interest in the Moon & Kerr Company at Virginia in the fourth wood area.

The St. Louis and its tributaries—chiefly the Floodwood, Whiteface, and Cloquet, drained a region of low rocky hills, lakes, and swampy flats that was dark with stands of timber. The Cloquet area, not too remote from Lake Superior, had attracted lumbermen even in the 1870's. Stumpage could be acquired cheaply, and the firstcomers dreamed of logging it, driving their cut down the St. Louis and marketing it in Duluth, already a thriving lumber center. The Knife Falls Boom Corporation was formed in 1871 to carry out this plan.

But nature was obstructive. Where the town of Cloquet would later rise, some thirty miles from Lake Superior, a slate ledge extended across the St. Louis. "At low water these rocks stood up like knives," recalled one man who knew the spot when it was all but wilderness. Knife Falls, as the place was called, was passable at high water, but the terrain below dropped sharply, the stream dashing in rapids past huge gray boulders and descending 573 feet in fourteen miles to Fond du Lac, whence it flowed lazily through an alluvial valley to Lake Superior. A few tests showed that most logs sent over the ledge were jammed or stranded along the rocky stream, while those that came through the rapids were so battered as to be unmerchantable.

The alternative was to center manufacturing above the rough water. In the late seventies the St. Paul & Duluth was being built up the St. Louis, and the area just above Knife Falls was the logical place for a plant. In 1879 a little sawmill was constructed there; it failed the next year and was taken over by the Knife Falls Lumber Company. That same year, C. N. Nelson, who had operated near Stillwater, constructed a mill a little farther upstream. He acquired land, erected an office and a hotel, and in general developed his property with energetic foresight.

The Knife Falls Lumber Company prospered so well that its owners in 1883 raised its capitalization, enlarged their mill, and contracted for great quantities of logs to be cut along the Floodwood. They also joined with Nelson in platting the town of Knife Falls, already a community of five hundred inhabitants. All signs for the future were auspicious. Up to now the logs contracted to the west and north had come down promptly on the spring or summer floods.

But throughout 1883 the water remained low, and the company waited vainly for its logs. This meant loss of lumber sales and cash essential to discharge the pressing debts. To avoid total ruin, the owners had to find a purchaser for their properties.

At this point Frederick Weyerhaeuser became a decisive factor in the situation. He had made a loan of $25,000 either to one of the contracting loggers or to the company itself. To protect his money, he must take over the tottering firm alone or get others to join in buying it. He had learned that the Davenport firm of Renwick, Shaw & Crossett was looking for a good investment in timber. He explained the situation to them, took George S. Shaw to Knife Falls, and helped arrange for the purchase of the company.[23]

A new corporation, the Renwick, Shaw & Crossett Company, was formed on February 1, 1884, under Iowa law. For their $25,000 loan, Weyerhaeuser and Denkmann took 250 shares, this amount being only 9 percent of the $277,000 paid in on a $300,000 capitalization. Renwick, Shaw, and Crossett each took 573⅓ shares, or $172,000 all told, and four other investors took 800 shares. In 1883 Shaw bought out his two Davenport partners and became the dominant stockholder.[24]

7

During the next few years the town of Knife Falls grew rapidly. A newspaper, the *Pine Knot*, appeared in 1883. By 1886 the town, its name now changed to Cloquet, could boast of four mills. Nelson had continued to prosper and in 1886 added a second mill, downriver from the first. In 1882 a new group, the Water Power Company, had built a mill just above the falls on an island, utilizing waterpower to operate its machinery. The Renwick, Shaw & Crossett Company became the Cloquet Lumber Company (1886) and in 1889 bought the Water Power Company's mill for $60,000. The Great Northern, the Northern Pacific, and the Duluth & Northeastern (primarily a logging road) ultimately all sent lines into the area.[25] By 1890 Cloquet had a population of 2,530 and was clearly destined to become an important lumber center.

Both Nelson and Shaw had sought to protect their investments by acquiring land on the south side of the St. Louis River, Shaw preempting what remained of usable terrain when he bought a large tract from the St. Paul & Duluth Railroad in the mid-1880's. In all the plots that they sold for residence or business purposes they inserted a clause forbidding the sale of liquor. However, William Dunlap of Carlton, a neighboring town, had acquired a large island lying opposite Nelson's lower mill and the original Cloquet Company mill. It was easily accessible to the south shore, and Dunlap sold lots indiscriminately. By 1890 the island contained a boardinghouse and saloons, some houses of prostitution, a village hall and a jail, stores, and a score of residences, together with the repair shops of the Duluth & Northeastern Railroad. Here the woodsmen who labored eleven hours a day, six days a week, at a wage of fifteen cents an hour, all congregated for diversion.

Cloquet was an uncouth community, like most others in northern Minnesota at the time, with mills and immense yards piled high with pine lumber, and with hills that were already becoming the sites of better residences. Water was drawn from wells, and no electric lights, sewers, or furnaces existed. From April to November the sawmill whistles each morning shook the community to life. When winter came, most of the men departed for the logging camps, and the town lay deep in snow until spring. But despite its primitive character, Cloquet was on the march toward a more stable existence.[26]

While Weyerhaeuser appeared as vice-president of Cloquet Lumber as early as 1885 and held that office for a dozen years, George Shaw, as chief stockholder, president, and general manager, was the dominant force in the company. He showed alertness and driving energy. When the high water of June, 1888, tore out the piers that held the logjams and carried many logs downriver, he started successful negotiations for stock in the boom company and for the purchase of the Water Power mill. He also took steps to acquire additional pinelands and in 1890 approved a large purchase by Weyerhaeuser, Rutledge, and Sauntry. Mineral discoveries were made on Cloquet land in 1892, and Shaw's concern for the future appears in his admonition to Weyerhaeuser in March: "I intend to invest all money received for our mineral interests in pine, so don't look for dividends." Altogether, 353,460,000 feet were acquired in 1891 and 1892 for $734,024, representing purchases from fifty-two individuals or companies.[27]

Yet Cloquet Lumber paid dividends, one of 8 percent being declared in 1886. On January 8, 1890, a 100 percent stock dividend raised capitalization to $600,000, and a second 8 percent payment was voted in addition. This action was followed on January 13, 1892, by a stock dividend of $400,000 raising the capital to $1,000,000.

In 1894 a fifth mill came to Cloquet. Samuel S. Johnson, a Canadian-born lumberman who had managed a mill in Barnum, Minnesota, had invested with two partners in extensive pine holdings on the St. Louis watershed. They organized the Johnson-Wentworth Company (capitalization $220,000) and built a modern two-band sawmill and a planing mill a little above Knife Falls. Elevated tramways carried the lumber to extensive yards. In 1899 Johnson acquired a majority holding in the company.[28]

8

But a far more strategic event was to transform the role of Frederick Weyerhaeuser in the town of Cloquet. In the fall of 1895, a Mr. Bacon, president of the Illinois Steel Company, called at the office of the lumberman and found his son Rudolph there. Bacon asked about the holdings of C. N. Nelson at Cloquet. Nelson was ill and wanted to retire. His lands held valuable iron deposits, which Illinois Steel wished to buy; but Nelson insisted on disposing of *all* his properties, and Bacon's company had no interest in timberlands and lumber mills. They hoped that Weyerhaeuser did. A full 600,000,000 feet of pine, the two mills, a commissary, hotel, and the St. Louis Boom and Improvement and the Knife Falls Boom companies were involved. On learning of this situation, Frederick Weyerhaeuser at once took an option.

Summoning George S. Shaw from Cloquet, Frederick Weyerhaeuser asked him what valuation he would put on the C. N. Nelson Lumber Company properties. Shaw named a figure, as Rudolph recalled later, "a little above what the option called for."

"If the Nelson properties could be bought for less than the figure you name, would you like to take an interest in the deal?" inquired Weyerhaeuser.

Shaw said that he would. As a result, the Cloquet Lumber Company took $100,000 worth of stock in a new corporation, Northern Lumber Company, which purchased the Nelson holdings for $1,900,000.[29] Other original subscribers were recruited from Weyerhaeuser's associates in other enterprises: Thomas Irvine, William Irvine, M. G. Norton, Artemus Lamb, Edward Rutledge, A. E. Macartney, and H. H. Hayden, who subscribed amounts ranging from $15,000 to $105,000. For a time Weyerhaeuser & Denkmann held 16,300 shares, worth $1,630,000. Northern Lumber began its life with a capital of $2,000,000 and a Wisconsin charter. Next to Weyerhaeuser and Denkmann the two largest stockholders soon were McDonnell & Irvine and the Laird, Norton Co.

Rudolph Weyerhaeuser, Frederick's second son, was sent to Cloquet to take over the management of the important new properties. "The only instructions that I had," he later remarked facetiously, "were to keep out of politics." He was eager to attack his new job but was worried as to how his fiancée, Louise Lindeke, daughter of a St. Paul merchant, would adapt herself to the life of a lumber town in the northern woods. He need not have worried. After their marriage in October, 1896, she quickly won a reputation as an excellent housekeeper and charming hostess.[30]

With the assistance of the experienced William Irvine, Rudolph took over the management of Northern Lumber, and in the fall of 1896 Frederick E. Weyerhaeuser, his younger brother, arrived to work under him. There was an immense amount of purchasable timber on the St. Louis and its tributaries, and Rudolph assigned Fred the task of buying what he could. The first large offer involved a 60,000,000-foot holding owned by a Detroiter. Fred went to St. Paul to consult his father, who told him, "Buy it."

"But I must take William Irvine with me," protested the younger Frederick. "I have never bought any timber."

"You can't begin younger, can you?"

"Then certainly I must take our attorney, Mr. N. H. Clapp, with me."

"Why?"

"I have never drawn a purchase contract and I will need his help."

"I thought you graduated from Yale College," observed his father dryly, "and you cannot draw a purchase contract!"

The neophyte bought the timber for $150,000, which he later thought may have been $25,000 more than Irvine would have paid for it, "but Father was determined that his sons should assume responsibility."[31]

The next year George S. Shaw died, and his stock in Northern Lumber was purchased by Weyerhaeuser & Denkmann from his heirs, who preferred cash to the part interest they might have had. Weyerhaeuser & Denkmann also acquired enough of Shaw's Cloquet Lumber Company shares to give it a 13½ percent interest in that firm. However, more significant was Frederick Weyerhaeuser's election as president and general manager of Cloquet, although H. C. Hornby now assumed the role of manager on the spot, paralleling Rudolph's position with Northern.

Thus the Weyerhaeuser influence became dominant in Cloquet. The group controlled four of the five mills and the boom companies. The situation was nevertheless somewhat confused, and a pooling of relationships and powers was in order if the activities of the town were to be conducted smoothly and efficiently.[32]

9

By the late 1890's Weyerhaeuser had taken a tripartite role in opening the hinterlands of Minnesota. Through Pine Tree and Mississippi River Lumber he and his associates controlled an immense stumpage in the Upper Mississippi area, while through Cloquet and Northern they held an even larger amount of pineland on the St. Louis watershed. They already owned considerable timber in the pine area lying still farther north. Through Mississippi River Lumber and Northern Lumber they owned boom facilities in the two great hinterland territories. Through Pine Tree, Cloquet, and Northern they had opened up the Upper Mississippi and Cloquet districts. Finally, Weyerhaeuser had found roles in Minnesota for three of his sons. As much as any one man can be said to have expedited modern lumbering in the remoter reaches of the state, he can be singled out as having done so.

NOTES

1. FEW Record, 468–470; MRLC Min. Bks. of Sept., 1888 and Nov. 19, 1889. Whitney, Canada-born, was a brother of Sir James Pliny Whitney, Prime Minister of Ontario. His associates in the St. Anthony Lumber Co. included E. M. Fowler and E. A. Pearson of Chicago, Arthur Hill of Saginaw, and Samuel Hill of Minneapolis (son-in-law of James J. Hill).

2. Larson, *White Pine Industry,* chaps. 1–4, 7, pp. 269–281 describes the original forests of Minnesota and aspects of the state's growth. See also Folwell, *History of Minnesota,* I, 1–13, *passim.* A party sent out by La Salle, under Father Hennepin, discovered the Falls of St. Anthony, later painted by George Catlin in the middle 1800's as one of a series of scenes in oil made for the French king, Louis Philippe. Catlin's painting of the Falls is reproduced in color in *American Heritage,* VIII, April, 1957, p. 13.

3. FEW Record, 543, 721–722; LN Papers, Letterbooks.

4. FW Papers, Young to F. Weyerhauser, July 19, 1892; *ibid.,* FW to Young, July 25, 1892; *ibid.,* A. Lamb to FW, Jan. 5, 1890; RDM Papers; Pine Tree Lbr. Co., Min. Bk. The cut was estimated at 287,995,000 bd. ft., later raised to 604,789,000.

5. *Miss. Val. Lbrmn.,* XVII, Jan. 31, 1890, p. 12; XVIII, Oct. 10, 1890, 1938; interview with R. D. Musser, May, 1954.

6. LN Papers, inc. corresp., RDM to Laird, Norton, May 20, 1891, and Peter Musser to W. H. Laird, May 13, 1891; FEW Record, 54–56, 459, 462, 574.

7. LN Papers, CAW to MGN, May 24, 1894; JPW Papers, FW to JPW, June 7–July 4, 1891; LN Papers CAW to Laird, Norton, Sept. 17, 1891, and other letters; Kasparek, "Logging and Lumbering," *Little Falls Herald,* May 6, 1938. Since numerous quotations are from LN Papers, inc. corresp., which comprise statements by Charles or Drew, no further citations will be made to them except for memoranda or reports.

8. LN Papers, inc. corresp., June–Sept., 1891.

9. Hotchkiss, *Lumber and Forest Industry,* 111–113, and Larson, 270–277; FW Papers, Ltbk. V., Young to FW, Dec. 29, 1890, and Young to C. H. Davis, Jan. 10, 1891; RDM Papers; FEW Record, 458–461. The Wright & Davis stumpage was estimated at 348,270,000 board feet, later raised to 417,924,000.

10. LN Papers, Ltbks.; MR Lbr. Co., Min. Bk.; MR Lbr. Co. Papers. Both Laird, Norton and the Mussers were already interested, along with Weyerhaeuser, in the Far West. Musser on May 13, 1891, wrote W. H. Laird that he proposed to go to Oregon on May 26 "to look over the lands I told you about," and hoped that Laird and M. G. Norton could accompany him.

11. JPW Papers, FW to JPW, April 10, 1893; FEW Record, 247, 486; MR Lbr. Co., Jnl. A, July 26, 1893, Jan. 1, and Dec. 21, 1894, and *passim.;* MGN Papers, MGN to R. L. McCormick, July 25, Oct. 26, 1893, and to FW, Nov. 14, 1893; W. H. Laird to C. A. Pillsbury, Feb. 28, 1894.

12. MR Lbr. Co., Jnl. A, Aug. 18, Oct. 4, and Dec. 27, 1894; LN Papers, H. C. Akeley to FW, June 10, 1895, and FW to Akeley, June 11, 1895; LN Papers, inc. corresp. 1891–1896, *passim.;* MR Lbr. Co., Min. Bk., 1895.

13. LN Papers, inc. corresp. and MGN Papers, Ltbks.; MR Lbr. Co., Jnl. A, 1895–1896, Min. Bk., 1897.

14. LN Papers, inc. corresp.; MGN Papers, Ltbk., II; Seattle *Daily Times,* Sept. 3, 1907; MR Lbr. Co., Minutes, Stockholders and Directors meetings,

1895–1899; Jnl. A. The company's stumpage was now about 300,000,-000 feet.

15. Pine Tree Lbr. Co. Papers.

16. FEW Record, 460; LN Papers, inc. corresp., 1891–1893, *passim.; Miss. Val. Lbrmn.,* July 21, 1893, pp. 6 ff.; interview with Albert Chadwick, June 3, 1954; RDM Papers; Little Falls Improvement & Nav. Co., Min. Bk., Articles of Incorporation; LN Papers, inc. corresp., "Logs Cut Season of 1893."

17. LN Papers, inc. corresp., 1893–1894.

18. Larson, 188; Kasparek, *loc. cit.;* LN Papers, inc. corresp., CAW to Laird, Norton, Aug. 8, 1895. The 1895 difficulties began in June but recurred in August. "Our log jam above our works still continues to be about as large as when Mr. Laird was up there," wrote Charles, but added that the logs were smaller than earlier in the year and easier to sort.

19. LN Papers, inc. corresp., *passim.; ibid.,* Peter Musser to MGN, July 15, 1893, and P. Musser to Swan R. Logging Co., May 10, 1895, and FW's Swan R. correspondence, May 27 to June 11. The Frederick Weyerhaeuser letters show his firm but pleasant touch in dealing with difficult situations.

20. Pine Tree Lbr. Co., Annual Report, with Treasurer's Report, Dec. 31, 1904; Pine Tree Lbr. Co., Min. Bk., May 5, 1897; LN Papers, inc. corresp., RDM to Laird, Norton, May 11, 1893. The money advanced by the stockholders 1892–1897 was absorbed in the issue of new shares in 1897 when capitalization was increased to $2,000,000.

21. RDM Papers, Charles A. Lindbergh, "Opinion on the Non-Payment of Exorbitant Taxes," dated May 16, 1896.

22. Kasparek, *loc. cit.;* FEW Record, 459; JPW Papers, CAW to JPW, July 26, 1891; RDM Papers and Annual Report files.

23. Larson, 7; FEW Papers, Fred D. Vibert to Hugo Schlenk, Feb. 2, 1953, and memorandum of Schlenk and H. C. Hornby to FEW, March 22, 1934; Northwest Paper Co. Papers, Minutes of Knife Falls Boom Corporation; Eldon W. Spoor Scrapbooks.

24. FEW Record, 429–432; Spoor Scrapbooks; address of H. C. Hornby at banquet honoring R. M. Weyerhaeuser, Cloquet, April 6, 1943; Cloquet Lumber Co. Min. Bk., 1884; the *Pine Knot* (Cloquet), Jan. 4, 1885; Hotchkiss, 581. There seems to be no doubt that F. Weyerhaeuser made his $25,000 loan in 1883, and Schlenk thinks it went to the company directly.

25. Spoor Scrapbooks and the *Pine Knot,* Jan. 2, 1923; Rector *Log Transportation,* 294–296; FEW Papers, Schlenk to FEW, Dec. 13, 1935; Schlenk Reminiscences; Renwick, Shaw & Crossett Co., Min. Bk. May 13, 1886; Cloquet Lumber Co. Min. Bk., Jan. 1927; H. C. Hornby, "Review of the History of the Cloquet Lumber Company."

26. The *Pine Knot,* April 6, 1928; Vibert to Schlenk, *op. cit.;* O'Meara, *The Trees Went Forth.* This novel gives a picture of early Cloquet, of which O'Meara was a native.

27. Renwick, Shaw & Crossett Co., Min. Bk., Jan. 14, 1885; FEW Papers, Schlenk to FEW Dec. 13, 1935, and Schlenk Reminiscences; Cloquet Lumber Co. Min. Bk., Jan. 9, 1889; Cloquet Lumber Co., Annual Reports; FEW Record, 432; FEW Papers, Geo. S. Shaw to FW, March 10, 1892.

28. Cloquet Lumber Co., Min. Bk., Meetings of Jan. 13, 1886, Feb. 1, 1890, and Jan. 13, 1892; FEW Record, 439–441; *Amer. Lbrmn.,* II, 37–40.

29. The FEW Record, 440, states that the Cloquet Lumber subscribed $100,-000, but the Minute Books show only $30,000, subscribed by Shaw personally.

30. FEW Record, 439–442; FEW Papers, remarks of R. M. Weyerhaeuser at banquet in his honor, Cloquet, April 6, 1943; Spoor Scrapbooks; Northern Lumber Co. Min. Bk.

31. FEW Record, 443–444.

32. FEW Record, 439, 444; Cloquet Lumber Co. Min. Bk., Jan. 12, 1898.

VIII

Whose Forests?

UNTIL AFTER the Civil War, the popular attitude of the nation toward its wilderness domain was that of a careless spendthrift. Nearly everyone, not excluding Frederick Weyerhaeuser and his friends, assumed that the American forests were illimitable and expendable. To many settlers, a wild tree was a challenge to the ax.

Early in 1868 a traveler published in *Harper's Magazine* an article on "The Minnesota Pineries" which accurately reflected this popular attitude. Its whole tone was one of thoughtless complacency in the destruction of woodlands. On one small waterway the writer had seen nearly five million feet of logs piled, in what he thought a splendid sight—for these logs could be converted into lumber at an average of $20 a thousand feet. The Upper Mississippi and the Rum River, with nearly a thousand lumbermen at work, floated to market every season "great argosies of wealth"—not far from a hundred million feet of logs. It was all a scene of glorious romance. The author even dilated on the pleasures of the loggers, well housed, well fed, and enjoying their adventures in the crisp winter air.[1]

Very different was the tenor of an article in the same magazine seventeen years later, when Grover Cleveland had just entered the White House: "Our Public Lands Policy," by V. B. Paine. Its opening paragraphs showed that a social conscience had awakened. "We read in the newspapers," Paine declared, "of gigantic land swindles by scheming speculators, whose audacity is equalled only by their success." As the government had lately been managed, he added, the General Land Department winked at any irregularity. If a fuss was raised, it hushed the matter up, issued new patents, "and in a twinkling, by a kind of legerdemain, vast areas of fertile prairie or virgin pine forest disappear within the capacious maw of some soulless, unapproachable, unknowable something termed a syndicate."[2]

Paine, a pioneer in magazine exposure, set the pattern for extreme statement and concentration on businessmen, instead of farmers, as the major offenders. He mixed well-ascertained facts with unsubstantiated rumor to buttress his charges. He detailed the frauds common under the Timber and Stone Act. Wealthy corporations would send employees and other agents to enter claims on 160 acres of valuable forest each, to be conveyed immediately to the company. Thus the government parted "with its choicest lands for the merest trifle to scheming speculators by unfair and unlawful means." He also had proofs for his assertion that numerous dishonest land registrars in the Lake States had, for a substantial consideration, patented away huge extents of timber and mineral land: "This has been done," he wrote, "for the benefit of favored syndicates, who were permitted to purchase for private entry, for cash, at $1.25 per acre, lands to which the general public were denied access by the known rules of the office, which required the lands to be proclaimed in market by the President, and to be offered at public auction."

Plainly, in the seventeen years between the two articles in *Harper's* some events or movements had aroused concern over the public lands in general and the forests in particular. What were they? Mr. Paine wished the government to act. What response did he get?

2

The American forest had always possessed a few champions who raised their voices against the reckless overcutting, piling, and burning, and the general improvidence of the pioneers. In colonial days men had protested against turning valuable oak and walnut groves into potash and pearl ash. The traveler Peter Kalm, for example, had objected to the denudation and erosion of good soil. Housebuilders and furniture makers long before 1800 had lamented the growing shortage of fine woods, and shipbuilders found tall white pine masts, once protected by the king's broad arrow, harder and harder to buy. In the early national era Fenimore Cooper wrote with genuine feeling of the destruction of the eastern forests. A contributor to the *North American Review* in 1817 declared that the rapid disappearance of southern live oak and New England pine made it necessary to economize what remained of these national treasures and to replace what had been thrown away.[3] And Horace Greeley from his Chappaqua farm raised a vigorous protest:

Were all the rocky crests and rugged acclivities of our country bounteously wooded once more, and kept so for a generation, our floods would be less injurious, our springs unfailing, and our streams more constant and equable; our blasts would be less bitter and our gales less destructive to fruit, we should have vastly more birds to delight us with their melody, and aid us with our not very successful war against devouring insects; we should grow peaches, cherries, and other delicate fruits which the violent caprices of our season and the remorseless devastation of our visible and insect enemies have all but annihilated; and we should keep more cows and make more milk on two-thirds of the land now devoted to grass than we actually do from the whole of it.[4]

For a quarter-century before the Civil War Solon Robinson, the ablest agricultural writer and editor of his day, advocated forest and soil conservation in numerous farm journals and newspapers. "If by some means the public mind of America cannot be induced to preserve and cultivate forest trees," he wrote as early as 1846, "the day is not far distant when we shall be as destitute of timber as many parts of Europe, where the want of it is distressing." But for fear of being told that it was not the legitimate business of government, he added, he would advocate the federal planting of groves of timber in the West.[5]

The Civil War and the industrial growth that attended and followed it required immense quantities of forest products. This fact and the rapid westward advance of railroads and town buildings gave lumber an enhanced value. Throughout the northeastern states, and particularly in upper New England and New York, forests had been thinned by 1870 to such an extent that the potential scarcity of timber alarmed many people.

In August, 1873, the most influential scientific body in the nation, the American Association for the Advancement of Science, met in Portland, Maine, where the destruction of forests in the region was painfully felt. Dr. Franklin B. Hough of Lowville, New York, was a delegate. A graduate of Union College, a regimental surgeon during the Civil War, and man of both literary and scientific talent, he had superintended the New York States census in 1865 and the national census of 1870. He had been impressed by the steady depletion of all natural resources. In his desire to enlist public support for conservationist measures, he found an enthusiastic ally in another delegate, George B. Emerson of Massachusetts. Both educator and naturalist, Emerson had headed a state commission that had published a long-famous work on the natural trees and shrubs of Massachusetts. Hough read a notable paper, "The Duty of Governments in the Preservation of Forests," in which he pointed out how far the United States had fallen behind other lands. At least eight European nations, and British India as well, had devised systems of managing national forests; a number of European countries had established schools of forestry. With Emerson's assistance, Hough induced the association to appoint a committee to memorialize Congress and the legislatures of the importance of action for woodland conservation.[6]

This committee included scientists of renown: J. S. Newberry of

Columbia, geologist and paleontologist; E. W. Hilgard, agricultural chemist; Asa Gray of Harvard, botanist; and Lewis H. Morgan, anthropologist. Within a half-year the group laid before Congress an urgent appeal. American timber was being rapidly exhausted, the waste was prodigious, no effort was being made to renew the supply, and such unchecked heedlessness must soon result in grave national injury—so the argument ran. A national commission on the subject should be appointed forthwith, to collect all the facts not only on forest spoliation but also on resultant flood damage and climatic change. Then the government could adopt proper laws.[7]

The memorial bore better fruit than had been anticipated. Congress created a Division of Forestry in the so-called Department of Agriculture, which as yet lacked Cabinet rank; and Hough was made head of the division. Although the division received a shabby pittance, only $60,000 in its first decade, Hough prepared three voluminous reports on subjects related to forestry and forest conservation.[8] To be sure, since he was only an informed layman and not a professional forester, these reports made no really original contribution to knowledge of the subject; they were valuable compilations of secondary facts, and nothing more. The same could be said of the report issued by Hough's successor, N. H. Egleston,[9] but the four volumes helped to educate the public.

Something also was done by the aggressive and independent Carl Schurz, who became Secretary of the Interior in 1877. Supported by President Hayes, he took a long, careful look at the nation's property under his care. He discovered an appalling amount of devastation and cheating. "I observed the notion that the public forests were everybody's property, to be taken and used or wasted as anybody pleased, everywhere in full operation. I observed enterprising timber thieves not merely stealing trees, but stealing whole forests. I observed hundreds of sawmills in full blast, devoted exclusively to sawing timber stolen from the public lands." This was an extreme statement, more fervid than exact; but Schurz obviously thought exaggeration necessary. Shocked, he proposed stringent laws.

Indeed, in his first annual report Schurz recommended that all timber lands still belonging to the United States should be withdrawn from entry under the homestead and preemption laws and that the purchase of lands with scrip be halted. In addition, he asked for an effective corps of federal agents to protect public-land timber and arrest malefactors.

The response was instant. Schurz was denounced by congressmen from the public-land states, abused by newspapers, and pelted by a storm of telegrams. He got no effective action. "I persevered, making appeal after appeal," he subsequently recalled. He spoke in public and private. "But I found myself standing almost solitary and alone. Deaf was Congress, and deaf the people seemed to be." Some laws were in fact passed, but they rather facilitated the theft of public timber than impeded it—and one of them legalized wholesale robbery.

Schurz had proposed that Congress "enact a law providing for the care and custody of such timber lands as are unfit for agriculture and for the gradual sale of the timber thereon and for the perpetuation of the growth of timber on such lands by such needful rules and regulations as may be required to that end." On these principles the nation later established its forest policy.[10]

But just what enactments did Schurz get? Congress on June 3, 1878, passed the Timber and Stone Act, providing that in California, Nevada, Oregon, and Washington anyone might buy 160 acres of surveyed public land, valuable chiefly for timber or stone and unfit for agriculture, at $2.50 an acre. On the same date it passed the Timber Cutting Act, which allowed settlers and mining interests to fell timber on the public domain for their own use without payment. Both were primarily the work of Far West members. It was under the first that the fraudulent entries described by V. B. Paine became common, great tracts passing into the hands of land speculators and corporations. It also contained a clause written by Senator A. A. Sargent of California exempting from prosecution any person who had stolen timber, or might thereafter steal timber, if he paid $1.25 an acre and swore that he had not cut the lumber for export. Few nations have ever stained their statute books with a law so blatantly condoning past crime and inviting future robbery. As for the Timber Cutting Act, it might have been excusable insofar as it let humble farmers and prospectors take a little mountain timber. But the chief beneficiaries proved to be mining corporations that cleared wide districts of valuable trees to make mine props.

Observing the success of the Far West in getting at the public resources, southerners felt a twinge of jealousy. Not that they had done badly thus far! Lawless exploitation of public timber had raged in parts of the South like a pestilence. Alabama trespassers had been especially bold and numerous, for ironworks as well as lumber mills had paid numerous ignorant employees to file claims as a cover for theft. Representative Hilary A. Herbert of Montgomery saw no reason why his section should lack the legal indulgences granted the Far West. He brought in a bill extending the Sargent immunities throughout the entire country.

Members from the Lake States, where the forests were now fairly well policed and measures for conservation were gaining wide support, protested angrily. They saw that Herbert's law would sharpen the competition from southern yellow pine. Representative Edward Bragg of Wisconsin declared that Herbert should call his measure "an act to license thieves on the public domain." Another Wisconsin member termed the bill a general jail delivery of criminals caught robbing the United States. But as southern and far western interests brought their peaveys into united play in a presidential election year, the measure rolled through (1880).[11]

The consequences of licentious legislation, lax administration, and meager appropriations for law enforcement were soon appalling. Railroads, stockmen, lumbermen, mining companies, and their attorneys and brokers became implicated in what seemed a vast conspiracy to loot the public domain. There opened what a reformer presently styled the era of "Fraud, Favoritism, and Fees." Overwhelming evidence accumulated that in the Far West and South particularly unscrupulous speculators, land monopolists, and exploitive corporations were consummating systematic frauds under the land laws. So wide and unblushing were the dubious practices that although Chester A. Arthur's administration had no reform hue, his Land Commissioner thrice implored Congress to give some attention to the subject, while in a number of states and territories he suspended the patenting of any tracts whatever.

3

More and more men, in fact, began to raise a cry for intelligent action. In California John Muir, exploring the forest belt of the Sierras, reported that five sawmills were biting into the Big Tree groves. Unable to hew down the giants, lumbermen were blasting them out with dynamite! After the Fresno and Kaweah groves had already been heavily damaged, a company had been formed to turn the magnificent stand on the north fork of Kings River into cheap lumber. Muir published in the Sacramento *Record-Union* of February 5, 1876, an appeal headed "God's First Temples," in which he emphasized not only the beauty of the threatened groves but also their importance to climate, an equable water flow, and soil conservation. He blamed millmen, campers, Indians, and above all sheepmen for ruinous fires that were "far more universal and destructive than would be guessed." The fibrous-barked sequoias were especially vulnerable. Wrote the indignant Muir:

> Whether our loose-jointed Government is really able or willing to do anything in the matter remains to be seen. If our law-makers were to discover and enforce any method tending to lessen even in a small degree the destruction going on, they would thus cover a multitude of legislative sins in the eyes of every tree lover. I am satisfied, however, that the question can be intelligently discussed only after a careful survey of our forests has been made, together with studies of the forces now acting upon them.[12]

Other men and groups independently joined in the demand for a comprehensive study of the problem. E. L. Godkin of the *Nation* editorially attacked the absurdity of the old land laws which had made a frank and honest purchase of public timberlands almost impossible. Major J. W. Powell asked for a rational classification of lands by type and an appropriate system of management and disposal for each class.[13] The National Academy of Sciences espoused the movement. It pointed out that the types of land designated by statute were so badly identified that the laws were unworkable or evaded. Coal lands worth $10 or $20 an acre, for example, were usually bought for $1.25 under a false label or taken by homestead and preemption entry. Valuable pinelands were obtained in the same way. The academy proposed that a geological survey should determine the geological structure and economic values of the public domain and that the Land Office, controlling the disposition, sale, and title of the lands, should call upon it for information to make a proper classification. This would largely cure what the *Nation* called a "disgraceful and senseless confusion."[14]

Congress, under the leadership of Abram S. Hewitt and others, did create the United States Geological Survey in March, 1879, and its first heads, Clarence King and Major Powell, began the work of scientific land classification. At the same time Congress established a Public Land Commission, which was to report on a codification of the laws relating to the public domain and on a system and standard for dividing public lands into arable, irrigable, forest, and other groups, with due regard to humidity, water supply, and other characteristics.[15]

This epochal report, in the shape of a huge document to be printed by Congress, was ready in 1880.[16] One of its proposals called for a repeal of the unhappy Timber and Stone Act passed two years earlier, and of all the old preemption laws. Codifying nearly 3,000 land laws Congress had enacted, the report urged the government to replace them by a new system specially adapted to the Far West. Early national legislation, it pointed out, had applied to the fairly homogeneous area of the Old Northwest; now much more varied statutes were needed for regions where semiarid grazing lands, densely forested hills, canyons useful only for mining, and sandy deserts made a rigid homestead approach look insane.[17]

Unfortunately, Congress did not respond to the Public Land Commission. Not only did it reject proposals in the early 1880's to revise the public land system; it even ignored the appeal of President Arthur's Land Commissioner for $400,000 to investigate frauds, and compelled him to reopen the land offices he had closed in areas where corruption and thievery were most prevalent. Powerful interests wished to continue the ramshackle old system. They did not deny that the West and South were filled with dummy entrymen, that ranchers were fencing in immense tracts of public land, that coal and iron companies obtained rich veins for a song by hiring or forcing whole communities to commit perjury; they just shrugged their shoulders. In state after state the original homestead entries were four or five times as numerous as the final entries, suggesting that wealthy men or corporations were using proxy claimants.[18]

Of course, a great body of honest opinion still believed the forests "inexhaustible." Nevertheless, the movement for reform steadily gained strength. The American Forestry Congress was founded in 1882 and began exponding the gospel of conservation. One of its leaders was J. Sterling Morton of Nebraska, who beginning in 1872 induced his state and others to celebrate an annual April day by general tree planting; he told the fourth Forestry Congress that as a result of this organized effort, seven million trees had been planted at one time.[19] Another leader was Charles Sprague Sargent, professor of arboriculture at Harvard, who as special agent of the Tenth Census published in 1884 a monumental *Report on the Forests of North America.*

This basic treasury of facts and figures, the first thorough survey of our forest resources, made it plain that the woodlands of the nation were being consumed at a startling pace. Sargent drove this fact home in a series of forestry bulletins. Of all the magnificent forests of white pine in Michigan, he wrote, there remained standing in 1880 only 35 billion feet board measure, which at the existing rate of consumption would last but eight years. In short, he predicted the imminent end of the Lake State forests—and every lumberman knew that he was correct.[20]

The situation in the mid-eighties, when Paine published his *Harper's* article, was growing too serious to be longer tolerated. As one Land Commissioner was shortly to put it: "A national calamity is being rapidly and surely brought upon the country by the useless destruction of the forests. Much of this destruction arises from the abuses of the beneficent laws for giving lands to the landless."[21] It was certain that the first reform administration in Washington would undertake sweeping measures.

4

Reform came when Grover Cleveland took the oath of office on March 4, 1885. His platform had promised the recovery of unearned railroad land grants and the preservation of the remaining public lands for true settlers. When he appointed a rugged, self-made Illinois attorney and former congressman, William Andrew Jackson Sparks, as Land Commissioner, alarm rose among corrupt land-grabbers and predatory corporations. In the House, Sparks had made a wide reputation for pugnacious independence and hostility to special interests. His passion for honest government and hard-hitting action sometimes carried him to the brink of fanaticism.[22]

Before he had been a month in office, Sparks was fiercely aroused. He had before him overwhelming evidence of what he termed unscrupulous speculation, unconscionable land monopoly, and outrageous robberies. Special agents, registrars, inspectors, federal attorneys, local officers, and private citizens poured in upon him reports and letters that exposed a widespread and persistent looting of the nation's patrimony. He and Cleveland were one in the feeling that a drastic purgation was needed. They made it clear that they would hold the land-grant railroads to a strict fulfillment of all the terms under which they had obtained liberal government donations and would institute suits for forfeiture wherever possible. They stopped final action on all homestead entries in seven states and portions of three others, comprising most of the remaining public domain; and Sparks put the entries in the hands of special agents for reports.[23]

The President also ordered General Sheridan to the Indian Territory to ascertain the truth about tribal complaints that various cattle companies had unwarrantably encroached on Indian lands. He then issued an order giving the companies forty days to remove their stock from the Territory and another order requiring ranchers to tear down all fencing on Indian holdings or on the public domain.

Meanwhile, Sparks recommended repeal of much of the existing land legislation, including the preemption acts. Like Secretary Schurz and the Public Land Commission, he wanted a complete new code for administering the public domain. Cash sales of public land, he declared, should be stopped, and they should be made available to actual settlers only. In his excellent annual reports in 1885–1886 he explained just what statutory changes should be made. But as conservatives controlled the Senate, Congress was immovable.

It soon became evident, indeed, that the Cleveland administration had tried to move too rapidly. A storm of opposition arose, astutely organized by railroads, mining interests, lumber companies, and others. From various parts of the South and West petitions and denunciations flooded Washington. Even prominent followers of Cleveland were offended; Abram S. Hewitt, who had an interest in a ranching corporation which had enjoyed "grass leases" from Indian tribes, thought that the President's orders had been too abrupt and rigid.[24] The suspension of land entries injured not only illegitimate but legitimate interests all the way from Kansas to Washington. A bill was introduced in the Senate to protect all such entries. Land reform and forest conservation thus became political footballs, the principles at stake being forgotten in partisan debate.

When in the fall of 1887 the tactless Sparks quarreled with Secretary of the Interior L. Q. C. Lamar over a railroad case and resigned, few lamented his exit. He had become a political liability, and a reformer of more suavity and shrewdness was needed. His departure ended the threat of a suit against Frederick Weyerhaeuser over a confused title to some "indemnity lands" originally granted to the North Wisconsin Railroad, just as it ended various other pending actions.[25]

Nevertheless, Cleveland and Sparks accomplished a great deal. As he departed, Sparks asserted with a note of triumph that 31,324,000 acres of public land, fraudulently obtained, had been retrieved by the government. When Cleveland left the White House in 1889, he declared with just pride that his administration had restored to honest homesteaders some 80,000,000 acres seized by "illegal usurpation, improvident grants, and fraudulent entries and claims." Under Cleveland, a new, able, and highly trained man, B. E. Fernow, was appointed to the place Hough had held as head of the Division of Forestry in the Agricultural Department. This was the first governmental recognition of a professional forester; for Fernow, a Prussian by birth, had been trained in the excellent forest academy at Münden and at the University of Königsberg. Congress at the same time (1886) gave the division, or bureau, a permanent integral place in the department, with statutory rank and its own appropriation.

Though Fernow's star was later to be eclipsed by a more brilliant luminary, Gifford Pinchot, his advent to the Washington office was an epochal event. Since coming to America in the centennial year, he had been a trailblazer in the cause of woodland conservation and scientific forest management. Indefatigably speaking, writing, and attending conventions, he had pleaded for schools of forestry; he had advised state organizations in planning legislation; he had become the leading scientific spirit in the American Forestry Congress; and he had published a short-lived but influential *Forest Bulletin* from New York. He had no direct charge of any forests. Like Hough, he could only educate, stimulate, agitate, and advise; but he had high hopes for the future.[26]

For it was plain that at last a new era was dawning. The bold measures of Cleveland and Sparks had dramatized the issue and aroused the nation to the magnitude of the natural wealth at stake. People even yet could not fully understand what was happening; they could not know, for example, that the 11,000 acres of Mesabi land which Frank W. Higgins (later Governor of New York) and the Higgins Land Company bought at public sale in 1882 for only $14,000 would be valued within forty years at $50,000 an acre;[27] but they had a glimmering of the truth. Though fertile parts of the Great Plains were rapidly settled from 1870–1890, most of the Mountain States and Pacific Northwest remained in the public domain.

How could these imperial holdings be protected? Only by such legislation as Sparks had recommended and such governmental vigilance as he and Cleveland exemplified. Just before Fernow took his place, N. H. Egleston published an official warning that since the Northern Pacific had built its line to Tacoma, lumbermen were "transferring operations from the nearly exhausted pineries of the lakes and upper Mississippi to the fir forests beyond the Rocky Mountains. The whole western coast of the American continent and the eastern coast of the Asiatic offers a limited market for the lumber of the Puget Sound region, and the lumbermen seem eager to reap the offered harvest."[28]

One object of conservationists was the preservation of the wooded parts of the national domain from reckless depredation and ruinous fires. They thought this aim could be accomplished by transferring the most valuable forests to the status of reserves, by stopping the violations and evasions of law, and by establishing adequate forest patrols. Already New York, in 1885, had created a forest preserve of 700,000 to 800,000 acres, chiefly in the Adirondacks and Catskills regions, and was steadily adding to it by purchase with the intention of enlarging it to 3,000,000 acres.[29] This action, realizing the dream of F. B. Hough, was finally taken through the efforts of Fernow, who wrote the law, State Senator Lowe, who carried it through the legislature, and Governor David B. Hill, who signed it. New York's ultimate policy of locking up the Adirondacks timber was unfortunate, but this initial step set an example to other states in the nation. Canada had pursued a far-sighted policy in protecting the Crown lands, and the province of Ontario had a fire-ranger system that had won envious praise.[30]

The other great object of reformers was the application of scientific forestry to such wilderness areas as might be reserved by state and federal action. In publicizing the value of such work the American Forestry Congress was invaluable. At its 1884 meeting F. P. Baker of Kansas caustically pointed out that "when we speak of the management of government timber lands we enter on a new field. There has been so far nothing that indicates the existence of a plan. . . ." Fernow, at the same meeting, outlined a program for a self-sustaining and profitable administration of all the government timberlands. It would soon pay expenses from the sale of ripe timber and afford additional funds for buying and reforesting wasteland. A number of educators—Sargent at Harvard, Edmund J. James at Pennsylvania, T. J. Burrill at Illinois—advocated scientific instruction in forestry, and here and there pioneer courses were given; at the Michigan and Iowa State agricultural colleges in the late 1880's, for example. No forestry school yet existed, but Fernow could write in 1891 that a system of forestry adapted to American conditions, political, climatic, and floral, was gradually taking shape.

The more intelligent and responsible lumbermen, by the time of Cleveland's reforms, were as anxious as anybody to promote judicious, legal programs of timber utilization. They knew that fraud and waste hurt their industry immeasurably. They realized that when abuses became widespread, the innocent would be pilloried along with the guilty. Diligent search has failed to show even one example of the use of dummy entrymen on public lands for the benefit of Weyerhaeuser or his associates. Again and again offers of false entry were made to these firms; they were always rejected. Yet when the heads of the California Redwood Company were indicted for fraudulent use of the Timber and Stone Act to obtain a hundred thousand acres of valuable forests; when the Montana Improvement Company was hailed into the courts because it had cut huge amounts of government timber with no warrant but the oral permission of President Arthur's Secretary of the Interior; when farmers, ranchers, and miners all over the country were attacked for timber grabbing by manipulation of the entry laws, it was certain that reputable firms would suffer. The larger companies were particularly liable to careless or malicious arraignment.[31]

The position of the best lumbermen was always clear and defensible. They bought large tracts of timberland, to be sure. But the government itself was responsible for the fact that these tracts were on the market. For legitimate public ends, it had granted princely domains to land-grant universities, railroads, Indian tribes, and other interests. Its objective was the rapid development and settlement of the country. Honest lumbermen had every right to purchase tracts and consolidate them. If they did not, weak lumbermen, greedy speculators, and companies whose one object was to cut with wasteful haste and get out would take them all.

Having obtained lands, the legitimate investor was under irresistible pressures to harvest ripe timber as soon as possible. The states with few exceptions had tax laws which made the cost of a long-term retention of growing trees prohibitive. Capital costs were heavy, interest had to be earned on the investment, and virgin timber could always be purchased at low prices. The states had practically no fire-prevention laws to protect lumbermen from sudden calamity. Nobody could predict the future course of the market, but the fear of such a drop as took place in the depression years 1893–1897 was always before the lumberman, impelling him to harvest his trees.

And meanwhile the growing nation, hungry for lumber, was itself impatient of any restrictive measures threatening to limit supplies or raise prices. In effect, society cried out to lumbermen: "Your job is to turn the forest into schools, churches, railway stations, factories, houses, fences; get on with it. At the same time, clear the land for the worthy farmer!" Down to the 1890's the nation, which itself held large tracts of timber, did not even begin to institute advanced conservation practices; indeed, it could not, for it contained no body of properly trained foresters. Nearly all the early land legislation of the country, as the Public Land Commission of 1879 and the National Academy of Sciences pointed out, was drafted with the object of promoting the interests of the farmer, and made no effort to provide a rational forest policy.

The better lumbermen could deny with asperity the charge that they were indifferent to proper protection of the forests. They could point out that the small farmer was by far the leading destroyer of woodland. They could show that forest fires, against which no effective public safeguards were raised until after 1900, ruined far more timber than the wasteful practices of the lumber industry. It was their duty, as some of them saw, to encourage conservation.

Conservation required both a set of scientific principles of timber culture and protection, and a great public movement to give force to them. Before 1900 the science of forest management was imperfectly developed except in a few Old World countries; neither the American universities nor the government had begun to develop its like in the United States. The great public movement to compel general use of sound forestry principles was unborn; it was just stirring in the womb. In due course the best lumbermen were to do their full share in developing conservationist practices and to offer the nation and states a partnership in conservation which these political bodies were sometimes slow to accept.

5

Six months after Benjamin Harrison became President, Carl Schurz electrified the American Forestry Congress in Philadelphia by a speech of impassioned eloquence. "The destruction of our forests is so fearfully rapid," he declaimed, "that if we go on at the same rate, men whose hair is already gray will see the day when in the United States from Maine to California and from the Mexican Gulf to Puget Sound, there will be no forest left worthy of the name." Who was guilty? The settler girdling giant oaks and elms; the miner laying waste a mountain slope to get a few sticks; the timber thief destroying more than he stole; the lumberman wasting more than he saved; the tourist, hunter, and prospector, lighting his campfire or pipe and setting the woods ablaze. Yet the final guilt attached to greater agencies. "It is a spendthrift people recklessly wasting its heritage. It is a government careless of the future, and unmindful of a pressing duty."[32]

From the Hudson to the Rockies, a severe pinch on the pocket nerve began to reinforce such words. America was preeminently a land of wood users. Every city and town, every factory and farmstead, was voracious in its demand for lumber. As population rose, so did consumption, for brick, masonry, steel, and glass were still but lightly employed. The railroads were equally insatiable. Gone were the days, lasting through the Civil War, when locomotives burned wood, but the requirements for ties were staggering. By the mid-eighties the nation's 150,000 miles of railway laid on nearly 400,000,000 ties, and Egleston estimated that it had required a forest area equal to Rhode Island and Connecticut to grow this supply. The annual renewal demanded 56,570,000 ties, the produce of 566,000 acres of trees. Other uses of wood were legion. Wood pulp now provided

most of the paper supply. The great city fires—Chicago, Boston, Baltimore—and the numerous forest fires from Peshtigo in 1871 to the Wisconsin and Minnesota holocausts of 1894, turned wide domains of wood
into smoke. Rising prices made buyers begin to think hard about wood
supply.[33]

Both President Harrison and his Secretary of the Interior, John W.
Noble, took a constructive attitude. They received memorials from scientific bodies on the urgency of forest conservation and an expert forest administration; they talked with leaders of the American Forestry Congress;
they stood ready to encourage proper congressional action. Harrison early
in 1890 laid before Congress a request from the American Association
for the Advancement of Science for the withdrawal of public forest lands
from entry or sale. Secretary Noble was anxious to make such withdrawal
possible. Major Powell of the Geological Survey opposed action, telling
Noble that the best course with the Rocky Mountain forests was to burn
them down and explaining with relish how he had himself once started a
fire that devastated a thousand square miles. But Noble happily accepted
Fernow's crisp rejoinder that under law it was the duty of the Secretary of
the Interior to protect the public domain against the vandalism of which
Major Powell had accused himself!

"I can still see the twinkle in the Secretary's eyes," wrote Fernow
later, "with which he met this short, pointed thrust, and the result was
gratifying. At midnight on March 3, 1891, the Secretary managed to get
a rider into a bill, then in conference committee, the rider giving power to
the President to set aside forest reservations. Thus, most important legislation, which changed the entire land policy of the United States, was enacted without any discussion, or, indeed, without direct participation in
framing it by either House or Senate."

The bill into which Secretary Noble inserted his momentous clause
was one entitled "An Act to Repeal Timber Culture Laws and for Other
Purposes." It carried out Sparks's recommendation for abolishing preemption, so long a cover for the grossest frauds; it also put a stop to the
farcical planting of a few scraggly trees ("timber culture") in order to reduce by two years the residence requirement in homesteading. Most western ranchers were now hostile to preemption and to homesteading generally; they had swung over to the support of Sparks's ideas. How did
Noble get his liberal provision for forest reserves accepted? Simply by
threatening that Harrison would veto the bill if it were not included. No
other rider added on the eve of adjournment has ever so benefited the
nation.[34]

With scanty public comment and singularly little Western opposition,[35] President Harrison in the fiscal year 1891–1892 established six

forest reservations, containing more than 3,000,000 acres. The first was the Yellowstone Timber Reserve in Wyoming; two were in Colorado, and a fourth was on the headwaters of the Pecos River in New Mexico, in the Santa Fe–Taos area. Harrison soon created nine more forest reserves, or a total of fifteen aggregating about 13,000,000 acres. Still Far West sentiment remained quiescent, probably because nearly all the proclaimed areas were distant from large settlements. Much the biggest was the Sierra Forest Reserve in California, of 4,100,000 acres, which preserved both scenic beauty and water values in a range largely difficult of access.

This western silence was the more remarkable because the creation of the reserves was accompanied by no provision for their management or utilization. The timberland was simply withdrawn from any form of legal development. The government protected its title, but nothing else; neither the forests from sporadic raids nor the people from lack of forest products. As Gifford Pinchot wrote later, the law of 1891 posed an impossible situation.[36] Under its blank, stony negatives, no timber could be cut, no grass grazed, no waterpower harnessed, no coal dug, no road built. Fernow's forestry division might and did print reams of material on the proper use of forests but had no authority whatever over these national woodlands.

It was not to be expected that the West would long accept such total occlusion of valuable resources. Nor could the government rest content with a paralysis that forbade even fire patrols. Senator Algernon Sidney Paddock of Nebraska offered a good bill for the protection and administration of the reserves, but it failed in 1892 because it was too elaborate.[37]

By the early 1890's also, a small body of educated foresters was at last becoming available. Some had been trained abroad, some in the scattered American university classes. The time was at hand when scientific forestry could be applied to the tangled wilderness; for as Pinchot, then newly trained in Germany, France, and Switzerland, always insisted, forestry in practice and forestry in theory are entirely different—"they are not even kissing kin." In North Carolina, George Vanderbilt, owner of the Biltmore Estate, had planned on the advice of Frederick Law Olmsted, to include a model farm, a model arboretum, and a model example of practical forest management.[38] Late in 1891 Pinchot agreed to manage Biltmore Forest, and here he trained foremen, crews, and assistants. Applications came in such numbers from ambitious young men that he had to answer them by form letter. Henry S. Graves, a Yale graduate of 1892, absorbed as much forestry as he could from Sargent and others at Harvard, and then went abroad to complete his work. The Pacific Coast was becoming interested. By 1900 there were perhaps four institutions where young men could obtain a respectable acquaintance with forestry principles.[39]

If proper legislation and appropriations could be obtained, these trained men could be used to staff an expanding system of forest reserves. More could be added from well-rounded forestry schools that various men already dreamed of founding. Numerous people now cherished Schurz's hopes that *all* the public lands containing forests could be reserved and put under a scientific management that would set an example to private owners.

6

Cleveland's reelection in 1892 restored to power an ardent believer in enlightened forest policies. He and such Democratic conservationists in Congress as Representative Thomas C. McRae of Arkansas were ready to work together for sound measures. The new Secretary of the Interior, Hoke Smith of Georgia, was enthusiastically with them.

The President immediately placed a challenge before Congress. He would create no more forest reserves, he announced in 1893, until laws were passed protecting those already in existence. "The time has come," he wrote in his annual message that year, "when efficient measures should be taken for the preservation of our forests from indiscriminate and remediless destruction." The next year he asked more emphatically for a comprehensive forestry system. Keepers and superintendents should be provided; and the nation should abandon the laws and policies "under which the government, for a very small consideration, is rapidly losing title to immense tracts of lands covered with timber, which should be properly reserved as permanent sources of timber supply."[40] McRae introduced a bill containing all the essential features of subsequent forest reserve legislation. But Congress, struggling with the silver question, tariff, labor troubles, farm discontent, and a terrible economic depression, failed to pass it. When 1896 opened, nothing had been done.[41]

At this gloomy moment Hoke Smith, urged by a number of men—Robert Underwood Johnson of the *Century Magazine,* Wolcott Gibbs, Sargent, Pinchot—took a constructive step. He called on the National Academy of Sciences, which had been incorporated by Congress with the duty of giving advice, when asked, to government departments, to answer certain questions. He wished to know whether it was practical or necessary to set aside the existing timberlands as reserves; whether the influence of forests upon soil and water conditions was vitally important; and what specific legislation was needed to remedy the current evils. "My predecessors in office for the last twenty years," Smith stated, "have vainly called attention to the inadequacy and confusion of existing laws relating to the public timberlands and consequent absence of intelligent policy in their administration, which will prevent proper development of the country."

Cleveland and Smith hoped that the report of the commission which the National Academy appointed to draw up its response might be ready in time to prod the winter session of Congress 1896–1897 into action.

This hope failed, for the report was not ready in time. But a great object was achieved nonetheless. The principal proposal made by the academy's commission was that the President should establish thirteen new forest reserves; and this could be done without congressional assistance. In February, 1897, as the last days of Cleveland's administration were running out, Sargent of Harvard wrote a letter in which he warmly advocated the creation of these reserves, descriptions of which had been written out by Pinchot. This letter reached the President's desk.[42] He eagerly embraced the proposal, remarking that the 165th anniversary of the birth of George Washington could not be more fittingly commemorated than by issuance of a proclamation "establishing these grand Forest Reservations." They were accordingly set aside on February 22, 1897, the last important public act of President Cleveland.

It was an act in which he took great pride. When a delegation from the American Forestry Association called to thank him, he had the three men shown in at once. They walked past a row of disconcerted politicians who had been waiting for an audience. "Take your time," said Cleveland. "There is no hurry. This is refreshing. It is the first time anybody has thanked me for anything for a long time. Let that bunch of favor-seekers rot in their chairs." He talked for more than an hour, explaining that he had deliberately established twice as many reservations as most men would have thought wise. "A Republican President will succeed me, and he will undo half of what I have done, so to be safe I have done aplenty."[43]

It is an unpleasant light that any sketch of American forest policy throws upon the workings of democracy. The people themselves were primarily to blame for a record of carelessness and neglect, for a general acquiescence in the spoliation of an invaluable part of the nation's wealth. To the very end of the century the story remained discreditable to the country, though the reasons were clearly discernible. Even a brief narrative, however, does show that once responsible leaders began a process of public education, they awakened a growing response, and that as the education broadened and deepened the response in time became irresistible. Just as no group made a worse record than the timber speculators and timber cutters of early days, so no group accepted the new attitude after 1880 with more enlightenment and public spirit than the really progressive lumbermen. They realized that the whole future of the industry depended upon the adoption of wise conservation measures, and threw increasing energy into their support.

NOTES

1. *Harper's Magazine,* XXXVI, March, 1868, 409–423. This complacent writer could have found in the Report of the Commissioner of the General Land Office for 1866 (p. 33) a warning that the Great Lakes region timberlands were "so diminishing as to be a matter of general concern."

2. *Ibid.,* LXXI, Oct., 1885, pp. 741–746.

3. *North American Review,* VI, March, 1818, pp. 368–382.

4. Greeley, *What I Know About Farming,* 146. Cf. William Cullen Bryant's fine contrast, in "An Indian at the Burial Place of His Fathers," between the well-watered land of forest days and the aridity that followed the felling of the woods:

   "The springs are silent in the sun;
   The rivers, by the blackened shore,
   With lessening current run;
   The realm our tribes are crushed to get
   May be a barren desert yet."

5. Kellar, *Selected Writings of Solon Robinson,* II, 37.

6. 43rd Congress, 1st Sess., Senate Exec. Doc. 28.

7. The memorial, dated Feb. 6, 1874, can be found *ibid.*

8. Hough was appointed Aug. 30, 1876. For his reports, see B. E. Fernow "Forestry Investigations of the Department of Agriculture, 1877–1898," 55th Cong., 3rd Sess., House Doc. 181.

9. Published in 1884, Egleston's volume dealt chiefly with tree-planting conditions in the prairie and plains states.

10. For Schurz's recommendations, see the *Annual Reports* of the Secretary of the Interior and the Land Commissioner, 1877, 1878, *passim;* for Hayes's support see Richardson, *Messages and Papers of the Presidents,* VII, 476. Schurz reviewed his work in his *Address Before the Amer. Forestry Assoc.,* Pa., Oct. 15, 1889.

11. In behalf of Herbert it can be said that he was deeply convinced of the necessity for a rapid economic development of the South and saw no reason why it should not stand on an equality with the Far West. He proved his independence of corporation influence by opposing a national appropriation for building the Texas & Pacific R.R. demanded by Alabama interests (*DAB*).

12. Bade, *Life and Letters of John Muir,* II, 57–60.

13. The *Nation* editorial, May 2, 1878, was inspired if not written by Powell, in charge of the U.S. Geographic and Geological Survey beyond the 100th meridian, and Powell reached the public through other channels.

14. See the *Nation,* Jan. 9, 1879, "The Proposed Reform of our Land and Scientific Surveys."

15. The commission was also to make general recommendations to Congress for land legislation; *Cong. Record,* 46th Cong., 1st Sess., 2339–2341.

16. Printed as 46th Cong., 2d Sess., House Exec. Doc. No. 46, and later summarized in Thomas Donaldson, *History of the Public Domain.*

17. Cf. Robbins, *Our Landed Heritage,* 289–290.

18. Robbins, *ibid.,* 240, gives figures for the years 1862–1882, when 522,112 original entries in eleven states became only 194,488 final entries. In Alabama the ratio was more than five to one, and in Washington nearly four to one. Of course, many honest homesteaders merely failed to meet their obligations.

19. American Forestry Congress, *Proceedings,* 1885. The Congress was founded after a visit to the United States by Baron von Steuben, a Prussian forester descended from the Revolutionary hero. It immediately

absorbed the American Forestry Association.

20. Sargent's *Report* is Vol. IX of the Tenth Census. He pointed out the fact that America had no school of forestry. Later, as editor of *Garden and Forest,* 1888–1897, he did much to encourage the systematic study of forestry.

21. *Report of the Land Commissioner,* 1891.

22. *Cong. Record,* 46th Cong., 3rd Sess., 211 ff., Dec. 20, 21, 1880, illustrates his bellicosity.

23. This was his famous order of April 3, 1885; see his annual reports for 1885, 1886.

24. See Nevins, *Cleveland,* 216–227; Nevins, *Hewitt,* 456–458.

25. On this threatened suit see Lillard, *The Great Forest,* 203. The North Wisconsin Railroad had a claim to the indemnity lands; it transferred them to another railway, the Chicago, Milwaukee, Minneapolis & Omaha; this latter line sold them to a Weyerhaeuser concern conditional upon the government giving final title; and Sparks contemplated an action for trespass. We know little else of the matter.

26. Rodgers, *Bernhard Eduard Fernow,* 108. Hewitt and Fernow had worked together in forming the New York State Forestry Association.

27. Robbins, 253.

28. Division of Forestry, *Report,* 1883, pp. 447–448.

29. N.Y. *Statutes,* 1885, Chap. 283; Longstreth, *The Adirondacks, passim.,* and Longstreth, *The Catskills,* Chap. XXII.

30. Rodgers, *Fernow,* 34–105. Ontario's fire-protection system dated nominally from 1878, effectively from 1886.

31. See Dunham's able Chap. XIII, "Timber Companies and Railroads Under Fire," in *Government Handout: A Study in the Administration of the Public Lands, 1875–1891.*

32. Philadelphia *Press,* Oct. 16, 1889.

33. Half the foreign travelers to the United States from Dickens to Chesterton commented on the universal dependence upon wood. The lack of it on the Great Plains until treeplanting programs became extensive was painful. In 1860 cordwood sold in Kansas and Nebraska for $7 to $10 a cord.

34. Fernow's dramatic statement concerning the bill contains minor inaccuracies. The Senate adopted the Act and rider Feb. 28, 1891, without comment. In the House Lewis Payson of Illinois, chairman of the conference committee, explained that the reserves would be principally on western watersheds to protect the water supply. Thomas C. McRae of Arkansas thought that the grant gave the President "extraordinary and dangerous power." Final adoption came March 2, 1891.—Cong. Record, 51st Cong., 2nd Sess., 3613 ff. For Fernow's account see Rodgers, *Fernow,* 154–156.

35. Robbins, 305. Robert Underwood Johnson in the *Century Magazine* did express interest in this legislation.

36. Pinchot, *Breaking New Ground,* 86–96.

37. Rodgers, *Fernow,* 195 ff.

38. Schenck, *The Biltmore Story.*

39. The University of Washington was one of the institutions to establish training in forestry (Rodgers, 218).

40. Richardson, *Messages and Papers,* IX, 454, 543.

41. The McRae bill encountered violent opposition from western members of Congress. One Oregon representative, who was later exposed as a common criminal, Binger Hermann, denounced it as "A Bill to Despoil the Forests." An almost solid phalanx of Washington, Idaho, Wyoming, and Montana members lined up against it, assailing it in opprobrious terms. McRae in his turn grew angry. "Whether intentionally or not," he declared, "you who oppose this bill are the aides of the monopolists who have had the special privilege of cutting government timber for nothing." Cong. Record, 53rd Cong., 1st Sess., 2341 ff.

42. The accounts of the intervention by the National Academy of Sciences given by Rodgers, *Fernow,* 220 ff., Robbins, 311 ff., Pinchot, 105 ff., and various other sources differ in detail as to what occurred, but agree in most vital respects.

43. Rodgers, *op. cit.,* 225–226.

IX

Timber, Labor, and Transportation: The Weyerhaeuser Role, 1870–1900

WEYERHAEUSER GROUPS in every step of their undertakings, from acquiring timberland to selling finished lumber, generally followed the pattern of the industry in the Great Lakes region. They were exceptional primarily in the extent to which they adopted co-operative action in purchasing timberland, driving logs down the various streams, and assembling them into rafts for delivery to downriver mills. Weyerhaeuser and his friends distinguished themselves not so much by their innovations in tools and techniques as by their administrative skill in organizing an industry that for generations had known neither planning nor economical management. In this connection the "growing financial strength of the company's stockholders," as F. E. Weyerhaeuser puts it, was invaluable. By 1900, through forty years of experience in the Lake States, they had evolved a comprehensive body of policies and practices.

2

Frederick Weyerhaeuser's preference for purchasing timber in large blocks gradually came to be accepted policy. Making the first such move with the Dwight and McGraw acquisition for the Mississippi River Logging Company in 1875, he followed it with numerous additions in Wisconsin and Minnesota. F. E. Weyerhaeuser, with a measure of filial exaggeration, observed: "Father almost forced the entire group of stockholders into these timber purchases that made most of them fairly wealthy."[1]

By 1882 Weyerhaeuser's policy of building large timber reserves was fully accepted by his associates. To initial large blocks he or others added lands within operating radius of established mills, and rarely did his judgment prove faulty. When his estimate *was* inaccurate, he usually arranged for disposition of the timber to other Weyerhaeuser firms, as he did after 1900 by selling Pine Tree Lumber holdings in northern Minnesota to the Virginia & Rainy Lake Lumber Company.

While Weyerhaeuser was buying large tracts for joint enterprises on the Chippewa, he and his associates were also investing in an almost bewildering variety of smaller ventures. Though he shared such ventures with a wider range of partners than any other single lumberman, cooperative action was general throughout the Lake States. Seldom did Weyerhaeuser or Weyerhaeuser & Denkmann hold more than a minority interest. He often shared ownership with McDonnell & Irvine, the Joyces, Moons, Rusts, and Youngs, though the most consistent co-investors in new ventures were the Laird, Nortons; Lambs, and Mussers. He "was willing to surrender his own interest today that the whole group might prosper tomorrow," said his son.[2] The policy of sharing also diversified his investments, and he often said that he preferred a one-sixth interest in six ventures to the whole of a single enterprise.

The late entry of the associates into every timbered area, and the fact that they purchased from earlier patentees, provided one valuable safeguard to their reputation. Since they paid firms like the Omaha Railroad and Wright & Davis comparatively high prices for lands acquired from the public domain, it was the original patentees who received such initial profits as were made. Weyerhaeuser and his friends cannot be accused of having robbed the people of either Minnesota and Wisconsin or the United States.

Weyerhaeuser and his associates never bought timber for speculation but for sawing and selling lumber. Activities on the Chippewa and St. Croix were mainly intended to provide logs for the downriver plants of firms in the Mississippi River Logging Company. Chippewa Lumber & Boom was also a means to that end. When circumstances indicated that lumber could be manufactured more economically nearer the stump than at Winona and points southward, the associates formed corporations, erected mills, and cut the white pine timber. Such was their course with timber purchased from the Omaha Railroad and with holdings tributary to Cloquet, Little Falls, and Rutledge.

In surveying possible purchases and supervising active operations,

Weyerhaeuser continued to make trips into the pineries, still making light of hardships. One night he and William Irvine bedded down in a large camp on the Chippewa, Weyerhaeuser in an upper bunk, Irvine in a lower. One tired lumberjack snored so loudly that the two visitors could not sleep. Suddenly the offender snorted, turned over, and was quiet. Weyerhaeuser leaned over the edge of the bunk and whispered, "Thank God, Villiam, vun is dead."[3]

But as new ventures multiplied, the Rock Islander was forced to delegate authority for management to a lengthening list of executives.[4] He could not be everywhere at once. He remained the acknowledged leader, but the rising group of company managers and other executives made important suggestions and often exercised so-called routine supervision in quite a creative way.

The Weyerhaeuser group deviated less from the norm of the Lake States lumber industry in managing timber and timberlands than in timberland acquisitions. For example, throughout Wisconsin and Minnesota most of the standing timber of the Weyerhaeuser group was logged by contractors, the common practice of the area.[5]

The advantages of such arrangements were numerous. Lumbermen were happy to escape investing in logging equipment and to leave the details of management to the contractor, who had a direct interest in using his labor force and equipment efficiently. Since the standing timber of numerous owners was often intermingled, it was advantageous to employ a firm with established camps, logging roads, landings, and other facilities to fell the trees of all owners in the vicinity. It seemed wise to managers of Weyerhaeuser firms to operate only a few camps on their own account, these being yardsticks to measure comparative costs for guidance in negotiating contracts.

Other rivers in Wisconsin and Minnesota never quite matched the Chippewa in the diversity of procedures employed in logging. During the season of 1885–1886, for example, thirty-two loggers were under contract with the Mississippi River and Chippewa Logging companies, and logs were purchased from twenty-six other firms. Only three company camps were maintained. In addition, forty-nine contractors logged and banked timber for various Weyerhaeuser interests and others. Chippewa Lumber & Boom and the Daniel Shaw Lumber Company tended to use their own camps extensively. The Chippewa River & Menomonie Railway Company operated camps of its own and also logged through contractors, conducting fourteen operations along five railroad spurs and two streams. The lumber companies at Eau Claire supervised ten camps of their own. The average output of all camps came to about 2,000,000 board feet per camp, although more than a third of them cut less than a million feet.[6]

On an increasing number of tracts purchased after 1880 the trees were so small, widely scattered, and remote from good driving streams that Weyerhaeuser companies began to rely more and more on logging railroads. Other lumbermen took the lead in Minnesota, but, as will be noted, Weyerhaeuser firms there soon owned logging railroads, too, such as Northern Lumber Company's Mesabe Southern Railway and Cloquet's Duluth & Northeastern. Other firms, including Cross Lake Logging, operated unincorporated lines.[7]

The advent of logging railroads did not eliminate the use of contractors, many of whom operated along spurs laid into the woods by common carriers. In some instances the railroads dumped logs into driving streams and in others carried logs all the way to the mill ponds, as at Cloquet in later years. In either instance they tapped areas remote from or inaccessible to creeks and rivers. High costs usually prevented small operators from undertaking such construction.

The logger agreed to cut and bank the logs at a negotiated contract price per thousand board feet, furnished his own equipment, hired the crews, and assumed the risks of the undertaking. Merchants extended credit for supplies, and timberland owners advanced funds for other operating expenses. The contractor was always paid in installments. For example, he would be given a dollar per thousand board feet during the winter as the logs were banked, another dollar when the camps broke up in the spring, and the balance during the summer or early fall. The final installment often provided his working capital for a new season.

The Weyerhaeuser interests gave favorable treatment to the reliable logger who did his work well. If he found that scattered timber, long hauls, unfavorable weather, or impassable terrain made his contract price too low, the associates often revised the contract. Most good loggers prospered, many investing their earnings in timberland or railroad construction.

If Weyerhaeuser firms ever introduced new techniques in logging, the sources examined failed to record them. As the bobsled replaced the "go-devil," horses almost entirely replaced oxen, and the crosscut saw supplanted the ax, Weyerhaeuser camps and contractors gradually adopted the new methods and tools. Similarly, Weyerhaeuser managers watched now unidentifiable loggers introduce iced roads during the dry seasons of the late seventies and then, as manufacturers produced mechanical rut makers, perfect the ice-grooved road in the eighties and nineties. In 1892 Ann River Logging extensively publicized the hauling of one load which totaled 31,480 board feet of logs. Though steam skidders, introduced in Michigan in the 1880's, never proved popular in Wisconsin and Minnesota, Weyerhaeuser loggers used the "jammers," a cranelike device that lifted logs first by horsepower and later by steam. Similar devices were used to load logs on railroad cars; in a report for 1903 Northern Lumber listed four, along with 219 horses and 34 log sleighs.[8] Traditional methods of logging continued to be the most satisfactory in the woods of northern Wisconsin and Minnesota.

The adoption of new techniques seldom meant a higher total of logs banked per manhour. Hauling on iced roads, for example, did not necessarily mean an increase in the output of a camp, since the logs were harvested a greater distance from the river and the work of loading, hauling, and unloading consumed the time of many men. During the 1900–1901 season one logging operation on the Chippewa involved a sled haul of four to five and one-half miles and required the use of twenty men and fifty horses, all at a price of a dollar a thousand board feet.[9]

The contract cost for logging and banking rose by about 25 percent during the last three decades of the century. On the Chippewa it hovered around $3 per thousand board feet during the 1870's, increased to $3.25 and then to $3.50 in the nineties, and finally to $4. In Central Minnesota, in 1893, Swan River Logging received $4.25 per thousand for cutting, hauling and driving logs into the Mississippi.[10]

These higher logging costs contributed to the rise in the price of Lake States logs occasioned largely by the lessening supply of timber. Running counter to the generally downward trend of prices in the country between 1865 and 1897, market quotations for logs in the Lake States more than doubled between 1870 and 1900. Members of the Weyerhaeuser group, as well as other purchasers, paid $5 per thousand feet in the early seventies, $5.25 by the 1874–1875 season, $5.11 in 1880, $7.45 in 1886, $9.20 in 1891, $10.65 in 1893, $8.00 or less during the depressed mid-nineties, and $10.90 by 1899.[11] The rapid rise was a powerful incentive for timber owners to cut every log that would produce a marketable board.

3

As late as the 1890's other considerations also pressed lumbermen to log off and dispose of timberlands. The danger of fire was increased by the growing number of settlers and the extension of railroads. Nothing could have demonstrated the menace more dramatically than the Hinckley conflagration in 1894. But prevention of fires was for various reasons so difficult that prudent owners hastened to harvest their trees. Norway and white pine, most in demand, seldom stood in concentrated stands but were scattered throughout the forest. As a consequence, men bought pinelands in noncontiguous tracts, and seldom indulged in extensive "blocking up." In the chaotically intermingled ownership by settlers and timbermen, individualists often refused to adopt a common program of fire prevention or to cooperate with the state authorities, if indeed the states made this possible.

In Minnesota the characteristic pattern of ownership contributed to the cut-out and get-out policy in still another way. In order to maintain reserves for a large mill, widely scattered forties had to be bought. The acreage of Pine Tree Lumber, for example, was dispersed over eight large counties comprising 20,000 square miles. As previously noted, lumbermen collided constantly with county tax officials, who expected to draw a large part of their funds from timberlands. In most instances the tax burden, though not high by modern standards, was heavy enough to hasten the conversion of the trees into logs, or, in the case of cutover lands, to cause their forfeiture to the government.[12]

More attractive investment opportunities elsewhere also influenced lumbermen. By the late nineties the timbered lands of the Far West and South beckoned so alluringly that lumbermen felt impelled to complete their operations in Minnesota and Wisconsin, take their earnings, and put them as quickly as possible into tracts that promised rich profits.

Dependent as they were on the market for lumber, Weyerhaeuser and his business friends, like other timber owners, abhorred any waste of merchantable logs. They salvaged much of the timber damaged in the Hinckley fire of 1894, though the decision meant flooding an already depressed market with additional lumber. During the fall of 1893, the managers of Pine Tree Lumber received a report that timber in the Swan River district had blown down and that the contractors, Wright & Davis, apparently chose not to log it. "There ought to be some way of reaching them," commented M. G. Norton, "and yet we are not quite sure whether under our contract we can compel them to put it in or not, but it is too bad to have such timber as that wasting and, more than that making it dangerous so far as fire is concerned, when it ought to be logged and put in."[13] Managers periodically made trips to inspect the cuttings and make certain that contractors left no merchantable timber.[14]

The question was: What was a merchantable log? As previously shown, the definition changed with economic conditions during the period from 1850 to 1900. While the early loggers selected only the choice white pine, the standards of size and soundness dropped with each passing decade, and by 1900 Mississippi River Logging Company took logs only five or six inches thick at the small end and 40 percent sound.[15] In northern Minnesota, where much timber was small and inferior, the mills eagerly took logs that would have been scorned by early lumbermen on the Black and the Chippewa.

Market conditions also led Weyerhaeuser, gradually and sometimes reluctantly, to fall in with a growing demand for species other than white pine. About 1875 Norway (red) pine began to be acceptable for bridge structures and other purposes requiring long timbers. Mississippi River Logging soon had numerous Norway logs in its drives. Some purchases of timber in the 1880's and 1890's contained heavy percentages of red pine, which was slowly accepted in boards for a variety of purposes. As far as is known, Chippewa Lumber & Boom and the venture at Park Falls were the only Weyerhaeuser enterprises to manufacture hemlock lumber, and that in limited amounts between 1904 and 1911.[16]

Tamarack was used for ties at Cloquet, cedar for fenceposts and shingles, and spruce for pulp by 1900. Weyerhaeuser's sole venture in hardwoods before 1900, that at Apollonia, proved unprofitable and was soon terminated.

To Lake States lumbermen, white pine was king, and they gave much thought to replenishing the dwindling supply. A publication of the University of Minnesota in 1896, "Rate of Increase on the Cut-Over Timber Lands of Minnesota," demonstrated that some lumbermen had an open mind toward practical forestry and clearly recognized the problems of growing white pine trees commercially. George S. Shaw of the Cloquet Lumber Company pointed out that small sapling pine left on good land would not be large enough to cut (twelve to fourteen inches) for sixty years and that on "poor sandy soil it would take much longer." One Minneapolis lumber executive thought it would be necessary to adopt the reforestation policy followed in northern Europe, planting the seed and protecting the young growth for many years from being destroyed by cattle and fire. He had noted that fires in cut-over lands destroyed the cones of pines, thus leaving the land free for occupation by poplar and birch.

Frederick Weyerhaeuser echoed these sentiments and added some of his own. "In my opinion," he said, "the only way to preserve the young pine timber in Minnesota is to make such laws as will be reasonably sure to keep all fires from destroying the young and growing timber, then reduce the taxes on all cut-over lands. What would be safer still would be to have all cut-over lands deeded back to the state at a small consideration." He obviously had no fear of state governments as leaders in scientific forestry, but he held firmly to one idea: "No one can hold cut-over lands and pay the present taxes."

These statements indicated the nature of the battle that was to be fought throughout Weyerhaeuser's lifetime and not terminated until after his death. He showed willingness to help work out a feasible conservation plan by agreeing to serve on the Minnesota State Forestry Board, created in 1899. And Weyerhaeuser firms retained their cut-over lands into the twentieth century in the hope of getting some "small consideration" for them.

4

What of the workers who cut, banked, and drove the logs? Members of the Weyerhaeuser group seem to have desired to be fair in terms of industry-wide practices at the time. They often exchanged information about "going wages," but almost never mentioned hours or other conditions of work, or gave thought to what labor policy could or should be. In this respect they were quite representative of businessmen in the United States at the time.

In retrospect it is difficult to understand why the workers in the woods and on the rivers did not receive more attention from magazine writers and novelists. The attire and vocabulary of the lumberjack, a name that gradually replaced "shanty boy" during the seventies and eighties, were as peculiarly a part of the American scene as those of the cowboy on the plains.[17] The speech was as distinctive as the checkered mackinaw, brightly hued shirts, heavy woolen socks covered by a boot pac, service-able mittens, and cap made of muskrat fur, knitted wool, or heavy flannel-lined material. In addition, the work of the woodsmen was linked dramati-cally to the growth of the nation and the fate of its immense forest areas.

The national origins of logging crews changed materially between the 1860's and 1900. Men of Scottish and French descent from Canada had been among the firstcomers in the pineries, together with others of Irish or English antecedents from Maine, Vermont, New York, Pennsyl-vania, and Michigan. In the later decades of the century, the first- or second-generation Swedes, Norwegians, Finns, Germans, and Poles made up more than half the men in the camps. The census of 1900 reported the population of Cloquet, which supplied the core of Weyerhaeuser logging crews, to be 17 percent Swedish, 14 percent Norwegian, 15 percent French, 14 percent Finnish, and 12 percent English.

The nucleus of the labor force in the woods consisted of steady men recruited from farms and sawmills. In obtaining capable hands, sawmill operators had an advantage over the contract logger; millowners at Chip-pewa Falls and Cloquet, for example, had better assurance of a supply of dependable workers than did the independent logger, who had to call on employment agencies specializing in itinerant labor.

From the ranks of the migratory workers, for the most part, came the men who gave lumberjacks the reputation of being a wild and unruly lot. Though nearly all of them scrupulously honored financial obligations,[18] some were boisterous and violent and others vulgar and uncouth. Most of them loved to brag, vying in tales of their superhuman exploits in eating, drinking, working, gambling, or fighting. These were the men who drank up their wages or dissipated them in brothels. Logging was one of the oc-cupations in which a wholesome family life was relatively difficult, but foolish spenders appear to have been in the minority. Chippewa Falls, Cloquet, and Little Falls now list among their best citizens numerous de-scendants of sober, hardworking family men who labored the year around in the woods and mills.

As the crews became larger late in the century, the crude one-room shanties of the fifties and sixties, roofed over with split poles, marsh hay, and earth, evolved into much better camps of several log buildings each. By the eighties the size of crews ranged from twelve or thirteen to two hundred, although the average was nearer twenty-five or thirty. The bunkhouse was a separate building, lined with tiered bunks, in which blankets were thrown over straw-tick mattresses. It was often overcrowded, badly lighted, and verminous. Before retiring, men still relaxed on the deacon seat, but their bench of hewn logs before a large black iron stove was an improvement over the open fire of the fifties with the smoke ascending through a hole in the roof. The cookhouse was a large building with a big iron range and long oilcloth-covered tables set with crude tin dishes and cups and rough cutlery. Washing facilities were primitive—often a mere trough and half a dozen washbasins. "The lumberjacks, I'm sorry to say," writes one who knew them well, "were not the cleanest people in the world. They would walk around in tobacco juice on the floor and climb right into their bunks. They didn't mind that at all."[19]

In large measure the success of a logging operation depended on the resourcefulness of foremen, who possessed absolute authority. They hired and fired the crews, supervised the work, selected camp sites, constructed buildings, laid out logging roads, procured supplies, assembled animals and equipment, built dams, and ministered to the sick and injured. Not the least important task was to make sure that the "bull cook" (chore boy) awakened the workers before daylight to consume a hearty breakfast. Music to the ears of foremen was the crunching of snow and jangle of harness in the crisp stillness of the winter dawn as the crews filed out of camp to their assigned day's work.

To maintain discipline, foremen set a number of basic rules. They allowed no liquor, no weapons, and no thermometer—for they assumed that the men would not complain of the cold if they did not know how cold it was. The cook scrupulously enforced a "no conversation" rule at mealtime; the men ate hurriedly and silently, without opportunity to grumble about the quality of the food or to quarrel.[20]

Second only to the foreman in influence over a camp was the cook. Hard physical labor in the brisk air of the northern pinewoods sharpened the appetites of men. A good cook helped to attract applicants, to maintain morale, and to increase the output of a camp. A bad one, as R. L. McCormick discovered in launching the North Wisconsin Lumber Company, often disrupted operations and caused men to leave.

In many camps the quantity and variety of the fare was as good as that found in many ordinary American homes at the time. The menu included roast and fried pork, flapjacks, baked beans, hash, beef stew, fresh bread, cookies, doughnuts, pie, cake, oatmeal, prunes, rice and raisin pudding, potatoes, and other vegetables. Many loggers grew vegetables.

Hogs and oxen foraged in the woods in the summer but were slaughtered in winter when refrigeration was no problem. Usually supplies were purchased from farms and stores and brought into camps over tote roads from the nearest railhead or river town.[21] The fare would have seemed wonderful to countless families in the South who subsisted on corn pone, blackstrap molasses, "grits," and salt pork, to frontiersmen in sod houses, or even to numerous city dwellers.

The hours worked depended on the weather and the season. As on the farm, men normally labored from dawn to dusk. In river driving all hands might charge furiously at the logs one week, working as long as there was light to see; the next week, if the logs were stranded by low water, the crews might do nothing but odd jobs at full pay. Excessively heavy snow or warm weather occasionally sent the men to the bunkhouses, for such weather made cutting and banking impossible. On the other hand, an occasional foreman exploited his hands, unprotected by any union, in ruthless fashion.

Wages in logging camps rose during the 1870's and 1880's, but then sank to a low level in the depression of the 1890's. During the years just after the Civil War payment for common labor ranged from $12 to $20 monthly, although it was usually $16. In the next two decades the "dollar-a-day" rate prevailed, much as it did for farm labor in the first few years of the twentieth century. Teamsters, loaders, and others with specialized skills received a little more than the $26 a month paid ordinary labor. Many foremen rewarded a dependable, hard worker by giving him slightly higher pay than others in his classification. The cook and camp blacksmith often received double the wage of common labor and sometimes as much as a foreman. Competent, honest scalers were so hard to find and retain that at the close of the seventies and later they received as much as $45 per month. River workers, who had more dangerous and disagreeable tasks than men in logging camps or sawmills, received $2 or more per day. By 1896 loggers' wages, always reduced in hard times, had fallen to about half the level prevailing before the crisis of 1893, but by 1900 would return to the level of the early nineties.[22]

Lumberjacks received their wages in a deplorably erratic fashion. They had no regular payday but were paid when they quit or at the end of the season. Deductions were made for clothing, tobacco, and other items obtained from camp supplies or the wanigan, and wages were not always paid in cash. The logger normally did business on credit and therefore might be obliged to withhold part of the wages until he himself was reimbursed for the season's cut. For that reason many loggers issued time checks, a kind of scrip, which could be discounted at banks or business establishments, though both employers and lumberjacks were protected by state lien laws.[23] In the industry as a whole all these practices, though sanctioned by custom, opened a way for flagrant abuses. Unscrupulous employers could charge excessive prices for goods sold at the wanigan, could make improper deductions, and could postpone payments in a way that worked cruel hardship. The Weyerhaeusers are reported to have always paid promptly and in cash.

Lumbering was a hazardous occupation. Falling trees, misdirected blows of the ax, panicky horses, or miscalculations in loading the logs could cause cuts, bruises, fractures, internal injuries, and death. At the rollways the men who had to start the timber on its water-borne journey might be crushed by tumbling logs. In breaking a logjam there was even greater danger of being struck down or drowned when the key log was dislodged and the mass of timbers began to move. A flying chip sometimes cost a man the sight of an eye; a hard fall might cripple him for life.

Given the hazards of logging and driving and the fact that employers were censurably slow to institute systematic safety campaigns, it is remarkable that serious accidents were so few.[24] Perhaps the main reason was that a large proportion of the lumberjacks and "river pigs" were young, physically tough men who knew their jobs, avoided risks, and in general took care of themselves. For example, the ability to ride logs, a skill surviving in birling, was practiced by few river pigs. Most log drivers were content to patrol the banks, wading in only to prod stubborn logs, or to move about in a flat-bottomed bateau. Although this sometimes capsized, the risk was small compared with that taken by daredevils who scooted about the river on logs, standing gallantly erect on steel-caulked boots with the aid of pike poles or peavies.

During the early years of the Lake States lumber industry the general practice was to "pass the hat" to aid the injured, and of course the hat often contained a painfully inadequate sum. Captain Henry, Weyerhaeuser's lieutenant in the woods on the Chippewa, was given blanket authority to write checks—we do not know how large—to injured lumberjacks.[25] Again Weyerhaeuser was simply following prevailing practice in the lumber industry.

He was a follower, not a leader, in adopting such new ideas as the hospital ticket plan—a simple type of hospital insurance that appeared in the lumber industry about 1875 and was soon widely utilized. Each worker was issued a ticket entitling him to medical care and hospitalization in the event of illness or injury. By 1889 hospitals in all the principal lumber centers participated in a plan under which millhands and woodsmen who paid fifty cents a month were entitled to twenty-six weeks of treatment for accident or illness.[26] The standard fee became one dollar a month, the employer paying half. Several Weyerhaeuser firms, among them Ann River Logging and the Chippewa River & Menomonie Railway, were early participants in the plan.[27] Not until 1947 did use of the hospital ticket cease in Cloquet, long after workmen's compensation legislation had superseded it in importance.

In spite of long hours, relatively low wages, and grim living conditions, a warm human relationship between labor and management often flourished in logging camps and on driving streams. The working force in any establishment, whether run by a Weyerhaeuser firm or by a contractor, was always small by modern industrial standards. Foremen and employers had little difficulty in getting to know each employee personally. They often shared his hardships and understood his problems.

Lumberjacks as a group were not unhappy, lonely, or downtrodden. They were physically fit men who enjoyed their rugged outdoor tasks and the sense of doing a job well. They were keenly aware of opportunities to rise in the world; often their employers had begun as humbly as themselves.[28] What gave the calling an irresistible appeal to hardy men was its adventurous and untamed-wilderness character; it had a lure comparable to the fur trapper's life, the prospector's, and the cowboy's. For many lumbermen the silent, stately pines set in a snow-covered landscape, the comradeship of camp life, and the exciting river drives in the spring had a powerful fascination. They would not willingly have changed their lot with any man.

The absence of clashes between management and labor in the woods does not mean that the conditions of work were acceptable to a majority of the lumberjacks. It suggests rather that, like farm laborers, railroad section hands, cannery workers, and other groups, the lumber workers found it difficult to take concerted action to improve their lot. Perhaps the freedom to leave camp if dissatisfied dulled the urge to organize; certainly the dispersal of the camps militated against it, and the remoteness of the lumber enterprises from cities prevented workers from learning methods of effective action. For that matter, strong labor organizations developed slowly everywhere in the United States down to 1900. Toiling under conditions sometimes good, sometimes very bad, no Weyerhaeuser lumberjacks struck in the woods for any purpose, and the only recorded strike on river drives was that previously noted as occurring in 1889 on the Chippewa.

5

While the Weyerhaeuser associates were conforming to the general pattern of behavior in the woods, they were showing ingenuity in handling logs on the rivers. The obstacles to efficient transportation on the Chippewa and other streams challenged the resourcefulness of the unassuming German-American and his business friends. Weyerhaeuser led the group in cooperation, planning, and systematic administration of many complex activities.

The system established on the Chippewa became the ideal. By getting control of key corporations and creating some new ones, Weyerhaeuser had instruments for improving the main stream and its tributaries with dams and cleared channels. Common ownership of improvements and joint drives largely equalized the costs of transportation for sawmill operators on the Chippewa and the Middle Mississippi. At both the Little Falls dam and Beef Slough the pooling of logs expedited the sorting process and minimized the competition in acquiring them.

On other streams the Weyerhaeuser group attempted to approximate the pattern of operations on the Chippewa but never fully succeeded in duplicating it exactly. Individual firms built most of the dams on the St. Croix and its tributaries, so Weyerhaeuser had to be content with leasing the St. Croix Boom Company as a means of erecting the Nevers dam and controlling the sorting of logs. On the Upper Mississippi the purchase of the St. Anthony Lumber Company and its subsidiaries provided the key to log handling, which was improved by control of several boom companies. At Cloquet, ownership of corporations with riparian rights and full powers for making improvements permitted dominance by the Weyerhaeuser companies in the driving and sorting of logs for adjacent mills.[29] But on none of these rivers was a log pool established before 1900.

In the early days rafts of logs or lumber were simply floated downstream, though small sidewheel steamers known as "coffee mills" began sporadic towing operations even before the Civil War. The era of steamboat rafting really opened in 1869. It was a response to the increasing hazards created by the erection of four new bridges across the Mississippi in 1868, which with the two already at Clinton and Rock Island made a total of six. Soon sternwheeler steamboats were pushing the rafts, steering them by lines running from a capstan on the deck. "The boat became a huge rudder, a rudder that also had propelling power."[30] The building of the first sternwheeler designed specifically for rafting logs by the Van Sants in 1870 has been noted. That family, competing with such specialists in steamboat transportation as Durant, Wheeler & Company of Stillwater and others, came to operate the largest line of rafting steamboats on the Middle Mississippi. Captain Samuel R. Van Sant, who began as an employee in the Weyerhaeuser & Denkmann mill at Rock Island, later became governor of Minnesota.[31]

Chancy Lamb, one of the most inventive of sawmill operators, shuddered at the losses met when rafts went to pieces on the heavy bridge piers and turned his attention to possible remedies. In 1874 he perfected a double-spooled steam capstan which answered the need, and within three years practically all of the log rafts were pushed by steamboats.[32]

At almost the same time another Weyerhaeuser associate, W. J. Young, was revolutionizing the composition of the rafts themselves. He is credited with the idea that the "brail" should supersede the "string" as the basic unit of the log raft.[33] Before 1880 the new method had been fully accepted on the Chippewa. Beef Slough became one of the world's busiest river ports,[34] recording 837 raft departures in 1888. As many as eighty-five steamboats pushed the brailed rafts in 1883 and seventy-five in 1890.

Lumbermen on the Middle Mississippi owned a substantial propor-tion of the steamboats on the river and often took families and friends on trips up and down the Mississippi. But the ownership was above all im-portant in assuring the downriver manufacturer that he would have his logs delivered when he wanted them at his mill.

Among Frederick Weyerhaeuser's early associates, Chancy Lamb ap-parently took the lead in operating raft boats, but others soon emulated him. The initial vessel in the fleet of C. Lamb & Sons, the *James Means,* was acquired before 1870. In 1873 the *Chancy Lamb* took a raft of logs from the Black River to Clinton, a news item because the logs were de-livered and the lumber manufactured and shipped by rail to Kansas City within a space of ten days.[35] The Lambs also owned at one time or an-other the *Lady Grace, Lafayette Lamb* and *Artemus Lamb,* which en-gaged in good-natured rivalry with the boats of W. J. Young, then the Lambs' main competitor in Clinton. At Muscatine the *Benjamin Hershey* competed with the *Silver Wave,* the *Le Claire Belle,* and the *Musser* (a late acquisition) of the Musser firm, though the latter fleet was operated with the Van Sants under a partnership arrangement in 1888 or earlier.[36] Sometime in the early 1870's Laird, Norton & Co. joined with Youmans Brothers in acquiring a little steamer called the *Julia,* and by 1890 had added the *Juniata* and the *Glenmont* to its fleet. Youmans Brothers & Hodgins was also operating the *City of Winona.*[37]

Weyerhaeuser & Denkmann depended on hired steamers until 1874, when it purchased an old sidewheeler snag boat, the *C. J. Caffrey,* from the federal government. It bought the *Stillwater* in 1879, and this boat remained in service for twelve years. The *F. C. A. Denkmann* and its twin, the *Douglas Boardman,* built for W. J. Young, came off the Diamond Jo ways in Dubuque early in 1881. The *Edward Rutledge* was acquired later. When the *C. J. Caffrey* was dismantled in 1893, its machinery was in-stalled in a new boat, the *F. Weyerhaeuser.*[38]

By that time Captain George Winans had made successful use of a small boat at the bow of a raft as an aid in steering it, and others had adopted the innovation. Laird, Norton's *Julia* and *Frontenac,* and a bow-boat called the *Satellite,* were pushing enormous log rafts about 1890.[39] Perhaps the largest log raft was delivered to the Weyerhaeuser & Denk-mann mill six years later by Captain Otis E. McGinley, who with the *F. C. A. Denkmann* and a bowboat brought down a raft 275 feet wide and 1,550 feet long, containing about 2,250,000 board feet of logs. In 1901 the *Saturn* and the bowboat *Pathfinder* brought down a raft of lumber 16 strings wide and 44 cribs long, comprising 9,152,000 board feet of sawed lumber with another million feet of shingles and lath piled on top. In twelve days the huge floating mass reached the Knapp-Stout wholesale yards in St. Louis. Since each crib of lumber measured 16 feet by 32 feet, the overall size was 270 feet by 1,450 feet (allowing space for coupling), or almost nine acres.[40]

As active participants, Weyerhaeuser and his friends played a notable part in the utilization of Lake States forests to 1900. If they showed limited ingenuity in cutting and banking logs, they displayed enterprise in timberland purchases and imagination in handling logs on the rivers. Their forte was in capably administering far-flung cooperative undertakings. Harmonious cooperative effort, however, could not be applied to manufacturing and marketing under prevailing circumstances.

NOTES

1. FEW Record, 190. See Chapters V–VI for timberland acquisition.

2. FEW Record, 116. See Chapter XI for transfer of timberlands from Pine Tree to the Virginia & Rainy Lake Company.

3. As told by Irvine to his adopted daughter, Ruth Irvine Richter.

4. Denkmann was fully occupied in Rock Island, though John Philip Weyerhaeuser gradually took over direction of the Rock Island Lumber & Manufacturing Company. Samuel Chinn, Thomas Irvine, and William Irvine acted as field managers on the Chippewa, John A. Humbird at Mason, R. L. McCormick at Hayward, Edward Rutledge at Rutledge, R. H. Chute at Minneapolis, and H. C. Hornby at Cloquet for the Cloquet Lumber Company. Some of these were associated stockholders; others (Chinn, the Irvines, Chute, and Hornby) were company managers, though they too became associates through purchases of stock. The second generation took over in the person of J. P. Weyerhaeuser at Lake Nebagamon, R. Drew Musser and C. A. Weyerhaeuser at Little Falls, and R. M. Weyerhaeuser at Cloquet in Northern Lumber.

5. Larson, *White Pine Industry*, 365; MR Lbr. Co. Papers, memo of agreement with Swan River Logging Co., Oct. 9, 1893, and Journal A, various entries.

6. C. H. Henry and F. Weyerhaeuser Notebooks, 1885–1886.

7. See J. C. Ryan, "Minnesota Logging Railroads," *Minnesota History*, XXVII, Sept., 1936, pp. 300–308, and the Railway and Locomotive Historical Society, *The Railroads of Wisconsin, 1827–1937*, Boston, 1937; Larson, 361–363. For examples of details, see annual reports of Cloquet Lumber Co. and discussions of the Duluth & Northeastern. See Chapter XIII.

8. Larson, 78, 176–177, 363–364; Rector, *Log Transportation*, 74–76, 194–200, 208–214; Fries, *Empire in Pine*, 27–28, 31–32, 34; Reynolds, *Daniel Shaw Lumber Co.*, 41, 43–44; *MVL&M* Feb. 7, 1879, p. 8, and Feb. 21, 1879, p. 4; *Nwn. Lbrmn.*, XI, No. 27 Feb. 16, 1877, p. 8;

XII, No. 26 Dec. 28, 1878; XIII March 8, 1879, p. 4; and XIV, No. 15 (April 12, 1879), p. 1; interviews with former lumberjacks and examination of photographs taken in the 1890's.

9. Reynolds, 56.

10. MR Lbr. Co., Journal A, various entries, 1893; FEW Record File, F. Weyerhaeuser Notebooks, 1870's; LN Papers, *passim;* Reynolds, 162; annual reports of firms on the Chippewa, St. Croix, Upper Mississippi, and St. Louis.

11. Most of these figures are for logs purchased on the riverbanks by the Mississippi River Logging Co. FEW Record File, F. Weyerhaeuser Notebooks and Expense Books; LN Papers, Winona, annual reports of MRLC.

12. See Fries, 175–178, 251; Larson, 342–344; LN Papers, 1868–1899, *passim;* Pine Tree Lumber Co. Papers, *passim.*

13. M. G. Norton Papers, Winona, Norton to Pine Tree Lumber Co., Oct. 5, 1893.

14. See W. B. Greeley, *Forests and Men,* 156, for comparison of forest waste caused by man compared with that attributable to Nature.

15. FEW Record File, Henry Notebooks; LN Papers, Winona, MRLC annual reports, 1874–1901.

16. LN Papers, Winona, MRLC annual reports; C.L.&B. annual reports, 1904–1911; Reynolds, 29.

17. See L. G. Sorden and Isabel J. Ebert, *Logger's Words of Yesteryears.*

18. Compare this generalization, based on study of labor conditions in Weyerhaeuser lumber towns and on interviews, with statements in Fred C. Burke, *Logs on the Menominee: The History of the Menominee River Boom Company,* 73–78.

19. Carl Henriksen, Reminiscences.

20. Fries, 229–238; Reynolds, 51–53.

21. Reynolds, 45; Fries, 27–29; Larson, 81–198; FEW Record; Reminiscences of C. H. Henry and Henry Turrish; interview on Aug. 17, 1953, with E. A. Miller, who began his career as a woodsman in northern Wisconsin.

22. Engberg, "Labor in Lumber Industry," 313–314, 320–323; LN Papers, *passim.* The census of 1880 states that the maximum number employed at one time in the lumber industry for that year in Wisconsin was 14,079, and the wages paid during that year aggregated $2,257,218. In Minnesota the maximum number employed was 3,772, and the wages came to $924,473. Succeeding censuses fail to give any comparable figures.

23. Engberg, 313–323; Fries, 27–28, 210; Larson, 182–185; LN Papers, Northern Pine Manufacturers' Association, *Proceedings,* Report of J. E. Rhodes, Secretary, Jan. 22, 1907.

24. See Engberg, 226–237, and accident report files, C.L.&B. Co. Papers, and Pine Tree Lumber Co. Papers. The Chippewa River & Menomonie Railway had only three fatalities among its workers during its lifetime.

25. FEW Record File, Henry letters; interview with J. C. Patience, June 10, 1954.

26. Engberg, 251–252.

27. LN Papers, Laird, Norton Co. to Chippewa Lumber & Boom Co., May 6, 1897; CL Co. Papers, labor contracts of C.R.&M. Rwy. Co., 1891, and H. H. Hayden to H. G. Chichester, April 15, 1897.

28. F. W. Kohlmeyer, "Northern Pine Lumbermen: A Study in Origins and Migration," *The Journal of Economic History,* XVI (Dec., 1956), pp. 529–537.

29. Minute books and reports of the various corporations.

30. Rector, 158. On the Van Sant rafting boat, see Chapter II, p. 20.

31. FEW Record File, Samuel R. Van Sant to W. A. Blair, Dec. 3, 1920; Larson, 95.

32. Rector, 160–161; Larson, 90–91; Blair, 83; *MVL&M,* I, Oct. 5, 1876, p. 8.

33. FEW Record, 139, Information from T. Irvine; LN Papers, Winona, BSM-BLD&T Co. rafting accounts for

1875–1877; Hotchkiss, 588; E. W. Durant, "Lumbering and Steamboating on the St. Croix River," Minn. Hist. Soc. *Collections,* X, pp. 664–665; Blair, 29–30, and *passim;* FEW Record File, F. Weyerhaeuser Notebook, 1879–1881; Fries, 55–56; Larson, 143–144; Rector, 151–152; *Nwn. Lbrmn.* XXI May 6, 1893, p. 2, data supplied by T. Irvine; *MVL&M,* IV (Sept. 26, 1879), p. 2.

34. Rector, 275.

35. *Amer. Lmbermn.,* II, p. 30; Clinton *Herald,* April 29, 1933; Blair, 293–303.

36. W. E. Downer and C. R. Musser, "Musser Lumber Interests," MS in possession of C. R. Musser of Muscatine in 1953; Blair, 293–303. Such other firms as Schulenburg, Boeckeler & Company, Dimock, Gould & Company, Burlington Lumber Company, J. S. Keator & Sons, and Standard Lumber Company—all associates of Weyerhaeuser by the mid-eighties— also had steamboats to serve their own purposes.

37. LN Papers, Laird, Norton & Co. to J. Turner, Feb. 20, 1879, and to T. Irvine, Nov. 26, 1879; Blair, 299– 303.

38. FEW Record, including Blair to FEW, Jan. 26, 1934; Blair, 293–303.

39. Winona County Hist. Soc., George Winans scrapbook, "Rafting on the Mississippi"; Gregory, *West Central Wisconsin History,* II, 831. Winans was born at Camanche, Iowa, on Jan. 8, 1839, and piloted his first lumber raft from Reads Landing to Dubuque on Nov. 1, 1857. From 1901 to 1916 he was employed by Weyerhaeuser in towing log rafts from St. Paul to Prescott.

40. FEW Record, 147, 150; Reminiscences of Captains Walter A. Blair and Fred A. Bill.

X

New Mills, New Markets,

1870–1900

O N JUNE 21, 1871, Delos R. Moon wrote his partner in Eau
Claire that the extension of railroads from Burlington, Clinton,
and Davenport was demoralizing markets in Missouri River
towns.[1] His voice was merely the first of many lamenting the uncertain
price situation in the midwestern lumber market. Seasonal and cyclical
fluctuations, railroad expansion, and the mechanization of mills accompanied a generally downward movement of prices until 1897. These events
reduced profits so sharply that lumbermen often worked desperately during this period to save their businesses. Weyerhaeuser and his associates
moved in the middle of the struggle—now leading, now following.

2

In such a loosely autonomous group as that headed by Frederick
Weyerhaeuser, each millowner made his own decisions on manufacturing
and marketing his product.

During the sixties, selling lumber was a simple process. Only one
product—white pine—was sold. Mill operators on the Mississippi sawed
their lumber, piled it for seasoning in the open air, and sent out price lists
to customers. Occasionally one partner would call on the buyers to collect
overdue bills and take new orders. Advertising was restricted to small
insertions in local newspapers, for there were no lumber periodicals. Mail
orders and purchases by dealers directly from the mill yards accounted
for most of the sales. Lumber virtually sold itself.

But during the seventies, Lake States lumbermen found their previously neat marketing pattern disrupted. New railroad construction, the long depression (1873–1879), new railroad rate arrangements, and the appearance of yellow pine timber from the South all posed new problems.

Railway construction—westward and northern extensions of such lines as the St. Paul & Pacific, Northern Pacific, the Winona & St. Peter, and the Omaha—opened new territories to settlement, creating an enormous demand for lumber of all kinds. Firms at La Crosse, Winona, Minneapolis, and points north prospered on sales encouraged by the railroad expansion in Minnesota and the Dakotas.[2]

But while some railroads expanded the market, others sharpened competition. In southern Minnesota, new southerly and southwesternly roads bisected the earlier east-west lines. The Winona & St. Peter was crossed by the Chicago, Milwaukee & St. Paul at Owatonna, the St. Paul & Sioux City at Mankato, and the Minneapolis & St. Louis at Waseca. In 1876 the first of these lines carried 54,272,000 board feet of lumber southward from Minneapolis, the second 33,453,000, the third 27,083,000—all into the immediate territory of Winona firms. Minneapolis mills could manufacture lumber as cheaply as those at Winona, and forced the latter to adopt an aggressive program to retain their markets.

Meanwhile, Wisconsin railroads were throwing still more lumber into the competitive scramble. As early as 1865 the Chicago & North Western connected Green Bay and Chicago, through Clinton, with the prime markets of Lamb & Sons, Young & Company, and David Joyce. An extension to Marinette in 1871 tied the heavily timbered Menomonie River basin, circuitously, to the same markets. In that year Tomah made rail connection with the St. Croix at Hudson and gained access to St. Paul in 1872.[3]

In 1877 the completion of the Wisconsin Central line from Milwaukee to Ashland on Lake Superior tapped hitherto untouched forested areas, encouraged the establishment of new sawmills, and brought additional lumber into glutted western areas. Quickly the Chicago, St. Paul, Minneapolis & Omaha worked out rate arrangements with the St. Paul & Sioux City and other connecting roads, enabling "Wisconsin lumbermen to compete with Chicago and older distributing centers for the Western market."[4]

In 1878 Laird, Norton & Co. received complaints from dealer-customers about cheaper lumber coming from Green Bay. The Winona firm could only reply: "You will keep abreast of your competition in the trade and hold your own, and if anything is needed on our part to help you if it gets too close we will help you out."[5]

While the Winona firms had to worry about competition from northern Wisconsin and Minnesota mills, Weyerhaeuser and his friends in Iowa and Missouri had to face a massive flow of lumber from Chicago wholesalers. Crossing the two states from east to west, six major rail lines carried loads from the nation's greatest lumber mart to points beyond the Mississippi. In 1876 Chicago received 971,416,000 board feet of lumber and boasted 110 wholesale and retail yards and 45 planing mills.[6] Carrying the product west, the roads took Chicago lumber through McGregor, Dubuque, Clinton, Davenport, Burlington, and Quincy. Sellers at those points could scarcely restrain their exasperation as they saw and heard the lumber-laden cars rumbling through their cities to seize a share of "their own" market to the west.

The Chicago shipments became positively menacing. In 1875 the Burlington alone carried out of the city a total of 176,459,000 board feet of lumber, more than the combined output of fourteen lumber-manufacturing firms in Minneapolis (137,769,000 feet), or the total production of the thirteen firms then associated with the Mississippi River Logging Company (166,318,000). The Rock Island transported 57,456,000 board feet westward the same year. Of course, no road carrying freight from Chicago moved all its lumber as far west as the Mississippi. But Chicago wholesalers were making tremendous sales and setting prices in markets recently "owned" by sellers along the Great River.[7]

Chicago distributors could sell more cheaply because they received favorable freight rates. Railroad managers desired to have full cars both east and west and, in view of low handling costs on long hauls, could afford to make lower tariffs for them than for short ones. In 1878 the carload rate on lumber from Chicago to Kansas City was $20, while that from Quincy to the same western city, not a third of the distance, was $36. Again, as the historians of Dimock-Gould observed, "because of unregulated railroad rate-making policies it was cheaper to ship by rail from Chicago 300 miles into Iowa than to ship by rail from Moline half that distance west."

Mississippi River lumbermen naturally considered such differentials discriminatory and demanded equally low rates. Out of a conference with several railroads in August, 1878, the sawmillers on the Upper Mississippi and its tributaries won through rates on lumber shipped west and south. And in 1879 the "Lumber Line" provided truly competitive tariffs, for the Omaha was a land-grant road and saw its salvation in hauling logs and lumber from land it sold. A rate war ensued. Though tariffs from such points as Davenport were lowered early in 1880, the fight still left the protesting distributors on the Middle River at a disadvantage because of added transfer costs.

In some cases, however, instead of protesting, the lumber companies leagued themselves with the railways. Thus Laird, Norton Co. chose to work closely with the Winona & St. Peter, its only rail line west. W. J. Young allied himself with the Chicago & North Western. Protests against the railways also abated during the prosperous years from 1880 to 1883, when satisfactory profits quieted the lumbermen on the Mississippi and the Chippewa until depression hit again.[8]

But those lumbermen who had no partnerships with railways, when prosperity ended, were once again galvanized into protest by new railroad policies. In February, 1884, the northern lines joined Chicago railroads in advancing all rates and establishing "competitive rate differentials." Mississippi River lumbermen protested, but the Chippewa firms did not rouse themselves until the temporary rates were declared permanent by the Bogue arbitral decision in May and the differential on shipments west was widened. Almost all Chippewa sawmillers then resumed rafting, and the outcry from newspapers against "discrimination" was loud. Restoration of the former charges on shipments from Eau Claire and Chippewa Falls in August, 1884, left lumbermen there content but gave no relief to the Weyerhaeuser firms and others on the Middle Mississippi.[9]

Meanwhile, the downriver millowners concluded that the fundamental difficulty lay less in railroad discrimination than in the overproduction of lumber and the general business stagnation. Mississippi River Logging Company firms held a meeting in Clinton on July 23, 1884, and resolved to shut down their mills earlier than usual, on September 15th, provided that seven-eighths of the mills in the region would do likewise. There is no evidence that this resolution, or a similar one in 1893 by the Mississippi Valley Lumbermen's Association, had much effect. Every sawmiller and logger seemingly operated on the principle that the only way to make money as prices fell was to increase volume of production.[10]

When prosperity returned in 1885, rail shipments direct from depleted Michigan and Wisconsin forests to Chicago were lessening; the Minnesota camps fed local mills chiefly; and shipments west from Chicago declined. However, new factors marred the profits picture for white pine lumbermen. As their forests were cut, the prices of their raw material rose, doubling between 1880 and 1900. Moreover, for the first time southern longleaf yellow pine lumber appeared as a strong competitor. Produced with low-cost timber and labor after 1875 it asserted its advantages in the South and by the early eighties was dominant as far north as St. Louis. By the late eighties white pine lumber, no matter how favorable its freight rates, could not hold its market for cheaper grades in areas north of St. Louis against the lower-priced yellow pine. In December, 1887, under pressure from northern lumbermen, managers of railroads lowered rates from Chicago to Kansas City to 18 cents per hundred pounds and later to as low as 8 cents for some classes. The most significant result was a reduction in rates by southern railroads on yellow pine lumber.[11]

While selling lumber at profitable prices during the prosperous period between 1886 and 1893, lumbermen on the Chippewa decided to try a new avenue for getting satisfactory freight rates to the West. They appealed to the Interstate Commerce Commission in 1890, and for some years that body seemed inclined to heed their pleas. But the Supreme Court in the Maximum Freight Rate Case asserted that the commission had no authority to set rates, and the Chippewa Valley lumbermen gained nothing on rivals in the race for favorable rate differentials.

Sawmillers on the Middle Mississippi never got relief, though they finally staged one abortive outburst. In 1895, hard-pressed by competition from the Minneapolis mills, they gathered on April 12th at Rock Island in response to an open letter from John P. Weyerhaeuser. There they created the Middle Mississippi Lumbermen's Association "for the purpose of protecting ourselves against unjust discrimination in freight rates."[12] Though geographic location, widespread depression, competition from yellow pine, and production in excess of demand were basic causes of their difficulties, they now struck out blindly, as the farmers did, against the one prime target, the railroads. But railroad executives, deep in depression also, could scarcely afford to give them a hearing.

In such an atmosphere not only Frederick Weyerhaeuser and his friends but lumbermen everywhere engaged in a terrific race for success or survival against narrowing profit margins. During the depressed seventies, for example, Laird, Norton Co.'s average price received on all lumber shipments dropped from $18.29 per thousand board feet in 1871 to $12.49 in 1879, or more than 31 percent. Upward movements in prices in the next few years resulted in a decline of shipments. Meanwhile, the price of logs, the basic raw material, was holding relatively steady around $5 per thousand, so that the decline in selling prices of lumber could mean acceptance only of smaller earnings per thousand feet.

With each succeeding year the squeeze on profits became ever more stringent. As already noted, the cost of white pine stumpage and logs at least doubled, while the average price received for lumber shipped by such a representative firm as the Rock Island Lumber & Manufacturing Company declined from $15.53 per thousand board feet in 1883 to $11.75 in 1897. If the price of all white pine lumber sold increased by 3 percent between 1880 and 1897, as one authority estimated, the profits must have accrued to lumbermen in eastern states, for competition in most of the Midwest was too strong to permit even this slight gain.[13]

3

Every lumberman, including Frederick Weyerhaeuser, had to decide how to combat the squeeze on profits if he wanted to continue in business. Clearly, protests against the railroads, even if successful, would be only palliative.

A whole series of remedies were available. A lumberman could establish mills along the new rail lines; Weyerhaeuser & Denkmann, in company with many associates, followed that path to profits in the White River Lumber Company, North Wisconsin Lumber Company, and numerous others. He could invest in Southern pine; the Rock Island partners did just that in 1882. And throughout the period, members of the Weyerhaeuser group directed their best efforts to procuring stumpage and timberland as inexpensively as possible along the northern rivers. By putting funds in ventures all over the Upper Mississippi Valley, Weyerhaeuser and his friends got logs at low cost, spread their risks and enjoyed the advantages, as well as the disadvantages, of almost every kind of location.

In addition to diversifying opportunities and risks, every able Lake States manufacturer of ability, including Weyerhaeuser and his associates, strove to reduce unit costs by expanding the size of his plant. Most commercial mills achieved greater volume year after year. To take one example, the shipments of the Rock Island Lumber & Manufacturing Company rose from 13,214,000 board feet in 1879, the first full year of operation, to 55,526,000 in 1897.

The creation of the Rock Island Lumber & Manufacturing Company in 1878 was itself a move to obtain the economies of larger production. The corporation acquired the mill of Anawalt, Denkmann & Company and the adjacent plant of Keator & Wilson, which converted many formerly unused boards into molding and other millwork.[14] And in 1888 Weyerhaeuser & Denkmann, to gain adequate log-holding facilities, purchased the mill of Renwick, Shaw & Crossett and operated it until it burned in 1901. The two mills of Weyerhaeuser & Denkmann produced about 77,000,000 feet of lumber in 1895, the two of Rock Island Lumber & Manufacturing approximately 40,000,000, though in 1898 the four together cut only 70,000,000.

In 1881, O. H. Ingram, as previously related, merged his Eau Claire firm (Ingram, Kennedy & Company) and its lands and mill with the wholesaling facilities of Charles Horton Lumber Company at Winona, and Dulany & McVeigh of Hannibal, in the new Empire Lumber Company, which later built a mill at Winona.[15] Ingram and his associates thus combined sawmilling and wholesaling, attempting to utilize advantages in several locations.

The output of the enlarged mills was increased by the installation of improved machinery. During the 1870's lumbermen on the Middle Mississippi and elsewhere put the latest technological innovations into general use. By that time a tough, pliable steel for circular saws capable of withstanding lateral and torsional strains at high speeds was available. The rotaries, although made of thinner steel, now wobbled less than formerly. The kerf on the improved 12-gauge saws amounted to no more than five-sixteenths of an inch instead of the earlier eight-sixteenths. And almost every commercial sawmiller of any size installed a double rotary; that is, one saw was aligned above the other, as the head saw for preparation of cants to be fed to the "gang," which often numbered as many as forty-six saws set in a sturdy iron frame and bolted to a heavy stone foundation.[16]

To keep pace with the hungry new rotaries and gangs, mill managers had to install a series of other improvements. A bull chain pulled the logs from the millpond to the log deck. Then steam-feed carriages with "dogs" (clamps), steam log turners, and setworks, one after another, assured the sawyer that the logs would be held rigidly against the headblocks on the carriage, that the carriage would be propelled and logs turned with great speed, and that boards would be of uniform thickness. Iron wheels and tracks superseded greased hardwood sliding carriages, but the wire rope wound on a drum (steam cylinders later) mercilessly jolted the carriage and its load.

As the output of the primary saws increased, the processes of edging, trimming, grading, and stacking were expedited. Double edgers, with an adjustable saw, and patent trimmers hastened the finishing process. Live rolls replaced manual offbearers at some stages of the sawing process, but additional men were hired to grade the greater volume of boards and transfer the lumber to the drying yard. Only a few, such as Union Lumber and Laird, Norton, installed dry kilns; the remainder preferred open-air drying. Planing mills, adopted first in the sixties and seventies by saw-millers on the Mississippi, were improved by better knives, which could turn out smooth boards at greater and greater speeds. Steam boilers were improved but occasionally exploded as a result of carelessness. Laird, Norton had such an experience in 1870.[17]

By the mid-seventies, when the first important lumber trade journals began to appear in the Lake States, advertisements clearly indicate that sawmill operators could buy from nearby manufacturers almost any type of equipment they needed. Several Weyerhaeuser associated firms bought direct-acting steam feeds from the Marinette Iron Works. E. P. Allis & Company of Milwaukee manufactured sawmill engines, circular and gang mills, edgers, trimmers, and other equipment. Allis "Improved Setworks" competed with those of a Milwaukee rival—Filer, Stowell & Company. With either machine a sawyer could turn out boards to the desired thickness, in gradations of one-sixteenth of an inch.

Purchases of machinery from local manufacturers cut freight costs to a minimum. The most widely known local producer of sawmill equipment was Frank McDonough of Eau Claire, who designed sawmill plants and installed a complete line of machinery of his own manufacture in numerous mills owned by members of the Weyerhaeuser group.[18]

Such firms supplied not only equipment but extensive service with most purchases. McDonough sent millwrights to set up and start the plants he built. Improvements in machinery came through suggestions from operators to the manufacturer. Observers from the manufacturing company saw improvements made by local millwrights, and adopted them. On many items a thirty-day trial was allowed. Many manufacturers of equipment permitted installment payments, thus helping lumbermen to buy their products more easily.

By the eighties, the band saw had won preeminence throughout the industry. It was a continuous sheet of steel with toothed edges, usually on one side but sometimes both, running on two wheels aligned one above the other. First given national publicity at the Philadelphia Centennial celebration of 1876, the new device was quickly adopted.

The band saw was a far-reaching innovation in sawmilling technology. The indiscriminating advance of innumerable oscillating saws in the gangs had worked against quality, and promoted waste. The gang did not permit the separation of good and poor grades of lumber or the detection of rot and other defects. Trimmers and edgers took a heavy toll, leaving many short and narrow boards that were hard to sell. With a band a skillful sawyer could turn the log and adjust the setworks to get the most high-grade lumber out of the log. Moreover, this new saw cut a kerf of a mere one-eighth inch, 75 percent less than the first circulars. In every respect the band conserved raw material and increased the overrun. These advantages more than compensated for a somewhat lower output per manufacturing unit than by rotaries, at least in the early stages of the band's adoption.

Spurred by disadvantageous locations and plummeting prices, sawmillers on the Middle Mississippi took the lead in adopting the band saw. In 1880 Lindsay & Phelps of Davenport installed the first band mill in the Mississippi Valley. Mechanically minded F. C. A. Denkmann and Chancy Lamb saw to it that their firms followed suit in 1884. A year later the Northwestern Lumber Company won primacy with the installation of a band mill in the Chippewa Valley, while Laird, Norton Co., building a new mill after a fire in 1887, also adopted the band, becoming the first Minnesota firm to do so.[19]

Indeed, Minneapolis sawmillers lagged sadly behind Laird, Norton and other Weyerhaeuser associates. They operated their antiquated plants as long as they would run or until they were destroyed by fire. Early in June, 1888, a party of some thirty Minneapolis lumbermen journeyed to Winona, which now boasted four "modern" sawmills. For the first time, apparently, the visitors witnessed the tremendous strides that had been made in sawmill technology. The plants were roomy and light; the laborers enjoyed the benefit of the latest labor-saving machinery. By this time modern establishments had electric lighting (at least in planing mills), automatic sprinklers, fire hydrants and pumps, corrugated steel roofing, and other improvements.[20]

Without doubt, the new plant of the Pine Tree Lumber Company epitomized the existing stage of sawmill technology near the end of the century. As earlier noted, this mill (built 1891–1892) had all the "latest" equipment. Two boilers and a Reynolds Corliss engine converted steam into mechanical power. The array of saws—two bands, steam feed and setworks, log turners, 42-inch gang, edgers, trimmers, shingle and lath machines—was driven by a 24-inch belt on a flywheel 12 feet in diameter. By 1895 additional machines were turning out molding, shiplap, and match stock. Behind each saw a system of rollers and chutes conveyed lumber to the next operation or to waiting carts. A blower system shot sawdust and shavings to the boiler room for use as fuel. Waste from the saws provided raw materials for lath, pickets, and other salable products.[21]

Between the iron-roofed, brick boiler-and-engine house and the shingle mill, jutting from the south side of the main structure, projected the bulbous top of the refuse burner. The slender iron smokestack beyond the long sorting shed, which formed the northern wing of the mill, identified the planing-mill engine room and electric-light plant. Adjoining the planing mill were the dressed-lumber sheds and loading docks. In the foreground the long tongue of the logway stretched down to the log-filled river, while in the background appeared row on row of stacked lumber.

Charles Weyerhaeuser personally studied the problem of piling lumber with a view to saving labor and improving quality. All the lumber was air-dried, his stockholders having voted against the installation of dry kilns. Skilled lumber pilers, working on contract, carefully placed each piece so that it would dry evenly. Piles reached a height of thirty-six feet or more. Each pile was grade-marked and dated. Wooden rails, some covered with strap iron, for tramways; wooden planking; electric lights fed by the company's power plant; water mains; and fire hydrants connected to the company's own pumping station all gave the yard the appearance of a town.

The advances in sawmill technology resulted in a marked increase in plant capacity and in production per man. With a muley saw of the 1850's, 25 men could turn out 5,000 board feet daily, or approximately 200 board feet per man. By the mid-seventies 100 men could process, with a double rotary and a large gang, 100,000 board feet daily, or 1,000 per man. The addition of more saws thereafter largely meant the hiring of more men, and the increase of productivity per man was not so noticeable after the mid-seventies. The band saw did not expand output of the headsaws, though in other respects it was a more efficient machine than the rotaries.[22]

Lumbermen passed on to workers a relatively small part of the gains from these technological improvements. Weyerhaeuser paid common sawmill labor—loaders, slab pickers, helpers—75 cents per day in the late fifties, $1.25 in the early seventies, and $1.35 in 1876. Sixteen years later sawmillers along the Mississippi had brought the pay for common labor to a high of $1.50 per day, though the rate on the Chippewa was ten cents less. Unskilled workers had their wages lowered to $1.10 per day during the depression of the nineties, but they rose again to former levels when prosperity returned at the end of the decade.

In truth, lumbermen in the Lake States, including Weyerhaeuser & Denkmann, usually gave concessions to workers on hours and wages only under pressure. The traditional hours of work were from 6:00 A.M. to 6:00 P.M., with an hour off for lunch—an eleven-hour workday. In the spring of 1876 some of the workmen at the Weyerhaeuser & Denkmann mill struck for higher wages. The management refused, and eventually the strikers returned to their jobs at the old rate of $1.35 per day. Late in July, 1877, the sawmill hands at Clinton asked for an increase in the common wage from $1.25 to $1.50 per day. They, too, met refusal, then struck, stormed the plants, piled lumber on the tramways, unhitched teams, and compelled the mills to close; but they won none of their demands.

In 1879 sawmill employees at Rock Island and Davenport asked for a ten-hour day with eleven hours' pay. Employers turned a deaf ear, whereupon crews at Weyerhaeuser plants quit work. The next day several hundred men and boys marched to Moline where they presented an ultimatum to J. S. Keator & Son and Dimock, Gould & Company. When the owners rejected it, the strikers forcibly turned off valves in the engine rooms. On Wednesday committees representing the strikers negotiated with millowners in both areas. Though some owners felt that the hours of work were too long, they refused to waive any part of their "right" to determine the wages paid and hours worked. A week later the mills were operating with no change in hours or wages.

Owner-managers began to yield more to labor pressure in the 1880's. "The most serious labor dispute the lumber industry was called upon to face in Wisconsin" occurred at Eau Claire in 1881.[23] Two thousand millworkers demanded a ten-hour day and, in defiance of local authorities, took possession of the plants. State militia restored order, and the men returned to work; but shortly afterward most of the Eau Claire millowners voluntarily reduced the workday. A slight depression in the mid-eighties abated labor demands for a time, but in April, 1886, with the brighter economic prospect, the call for a ten-hour day became widespread. Journalists took up the cause of unorganized labor. Soon lumbermen started to yield. Laird, Norton began the ten-hour day in that year but kept the basic daily wage of $1.25. Other mills retained the eleven-hour day and increased wages for the unskilled worker to $1.37½.

Intermittent labor pressure and prosperous conditions brought about wide acceptance of the ten-hour workday and the $1.50 daily wage along the Mississippi by 1892, though, as noted, Chippewa sawmillers elected

to keep their rate at $1.40. At Little Falls, Pine Tree Lumber started oper-
ations with a ten-hour workday, and raised it to eleven when burned-over
timber had to be converted into lumber after the Hinckley fire, but later
returned to the shorter day.

By 1898 most mills had restored wage levels of the predepression
years, but many workers were dissatisfied. At Chippewa Falls, efforts of
the American Federation of Labor to organize sawmill employees resulted
in a strike, closing the Big Mill in the same week the Spanish-American
War broke out. The manager wired to Frederick Weyerhaeuser for advice,
as noted elsewhere. Weyerhaeuser's threat to "let the logs go down the
Chippewa" ended the strike. It showed also that Weyerhaeuser had no intention of sharing fundamental decisions with his workers.[24]

If accidents in the Big Mill at Chippewa Falls were representative,
workers could scarcely have cited the hazards of the sawmill as important
reasons for demanding higher wages and shorter hours. Most injuries were
minor. Two-thirds of those reported by the Chippewa Lumber & Boom
Company during the five-year period 1892–1896 were mere cuts and
bruises. The saws accounted for 18 percent of the injuries, moving belts
and shafts for another 10 percent. Flying pieces of bark, boards, and
broken sawteeth caused others, while strains, sawdust in eyes, and infec-
tions from slivers similarly led to loss of working time. The most serious
accident, recorded in April, 1896, resulted in a back injury. No fatalities
were reported during these years. And the hospital ticket plan, used in the
mills as in the woods, took care of injuries in most instances.[25] While sawmill safety undoubtedly fell short of J. P. Weyerhaeuser's ideal, that children should be able to play in a mill without danger, the record would
probably compare favorably with those in many occupations, including
farming.

A variety of explanations have been advanced for the failure of the
worker to reap the full rewards of mechanization. Organized labor
throughout the United States had made only limited headway and had
rarely invaded the lumber mills. Again, workers were scattered in small
towns throughout the Lake States. Each sawmill manager had the power
to hire, fire, and set wages and hours. The unrestrained competition,
narrowing profit margins per unit, and the large number of firm failures
all bolstered the determination of owner-managers to keep wage levels
from rising. Each sawmill manager carefully compared his own terms with
those of his competitors in his vicinity. It seemed natural to him to apply
the low wages and long hours of the local farms to those of lumbering.
Also, the owner-managers stubbornly fought to hold their increased earnings and the power to control their work force; nobody gives up either
power or pelf until compelled to do so.

Even though the workers' wages rose slowly, real wages increased more than money wages. The long downward trend in prices between 1867 and 1897 meant that workers whose wages had risen from $1.25 per day to $1.50 gained more in housing, food, and clothing than the difference in the figures implied. With such incomes, meager as they were, thrifty workmen built substantial homes out of low-cost pine lumber, raised large families, fed them with low-cost food, and celebrated weddings, anniversaries, and christenings.

4

Despite their gains from technological advances, investments in stumpage, the rise in timber values, and the small concessions to labor, sawmillers would still have faced insolvency if they had not been able to market their product against strong competition and narrowing profit margins.

One obvious way to increase sales was to push into newly settled territories as these were reached by the railroads. As early as 1870 W. J. Young & Company had branch yards in Council Bluffs and Omaha. By 1877 Weyerhaeuser & Denkmann and the Rock Island Lumber & Manufacturing Company were sending their lumber as far west as the foothills of the Rockies and as far south as Texas. Cloquet firms took advantage of the building of the Canadian Pacific Railroad to sell heavily in Manitoba. And they shipped a large proportion of their products into the Red River Valley and the Dakotas along rails laid by the Northern Pacific and the lines that had become the Great Northern Railway Company by 1890.[26]

The alacrity with which Weyerhaeuser firms accepted the practice of direct rail shipments varied with the location of the mills. Along rail lines in Wisconsin and northern Minnesota shipment to market by this means was accepted at once. Along the Chippewa, the cheapness of water transport of lumber to downriver wholesalers deferred the adoption of the new practice for several years. But in the late seventies, when rafted lumber fell to as low as $7 per thousand feet at Dubuque, Hannibal, and other points, a few sawmillers added planing equipment to their mills, built spur tracks, and laid out yards. Not until 1883 did Chippewa Lumber & Boom's Big Mill have planing, yarding, and shipping facilities. The managers discovered by 1885, though initial transfer costs were less by water than by rail, that earnings on direct shipments by rail exceeded those sent by water by 34 cents per thousand. Still, the Knapp-Stout and Daniel Shaw firms continued to float lumber downstream, the latter sending out its last raft shortly after 1900.[27]

However, the most imaginative of the firms associated with Frederick Weyerhaeuser were to be found in Winona. Laird, Norton & Co. decided in the 1860's to build its market along the Winona & St. Peter Railroad, across southern Minnesota and into the Dakotas. It pioneered in starting retail "lineyards" along the railroad line, the first two at St. Charles and Rochester, Minnesota, in 1864. Later, Youmans Brothers followed where Laird, Norton had led. Soon it became the policy of many firms in the Midwest to use this method of retailing their produce.

Not until after the depression of the seventies began to lift and direct competition from sawmillers in Minnesota and Wisconsin became onerous, did Laird, Norton rapidly expand its lineyard system. Only three new yards were started between 1872 and 1877; but as sales improved and the rails of the Winona & St. Peter were pushed west, the Winona firm established three yards in 1878 and twelve more in 1879. Twenty-eight additional outlets were created in the 1880's. Youmans Brothers & Hodgins provided active competition in more than a dozen Minnesota towns and in several Dakota communities.[28]

Other firms associated with Weyerhaeuser were slower in starting retail yards. On January 12, 1887, the Rock Island Lumber & Manufacturing Company appointed E. H. Anawalt as manager of its newly organized retail yard system in Kansas and Nebraska. Anawalt acquired some twenty yards in the hope of profiting from a building boom then in progress. The bright prospects proved illusory. The yards were managed from Wichita, far from the Rock Island mills, competition was sharp, the boom collapsed, and the depression of the nineties ended any hopes of profit. Moreover, stockholders criticized the aging manager for using the yards to advance his sons at a time when the books showed too much red ink.

In the depressed nineties Frederick Weyerhaeuser had another opportunity to enter the retail-yard business. Early in the decade he had become a partner of John C. Hill, former office man at Chippewa Falls, in a venture in logs, lumber, and retailing. John C. Hill & Company, unable to weather the depression, was reorganized as Weyerhaeuser & Company in 1894 and incorporated as F. Weyerhaeuser Co. in 1901. As a result, the earnings of a few yards in southern Minnesota financed for many years Frederick Weyerhaeuser's central office force in St. Paul.[29]

Creating a lineyard system inevitably brought the owners, at least before the passage of the Interstate Commerce Act in 1887, into bargaining relationship with railroads. As long as sawmillers like Weyerhaeuser & Denkmann sold their products to retailers f.o.b. mill, they would not be involved in the questions of rebates and drawbacks, then universal in the railroad industry. But Laird, Norton, with its many lineyards, naturally sought the best possible locations on sidings and spurs, and in negotiating with the railway company naturally asked for rebates, and got them. Numerous letters to managers requested a list of freight costs so that the rebates might be collected.[30] Indeed, Laird, Norton did well enough to be highly satisfied with "our railroad," the Winona & St. Peter, for they opposed moves by the Chicago, Milwaukee & St. Paul to equalize rates with other distributing points in the late seventies.[31]

But millowners, whatever their location, the cost of logs, and their productive capacity, had other avenues for marketing lumber: they could improve selling techniques, expand advertising, form voluntary associations to stabilize prices and systematize grading, and vary credit and prices according to the market. Members of the Weyerhaeuser group used all these methods.

During the 1870's lumber manufacturers began to solicit sales much more actively. A member of the firm or an important official devoted at least part and sometimes all of his time to calling on retailers. Orrin Holt, bookkeeper and office manager, performed the function for Weyerhaeuser & Denkmann; W. H. Laird and later R. L. McCormick for Laird, Norton & Co.

By the mid-eighties most of the larger lumber manufacturers were employing traveling salesmen, first used extensively by lumber wholesalers in the depressed seventies. In 1880 one lumber journal noted that drummers and commission men were being employed by mill operators, sometimes on a part-time basis. With the extension of railroad facilities competition became so strong that after 1882 "the bulk of the distributive trade of the north" was "carried on through the medium of traveling solicitors." Lindsay & Phelps of Davenport provided one oustanding exception; it never employed either traveling salesmen or commission men.[32]

By the end of the century, most Weyerhaeuser companies were employing a sales manager and not less than three traveling salesmen. Their competitive weapons were price lists, a *Russell's Railway Guide,* a stock sheet, an order book, a credit-rating book, a mileage book, some expense money, and their talents as salesmen.

Numerous small concerns lacked resources to support a sales department and fell back on commission agents. A few Weyerhaeuser companies used these as well as salesmen. Some of the agents, known as "scalpers," sold lumber for a number of manufacturers and were devoted to none, were interested in quick turnover of inventory and immediate commissions, and often disposed of only the lowest-priced items in each stock. In depressed times, wholesalers as well as manufacturers sometimes authorized them to sell without reference to price lists. As late as 1902, the Chippewa Lumber & Boom Company marketed 58 percent of its lumber through commission men, and only 23 percent by mail order and 19 percent by traveling salesmen.[33]

During the 1870's, as trade periodicals appeared, Lake States lumbermen began to have good sources of information about their industry and an effective medium for advertising their wares. The *Michigan Lumberman,* published in 1873 at Grand Rapids, became the *Northwestern*

Lumberman a year later and appeared under that title and a Chicago address until 1898. The *Mississippi Valley Lumberman & Manufacturer* (later *Mississippi Valley Lumberman*) started a career in Minneapolis on August 17, 1876, which has not yet terminated. *The Southern Lumberman* first came out in 1881 at Nashville. *The Timberman,* founded in Chicago in 1885, was merged with the *Northwestern Lumberman* in 1898 under the title *American Lumberman.*

To emphasize the quality of lumber was almost impossible prior to 1900. Some of the Weyerhaeuser group did adopt dry kilns, but most of them relied on careful air drying to produce lumber of low moisture content. Planing machines were improved and the finish of boards was undoubtedly much better in 1900 than in 1860 or 1870. But such improved quality as might be achieved by the band saw, more attention to drying, and improved planing machinery was offset by a marked decline in the quality of logs received after 1890.

Numerous cooperative endeavors in the lumber trade had blossomed in the 1870's and 1880's, most of them to wither away. The Chicago Lumbermen's Exchange had been organized in 1869 but achieved little until a new secretary began compiling statistics of receipts and shipments in 1874. Little success met the lumber exchanges and boards of trade organized in the depressed mid-seventies by local businessmen at Davenport, Moline, Muscatine, Rock Island, Minneapolis, and Stillwater. The National Association of Lumbermen, created in 1874 to curtail production as a means of stemming the postpanic decline in prices, proved completely ineffective for lack of support.

In fact, not until 1881 were lumbermen able to create even a mildly successful trade association—the Northwestern Lumber Manufacturers' Association. For many years the organization remained relatively ineffectual, although its secretary-treasurer, George S. Long, later became one of the most remarkable executives in the history of Weyerhaeuser enterprises. In 1884, when prices were again falling, members voted to curtail production, but, "You couldn't bind them to any agreement with a log chain," one delegate to the meeting raspingly informed O. H. Ingram.[34]

The first outstanding achievement in the cooperative regional lumber trade effort—the Mississippi Valley Lumbermen's Association—was founded on September 1, 1891. Members of the Weyerhaeuser group took an active part in its creation and work. William H. Laird and William Irvine became its first vice-presidents and R. L. McCormick its first treasurer. Among the directors were Frederick Weyerhaeuser, George S. Shaw, W. J. Young, Jr., and George H. Atwood. W. H. Laird held the presidency for several years during the nineties, and Sumner T. McKnight of the Northwestern Lumber Company at Eau Claire was chosen vice-president in 1894.

Frankly admitting that they were organizing for the purpose of establishing "more nearly uniform prices," founders of the association immediately set up committees to deal with grading, price lists, and railroad rates. The last unit accomplished nothing, and the association found that it had to standardize the grading of lumber before it could make judgments about uniform prices. As early as 1873 the Chicago Lumbermen's Exchange had adopted grading rules, which in the ensuing years were followed to some extent throughout the Lake States. But too many lumbermen disregarded the rules, and the price lists became practically meaningless. As early as 1881 the editor of the *Northwestern Lumberman* observed the "Babelic confusion regarding grades." He urged that the "same grade board should have the same name in one market that it does in another" and that "the different markets should have the same inspection rules for determining the grade." By 1884 Minneapolis grading rules had been "so kicked, cuffed, knocked and mutilated that the fond parents of the system would not know their offspring."[35] Each sawmiller tended to grade his own lumber, and both wholesalers and retailers sorted and manipulated grades to gain every advantage that they could.

In 1890 the Northwestern Lumber Manufacturers' Association had appointed an inspection committee to visit all large plants in the region and to compare grades with the Meginn Rules for Lumber Inspection used by most Chicago wholesalers. The committee found wide discrepancies from town to town throughout the Northwest. Because manufacturers left grading largely to distributors, George S. Long later observed that "quite a few of the early operators were able to pile up excellent margins by reason of cheap timber, cheap logging, and cheap manufacture and yet threw away very comfortable fortunes by not sorting and selling the lumber with the same businesslike care that they had given to buying timber."[36]

Since the Mississippi Valley Lumbermen's Association had been formed with uniform grading on a regional basis as a central objective, it took the Northwestern group's report and started to draw up a set of rules. Action was delayed for almost five years by the necessity of getting agreement among a host of producers, by the demoralization of the market after the panic of 1893, and by a lawsuit.

Hardly had the MVLA been organized when it was indicted for price fixing in violation of the Sherman Antitrust Act of 1890. Several Weyerhaeuser associates testified at the trial, held in the Federal District Court in St. Paul in 1892; among them were William Irvine, W. H. Laird, S. T. McKnight, and Frederick Weyerhaeuser. The judge exonerated the lumbermen, but the citizens of Minnesota then brought the issue to the Minnesota legislature, which in 1893 devoted much energy to an investigation of lumber prices. The point of attack was the association's price list, which suggested combination for illegitimate regulation of prices.[37] Though nothing came of this inquiry, it and the lawsuit marked the beginnings of public concern over the industry's alleged price fixing.

At long last, on February 20, 1895, the MVLA adopted a well-conceived set of grading rules with eight categories. Each category had subdivisions, some as many as nine, and each grade had detailed specifications. No. 1 Common Boards and Strips included, for example, "all sound, tight-knotted stock whether red or black knots, free from very large, coarse knots or any imperfections that will weaken the piece. This grade should be of a character fitting it for any ordinary use except finishing purposes. Sap, knots, and a small amount of shake are admissible if they do not affect the general utility of the piece."

The success of the rules depended on the Chairman of the Bureau of Uniform Grades and on rigid inspection. Fortunately, the association chose George S. Long as the chairman, and he selected E. M. Warren of Chicago as chief inspector. By 1897, and not until then, inspection practices were proving extremely effective. Skilled lumber graders periodically visited each plant to determine whether the lumber was below, over, or "on" grade. The rules were revised and reprinted from time to time, a fourth edition of 15,000 copies appearing in 1901.[38] And the system was continued by the successor of the MVLA, the Northern Pine Manufacturers' Association in 1906.

Several other lumber associations sooner or later found the grading system of the MVLA worthy of emulation. Among them were the Northwestern Hemlock Manufacturers' Association and the Western Pine Association. By World War I producers of southern pine lumber were making almost as many grades as northern white pine manufacturers. Indeed, according to a leading textbook authority on the American lumber industry, "nearly every association has copied these [MVLA] rules to a greater or less extent, both in nomenclature and description of grade."

As to influencing prices, the Mississippi Valley Lumbermen's Association accomplished nothing measurable through 1897 and probably little thereafter. Price lists were industriously circulated, but average prices received by the Rock Island Lumber & Manufacturing Company dropped from $15.17 in 1893 to $11.75 per thousand board feet in 1897. Similar figures for Pine Tree were $13.12 and $9.95. And after 1897 the impact of price lists must be considered in conjunction with the effects of the higher schedules on lumber imports in the Dingley tariff of 1897, the upward trend in prices throughout the economy, higher costs of all supplies, rises in prices of white pine timber as a result of growing scarcity, higher wages for labor, and higher logging costs. Contrary to claims made by officers of numerous lumber trade associations about their price-supporting activities, the upward movement in prices for white pine lumber can only be explained in terms of these factors.[39]

Laird, Norton policy on lineyards indicates what made for successful

Frederick Weyerhaeuser

Frederick Carl August Denkmann

Log jam on the St. Croix River, in 1888, containing an estimated 200,000,000 board feet.

(TOP) Northern Wisconsin logging camp in 1860's.

The bunkhouse, the "home" of the early logger who worked a rugged 10- to 12-hour day.

Weyerhaeuser and Denkmann Rock Island mill.

The Frederick Weyerhaeuser family's first home in Coal Valley, Illinois, purchased in 1859.

William Harris Laird

James Laird Norton

Matthew George Norton

Chancy Lamb

W. J. Young

Thomas Irvine

Edward Rutledge

O. H. Ingram

The steamboat C. J. Caffrey *towed log rafts down the Mississippi River.*

Summer or winter, the woods of Wisconsin were a challenge to Frederick Weyerhaeuser (2ND FROM RIGHT).

The Wannigan (cookhouse) followed the men driving logs down the Chippewa River.

Wood Indian and Little Falls Dam, at Holcombe, Wisconsin, built in 1880 by Weyerhaeuser and his associates.

J. P. Weyerhaeuser

R. L. McCormick

John A. Humbird, Sr.

William Irvine

C. A. Weyerhaeuser

R. Drew Musser

R. M. Weyerhaeuser

F. E. Weyerhaeuser

(ABOVE) *The Cloquet Lumber Company mill, in which Weyerhaeuser and Denkmann purchased an interest in 1883.*

The Johnson-Wentworth Company mill, purchased jointly by Northern Lumber Company and Cloquet Lumber Company in 1902.

Peter M. Musser

A. W. Laird, Frederick Weyerhaeuser, and P. M. Musser at Potlatch logging camp.

H. C. Hornby

George S. Long, Sr.

A. W. Clapp

E. W. Davis

The Northwest Paper Company mill at Cloquet in 1899.

Cloquet before the disastrous fire of 1918.

Cloquet after the fire; almost completely reduced to ashes.

Weyerhaeuser Timber Company directors and stockholders at annual meeting in Tacoma in 1900.

STANDING LEFT TO RIGHT:

Horace Rand, William Carson, W. L. McCormick, H. H. Irvine, C. R. Musser, F. C. Denkmann, R. M. Weyerhaeuser.

SITTING LEFT TO RIGHT:

George S. Long, Sr., Frederick Weyerhaeuser, F. S. Bell, P. M. Musser.

Everett Mill "A" in 1903, a year after its purchase, was Weyerhaeuser Timber Company's first venture into Northwest sawmilling.

marketing in lumber between 1870 and 1900. New yards, established in recently settled territories, for a time usually had no competition. They stocked a full line of building materials. Control of selling prices lay in the Winona office, a condition not realized by wholesalers disposing of their product to independent retailers. After 1879 all lineyard managers made weekly reports of daily sales and other data on a printed form. They also sent to the home office a monthly report of accounts outstanding. The administrative objective of the firm as stated in 1879 could be accepted today: "Not to have too much red tape or complexity of reports, and yet such as that we will constantly have before us what they are doing." Traveling representatives of the firm exercised on-the-spot supervision of lineyard managers. By 1884 improved accounting methods made possible reliable end-of-month reports and annual summaries.

Both lineyard managers and independent retailers tended to be "liberal" in extending credit; it was almost an imperative in effecting sales. Yet prudence and caution were watchwords of the Laird, Norton firm. Its policy was to make a 5 percent discount for cash in thirty days and to charge interest on all accounts beyond that time. "You will suit us by making no time sales but hold for cash or what will be short time," wrote Laird, Norton to the Owatonna manager in 1879, "and if necessary to do so, make a discount enough to bring in the cash."[40] Mortgages, personal notes, and chattel mortgages were accepted for building materials sold on credit by yard managers. Open book accounts they tried to keep small and then not to run over sixty days without conversion to a promissory note.[41] So many schoolhouses were built on credit with Laird, Norton lumber that occasionally bundles of bonds (usually $400 in amount at 12 percent interest) were sent to agents for collection from surrounding districts. School districts almost universally were laggard in making payments, and money due for lumber sold to build churches was almost as difficult to bring into the till.

Occasionally, often in depression years and usually at points where union was thought necessary to meet competition from lumber shipped from Minneapolis and Wisconsin, Winona firms agreed on price lists or on a division of the market. In 1884, for example, Laird, Norton, Empire Lumber, and Youmans Brothers & Hodgins decided to divide equally their share of the Rochester market as a means of meeting "outside" competition. During the 1880's several such "local pools" were arranged by yard managers with the full approval of Laird, Norton, but after the passage of the Sherman Act in 1890, no agreements were written. "We cannot sign the agreement," the firm wrote one man in 1895, "but we should expect to live up to a verbal agreement that you might make regarding prices." Most such pacts were little more than truces between general price wars.

But by the 1880's even liberal credit and price manipulations failed to provide the answers for the Weyerhaeuser firms. Competition from southern pine lumber in Missouri, Kansas, and Nebraska became so strong that resort to new methods was imperative. Already noted previously were the failures of the lineyards owned by J. C. Hill & Company in Minnesota and the Rock Island Lumber & Manufacturing Company in Kansas and Nebraska.[42] As early as 1894 M. G. Norton recommended that some of the associated firms try to expand sales in eastern markets. A few did so, starting shipments to Pittsburgh by way of Tonawanda (near Buffalo), and finally the Cloquet companies acquired a yard there in 1906.[43]

Statistics of lumber production in 1899 indicate the relative position attained by the Weyerhaeuser group in the Lake States industry, including those firms owning mills independently of Weyerhaeuser himself. In the St. Croix Valley, mills of the associates sawed 26.6 percent of the subregional total, a figure that may be compared with the group's 26.7 in northern Minnesota, 18 percent on the Mississippi above Minneapolis, none in Minneapolis, 84 percent along the Omaha Railroad in Wisconsin, and 53 percent on the Chippewa. Of the total softwood production reported in the Federal Census for Minnesota and Wisconsin, however, mills of the associates accounted for little more than 12 percent, 9 percent if Michigan production is added, or slightly less than 11 percent of the total output in the six states where all their mills were locted. Comparable percentages for white pine alone were 15.6, 12.2, and 16, respectively.[44]

Although members of the Weyerhaeuser group thus attained a relatively small percentage of total output in their area, they set a successful record of financial management. In the log pools, funds were raised annually, as noted, by standardized calls, and earnings were left in the business for a long period of time. Mississippi River Logging paid no dividends for twenty years. The Weyerhaeusers, Mussers, Laird, Nortons, and others contributed funds for initial investments in timber and mill construction, then left earnings in the firms for further purchases of timber or as working capital. Only after a period of ten years or more did they begin to authorize the payment of dividends, usually when original costs of both timber and mills had been written off. Modified only slightly in 1896, such primitive accounting, with only occasional trial balances and annual balance sheets, answered the needs of lumbermen and *in toto* recorded an impressive accumulation of capital between 1860 and 1900.

Frederick Weyerhaeuser and his friends must also be accorded an important role in the general history of the forest-products industry in their area. As manufacturers of lumber they had contributed notably to the building of the Upper Middle West. They had also furnished sizable amounts of capital for use in that area. The first historian of the lumber industry in the Old Northwest estimated that, during the sixty years through 1897, the lumbermen of Michigan, Minnesota, and Wisconsin had "enriched the nation" and "added to its development" the sum of $4,196,428,262, an amount exceeding by almost 50 percent the cost of the Civil War to the North, and triple the value of all gold ($1,300,000,-000) produced in California between 1848 and 1897.[45] Much of this capital, including a large part of that held by the Weyerhaeuser group, went into developing the forest-products industry in the Pacific Northwest, a smaller portion to the South.

NOTES

1. Bartlett Papers, Moon to Porter, June 21, 1871.

2. See Riegel, *Story of Western Railroads,* for a comprehensive analysis.

3. Larson, *White Pine Industry,* 107–108, 110–111; LN Papers, corresp., 1878–1879.

4. Fries, *Empire in Pine,* 86–87 (quotation); Gregory, *West Central Wisconsin History,* I, 379; Bill, "Reminiscences," *Burlington Post,* June 14, July 5, 1930; *Nwn. Lbrmn.,* XI (April 27, 1878), p. 5.

5. LN Papers, Laird, Norton & Co. to J. Swenson, Sept. 21, 1878.

6. 55th Cong., 2nd Sess., House Doc. No. 277, Serial No. 3679, 100–101; *MVL&M,* I, No. 20, Dec. 29, 1876, p. 8; Hotchkiss, 685.

7. Larson, 122; *MVL&M,* III (Feb. 28, 1879), p. 3.

8. *Railway Age,* V, Feb. 26, 1880, p. 103 (quotation); *MVL&M,* IV (Feb. 20, 1880), p. 4; Fries, 87, 94; LN Papers, corresp., Sept.–Dec., 1879; Sieber, "Sawmilling on the Mississippi," Chaps. VII–VIII.

9. Fries, 93–96. For reactions of the industry to the rate controversy, see *MVL&M,* "Weekly Trade Reports," March 20, July 24, Sept. 25, and Nov. 20, 1884.

10. *MVL&M,* "Weekly Trade Reports," July 24, Sept. 25, Nov. 20, 1884, Sept. 24, 1885, Jan. 22, 1886.

11. *MVL&M,* XIII (Feb. 24, 1888), pp. 8–9; *Amer. Lbrmn.* (Jan. 6, 1906), p. 21.

12. Fries, 95–98; FW Papers, correspondence, April–May, 1895; Preamble of Middle Mississippi Lumbermen's Association, printed pamphlet, April 12, 1895; *Minneapolis Journal,* April 7, 1907.

13. LN Papers, Winona, Record Book; MRLC, annual statements for the 1870's; JPW Papers, A. B. Du Von to JPW, July 20, 1908; Wilson Compton, *The Organization of the Lumber Industry,* 91.

14. JPW Papers, A. B. Du Von to JPW, July 20, 1908; Rock Island Lumber & Manufacturing Co. Min. Bk., 1878–1880.

15. FEW Record, 111; *Amer. Lbrmn.,* Jan. 21, 1899, p. 29; Hotchkiss, 626, 629–631, 584, 494–497, 564, 570. Ingram also had interests in the Rice Lake Lumber Co., the Wabasha Lumber Co., Hudson Saw Mill Co., and Fort Scott (Kans.) Lumber Co.

16. F. H. Gilman, "History of the Development of Sawmilling and Woodworking Machinery," *MVL* (Feb. 1, 1895), 59–63; FEW Record, 71–72; *MVL&M* (Feb. 22, 1878), p. 1.

17. LN Papers, 1870.

18. See advertisements in *MVL&M,* 1876 onward; FEW Record File, Hauberg, "Weyerhaeuser & Denk-

mann"; LN Papers, *passim.* Advertisements often included lists and testimonials of firms using the equipment emphasized.

19. Gilman, 62; Hotchkiss, 481, 588, 602; Larson, 152, 158; *Amer. Lbrm.,* I (May 6, 1899), p. 1.

20. *Miss. Val. Lbrmn.,* XII, Sept. 16, 1887, p. 6; Nov. 10, 1880, p. 2, 4; XIII, June 15, 1888, p. 2; R. D. Musser Papers, M. G. Norton to Pine Tree Lumber Co., Nov. 2, 1897.

21. R. D. Musser Papers, contracts.

22. Larson, 29–52, 147–164; Hotchkiss, 653–659; Noah Shaw, "Early Reminiscences of Saw Mill History," *MVL,* XXVI (Feb. 1, 1895), p. 69; Gilman, 63–68.

23. FEW Record File, FW Time Book, 1858–1865; J. P. Weyerhaeuser to F. Weyerhaeuser, April 27, 1876; *MVL&M,* I, March 16, 1877, p. 2; *ibid.,* Aug. 3, 1877, p. 3; *ibid.,* IV, July 25, 1879, p. 2; Wickstrom and Ainsworth, *Always Lumber,* 129; Fries, 204–220; Engberg, *passim;* Fries, 212–213.

24. FEW Record, "Reminiscences" of W. Irvine; JPW Papers, A. J. Taylor to J. P. Weyerhaeuser, July 16, 1898.

25. CL&B Co. Papers, Accident Report Files.

26. *MVL&M,* I (March 16, 1877); Cloquet Lumber Co. and Northern Lumber Co. Papers, annual reports; Sieber, Chap. VII.

27. *MVL&M,* III, Aug. 9, 1878, p. 4, and IV, July 18, 1879, p. 4; CL&B Co. Papers, MHS, Annual Report for 1885; Reynolds, 104.

28. LN Papers, Ledger, 1864–1865; Charles Towle, "The Winona & St. Peter Railroad," *Weekly Philatelic Gossip,* LXIII, Jan. 12, 1957, p. 606; W. E. Downer and C. R. Musser, "The Musser Lumber Interests"; LN Papers, Ledger, 1864–1888; Larson, 109. Between 1856 and 1871 the Musser family operated combination wholesale-retail yards at both Muscatine and Iowa City, but these were not lineyards, and no extension of the jointly operated yards was made. W. J. Young & Co. began some line-

yards in the 1860's but closed all of them by 1882 (Sieber, Chap. VIII).

29. JPW Papers, Anawalt to JPW, Nov. 27, 1887; and correspondence between JPW and auditors H. M. Temple, Charles Esplin, and others; Rock Island Lumber & Manufacturing Co. Min. Bk., 1878–1900; FEW Record, 439–440; FEW Papers, correspondence; interview with Charles McGough, April 21, 1958.

30. LN Papers, Laird, Norton Co. to G. H. Ellsbury, June 4, 1886; to G. H. Prior, June 4, 1886; to David Connors, Nov. 13, 1886. This was merely one of many requests for rebates.

31. LN Papers, Laird, Norton Co. to J. Swenson, Oct. 28, 1877; to M. L. Joyce, Sept. 5, 1879; to Marvin Hughitt, Dec. 10, 1879; to H. R. McCullough, Dec. 24, 1879.

32. FEW Record, 71, 73, JPW to FW, April 27, 1876, Oct. 4, 1877; LN Papers, 1870's, *passim.; MVL&M,* V, Aug. 27, 1880, p. 41; Hotchkiss, 601.

33. JPW Papers, Taylor to JPW, March 13, 1899; D. H. Bartlett, Reminiscences; interviews with N. D. Woodworth and J. C. Patience at Little Falls; CL&B Co. Papers, MHS, Annual Reports for 1902; O. M. Butler, "Distribution of Softwood Lumber in the Middle West: Wholesale Distribution," United States Forest Service, Report No. 116, Washington, D.C., 1917.

34. Ingram Papers, A. G. Van Schaick to Ingram, June 30, 1884, cited on Fries, 133; Hotchkiss, 309, 680, 683; Wickstrom and Ainsworth, 103; Larson, 108; *MVL&M,* I, Oct. 5, 1876, p. 4; *ibid.,* I, Sept. 28, 1876, p. 4; *ibid.,* I, Dec. 29, 1876, p. 4; *Nwn. Lbrmn.,* Sept. 24, 1881.

35. *Nwn. Lbrmn.,* Sept. 24, 1881, *MVL&M,* VIII, April 25, 1884, p. 21. In 1884 the Missouri and Arkansas Lumber Association had adopted rules dividing lumber into three broad grades—Dressed and Matched Flooring, Step Stuff, and Boards

(Stanley F. Horn, *This Fascinating Lumber Business*, 216).

36. Long Papers, Tacoma, Long to E. W. Backus, Aug. 3, 1925; report by J. S. Funk and A. A. Fiero, Inspection Committee, July 8, 1890, reprinted by Long, July 15, 1925, copy enclosed in letter from A. N. Frederickson to Wendell Link, April 20, 1953.

37. Larson, 391.

38. Association Standard Grades of White Pine Lumber reported by the Bureau of Uniform Grades and adopted by the Miss. Valley Lumbermen's Assoc., Feb. 20, 1895, pamphlet in historical collection of Weyerhaeuser Sales Co.; *Proceedings* of the 10th Annual Meeting of the MVLA, Feb. 19, 1901.

39. N. C. Brown, *The American Lumber Industry*, 81; *White Pine Standard Grading Rules*, published by the White Pine Bureau, St. Paul, 1917; Long Papers, Tacoma, L. S. Case to W. H. Boner, May 8, 1918; Bureau of Corporations, *The Lumber In-* dustry, IV, 12; Larson, 392; Pine Tree Lumber Co. annual reports; JPW Papers, A. B. Du Von to JPW, July 20, 1908; Compton, 131–132.

40. LN Papers, W. H. Laird to R. L. McCormick, Nov. 12, 1879; Laird, Norton & Co. to J. H. Potter, Sept. 9, 1879.

41. *Ibid.*, Laird, Norton Co. to C. E. Childs, Sept. 28, 1889.

42. The Hill & Company yards were taken over by F. Weyerhaeuser Co. and later by the Rock Island Lumber Company. Rock Island Lumber & Coal Company bought the Kansas yards, the others in that string going to Rock Island Lumber.

43. M. G. Norton Papers, Winona, Norton to R. L. McCormick, Aug. 20, 1894; annl. repts. of CL&B Co., and Pine Tree Lbr. Co.

44. *Amer. Lbrmn.*, Jan. 13, 1900 and Steer, *Lumber Production in the United States, 1799–1946*, 11.

45. Hotchkiss, 641.

XI

Last Years in Minnesota

B Y EARLY 1897 the Pine Tree Lumber Company was paying off its indebtedness, and by late 1899, in the economic sunshine of the McKinley administration, had worked free of it. On December 26th Drew Musser wrote to Laird, Norton that "in accordance with the request of a majority of the members of our board we have this day made a 10 percent dividend payment in cash."

This act began an almost continuous period of prosperity for the Weyerhaeuser firms in central Minnesota. In 1900 and 1901 Pine Tree repeated the 10 percent dividend; in 1902 it paid one of 70 percent. On May 6th of the following year the treasurer could report that dividends to date now equaled the "entire investment of capital stock." A further 20 percent payment was made later the same year.[1]

Pine Tree was now sawing from 70,000,000 to 93,000,000 feet of lumber yearly, aside from lath and shingles. Its stumpage remained impressive; purchases in 1899 and 1901 kept the total high. When Charles Weyerhaeuser in December, 1903, made a successful bid for Indian reservation timber at public auction, he added an estimated 255,000,000 feet to Pine Tree and Mississippi River Lumber Company reserves. In 1906 Pine Tree's stumpage still stood at 636,000,000 feet. A cooperative arrangement with Cloquet for selling lumber in Chicago was in force, and late in 1904 Drew Musser wrote Frederick Weyerhaeuser that this was "a very satisfactory and successful undertaking."[2]

Meanwhile forces were at work that would round out the activities of Pine Tree and relate them importantly to the Mississippi River Lumber Company. One such force was the eagerness of Drew and Charles, as soon as they saw daylight ahead for Pine Tree, to expand their operations. Like captains coming late into a military campaign, they were determined to make up for lost time and distinguish themselves in action. Frederick Weyerhaeuser, always ready for bold ventures if sound, did not curb them, and they won support also from Peter Musser and Laird, Norton. One of their projects, the Northwest Paper Company, found a location at Cloquet, and will be dealt with later.

Another was the formation of the Immigration Land Company (1898), a corporation capitalized at $20,000, which was to sell the cutover lands of Pine Tree. Already employed in Wisconsin, the device, hoped its young promoters, would yield modest profits, settle farmers on the cutover lands, and lift a severe tax burden on idle acres from Pine Tree's shoulders. The first years of operation brought brisk sales and seemed to justify the hopes of the founders.[3]

Still another step, not however primarily attributable to Drew and Charles, was the joint purchase of stumpage with the Mississippi River Lumber Company, already noted. Acting together, the two organizations could buy freely, acquiring larger holdings than either could purchase alone.

The next project of Charles and Drew developed from their search for new stumpage. They had looked everywhere for timber, even in northern Minnesota, and as a result became aware of the Duluth firm of Kehl and Deary, which bought and sold timber in the north.

One day early in October, 1898, William Deary called upon them. He was the field expert of the firm, Kehl the office head. A rough lumberman, Deary impressed the Pine Tree managers with his vigor and ability. "Mr. Deary seems to be a fair-minded man," wrote Drew to Norton, "and he feels he can do us some good."

The relationship soon led to the incorporation of the Northland Pine Company on July 15, 1899. Capitalized at $100,000 as a Minnesota firm, it represented a merger of the Kehl and Deary interests with the Weyerhaeuser group, the latter holding 75 percent of the stock. Kehl was president, Deary general manager. He continued to buy stumpage, and by September 12th had acquired 105,943,000 feet at an average cost of $1.56 per thousand.[4]

Northland was buying northern Minnesota stumpage almost exclusively and selling to Canadian mills or in the Duluth area. Some of its holdings were of potential use to Pine Tree. However, in April, 1900, the directors sent Deary at company expense on an abortive trip through the South. He and Kehl also visited the Far West and at the meeting of October 12th reported enthusiastically on white pine stands in Idaho. The minutes note that "after J. B. Kehl told the company of the timber he had recently seen in Idaho, the stockholders' meeting was adjourned." It was a vote for the Far West, and may not have been a wise one. F. E. Weyerhaeuser said later, "Almost any investment in southern pine lumber made in 1900 by competent lumbermen would have been exceedingly profitable. . . . On the other hand Idaho, with very few exceptions, brought enormous losses if not financial ruin to every important operator."[5]

Deary continued to operate in Idaho, but in 1903 his acquisitions were merged with those of Henry Turrish in the Potlatch Lumber Company, Northland stockholders holding four-fifths of the stock. Meanwhile, Northland's Minnesota properties were sold to Pine Tree on April 9, 1902, for $450,000. In 1903 little was left of Northland but its corporate entity.[6]

2

In 1898 the Mississippi River Lumber Company was still operating on a reduced scale, cutting less timber than it bought. But with 1899 it resumed volume activity, logging more than 46,000,000 feet and selling 52,411,000, and continued this scale of operations. It met the usual difficulties in the making of log drives, and was reviled as "the syndicate."

Meanwhile the company revived its original dream of establishing its own manufacturing facilities. In 1904 it acquired jointly with Pine Tree the moribund Northland Pine Company, and soon sold to it the Cross Lake Logging Company and the Northern Mississippi Railway·Company. These properties gave Northland facilities for cutting timber on Indian reservations, and for transporting its logs to the Mississippi, whence they could be sent downstream to Minneapolis. With a mill in that city it could convert them to lumber.[7]

To acquire one, negotiations were renewed with the Backus-Brooks Company, which had previously offered its mill, but at a price considered too high. Drew Musser attributed this step to Frederick Weyerhaeuser. "It was largely due to his advice that the mill was purchased," he wrote soon after the event. Charles Weyerhaeuser conducted the negotiations, and in March, 1905, Backus sold the mill, office, houses, and barns for $155,000, along with 23,000,000 feet of logs, for which an additional $345,000 was paid. According to Drew, the mill "was very efficient with machines that were speeded up to produce lumber profitably." In 1905 Frederick Weyerhaeuser succeeded Chute as president, the latter becoming general manager. However, the assistant manager, C. A. Barton, soon showed outstanding abilities and became the actual director of operations.[8]

The new company moved into action rapidly. On April 11, 1905, the sum of $875,000 was levied on stockholders for "sawmill operations." Including the money paid for Cross Lake Logging and the associated railroad, a total of $1,275,000 was advanced. Northland bought 8,058,-000 feet of logs from Pine Tree and during the season cut 44,000,000, half of which reached Minneapolis that year. Barton continued on approximately this scale through the ensuing four years. By agreement with Pine Tree, Charles E. McGibbon was employed to sell the lumber of both companies. By 1908 the $1,275,000 advanced by the stockholders had been repaid, and in that year the new company declared a first dividend of $300,000.[9]

As Northland rose, Mississippi River Lumber declined. It had now abdicated as a buyer and seller of timber, dropping sharply from 27,268,-000 feet of logs banked in 1904 to 3,363,000 in 1905. By 1909 its stumpage was completely disposed of. It controlled its three boom companies and a few other minor operations.

In 1912, to escape disadvantages of the Iowa tax system and better their political position in Minnesota, the stockholders organized the Mississippi Lumber Company, a Minnesota corporation capitalized at $235,000. Shares in the new firm were distributed to the stockholders of the older one in exact proportion to their holdings in the latter. Mississippi Lumber then began to liquidate its properties of River Lumber, though for legal reasons the latter continued a paper existence.

Meanwhile, Mississippi Lumber took on liquidating characteristics. Typical were the sales of cutover lands and the boom operations. Some gains were realized from the land sales ($212,210) from 1912–1918, but the trend was toward a deficit operation, which soon became chronic.[10]

As to the boom companies, during the 1900's they showed encouraging profits, which after 1905, as the supply of logs diminished and was mostly carried by rail, rapidly fell off. When by 1919 the flow of logs ceased altogether, the chief value of riparian rights held by the boom companies lay in their use by power corporations. This condition had been anticipated, and from 1910 on agreements were made for eventual sales. Thus the Mississippi River Electric Power Company (later the Northern States Power Company) in 1917 took over the entire properties of the Mississippi & Rum River Boom Company for $75,000. In similar fashion other subsidiaries of Mississippi Lumber were sold.

One, however, maintained its existence. When Weyerhaeuser and his group made the original purchase of the St. Anthony Lumber Company, they acquired half-interest in any mineral rights in the properties. Within a few years it became clear that such rights were potentially valuable; and on January 10, 1896, the Mississippi Land Company was incorporated (capitalization, $15,000) to hold title in such tracts as showed promise of iron or other deposits and to lease and develop them. Mississippi River Lumber held half the stock, E. C. Whitney and his associates the remainder.

From that time forward leases were made by the Mississippi Land Company to various mining firms. As time passed, low-grade ore, at first despised, became valuable, and the firm still continues to be active.[11]

3

After 1907 Pine Tree and Northland were engaged in cutting the last timber in central Minnesota and manufacturing lumber at Little Falls and Minneapolis. Neither firm could maintain a production comparable with that of companies in the northeastern corner of the state. In 1913 Northland sawed 74,000,000 feet and Pine Tree 37,000,000, but in the north the Virginia & Rainy Lake Company produced 170,000,000. These figures reflect the impending exhaustion of the central Minnesota forests and the richness of the northern resources.[12]

During these years Pine Tree and Northland drew heavily upon the timber of Indian reservations. The 1903 purchase by Charles Weyerhaeuser proved to be much greater than estimated. In 1910 he obtained another 65,000,000 feet, and Northland bought the stumpage on Indian lands held by the Thief Falls Lumber Company (59,211,000 feet), while both Weyerhaeuser companies from time to time picked up small amounts from Indian or white owners. In 1909 Pine Tree, Mississippi River Lumber, and Northland jointly acquired a large tract from the Minnesota and International Railway—about 311,000,000 feet, of which Pine Tree got 255,000,000. In 1910–1911 Northland acquired 172,766,000 feet, some from Pine Tree and some in connection with the purchase of a mill from the Carpenter-Lamb interests. As already noted, Pine Tree on occasion sold stumpage to Northland as being the better company to handle certain tracts. Several transfers, including one just mentioned, occurred in 1910–1911.[13]

From 1907 on, Pine Tree logged an average of 32,020,000 feet a year, and sawed a considerably larger amount—45,000,000 feet on the average. This was less than its performance in the late 1890's (about 70,000,000 feet a year); but the smaller volume of business was done at a good profit, and there were additional gains from the sale of stumpage that the company decided not to log.

Even before the Mississippi River Lumber Company had organized a Minnesota corporation to take over its assets, Pine Tree had escaped Iowa taxation and rid itself of the stigma of being an "alien" corporation by forming on December 28, 1909, the Pine Tree Manufacturing Company, a Minnesota firm. It replaced the original Pine Tree Lumber Company, an Iowa unit. Capitalized at $380,000, the new organization had the same officers and stockholders, acquired all the properties of the original Pine Tree, and carried forward its work without a break, including the local retail operations of the Morrison County Lumber Company organized in 1907.[14]

Necessary administrative changes occurred after the death of Pine Tree's president, Peter Musser, at Muscatine, Iowa, on September 28,

1910. By his eighty-fifth year, Musser had presided over the company for the full twenty years of its life. According to a memorial adopted by the stockholders on May 3, 1911, he was "far-sighted in business matters, not through intuition, but because of the study and thought he put upon all of them." At a meeting on May 19th to choose a new president, Charles Weyerhaeuser vainly urged both Drew and P. M. Musser to accept the post, and almost two years later, on April 15, 1913, reluctantly took it himself! He retained his post as manager. He had exercised his new responsibilities for less than a year when Frederick Weyerhaeuser died in 1914. The old guard was passing, and the young men of 1890 were now in full charge of the enterprise they had carried through early years of adversity to full success.[15]

When the Virginia & Rainy Lake Company sought additional timber in 1908, Pine Tree at first refused to sell 225,000,000 feet of stumpage in St. Louis County. In 1909 and 1912–1913 it did, taking in payment cash, notes, and shares; in 1916 Pine Tree reported holdings of 9,190 shares of Virginia & Rainy Lake stock valued at $125 per share.

Many Pine Tree stockholders were eager to close out their investment, and on January 7, 1913, Charles Weyerhaeuser sold to the Crookston Lumber Company for $1,800,000 an acreage with an estimated stumpage of 217,704,000 feet. This sale shortened the life of the firm by about eight years.

Carrying out a suggestion of Frederick Weyerhaeuser made in 1908 when he was a member of the State Forestry Board, Pine Tree offered to donate 3,000 acres in what is now Itasca State Park to the state, reserving the right to cut trees more than eight inches in diameter, breast high. The offer was accepted.

An act of April, 1911, also permitted the donors to reserve mineral rights. With the formation of the Crow Wing Land Company six months later, Pine Tree took steps to hold and lease iron-ore deposits near Crosby, Minnesota. Further deposits were protected through the Immigrant Land Company, the unit controlling cutover tracts.

With 1916, Pine Tree and Northland moved into the final stages of active life. A distribution of $1,332,800, mostly from liquidation of assets, marked that year for Pine Tree. Then came a rapidly diminishing cut of timber, and on April 12, 1920, Charles Weyerhaeuser reported that in October, 1919, the last log had been sawed and that the company was now shipping its remaining lumber "at prices better than ever received before." The remaining Northland mill sawed its final log in the summer of 1919 (it was the last Minneapolis mill to close), and ceased lumber shipments in November, 1920. The firm had disposed of its Twin City retail yards, acquired in 1915 from the Shevlin-Carpenter interests, to Thompson Yards as of January 1, 1919. Both operations had terminated at almost the height of a boom. The timing could not have been better.[16]

The three Weyerhaeuser lumber companies operating in central Minnesota had all been successful in carrying through their undertakings, and all profited on a more than generous scale. By 1922 Pine Tree, which almost twenty years earlier had paid all its debts and returned 100 percent on the original invested capital, had paid its stockholders an additional $11,463,395. Up to 1910 the Mississippi River Lumber Company paid no dividends, but during the next eight years distributed $3,958,750— more than twice the original investment. Northland declared dividends totaling almost $1,000,000 by 1903, and between 1908 and 1925 paid out $6,900,000 more, largely reflected in the earning statements of its two parent corporations.

As was usually true of their enterprises, the Weyerhaeusers were in no case exclusive beneficiaries of these returns. In 1890 Frederick Weyerhaeuser held about 11 percent of Pine Tree stock, in 1893 12½ percent of Mississippi River Lumber shares, and in 1905 he and two of his sons, directly or indirectly, owned but 25 percent of those of Northland. Subsequent changes altered these proportions little. But with their associates, chiefly the Denkmanns, Laird, Nortons, and Mussers, the Weyerhaeusers profited notably. Theirs were the rewards of shrewd and daring use of opportunities, sound management, and of cooperation between their companies. These had never abused their advantages, and while no boldly progressive measures marked their work in milling, labor relations, or forestry, they had sown the seeds of cooperative marketing, and gained experience with cutover lands that would count in the future development of a constructive reforestation policy.[17]

4

"Estimate of standing white pine in Minnesota 20 to 30 billion board feet," ran a Laird, Norton memorandum in June, 1897. The appraisal was not unduly optimistic, and more than half of the total lay in the northeast, then the least-logged area of the state, with Cloquet as its center. When Rudolph Weyerhaeuser arrived there in 1896 to manage the Northern Lumber Company, uncut timberlands lay to the north, northwest, and northeast, still little charted and difficult of access.

"When I went to Cloquet," he recalled later, "Mr. Shaw [of the Cloquet Lumber Company] was the only person I knew there." In November, 1897, death removed this tie, but Rudolph had meanwhile become acquainted with H. C. Hornby of the Cloquet Company and S. S. Johnson of Johnson-Wentworth. He also met a lawyer resident in nearby Carlton, a quiet, able man named Henry Oldenburg, then not quite forty, who was soon to become a guide for the Weyerhaeuser interests.[18]

With the acquisition of the Nelson properties, the Weyerhaeuser influence became dominant in Cloquet. The family investment in Cloquet Lumber was relatively small, but after Shaw's death Frederick Weyerhaeuser had become its president and general manager; and the stockholders in January, 1898, voted to follow the Weyerhaeuser policy of acquiring additional timberland "if tributary to the Cloquet mills." Hornby became de facto manager. Meanwhile, in the Northern Company Weyerhaeuser & Denkmann held 16,300 of 20,000 shares, and Northern controlled the boom companies. It would cooperate increasingly with the Cloquet Company.[19]

Cloquet was now a thriving town of six thousand inhabitants, its houses clustering about the five mills. Many of the dwellings were primitive. Stumps still studded a number of streets, and the entire town smelled and looked of lumber. Lumber exerted an economic domination. "Everything here depends on the mills for support," wrote a new teacher to her parents. "The principal store is the Company store, the principal hotel the Company hotel, many of the homes are Company houses." True, noncompany establishments competed for the worker's patronage, and he was free to build his own house. But Cloquet was a lumber town, carved out of swamps, rocks, and forest, and its people lived by the mills.

For business, the year 1896 was poor, with sagging prices for lumber; but conditions improved in 1897. In 1898 the two companies together sawed 108,516,000 board feet, and surpassed this figure in 1899 with 147,687,000.[20]

Of the Cloquet Company's mills, the steam-driven plant opposite the eastern end of Dunlap Island was the larger, with three bands, one double-cutting; the "water mill" near the falls had two bands and a gang. The Northern Company's Lower Mill, opposite the western tip of Dunlap, was somewhat larger than the Upper, which lay a little east of Posey's Island. The Johnson-Wentworth plant, as noted, was opposite the falls, and thus farthest downriver of any of the five mills.

While ready from the start to cooperate in certain matters, Rudolph and Hornby each quickly showed a determination to make the record of his own company outstanding. Each commanded two mills, with a total capacity about equal. Hardly more than a fifth of the stock of the two concerns was in identical hands, so that they mainly served different groups of owners. Both managers had had practical experience, Hornby perhaps more, for he had worked up from the bottom. David H. Bartlett, who knew both men, calls Rudolph "a very keen operator," who knew markets and men and could "select the right men to do the jobs." Hornby he found "very quiet," but also shrewd in handling his employees, "a driver, a very keen businessman." All who knew Rudolph agree that he could speak with biting sarcasm, sometimes jocosely, but always with effect.[21]

Since his arrival Rudolph had purchased logs from William O'Brien, a timber broker and logging contractor. O'Brien had insisted on using the St. Croix instead of the Scribner log scale, which the Weyerhaeusers preferred. In 1900 O'Brien described the timber areas he would cut, Northern to buy the logs. Rudolph agreed, but stipulated that the Scribner scale be used. O'Brien refused, saying he could sell to others on his own terms. "I doubt it," snapped Rudolph, and negotiations were broken off. "It was shortsighted on our part, which we realized later on," Rudolph confessed in 1935. Only fifty cents a thousand board feet was involved.

O'Brien went to Michael J. Scanlon, a prominent Minneapolis lumberman, who promptly built a large mill a few miles below Cloquet. He bought from O'Brien, Cook & Turrish, and others, and not only took logs and stumpage the Weyerhaeuser companies might otherwise have had, but also complicated the task of the boom companies by dumping a new category of logs on the crowded St. Louis River.

Another result of Rudolph's mistake was a menacing logjam, which, however, had one compensatory effect for the Weyerhaeuser companies in that it discouraged the owner of the Johnson-Wentworth Company. "I was on the log jam above Cloquet with Mr. Hornby and Mr. S. S. Johnson one day," Rudolph stated later, "when he told us that he would like to sell out his going business. . . . He gave us an option on his property for two weeks."

The sale was made in November, 1902, for $2,535,622, with Northern and Cloquet Lumber assuming joint ownership. Johnson managed the company for a year, then pleaded ill-health, and on December 1, 1903, Joseph R. Wilson took over. He was a "rough and ready operator," hard, resourceful, driving. He made the rivalry between the Weyerhaeuser companies three-sided, and asked no favors of Hornby or Rudolph.[22]

Meanwhile the companies had been acquiring stumpage to maintain their reserves. The most notable purchase was one by Northern in 1900 of 31,348 acres from the Northern Pacific and other holders. While title litigation for these lands plagued the company for sixteen years, for $686,586 it acquired 235,000,000 feet of rich and well-located timber.

Johnson-Wentworth came into the Weyerhaeuser fold with 377,000,-000 feet of logs and stumpage. However, all three companies were soon to profit in stumpage as in other matters by a policy of more intensive cooperation.[23]

5

The situation invited teamwork. There was first of all stumpage. In St. Louis and Lake counties much forested land was still available, some in the hands of wealthy speculators and railroads, some on state and Indian lands, and the rest held by farmers or small lumber companies. The question of the far-northern areas was a moot one. In 1903 tracts there did not seem to be "tributary" to Cloquet, but with better rail facilities and higher lumber prices they could be, and Weyerhaeuser firms bought timber there when they could get it cheaply.

As we have seen, F. E. Weyerhaeuser had already been buying stumpage for Northern, and in 1905 he and George F. Lindsay set up an office in Duluth to purchase for the three Cloquet companies jointly. They soon justified themselves by the acquisition of 550,000,000 feet of timber in northern St. Louis county for $3,360,000, though much of this lay so far north that it was later transferred to the Virginia & Rainy Lake Company. Meanwhile, Weyerhaeuser and Lindsay had been buying small tracts that helped maintain the reserves of the Cloquet corporations.

In 1908 the three companies held 1,500,000,000 feet of uncut timber, Northern 915,518,000 feet, Cloquet 412,000,000, and Johnson-Wentworth 224,311,000. Undoubtedly the willingness to buy jointly had helped to provide all three firms with reserves for the future.[24]

In logging, the companies operated with considerable independence, but soon found an increasing area of activity in which they could work together. The character of logging near Cloquet was basically the same as in Wisconsin or central Minnesota, but it was altered sharply by the character of the country, which encouraged the use of logging railroads.

Each company maintained its own camps, which averaged from three to seven per company but varied from year to year. Individual logging contractors were also employed, but company camps did the greater part of the work, and at a somewhat lower cost.

Northern Minnesota bore some heavy stands of timber that in general were inferior to the forests of the Chippewa or the St. Croix. The poorer land and the frequent lakes and swampy areas (where only cedar and tamarack grew) tended to thin out the stands of white pine and to make for smaller trees, while the farther north the loggers went, the more expensive became the transportation of logs. When winters were mild the difficulties were much increased, for a firm freeze was essential to the heavily laden sleds. Again, because of slight variations in level and smaller streams, driving on all rivers but the St. Louis was tricky, and even the St. Louis proved less than satisfactory.

It would be pleasing to record that with the increasing mechanization of the country the handicaps of boggy terrain, scattered timber, and feeble streams were overcome by new machines, but in the main such was not the fact. The tractor was not yet dependable, and both the steam log hauler and the steam skidder, used effectively elsewhere, functioned poorly in the swampy land and scattered stands of the north. A steam scow, the *Morris Irwin,* made a far better showing, chiefly at rollways on the St.

Louis itself. On this vessel an upright steam engine powered a drum and steel cable. With the scow anchored to a stump on the bank, the cable was fastened to a key log in a jammed rollway. With a whir the drum quickly pulled out the log, and a hundred others showered after it down the inclines to the river. This device replaced scores of men with peavies. Similarly, mechanical loaders speeded and cheapened the piling of logs on railroad cars.

In general, however, the camps depended on simple standard equipment and the brawn of their men. The camp buildings were much like those in Wisconsin or central Minnesota. Horses and mules, pulling heavy loads over iced runways, negotiated the difficult terrain more easily than cumbersome steam haulers. Two sawyers wielding an eight-foot crosscut saw with handles at either end, with double-bitted axes, wedges, a mallet, and a bottle of kerosene to clean a gummed blade, quickly brought down lordly trees and sliced them into logs that were hauled down a skidway to a log deck, loaded there on sleighs, and with explosive whips hauled to rail or river landings.[25]

The unsatisfactory character of the streams often made driving difficult. In low water, the logs dug into sand or against rocks, or slid toward the banks, building up jams. To be sure, with high water a drive could go like a yacht in a favoring breeze. Waters released from numerous dams helped to maintain such parades. But in a period of drought those stimulants could be as futile as an injection administered to an already dying patient.

Driving on the St. Louis and its tributaries had been done since the 1890's by the St. Louis River Dam & Improvement Company, which in 1899 acquired a right to control the earlier Knife Falls Boom Corporation. Northern acquired both companies from Nelson in 1896. In 1900 Cloquet Lumber bought a half-interest in them for $30,000. Thus, joint operation was complete in transportation by water.

But even before 1900 the logging railroads had begun to play a role in transportation. Northern's Mesabe Southern Railway (capital, $240,-000) ran from a point well up the St. Louis then known as Kinross, some fifty miles north by northwest from Cloquet, almost due north for 28 miles toward Mountain Iron. A dozen miles of spur tracks helped to tap an extensive region in the westward area of the timberlands then being logged. The road hauled from 20,000,000 to 45,000,000 board feet of logs annually, bringing them to the river (whence they floated down to Cloquet). In 1903 it possessed 6 locomotives and 138 railroad cars.

In 1898 Cloquet Lumber also incorporated a logging railroad, the Duluth & Northeastern (capital, $50,000), which operated in the eastern section of the forested areas. It ran from Island Lake on the Cloquet River northeastward to Hornby, a point on the Duluth, Mesabe & Iron Range

Railroad. While the Mesabe Southern operated in the westward areas of timber and the Duluth and Northeastern in the eastern, access to the central territory between the two was provided by the St. Louis and Whiteface rivers, and the Canadian National Railroad.[26]

The Duluth & Northeastern operated a main line of 27.6 miles, and eventually 19 miles of spur lines. It used 64 railroad cars. In 1904, because of the unreliability of the Cloquet River, the line was extended from beyond Island Lake directly to Cloquet at a cost of $256,177. In the same year Cloquet Lumber exchanged with Northern Lumber a half-interest in the road for a half-interest in the Mesabe Southern. Thus the two companies pooled their railroad facilities, and all transportation units were operated cooperatively, as were certain logging agencies.

An equally important step in cooperation was taken in 1903. The Cloquet and Northern companies now entirely owning Johnson-Wentworth, the St. Louis River Logging Company (renamed the St. Louis River Mercantile Company in 1905) was formed to "pool" and sort the logs of all firms. This agency scaled the logs both at river landings and just before their arrival at Cloquet, and also supervised their distribution.[27]

Cooperation in the production of logs was extended through such subsidiaries as the Cloquet Tie & Post Company, which dealt with trees and products the main companies could not handle. For example, cedar and tamarack were an embarrassment to loggers of white pine. They were the copper residue in gold ore, and most veteran woodsmen disdained them as "brush." But because the demand for tamarack ties and cedar poles was active, Cloquet Tie & Post logged the trees, which in the boggy lands of the St. Louis were numerous, and profitably manufactured the products.

Similarly, the three main companies united to handle the retail store problem. In October, 1907, the separate stores they had operated were consolidated into one; and in theory the Companies' Store could command a greater volume of business, effect economies, and show consequent profits. Actually, results did not equal hopes, and after the 1918 fire the store was never revived.

Finally, experiments were made in joint selling. Not only did Robert Starrs in Chicago serve both the Cloquet companies and Pine Tree; there was also a common sales office for the former established in Minneapolis in 1907, with W. E. Thomas in charge. In the same year Northern and Cloquet Lumber invested jointly in the Eastern Lumber Company at Tonawanda, New York, on the Niagara River ten miles west of Buffalo. It served as a distributing center for lumber sold in the eastern states. The experiment made in 1916 in the state of Iowa, which was the germ of the Weyerhaeuser Sales Company, also commanded the support of the Cloquet companies and served them well.[28]

6

Into this tidy pattern of Cloquet activity there intruded two other companies in which the Weyerhaeusers and their friends had large holdings. The first to appear was the Northwest Paper Company, organized on May 2, 1898. Actually, it was a project of Charles Weyerhaeuser and Drew Musser, adopted on the persuasion of C. I. McNair of Little Falls, an experienced manufacturer of newsprint there. With the two Pine Tree managers he visited Cloquet in 1897 to inspect a site on the St. Louis River owned by the Northern Lumber Company. It lay a short distance downriver from Cloquet's "Water Mill." In F. E. Weyerhaeuser's words, McNair "convinced Charles and Drew that a dam across the St. Louis River could be built for some $50,000, a newsprint paper mill for $100,-000, and that satisfactory dividends would soon be forthcoming."

The young managers drew into the undertaking E. M. Hoover, sales manager of Pine Tree, E. P. Denkmann, William and C. R. Musser, the Laird, Norton Co., and Frederick E. and Rudolph Weyerhaeuser. In 1899 the older Weyerhaeuser himself took some stock. A company was organized under the laws of West Virginia with a capitalization of $150,-000, raised a year later to $250,000. Of this the Weyerhaeusers and Denkmanns held 36 percent and the Mussers 22 percent.[29] The dam was built, a newsprint mill erected, and in 1903 a supplementary pulp mill was constructed at Brainerd on the Upper Mississippi. The young company prospered mildly.

Since the stockholders knew nothing about the paper business, management was left to McNair, who, according to his cousin W. K. McNair, was "a quick thinker and talker, a real manager of the old stamp." He favored paying for expansion largely out of earnings. Stockholders were asked to subscribe only $50,000 to help build the Brainerd plant, raising the paid-in capital to $300,000 by 1903. Of $799,931 earned to September 30, 1910, only $225,000 went to dividends, most of the remainder being devoted to plant expansion. The extensive growth in investment was reflected on October 1, 1910, when all rights and properties were merged in the Northwest Paper Company, a new $1,000,000 Minnesota corporation.

However, two of McNair's policies involved his company in difficulties. In order to compete effectively with the International Paper Company, Northwest Paper and several other midwestern firms created a joint marketing unit, General Paper Company, which was dissolved by court order in 1906. McNair took this reverse in stride. But his practice of buying logs rather than acquiring timberlands led to an embarrassing shortage of spruce, of which, according to Charles Weyerhaeuser, rival companies had bought "at least 75,000 acres in the back yard" of Northwest. McNair felt compelled to erect a sulfite plant for the manufacture of book paper, which did not require so much timber, and that not necessarily spruce. This new plant went into production in 1915, and, to finance it, an increase in capitalization to $1,500,000 was necessary. With further expansion in 1922 the total rose by another million. The company continued to make newsprint, selling its surplus pulp to other firms. Up to World War I Northwest Paper paid irregular but considerable dividends and in general showed a good record.

But with every year further plant expenditures were required, such as those in 1922 for facilities essential to the making of book paper. While the stockholders had steadily drawn profits, they had been called upon to invest far beyond their expectations and seem to have felt the exasperation of men who put their money into an activity they do not know (papermaking and lumbering then had little in common), and must stand by while others conduct the enterprise they are financing.[30]

The second corporation that involved the Cloquet lumber companies resembled Northwest Paper in that, while a lumber firm, its chief ownership and entire management were in non-Weyerhaeuser hands. It involved stumpage already acquired in the far north by Pine Tree, Northland, and the three Cloquet companies that seemed too remote for them to handle.

In the 1890's Frederick Weyerhaeuser and F. C. A. Denkmann had invested in the Moon & Kerr Lumber Company at Virginia, the chief town in the northeastern corner of Minnesota. They held 27½ percent of its stock, and profited modestly from the small mill it operated, until this was burned down in June, 1900. As a result of this loss and certain legal difficulties, the Moon & Kerr Company was liquidated, and Northern acquired its logging outfit and much of its stumpage.

Other lumbermen held timberlands in the far north, two of them being William O'Brien and Wirt Cook, who together owned a mill at Virginia and in 1905 incorporated the Virginia & Rainy Lake Company with a capitalization of $2,000,000. Edward Hines, owner of a lumber company bearing his name and already prominent in the industry because of his shrewd and bold marketing tactics, controlled less stumpage in the region. As noted earlier, he had bought certain north Wisconsin properties and had a gift for consolidating scattered holdings.

Hines now proposed a merger of all the chief northern Minnesota properties, into which he would put several million dollars in cash. Frederick Weyerhaeuser had confidence in him. Northland and Pine Tree wanted to dispose of their far-northern stumpage, and the three Cloquet companies were ready to put in theirs. Virginia & Rainy Lake Company soon raised its authorized capitalization to $10,700,000. At the last minute Pine Tree held off, but, as noted, came in later. The stock was held about a third by Cook & O'Brien, a third by the Weyerhaeuser companies, and a third by Hines.

It was an unwieldy but impressive monster that attacked the timber of the far north. The Cook & O'Brien mill at Virginia was included in the merger, and Hines built another, the two providing a capacity of more than 100,000,000 board feet a year. Logging railroads tapped the scattered forests, and Weyerhaeuser supplied Hines with an able logging superintendent in Frank H. Gillmor, who formerly ran the Mesabe Southern. The Weyerhaeuser companies seemd likely to draw substantial profits from the new project, but unfortunately it proved to be unwieldy and inefficient.

There were internal dissensions. "On one occasion at least," wrote F. E. Weyerhaeuser, "Mr. Hines carried a gun in his pocket, fearing physical violence from Wirt Cook, William O'Brien's partner." Cook alleged that Hines was guilty of improper business practices, which the latter denied. The directors supported him. Another difficulty was Hines's tendency to control everything himself. He resented suggestions, even from the Weyerhaeusers. He insisted on "cutting clean," and logged much worthless timber at high cost.[31]

It is true that anyone managing the Virginia & Rainy Lake Company would have faced formidable difficulties. Much of the stumpage had been priced high, the timber was scattered, and the logging costs were greater because of the remote work areas. Finally, transportation in general was more costly.

Yet Hines seems to have compounded his difficulties by his logging methods, as noted, and also for a time by his milling operations. He sawed his lumber "fat," and his overrun was only 44.8 percent as against the Cloquet Companies' 69.71 and 72 percent. Shocked at these figures, Hines furiously set himself to improve the work at his mills; and the results, visible in 1918, were encouraging.

Nevertheless in the end the entire enterprise proved disappointing. Operations were closed out in the late 1920's, and F. E. Weyerhaeuser stated some years later that the associates "just about got their investment back and perhaps a very low rate of interest beside." But as the operation ran out, he recognized it as a failure. "The outcome of our Virginia and Rainy Lake investment is something of a wallop between the eyes," he wrote Hornby early in 1928.[32]

7

Up to the fall of 1918 the Cloquet companies had proceeded vigorously with the logging and manufacture of their stumpage. American participation in World War I had affected them little (see Chapter XVIII). The managers were now expecting to complete all operations in several years. Hornby set the terminal date for Cloquet Lumber and Johnson-

Wentworth at November 1, 1920. The latter firm had practically exhausted its stumpage, and Cloquet had only an estimated 105,531,000
feet remaining. Northern, with 482,254,000, could expect eight years of
activity. The end of lumbering at Cloquet was in sight.

The summer of 1918 in northern Minnesota had been hot and dry.
In the fall, frosts had killed the grass and colored the leaves of deciduous
trees. The morning of Saturday, October 12th, was fair and mild with a
light breeze—a typical Indian-summer day. To the north and west of
Cloquet, a smoky haze edged the horizon, evidence of small fires in the
distance, some lighted by settlers clearing the land, and several doubtless
burning at Milepost 62 on the Great Northern tracks near Brookston,
some twenty miles northwest of Cloquet, where section crews had left
smoldering piles of old ties to burn themselves out. No one in Cloquet
worried about such fires. They were "endemic," and most people felt that
they cleared the brush and even helped improve the land for farming or
grazing. Some second-growth woods about Cloquet had been burned
over the preceding year. The mills continued their usual activity and the
town its business.

But with afternoon the light breeze of early morning rose to a gale.
It blew from the northwest, and soon "clouds of smoke began to roll up
over the treetops and the air became acrid with the smell and taste of
burning wood." The ground cover of weeds, brush, and dead leaves invited the spread of the flames, which were coming down the river valley,
beyond control by the small bands of rangers and their volunteer helpers.
Reports of raging fires now reached the town, and a trainload of refugees,
some blackened and blistered, some weeping, arrived from Brookston;
still, the mills continued to run steadily all afternoon.

With sundown the wind increased in fury and the fires marched on
Cloquet like a "tornado of red death." The blaze suddenly came in from
the west through a ravine where Northern had piled boards from the
Upper Mill. These the wind lifted, burning, and flung like so many
torches across the town. The fire departments of both the mills and the
town felt themselves helpless and telephoned inhabitants to leave at once.
The exodus began, some people in automobiles, some on foot, and many
in a two-coach passenger train to Duluth. Baggage was forgotten as a
gust of terror swept the town. Lawrence Fawley, local agent for Great
Northern, commandeered on his own authority every locomotive and
every passenger and freight car in the area, and packed them with people.
He himself left on the last train. At eight o'clock the sawmill whistles
sounded a shrill alarm just before electricity failed and the town was left
in darkness except for the glare of the flames.[33]

Some men remained. Rudolph Weyerhaeuser arrived at 6:45 P.M.
and joined H. C. Hornby, H. G. Stevens, Joe Wilson, and others in a

desperate effort to save mills, shops, barns, and horses. They performed prodigies. "I do not think there were ten people left in the town during the night," wrote F. E. Weyerhaeuser two weeks later, "and these ten men saved about half the industrial portion of the town." (One wonders how much more could have been done if fifty additional volunteers had remained.) Hornby, Stevens, and others, forming a bucket brigade, preserved the Cloquet Lumber steam mill on the south shore. They checked the fire at a crucial point on the island before it reached the waterpower mill. Had the conflagration spread farther, it "would have carried with it the destruction of all the balance of the industrial section of Cloquet." Northern's two plants, farther up the river, were completely consumed, along with its planing mill, shops, barns, and 70,000,000 feet of lumber.

Thanks to Hornby and his fellow workers, the Johnson-Wentworth mill and planing mill were saved, and the Northwest Paper Company plant was fortunately jumped by the fire; but Cloquet Lumber lost its offices, barns, warehouses, planing mill, and most of its lumber, while Johnson-Wentworth had two large barns and some warehouses destroyed. The Cloquet Tie & Post Company buildings, the Companies' Store, and the offices of the St. Louis River Mercantile Company were all burned to the ground.

With morning the full effect of the conflagration was starkly revealed. Except for the three mills, the Johnson-Wentworth planing mill, five or six small residences at the eastern end of the town, one school building, and a group of saloons on Dunlap Island, the place was one black, smoking bed of ashes. Darkened stone foundations, strings of twisted metal, and charred stumps of trees alone gave grim evidence of what had vanished.

Yet in one sense Cloquet was lucky: only four of its 9,000 inhabitants were killed, while in neighboring villages people had perished by the hundreds. Altogether, 453 persons in the region had died in the flames, while 85 more later succumbed to burns. Some 1,500 square miles had been swept by fire, 11,382 families registered with the Red Cross as homeless, 2,100 received treatment for injuries. More than 4,000 houses, 6,366 barns, and 41 schoolhouses were destroyed.[34]

The homeless had been generously received in little Carlton, in Duluth and Superior, where churches, schools, and auditoriums had become temporary homes. On Sunday the 13th, the National Guard arrived in Cloquet and placed it under martial law. But almost simultaneously the workers from the various mills reported for work, some with their families. With a faith as simple as the hordes of twelfth century children who poured across Europe on their fantastic crusade, they never questioned that Cloquet would rise from its ashes, and their homes and work with it.

What should be done? Officials of the three companies, regarding their work as almost finished, were shaken by this manifestation of loyalty and confidence. Two men promptly spoke out for reconstruction: the lawyer Henry Oldenburg and H. C. Hornby. "Personally I was down and out and ready to give up," confessed Rudolph Weyerhaeuser years later. "Mr. Hornby was the man that brought Cloquet back. He had the foresight and energy and enthusiasm to carry on." Oldenburg with quiet conviction also insisted that Cloquet must be revived.

Even while the matter was debated, reconstruction went forward. Hornby organized crews of men and set them to erecting temporary shelters and facilities for feeding the workers who were returning hourly. Wilson started his mill and planing mill to meet the demand for lumber, feeding his crews on canned goods and frankfurters heated by engine-room boilers until cooks came in from the logging camps.

By December the decision had been taken to go on. Money was available, both from company funds and the insurance companies, who paid promptly. A shortage of carpenters was partly met by volunteers from Duluth who worked Sundays. "The great problem confronting us at the present time is how to house our men," wrote Rudolph to F. C. Denkmann on November 15th. Temporary bunkhouses and cook shanties served. Families also lived in shacks or roofed-over basements.

After a winter of cold and influenza (which swept the nation and did not spare Cloquet), spring saw the reopening of Cloquet Lumber's steam mill (the water power mill had been operating). Difficult negotiations resulted in a program by which the mills for a time would be operated jointly. They would use Northern's stumpage until it was exhausted; then that company would buy the Cloquet Lumber mills. Oldenburg drafted the agreement.

Meanwhile, the work of rebuilding Cloquet went forward. The government relaxed war restrictions on building materials; on company pay the workers erected their own houses, bonds were issued for a new city hall and waterworks, and the Park Board purchased 5,000 elm, maple, and other shade trees. New homes for merchants and officials sprang up.[35]

Sentiment had outweighed business, as Rudolph wrote to his brother John. To be sure, the companies had funds, and there was a further prospect of remuneration from the government, then operating the railroads, for strong evidence pointed to the fires at Milepost 62 as the chief cause of the great conflagration. More important, once the officials had accepted their task, they saw a sound economic possibility for the new Cloquet. In fact, the decision of 1918, together with the attention given to processing waste products (see origins of Wood Conversion Company, Chapter XIX) and the operations of Northwest Paper, amounted to nearly full utilization of the available trees for the first time in Weyerhaeuser history.

After the fire the companies, while continuing as separate units, pooled many of their activities, particularly logging and to an extent the manufacture of lumber. Northern paid half of the $519,956 required to rehabilitate Cloquet's steam mill, and to replace the old waterpower plant a new one jointly owned was constructed, operated by Northern, at a cost of $387,000.

The stumpage available was mostly Northern's, but was supplemented late in 1919 by the purchase of tracts in Cook County. Lying far to the northeast, this timber was poor and remote, but Hornby was eager to acquire additional acreage even if the profits to be made were doubtful.

In addition to their regular task of manufacturing the poorer logs they now received, Cloquet and Northern agreed to furnish pulpwood to the Northwest Paper Company in exchange for stock, but the records do not disclose that this was ever done. They also gave close attention to by-products—lath, crating, molding, wood refuse, and so forth, and in 1926 Northern, although sustaining a loss of $52,940 on its lumber, realized a clear profit of $60,902 on its by-products, thus showing an overall net gain of $8,412![36]

The town was now less dependent on lumber mills than it had been. The Wood Conversion Company, to be dealt with later, had begun manufacturing in 1922, and other firms making such wood products as matches, toothpicks, throat swabs, and tongue depressors had come into being. The Northwest Paper Company had steadily expanded, and was acquiring facilities to produce a wider range of products. Particularly it was seeking to develop a range of quality papers. In 1920 it employed 730 men, mostly in Cloquet. Toward the end of the decade it would supply jobs for almost half the families of the town.[37]

By 1928 the lumber mills were nearing the end of operations. Northern's stumpage had "shrunk," chiefly as the result of forest fires, and while considerable scattered timber was uncut, the two firms were not inclined to handle it. For the entire decade Cloquet Lumber had earned only $126,188 from the manufacture of lumber, although it received dividends from outside investments. On January 13, 1928, Rudolph Weyerhaeuser therefore proposed that the operations of all the companies be combined and that Northwest Paper, as the most active firm, take over the properties of the others.

As the plan was carried out on December 31, 1928, the two lumber companies each accepted 46,700 shares of Northwest Paper stock ($100 par) for their properties. The paper company's capitalization, increased in 1924 (by $1,500,000) and 1926 ($1,000,000), was now raised from $5,000,000 to $15,000,000. The two lumber companies now held 66.5 percent of its stock and the Weyerhaeusers 13.7 percent, the Mussers 7.3 percent, and the Laird, Nortons; the Denkmanns, the McNairs, Hornby, and others still smaller percentages.[38]

Logging and manufacture of the small amount of pine lumber to be produced was thus taken over by the paper company. The assumption had been that most of the remaining stumpage could be used for its operations, for spruce, poplar, cedar, birch, and tamarack were everywhere intermingled with pine. Unfortunately, the timber proved to be less than estimated, of poorer quality, and very expensive to cut and transport. Moreover, the Great Depression was about to begin.

Northwest Paper was the less able to meet the situation because of administrative difficulties. C. I. McNair, who had managed it into the early 1920's, had begun to fail in health just as the expansion of manufacturing facilities was undertaken in order to produce new types of pulp and paper. He resigned in 1924, and Rudolph Weyerhaeuser, as president, reluctantly took over the task of manager as well. He was, of course, directing Northern, was active in the guidance of other Weyerhaeuser companies, and soon chose a successor. He felt that Irving McNair, the able son of the former manager, lacked the experience for the post, and turned to William H. Kenety, who, while untrained in the pulp and paper business, was a seasoned forester whose tact and general ability promised that he might become an able leader. In 1928 Hornby became president, succeeding Rudolph.

Unfortunately, in the course of expansion the company had also encountered technological problems that had proved difficult of solution and continued to require expensive alterations in and additions to the plant. Furthermore, various properties and activities that had come with the consolidation continued to cause confusion and expense. The depression brought losses and financial crises. Hornby, though an able lumberman, was not qualified to deal creatively with the situation, and Kenety, although also able, lacked the full knowledge and authority to cope with it as it worsened. The directors, hopeful of improvement, as yet took no action.

Of course, the period was a difficult one for all business, and Northwest Paper had exceptional problems. Still, in comparison with other firms in its field, its showing was incredibly bad. In 1934, while most of its competitors counted modest profits, it sustained a loss of $580,069 in paper operations, on net sales of $3,783,706. Its directors must have been aware that the Weyerhaeuser Timber Company's pulp plants on the Pacific (although in different conditions) were earning $16.17 per ton and demonstrating that a successful enterprise in the pulp and paper field could be conducted under Weyerhaeuser auspices.[39]

Meanwhile in May, 1932, at the insistence of the creditor banks holding $1,500,000 of frozen loans, the stockholders had reduced the par value of the 150,000 shares of common stock from $100 to $25 ($15,-000,000 down to $3,750,000) and had issued 209,033 shares of 6 percent, $25 par value cumulative preferred stock ($5,225,825) to other noteholders (practically all stockholders) in order to make a statement more acceptable to the banks. But the situation had continued to deteriorate. The common stockholders shortly lost their voting rights because these went, by the terms of the new shares, to the holders of preferred stock when the company failed to pay dividends on common stock.

In 1934 the directors began to consult experts in the paper industry concerning their problems. They concluded that they had no choice but to change management and to seek an experienced paper-company executive to put the firm back on its feet. A committee composed of F. K. Weyerhaeuser, John M. Musser, and George R. Little (of Laird, Norton Co.) was assigned the task of finding such a man. They reported their conclusions at the annual meeting in May, 1936, and suggested Stuart B. Copeland, vice president of Eastern Manufacturing Company of Bangor, Maine, as their first choice for a new executive.[40]

Negotiations were opened with Copeland, and on July 1, 1936, he was named president and general manager. A graduate of the Massachusetts Institute of Technology, and an engineer and executive in the industry for more than twenty years, he had the full experience which his new and difficult task required. He was well known in the pulp and paper field, having been vice president of the American Paper and Pulp Association, president of the new U.S. Pulp Producers Association (founded in 1933), and a director of the Writing Paper Manufacturers Association.

The selection of Copeland, an outside professional manager, was the beginning of vigorously independent action by Northwest Paper. For some months he made few changes. He recommended increasing the electric power capacity of the Brainerd plant to permit year-round operations (depending chiefly on waterpower, it had been closed for some months every year), installed an adequate cost system, carefully watched costs in all operations, liquidated unproductive properties, and began to eliminate a number of the products manufactured, for the range and number of these had been great, with various unprofitable items. Copeland worked toward a concentration of quality products. He also gave immediate study to the labor situation. By a series of conferences he promoted an atmosphere of understanding, adopted suggestions by workers, in December, 1936, made a small wage increase, and on May 6, 1937, signed a contract with the three A.F. of L. unions that further increased wages and established harmonious relations between the workers and the management. This was a highly important act, for labor during the past three years had been restive and resentful. Soon afterward Copeland announced a reassignment of executives to define lines of authority more clearly.[41]

The effects of pruning activities, the labor settlement, and the executive realignment were reflected in a modest profit of $95,141 for 1937, the first since 1928. However, the 1938 recession, with a drop in the price of paper, brought two more deficit years. These were the last the company has known to date. It wrote a small profit in 1940, realized $1,376,283 in 1941, and gradually built the totals to higher figures.

The real turning point in the company's financial rehabilitation came on December 31, 1940. At that time Copeland was able to effect by voluntary agreement of loan creditors and stockholders a realignment of the company's debt and capital structures; this new arrangement fairly recognized relative equities and at the same time gave the company a chance to establish itself on a sound financial basis through orderly debt retirement if reasonable earnings could be developed.

Careful financial management meanwhile steadily reduced a large interest-bearing debt, and in 1945 the company paid its first dividends in twenty-four years—$224,796. By 1948 dividends had been more than doubled, the debt (scheduled in the December 31, 1940, agreements for retirement over the period through 1960) was completely retired in 1949, and the company's surplus, which temporarily became a deficit in 1939, mounted steadily. Retained earnings stood at $25,538,373 at the end of 1959. Copeland and his associates had transformed an insolvent organization, which threatened the stockholders with immense losses, into a sound, prosperous, and expanding company with 2,000 workers and an assured position in the industry. It was a miracle, but its magic sprang directly from the long experience, full knowledge, and sound judgment of the man who directed operations and who, upon his retirement in 1957, turned them over to Harry T. Kendall, Jr.,[42] long the right hand of Stuart Copeland and son of one of the architects of the Weyerhaeuser Sales Company.

Weyerhaeuser executives have debated as to whether Northwest Paper was a cause of loss to the lumber companies who owned it, or they to it. The firm's capitalization was indeed scaled down, with more than a $6,000,000 shrinkage in the value of Cloquet and Northern holdings. On the other hand, Paper Company employees felt that the 1929 agreement had led directly to many of their depression difficulties. One answer is that during the 1930's all firms would have suffered in any case.

Even noting the losses on Northwest Paper prior to 1940, stockholders in the Cloquet companies could reflect that the town had been a pearl of great price. The Cloquet Lumber and Northern companies were immensely profitable, a fact largely attributable to the spectacular rise in timber values as white pine became scarcer and scarcer. During the four decades between 1895 and 1936, Cloquet Lumber distributed a magnificent $12,694,000 to its stockholders. Northern paid its first dividend in 1898, and with liquidation items its total payments up to 1936 reached a fabulous $25,240,123. The earnings of the two firms of course embraced those of Johnson-Wentworth, which channeled $4,046,660 to them.[43]

Funds from the three lumbering operations moved through the hands of stockholders into western investments early in the century and helped to sustain shaky enterprises in Idaho as well as Northwest Paper and Wood Conversion later.

Meanwhile, the Cloquet and Northern companies lived out paper lives. Northern was dissolved in 1945, but Cloquet Lumber remained in existence because of potential value of low-grade mineral lands that it held. And Northwest Paper, Wood Conversion, and the town of Cloquet still continue to live and thrive—testimonials to the confidence of Weyerhaeuser executives in wood products and to the soundness of their decisions over the years.

NOTES

1. LN Papers, Ltrbks. for May–July, 1897; Pine Tree Lbr. Co., min. bks., 1903–1904.

2. *Ibid.*, annl. reps.; FW Papers, FW to Peter Musser, Aug. 20, 1907.

3. R. D. Musser Papers, Immigration Land Company, annl. reps.

4. LN Papers, inc. corresp., R. D. Musser to Laird-Norton, Oct. 7, 1898, and others; Northland Pine Co. Papers, 1904; FEW Papers, Arts. of Incorpn., Northland Pine Co., and Min. Bk., Directors' Meeting, Sept. 12, 1899.

5. FEW Record, 496; LN Papers, Ltrbk.; Northland Pine Co., Min. Bk., April 2, Oct. 12, 1900; FEW's statement about Idaho is an extreme one, with which some authorities would disagree.

6. Northland Pine Min. Bks., 1902–1903.

7. Miss. R. Lbr. Co. and Northland Pine Co., annl. reps., 1897–1904; *Miss. Val. Lbrmn.*, March 23, 1894, p. 248; FEW Record, 475, 499. Exact descriptions of the No. Miss. Railway Co. and the Cross Lake Logging Co. do not appear in source materials, but they were clearly logging and transportation units, respectively.

8. FEW Record, 499–500; R. D. Musser Papers, Contracts, Backus-Brooks and Northland, March 1, 1905; LN Papers, Ltbk; Northland Pine Co. Papers, 1905; Potlatch Lbr. Co., Corresp., 1905.

9. Northland Pine Co. Papers, ledger entries; R. D. Musser Papers, Annl. Rept.

10. Miss. R. Lbr. Co. Papers, annl. reps.; FEW Record, 476–477.

11. *Ibid.*, 476–477, and 488–494, St. Paul Boom Co. Papers, annl. reps.; Miss. Lbr. Co. Papers, Min. Bk., Special Directors' Meeting, Nov. 10, 1919; Northwest Paper Co. Min. Bk., Stockholders' Meeting, Nov. 22, 1910.

12. R. D. Musser Papers, Production Statistics, White Pine Bureau; Hotchkiss, *Lumber and Forest Industry,* 572; Larson, *White Pine Industry,* 246, 256.

13. Pine Tree Lbr. Co. Papers; Northland Pine Co., min. bks. and annl. reps.; 1904–1912; Miss. R. Lbr. Co., Journal B.

14. Pine Tree Lbr. Co. and Pine Tree Mfg. Co. Papers, annl. reps., 1907–1920.

15. Pine Tree Mfg. Co. Papers, min. bks., May 3, May 19, 1911, April 15, 1913, and April 14, 1914.

16. Pine Tree Mfg. Co. Papers, min. bks., annl. reps., 1910–1920; JPW Papers, CAW to F. C. Denkmann, Feb. 26, 1919, and CAW to F. S. Bell, Nov. 13, 1920; Northland Pine Co., Genl. Ledgers A. & B., Dec. 3, 1920, and memo of agreement, CAW and T. L. Shevlin, Feb. 1, 1915.

17. Pine Tree Lbr. Co., Pine Tree Co., Miss. R. Lbr. Co., and Miss. Lbr. Co., mins. and annl. reps., 1909–1922.

18. LN Papers, Ltrbk., June 1897, 214–217; FEW Record, Memo, RMW to FEW, 441.

19. Cloquet Lmbr. Co., Min. Bks., Nov. 9, 1897, Jan. 12, 1898. Up to Shaw's death, W&D apparently held 9 percent of Cloquet stock; after it they purchased stock from the heirs, and by 1906 held between them 21 percent.

20. A. N. Frederickson, Reminiscences; Spoor, Scrapbooks; Cloquet Lumber Co., Northern Lmbr. Co., annl. reps.; JPW Papers, RMW to JPW, July 9, 14, 1897; LN Papers, Ltrbk., LN to RMW, July 9, 17, 1897; FEW Record, 443–444.

21. Frederickson, Bartlett, Schlenk, in their reminiscences.

22. Cloquet Lbr. Co., Northern Lbr. Co., annl. reps.; FEW Record, 442–443; Bartlett, Reminiscences; interviews with Spoor, Schlenk, and others. The St. Croix scale somewhat favored the seller, the Scribner scale the buyer of logs.

23. Cloquet and Northern Lbr. Cos., annl. reps.; FEW Papers, FEW to RMW, Aug. 19, 1905; ibid., Schlenk to FEW, Sept. 9, 1916.

24. FEW Papers, FW to William Irvine, Oct. 15, 1902; Cloquet Cos., annl. reps., 1903–1908; Johnson-Wentworth annl. reps., 1908, memo of Joe F. Wilson to FW, May 30, 1908.

25. Cloquet Cos., annl. reps., 1896–1918; Rector, *Log Transportation in the Lake States Lumber Industry*, 238–244; FEW Record, 305; *Minneapolis Journal*, Nov. 27, 1919, April 27, 1913; *Amer. Lbrmn.*, Aug. 3,

1907, pp. 59–60, 66; interviews with former logging superintendents and workers.

26. Duluth & Nestn. annl. reps., 1898–1904; *Minneapolis Journal*, Nov. 11, 1899; Knife Falls Boom Corporation Min. Bk., 1871–1880; St. Louis River Dam & Improvt. Co., Min. Bk., 1889 ff.; Northern and Cloquet Lbr. Cos., annl. reps.

27. Cloquet Lbr. Co., annl. reps., 1898–1918; *Amer. Lbrmn.*, Sept. 19, 1908; interviews with Schlenk, McGough, Spoor. The *Lumberman* article gives a vivid description of the sorting works. The firms disputed over the years concerning the quotas of logs handled. These for Northern, Cloquet, and Johnson-Wentworth were supposedly to be put in on a 40–40–20 basis, but these percentages were not kept, and Johnson-Wentworth often purchased logs from the pool at less than their actual cost (e.g., logs that cost $14 for stumpage and $6 for logging were charged at $14). Why this was permitted is not clear; of course, the other companies were co-owners of Johnson-Wentworth, and eventually got their return in dividends.

28. Garfield Blackwood, "History of Lumbering at Floodwood, Minnesota," and *Minneapolis Journal*, Nov. 26, 1903; Cloquet Tie & Post Co., Min. Bk., Charter; The Companies' Store, Inc., min. bk.; Northern Lbr. Co., min. bk. May 10, 1907 (Tonawanda); FEW Papers, Pressbk. 10, FEW to Wm. Deary and T. J. Humbird, June 4, 1907 (Minneapolis Sales Office).

29. FEW Record, 448; Northwest Paper Co., Min. Bk. FEW in his Record sets the original capitalization at $250,000, but the Minute Book puts it at $150,000 and states emphatically that it was raised to $250,000 in 1899. At this meeting FW pledged 200 shares, RMW, CAW, and FEW each took an additional 140, E. P. Denkmann 50, Laird, Norton 125. The original capitalization had been fixed at a permissive $500,000.

30. Northwest Paper Co., Min. Bks.; W. K. McNair, Reminiscences; FEW Papers, CAW to E. M. Hoover, Nov. 1, 1912; Northwest Paper Co., annl. reps., 1911–1922. The sulfite plant was built in 1915. After 1907, no dividend was paid until 1911 ($46,-350), but this was one of five, amounting through 1918 to $258,-734.

31. FEW Record, 452–454; Gillmor Papers, Frank H. Gillmor to Lucile Kane, Dec. 30, 1947; FEW Papers, Cook to FEW, Feb. 7, 1911; Va. & Rainy Lake annl. reps., 1906–1918. Cook's interest was bought out at the time the directors supported Hines.

32. FEW Record, 454; Cloquet Cos. and Va. & Rainy Lake Co., annl. reps., 1916, 1918; FEW Papers, corresp., 1917–1928; JPW Papers, CAW to JPW, March 14, 1919.

33. Cloquet Cos., annl. reps., 1917–1919; Pine Knot, Oct. 18, 1918, and Oct. 10, 1919; St. Paul Pioneer Press, Oct. 5, 1926; Duluth Herald, Oct. 12, 1938; and Holbrook, Burning an Empire.

34. Cloquet Cos., annl. reps., 1918–1920; FEW Papers, FEW to Frank E. Lord, Oct. 31, 1918; JPW Papers, RMW to JPW, Oct. 21, 1918; Pine Knot, Oct. 10, 1919; Duluth News-Tribune, Oct. 12, 1926, Oct. 6, 1935.

35. FEW Record, 451–452; Address of RMW at banquet in his honor, April 6, 1943, Eldon W. Spoor Scrapbks.; Pine Knot, Oct. 10, 1919; JPW Papers, A. W. Laird to JPW, Oct. 19, 1918, and RMW to F. C. Denkmann, Nov. 5, 1918; Cloquet Lbr. Co.,

Mins., Hornby to Stockholders, Feb. 22, 1919; FEW Papers, RMW to F. S. Bell, Feb. 11, 1919.

36. Cloquet Cos., annl. reps., 1919 ff., and particularly 1926–1927.

37. JPW Papers, RMW to JPW, Oct. 21, 1918; Northwest Paper Co., Time & Payroll Book, annl. reps. Employees by 1926 probably numbered 1,000; in 1938 the company employed 1,334 persons, 1,151 in or about Cloquet.

38. Cloquet Cos., annl. reps., 1928–1929. Assets of the lumber companies included timber, valued at $1,884,652, mills, logging railroads, and stocks in various companies.

39. Northwest Paper Co., annl. reps., 1924–1934; Moody's Manual, 1934; FEW Papers, JPW, Jr., to the Exec. Com., WTC, June 8, 1934.

40. FEW Papers, corresp., 1932–1936; Northwest Paper Co., annl. reps., 1932–1936.

41. Northwest Paper Co., annl. reps., 1936–1939; FEW Papers, John P. Burke to S. B. Copeland, Jan. 16, 1939; Copeland to Burke, Jan. 20, 1939; Eldon Spoor Papers, copy of address by Copeland to Cloquet Commercial Club, Jan. 4, 1939.

42. Northern and Cloquet Lbr. Cos., annl. reps., 1930–1946; Northwest Paper Co., annl. reps., 1936–1955; interview with W. K. McNair, May 1956; Schlenk, Reminiscences.

43. All Cloquet Cos., annl. reps., 1895–1936. The sum of $4,046,660 for Johnson-Wentworth covers its entire life, and was the return on $1,267,-811 invested in it by Cloquet Lbr. and Northern in 1902.

XII

Opening a New Empire

O N FREDERICK WEYERHAEUSER'S removal to St. Paul in 1891, he
found that the enterprising James J. Hill, then building his Great
Northern to Puget Sound and soon to take a hand in the reorganization of the Northern Pacific, was one of the oldest citizens. Hill had
arrived in St. Paul in the summer of 1856 when the little town had fewer
than five thousand people. The two men soon became close neighbors, for
in 1893 Weyerhaeuser bought the house at 266 Summit Avenue, where he
lived the rest of his days, and Hill owned the house next door. The rugged
business captains admired each other, became fast friends, and spent
many evenings in talk.

To Weyerhaeuser the intimacy carried one slight penalty. He had the
habit of going to bed early and rising about dawn; Hill kept midnight
hours and slept late. As Hill sat and chatted, Weyerhaeuser in his easy
chair would grow drowsier and drowsier. His family watched with amusement as he nodded, dropped off to sleep, and awoke with a start. Absorbed in his monologue, Hill paid no attention.

But these evenings at the Summit Avenue fireside above the Mississippi left their mark on lumber history. For Weyerhaeuser heard all about
Hill's railroad plans, discussed the immense timber holdings of the Northern Pacific and other lines, and learned of certain financial exigencies that
might require the sales of great blocks of forest.[1]

2

By 1890 most of the virgin forests of the Great Lakes area were cut
over, the census was prematurely announcing the end of the frontier, and
protests against timber-cutting on the public domain were gaining volume.

Lake States lumbermen, including Weyerhaeuser and his friends, looked about for new sources. They saw that two regions, the South and the Far West, offered large opportunities.

The South had attracted lumbermen as soon as the repeal of the Southern Homestead Act in 1876 opened its forests to unrestricted cutting. Speculators, in general, moved in first, picking up pine tracts for as little as $1.25 to $3.00 an acre and hardwood forests at $5 to $10. On their heels came hungry millowners from the East and Midwest, eager to obtain large holdings for immediate use or as reserves. Before long, two Michigan lumbermen, Nathan Bradley and C. F. Hackley, held between them more than 200,000 acres; Daniel F. Sullivan, from England, became known as the lumber king of Florida; and the Pennsylvanian H. J. Lutcher was reported at one time to own 1,500,000 acres in Texas and western Louisiana. Although by 1890 public-spirited southerners felt that far too much of their timber had passed into northern hands, opportunities for further acquisitions still existed and increased with the hard times after 1893.

All of the cotton belt except certain coastal prairies and marshy lands had originally been forested as far west as Texas, and much of it was still wooded. The longleaf yellow pine covered immense stretches—so immense that during the decade after 1910 great areas of virgin forest were still being logged over at the rate of 5,000,000 to 10,000,000 acres a year.[2] On upland plateaus or hills grew oaks, hickories, tulips, black walnut, and pecans. Swampy districts yielded cypress, which was especially valuable for water-resistant uses. As the Nashville, Chattanooga & St. Louis Railroad began advertising itself as the Great Lumber Route, and as coastal vessels carried large cargoes of pine and hardwood out of southern ports, lumbermen in the Lake States awoke to a brisk new competition.

Exploration of the southern possibilities was needed, and the Mussers and other friends were quite willing to undertake it. But for several reasons Weyerhaeuser hung back. He feared the heat and malaria of the South would make it unsafe to transplant northern superintendents and skilled labor, he preferred white pine to yellow, and he kept a lingering memory of Civil War antagonisms. The idea that some members of his family would have to live in the South was repugnant to him. He made his first trip there in December, 1894, in a distrustful mood.

E. W. Durant of Stillwater arranged the journey on two special cars of the Illinois Central, the party including various lumbermen and friends. Memphis businessmen gave a dinner in their honor that thawed most of Weyerhaeuser's Civil War feeling, and at Vicksburg a call by General William Porcher Miles, an old Confederate warhorse now the soul of genial courtesy, completed his conversion. When, taken to a large mill in the Yazoo delta, Weyerhaeuser saw healthy men processing the finest white oak timber, he called Durant aside. "I think I would better take back my ideas of this southern lumber and the people," he said.

Near New Orleans the party paid visits to some cypress forests and mills that equally impressed him. Finally a group of cypress holders made a proposal: They would sell their pooled properties of about two and a half billion feet of standing timber at $1 a thousand feet, with mills and equipment thrown in. Weyerhaeuser, as usual, was full of hearty friendliness and told some favorite anecdotes. But $2,500,000 was a large sum in those hard times, and he did not buy.[3]

Two years later another large group, including Weyerhaeuser, O. H. Ingram, W. H. Laird, and a dozen others, were taken south by a New York promoter, Hugh Bellas. Though the election of McKinley had just improved the economic atmosphere, the South was still gripped by depression. Timber and sawmills were for sale at bargain prices. In fact, many millions of acres of choice yellow pine could be had at $5 to $8 an acre.

This time Weyerhaeuser was genuinely tempted. He saw that the timber was choice, the logging costs were reasonable, and the market was showing signs of revival. Many tracts were sufficiently near tidewater to supply an export trade. Returning from Texas, the party held a final meeting with southern owners in New Orleans. Weyerhaeuser, glancing around the circle, boldly announced that he would invest a million dollars if others would join him—but not a man spoke up. "Unfortunately," comments his son, "there seemed to be nobody available among father's associates to manage so great a property."

3

Weyerhaeuser later participated in several southern enterprises, though only one possessed long-lasting magnitude. In 1882 he had become a minor stockholder in the Lindsay Land & Lumber Company owning pinelands in Arkansas. The initiators were a long-time associate, Charles R. Ainsworth of Dimock, Gould & Company, and James E. Lindsay[4] of Lindsay & Phelps, a lumber firm in Davenport. Weyerhaeuser & Denkmann joined those families and others in an original investment of $159,-600, later expanded to permit holdings of almost 70,000 acres.

Though stockholders of Northland Pine Company had accepted William Deary's adverse reactions to investments in southern timber in 1900, the next year Weyerhaeuser found that George F. Lindsay and Morris N. Richardson, sons of the Lindsay Company's founders, had become completely enamored of an untouched tract of 54,000 acres of longleaf yellow pine. This "Brown tract" was intermingled with 56,000 acres owned by other interests and adjacent to a holding of Isaac M. Stephenson, later senator from Wisconsin. Weyerhaeuser, who had great faith in the two young men, looked into the matter. He saw a gently rolling landscape studded with magnificent trees, just thick enough, with no underbrush and no hardwood—"the most beautiful piney woods picture that I ever saw," according to one observer.

The upshot was that Weyerhaeuser & Denkmann and the Laird, Norton Co. joined the Lindsay, Richardson, and Ainsworth families in organizing, on May 4, 1901, the Southern Lumber Company of Louisiana. Capitalized at $1,000,000, the new firm took over the timberlands in central Louisiana. Subsequent small purchases raised the total holdings in that state to 130,000 acres (an estimated 1,300 million board feet), plus another 40,000 acres in southern Arkansas purchased largely from Lindsay Land & Lumber.

Partly because the holdings lay in two states, in 1902 a new corporation was formed in Arkansas, and the Southern of Louisiana was renamed Southland Lumber Company. Southland remained a landholding firm of commonplace history, never manufacturing lumber but selling logs and timber to local mills and completing the disposal of its lands—very profitably—in 1927. On an original investment of nearly $1,500,000 the stockholders received back $10,237,400 after all charges.[5]

But the new $750,000 Arkansas corporation, Southern Lumber Company, began a long and interesting history with Frederick Weyerhaeuser's designation of his son Frederick E. as head. "I had the thrill of a lifetime," later wrote Fred, when his father, "returning from Rock Island, told me I had been made president of the Southern Lumber Company and was expected to oversee the building of a mill in the South." Fred found a good site, then brought an old mill from Wisconsin and reconstructed it at Warren, Arkansas, with new machinery. The company took first a half-interest in and later full ownership of the Warren & Ouachita Railroad, a logging line that connected with the Rock Island system. It bought Southland's Arkansas lands and made useful exchanges of timber with a neighboring company. Altogether, with Fred as its chief and members of the Denkmann and Lindsay families as dynamic aides, the Southern Lumber Company became a flourishing organization.[6]

The elder Weyerhaeuser took a keen interest in it and greatly relished several visits to Warren. Writes Fred:

One Saturday morning as he was there the mill was running with a very short crew. The colored men never liked to work on Saturday, if they ever did. The mill was cutting on an order for small timbers which were literally being dumped out of the back end of the saw floor, and left in hopeless confusion, as there were no men to pile them. Father did not like the way it was being done; went over to the green chain, on which the ordinary lumber was moving out of the mill, took three big Negroes with him, and in a short time had the timbers properly piled. On going up to the office he told me and Harvey Clapp, who without his knowledge had seen what took place, that he never saw better workmen—better than the Swedes in Minnesota. When pressed to tell what he had done for the Negroes, he finally admitted that he gave each of them a dollar.

After a slow start through 1904, managers of Southern of Arkansas easily surmounted a series of difficulties and began to make an impressive record. In 1904 the company issued $300,000 in mortgage bonds, the only Weyerhaeuser firm ever to do so, to finance expansion, and retired them in four years. Small dividend payments began in 1907, and the makeshift mill was rebuilt a year later. Within two years after General Manager N. H. Clapp's unexpected death in 1910, another man had been trained to fill the position. A second mill was erected in 1915, which initiated a ten-year period of great productivity. By World War II returns to stockholders on an original investment of about $1,000,000, and exclusive of plowed-back earnings, had reached approximately $10,000,000, which was divided among the Lindsays, Denkmanns, Ainsworths, Richardsons, Weyerhaeusers, and others.

Members of the group also became interested early in the century in various other southern enterprises, though Weyerhaeuser had a part in only one of them. As he had taken the train for the North after his inspection of the "Brown tract," he remarked to Morris Richardson: "Well, Morris, try to look up another fine tract like that." He found none, but others did—in the holdings of the Calcasieu Pine Company, a concern belonging to Isaac M. Stephenson. Laird, Norton Co., the Mussers, and others joined Weyerhaeuser in a reorganized corporation (total investment $2,700,000) managing this handsome Louisiana property. It held its longleaf timber for a decade, and then, under the guidance of F. S. Bell, son-in-law of W. H. Laird, gradually sold all its lands, distributing a total of about $8,900,000 to stockholders by the time the corporation was dissolved in 1927.[7]

Other southern explorations were made with little result. In spite of the impressively high returns on all the yellow-pine ventures, Weyerhaeuser abandoned the southern area to the Denkmanns, Joyces, Lindsays, and Richardsons. Long decades were to pass before the Weyerhaeusers and other friends put down any but peripheral roots in the South, for the Pacific Northwest was now to command their major interest.

4

As early as 1885 Weyerhaeuser had paid passing attention to the rich timber stands on the Pacific slope. In that year the Northern Pacific Railroad offered him timberlands and a millsite at Tacoma, but the overture was turned down. A year later he, Peter Musser, and others took an option, never exercised, on about 80,000 acres of Douglas fir near Tacoma. On several early trips to California he evinced a mild interest in the redwoods. Consumption of redwood lumber had grown so slowly over the years, however, that he made no purchases. When in 1891 he took a group of friends on a pleasure jaunt to Alaska, Henry C. Davis of the Northern Pacific helped make arrangements; on their return they visited the Puget Sound area, and we may safely surmise that Davis mentioned the railroad's timber holdings. He may even have dwelt on them.[8]

Nevertheless, Weyerhaeuser and his friends for some years gave the Far West a very gingerly look. They considered a tremendous land grant of 850,000 acres that the government had made in 1864 to the Oregon Central Military Road Company. To be sure, it was not a very attractive prospect; a meandering ribbon of odd-numbered sections along a wagon road stretching from Eugene over the Cascade Range and across Oregon by marsh, desert, and forest to the eastern boundary. After taking the option in 1890 and debating the purchase in 1893, they decided adversely.[9] Following his Alaska trip Weyerhaeuser talked with the editor of the *Northwestern Lumberman* so conservatively that the journal predicted: "It will be a long time before he will plunge very deeply into lands or manufacturing at Puget Sound." Until the end of the decade he did no more than take a part share in some minor companies.

The Northwest, however, was developing fast. Several midwestern lumbermen invested there in the eighties and nineties. The completion of James J. Hill's Great Northern to Seattle and Everett and his setting of a 40-cent rate on lumber to St. Paul in 1893, the rush to the Klondike goldfields in 1897, the ensuing Seattle boom, the spurt of the salmon industry under business consolidation, the westward migration of farmers and fruit growers, and the return of national prosperity while Spain sued for peace and imperialism became an issue, changed the scene entirely.

When a fine body of timber became available in the Skagit and Sauk River district of northern Washington, and Lindsay & Phelps invited Weyerhaeuser & Denkmann to join in buying it, they responded favorably. The Sound Timber Company was organized late in 1899 to manage the tract, and they took half of the stock issue of $600,000. Meanwhile, a year earlier the Weyerhaeuser group had entered the Coast Lumber Company (1898–1903) which specialized in shipping shingles from Puget Sound to St. Paul during the spring season when the Great Northern had a plethora of empty cars. Hill got the needed traffic; the group got low freight rates.[10]

Then in 1900 came a transaction that startled the West and heralded a new era in the lumber history of North America. The Weyerhaeuser office announced the purchase from the Northern Pacific of 900,000 acres of timberland at $6 an acre, one of the largest single land transfers in American annals. The Northern Pacific was now to a great extent under

Hill's influence. He badly needed ready money for the redemption of a bond issue. Of the purchase price of $5,400,000, $3,000,000 was to be paid down at once and the rest in eight semiannual installments at 5 percent interest. On January 3, 1900, the papers were signed by Weyerhaeuser and the railroad's land agent, William H. Phipps. It need not be said that the financial resources of the Weyerhaeuser group were strained by such an effort. According to one man's memory, "it took practically all the lumbermen on the upper Mississippi River to raise the money." Many friends refused the risk. As a result of weeks of quiet labor, a considerable group of the familiar associates joined hands. Weyerhaeuser & Denkmann agreed to subscribe for $1,800,000; the Laird, Norton group $1,200,000; R. L. McCormick, S. T. McKnight, and O. H. Ingram $350,000 each; and nine others smaller amounts.[11]

A little later this purchase was to seem a colossal bargain. The Bureau of Corporations within a dozen years estimated that in terms of the probable cut the price was only ten cents a thousand feet.[12]

Nevertheless, at the time many thought the investment exceedingly speculative. When the directors held their first meeting in the rambling, vine-covered, comfortable old Tacoma Hotel overlooking Commencement Bay, some of the eleven men had apprehensive thoughts. They knew that lumbering in the Puget Sound regions was still in a primitive stage. Oxen dragged the heavy logs on greased skid-roads for short distances from stump to railroad or stream. Logging over long distances, by railroads pushed out into the woods, or by donkey engines, was yet in its infancy. White fir and hemlock, abundant in the Sound area, were then commercially worthless, and even Douglas fir was still used in the East as a structural timber alone. The Panama Canal was only a dream, and ocean freights via Cape Horn or Suez seemed cruelly high. The fire hazard in the forests was great—every autumn brought its fires; and when Weyerhaeuser quoted a sage lumberman as saying, "If half the timber burns, the other half will be twice as valuable," he seemed whistling to keep up his courage. Over the years, coastal lumber mills had seldom paid well. Three millions now had to be paid on the nail, in hard cash—and when would some of it begin to come back?

In short, so great a purchase required courage. A decade later George Long, the Weyerhaeuser manager in the area, recalled that in this very year the London & San Francisco Bank, one of the richest corporations on the coast, sold ten thousand acres of choice timber near Centralia —much finer than the average sold by the Northern Pacific—for $9 an acre "and were exceedingly glad to have the opportunity." About the same time the Tower Estate lands, 40,000 acres in Washington, were offered at $8 an acre without takers.[13]

Nobody, moreover, knew except in the most general way what timber the tract held. The railroad had cruised about three-quarters of it from three to five years earlier, but the remaining quarter had never been examined. The Weyerhaeuser group had no available cruisers. Indeed, any full inspection would have required several years.

Company officers in the first six months made some sampling surveys that appeared depressing, for they indicated that on a good deal of the unexamined land the stands were only a quarter or third of the stand on examined tracts. A 640-acre block supposed to contain 3,200,000 feet turned out to have only 50,000, while of 220 other sections inspected 74 had less than 6,000 feet an acre.[14] "I have tried not to be at all prejudiced in this matter," reported the manager in June, "but cannot get away from the conviction that on the so-called unexamined lands we have been imposed upon, and that there has been given to us a large quantity of isolated, scattering timberless tracts of land which it will never pay us to log."[15] He learned that the Northern Pacific had just offered 18,000 acres through a real-estate firm at $1.90 an acre. Indeed, all its lands had been on the market at $6 or less. The railroad, he thought, ought to make some adjustment.

Nevertheless, Weyerhaeuser and his friends were hopeful that the future would justify the purchase. As the last important stands of Eastern pine melted away, the values of Douglas fir must rise. A movement westward was always congenial to Americans. Thinking of the vast extent of the forest, Weyerhaeuser remarked: "This is not for us, nor for our children, but for our grandchildren." The tract's manager on the whole took an encouraging view. The timber, he wrote, will cast an impressive shadow when it gets out into the sunlight; "there is a great lot of it in every conceivable direction."[16]

When several of the directors became seriously concerned about the density and quality of some of the timber they had purchased, they discussed the possibility of abandoning the ownership by discontinuing the payment of taxes. With a shrewd twinkle, Frederick Weyerhaeuser suggested a motion deeding such abandoned lands to him—which effectively ended the discussion.

It quickly became plain that the lumber industry shared this optimism. The prevailing prosperity and the Weyerhaeuser purchase loosed a flood of speculative activity in Northwestern timber investment. Since everyone trusted Weyerhaeuser's judgment, a host of lesser capitalists followed in his wake. As they scrambled for Washington and Oregon stumpage, prices rose, and land that could hardly have been given away a few years earlier was presently changing hands at $10 an acre or more. Public statements by Theodore Roosevelt and Gifford Pinchot warning the country of an impending timber famine soon accelerated the movement. The trust movement was at its height, great new corporations and mergers were being arranged, Wall Street was exuberant, and factories and farmers alike felt a renewed prosperity.[17]

The land boom and the purchase of large tracts by other capitalists brought about a marked change in the pattern of timber ownership in the Pacific Northwest. When the government in 1864 had made its huge land grant to the Northern Pacific, 25,600 acres a mile through the territories and 12,800 acres a mile through the states, most people presumed that the railroad would sell to small holders.[18] The difficulty was that such sales would have been protracted over many decades, and in 1900 the railroad needed large sums of money immediately. Nevertheless, many small purchasers did acquire timberland, especially close to tidewater.

Now the boom divided control of the forests of Washington, Oregon, and Idaho very sharply between two groups: on one side a few, at most twoscore, of really large owners; on the other side, thousands of small ones. Many of the latter naturally feared that the "big fellows" might control lumber output, stumpage prices, and marketing in an unjust way. The small owners themselves, however, showed certain weaknesses. Owning from 500 to 2,500 acres, often scattered and inconveniently placed, they lacked the capital and experience to harvest timber efficiently. Later, when conservation became an issue, they did not have the means or the inclination to adopt sound forestry policies.

This was an unhappy situation, produced primarily by public policy, and characteristic of the headlong growth of the American nation. The tremendous land grants to the transcontinental railways made inevitable the transfer of princely domains to a few large possessors. Naturally the railroad heads were anxious to sell to men and firms with capital for the large-scale conversion of timber into freight. Both the large and the small holders included some who bought for a speculative rise, looking for a juicy unearned increment.

Four broad factors must thus be considered in the early years of the Weyerhaeuser interests in the Northwest: the steady general growth of that rich region; the continued boom in timberlands, with natural checks and fluctuations, bringing prices by 1912 to a higher point than they were to reach again for decades; friction between large and small holders; and the tendency of some politicians to make capital of that friction.

5

At an early meeting of incorporators it was proposed that the company controlling the new properties should be called Weyerhaeuser Timber Company, and the name was adopted over the protests of Weyerhaeuser himself. He was chosen president and W. H. Laird vice-president. A search had already begun for a manager. Few if any could have guessed how fortunate they were when the choice fell on a tall, lanky, Lincolnesque

Hoosier named George Smith Long,* whose appointment the directors ratified on February 9, 1900.

Long was well known in the industry for his experience, keen intelligence, and gift for managing men. Born near Indianapolis, where his father operated a small mill, after leaving school he went to work for a hardwood manufacturer. After a year or two his employer sent him South to search out stands of hardwood timber and stocks of hardwood lumber for the Indianapolis mill. Then, rebelling against the southern climate, he found a place in the Eau Claire mill of Northwestern Lumber Company in 1884, rapidly rising to be yard foreman and then sales manager. An expert judge of lumber, he led a movement to standardize its grading by the pine mills of the Lake States. When the Weyerhaeuser group approached him, he had just accepted a position with a Madison, Wisconsin, firm, who made him manager with the right to buy ownership. Bidding rather high for him, the Weyerhaeusers offered $5,000 a year, plus a $100,000 block of stock which they enabled him to buy on credit.

They never made a better decision. "When I came out to the Coast to take charge of the Weyerhaeuser Timber Company," Long wrote, "their business was solely and strictly timber lands, and what I did not know about that would fill a book." He meant Douglas fir lands. "I had no conception of even what townships and ranges meant, had never been in the woods in my life, did not know how to find a section corner, had never attempted to estimate a quantity of timber, did not know anything about its value, why one tree might be worth more than another, and absolutely knew nothing about logging; and here I was confronted with a job where I was expected to tell others what to do!" However, he learned fast, and showed a wise grasp of basic policies.[19]

The first of these policies, learned from Weyerhaeuser himself, was the rapid continuing purchase of good timber lands in Washington and Oregon while they were still cheap. The second was the steady "blocking up" of the lands for efficient care and logging; inasmuch as the Northern Pacific had received alternate sections on both sides of its line and had sold spottily in some tracts, the interstices had to be filled. A third policy was management of the lands to offer as much aid, and as little offense, to small lumber interests as possible. Long gave existing mills, which had been used to buying Northern Pacific timber, an informal allocation of lands that would be sold to them at reasonable prices; and he saw that other small mills got timber at fair rates.

Long and the directors had to acquaint themselves with the special traditions of Pacific Northwest lumbering, reaching back to a primitive mill at Fort Vancouver in 1827 and Marcus Whitman's waterpower mill

* Long always signed himself "Geo. S. Long," and insisted on being referred to in print in this fashion.

at Walla Walla in 1838. The first settlers on the coast had demanded boards. The gold rush, the spurting growth of California towns and mining camps, the rise of San Francisco, and the repeated fires in that city stimulated the northern sawmills. Because the Columbia River bar was dangerous, traders preferred to come into Puget Sound for lumber, and the industry expanded more rapidly there than around Portland. The pioneer firm of Pope and Talbot, two enterprising Maine lumbermen who brought efficient machinery around Cape Horn and used it to convert shoreland trees into beams, boards, and shingles, planted their first mill at Port Gamble in 1853 and gained renown before the Civil War. They had efficient imitators. Before Appomattox, steam mills had rapidly replaced cruder types, and a brisk export trade had developed to the Hawaiian Islands, Australia, and South America.[20]

The pattern of lumbering in the Puget Sound region and elsewhere in the Washington-Oregon country west of the snowy crests of the Cascades had been fixed partly by methods brought in from the East, partly by geographic conditions, and partly by the peculiar qualities of the trees. It was the trees to which Long had to give most intent study.

Though men were slow to appreciate it, the Douglas fir wilderness of western Washington and Oregon, covering 55,000 square miles, was one of the treasure chests of the nation. Even when Pope & Talbot had grown rich, it was practically a virgin forest. Mile on mile, county on county, it stretched from level bay to high-hipped mountain, from river canyon to lava ridge, carpeting shoreland flat, valley, and peak with an almost unbroken mantle of green.

And what a noble carpeting! David Douglas, the Scottish naturalist who gave them their name, described the great firs as among the most striking and graceful objects in all nature. Many soared from 250 to 280 feet into the air, clear of branches for 150 feet above the ground. The massive dark-gray trees, as straight as columns of a temple, were often eight to ten feet in diameter. Growing thickly, they struck the beholder by their perfect symmetry. The lower branches were shrouded in gloom, but high aloft they lifted perfect pyramidal crests, bright green-yellow in the sunshine. Sometimes they alone were the forest; as elevation rose in the Cascades, they made room for red cedar and Sitka spruce on lower levels, for hemlock and white fir at higher points.[21]

Near the Pacific, and especially on the Olympic peninsula, where western winds brought in drenching rains for most of the year, the mighty firs rose out of an almost impenetrable jungle of huckleberry, blackberry, salal, grape, and other underbrush rooted in rich muddy soil. Here the lumberman had to meet difficulties hardly known in the East. Into the untracked wilderness went the swampers, hewing out paths and roads. After them came fallers ready to meet the special problems of the Douglas fir. Its deeply furrowed bark was so gum-filled and tough-fibered at the base that hard leathers would have been easier to cut.

The fallers drove springboards into notches six to ten feet above the earth. Standing with calked boots on these swaying planks, two would cut in unison, one with a righthanded and the other a lefthanded swing. First a deep gash would undercut the side toward which the tree should fall; then by ax and saw they would go through the heartwood on the opposite side. The lumberman found the perils of his high, narrow stance more than offset by its resilience, the board absorbing much of the shock from the strokes. For years it was difficult to convince newcomers, looking at the high stumps, that the trees had not been cut in winter by men standing on the crust of deep snows.[22]

The first loggers in the Puget Sound country felled the trees nearest navigable water without inquiring too narrowly into the question of government or private ownership. In the early decades, sawmills usually rejected any logs of less than sixteen inches in diameter, a rule which meant that much valuable timber was left standing.

The tremendous size of the bigger fir logs compelled the adoption of new handling methods. For short distances, some hardy pioneers managed to roll great timbers, such as ship spars, by log jacks and peavies, to the water—using bands of Indian helpers. Lumbermen covering greater distances turned to skid roads and long teams of oxen. A fairly smooth roadway was made, and at intervals of perhaps ten feet, large logs or skids were set transversely across it; a trough was cut in the middle of each skid and was well greased with fish oil or some other fat. Teams of from four to ten yoke of oxen, which often included powerful bulls for wheelers, then could drag even a very heavy log down the skidway. A log 24 to 30 feet long was a good average. However, one veteran bullwhacker is quoted as saying that in early Puget Sound days he had hauled logs intended for masts that reached a length of 120 feet.[23] To be economical, a skid road was never more than two miles long.

The management of oxen, popularly called bull teams, was a woods craft learned only by hard experience. They had to be driven gently but firmly and watched carefully to prevent them from injuring themselves. Each driver was accompanied by two men: a hook tender, who made up the load, saw that the logs were properly chained together and dealt with any impediments en route, and a hand skidder, who made the chains perfectly secure by using a heavy maul to drive clamps or dogs into the logs. The skid road terminated in some river pool or harbor cove, where the logs floated inside booms until wanted. Sometimes they were formed into rafts, rivaling any in the Lake States, to be towed to the mills. Before the Civil War Pope & Talbot had a tugboat, the *Resolute,* puffing about Puget Sound.[24]

By the time George Long reached the coast, the export trade in lumber had attained considerable proportions. It had its romantic as well as practical side. Lumber ships nosed into Puget Sound, Grays Harbor, and if they could pass the bar at the mouth, the wide lower reaches of the Columbia. The majority in the early days had been schooners, but after them came brigs, barks, even a few clipper ships, and finally countless steamers. Sawed timber was taken to Australia for the mines and cities, to Mexico for ranch houses, to Argentina for making cattleships, and to Europe for every possible use. One notable shipment of fifty-foot timbers, six inches square, wrapped in burlap, went to Cecil John Rhodes in the 1890's to build a grape arbor at his Groote Schur house near Capetown.

Long and his Weyerhaeuser associates heard many stories of how sailors had been used in the old lawless days to help greedy lumbermen swell their timber holdings. The Timber and Stone Act of 1878, as we have seen, granted every actual or intending citizen the right to buy 160 acres of forested land at $2.50 an acre. Some lumber companies or individuals owning vessels had sent their sailors ashore, where each laid claim to his quarter-section and later transferred it to his employer. One prominent timber grabber was quoted as saying that he never acquired land far from salt water because he was "afraid them sailors would get lost."[25]

Long did not need to be told that overproduction had been an intermittent ailment of the Pacific Coast Lumber industry. The panics of 1873 and 1893 had left a debris of bankrupt or anemic lumber firms in the Far Northwest. Movements to restrict output had gained headway in every depressed period and then flagged as prosperity returned.

The industry, however, was gaining in stability. As mills grew, better machinery was installed, planing was improved, and finer grades of lumber produced. Washington, where the mills were bigger though less numerous than in Oregon, forged to the front. New filaments of railroad shooting through the mountain belt and the Pacific States naturally widened the market for Coast lumber. Not until the Chicago, Milwaukee & St. Paul was finished to Seattle in 1909 and the Western Pacific was completed from Salt Lake City to San Francisco in 1911, did the railroad expansion cease. Hill, Harriman, and others worked hard to bring settlers to the West, and every new settlement needed lumber.[26]

If the Weyerhaeuser pioneers did not know that the Douglas fir forest presented an acute fire hazard, they were quickly told. Late summer and fall, the "fire months," often brought droughts that dried out the woods. The dense undergrowth, the heavy resinous content of the trees, the windrows of down timber in some spots, turned any shaft of lightning into a fierce conflagration. The earliest records of the Washington country spoke of great forest holocausts. "The country around us is all on fire," runs a journal kept by the British garrison of Fort Nisqually in August, 1835, while an entry for October, 1836, reads, "The weather is gloomy from the smoke around us."[27] When careless loggers began leaving brush heaps in the woods, and locomotives came to scatter sparks, the danger was compounded. Some settlers, moreover, anxious to clear the ground for cultivation, thought nothing of touching off large wooded tracts to give themselves wheatfields and bean patches. Others felled acres of lordly trees, heaped them in the cleared area, and consumed them in a roaring bonfire.

Lumber interests as yet had made little systematic effort to restrict fires. The Timber Company directors and Long, with such a broad domain to watch and ward, soon marked out this field for attention. They well knew that they would have to use the legislature for a fulcrum.

6

Long established offices in the Northern Pacific Building in Tacoma, where he could keep in touch with the land department of the railroad. In learning the Weyerhaeuser administrative routines he had sound instructors. The experienced F. S. Bell lingered on after the first directors' meeting to teach him to keep records under the accepted system. The burly, genial, full-whiskered R. L. McCormick was also an adviser, and later, as secretary and efficient co-worker, he was to take up his residence in Tacoma.

Long quickly found his feet. He asked elementary questions unblushingly, studied all the cruisers' reports, pumped veteran coast lumbermen, and made laborious excursions into the company holdings. The office force at first consisted only of himself, a Weyerhaeuser employee from Minnesota named Hugh Stewart, who served as office manager and bookkeeper, and a woman hired as secretary and map maker. Some two years later, when the land transfers became burdensome, an experienced abstractor of titles, J. R. Peetz, was also employed. This force of four soon was supervising much more than a million acres, though a field force of nine or ten was needed as cruisers, landlookers, fire watchers, and general business agents.[28]

Originally Timber Company stockholders had hoped to build large sawmills and manufacture lumber extensively, though they took care to make the manufacturing clause in the 1900 contract "as easy as possible" on themselves. Manufacturing lumber was their business; they were under implied obligation to the Northern Pacific to produce lumber as freight; and they wished to catch up any slack in Lake States lumbering. After all, the timber resources on their purchases, by Northern Pacific estimate, would have meant only twenty years of operation at the rate reached on the Chippewa and Mississippi rivers. The railroad estimate was much too low, but no one knew this.[29]

A variety of factors, however, compelled the abandonment of their earlier plan and a concentration on new land purchases instead. Long and the directors found that there was already a surplus of lumber manufacture in the Far Northwest. A salesman by experience, he naturally perceived that entry into manufacturing would further have depressed the prices of lumber and standing timber. A more important element involved public relations. The Weyerhaeuser Timber Company had entered the Pacific Northwest under a cloud of suspicion. So wealthy a corporation, holding so vast an acreage, generated antagonism by its very size. Farmers and stockmen feared that it would lock up lands they needed or desired. Small millowners dreaded the ruinous competition it could offer. Citizens in general apprehended that it, alone or in partnership with the Northern Pacific, might enter politics. It seemed wise to move cautiously and show that these fears were unfounded.

The directors accordingly waited before attempting large-scale manufacture, and while they did so, Weyerhaeuser in 1904 had a serious illness. Afterward, under his doctor's orders, he restricted his business activities so that his influence was no longer thrown so strongly on the side of energetic action. Meanwhile, the rapid rise in the value of fir encouraged Long in the sale of timber to be logged by others.[30]

Thus for its first dozen years the company carried on only a modest manufacturing venture as a pilot project. Statistical information on logging and manufacturing was needed to enable the company to appraise accurately the timber it held. Numerous men and firms offered it either sites or existing sawmills. Long rejected all proposals until the directors had decided that Everett was an advantageous place to begin. This was the city on Puget Sound thirty-three miles north of Seattle which Hoyt & Colby, investing part of John D. Rockefeller's surplus capital, had founded in 1891–1893, and tried to build into an important lumbering, farming, and mining center. A station on the Great Northern, it had grown by 1900 to about 8,000 population. Rockefeller had liquidated some properties and put others in the hands of an improvement company, from which the directors in the summer of 1900 bought an 80-acre site, only to turn almost immediately to other possibilities. After considering several properties, in 1902 Weyerhaeuser Timber acquired from the Bell-Nelson Mill Company of Everett a dilapidated sawmill, a minor amount of timber, and some logging equipment, paying $243,000 in all.[31]

Nearly $5,500,000 paid for land and less than $250,000 for a mill! Long had no illusions about the character of the plant; he knew that with its old circular saws, poor planer, and inadequate kiln, it was hardly even third-rate. It would have to be rebuilt, he curtly informed St. Paul, and during the early part of 1903 it was. New equipment made it a "pretty snappy little sawmill," turning out 50,000,000 feet a year.[32]

As such, it served its purpose in providing the company material for making a fair appraisal of timber and a good deal of varied experience not only in manufacture but also in labor relations, shipping, and marketing. Of all these problems, marketing offered the most difficulty. So many mills of the Far Northwest were producing lumber for the "cargo market" —that is, ocean shipment to various points—that they had oversold their customers, and some control over exports seemed needed.

The millowners therefore agreed on a pool, establishing a cargo association that fixed definite quotas for each shipper and penalized any firm that exceeded its limit. Its rules became effective January 1, 1902, to last for two years.[33] But like most pools in all industries, this one worked badly, especially after a price decline that began in 1903 placed a premium on infractions. As each mill again began fighting for its share of the "cargo market," nearly all the small firms in Washington and Oregon were plunged into difficulties. Competition for the rail trade in the mountain and plains states was equally keen. A number of small mills around Centralia, Washington, banded together to form a sales agency, the Lumber Manufacturers Association, and the Weyerhaeuser mill had to meet its rivalry. Altogether, the Everett mill, using C. R. McCormick & Company of San Francisco as its shipping agent and A. Marshall of Minneapolis for the rail trade, found difficulty at times in disposing of its product.

Indeed, the Pacific Coast lumber-milling industry barely kept its head above water in the period 1900–1905. Not until the summer of 1906, when the San Francisco earthquake and fire brought a demand for lumber, did it operate on a comfortably profitable level. This fact and others explain the early delay of Long and the directors in entering large-scale manufacture. E. M. Warren, the mill manager at Everett, was content to do his logging, sawing, and marketing at a sober, steady pace.

7

But Long, catching Weyerhaeuser's enthusiasm for timber purchasing, energetically pushed the acquisition of more land. For this action there were two main reasons. He had to carry on buying in order to "block up" the holdings for efficient management and logging—a labor requiring anxious care and great tact; and he wished to obtain desirable tracts while prices were still relatively low. Weyerhaeuser had declared in March, 1900, that the policy would be to fill out the checkerboard properties by taking "all the adjoining land which has timber and can be bought reasonably." But what was reasonable? The directors gave their interpretation when they decided in May that $0.35 a thousand feet was enough to pay, and authorized Long to spend $1,000,000 at that price.[34]

Because the land boom filled Washington and Oregon with speculative buyers offering equal or larger sums, Long at first made slow progress. The rival purchasers came from all over the Lake States. Some of them, like the Dempsey family, who acquired land west of Mount Rainier, and the veteran Saginaw lumberman Joseph Fordney, who had recently gained a seat in Congress, commanded plenty of capital. Long reported in June, 1900, that hundreds of men seemed to want "a little Washington timber," and in October that "Portland is full of scalawag timber brokers."[35] He and his associates watched for large tracts, but 10,000 acres that they snatched from the London & San Francisco Bank for $96,000 was their only early prize. They scanned the local newspapers for advertisements and enlisted small real-estate dealers. They offered special incentives to agents, such as a $100 bonus to an Eatonville "looker" for every purchase he helped effect. But in the first year the company obtained only about 35,000 acres, for which it paid slightly more than the $0.35 figure.

It was obviously necessary to offer higher prices, and in the spring of 1901 Long began to bid $0.50 a thousand feet. That year he succeeded in buying one fairly large tract. Just north of the mouth of the Columbia, looking over it to the historic town of Astoria, two Washington counties, Pacific and Wahkiakum, slope to the rugged coast, in part separated by the Nasel River. Here a lumber company owned a valuable stretch of timber with a boom and a decrepit sawmill. Long bought the whole property for $78,500.[36] Meanwhile, he pursued his consolidation program throughout the areas bought from the Northern Pacific. In the Grays Harbor–Thurston County district west of Rainier and in Clarke and Cowlitz counties, he obtained pieces with stands of from 50,000 to 100,000 feet an acre, some of the richest timberlands on the globe. Various buyers here, wishing to control what threatened to become a runaway market, seem to have attempted to form a united front of large timberland purchasers, who would apportion the available acreage among themselves and pay only reasonable rates.

Had this mutual buying agreement worked, it would have been open to attack on ethical if not legal grounds, but of course it failed to work. Jealousies continually developed among members of the group, some of whom violated their pledges, and outsiders took advantage of the situation to offer just a little more than the associated bidders. But while the combination still had a paper existence, the Weyerhaeuser Timber Company did acquire one considerable holding, the Bliss tract, in the Clarke-Cowlitz area.[37]

The buying of small intermingled timber lots was accompanied, much to the advantage of public relations, by what amounted roughly to land-trading activities. That is, Long readily sold some company lands that did not fit into his plans, especially when such sales facilitated buying in more advantageous places. Obviously, it would never do for the Weyerhaeuser Timber Company to gain the reputation of an avaricious monopoly, which held all it owned by a grip of death and continually tried to pry loose what others controlled. Particularly must small loggers and petty sawmill owners, whose very lives depended on timber supply, be granted fair opportunities to buy. Long made his first sale as early as June, 1900, reporting that he hoped the transaction would open the door to a purchase of 3,000 or 4,000 acres. Such sales became numerous, aggregating by the end of 1904 about 35,000 acres of timber rights or forest.

These transactions effected a double object. They blunted the edge of popular suspicion of the Weyerhaeuser interests, and they also made a fair profit. The 35,000 acres sold contained an estimated 1,163,500,000 feet of lumber. As they fetched $940,000, the company had made what seemed a large profit; and although the margin was less than it appeared— for interest, taxes, and management costs had to be considered—it was liberal.[38]

Timber prices rose so steeply in 1904 that the company slackened its buying and spent only $60,000 that year. A substantial number of directors favored stopping purchases entirely in the delusive hope of lower prices later. While Long, who still believed—quite soundly, as time showed—in buying timber in selected areas, was obtaining what he could in Washington, Weyerhaeuser himself had made one more tremendous acquisition, this time in Oregon. Very possibly this was the fruit of more late-evening talks with Hill beside the fireside in St. Paul. At any rate, when the Northern Pacific in the summer of 1902 suggested to Weyerhaeuser that he might get 200,000 acres, more than half of it already patented, at $5 an acre, he snapped the offer up in a two-line letter: "Your favor of yesterday at hand. We will take the Oregon lands according to your option."

The directors' retardation of purchasing was later considered a mistake. Nevertheless, it left the Weyerhaeuser Timber Company in possession of so large an acreage that a breathing spell might well have seemed proper. In January, 1905, at the end of its first five years, it owned nearly 1,500,000 acres costing almost $9,500,000.[39]

In turning to the Pacific Northwest, the Weyerhaeuser group had built better than it knew. It had bought at the right moment, as the nation completed its turn from depression to prosperity, and the Pacific States began growing faster than ever. It had acquired one of the richest timber areas of the planet; an estate which made possible large-scale operations for decades to come—indeed, with proper conservation practices, for perpetuity. Partly by luck, it had found in Long a manager who had not only judgment and vision but also a gift for making friends and for public leadership. It had cruised and blocked up its checkerboard holdings. Though it had bought and rebuilt a weak mill at Everett and had thus learned much about sawing and marketing Douglas fir, not to mention log values, the delay in manufacture was disappointing to some stockholders and was to result in embarrassments not yet foreseen. But this apart, no one could deny that the group, and particularly Frederick Weyerhaeuser, had matched bold vision with energetic action.

NOTES

1. FEW Record, 390–395; Pyle, *The Life of James J. Hill,* II, 2–48.
2. Lillard, *Great Forest,* 185–187 with references; *Statistical Abstract,* 1951, 648–661; Smith, *North America,* 266–268. The South in 1945 still had a total forest area of nearly 190,-000,000 acres, much of it of course second growth.
3. FEW Record, 38, 398–402. Durant believed that if Weyerhaeuser had made the $2,500,000 investment in cypress, in ten years it would have become worth $25,000,000.
4. FEW Record, 520–528; FEW Papers, C. M. Cochrane to FEW, Jan. 23, 1936; Hotchkiss, *Lumber and Forest Industry,* 600–602; memorial volume to James Edwin Lindsay (1915), reprinted from *Appleton's Cyclopedia of American Biography; Amer. Lmbrmn.,* I, 351–354. Weyerhaeuser was especially attached to Lindsay, a devout Baptist who had learned lumbering at his father's mill in Schroon, N.Y. Morris N. Richardson gives an interesting impression of Weyerhaeuser: "As he came into a meeting, with a gentle twinkle in his eyes, a little shoulder shrug, cordial to all and showing interest in every way, he created a spirit of real friendliness toward everyone."

5. FEW Papers, Cochrane to FEW, Jan. 23, 1936; FEW Record, 528–530. Southland, with FEW as president, made its two largest sales of timberland in 1916.
6. FEW Record, 530–538; FEW Papers, Cochrane to FEW, Jan. 23, 30, 1936; Southern Lumber Co., Min. Bk., Jan. 28, 1902, Dec. 7, 1928. Weyerhaeuser and Denkmann interests each held $107,900 of stock in Southern Lumber. Only $608,700 of the $750,000 was paid in.
7. Southern Lumber Co. Min. Bk., *passim;* FEW Papers, FEW to C. H. Davis, Dec. 3, 1906; July 10, 27, Sept. 23, 1908; FEW to FW, Sept. 24, 1906; G. F. Lindsay to FEW, April 16, 1929; Z. K. Thomas to FEW, Dec. 24, 1936; (Warren) *Eagle Democrat,* April 5, 1951; C. M. Cochrane to FEW, Jan. 23, 1936; FEW Record, 535–547; WTC Papers. F. S. Bell and F. H. Thatcher of Laird, Norton Co. on a chance visit to New Orleans saw the Calcasieu tract, and liked it. The company was reorganized by the new owners in Nov., 1902, Weyerhaeuser & Denkmann and Laird, Norton each subscribing for 217 shares out of 3,000. In 1911 the assets passed to the Calcasieu Timber Co. with Bell as president.

8. Coman and Gibbs, *Time, Tide and Timber,* 214–215; FEW Record, 398, 543.

9. FEW Record, 732 ff.

10. Coast Lumber Co. Min. Bks.; FEW Record, 419; Coman and Gibbs, 215. The Shingle Weavers had an old industry on the Pacific Coast and had formed a union in 1890. See Johansen and Gates, *Empire of the Columbia,* 470.

11. WTC Papers; G. W. Dulany, Jr., Reminiscences; Ingram Papers, W. H. Day to O. H. Ingram, Nov. 7, 1899. Of the secret negotiations preceding the contract we know little, except that Hill's original price was $7 an acre, while Weyerhaeuser at first offered $5. Phipps left the Omaha for the Northern Pacific in 1894.

12. Bur. of Corps., *Report on Lumber Industry,* I, 208 ff. The Bureau admitted that in some Washington areas timber had found no sale whatever, and the Weyerhaeuser purchase gave Chehalis County forests a value for the first time.

13. Long in *Miss. Valley Lbrmn.,* April 22, 1910.

14. Long Papers, Long to S. T. McKnight and F. S. Bell, Feb. 28, May 22, etc., 1901.

15. *Ibid.,* Phipps of the Northern Pacific refused to make any adjustment except to correct manifest errors.

16. *Ibid.,* Long to F. S. Bell, June 5, 1900.

17. Johansen and Gates, 463, remark that high as the boom prices seemed, they were in general economically justified, for the timber market kept on rising until the First World War.

18. The Northern Pacific in all received about 44,000,000 acres stretching from Superior to Puget Sound; the Union Pacific, Southern Pacific, Santa Fe, and other roads received similar grants. A full half of the Northern Pacific stumpage lay in the state of Washington.

19. FKW Reminiscences, 40 ff., offers a good characterization. See also Long's reminiscent letter to FEW dated Oct. 6, 1919, FEW Record, 650 ff.

20. Coman and Gibbs, 3–128; C. H. Carey, *History of Oregon,* I, 244, 257.

21. WSC Papers. R. B. Fehren of the WSC wrote an excellent account of the Douglas fir. See also McCulloch, "The Cascade Forest" in Peattie, ed., *The Cascades,* 171–213.

22. Snowden, *History of Washington,* IV, 262, 363. Morgan in *The Last Wilderness* publishes a frontispiece illustration of loggers in 1902 felling from springboards a Douglas fir 14' 11" in diameter inside the bark.

23. Holbrook, *Green Commonwealth,* quotes Forbes in a masterful description of skid roads and bull teaming. The West Coast Lumbermen's Association has good photographs of oxen at work with huge logs.

24. Morgan, *The Last Wilderness,* 81; Coman and Gibbs, 67.

25. Morgan, 79.

26. Riegel, *The Story of the Western Railroads,* 278 ff., 318.

27. Snowden, *History of Washington,* IV, 363; Morgan, 6.

28. WTC Papers, directors' minutes and salary records.

29. Ingram Papers, FW to O. H. Ingram, Dec. 11, 1899; FEW Record, 683, 701. Actual stumpage of the original 900,000-acre purchase was at one time computed at just under 17,000,-000,000 feet. This was probably an understatement. Early in the 1900's only the biggest and best fir timber would have been counted, while hemlock and white fir would have been left out of the computation as unsalable.

30. FEW Record, 701.

31. Nevins, *Study in Power,* II, Chap. 30; WTC Papers, Miscellaneous Contracts; FEW Record, *ut supra.*

32. FKW Reminiscences.

33. *The Pacific Lumber Trade Journal* for some years had pressed for better organization within the industry, and reports such activities fully. See also Moravets, *Lumber Production in Oregon and Washington, 1869–1948.*

34. WTC Papers, Directors' Min. Bk. A, 16 ff.

35. Long Papers, Long to FW, Oct. 2, Nov. 1, 1900; *ibid.*, Long to O. H. Ingram, Nov. 1, 1900.

36. *Ibid.*, Long to McCormick, Sept. 26, 1901. The mill was worthless, but the boom was used.

37. Long Papers, Long to Laird, Norton, Nov. 13, 1901. Some devastating forest fires in 1902 promoted a certain amount of combined action by the large companies in salvage operations. With these fires and their results we deal later.

38. FEW Record, 667–669; WTC Papers, statistics.

39. FEW Record, 661–662; WTC Papers, statistics. Because the NP failed to patent some of the Oregon lands, the total purchase by WTC amounted to only 172,492 acres.

XIII

Growth on the Pacific

ONE DOMINANT NOTE in Weyerhaeuser activities on the Pacific Coast during the decade before the World War was geographical expansion. The associates not only continued buying timberland in large quantities but bought it over a widening area. The initial holdings had lain chiefly in the Douglas fir region west of the Cascades in Washington, some of them close enough to sound or ocean for loggers on quiet days to hear the faint diapason of a steamship whistle. Indeed, most of the domain continued to lie in Washington.[1] Large purchases were soon made, however, not only in coastal Oregon, but in a region about Klamath Lake lying east of the Cascades and dipping down into northern California, rich in some types of timber unfamiliar to Timber Company stockholders.

While new lands were thus acquired, until 1915 the manufacture of lumber remained a secondary activity. Save for the barometer mill at Everett, the Weyerhaeuser Timber Company left that activity to others. Though it was understood when the company was organized that such postponement would be necessary, it grieved Frederick Weyerhaeuser. In the abortive effort of the northwestern industry to form a selling pool in 1902–1903, the Timber Company was allotted only 1.6 percent of the market. Long, attending a final meeting of pool directors in the fall of 1903, was irked by the apparent contempt in which his concern was held. "We do not one bit like the way in which they sneered about the W.T.C.," he exploded, "and the quicker we let them know that we have a right to do business, the better it will be."[2]

While Long concentrated on purchases, he continued to sell timber to local manufacturers. He sold partly to keep them prosperous but chiefly for much-needed revenue for his own firm. And he kept his firm solvent while others were failing.

2

One of the most dramatic events in the early history of Washington lent a strong impulse to this sale of timber. The last days of August and first fortnight of September, 1902, were hot, clear, and dry. The forests became tinder. On September 11th a high wind swept down from the north and east, blowing hour after hour. Almost simultaneously a score of blazes were roaring, all the way from Lyman in northern Washington to central Oregon, and from the Cascade peaks west to Willapa Bay and Grays Harbor. Some 700,000 acres were burning at one time.

"At this hour 2 P.M.," George Long wrote Weyerhaeuser on the 12th, "the city of Tacoma is practically in a state of semi-darkness, the sky having a pinkish overcoat and the general effect is exactly that of the reflection of a big fire at night." As he wrote, Portland, Vancouver, and other cities were engulfed in smoke. Ashes fell in them to half an inch or more in depth. A score of villages and settlements were destroyed, while hundreds of farmers and loggers saw their buildings and equipment licked up by the flames. The death roll was later put at thirty-five.[3]

Never were forest fires—110 in all were counted—more spectacular. Men on the uplands could see them raging as far as the eye could reach: billowing rolls of smoke, fold over fold, white at the bottom, gray as they rose higher, and black at the top until they merged with the clouds. Seen nearer at hand, the arcs of fire were jagged scythes of flame eating into the wilderness. The leaping red-and-white tongues raced across roads, wiped out streams, encircled and drank up ponds. Roaring like tornadoes as they marched, the larger conflagrations scorched everything far to right and left of their paths. Bears, deer, and wildcats fled frantically to clearings and lakes. Sixty-odd farmers, prospectors, and lumbermen in one part of the Lewis River Valley got to Trout Lake, put off in hastily improvised rafts, and stayed in deep water for forty-eight hours. Some unfortunates were caught—a wagon party left only the iron wheeltires, metal rings of neck yokes and tongue, and blackened skeletons of men and horses to show where they had been overtaken; a woman trying to rescue her cherished Singer sewing machine became only a few charred bones near its scorched frame.

Ironically, a place that was left unharmed gave its name to this great "Yacolt Burn." A hamlet of fifteen buildings, the terminus of the Portland, Vancouver & Yakima Railroad then being built, Yacolt apparently lay in the path of destruction. Its terrified inhabitants fled to a creek, sheltered there all night, and came back to find every structure in the village intact except that the paint on the walls had blistered.

When experts computed the damage for the entire catastrophe, they set the immediate loss at $13,000,000. The indirect losses, however, came to vastly more: young growing timber had been swept away, the soil bared to erosion, a haven provided for insect pests, and the productivity of a large area checked. Next year, tardily and inadequately, the Washington legislature provided for a forester and a chief fire warden. It would soon have to do more.

Long faced a stupendous problem in salvage. "All told," he wrote O. H. Ingram three months later, "in the Columbia River district, in Clarke and Skamania Counties, there are somewhere between one and one-and-a-half billion feet of burnt timber, but the present indications are that not more than one-third of it will be saved; we hope to save all of ours."[4] The task was urgent, for the charred trunks would rapidly deteriorate. Some 20,000 acres of the company's lands had been burned over in Clarke County alone, and other large tracts in the shadow of Mount St. Helens.

Thus the "burn" had the effect of temporarily swinging the emphasis of Weyerhaeuser operations from Everett and Puget Sound to southern Washington and the Portland area. Plans had been considered for erecting a second mill at the barge works in Everett. Frederick Weyerhaeuser now counseled building it near the "burn" instead.[5] Various sites were studied, one at Yacolt, about thirty miles northeast of Portland, and one at St. John's in the Portland suburbs being the most important. When Long decided that St. John's was the better point, ground for a mill on the Willamette River there was purchased. Meanwhile, transportation at reasonable rates had to be arranged; R. L. McCormick obtained from the Northern Pacific, which owned the Portland, Vancouver & Yakima spur, a reasonable scale of charges on logs from Yacolt to the mill.[6]

Once he had established camps in the spring of 1903, Long insisted on speed in logging. "The great big word we ought to have before us in connection with this burned timber district is HASTE," he wrote in March, 1903; "haste all the way down the line. . . . I think we are too slow."[7]

Logging a burned forest is an exceptionally dirty, toilsome undertaking. Dead timber hardens until it resists the saw almost like rock; many badly damaged logs have to be discarded; a litter of fallen branches and snags interferes with men and animals; ashes and charcoal blacken the workers like miners. So in the Yacolt area lumbermen swore, teams struggled, and choppers blunted saws and axes, as they sawed useful timber. To make the situation worse, a pall of declining prices hung over the whole Northwestern lumber industry during 1903–1904. Many sawmills were being thrown on the market by owners who could no longer afford to run them. As it became evident that the area had a plethora of mills and that a new competitive unit would be uneconomic, building plans at St. John's went by the board. Only a log boom was used there.

The first summer saw the Timber Company working jointly with the

C. H. Davis interests through a specially created logging company that
sold chiefly to two Portland millowners. After much hard work in establishing roads and camps, production rose so that by November the partners
were pouring a steady stream of logs into Portland. But their activities
were embarrassed by the crazy pattern of holdings, and finally their
respective lands were merged in the Clarke County Timber Company
(1904) with a capital of $300,000 equally divided between the Weyer-
haeuser and Davis interests. Though officers anticipated that it would
rapidly complete its logging and expire, actually it was to endure for almost a generation, and under the urge to increase its profits it was shortly
acquiring green timber to log! A jointly owned boom company was also
formed.[8]

Long similarly joined with Russell A. Alger and other Michigan
men in saving burned-over timber along the Coweeman River, near the
foot of Mount St. Helens.[9] Contract loggers were put to work cutting trees
and rafting them to the Columbia. In other fire-damaged areas, Long
sold the standing timber to lumbermen already working in the localities.
The incomplete nature of the records, for salvaging was a rough-and-ready
business and numerous companies were involved, makes any precise statement of the timber saved impossible. Altogether, it aggregated more than
a half-billion feet. Log prices were $5.00 a thousand feet or less in 1903–
1904 and hovered around $5.50 in 1905. Inasmuch as the costs of cutting
out logs were especially heavy and the Northern Pacific charged $1.50
a thousand feet for transportation from Yacolt to the mills, net returns
were small.[10] The "Yacolt burn" had struck the company a heavy blow,
and thereafter neither Long nor the other officers ever forgot that fire was
their most deadly enemy.

3

The reasons why the Weyerhaeuser interests did not buy or build
new mills in the Puget Sound and Portland areas were numerous. Uncertain market conditions, reluctance to injure small local mills, emphasis
on sale of logs, and employment of capital in land acquisition all continued to be effective to the eve of the First World War.

Another factor in this policy is difficult to measure but was important. Frederick Weyerhaeuser's ideas came in conflict with those of the
conservative F. H. Thatcher. Of all the second-generation directors he had
much the most forceful personality. He earnestly opposed an early expansion of manufacture by the Weyerhaeuser Timber Company as impolitic.
Weyerhaeuser favored the policy of building mills. Under his encouragement the directors at one time or another in the first four years authorized
a new mill at the barge property in Everett, one at Grays Harbor, and one

in the Portland district. In one instance he asked Vice-President W. H.
Laird to take the chair in order that he *himself* might personally introduce
and speak for a resolution authorizing new mills. But Thatcher and others
urged successfully that the company remain primarily a timber-holding
concern.

Moreover, in George S. Long, Thatcher had a halfway ally, though
their reasons for opposing extensive manufacturing were different. Long
did not object to expansion; indeed, he favored the extension of Weyerhaeuser enterprises. But he was by training a salesman. "I knew nothing
about machinery," he said, "nothing about a sawmill. . . . In other
words, I had a one-sided education in the lumber business, which per-
tained solely and simply to the lumber itself after it was manufactured."
Knowing the market in the early years of the century, Long did not think
that lumber prices warranted entry into manufacturing.

F. E. Weyerhaeuser in retrospect asserted that the company would
have made greater progress had the commitment to manufacturing been
promptly taken. In the first thirty years of its history, he argued, much
of its stumpage was manufactured by mills much smaller and less efficient than those the company could have built—mills often unable to give
their product proper finish and standardization or to launch a program
of publicity designed to help lumber compete with its many substitutes.
He believed that a proper supply of timber for competitive mills could
have been provided while the company's own manufacturing facilities
were developed. Had its directors so acted, certainly they would have
armored it against charges that it was "locking up" forests for price rises.
Some outside timber holders of the Northwest have agreed with Frederick
E. Weyerhaeuser on most of these points, but opinion inside the company
remains divided.[11]

Production by the single small Everett mill, however, did show a
decided expansion as the Timber Company improved its equipment. Just
over 28,000,000 feet in 1902, the volume rose to more than 38,000,000
feet in 1905 and 39.7 million in 1906. And progress became still more
rapid when William H. Boner took the managership in the summer of
1907.[12] Born in a log cabin in Missouri, of Scotch-Irish ancestry, he had
devoted his life to lumber and had become a close friend of O. H. Ingram
of Eau Claire. Just over forty when he took the Everett position, a big
burly man of strong character, he was at the height of his aggressive vigor.
With Long and the directors behind him he greatly improved and enlarged
the mill, putting in gang saws and other machinery, reducing saw kerf
and sawdust, and replacing horses by tractors. In 1909 production rose
to nearly 49.5 million feet, in 1912 to nearly 69.7 million, and in 1914
to more than 79.2 million. The finish of the lumber was meanwhile

bettered. New kilns permitted the mill to dry larger quantities of lumber, lowering freight costs and giving consumers stable materials.

Boner was justly proud of doubling the mill output in seven years. He kept a somewhat rough cost-accounting system, watched expenses carefully, and boasted of the savings he effected. "Somehow," Long replied to one such boast in 1912, "I am of the opinion that your reduced cost in manufacture arises very largely from the increased facilities for making more lumber and the increased power, rather than from any notable increase in the efficiency of your men. Nevertheless, it is grateful and satisfactory to learn that the cost is reduced, by whatever means it is obtained."[13]

Boner's responsibilities included not only direct management of the mill, but general oversight of the woods superintendent of the Weyerhaeuser Logging Company as well as of transportation, labor relations, and marketing. He kept alert for new ideas, and never forgot that his employees were human beings. "I have been reading up on this Scientific Management," he wrote Long in 1913, "and have had my mind set on lines of efficiency and not cheap labor."[14] Few details escaped him. He knew all about freight rates, shipping costs (the Timber Company owned shares in several vessels), the demands of farmers for silo materials, contract loading, and insurance.

The mill up to the World War turned out chiefly dimension, timbers, and flooring lumber. About a tenth of the product was sold in the local Northwest market, while something over another tenth went into the export trade. California took a substantial slice. In the years 1905–1910 about three-fifths of the output went to markets by rail, and most of that to the Dakotas, then rapidly filling with population. In 1910 Boner boldly invaded Nebraska. The principal salesman was Albert Marshall, an efficient, likable, experienced man who operated from Minneapolis.

Naturally, as demand and production grew, the strain on northwestern railroad facilities increased. In 1904 some 44,000 cars were needed to haul the 705,000,000 feet of lumber that left Washington by rail; in 1905 some 65,000 cars were demanded for the 1,300 million feet.[15] Severe pinches occurred; in August, 1906, for example, the Everett mill was unable to fill its orders by rail, and two months later its manager reported that he had not had a Northern Pacific car in his yards since the 20th of September. Other manufacturers were in the same fix, and they filled the *West Coast Lumberman* with articles and editorials denouncing Jim Hill.

The wrathful millowners turned in various directions for relief. For one thing, they persuaded the Washington and Oregon legislature to pass demurrage laws, penalizing the railroads for failure to deliver cars as ordered.

More effectively, they turned to the ocean. For one reason, they

believed that railroad rates on lumber were extortionate—particularly
after the lines in July, 1907, announced a raise in tariffs from the coast to
Denver, St. Paul, and Chicago.[16] For another, they realized that the hour
when the Panama Canal would be open steadily approached and would
give them cheap access to the East. The Weyerhaeuser interests relied
on Charles R. McCormick & Company, San Francisco wholesalers, for
reaching the cargo and Californian markets. When the *Yosemite,* a Mc-
Cormick ship in which the Timber Company had bought a small interest,
made its first voyage in 1907, it netted more than $2,000 in profits.[17] This
experience encouraged Long to take another small interest in the steamship *Yellowstone* and the schooner *Shoshone.* He, like others, was for
playing ocean transportation against rail transportation. And by 1911 he
was insisting, in letter after letter to Boner and F. E. Weyerhaeuser, that
they must soon open eastern coastal lumberyards.[18]

The struggle for markets had always to be strenuously waged. If
Dakota farmers had a bad crop year, as in 1912, they bought no lumber.
If railroad building flagged in the Northwest, as in 1910–1912, demand
for ties and boards suffered. If New York banks curtailed credit, lumberyards all over the map restricted their business. "Before 1904," some men
said in Tacoma and Portland, "lumber sold itself; after that year it had
to be sold." The Timber Company had an alternation of bright years and
dark—the brightest season just after the San Francisco fire of 1906, the
gloomiest just after the autumn panic of 1907.

4

The earthquake and three-day fire which in April, 1906, devastated
the business center and some adjacent districts of San Francisco cost 500
lives, destroyed buildings valued at $105,000,000, and damaged addi-
tional property to the extent of $300,000,000 or $400,000,000. Many
structures were dynamited to stop the spread of the flames. Charles R.
McCormick & Company wrote Long immediately afterward that their
office but not their records had been lost and half their lumberyard ruined.
But even while the ashes were hot men began to rebuild the city.

Inevitably the emergency caused a swift rise in costs. Wages of
skilled labor reached the then extraordinary level of $12 a day, freight
and drayage charges broke bounds, and the prices of all kinds of materials
soared. Nevertheless, reconstruction proceeded so steadily that within
three years it was almost completed.

Long knew that his industry would become one of the targets of
attack. "I anticipate," he wrote, "that the result of this will be a great
howl from San Francisco about the advance in the price of lumber, taking
advantage of their disaster."[19] He expected also a demand for tariff-free

lumber from British Columbia. Lumber prices indeed rose, but they had begun their upward movement all over the country early in the year. Frederick E. Weyerhaeuser in St. Paul had written a Saginaw friend on February 15th, two months before the earthquake, that the associates' trade in January was thrice that of a normal month and that the demand remained "astonishing."[20] Prices of logs on Puget Sound had risen by from half a dollar to a dollar a thousand feet; for one small tract of timber bought a year earlier Long had been offered six times what he paid.

He had additional reason for resenting a charge of profiteering in that he made some effort to hold the line. When companies such as Benson Logging raised the price of logs on May 1 to $10 a thousand, the managers of the W.T.C. kept theirs at the $9 level until June 1st and then raised the price only to $9.50, effective for three months to come.

The San Francisco fire thus simply accelerated an upward movement already strongly under way. High prices, declared Long, were mainly the result of prosperity, expansion, and consequent demand in all sections. He noted that loggers' wages had risen $1 a day within a year and millmen's wages $2, while transportation costs had gone up. "In other words, the advance in lumber reflects an increase to the owner of stumpage of about one-seventh of the increased cost of lumber."[21] The advance, however, kept on—and of course the general rise added immensely to the value of timberland which the W.T.C. group had bought at $6 an acre.

The boom reached its apex midway in 1907, receiving an additional stimulus from a destructive earthquake at Valparaiso in 1906–1907. Rising prices naturally resulted in a spectacular increase in the number and volume of West Coast sawmills. While in 1905 the Pacific States had 557 mills, the spring of 1907 found 1,036 rolling forth dimension, timbers, flooring, siding, and shingles. For a time, capacity was strained to the utmost. One lumber journal reported that the Everett mill was running thirty hours a day! Its production of more than 82,000,000 feet in the two years 1906–1907 reflected the exceptional demand.

Prosperity for a time was an eagle that perched on every millstack, but Long realized that it might swiftly fly away. Noting in the fall of 1906 that real estate, timberlands, logs, and lumber had all gone up by about 50 percent, he added: "The inflated prices can hardly last, especially on logs and lumber." Early in 1907 the national skies began to cloud. A sharp break in stocks in February caused Jacob Schiff to declare that the country was "suffering from an excess of prosperity which is simply overwhelming us," an explanation which perhaps appealed to lumber interests facing grave car shortages. Men began talking of a "rich man's panic" arising from the forced sale of stocks by capitalists who had borrowed too heavily.[22]

The slump in the second half of 1907 soon approached a collapse.

Continued financial flurries in the East, culminating in the trust-company and bank panic of October and in emergency Treasury measures the following month, played a part. Lumber orders from California, which at one time had taken about 35 percent of the Oregon-Washington cut, fell heavily. Local demand in the Northwest by mid-November was down two-fifths. The Dakota trade was hard hit, and the financial condition of many dealers became so shaky that Marshall was directed to sell only to those with "absolutely gilt-edged credit." Three Portland banks went under in as many months. One result was that millowners there could no longer pay the Clarke County Timber Company for logs. Other debtors of the Weyerhaeuser interests began asking for extension of their notes. Clearing-house certificates soon took the place of regular money all over the region, for bankers either had no specie or locked it up to forestall runs. Charles R. McCormick reported on November 7th that he doubted if he could find $50 in currency to send out of San Francisco. At the Everett mill Boner had to meet his payrolls in certificates. Many small sawmills quickly became insolvent and closed, Washington alone losing 110 by the year's end.[23]

The depression maintained its paralyzing grip during the first half of 1908. When Boner closed the Everett mill in December for the annual overhaul, he little realized that it would remain silent four months and that he would begin again only because he had 4,000,000 feet of teredo-infested logs in the water. Marshall, selling lumber in the Dakotas at $3 below list prices, found himself undercut by southerners disposing of their products at almost any price simply, it was believed, to pay interest on the short-term notes or bonds with which they financed their logging. In February, Long heard of a San Francisco speculator who bought random cargo on the Columbia at $6 a thousand for good lumber and placed another order at $7.50—prices simply indecent. "There absolutely seems to be no bottom to the price of lumber," wrote Boner in May. The Timber Company, its files filled with letters from debtors begging for deferments, continued to extend the time for payments on notes. Fortunately, the export market, now absorbing about 15 percent of the company's production, remained firm.[24]

Labor took hard buffets in this general tumble, for canneries, shipyards, flour mills, and slaughterhouses as well as the lumber industry had to restrict activity. In the fall of 1907 the Timber Company was discharging some cruisers, closing some logging camps, and following its competitors in making 20 to 25 percent wage cuts. Common laborers at the beginning of 1908 were glad to get $1.75 a day in the Northwest, and discontent was making them radical-minded. Believing that the company was paying wages higher by a quarter than its rivals, Long pressed Boner for further cuts, and got them. He also wrote his agent at Yacolt to drop the less efficient loggers in that district from the payrolls, for the men would work harder if they knew their jobs were insecure—labor would not be so independent![25]

While Weyerhaeuser Timber apparently did more for its employees than many other firms, the general attitude toward workers at that date was callous by subsequent standards. Commenting on the wage reductions and unemployment, the *West Coast Lumberman* complacently remarked in December that northwestern hands would meet little real hardship because the climate was mild, firewood was available for the mere gathering, and "when the tide is out the table is spread"—that is, they could dig clams!

In the latter half of 1908, and especially after the election of Taft encouraged business, the economic situation improved. In the early spring of 1909 Long was able to give the directors an encouraging report. Despite the fact that nearly two-thirds of Washington lumber was sold at cost, the Everett mill was making $0.50 a thousand on lumber cut from logs bought in the open market. Meanwhile, the Clarke County Timber Company was netting $3.00 a thousand on logs sold in the still weak Columbia River market. As government analysts later commented, the wails uttered by various large companies—the Weyerhaeuser group just groaned privately—were not justified. Any manufacturer who had bought timber during the boom lost money. "But nearly all the mills of any importance were cutting timber which they had bought years before at low prices and were losing only in the sense of making less than the boom had led them to expect." Prices of timberland, significantly, never declined at all.[26]

The main activity of the Weyerhaeuser interests in the decade before 1914 remained the acquisition of timberlands, a detailed account of which is unnecessary. By the beginning of June in 1914, just before Serajevo, the Timber Company had raised its total holdings to 1,982,000 acres. It had paid an average of $8.80 an acre, or a total of nearly $17,500,000, and it estimated its mature timber at well over 41,000,000,000 feet. In Washington (1,514,000 acres) the most important additions were interstitial purchases to round out the tracts. Almost 400,000 acres lay in Oregon and nearly 50,000 in California. By all odds, the most striking addition to the empire was in the Klamath Lake area.

The physical geography of this region is as interesting as its natural beauty is unforgettable. The so-called Klamath Mountains lying between the Willamette headwaters on the north and the Sacramento headwaters on the south are misnamed. This wide rugged district is really a plateau, which slopes from an elevation of about five thousand feet on its eastern side, just under the Cascade range, to about two thousand feet on the western side, fronting the Pacific. The waters from the Cascades flow down to the sea in a series of rivers—the Klamath, Rogue, Coquille, Umpqua—which, after carving grim canyons through the more rugged parts of the terrain, open as they approach the coast into wide, rich valleys. The Klamath River is the outlet of Klamath Lake in south central Oregon.

When Frémont skirted this country in 1843, following the eastern foot of the Cascades and admiring magnificent peaks from Mount Rainier to Mount Hood, he described the eastern river canyons matching those on the west—"narrow and chasm-like valleys generally sunk a thousand feet below the surface of the plain." He was struck by the immense forests everywhere. "The timber was uniformly large," he wrote of the Fall River Valley, "some of the pines measuring twenty-two feet in circumference at the ground and twelve or thirteen feet at six feet above." Visiting Klamath Marsh, just north of Klamath Lake, the Pathfinder traveled on south and east through a district still heavily forested.[27]

The nature of this rich forest country requires special explanation. Klamath Lake lies close to the Cascade Range divide, with the snow-tipped peak of Mount McLoughlin, nearly 9,500 feet high, in full view from its waters. This divide separates two entirely different lands. On the east is a high, russet, semiarid region of spacious views, rough lava flows, and open woods; on the west are green valleys, thicker timber, and cooler, moister air, though the terrain is less tangled with bushes than the rain-drenched coastal woods. Two busy highways today roughly parallel the divide, Number 99 on the more heavily populated western slope, Number 97 on the dry, rolling, thinly inhabited eastern side. Most tourists are too busy thinking of the scenery or sports—the icy mountain cones; the exquisite colors of Crater Lake, the wide collapsed heart of a volcanic mountain now filled with crystal-clear aquamarine water; the Klamath beaches covered fall and winter with great flocks of white pelican; the rainbow trout and salmon of the lakes and streams—to pay close attention to the sharp differentiation in trees. If they did, they would see that on the western slopes stand hemlock and above all Douglas fir, while the eastern slopes are distinguished by sugar pine and ponderosa pine.

The ponderosa, with its yellow scaly bark picturesquely fissured into irregular plates and ridged by deep black furrows, was long miscalled western yellow pine. It was also underrated. Prolific, able to withstand drought and resist fire, capable of crowding out varieties like sugar pine, its stand in the region rated second only to that of Douglas fir. For lumber its merits almost equaled those of white pine. Its even cell structure, straight grain, freedom from excessive pitch, and toughness adapted it for building, millwork, furniture, and posts alike. It dried more easily than most softwood, and thus came to market better seasoned. It took paints and varnishes well and had a high insulating value. As it was especially knotty, for growth in open park-like groves encouraged heavy limb development, it made excellent wall panels. Nearly half of the whole national stand was in Oregon and California; indeed, Oregon had a larger area of ponderosa than of Douglas fir.[28]

The Weyerhaeuser feat in acquiring a great storehouse of Douglas fir in Washington was now to be followed by the acquisition of a storehouse of ponderosa pine in Oregon and California. Climate and soil vitally affect the quality of ponderosa. The Klamath region yields softer, whiter wood, available in larger widths than the stands in eastern Oregon and southern Idaho; and Klamath was to become the chief center of its manufacture.

Here it was that Frederick Weyerhaeuser again proved his shrewd foresight. He and his associates heard in 1903–1904 that good timberlands could be had southwest of Klamath Falls. On investigation, he learned that several different groups held land there in such an inextricably confused pattern that purchase from any one would lead into a legal morass. One owner was the Pelton-Reid Sugar Pine Company with 16,000 acres; another, the Pokegama Sugar Pine Lumber Company with 10,000; another, William R. Thorsen of San Francisco. The only safe course was to buy out a number of the owners at one time. It is evidence of Long's skill in negotiation that he brought order out of the prevailing confusion and by the spring of 1906 was able to report that he had acquired for the company about 49,000 acres of forest.[29]

This feat took place just in the nick of time, for the San Francisco fire and other factors brought a brisk boom in Klamath timberlands. Moreover, hard on the heels of Long's purchases came an announcement by the Southern Pacific that it would build north from Weed, California, to Klamath Falls. This news had a double significance. It meant that the little Klamath Lake Railroad, which linked the Southern Pacific at Thrall, California, with the village of Pokegama in Klamath County, would lose most of its importance. The 24-mile line, with one locomotive, thirteen cars, one engineer, one conductor, and a third-rate hotel at each terminus, was a curiosity. But as it was an interstate road, it could not be dropped without federal consent.[30] The Southern Pacific announcement also meant that land values would advance along the new line and at Klamath Falls. If Long was to add to his domain of sugar pine and ponderosa, he must move with diligence.

Long hoped to round out his purchases to at least twice his original 49,000 acres. He had written Frederick Weyerhaeuser that he saw "a possibility of assembling in one mass on the Klamath River plateau an aggregation probably of 100,000 acres of sugar and yellow pine, where the logging conditions strike us as being particularly good, the quality of the timber most excellent, and everything extremely favorable for handling the sugar and pine." A few examples will show his activity in 1906. He paid $250,000 for a small sawmill (which he scrapped) and 4,100 acres of timber. He bought the 8,300-acre Dorr tract; the 20,000 acres of the Bray family. Some offerings he rejected because of price or remoteness. He was now willing, however, to pay $20 to $24 an acre for pine timberland.

Competition spurred him on. "There are dozens of commission men and land locaters and speculators," he wrote, "who are trying to get options all through that country [Klamath] with the view of unloading the lands on us or some other buyer." When a Chippewa Falls group tried to charge him double prices, he dealt with them firmly: "We have purchased about 50 claims completely surrounding them at prices varying from $2,000 to $3,500 and in one or two instances as much as $4,000, where the claims had three million feet or more of timber." By late summer in 1906 he felt satisfied with his progress: "We are having a run for our lives in that district, but are doing business, and think we are quite a little ahead of the other fellows." The total purchases for the months of July–October came to 40,000 acres.[31]

Partly because investors and speculators pushed land prices to steep levels and partly because the W.T.C. seemed to some directors to be growing too fast, various attractive stretches of timber were declined. The wide holdings of two men named Booth and Kelly, some 137,000 acres, on which Long and McCormick temporarily held an option, were finally let slip. When W.T.C. cruisers reported that they contained only two-thirds the timber which Booth and Kelly had claimed, the company proposed to pay no more than $2,812,500, which the owners refused. Conservative directors breathed a sigh of relief, but F. E. Weyerhaeuser believed that a splendid opportunity had been missed. Another major holding which the W.T.C. rejected as overpriced was the Hopkins tract west of Klamath Falls. While the company hesitated over a figure of $2,500,000 set in 1905, the shrewd Pennsylvanian who owned it raised his demand to $3,000,000 in 1906 and $3,500,000 in 1908.[32]

The sellers' market continued until the panic and depression of 1907, which, as noted, ended it abruptly. But when in the spring of 1909 a timber broker offered Long nearly 60,000 acres owned by the Manistee Lumber Company, he was willing to consider it. Nearly a year was spent in cruising and in negotiations. The upshot was that in January, 1910, the company paid $20 an acre for the property, of which roughly a third was in the ponderosa land of Oregon and two-thirds in California. The price was good for the time and place. Part of the holding, however, had figured in an earlier scandal. A muckraking writer, S. A. D. Puter, in his book *Looters of the Public Domain*, virtually confessed that he had fraudulently acquired 17,280 acres of it by the use of dummy entrymen, later selling it profitably. Of course such frauds argued both private criminality and a most culpable federal negligence.[33]

Altogether, before the First World War the Weyerhaeuser group obtained in the ponderosa and sugar pine region of Oregon around Klamath Lake and River a total of 255,000 acres, which cost $4,422,500. This stood quite apart from their 141,000 acres in the Douglas fir country of Oregon.[34] The pine holdings would be more than adequate, in due time, for the establishment of a notable manufacturing business at Klamath Falls.

6

Long's correspondence makes it clear that he grew into a mature, careful, experienced administrator, expert in managing every part of a complex business, one of the best business executives in the country. He had a gift for inspiring affection. Tall, thin, in his neat dark suit, stand-up collar, black cravat, sharp bespectacled eyes, and air of quiet self-possession, he looked (except for his cigar) like a severe schoolmaster. But his deeply lined face easily crinkled into a smile; his endless fund of stories delighted every circle. Everybody trusted his growing knowledge and deep insight.[35]

From his Tacoma office he had to look after almost everything. In the first instance, he guided the timber-purchasing program. This meant that, with the assistance of Minot Davis after 1910, Long had to train cruisers to appraise stands accurately—he wrote that Wisconsin cruisers were more honest than Washington cruisers but had to be taught by a half-year's work as compassmen. He had to make sure of large contiguous blocks, negotiate warily, and make arrangements for short-term financing. He had to take precautions against trespassers and timber thieves, a problem that he had inherited from the Northern Pacific Railroad. One of his worries after 1907 was about squatters on lands the company had obtained from the Oregon & California Railroad Company, for rumors got about that the federal courts would invalidate the O.&C. title, while Senator C. W. Fulton of Oregon introduced a forfeiture bill, so that numbers of land-hungry men drifted into the area. Long had to keep a watchful eye on state and local taxes, a problem discussed elsewhere. By 1908 he and other lumbermen had hired an expert investigator of taxes and public spending, O. Bystrom, who never appeared before boards of equalization but collected information assiduously.

Long had also to concern himself with grub-infestation and various timber diseases. He had to warn campers not to set fires and persuade the railroads to watch locomotive sparks. He had to make decisions, with approval from his superiors, on the W.T.C. purchase of shares in steam-

ships and schooners. It was his responsibility to work out leases on coal
lands, for which the company got fifteen cents a ton royalty, and to give
grazing permits in the Klamath area to sheepherders who in 1908–1909
paid four and a half cents an acre. Every aspect of labor relations was his
province: the medical care of employees, the support of the Yacolt hospital, the fixing of wages. In these years he took the initiative in employing
E. T. Allen, an able district forester, to organize all the existing forest-fire
patrol associations of the Pacific Northwest, then thirteen in number and
steadily increasing, into a regional body uniting federal, state, and private
timberland interests for purposes of conservation.[36] Long frequently gave
the press informative interviews on matters of public interest, appeared
regularly at lumbermen's gatherings, and made himself an effective
speaker.

In the battle against forest fires he became one of the principal northwestern leaders. Down to 1902 more timber in the Pacific States had been
burned than logged. The embers of the Yacolt fire that year had not
cooled before he was in the field with demands for organized action. He
wrote Victor Beckman, editor of the *Pacific Lumber Trade Journal,* on
September 20th asking the magazine to poll lumbermen on the best
methods of preventing fires and on the state legislation needed, promising
that the W.T.C. would pay for the work. An identical letter went to
George Cornwall, editor of the *Oregon Timberman.* The myth that the
humid coast forests would never be the scene of huge conflagrations like
those in the East was dead, he declared; so was the myth that fire would
not run in green timber, for in the Coweeman Valley a quarter of a billion
feet of green forest had burned. The State of Washington might lose its
500,000 acres of timber on school lands; every tree burned meant a sheer
loss of taxable values and railroad freight, while the housebuilder and
furniture maker were gravely injured. "I thoroughly believe," he wrote,
"that we will have greater fires in Washington in the future than we have
had in the past, unless something of a more vigorous nature is done to
guard against such disasters."

The Northwest, Long kept repeating, must study the fire laws of
states like Minnesota and Pennsylvania. It should insist on safeguards
when loggers burned their slashings, should see that locomotives installed
spark arresters, and should educate hunters, fishermen, and other campers.
"Thoughtlessness may destroy Washington's greatest source for future
development and prosperity." Late in October he met with Oregon lumbermen who appointed a committee to draft a fire-control bill to be laid
before the next legislature; and he took simultaneous steps to have Washington lumbermen hold a similar meeting.[37]

It was partly because of his efforts that Washington, though moving
at first slowly and clumsily, in time took national primacy in work for

forest-fire prevention. The law of 1903 was ineffective. But two years later the legislature passed a new act establishing a state board of forest commissioners empowered to appoint county wardens and deputies as enforcement officers. As the appropriation made was only $7,500 for two years' work, the legislature shortly authorized the State Fire Warden to solicit gifts from private interests. In 1906 a long list of timber, lumber, and logging companies contributed $9,650, of which $4,000 came from the Weyerhaeuser Timber Company. The state laws were continuously tightened. A closed season (May 1–October 1), in which all fires without permit were forbidden, was in time established; timber owners were made responsible to their neighbors for any blaze starting on their land; firefighting equipment was accumulated; and the number of wardens on patrol eventually rose into the hundreds.

Meanwhile, Long became the principal leader in a cooperating private organization, the Washington Forest Fire Association. In 1908, under his captaincy, owners of some 2,500,000 acres in the state met, elected officers, levied an assessment of two cents an acre for costs, and began collaborating with the State Forestry Department. Long was president, and George C. Joy, who later became State Supervisor of Forestry, was Chief Fire Warden.

By 1913 the association was spending nearly $45,000 annually, had a patrol force of eighty men busy throughout the summer, was urging compliance with a set of practical rules for all logging camps, and was giving close supervision to the disposal of slash by lumbermen and ranchers. That happened to be a year of few fires. Yet association rangers extinguished or helped extinguish some six hundred, nearly a hundred of some magnitude. The association that year undertook a new type of effort, the construction of fireguard trails in zones of special danger. This meant the felling of all dead trees and snags over a stretch thirty to forty rods in width and the clearing of a roadway ten to fifteen feet wide of all logs, brush, and leaves, so that it would be possible to stop a fire on this strip of open land.[38]

When World War I came, however, much remained to be done. Oregon in 1904, prodded by Long, Ben Ames, and other managers of timber properties, had established some elementary protections and required every timber owner to pay his share of costs on an acreage basis. Five years later the state had created its own forestry department. However, it never appropriated enough money; in 1908, for example, Long offered $4,000 to help meet a shortage of $8,000 on condition that other lumber interests would pay the remaining half. Washington also pinched its pennies for many years. What Long called the "characteristic graft" of northwestern government occasionally crept into the state organizations, so that one potent reason for forming the Washington Forest Fire

Association was to combat it. Altogether, in 1914 progressive leaders felt that only a beginning had been made.

7

The most important decisions on policy that the Timber Company made just before the war were all interrelated: to begin paying dividends, to slacken the pace of land purchasing, and to inaugurate manufacturing at Everett on a larger scale. Money distributed in dividends could obviously not go into timberland, while a decision that the northwestern domain had reached its full size meant that the time had come for its intensified use.

After a decade with no returns, the stockholders began to exert a tremendous pressure on Long. They were acutely conscious that they had put $12,500,000 into stock. At the annual directors' meeting early in 1910 a resolution to pay dividends when enough money accumulated was passed unanimously. Frederick Weyerhaeuser himself shared the general sentiment. "If our receipts continue about as they have," he wrote Long on September 20, 1910, "don't you think we would be justified in making say four 1 per cent dividends a year?" He thought they might begin at once.

Long, however, demurred on several grounds. The Timber Company was paying heavy tax bills—a total of $906,000 for the three years 1907–1910; in partnership with the Tacoma Commercial Club, it was erecting a handsome office building in Tacoma that would cost it $100,000 that year and more the next; it was still laying down cash for Northern Pacific lands, and it needed more money for the Thorsen purchases. He explained also that the lumber business was poor, "a steady drag at low prices."[39]

But in 1911 even the cautious Long could not withstand the pressure, and the first dividends went out—2 percent for the year on the capital, still $12,500,000. Next year 4 percent was paid. The market had improved, the Everett mill now sawed nearly 70,000,000 feet of lumber, and improvements in drying and shipping practices helped raise the profit. "People out here," Long wrote after Wilson's election, "are not at all disturbed at the results, most of us think that we will have a pretty good administration even if it is Democratic"(!)[40] In 1913 the profits justified dividends of 14 percent and in 1914 of 4 percent. Then they stopped until the last year of the war; earnings were used to pay taxes and to finance expansion of manufacturing plants.

For the diminution of land purchases, various reasons existed beyond the wish to pay dividends. Some stockholders thought the holdings great enough. Several years earlier F. S. Bell had written Long: "We feel conservative about expanding a company which is already large and somewhat vulnerable." Perhaps by "vulnerable" he meant open to public criticism as well as economic vicissitude. At any rate, by the date of Wilson's election such criticism was certainly swelling. The Bureau of Corporations in the report by Herbert Knox Smith, treated elsewhere, arraigned the major owners of timberland as inert monopolists waiting greedily for huge unearned increments. "The largest holders are cutting little of their timber," it declared. "They thus reserve to themselves the incalculable profits which are still to accrue with the growth of the country. . . ." This official charge coincided with the grumbling of would-be timber buyers about "lumber hogs." The fact that the price of timberland was at a peak in 1912–1913, which it would not attain again for a generation, lent energy to these fulminations.

The imminent opening of the Panama Canal and the growing exhaustion of timber in the older states were among the factors that made enlarged manufacturing facilities in the Puget Sound region desirable. Throughout 1913 Long and Boner, with the St. Paul executives, were studying plans. In May, 1914, work began on a huge electric sawmill, to be called Mill B, on the river side at Everett—and with that opened a new chapter in the history of the operations in the Pacific Northwest.

NOTES

1. Weyerhaeuser's purchase of about 200,000 acres of Oregon lands in July 1902 was west of the Cascades.
2. Long Papers, Warren to Long, Oct. (no day), 1902.
3. See Johansen and Gates, 602; Holbrook, *Burning an Empire*, 110–114; Portland *Oregonian*, Sept. and Oct., 1902, and numerous letters to Long in Long Papers. W. S. Lysons wrote Long on Sept. 15, 1902: "I have talked with several people from the Coweeman and they all agree that the newspaper accounts of the fire are very much exaggerated." But this was one locality.
4. Long Papers, Jan. 28, 1903.
5. FEW Papers, FW to Long, Dec. 30, 1902.
6. FEW Record, 706–708. Weyerhaeuser at first favored leasing the Yacolt spur, but Long preferred making the railroad responsible for maintenance and operation. It is clear

that St. Paul granted him a large measure of control over operations.
7. Long Papers, Long to FEW, March 12, 1903. Very little hemlock or cedar was salvaged from the burn.
8. Long Papers, Long to Davis, May 27, 1903, and Long to Weyerhaeuser, June 18, 1903. The Portland manufacturers were the Peninsula Lumber Co. and Portland Mill Co. Decisions first for and then against mill-building can be traced in the directors' minute books. The two special companies were the Twin Falls Logging Company and the Lake River Boom Company.
9. This joint operation was the Coweeman Driving and Rafting Co., bought late in 1904. See Long Papers, Oct.–Dec., 1904.
10. See review of prices in WLB Co. Papers, Boner to Long, Feb. 18, 1908.

11. FEW Record, 702–703, treats this matter.

12. Warren's health had failed. See Long Papers, James Gowen to Long, July 11, 1907. Boner was soon paid $6,000 a year plus 5 percent of net mill profits.

13. *Ibid.*, Long to Boner, Jan. 12, 1912.

14. WLB Co., Papers, Boner to Long, March 24, 1913. J. L. Bridge, working out of Tacoma, had direct charge of the woods camps of the Weyerhaeuser Logging Co.

15. Figures from *WC Lbrmn.*, Feb., 1907, 357. The car requirement rose to 66,000 in 1906. Marshall covered sales in North Dakota and Minnesota; J. M. Barber covered Montana; and from 1910 J. C. Summers sold in Nebraska.

16. The zone rate to the Dakotas in 1904 had been 40 cents and the rate to Omaha 50 cents; lumbermen that year had wished to extend the 40-cent territory clear to the Missouri River. They changed the old slogan "Fifty-four forty or fight" to "Forty or fight." On Nov. 1, 1907, the rates to the points named went to 60 cents. In 1908 the Interstate Commerce Commission slightly reduced the tariffs. See the annual reports of the Commission for background.

17. Long Papers; Long wrote McCormick, Aug. 7, 1906, "This is a good send-off."

18. For example, *ibid.*, Long to FEW, Feb. 23, 1911, suggested a study of the possibilities of lumberyards at New York, Boston, or Philadelphia.

19. *Ibid.*, May 15, 1906. The *Yosemite*, then just being completed, was undamaged.

20. FEW Papers, FEW to C. H. Davis.

21. Long Papers, Long to C. R. McCormick, F. P. Deering, and others, July 31 and early Aug., 1906.

22. *Ibid.*, to S. T. McKnight, Nov. 30, 1906; *Nation*, LXXIV, 1907, pp. 122–123, 253.

23. The depression can be fully traced in the Long Papers, the WT Co. Papers, directors' minutes, and the annual reports 1907–1908.

24. Long Papers, Boner to WTC, May 22, 1908, and Feb.–May, 1908, *passim*. Better close the mill than take such prices, wrote Long. Boner (July 30, 1908) later ordered Marshall to stop selling at the ruling prices.

25. *Ibid.*, Nov., 1907–March, 1908, *passim* and Long to P. Connacher, Nov. 11, 1907. Letters and memoranda in the files of the Cowlitz County and other logging companies indicate Weyerhaeuser paid more than the scale recommended by the Loggers' Association.

26. U.S. Bureau of Corporations, *Report on the Lumber Industry*, I, 38–39; Long Papers, Long to P. J. Bernard, Nov. 8, 1907.

27. Nevins, ed., *Frémont, Narratives*, 308 ff., 485 ff.

28. Cf. Heald, "Cascade Holiday," in Peattie, ed., *The Cascades*, 107 ff.; U.S.D.A. Yearbook, *Trees*, 800–802; WSC Papers, Report by W. B. Fehran to WS Co. on Ponderosa pine.

29. Long Papers, Long to F. P. Deering, Dec. 16, 1905; Long to F. S. Bell, March 27, 1906.

30. On the Klamath railroad see Long Papers, F. P. Deering to Long, May 19, 1911; and Long to Bell, April 26, 1912. Ensuing quotations are from the Long Papers.

31. Long Papers, May–Nov., 1906, and especially Long to FW, Oct. 26, 1906.

32. The annual reports 1905–1914 and Long's letters give reliable statistics on purchases, sales, and aggregate holdings.

33. Puter was given a two-year jail term for his part in Oregon land frauds, emerging in 1907 to collaborate with Horace Stevens in the book named. In his introduction Stevens speaks of "Weyerhaeuser with his tainted timber wealth," and James J. Hill "with his Rainier Mountain Forest Reserve steal," but the text contains nothing whatever on Weyerhaeuser.

34. Figures in FEW Record, 683 ff.

35. Secondary materials on Long are few; but James Stevens offers in his Reminiscences valuable material sup-

plementing the letter files. See also the *Amer. Lbrmn.*, July 6, 1929, especially the article "A Genius in Foresight and Organizing Skill."

36. This body became known as the Western Forestry and Conservation Association, organized at Spokane in 1909. By 1913 it included thirty associates for forest fire patrol work. See its pamphlet, *Forty Years of Western Forestry.*

37. Long Papers contain the voluminous correspondence on this subject, especially for the period June 27–Nov. 8, 1902. See also Joy, "The Fight With Fire," *WC Lbrmn.*, LIV, May 1, 1928, p. 648. The Portland *Oregonian* and other newspapers took important parts in the effort.

38. See Washington State Forester and Fire Warden, *Reports,* 1907–1914. Oregon State Forestry Department, *Reports,* 1909–1914; Chief Forester,

U.S. Forest Service, *Reports,* 1903–1913; files of lumber periodicals. The Washington Forest Fire Assn., with offices in Seattle, issued annually a well-printed and illustrated report. Long was partly responsible for drafting a model law to meet Oregon's forest-fire problem.

39. Long Papers, Long to FW, Sept. 24, Dec. 28, 1910; Long to O. H. Ingram, Dec. 28, 1910; WTC Annual Report, 1913. The office building cost the company just under $300,000 in all. At a later date the Timber Company bought the other half-interest in the building. Authorized capital of the company was $15,000,000, but the additional $2,500,000 was not used, and the authority was canceled in 1914.

40. Long Papers, Long to F. H. L. Cotten, Nov. 11, 1912.

XIV

Idaho: Promises and Realities

Nowhere in the Far Northwest did the Weyerhaeuser group cherish brighter hopes at the beginning of the century than in Idaho. Their enterprises in that land of peaks, canyons, lava beds, sagebrush barrens, fertile valleys, and towering forests included a preposterous mountain railroad, fantastic adventures with logs on precipitous streams, flume building, a mill fire, lawsuits, and one of the most remarkable company towns in the annals of lumbering. But in the forty years after 1900, more disappointment than success was recorded.

No state has more illogical boundaries than Idaho. It is a great solid rectangle of territory, based on Nevada and Utah, atop which is superimposed a jagged wedge running far north between Montana and Washington to reach the Canadian boundary. A lumberman might compare it to a square stump with a big splinter of the original trunk jutting upward at the top.

This curiously shaped state would be awkward enough if it were physically all one piece, but instead it is cut into sharply differing districts. The Salmon River, churning from east to west through a deep gorge filled with rapids, cataracts, and whirlpools, so effectually separates north Idaho from south that, until the painful construction of a north-south highway in the period between the two world wars, travelers had to make circuits into adjoining states to get from one section to the other. The Salmon rises in the snowy heights of the Sawtooth Range and for almost its whole length dives amid abrupt peaks, deep tributary gorges, and tracts of almost inaccessible Douglas fir, larch, cedar, white pine, ponderosa, and Engelmann spruce. The continental United States has no wilder land.

Three different parts of Idaho were to interest the Weyerhaeuser associates: two north of the Salmon River canyon and one south. The most beautiful and most difficult was at the very top of the Panhandle, just below the Canadian line. Here lies the country of the Kootenai River, Lake Pend Oreille, and Lake Coeur d'Alene, an American Switzerland, Vardis Fisher has called it, with dense forests, high mountain valleys, and racing streams. The dark mantle of timber is kept moist by frequent rains in summer and snows up to twelve feet deep in winter. Winds from the Pacific give the district a milder climate than the Rockies farther south, and chinook winds often melt the drifts into sudden torrents. At the very top, the Kootenai and the Clark Fort of the Columbia foam across the Panhandle. Farther down the St. Joe and the Coeur d'Alene flow into the lake of the latter name. Here grow Douglas fir, white fir, spruce, ponderosa, lodgepole pine (commonest of all Idaho evergreens but hardly commercial), red cedar, larch, and the western white pine, aristocrat of the woods, sometimes reaching two hundred feet in height.[1]

Farther south, but still north of the Salmon, lies the gentler country of the Clearwater River, which empties into the Snake, the two streams cradling Lewiston in their fork. The cold, rapid Clearwater has branches —Potlatch and Orofino creeks, and the North, Middle and South forks. This river system extends completely across Idaho, draining the Bitter Root Range. It was on the Clearwater that the Reverend Henry H. Spalding planted his pioneer mission among the Nez Percés in 1836. It was near Lewiston that one of the first gold-mining rushes developed and in Lewiston that the first territorial government was established in 1863 in a one-story wooden shack with a false front.[2] In Lewiston, too, appeared Idaho's first newspaper, the *Golden Age,* 1862–1865.

The third area in which the Weyerhaeuser group acquired interests lay below the Salmon. Just north of the great bend where the Snake becomes the boundary line with Oregon, three small rivers, the Boise, the Payette, and the Weiser, flow into it. In the so-called Boise Basin gold had been discovered in 1862. Noisy, lawless mining camps—Placerville, Centerville, Bannock (later Idaho City)—rose and fell. Boise succeeded Lewiston as the capital and in 1887 became the terminus of a branch of the Union Pacific system. By 1900 the lower valleys of the three small rivers were showing the promise they have since redeemed as a rich fruit and grain district, famous for cherries and apples. But higher up, the streams led into tremendous reaches of ponderosa, white fir, larch, lodgepole pine, and Engelmann spruce, the characteristic Idaho trees.

Idaho was still an untamed country when the century began. Much of it, for that matter, was wild even when World War II opened, with lakes that had never been described and streams never mapped. Though large tracts of timber had been cut by 1940, still larger stands could apparently never be reached and harvested.³ If Weyerhaeuser and his co-investors had known what lay before them, they would not have raced into the state.

2

For the Idaho story begins with a race. In August, 1900, two rival timber experts, each with a crew, were exploring the upper Clearwater Valley for white pine. The agent for wealthy lumberman W. E. McCord of Chippewa Falls, Wisconsin, was named Bussell. The other, an agent for Frederick Weyerhaeuser and some friends, was a Maine Yankee by birth and a Michigan man by experience named Charles O. Brown. Each expert knew that a body of desirable timber lay in an unsurveyed area within the bend of the North Fork. The first to make the selections, fix the legal boundary lines, file descriptions at the federal land office in Lewiston, and offer payment would get the timberland. Success might hang on an hour of time.

By the summer of 1900 a number of important lumbermen in the Middle West had awakened simultaneously to Idaho's possibilities. At the Chicago World's Fair in 1893 Weyerhaeuser saw a graphic display of the state's splendid reaches of timber. Charles O. Brown had heard of them, too, and in 1894 had moved west to the Clearwater region, where his son Nat and his son-in-law, Theodore Fohl, joined him. The three cruised the forests and selected extensive timberlands for the state. They realized that large capital would be needed for any private lumber enterprises. By occasional letters, Brown encouraged Weyerhaeuser—and also J. A. Humbird, active in the White River Lumber Company with the Rock Islander, in the general idea of an Idaho investment.

In 1900 the idea suddenly crystallized. Humbird and Weyerhaeuser bought Mount Rainier scrip from the Northern Pacific for approximately 40,000 acres, paying about $250,000, sent it to Lewiston, and dispatched an agent to the Clearwater to spur on the two Browns in choosing and filing land claims.⁴

The two crews, Brown's and Bussell's, finished their surveys of overlapping tracts the same September afternoon. Bussell was the first to start for the railhead at Orofino. Nat Brown, chosen for his youthful vigor, set out after him on horseback. The forest was dense and the trail steep; darkness came on with a drizzling rain. Brown's only light was a "palouser," or gallon lard-pail with a tallow candle stuck through its side. The young man spurred at dangerous speed along rugged divides and rocky creeks. After midnight, having covered nearly twenty-five miles, he reached a rancher's house. The smell of fresh steaming coffee apprised him that Bussell was inside refreshing himself. Stealthily entering the stable, Brown found a fresh horse waiting there, hastily saddled it, turned both his own and Bussell's jaded horse loose, and galloped off. He was ahead!

Even so, Nat Brown felt unsafe, for he knew that McCord had a locomotive with steam up at Orofino ready to speed Bussell down to Lewiston. Brown himself would have to take a slow local passenger train later that morning. Galloping into town at daybreak, Nat went to Paine's Hotel, put his horse in the livery stable, and accosted Paine. "Is my engine ready?" he demanded. "Yes," responded Paine, "and I have a letter in the hotel office authorizing you to use it." As he handed over the letter, Paine added: "You don't look as old as I expected you to be." Boarding the locomotive, Nat reached Lewiston around seven, hunted up the holder of the scrip, and spent two hours copying out the boundary descriptions from his minutes taken in the woods. The moment the land office opened he was ready to file. He was just completing the task when McCord, who was expecting Bussell, hurried in. Nat's record of this confrontation is a magnificent understatement: "He seemed greatly surprised and agitated."

Thus a foundation was laid for the Clearwater Timber Company, organized under Washington laws on December 13, 1900, with its head office in Tacoma and an original capital stock of $500,000. J. A. Humbird was the first president, Weyerhaeuser vice-president, and John E. Glover, a lumberman from New Richmond, Wisconsin, secretary. A dozen years later the capital was increased to $3,000,000, and to $6,000,-000 in 1924, then to $9,000,000 in 1926. As owner of one of the finest bodies of Western white pine in the nation, acquired at from $6 to $7 an acre, the company seemed almost certain of rich profits. Additional purchases were made from time to time, until it held about 220,000 acres by 1927, with well over 2,000,000,000 feet of white pine and an equal amount of other species.

But instead of profits, the operation showed heavy losses for years. Income was negligible, while carrying charges from 1913, when careful accounts began to be kept, to the opening of the sawmill in 1927 amounted to $2,395,337. Taxes alone totaled more than $1,000,000 for the period.[5]

Simultaneously, the Weyerhaeuser associates invaded the Pend Oreille-Kootenai district in the northern part of the Panhandle. Here the Northern Pacific threads across the state on its way from Missoula, Montana, to Spokane. Early in 1900 the railroad's land commissioner, William H. Phipps, had called the attention of Weyerhaeuser and Humbird to the white pine in this district. Edward Rutledge became interested, and after sending out a crew of Wisconsin timber estimators, followed in person with Frederick E. Weyerhaeuser. The pair long remembered how they

got off the train at Sandpoint after dark, found the local hotel jammed by
a ball, sat up all night in the station, and at dawn received the congratulations of men driven out of their rooms by the abundant insect life. Inspecting the pine, red fir, larch, and cedar of the Priest River Valley, they
decided it was worth buying. Since the Northern Pacific estimators were
Douglas fir experts who saw little value in this Idaho timber, the Weyerhaeuser associates were able to get the first tracts on extremely favorable
terms.

The upshot was a swift burst of activity. Humbird, Rutledge, and
Weyerhaeuser & Denkmann took over the Sandpoint Lumber Company,
which owned a single-band mill in the hamlet of that name and an ap-
purtenant body of timberland. They vested the properties of this concern
and the Priest River timber purchased from the Northern Pacific in the
new Humbird Lumber Company, organized December 6, 1900, with a
capital of half a million and head offices at Tacoma. J. A. Humbird, president of the new company, took hold with energy. As already noted, he
and Weyerhaeuser sent his promising son, T. J. Humbird, to Sandpoint
as manager on a salary of $3,000 a year.

The young man justified the high expectations held of him. He converted the Sandpoint mill to a two-band operation, and when it was
burned in 1907, rebuilt it with improvements. Four years earlier he had
purchased an old single-band sawmill at Kootenai, five miles away, and
greatly bettered it. At Sandpoint and Kootenai he provided ample log-
storage facilities in the shore waters of Lake Pend Oreille. Much later
(1917) he bought another single-band mill on the Pend Oreille River in
Idaho opposite Newport, Washington. Wise purchases of timberlands, especially one from the Northern Pacific in 1910, provided ample logs for
the three mills.[6]

T. J. Humbird, in short, made an enviable name for himself in the
annals of the Weyerhaeuser group and gladdened the heart of his father
until the latter's death in 1911. From the initial operation of the Sandpoint mill in 1902 to the cessation of sawing by all three plants of the
firm in 1931 their combined output totaled 2,052,486,000 board feet.
The consistent earnings of the Humbird Lumber Company, its paid-in
capital having been raised to $1,000,000 in 1904, was long the only
bright spot in the general Idaho gloom.[7]

In sharp contrast to Humbird's record stood that of another north
Idaho enterprise, the Edward Rutledge Timber Company. Fired with enthusiasm for Idaho white pine in the watersheds of the St. Joe and St.
Maries rivers, during 1901 Rutledge agreed to buy from the Northern
Pacific up to 29,440 acres (only 25,520 actually deeded) of its unsurveyed lands for Weyerhaeuser & Rutledge. By 1902 Charles A. Weyerhaeuser also became so enamored of white pine prospects in the same

general area that he and William Deary joined other groups in purchasing state timberlands, their share being approximately 30,000 acres. As we have seen in Chapter XI, this went to the Potlatch Lumber Company. Rutledge put his holdings into a new Washington corporation, the Edward Rutledge Timber Company, organized in October, 1902, with an authorized capital of $200,000 and Rutledge as president. He took 675 shares, the Weyerhaeusers 1,225, and the general manager, Frank J. Davies, 200.

Davies, a former employee of the Northern Pacific, plunged into buying more timber, consolidating holdings into blocks, and preparing to build a mill. By the end of 1916 acquisitions of land had mounted to 116,650 acres, some of which had been sold and a few hundred logged. Salvage of trees damaged by fires in 1910 and 1913 had led to most of the logging, and annual fire threats had caused Davies to take an active part in voluntary associations for timber protection. Extensive logging began in 1915, the year the directors appointed Huntington Taylor, son of a president of Vassar College and an undergraduate friend of Rudolph Weyerhaeuser, to apply his mill experience acquired at Cloquet to the erection of a plant at Coeur d'Alene. To bring logs from Marble Creek, the area of the company's best stand of white pine, Davies built a wooden flume. Though this construction was ultimately replaced by a railroad, it served for a time to convey the logs across the intervening county to the St. Joe River. They were then driven to Lake Coeur d'Alene and towed to the mill, which began sawing April 1, 1916, and averaged a cut of more than 45,000,000 board feet per year for its first five years.

In spite of the promising performance up to 1920, Hunt Taylor, who became general manager in 1917, never succeeded in making the Rutledge Company profitable. Tax assessments and tax rates both seemed high to him, and interest charges were undoubtedly heavy for the size of the operation. Even after $2,300,000 of outstanding loans had been converted to shares in 1917, the long-term debt remained at $1,189,010 and rose to a peak of almost $5,000,000 six years later. Investors received not one single dividend from 1902 through 1930, when the mill and lands were taken over by Potlatch Forests, Inc.[8]

Northern Idaho provided still another unsatisfactory showing by a Weyerhaeuser enterprise—the Bonners Ferry Lumber Company. This corporation was formed late in 1902 in Wisconsin to take over some 13,000 acres of timberland, logging contracts, a mill site, sawmill machinery, and riparian rights at Bonners Ferry on the rushing Kootenai River. The properties had been acquired by two men from New Richmond, Wisconsin. One of the group of investors was a business friend of Frederick Weyerhaeuser, and ultimately interested him in the project. The initial capitalization of $220,000 was raised to $332,000 in 1905. A year earlier the one-band mill had begun sawing white pine, ponderosa, fir, and larch in a setting of exceptional beauty. "The land spreads out in all directions like a great green carpet," later wrote a contributor to a company newspaper, "flecked generously at this time of year [fall] with the gold of tamaracks disrobing for a winter's sleep. The folds of the forest carpet form deep valleys over which the mountains tower in quiet dignity, outlined in sharp, rugged grandeur against the sky." It was a scene of exceptional grandeur.

The beauty of the district turned out to be the only advantageous element in the situation. Everything went contrary to hopes and plans. Driving logs down the rocky and rapid Kootenai was difficult, but the Great Northern, the only railroad in the region, could not carry logs through tunnels, and confined its log-hauling services to short transfers. Facilities for holding logs at Bonners Ferry were inadequate, even with the aid of a fin boom, and flood waters at times inundated the drying yard. The dry kiln was not large enough to handle all the mill throughput. The mill itself burned in 1909 and was rebuilt with two headrigs. This change necessitated heavy outlays in timber to provide enough logs for the mill. An investment of more than $200,000 in Canadian timber tributary to the Kootenai ultimately was lost when Canadian authorities refused to allow logs to be transported across the boundary. Other timber holdings were inefficiently scattered on streams along the Great Northern line from Eureka, Montana, to Bonners Ferry and still farther northwest along the Kootenai. Freight rate differentials operated against the company, which sent its lumber into Montana and the Dakotas, and efforts to minimize the differentials were never successful.

Earnings never measured up to expenses. Before the opening of the first mill in 1904, the managers had already borrowed, and the debt piled up year after year; the borrowing limit had been raised to $1,500,000 by 1911. The only advantage to the Weyerhaeusers was that they supplied the bulk of the loans at 6 percent interest.

Time after time after 1913 members of the Weyerhaeuser family proposed to take their loss and discontinue operations at Bonners Ferry. On each occasion, however, either a director or R. H. McCoy, who bought some shares at the time he became general manager in 1906, pointed to favorable prospects for the future. Production rose from slightly less than 13,000,000 board feet in 1904 to more than 50,000,000 in 1913, the peak year, then tapered off before coming to a stop shortly after McCoy's death in 1926.[9]

3

Not far north of Lewiston and the Clearwater a little river, the Palouse, rises in the Idaho mountains and flows across the Washington boundary to join the Snake. One of its tributaries is called Potlatch Creek. The Palouse-Potlatch forests and the Clearwater forests must be distinguished, though they lie in juxtaposition and at points seem to merge. Here in the Palouse basin was to rise the most ambitious of the early Idaho enterprises, the Potlatch Lumber Company. "There was an atmosphere of importance and superiority about it, a sort of grandiosity that at times seemed to annoy father," wrote F. E. Weyerhaeuser. "It enjoyed its full share of newspaper publicity."

After making the initial purchases on the Upper Clearwater, through the Northland Pine Company the Weyerhaeuser group competed with many others in buying state timber at auction sales in 1901 and 1902. William Deary as president of Northland and J. B. Kehl as manager then turned to buying homesteaders' claims and other lands in the Palouse-Potlatch area. Henry Turrish of the Wisconsin Log & Lumber Company was the chief competitor, though by 1902 Deary and Turrish were buying state timber jointly. By this time the second generation of Weyerhaeusers, Mussers, Lairds, and Nortons was actively on the stage. Apparently at the suggestion of R. D. Musser at a meeting in St. Paul, representatives of the various families agreed to combine their Palouse Valley undertakings in one company for more effective purchasing and ultimate manufacturing.

The result was the incorporation, in March, 1903, of the Potlatch Lumber Company, initially capitalized at $3,000,000 and later raised to $8,000,000. Charles Weyerhaeuser was elected president, Henry Turrish vice president, and Clifton R. Musser, son of Peter M., treasurer, with William Deary as general manager and F. H. Thatcher of the Laird, Norton Co. as the prime legal adviser.[10] As earlier noted, the assets of Northland Pine were transferred to Potlatch Lumber for almost $930,000 and those of Wisconsin Log & Lumber for about a quarter as much, both at about 100 percent above original cost. The new firm quickly absorbed some smaller concerns, notably the Palouse River Lumber Company at Palouse, the mill and timberlands together costing about $265,000.

From the outset Deary was general manager. His dynamic energy and imperious temper made him almost as dominant in its policy as was the sagacious George Long in controlling the Weyerhaeuser Timber Company. Men agreed that a great mill would have to be built, but differed as to the site. An early officer relates a story that, if inaccurate in detail, is true in spirit:

A group of directors were seated around a table in a second-floor office above a store in Moscow, Idaho. The room was heated by a pot-bellied wood-burning stove. It was March, and those Idaho springs were bad. The decision these men were trying to make was where the big sawmill would be situated. Sometime during the session Mr. Deary came in from the woods. He pulled

off his boots and was warming and drying his feet and stockings beside this
stove, when he heard the group at the table just about decide to put the mill in
Moscow. He jumped up barefooted, went to the table where the map was spread
out, picked up a lead pencil, and said in his thick Irish brogue: "Gintilmen,
there isn't enough water in Moscow to baptize a bastard! The mill'll go here."
He punched a hole in the big map, and the hole, strangely enough, was exactly
where the mill site of the Potlatch Lumber Company is today, over the Moscow
Mountain, on the Palouse River. Mr. Deary of course was familiar with the
map.[11]

Deary bought the site of the mill and of the future company town of
Potlatch from independent timber owners and ranchers. Beams and lumber came from the Palouse River Lumber Company mill, which he ran
full tilt.

The directors hired W. A. Wilkinson of Minneapolis to plan and
erect as good a sawmill as any in the country. In the fall of 1905 work began on a structure 70 feet high, more than 100 feet wide, and nearly
300 feet long, with a large steel-framed planing mill, a powerhouse, and
a lumber shed adjacent. A Corliss engine with a flywheel twenty-four feet
in diameter drove the machinery, which had a capacity of 135,000,000
board feet per year. The lumberyard, covering sixty-five acres, had forty-
five miles of track for its locomotives and cars. Four band saws, a gang-
saw with forty-six blades, and four double edgers turned the logs from the
great pond into lumber. The dry kilns and sorting shed were of the latest
design. Altogether, the 125 employees present on September 11, 1906,
when Charles Weyerhaeuser, Deary, C. R. Musser, and others set the mill
in motion, had reason to take pride in its completeness and modernity.[12]

These employees, the teamsters, woodsmen, and others had to be
housed, and on two wide-topped hills overlooking the plant the company
built the town of Potlatch with astonishing speed. Deary and his kindly,
public-spirited assistant manager, A. W. Laird, regarded this town planning as a special challenge. When the mill opened, 128 dwellings were
occupied, 35 more were nearly finished, and plans for another 40 had
been accepted. Before long a grade school, high school, hotel, two
churches, and a capacious two-story general store, built of brick, were
ready. For single men two large boardinghouses were provided. One two-
story brick building afforded quarters for a bank, post office, and "opera
house." The main street was soon macadamized, and wooden sidewalks
were laid.

Company towns have a bad name in the United States, but all accounts agree that in its first fifteen years Potlatch was attractive, efficiently
managed, and quite free from any exploitation of the workers in rents or
prices of necessities. Later it declined. After the First World War visitors
found the houses deteriorating, the hotel poor, and the roads out to

Spokane and Pullman almost impassable in winter. After World War II, when the tenants were allowed to buy houses on generous terms, the town improved.[13]

Much of the timber in this wide Clearwater-Palouse-Potlatch area was of the highest quality. One long-famous tree, "The King of the White Pines," on land first taken by Theodore Fohl, was 207 feet high, measured six feet nine inches across the butt, and yielded nearly 29,000 feet of lumber when brought to the Potlatch mill late in 1911.

To bring this attractive timber from the hills and to ship out the finished product, it was necessary to build a railroad. The Washington, Idaho & Montana Railway Company, a million-dollar Maine corporation, was organized in March, 1905. This 45-mile road ran from Palouse, Washington, through Potlatch eastward to Bovill, where it met the Chicago, Milwaukee & St. Paul when that line was eventually completed.[14]

Construction of the W.I.& M. road in 1905–1906 was rapid, and through trains began running in 1907, making flag stops at towns bearing the names of various colleges: Wellesley, Harvard, Yale, Princeton, Stanford, and others.[15] The railroad stimulated not only lumbering but agriculture and even a little mining. It was soon hauling a heavy tonnage of logs, boards, poles, grain, vegetables, and livestock. Logs came down the railroad to the mill; lumber went out on it to the Milwaukee and the Northern Pacific lines. Photographs in the early years show a train of heavy logs cautiously backing down a 12 percent grade, a much larger train of more than a hundred 41-foot flatcars bringing 1,100,000 feet of logs into Potlatch, and steam derricks loading logs from sidings upon cars.

Before 1905 Weyerhaeuser had vainly attempted to persuade executives of the Northern Pacific, a branch of which passed through Palouse, to build the road as a feeder. When the Milwaukee began building through northern Idaho, however, the attitude of the Northern Pacific men sharply changed. Weyerhaeuser had agreed with the Milwaukee's leaders not to sell the W.I.& M. railroad for ten years and to erect a new sawmill at Elk River (built in 1910) to provide more freight. He was not a little astonished, as F. E. Weyerhaeuser tells the story, when President Howard Elliott of the Northern Pacific called at his office in August, 1908, and offered to buy the Washington, Idaho & Montana. Weyerhaeuser explained that he had promised the Milwaukee not to sell it for at least a decade. To this statement Elliott replied that the Northern Pacific would at once construct a line parallel to the W.I.& M. Frederick Weyerhaeuser's face expressed astonishment, swiftly followed by amusement. He called the bluff in a crisp sentence:

"Good, Mr. Elliott! We will give you half of our right of way, and let you use our bridges as far as Potlatch."

Elliott finally offered to pay a total of $2,500,000 in principal and

interest for the W.I.& M., exclusive of the rolling stock. Frederick Weyerhaeuser and the Mussers were very favorable to the sale if the agreement
with the Milwaukee could be changed, F. C. Denkmann less so, and the
Laird, Norton group opposed. Potlatch Lumber continued to own and
operate the railroad in spite of the fact that the Northern Pacific refused
to grant it joint rates until 1922.[16]

Despite its holdings of timberland, reaching about 170,000 acres by
1920,[17] its finely equipped sawmills, its railroad, and other modern facilities, the Potlatch Lumber Company disappointed its owners. It paid
no dividend until 1911, when stockholders got 3 percent. During the war
payments rose to 10 percent. The total for the first twenty years, however, averaged only 3.6 percent a year, a small figure for an industry so
full of risks.

D. T. Mason, who made a careful study of the lumber industry in
the Inland Empire for the years 1909–1914, states that lumbermen agreed
that the business should yield at least 12 percent on investment, or it was
not worthwhile. Studying thirty-odd companies, he found that their actual average net earnings for the period varied from zero in 1914 to 3.2
percent in 1909, the best year. The Potlatch Lumber Company thus did
better than most of its competitors.

Mason's study proves, however, that the whole region stood in an unfavorable position. "Conditions up to the middle of 1915," he writes,
"were becoming worse so rapidly as to threaten serious damage to the
interests of the industry and the public alike."[18]

Frederick Weyerhaeuser used to say ruefully that the name Potlatch,
which signified an Indian feast marked by lavish gifts, was appropriate,
for the giving of money to the company never ended and little came back.
Other stockholders complained still more bitterly. In time it became
plain that serious errors of policy had compounded the difficulties imposed by basic conditions. Deary, a good logger and able woodsman,
knew little about the manufacture and sale of lumber. A. W. Laird, a
banker by training, was inexpert in most problems outside his office
routine.

Their most serious mistake in the long run was in their policy of
"cutting the timber clean." In the mixed stands of the northern Rockies,
the relatively abundant white fir, larch, Engelmann spruce, inland cedar,
and lodgepole pine were much less salable than the white pine, Douglas
fir, and ponderosa pine. Selective cutting, with careful preservation of
seed trees of the better species, would have been wise. Deary and Laird,
however, believed in taking every sizable tree, whether it carried a profit
or a loss. This was a natural result of their early training in the Middle
West, where almost every tree did have value by 1900.

Deary once took Rudolph Weyerhaeuser to the top of a high hill up which he had built a costly logging road. The slopes held little but larch and red fir. Obviously the whole tract should have been left standing, for to cut it meant a loss of $10 or $12 per thousand feet. When Rudolph pointed this out, Deary replied, "We cut everything as we go." This was the attitude at the time of most Idaho lumbermen of similar antecedents.[19]

Laird's motivation was more complex. Proud of the community he had helped create, he frankly avowed that his purpose was to keep the establishment running as long as possible. To some stockholders, he seemed to think of the community first and the company's finances second. Any idea that the cream of the timber might be skimmed off in a few decades and the mill moved would have horrified him. The time came in 1922 when the irritated directors asked the manager to experiment in cutting only white pine and perhaps the best of some other woods. Because Laird, Deary's successor as general manager, could not control his logging bosses, this resolution came to nothing.[20]

On the whole, however, Deary and Laird carried a tremendous burden with far more ability than some dividend-hungry stockholders seemed to comprehend. "I have been crowded pretty hard," Deary wrote F. H. Thatcher in 1905.[21] That summer he was overseeing the construction of the first sections of the W.I.& M. railroad; helping build the Potlatch saw-mill and company town; running the Palouse sawmill; buying timber-land; and keeping an eye on the chain of sixteen retail lumberyards that the company had bought and was expanding in the Inland Empire. He did his best to improve the Potlatch mill. He played a major part in sustaining the fire-patrol work of the Potlatch Timber Association. With Laird, he dealt successfully with labor troubles, minor until World War I days. With Charles A. Weyerhaeuser, he built (1909–1910) the electrically-driven Elk River mill, which, through no fault of his, proved unprofitable.[22] Laird, meanwhile, was virtual city manager of Potlatch, and, as such, diligent and tactful.

No managers, however capable, could cure the fundamental difficulties. The unexpectedly high capital investment, $8,000,000 in shares and $3,557,178 in loans by 1920, was certainly one adverse factor, for the volume of business could not be made consistent with costs. Another difficulty lay in the maintenance of the town, which with its schools, churches, YMCA, and other activities, was costly in time and money. The severe winter climate was an impediment, deep snow shutting down the Elk River mill for months every year. A minor source of worry, little regarded as yet, appeared in insect pests, especially the pine beetle, fir beetle, tussock moth, and spruce budworm.[23] The Idaho land laws, requiring that timber sold by the state be removed within twenty years, after which any remaining stands reverted to it, were so vexatious that unremitting efforts were made to modify them. As noted elsewhere, the Weyerhaeuser interests retained William E. Borah to deal with some of their legal problems. Meanwhile, freight costs penalized this mountain area in competition with other sections.

"There is no doubt in my mind," wrote R. M. Weyerhaeuser in 1921, "that Idaho is entirely out of the running with the South running ten hours a day at fifteen cents per hour and with freight rates 15 percent less than from Idaho to Chicago. I think it is important that the transcontinental lines serving Idaho be advised of this fact."[24]

4

The early undertakings of the Weyerhaeuser group in southern Idaho —Barber Lumber Company on the Boise River and Payette Lumber & Manufacturing Company on the Payette—present the same general patterns as those in the north: bright initial hopes, extensive acquisition of timber, unexpected difficulties in logging and transport, failure of manufacture to justify investment, heavy assessments on stockholders, and a growing sense of frustration. Not until a merger of the principal companies was effected in 1913 did the situation offer substantial promise in place of hazy mirages.

Barber Lumber Company, a Wisconsin corporation with an authorized capital of $150,000, was organized in July, 1902, by James T. Barber, William Carson (son of the first lumberman of that name), C. W. Lockwood (a brother-in-law of Carson), and brothers C. D. Moon and Sumner G. (Jack) Moon. Through their firms—Northwestern Lumber and Valley Lumber companies of Eau Claire, Wisconsin, and Burlington, Iowa—all had been associated with Frederick Weyerhaeuser in Chippewa River operations. But he took no part in starting the enterprise in Idaho, of which Barber was president and Jack Moon secretary. The firm grew out of the purchase, in March, 1902, by Barber and Jack Moon of 25,000 acres of timberland on Grimes and Moore's creeks, tributary to the Boise. The seller was Frank Steunenberg, later governor of Idaho and the victim of a famous murder by an agent of the Western Federation of Miners.[25]

Barber and Jack Moon had to modify almost every plan made for their new firm. They expected to drive logs down the streams to a mill they would build at Boise but soon found this impractical. They then erected a two-band mill and a town, called Barber, six miles north on the river. By 1906 construction was completed, including a dam and a small electric power plant. Meanwhile, Barber and Moon had experienced difficulty in finding competent loggers and even more in driving Grimes and Moore's creeks. Heavy snows choked off logging in the depths of winter; timber had to be cut one season and driven downstream the next, with the result that ponderosa logs stained blue to such an extent that the lumber from them had to be graded low. During the early gold rush placer miners had washed tremendous quantities of mud and sand into the streams and over the flat areas. To be sure that the logs would not be buried in mud or stranded on the innumerable bars, they had to be driven at extremely high water, which carried silt into the Boise River to settle in the log pond behind the dam at the Barber mill. Moon had thought Moore's and Grimes creeks drivable; "Experience proved that my judgment was very bad," he acknowledged in 1937.

In fact, as early as 1906 it was plain that a railroad would have to be built from the mill to the timber. Accordingly, the company hired a man to survey a route and in 1907 got an Idaho charter for the Intermountain Railway Company, the line to run from Barber to Centerville.[26]

This need for a railroad pinpointed the weak financial position of the lumber company. To add to timber holdings and to build the mill, subscribed capital had reached almost $1,000,000 by 1905. In less than a year stockholders were so embarrassed that they turned to the Weyerhaeusers and Laird, Norton Co. for aid. Neither group was willing to lend money, but each bought 1,500 shares at $135 per share ($405,000) as a part of a decision to increase capitalization to $1,500,000. F. S. Bell represented all the new investors on the board of directors and soon discovered that more funds were needed. A relatively large sum was required to construct the railroad into the timber. At the same time, in order to justify such a large expenditure, managers would have to add to the 61,000 acres held in August, 1906. The state had some lands near timber owned by Barber Lumber, but the State Land Board had appraised it at such a high figure that Barber and Moon were reluctant to consider the purchase even if they had the money. In June, 1907, the stockholders decided to postpone indefinitely the purchase of state timber and the construction of the railroad.[27]

Money was getting tighter as the crisis of 1907 approached, but the trigger for the decision to put off action on the timber and the railroad was an investigation of Steunenberg's murder. A federal grand jury was convened in Boise in March, 1907, in connection with an indictment of William B. Haywood of the Western Federation of Miners for complicity in the crime. In the course of the proceedings the murdered man was called a timber thief. In April the United States District Attorney, partly for personal reasons, then secured indictments, later made joint, of Steunenberg, Barber Lumber, and William E. Borah (the company's attorney) for conspiracy to defraud the government in acquiring timberlands. Barber, Moon, and numerous dummy entrymen were also named in the joint indictment, though Borah alone insisted on a separate trial and won acquittal in the fall of 1907. The time was certainly not ripe for further expansion of activity.

In July, 1908, William Carson, recently chosen as president to replace Barber, announced suspension of operations of the mill. "We cannot go on," he told reporters, "until all these controversies with the government have been cleaned up. Aside from any other considerations we cannot, during the pendency of these matters, continue our negotiations with the state for timberland that we must have in order to conduct our business here in a profitable manner. Unless we can build a railroad into the timber, the business cannot be satisfactorily conducted, and without the holdings of the state referred to there would be no use building a railroad."[28]

By that time the stockholders had agreed to raise the authorized capital of Barber Lumber another $500,000. Actually, only 30 percent of the amount authorized was subscribed, and the remainder was later rescinded. After the expenditure of the new funds for properties of two small lumber companies, chiefly for their timber, Barber Lumber's total investment exceeded $1,600,000, of which only $50,000 was in the form of loans from stockholders.[29] Prospects for successful operations were dark indeed and would remain so until legal and economic obstacles could be removed.

Not until 1912 was the legal hurdle removed. Lower courts consistently took the position that there was no evidence that Barber, Moon, or their company had knowledge of any frauds committed by those men who had transmitted lands to Steunenberg for sale to the Barber Lumber Company. The case finally went to the Federal District Court at San Francisco, and in February, 1912, the names of the company and its officers were cleared of the charge of conspiracy to defraud the government. The *Idaho Daily Statesman* noted that the decision meant much to Boise, for if the company's plans for expansion were consummated, upward of 1,500 men might soon be employed in the woods and in the mill.[30]

Unrecorded by the reporter was the fact that successful operation hinged on the building of a railroad, the purchase of state timber, and a merger with Payette Lumber & Manufacturing Company, whose stockholders had to be assured that such a merger was to their advantage. In truth, at one stage the affairs of that firm had reached almost as formidable an impasse as those of Barber Lumber, but in 1912 the prospects of the enterprise on the Payette were much brighter than those of its sister on the Boise.

Payette Lumber & Manufacturing was chartered in Minnesota in December, 1902, with an authorized capital of $500,000. It took over stumpage and timberlands in the Payette Basin acquired by William Deary for Northland Pine and Henry Turrish for Wisconsin Log & Lumber companies. The nucleus was 32,904 acres of state stumpage bought for $183,620 on November 10, 1902. During that same year Deary had Cobban & Casey, land brokers, buy and place scrip on various other lands, and also arranged to purchase some tracts held by that firm. Deary, blocking up holdings in the Payette Valley, proceeded on the conviction that "if a little of this timber is a good thing, a whole lot of it would be better." The Musser and the Weyerhaeuser groups (the four brothers) each owned 30 percent of the first stock issued. William Musser, son of Richard, became the first president and most active stockholder in the company. The secretary and first general manager, F. W. Kehl, was replaced in 1904 by E. M. Hoover, who had learned the lumber business as a salesman in the Pine Tree Lumber Company at Little Falls.[31]

Hoover did his work well. He picked up valuable timber year after year, usually at relatively low rates. Total holdings on May 1, 1905, amounted to 98,000 acres of timber, estimated to yield 935,056,000 board feet, of which 680,000,000 was ponderosa. Average cost was calculated to be 63 cents per thousand. By the end of 1913 Payette Lumber & Manufacturing owned 153,000 acres, estimated to cut 1,485,000,000 board feet at an original cost of $1,096,000. Though additional general expense items had reached $120,000 by that date, and the company had paid another $185,000 in taxes, Hoover had labored diligently to keep expenses to a minimum and to keep appraisals for tax purposes as low as possible.[32]

Through no fault of his own, Hoover experienced greater difficulty in providing for transport of logs than in acquiring land. Because a few small batches of logs had already been driven down the Payette, Deary and Will Musser concluded that, with the addition of dams and other improvements, large quantities could be handled. A franchise for improving the river was acquired. Hoover then had the task of supervising the building of a dam at the head of Black Rock Canyon on the North Fork and an eighteen-mile road along that stream to Smith's Ferry. By 1908, after annoying difficulties with contractors, the tasks were finished at a total cost of $150,000. But before Payette Lumber & Manufacturing floated a single log downstream, careful inquiry convinced the officers that the rocky Payette would broom many logs entrusted to it.[33]

Nevertheless, the expenditures for improving the Payette may have been partly justified, as Hoover later thought. They probably persuaded the Oregon Short Line, a part of the Union Pacific system, that Payette Lumber & Manufacturing seriously intended to bring logs from the forest to a mill at Emmett or somewhere in the vicinity. Both logs and lumber would provide lucrative traffic. Perhaps an even greater pressure on the Oregon Short Line was recurring reports of competitive building into the area by the Chicago & North Western, the Burlington, the Northern

Pacific, and the Milwaukee lines. In any case, in 1911 the Short Line began extending its rails northward to the Payette Lakes. Within two years
Payette Lumber & Manufacturing could be sure of getting sound logs at
reasonable cost from its lands to Emmett, where plans had already been
made to erect a sawmill.[34]

As early as 1910 Hoover had also surmounted a legal obstacle. The
state stipulation that all purchasers of state timber had to log off the lands
in twenty years constituted a threat to the entire plan of operations contemplated by Hoover and William Musser. Having failed to get an extension of time, in 1909 Hoover purchased the land itself—10,406 acres
at $10 per acre. Although the state authorities then claimed that so large
a single purchase was contrary to law, on February 4, 1911, the Idaho
Supreme Court decided that the purchase by Hoover was valid.[35] Payette
Lumber & Manufacturing could begin logging and milling as soon as the
railroad was constructed.

Meanwhile, owners of the Barber Lumber Company had begun to
feel renewed hope for the future success of their firm. Early in 1911 the
federal Reclamation Service started work on the Arrowrock Dam, seventeen miles from Boise, as part of an irrigation project. To facilitate construction, the government had to build almost twelve miles of railroad
from Barber Junction on the Oregon Short Line to the dam. Both Carson
and Hoover immediately foresaw that after the dam was completed the
Reclamation Service would not need the rail line and might sell it at a
reasonable price; this purchase would give Barber Lumber a low-cost
section of the railway needed to run from its mill to its timber. Acting on
this prospect, Carson reopened negotiations for buying the controversial
state lands on Grimes Creek.[36]

As the clouds over the Barber Company began to lift, during 1912
and 1913 its stockholders engaged in a flurry of negotiations for a
merger with Payette Lumber & Manufacturing Company. Various investors had proposed such a scheme as early as 1905. Operating in the
same general area and facing similar problems, the two firms could advantageously unite. One powerful company might hire better managers
than two relatively weak ones; and such a company could speak with
greater authority in the legislature, which lumbermen continuously but
vainly besought for an amendment of the restrictive law under which all
uncut timber was forfeited to the state at the expiration of twenty years
from purchase.

Until 1912–1913, however, agreement to merge the companies had
always foundered on the rock of values to be assigned the properties.
Both firms had groups of stockholders who thought the shares of the other
were too highly priced. Will Musser and William Deary were particularly
obdurate in opposing union of their strong company with the weak Bar-

ber enterprise. By 1912 F. H. Thatcher decided that a merger would be highly advantageous to the Laird, Norton group, and induced Henry Turrish to try to convince his good friend Deary that the proposal was sound, providing the Payette properties were valued at least twice as high as those of Barber Lumber. For a short time the death of Deary early in 1913 left the stockholders stunned and apathetic, but Thatcher recovered quickly and finally found Will Musser agreeable, having already persuaded M. G. Norton, hitherto reluctant to give his approval.[37]

Now only one obstacle stood in the way of agreement. Without the acquisition of the state lands so long desired by Barber, the merger could not be consummated. Carson spent two years setting the stage for the auction. He finally convinced the governor, members of the State Land Board, and other officials that the appraised price of $150,000 on the 12,000 acres was too high and promised that, if they would accept a bid of $100,000, his company would build a railroad and begin sawing lumber as soon as logs were available at the mill. In view of the required outlay for a railroad, officers of the company assumed that no other firm would be in the running. With high expectation they made the $100,000 bid on October 25, 1913, only to have a competitor offer $101,000. Fortunately, the "intruder" failed to abide by certain technicalities of the sale, could promise neither railroad nor immediate production of lumber, and so lost the lands to Barber Lumber under a decision of the Supreme Court of Idaho.[38]

Before that favorable decision, always confidently expected, had been handed down, stockholders of Barber and Payette had formally agreed to the merger and created the new firm. On the day before Christmas, 1913, the Boise Payette Lumber Company was incorporated in Idaho. It bought all the stock and property of Payette Lumber & Manufacturing for $3,000,000, those of Barber Lumber for $1,000,000, the price for the latter being 72.19 cents on the par value of the stock issued. Since the authorized and paid-in capital of Boise Payette was $7,000,000, the new firm had fresh funds to the amount of $3,000,000 for employment as working capital.[39] Almost a third of the amount was to be spent on a large new mill at Emmett, which became active in 1917.

The question of a manager gave the stockholders of the new company some perplexity. E. M. Hoover, who for a decade had done very well in running the Payette company, expected to be promoted. However, he was primarily a salesman and knew little at firsthand either of logging or of sawmill operations. Boise Payette stockholders also felt that they owed a debt to C. A. Barton, who had been conspicuously successful as manager of the Northland Pine Company, now approaching its end.

Not only did Barton have a thorough knowledge of accounting, logging, and manufacture, he was a very superior executive. A polished gentleman of likable personality, devoted to his church—he had been an active Presbyterian in Minneapolis—and kindly with his "boys," he had a quick, clear mind and made decisions unhesitatingly. As of January 1, 1914, he became vice-president and general manager at a salary that was soon lifted to $15,000 a year, with generous stock-purchase rights. Though Barton clashed with Hoover as sales manager, who soon resigned, no better choice could have been made at the time; throughout the World War years, and just afterward, his record was outstanding.[40]

Officially, Boise Payette began operations on March 9, 1914. Three weeks later Barton began construction of the Intermountain Railway running from Arrowrock Junction to Centerville. It began operations on May 1, 1915. Two years later the Boise Payette Company struck the anticipated bargain with the Reclamation Service, buying the Boise & Arrowrock Railroad for $70,000. Logging and sawing were initiated in 1915, the mill turning out 23,327,000 board feet of lumber in that year and 42,587,000 the next. When the new Emmett mill swung into operation in 1917, the output of the company jumped to 132,000,000 board feet and averaged 123,000,000 from that date through 1923. In the latter year total investment in the Barber plant, including a box factory, amounted to $662,000 and that in the Emmett mill to $953,000.[41]

The facilities by this date were good and the properties relatively well balanced. Timber purchases had been made from time to time, so that by 1923 the original Boise Payette holdings of an estimated 2,432 million board feet set in 1913 had been raised to 3,330 million. The war years and immediate postwar boom had given a breath of life to Boise Payette Lumber Company, and, though a disastrous recession had occurred in 1920–1921, net earnings of $901,000 two years later, or 10 percent on issued capital stock, must have seemed eminently satisfactory.

Much of the company's prosperity stemmed from its system of retail yards in the intermountain area—Idaho, western Wyoming, western Colorado, and eastern Oregon. Barton had had a limited but successful experience with retailing as manager of the Northland Pine Company. He now observed the unfavorable position of Inland Empire mills with reference to both the midwestern markets and those supplied by coastal plants. He proposed to assure sales, as far as he could, within the intermountain region reached by rail from his mills. Accordingly, in 1915 he and key directors agreed that an extensive system of retail yards should be established for Boise Payette. C. W. Gamble, an efficient yard manager, was employed. Purchases of yards began in 1915, the total reaching 72 by 1920, most of them catering to farmers in rapidly growing irrigation districts. A design and architectural service, offered free, enhanced sales.[42] Earnings from the yards contributed materially to the success of

Boise Payette in its early years and during the 1920's and 1930's constituted the major portion of its net income when it had any at all.

Inevitably, Boise Payette suffered the disabilities common to most lumber companies in Idaho. Barton and James Long, his logging superintendent, followed the same "cut clean" policy as Deary, so that much of the inferior timber taken out was unprofitable. The mixture of many species added to the disadvantages. Labor costs and railroad rates put Inland Empire lumber in an unfavorable competitive position in the Middle West vis-à-vis southern pine, as already noted. Fir lumber had the advantage of going east via the Panama Canal. Midwinter snows made logging costs extremely high. Dividends from earnings on the Barber and Payette enterprises (later Boise Payette's) from their inception through 1931 amounted to only 38 percent of capital invested. By 1937 the three firms had distributed to stockholders a total of only $3,642,000 from earnings as against $21,744,000 that they had paid to the railroads, not including their own lines, in freight costs.[43] It seemed to the investors at times that they were operating their business for the benefit of everybody —the state with its tax bills, the railroads, labor, consumers—except themselves. They had proved that Idaho was a special and very risky area for lumber enterprises.

5

It would be a mistake to measure the Idaho results in money alone, a mistake that enlightened members of the Weyerhaeuser, Musser, and Laird, Norton groups, and sagacious executives like T. J. Humbird, A. W. Laird, and C. A. Barton were not allowed to commit. They could see that if they were not making profits, they were helping to build a commonwealth.[44] When Palouse, Washington, offered a donation to William Deary to further the Weyerhaeuser enterprises in the Palouse-Potlatch area, the citizens were expressing a sense of the benefits to be gained from a lumber industry. When Boise applauded the promise of William Carson that once the Barber interests were free of litigation they would raise their investment to three million, the city was expressing the same feeling.

One community in particular, Potlatch, reflected credit upon the executives who built and maintained it—especially A. W. Laird. To make money was of course Laird's first concern, but he wished also to make Potlatch an attractive town, with contented employees. "Life here is somewhat crude, and will be for a while yet," he wrote a friend in 1907, but he steadily reduced its crudities and enlarged its amenities. The central square became a recreation ground as well as park, and in time a four-hole golf course adorned it. Shade trees—elm, maple, ash—grew high. The Union Church for Protestants and the Catholic Church became centers of a pleasant social life. Even before the company built a large hall in town equipped as a gymnasium, sports were vigorously promoted, and the Potlatch baseball team was renowned throughout the Inland Empire. Rentals of houses were kept low; the company heated the community hall; in wartime it dug and harrowed garden plots for the residents. A neighborly spirit pervaded the community. Many workers, enjoying the abundant hunting and fishing in the country about, regarded Potlatch as the most delightful of towns.

Nevertheless, from the business point of view, Idaho was extremely disappointing. To be sure, officers of the various companies knew that they were writing a more adventurous record than in any other state. To watch men running logs in the torrential Kootenai, operating the Marble Creek flume, firing the huge Corliss engine at Potlatch, or bringing a trainload of logs behind the Shay locomotive down the steep grades of the Intermountain Railway was to realize that lumbering could indeed have a great deal of romance. At the same time, adventure and the creation of a model town, even a share in building a state, were from the investors' standpoint small consolations for sinking the earnings from lumbering in the Middle West and South in operations that yielded no dividends and sometimes even lost money.

NOTES

1. White pine was found in the moister, higher country, while ponderosa pine did best in the dryer country. Lodgepole pine did find a commercial use early in the century for telephone and telegraph poles.
2. C. J. Brosnan, *Hist. of the State of Idaho*, 187–189. Idaho Territory, as created in 1863, covered most of the present-day Idaho, Montana, and Washington, with an area of more than 325,000 square miles. The Indian name, literally translated, means "Behold, the sun coming down the mountain."
3. W.P.A., *Idaho: A Guide in Word and Picture*, 178–179.
4. FEW Record, 548–561, citing E. N. Brown to FEW, March 23, 1937. Under the Mount Rainier Park Act of March 2, 1899, the Northern

Pacific relinquished to the government large tracts and received scrip for land selections good in six states; Donnelly, *The Facts About the N.P. Land Grant*.
5. FEW Record, 585–594, citing E. N. Brown to FEW, March 27, 1937; Clearwater Timber Co. Min. Bk.; CTC Papers, disbursement calculations, 1927. The ethics of this appropriation of his rival's horse and locomotive did not greatly trouble Nat Brown. After this episode, in October, 1900, Weyerhaeuser, his son Charles, Humbird, Glover, and the two Browns made a trip through the Clearwater and Potlatch forests. The party liked the timber they saw so much that they decided to place scrip on all unappropriated lands carrying ten thousand feet or more of old-

growth white pine per acre. "The night we arrived in Pierce on our return," writes Nat Brown, "the Clearwater Timber Company was practically formed, and named, in the old sitting room of the Pioneer Hotel."

Weyerhaeuser & Denkmann subscribed for 1,667 shares, J. A. Humbird and J. E. Glover 1,250 each, Rutledge for 832, and George S. Long for one. Glover sold his shares and resigned from the company in 1904, members of the Weyerhaeuser family buying all the shares except 175 taken by Humbird.

6. Material in FEW Record, 562–568, is supplemented by other FEW Papers. One of the authors talked with T. J. Humbird in Spokane in 1953 and another with his son, John A. Humbird, in Vancouver in 1956. The latter permitted the authors to extract data from his manuscript history of the Humbird Lumber Co.

7. FEW Papers, T. J. Humbird to FEW, Feb. 17, 1937, and enclosures; J. A. Humbird to FEW, Feb.4, 1937.

8. Edward Rutledge Timber Co. Papers (Coeur d'Alene), including Min. Bk. and correspondence; R. D. Musser Papers, 1901–194; LN Papers, Winona, 1902–1904; FEW Papers, 1902–1934, passim; FEW Record, 600–609.

The Rutledge Company owned shares in the St. Joe Improvement Co., which drove logs on the river of its name, and the St. Joe Boom Co., which sorted logs before they were towed across the lake by the Red Collar line of steamers. The Rutledge firm also bought the latter in the late twenties.

9. Family Tree, Oct., 1948; Salesmen's Log, July 7, 1922; FEW Papers, incoming and outgoing correspondence, 1905–1934, passim; "Statement of Production and Shipments" by Weyerhaeuser mills, 1900–1927; Bonners Ferry Lumber Co. annual repts., 1903–1926, and timberland bks. (at Coeur d'Alene); I.C.C. Docket 6710. Frederick Weyerhaeuser acted as president of the Bonners Ferry Lumber Co. until 1912, when J. P. Weyerhaeuser took the helm.

In 1913 F. E. Weyerhaeuser persuaded President C. R. Gray of the Great Northern to reduce tariffs on lumber from northern Idaho points into Montana and the Dakotas, but the Montana Railroad Commission immediately adjusted rates in Montana enough to maintain the formerly favorable differentials for sawmillers in that state.

10. FEW Record, 580–581. To finance early activities, the original capital stock of $3,000,000 was raised on Oct. 2, 1906 to $6,000,000 and then to $8,000,000 on May 14, 1907.

11. Maxwell W. Williamson, Reminiscences.

12. A full acount of the plant and its opening is given in the Palouse Republic of Sept. 14, 1906. See also the undated illustrated booklet entitled "Potlatch, Idaho."

13. "There was a lot that might have been improved in 1923–25 when we lived there," Frederick K. Weyerhaeuser wrote the authors (July 2, 1958). "The hotel was terrible, and during bad weather the roads out to Pullman and Spokane were almost impassable." In the late 1940's he and Norton Clapp, as directors of Potlatch Forests, Inc., initiated action for sale of the houses to residents. The town soon became attractive again.

14. Brosnan, 294. The Chicago, Milwaukee & St. Paul Railroad Co. opened through freight service from the Missouri River to Puget Sound in May, 1910.

15. FEW Record, 577–579; LN Papers, Winona, 1905–1927, passim; FEW Papers, 1905–1937, passim; JPW Papers, 1905–1906.

F. H. Thatcher was president of the railroad company, F. E. Weyerhaeuser vice-president, and C. R. Musser secretary. Because the directors feared the Interstate Commerce Commission might decree that a railway owned by a lumber company was simply a plant facility and not a common carrier, Thatcher was entrusted with the organization of a holding company, the Inland Improvement Company, a West Virginia corporation of nominal capital. He did so in Jan., 1907, and for many years, with a capital of $9,900, held W.I.&M., capitalized at $1,000,000.

16. FEW Record, 577–579; FEW Papers, FEW to CAW, Aug. 18, 1908; FEW to P. M. Musser, Aug. 31, 1908; LN Papers, Winona, J. G. Woodworth, vice-president of traffic of the NP, to A. W. Laird, Jan. 5, 1921.

17. Potlatch Forests, Inc. Papers, Financial Records. As the company both bought and sold from year to year, precise figures would require long tables. A careful valuation report of 1920 showed that the firm had 143,000 acres of timberlands, 27,500 acres of cutover lands, and a total of 4,426 million feet of timber.

18. Mason, "The Lumber Industry in the Inland Empire" (MS, Univ. of California doctoral dissertation, dated June 15, 1916), pp. 2–10, covers the economics of the industry.

19. FEW Record, 579–585. An article in the *Timberman* Dec. 1928, p. 142, stated that since it began logging in 1903 the Potlatch Lumber Company had cut 2,679 million feet of lumber. Of this 39.16 percent was Idaho white pine; 16.97 percent ponderosa; 5.29 percent Western red cedar; and 38.58 percent mixed woods.

20. LN Papers, Winona.

21. LN Papers, Letterbox W.I.&M. Ry., July 16, 1905.

22. Deary had to see a brickmaking establishment built at Potlatch; to order railroad cars capable of rounding a 10 percent curve on steep grades; to provide log loaders and deal with a mass of similar details. By the fall of 1905 the Potlatch Lumber Company had established retail yards at sixteen towns and cities in Idaho and eastern Washington.

See the LN Papers, Potlatch Lumber Company letterboxes, 1905–1909.

23. PFI Accounts. Mr. F. K. Weyerhaeuser wrote to authors, July 2, 1958: "I can remember father wondering about a white butterfly in the Clearwater woods in the 1920's, but nobody knew what to do about it."

24. LN Papers, Winona; FEW Papers; RDM Papers.

25. Boise-Cascade Lumber Co. Papers (hereinafter cited BC Papers), "Records of the Barber Lumber Co.," a book containing copies of the articles of incorporation, meetings of the stockholders and directors, stock subscriptions, bylaws, and other data; Barber Lumber Co. Minute Book; certified copy of articles of incorporation of Barber Lumber Co.; *U.S.* v. *Barber Lumber Co. et al.,* 194 Fed. 24–36, summary of facts; FEW Record, 617–622, quoting the purchase contract of March 12, 1902.

26. Long Papers, Long to Carson, Feb. 28, 1905 (loggers); Boise *Evening Call,* Dec. 10, 1904; FEW Papers, FEW to CAW, Aug. 31, 1906; BC Papers, Records of Barber Lumber Co.; Moon to FEW, April 24, 1937, in FEW Record, 622; LN Papers, Winona, July 6, 1907.

27. BC Papers, "Records of Barber Lumber Co."; FEW Papers, FEW to CAW, Aug. 6, 11, 31, 1906. In Sept., 1906 the directors decided to buy the 375 shares of Barber Lumber in Frank Steunenberg's estate at $135 a share.

28. *U.S.* v. *Barber Lumber Co. et al.,* 194 Fed. 24–25; *Idaho Daily Statesman* (Boise), July 26, 1908 (quote).

29. LN Papers, Winona, F. S. Bell to M. G. Norton, March 9, 1908; BC Papers, "Records of Barber Lumber Co."

30. Marian McKenna, *William E. Borah;* 194 Fed. 24–36; *Idaho Daily Statesman,* Feb. 20, 1912.

31. BC Papers, certified copy of articles of incorporation, Payette Lumber & Manufacturing Co., Dec. 9, 1902; FEW Record, 625–631, quoting letters from FEW Papers, E. M.

Hoover to FEW, April 23, May 23, 1937; LN Papers, Deary to F. S. Bell, Oct. 10, 1902 (quote).

For his Record FEW could not locate the minute book and other early papers of the Payette Lbr. & Mfg. Co. The organizational meeting was held in Jan. 1903. In addition to Musser, the first officers were Turrish as vice-president, F. W. Kehl, secretary, and R. D. Musser, treasurer.

32. LN Papers, Winona, Statement of Payette Lbr. & Mfg. Co., May 1, 1905; FEW Record, 631.

33. LN Papers, Winona, Deary to CAW, June 25, 1903; Hoover to Thatcher, Dec. 2, 1905; Borah to Hoover, Nov. 23, 1905; BC Papers, contracts between Payette Imp. & Boom Co. and contractors for building road and dams; FEW Record, 626–627.

Payette Improvement & Boom Co. was a $50,000 Minnesota corporation. The building of the dam made it impossible for local residents to ford the stream. When a toll road was built on the top of the dam, they protested to the State Land Board, but the right to collect tolls was sustained.

34. LN Papers, Winona, W. Musser to Thatcher, Oct. 28, Nov. 27, 1905; Thatcher to C. R. Musser, Nov. 16, 1905; Thatcher to Hoover, Nov. 16, 1905; R. D. Musser Papers, Hoover to Thatcher, Feb. 3, 1909; FEW Papers, Hoover to FEW, Feb. 8, 1910; *Idaho Daily Statesman,* Feb. 8, 1910; JPW Papers, Hoover to JPW, Feb. 3, 1912; FEW Record, 627–629; BC Papers, contracts of Payette Lbr. & Mfg. Co. with the Idaho Northern and Oregon Short Line, 1911–1913.

35. *Idaho Daily Statesman,* Dec. 15, 1910; *State of Idaho* v. *E. M. Hoover,* 19 Idaho 299–304.

36. JPW Papers, Carson to JPW, Feb. 17, 1911; LN Papers, Winona, Hoover to Carson, Feb. 3, 1911; Carson to F. S. Bell, July 24, 1911; BC Papers, "Records of Barber Lumber Co.," annual meeting of stockholders, July 19, 1910. At the 1910

meeting counsel for Barber Lumber was authorized "to settle all differences arising [*sic*] between our Company and the Centerville Mining & Milling Company," which claimed over 1,000 acres of Barber Lumber's scripped lands were really mineral lands.

37. R. D. Musser Papers, C. R. Musser to R. D. Musser, Nov. 18, 1905; JPW Papers, JPW to Carson, Feb. 11, 1908; LN Papers, Thatcher to Norton, April 3, 1912, April 8, June 8, 1913; Thatcher to Carson, May 14, 1913; Carson to F. S. Bell, Jan. 13, 1915.

38. FEW Papers, Carson to FEW, July 14, 1913; Carson to JPW, July 19, 1913; Lyon Cobb to FEW, Sept. 8, 1913; transcript of hearings before State Land Board, 1913; Lyon Cobb to JPW, Sept. 17, 1913; Hoover to W. Musser, Sept. 29, Oct. 25, 26, 1913; Cobb to Thatcher, Nov. 29, 1913; *Idaho Daily Statesman,* Oct. 26, 1913; LN Papers, Carson to Thatcher, Nov. 25, 1913; Thatcher to Carson, Dec. 8, 1913; Carson to F. S. Bell, Dec. 3, 1913; Cobb to Thatcher, Dec. 24, 1913; BC Papers, "Records of Barber Lumber Co."

39. BC Papers, Boise Payette Lumber Co. Min. Bk.; "Records of Barber Lumber Co."; FEW Record, 633–635. Laird, Norton Co. with 8,490 shares out of the first 40,000 was the largest single stockholder in Boise Payette, but the Musser group had 9,350 shares and five individual Weyerhaeuser holdings amounted to 12,160 shares.

In 1918 to retire loans made by stockholders for expansion of properties, the authorized capital of Boise Payette was raised to $10,000,000, though only $2,000,000 was subscribed. Hoover and Turrish failed to add to their holdings at that time. Barber Lumber Co. was finally dissolved in 1930.

40. Interview of F. W. Kohlmeyer with Mrs. G. A. Morse, C. A. Barton's daughter, Sept. 29, 1954; F. W. Hewitt, Reminiscences; FEW Rec-

ord, 635–636; Hewitt gives a glowing account of Barton's managerial
skill. Conversations of the authors
with company veterans suggest that
Hoover believed Barton, and probably some directors as well, had
treated him badly.

41. Boise Payette Lumber Co. Annual
Report, 1923, 4–7; "Statement of
Production and Shipments" of Weyerhaeuser companies; BC Papers, Intermountain Railway Co. file. The
railroad was capitalized at $400,000,
though total investment in the road
amounted to $1,037,499.

42. Boise Payette Lumber Co. Min. Bk.;
Boise Payette Lumber Co. annual
repts., 1914–1920; BC Papers, folder
on early financing of the company,
chiefly correspondence between Boise
Payette and FEW, 1916–1918; FEW
Papers, FEW to Barton, March 30,
1915; F. H. Gilcrest to FEW, May
7, 1915; FEW to Gilcrest, May 10,
1915; Barton to FEW, May 17, Oct.
18, 1915; Aug. 1, 1916; Carson to
FEW, Aug. 5, 1915; LN Papers,
Winona, Carson to Bell, Aug. 5,
1915; John Kendall to Bell, Sept. 23,
1915; Barton to Bell, Oct. 18, 1915;
Nov. 7, 1916 (had 62 yards by this
date); *The Log,* Feb. 1920.

43. FEW Record, 637.

44. This was especially true of Laird at
Potlatch, Taylor at Coeur d'Alene,
and Barton in Boise, each a pillar of
his community; the authors have
talked to numerous townsmen of all
three places.

XV

Manufacturing and Marketing

in the Northwest

A PARTY of Weyerhaeuser executives, traveling to Tacoma for the
annual meeting of stockholders, gathered at Everett on April
29, 1915, to inaugurate the new Mill B constructed on the old
Barge Work Tract on the shores of the Snohomish. George S. Long, his
high collar jutting up to his chin, stood ready at the switch of the big
chain as Earl M. Rogers, the mill superintendent, checked the line of incoming logs. At his signal, Long turned on the current and put the chain
in motion. As the first fir log rolled toward the big double-cutting band,
F. S. Bell, who had come in from Minnesota, started that mechanism.
Charles A. Weyerhaeuser and W. H. Boner, the local manager, set the
edger and the large fifty-four-inch gang saw in motion.

Cheers went up from the skeleton crew as the first boards moved out
toward the timber deck. Boner then led the party through the 400-foot,
entirely electrified main mill, capable of cutting in 8 hours 400,000 feet,
and out into the big yard with its 20 miles of tracks. The impressive
works were located on 80 acres, 30 of them enclosed. Included were dry
kilns, a planing mill, a remanufacturing plant, and a dry lumber shed, all
with the most modern facilities. The party, lunching in the mammoth
lumber shed, heard George Long extol the promise of Everett and the
Pacific Northwest. Thus, reported the *American Lumberman,* opened
"one of the largest and most up-to-date sawmill plants in the United
States."[1]

2

After fifteen years on the Pacific Coast, the Weyerhaeuser Timber Company had thus launched a large-scale program of manufacturing. It had fulfilled the original intention of Frederick Weyerhaeuser, who as his son later testified with reference to the Northwest, "always thought of a purchase of timber in terms of future logging and sawmill operations."[2] What considerations had moved the company directors to undertake such expansion, reversing the previous opposition of F. H. Thatcher and the conviction of George S. Long that conditions on the West Coast did not promise well for a drastic increase in sawmill facilities?

The early history of the mill the company acquired in 1902 has already been outlined. As Long had noted before its purchase, it was then "not a first class one by any means," but the great improvements made had lifted it to a high level of efficiency. Among the factors that moved the directors to sanction the building of a second and much larger plant, the performance of Mill A seems to have been the most influential, though the opening of the Panama Canal was not an unimportant consideration.

The time was not a happy one for most West Coast manufacturers. Average lumber prices had been low in 1911 at $11.05 per thousand, and while they rose in 1912 to $11.58, there was no prospect of a further sharp increase. Actually the market continued uncertain or depressed, and early in 1915 Austin Cary, a United States Forest Service expert, after an extensive survey gave figures that showed the average cost of production to be greater than what was usually received for finished lumber. "It is no surprise to us," wrote J. H. Bloedel, president of the West Coast Lumber Manufacturers' Association to his members in sending out Cary's report.

The future of Far West lumbering in 1913–1914 looked more promising than its present. The whole area was growing, and its people would need lumber as surely as a healthy family of children would need clothes and shoes. The Panama Canal was completed and would offer cheap transportation by water to the East. Finally, the lessening output of the Lake States meant that white pine could no longer supply sufficient lumber to the Middle West, and western fir was already finding a market there. Long, appraising the situation in 1909, had written O. H. Ingram that the time to manufacture in quantity was "about the time when the Panama Canal is finished," and by 1913 this conviction was fortified by what Boner was accomplishing.[3]

For Boner was making money at Everett. By working from a low-cost inventory, sawing carefully to get the best-quality lumber and the greatest possible quantity from every log, shipping his product fully seasoned to cut down freight costs, and establishing a reputation for prompt delivery, he had prospered where others were struggling to break even. In 1913 he had shown a net profit of $194,779, and Long told his stockholders in his 1914 report: "The good showing of the Everett mill proves that we can profitably enter the manufacturing business." He also pointed out that the company could now take profits on a full cycle of activity: the cheap acquisition of stumpage, the extension of logging, and manufacturing commensurate with the firm's vast timber holdings.[4]

Two other factors had exerted an influence on the director's thinking. One, the federal income tax authorized in 1913, and first applied formidably in 1916, tossed an element of uncertainty into the situation. The problem was to reach agreement with the government on the valuation of the company's timberlands as a base for calculating costs, which in turn would be a prime factor in establishing earnings to be shown for the Timber Company. Appraisal was difficult, the negotiations with governmental authorities protracted. In the annual report of 1917, for the first time, Weyerhaeuser Timber was able to list the appraised value of its timberlands—$87,450,328—covering an estimated stumpage of 59,000,-000,000 board feet on 1,798,369 acres.[5]

The second factor was the desire of the Weyerhaeuser family and some other stockholders, as already noted, to raise the company's manufacturing activity to a volume comparable with its forest holdings. As pointed out in Chapter XIII, Weyerhaeuser Timber had been accused of acquiring timberland merely to sell it later at a big profit. Conscious that the charge was false, F. E. Weyhaeuser in particular wanted to kill it once for all by logging and milling on an impressive scale. He felt, too, that the erection of Mill B (and additional mills elsewhere later) would represent the fulfillment of an implied pledge made at the time of the original purchase from the Northern Pacific. However, the demonstration by Boner that manufacturing would pay made the pledge easy to redeem and brought stockholders who might otherwise have been opposed into agreement.

The design and construction of the mill were put, by a contract of March 14, 1914, into the hands of Arthur B. Pracna of Seattle. In his organization was a highly gifted young engineer and designer, Albert H. Onstad, who apparently took a part in planning and erecting the plant. This, his first contact with the Weyerhaeuser Timber Company, was to mark the beginning of a long and fruitful association.

The work had scarcely begun when World War I broke out late in July, 1914. For a time it affected adversely all American business activity, and lumbering in particular. Company directors were apprehensive as to the manufacturing program. "The size of the new plant at Everett rather staggers me," wrote F. E. Weyerhaeuser in December. Long himself, while concerned, staunchly held to his program. "It looks like sheer foolishness to build more mills," he conceded in a letter to O. H. Ingram on December 4, 1914, "but we got well under way at Everett before the war happened, and we will, of course, complete the mill." However, when the plant was unveiled on the opening day, marketing conditions remained discouraging.

If the directors had doubts, Long had none. Committed to the new manufacturing program, he pushed ahead with it vigorously. He had ample confidence in Boner and in the rewards to be reaped from the full cycle of lumbering. Boner in turn pursued his tested policy of sawing to get quality lumber, pushed sales in the Middle West, and found himself justified by the outcome. For the first half-year of 1916, Mill A showed a profit of $101,723 and Mill B one of $164,097. The full year of 1917 recorded results even more gratifying: $315,971 net for Mill A and $606,036 for B. Moreover, the manufacturing costs of the new plant stood at a dollar per thousand feet lower than those of the older one. Long could comment with an undertone of exultation: "It certainly looks like it had paid to build the new mill."[6]

3

Meanwhile the Weyerhaeuser Timber Company had taken another step in expansion by deciding to build a mill at Snoqualmie Falls on the Snoqualmie River. The site lay some forty miles south, southeast of Everett, on a branch of the Snohomish. Weyerhaeuser Timber and the Grandin Coast Lumber Company both owned large tracts of intermingled timber in eastern King County, and after extensive negotiations, in 1914 the directors of the two firms had voted to merge their holdings and to log and mill together.

The compact was made in June and affected almost 45,000 acres of stumpage. That month the Snoqualmie Falls Lumber Company was formed, Weyerhaeuser Timber owning 67.5 percent of the stock. George S. Long became president and O. D. Fisher of Grandin Coast the vice-president. The choice for general manager fell upon W. W. Warren, an experienced lumberman and Fisher's brother-in-law. He had worked with the Missouri Lumber & Mining Company (a Fisher firm) of Grandin, Missouri, and later had for years managed its operations in Louisiana. Just past forty, he was a modern-minded executive of whom both F. E. Weyerhaeuser and George S. Long warmly approved.[7] The appointment came as the construction of Mill B at Everett was well under way.

Warren wanted to start the Snoqualmie Falls project at once, but stockholders of the two owner-companies were wary of further expansion in a troubled period. Captain J. B. White, vice-president of Grandin

Coast, wrote to Long: "It is sometimes a good time to build a mill when times are dull, but one wants to see a ray of hope ahead." Both F. S. Bell and F. E. Weyerhaeuser advised caution. Long replied to the latter: "Like you, we have all felt that we would wait and see just how our Everett mill started off, and wait for skies to clear a little before we attempt to construct anything at Snoqualmie Falls." This was in December, 1914.

By the next fall the skies had begun to clear, and Warren discussed with Pracna the design of a mill for the new enterprise. Pracna wanted a fee of $1,400 a month, which Warren thought much too high. However, in December, 1915, A. H. Onstad left the Pracna organization, and Long took him on the W.T.C. payroll at $4,000 a year. He then suggested that Warren employ Onstad, and, although the construction at Snoqualmie was not begun until the fall of 1916, the mill designer at once began a study of the problems to be faced there.[8]

It was his first assignment as a Timber Company employee, and apparently the first big undertaking he had directed. It was a formidable one. By now two mills were in contemplation, the larger for the manufacture of fir lumber, and the smaller for cedar, and, as it proved, for hemlock. A shingle mill, while separate, was a related unit.

The site lay on a flat by the river, with ample room for all the mills, sheds, offices, and yards. It was possible to develop a large storage pond for logs, and two railroads were available to carry away the lumber. In addition to the extensive plant, however, Onstad was responsible for laying out and constructing a town with a large modern store, an imposing hotel—boardinghouse, and dozens of bungalows for employees. These buildings were located on a hill above the mills, "on a winding boulevard sort of road tucked in among trees." Most of the lumber was furnished by Mill B at Everett.

By the end of 1916 the town was half built and the fir mill under construction. Like Everett Mill B, the plant was modern in layout and equipment, operated by a 4,000-kilowatt turbine and employing electric engines to transport lumber to the planing mill and the yards. Although scheduled for completion by July 1, 1917, the growing scarcity of labor after the American entry into the war and the widespread strike of July, 1917 (see Chapter XVIII), slowed the construction. The fir mill was completed in October but did not begin operations until the first week in December. It had a capacity of 200,000 feet of lumber a day. The cedar and shingle mills were ready in the spring of 1918.

When 1917 closed, the fir mill had sawed 3,075,617 feet of lumber and quickly increased its output. In September, 1918, Warren could claim a monthly production of 10,000,000 board feet on two eight-hour shifts. The shingle mill was turning out 300,000 shingles a day. Long's purpose was "to get all the good lumber possible out of a log before we ever make a shingle and then to make the best shingle we can of what is left."[9]

To assist Warren, F. R. Titcomb, son-in-law of J. P. Weyerhaeuser, joined the Snoqualmie Falls staff on his return from the war. Charles H. Ingram, a grandson of O. H. Ingram of Eau Claire, was another recruit.* Both in turn were later to manage the plant. S. P. Johns, Jr., handled sales, while Guy Rogers acted as mill superintendent.[10]

Thus with Everett's Mill B and Snoqualmie Falls, the Weyerhaeuser Timber Company had established a manufacturing program fully worthy of its large timber holdings. But it would have to develop two activities already initiated with mixed results: the logging of the timber for its mills and the marketing of its increasing volume of lumber.

4

As previous chapters have indicated, in its earlier years Weyerhaeuser Timber had followed a vigorous policy of timberland acquisition. By the end of 1916 it had acquired title to 2,013,404 acres, for which the total outlay had been $28,896,689.

However, purchases had been sharply curtailed in the second decade of the century. Prices of timberlands and taxes had both risen, discouraging all but the more strategic acquisitions. In 1910 the company bought 52,000 acres but sold 21,181. It was to buy still more carefully. Such a policy was not confined to W.T.C. By 1920 the United States Forest Service would report that "the carrying charge on long-term timber investments, which may double the capital cost of stumpage every seven or eight years, has largely halted the movement for building up enormous speculative timber properties which was in full swing prior to 1910."[11]

Neither Frederick Weyerhaeuser nor George S. Long had ever thought of the Weyerhaeuser Timber Company as an owner of "speculative timber properties," since their eventual objective was manufacturing; but with the second decade purchases were made only when, as F. E. Weyerhaeuser put it, "a very attractive proposition" was offered. Furthermore, buying was now to be related to definite projects. For such ends the company was still willing to make large acquisitions. In 1911 it considered buying a 42,000-acre tract held by the Walker family near Klamath Falls, Oregon. The land lay in California, but near extensive Weyerhaeuser holdings that in time would be logged and milled. However, the directors considered the price, $1,600,000, too high, and authorized F. E. Weyerhaeuser, who was conducting the negotiations, to offer but $1,000,000. The land eventually went to the company's competitor,

* Mr. Ingram always signed himself "Chas. H. Ingram," and liked to be referred to in print in that way.

Long-Bell. The episode showed the wariness of the stockholders, and they were vindicated later to the extent that they bought some of the stumpage for less than Long-Bell paid for it.

In 1917 the world conflict checked what might have been the normal course of land acquisition. "The whirligigs that have been brought about by war conditions," wrote Long on April 30th of that year, "have led us to abandon all idea whatever of the purchase of timberlands." However, with the coming of peace buying was resumed, and the 38,500-acre Hopkins tract in Oregon was acquired in October, 1920. Long convinced Thatcher that the purchase represented a good risk for resale, and not necessarily a commitment to manufacturing.[12]

Meanwhile the company had been selling certain timberlands to finance the construction of its new mills and to dispose of peripheral properties that did not fit in with logging and manufacturing operations. By 1917 the total net reduction in the stumpage to which the Timber Company had acquired title since 1900 exceeded 215,000 acres.

The expansion of logging in the second decade of the century was notable. Weyerhaeuser logging operations on the coast had previously involved, in large part, efforts to salvage burned timber. As noted, after the Yacolt fire in 1902, the Clarke County Timber Company and the Twin Falls Logging Company had been formed to cut the charred timber on company lands. This was not the Timber Company's first logging venture, but of necessity it was an extensive operation. Two other enterprises that followed also dealt with fire-stricken woods. In 1905 the Cowlitz County Logging Company, in which the Weyerhaeuser Timber Company owned half the stock, was organized to log seared timber on the Coweeman River; while in 1910 the Mineral Lake Logging Company was also formed to work at first on fire-ravaged land. As to Mill A, the management soon discovered that it was cheaper to buy raw material on the open market than to do its own logging. Up to the First World War, Mill A was still buying most of its logs in this fashion.[13]

The limitation of logging in the company's earlier years was a wise policy. It not only permitted independent logging firms to prosper, thereby promoting good will in the area, but also enabled the Timber Company to raise cash through sales made especially profitable by the marked increase in the market value of its standing timber. Average quotations for Douglas-fir stumpage rose from $0.25 per 1,000 board feet in 1900 to $1.50 in 1914. The cost of living in the United States had increased in these years, but while with 1900 as a base year equaling 100, the general index rose to 125, the cost of Douglas-fir stumpage increased sixfold! Other large timber owners on the coast who began manufacturing often followed the Weyerhaeuser Timber Company's policy of purchasing logs in the open market instead of cutting their own stumpage. It was the small owner in need of an immediate return who logged his timber at once.[14]

But with the second decade of the century the costs of maintaining large holdings were rising, and the need to cut them seemed to be imperative. Moreover, the expansion of manufacturing required a larger and larger supply of logs. Clarke County Timber completed the logging of burned timber and in 1916 was cutting green trees. The Timber Company became part owners of the Mud Bay Logging Company (1910) and the Cherry Valley Timber Company (1912), both ventures proving profitable. Other enterprises were carried on. Several years after James Bridge became general manager of the Sound Timber Company (1913), that firm undertook logging, beginning operations late in 1917. It did no manufacturing but sold logs on the open market, a substantial portion going to the Everett mills.[15]

The Snoqualmie Falls Lumber Company had commenced logging operations while the construction of its mills was going on. In 1915 its first railroad camp cars, fitted with steam-heated sleeping compartments, were available for its logging crews. These cars could be moved from site to site. More important, an attempt was made to use electricity in logging: an experimental electrical donkey engine was purchased and other devices were carefully investigated.

While this marked the first use of electrical equipment in logging by a Weyerhaeuser company, the practice was not new. As early as 1903 T. H. Brew of the Morse Manufacturing Company at Puyallup, Washington, had erected an electrically operated skid haul that pulled logs from distances in the woods as great as two thousand feet. But electric-power operations were undertaken by Snoqualmie on a scale never before attempted. By 1920 the entire skidding work of the company was electrified. According to Warren, it was "a wonderful success," which "has . . . justified our faith, hopes, and expectations." Later the use of electric equipment revealed defects not evident at first, but for the moment Snoqualmie was the innovator, blazing a path to more modern methods.[16]

5

By 1915 the long primary period of westward expansion in America, with a demand for lumber that simplified its sale, was drawing to an end. Many cities had been built; the railroad lines that consumed millions of feet for ties, stations, tanks, and warehouses had been all but completed. The output of lumber was now so large that manufacturers were competing frantically for the market, while wood substitutes like steel, asphalt, and concrete—to be discussed later—were reducing the per capita demand for wood products in general.

The early sales of Mill A at Everett had been mostly to wholesalers. Then in 1908–1909, under sales manager Robert Hunt, the mill began to solicit retail lumber dealers, and a few salaried salesmen were assigned to midwestern markets. By 1914 Hunt had a force of seven. Because railroad freight rates were too high to permit fir to compete in eastern markets, the salesmen operated solely in the Far West and the Middle West.[17] Only 9 percent of Mill A lumber was sold locally from 1902 to 1915.

Cargo shipments, accounting for 29 percent of total sales, were made to California and various ports in Alaska, South America, Australia, and the Orient. None before 1914 went by water to eastern United States. As already noted, Weyerhaeuser shipments to California were handled by Charles R. McCormick, who operated his own ships. In foreign trade the larger shipping lines, such as W. R. Grace & Company, or sometimes the ultimate buyer, would act as agents or solicit bids. American, English, and other ships carried Everett lumber. The Timber Company owned no vessels of its own, but as early as 1905 had started to buy stock in McCormick's steamship ventures.[18]

In laying plans for the new mills at Everett and Snoqualmie Falls, Long, Boner, and Warren realized that marketing required renewed attention. The methods adequate for one mill were inadequate for three. In retailing and wholesaling, and in overseas, midwestern, and eastern markets, new challenges must be met.

In 1914, for the first time, Atlantic markets seemed on Everett's doorstep: the Panama Canal was open, and at moderate rates ships could carry fir to New Orleans, Baltimore, or Boston. Unfortunately, just as the promise for the future brightened, the war in Europe closed the canal to civilian shipping, and the East seemed as remote as ever.

But if the hope of penetrating eastern markets must now be deferred, this fact only made the necessity to find other outlets for fir the more urgent. As Long had said in 1915, the market early in that year and in the preceding one had been "groggy." Never before had the margin of profit for the Timber Company been thinner, and by April, 1915, orders had fallen off almost a third. Larger outlets for Weyerhaeuser products would have to be found.

To encourage exports, the Timber Company in May, 1915, became a member of the Douglas Fir Exploitation & Export Company. Formed in 1913 by California lumbermen, this agency, which first became active in 1915, sought to book orders, correct adverse publicity about Douglas fir, send samples of the wood to distant corners of the globe, and in all possible ways expand the fir market. It operated on a 2½ percent commission for all lumber handled. By October, 1916, it had recruited 38 of the 60 Pacific Northwest mills that exported lumber. Boner that year became a member of the company's board of directors. However, the war hurt the cargo trade badly, and by 1917 this had fallen to half the prewar level.

Weyerhaeuser Timber membership in the export company was renewed annually, but in some years Long and Boner used the organization little, handling their own exports. They found the larger agency useful only when markets were poor. While in subsequent years the Weyerhaeuser foreign trade would rise, its domestic trade would rise more rapidly. Here the real progress in marketing would be made.[19]

As W.T.C. directors and officials, including Long, studied export possibilities, they also studied the markets to be reached by rail. Rates on coast lumber to midwestern points, though not so low as shippers desired, were now low enough (55 cents per hundredweight to Chicago) to permit effective competition. White pine was *the* quality wood, and the freight charges on yellow pine, while lower than those for fir, gave the latter a chance to fight for the market.[20]

Just before Mill B opened at Everett some of the directors in St. Paul had taken the step of acquiring a controlling interest in an important retail chain called Thompson Yards. Boner had become vice-president of this organization.

Still relatively modest in size, this system of yards had been created and promoted by a dynamic resident of the Twin Cities, George Thompson, who was applying the merchandising ideas developed by big chain stores and mail-order firms that had arisen since the Civil War. His was essentially the same formula as that later used successfully by J. C. Penny. He studied typical communities, found a solution for selling to them, and multiplied the answer. He was a persuasive salesman. "He was a dreamer," says one of his former employees who knew him well. "He was ahead of his times so far as merchandising was concerned." He provided customers with acceptable plans for houses, stores, or farm buildings. He bought lumber in quantity. Learning that the Weyerhaeusers were interested in acquiring additional retail outlets (they had bought the Shevlin yards in 1915), Thompson talked persuasively with F. E. and Charles Weyerhaeuser, proposing that they take over his chain. Long, at first favorable, later became doubtful, but the other stockholders, including John P. Weyerhaeuser, the new president of W.T.C., wanted to buy, and on March 29, 1915, Long signed the purchase contract.

The employee quoted above says that "Thompson came bustling into the office and walked straight to my desk and hit it with a resounding whack and said, 'By golly, we're Weyerhaeuser!' " He had been elected president and general manager of the new organization, which, over Long's protest, he succeeded in naming Thompson Yards, Inc. It was capitalized at $1,000,000, all of which the Weyerhaeuser Timber Company paid in for about 60 retail yards. Thompson received a salary of

$12,000 a year, a $250,000 stock interest, and operated along the lines he had already followed. During 1915 he added six new yards to the chain and planned to expand it more vigorously in 1916.

Boner came to Minneapolis in October, 1915, and tried to persuade Thompson to dispose of a hundred carloads of fir in that city. The market did not permit such a sale, but Thompson worked hard to handle the Everett product. By 1916 he was taking a third of the Timber Company's production.[21]

In the meantime, the Minnesota associated companies, as noted elsewhere, had united to launch the informal Weyerhaeuser Sales Company, which sent salesmen to independent retail yards and individual corporations. Boner and Hunt saw possibilities in this organization as another outlet for their products, and in October, 1916, the Sales Company began to handle the output of the two Everett mills in their marketing territory: Wisconsin, Illinois, Iowa, Kansas, Wyoming, Colorado, and Minnesota.

One difficulty had to be met. According to Hunt, "Louie Case [manager of the Sales Company] was a pine man and Louie Case worked hand in glove for pine, pine, pine." Boner, Hunt, and other West Coast men stood up staunchly for fir and gradually made headway. Long was patient, urging Boner to send out lumber that would show fir at its best. "The fir industry," he said in 1917, "is a great big slumbering giant." He had faith that the lumber would win increasing recognition, and gradually it did.[22]

Meanwhile, Thompson carried out his plans for expansion. On that policy at this stage there was rather full agreement, although Long wanted fewer yards in North Dakota and more in the fertile belt of southeastern South Dakota, southern Minnesota, and Iowa. In the latter area, in contrast with the one-crop economy of North Dakota, there was a diversified one of corn, hogs, dairy cattle, and small grains that made for dependable income regardless of weather conditions. F. E. Weyerhaeuser and F. S. Bell agreed to the concentration suggested, and Thompson heeded this advice to an extent, acquiring 39 new yards in 1916.[23]

The years 1917 and 1918 saw still greater expansion. The directors were "high" on Thompson and his methods. When an opportunity came to buy the 54 Queal Yards, in Iowa, South Dakota, and Minnesota, George S. Long was doubtful. He admitted that for the $339,500 asked the yards were a bargain, but the situation in Europe looked bad, and he frankly confessed to having "cold feet." The other directors did not, and the purchase was made. To finance expansion, Thompson Yards increased its debt to about $2,350,000, much of it owed to W.T.C. and other Weyerhaeuser firms; the lenders accepted new stock when capitalization was raised to $3,000,000. Altogether, in 1917 Thompson acquired almost 90 yards, about doubling the number he held at the beginning of the year.[24]

In 1919 outlays were made for two additional properties. One comprised the seven yards of the Northland Pine Company, which was now ending all logging and milling activity. The other was an eighteen-acre site in the Midway District between Minneapolis and St. Paul, which was to serve as a distributing yard for W.T.C. lumber. Long, envisaging a far greater sale of fir in the area than had ever been realized for white pine, was particularly eager to acquire this land. F. E. Weyerhaeuser thought the asking price of $150,000 excessive "for real estate on which to pile lumber." However, on September 4, 1919, the tract was bought for $130,000.

The Twin City Yard of Thompson Yards started as a giant retail outlet, and in 1921 entered on wholesaling activities. Thompson built a stable with varnished stalls, central heating, and a sickbay for his dapple gray teams with "fancy harness" that delivered lumber throughout the area, and became a symbol of his ostentatious conduct. The distributing center in turn became representative of his large-scale dealing in lumber, and his slogan: "Any species, any grade, any size, any time, any place."[25]

The growth of the Weyerhaeuser Sales Company, the other outlet for Everett lumber, is outlined in Chapter XVII. Incorporated in December, 1919, it made arrangements with the Timber Company, Snoqualmie Falls, and the Idaho firms to sell all their output not handled by Thompson Yards.

Friction quickly developed between Thompson Yards and the Sales Company. The latter found that independent retail dealers were hostile to Thompson, whom they considered "a price cutter and a pirate." F. K. Weyerhaeuser, who knew the situation fully, believed later that "the Weyerhaeuser Timber Company and the Weyerhaeuser Sales Company probably lost more business from competitors of Thompson Yards than they ever gained by the ownership of Thompson Yards." An important factor in the general situation was that Thompson gave his retail outlets little independence (for example, prices were set by the central office and all records were kept there), so that they could not deal effectively with local conditions. Thompson persisted in his flamboyant advertising, claiming to sell at practically wholesale prices. This uneasy situation was to persist for several years.[26]

The markets in 1919 and 1920 were excellent, and Thompson continued his policy of rampant expansion. By 1920, at the peak of his activity, his firm controlled 193 yards. Their sales reached the impressive figure of $13,891,285.

But Thompson's financial position was daily becoming more precarious. He had built up an immense inventory of unsold lumber, and his accounts with the Everett mills and elsewhere were steadily growing.

When pressed for funds, he borrowed from Weyerhaeuser Timber, and early in 1920 owed a menacing total of $5,000,000. Just at this time came the first signs of the 1920–1921 depression, and the desperate character of Thompson's situation soon became clear. He could not dispose of his vast inventories except at prices that meant appalling losses.

A number of factors that worked against the Yards had been at play for some time. The animosity of independent retail dealers, already noted, was one. This built up resistance to Weyerhaeuser Sales Company efforts as well as to those of Thompson's outlets. Another adverse factor was partly the fault of the mills, for they were pressing lumber upon Thompson, especially straight cars of surplus items, which he accepted but could not sell. Again, to stimulate business Thompson financed a number of speculative builders. Some of them failed, and the Yards had to take over and complete the houses the builders had started. Thompson Yards was administered in a bold and expansive manner, credits were not watched, and bad debts were accumulated. It was felt (and here again the Weyerhaeusers and their associates were in part responsible) that the main objective was to market lumber rather than to earn an adequate return upon the large investment that had been made.[27]

The "hypnotic influence" of Thompson's personality, as F. S. Bell later put it, was undoubtedly the strongest factor in permitting a dangerous situation to grow worse. Thompson was always confident, optimistic, convincing. But the responsibility for what was occurring and would occur must be placed on the directors, who had sufficient warning to take stern measures early in 1920. It was of course not yet certain that the boom would suddenly collapse, but the general situation and the particular condition of the yards both indicated the need for caution. Yet on February 24th, when Thompson asked W.T.C. for $300,000, the amount was promptly forwarded to him, and in the next sixty days Thompson procured advances totaling $1,200,000.

Long, however, was now alarmed and requested a conference of the directors. Thatcher suggested a reduction of the total investment in the Yards. Still nothing was done, and in December Long felt that the affairs of the yards were as important "as any other thing before us." By 1921 matters naturally had worsened, and at the end of that year even Thompson felt that the company had "expanded sufficiently for the present."

The remainder of the unhappy episode may be summarized. In July, 1921, as a temporary solution, capitalization was raised from $3,000,000 to $6,000,000. Thompson continued to exude confidence, and now sought permission, which was tacitly but not formally given, to engage in wholesaling activities. The directors still had confidence in him and wanted to assist him. They recognized that the depression had wrecked many apparently sound concerns and remembered his early success. But finally it became evident that firm and close control was essential. H. H. Irvine became chairman of an Executive Committee appointed by the directors to investigate and improve the situation; examination revealed activities on Thompson's part that showed both speculation and extravagance; and eventually Thompson's resignation was accepted. Under John Kendall, who had already taken over much of Thompson's authority, there began a complete overhauling and pruning down of Yards activities to which independent dealers had objected.

The Yards were continued as Weyerhaeuser outlets, and in the long run served well both the Timber Company and other firms. But the losses incurred through the misplaced confidence and inertia of the directors were tremendous. In 1921 alone, a depression year, the Yards showed losses, primarily on inventories, of $2,000,000. The closing down of unprofitable yards meant further losses, and bad debts ultimately added to the total. By 1925 the capital had been impaired by more than $4,000,000.[28]

Meanwhile, plans had been made to develop marketing on the East Coast, and they were destined to achieve far more satisfactory results. In 1914 Long, Rudolph Weyerhaeuser, and W. L. McCormick had spent three weeks inspecting potential sites for a distributing terminal on the eastern seaboard. They visited Boston, New London, Philadelphia, Baltimore, and other places but did not find what they wanted. It was on the way home that they had discovered the Midway site. Hornby, Rudolph Weyerhaeuser, and F. E. Weyerhaeuser argued for making this a central marketing office for eastbound lumber, which would use Tonawanda (on the Niagara River near Buffalo) as a center whence shipments could be made direct to western New York, Pennsylvania, and Ohio, and by lake and Erie Canal to the East Coast.

Long, however, reserved judgment, for he was still thinking in terms of the Panama Canal. He realized that when peace came this route would provide the best means of penetrating eastern markets. His view prevailed, and finally, in the midst of the war (1917) Weyerhaeuser Timber found 73 acres for a yard at Baltimore, which it purchased for a total of $85,475. The area, lying on Chesapeake Bay opposite Fort McHenry of "Star-Spangled Banner" fame, fronted on deep water, provided ample piling room, and was served by three railroads, whose rates from there to points on the East Coast were not exorbitant.[29]

The development of the site would have to wait for the war to end. But with peace Colonel James E. Long, brother of George, was appointed by the directors to manage the new operation. On September 24, 1919, the first cargo of Weyerhaeuser fir lumber was shipped on the S.S. *Mannahocking* to the Baltimore Yard to be used to construct the sheds. This was the beginning of a stream of Weyerhaeuser lumber that would flow eastward through the Canal.[30] The choice of James Long to manage the Baltimore Yard was doubtless influenced by the brilliant record made by his brother in the Far West, but his own record had proved him to be an able executive in the lumber field. He had served as general manager of the F. B. Dubach Lumber Company of Louisiana, as a sales agent in St. Louis for a large group of mills, and in various capacities in Mexico, Brazil, and Argentina. In World War I he rose to be colonel and acted as purchasing agent for the 10th and 20th Engineers, the so-called Forestry Battalions of the overseas army.

Constructed between 1919 and 1921, the Baltimore Yard plant was built in anticipation of the day when, as many lumbermen thought, southern forests would be greatly reduced and the East would become dependent on the Pacific Northwest for its principal timber supply. It had a storage capacity of 75,000,000 feet, and from it deliveries could be made in twenty-four hours to hundreds of dealers and in two to four days to many hundreds more. Essentially, it was an arm of the Everett mills, absorbing their production and turning the eastern seaboard into a regional market for Everett.

The new plant was equipped with a receiving station built along the waterfront. The larger timbers were dumped into the channel and afterward drawn up a slip to the timber sorting dock, where they were loaded on flatcars and hauled to the site. Most lumber was unloaded on the pier, where a narrow-gauge railway extending from the side of the vessel carried it to a huge sorting shed. There the lumber was assembled according to thickness, grade, width, and length. Small railroad cars carried it to specialized sheds, mostly for storage, some for remanufacturing. The entire operation was electrically powered. No other yard in the world had comparable facilities for handling lumber.

By the end of 1921 the total expenditures came to $928,148. "These costs seem alarming and they are," George S. Long declared in the Weyerhaeuser Timber Company report for 1921. But the potential rewards in providing a great new outlet for western fir more than offset the risk of the undertaking.[31]

In the years to follow, East Coast operations and the activities of the Weyerhaeuser Sales Company would expand impressively. The family directors had made a costly mistake in failing to curb Thompson, but they made no mistake with the Baltimore Yard or with the Weyerhaeuser Sales Company. Both would in time prove invaluable. By developing foreign markets for lumber, by helping to multiply retail outlets and coordinate sales activities, and by penetrating eastern markets, the Weyerhaeuser Timber Company had proved its ability to plan and to act.

By the close of the decade, Weyerhaeuser Timber was fully pledged to a manufacturing program; it had logging operations under way on large tracts of timberland; its marketing procedures gave convenient service to consumers. In summarizing its record from the time of the 1914 Bureau of Corporations report to 1920, a Forest Service writer recognized that the company "has sold approximately 250,000 acres, chiefly to operating companies, and has itself become a large timber manufacturer."[32] Never again could government officials hurl the accusation "speculative holder" at the Weyerhaeuser Timber Company. Indeed, with the 1920's Long was to push his growing organization into a strong position among the chief manufacturers of the industry.

NOTES

1. WTC Annual Report, 1915; *Amer. Lbrmn.*, May 8, 1915, p. 39, and Nov. 28, 1914, p. 50.

2. FEW Record, 700.

3. *Amer. Lbrmn.*, April 3, 1915, p. 46; Long Papers, Long to Ingram, Dec. 4, 1909.

4. WTC Annual Report, 1914; *Amer. Lbrmn.*, April 24, 1918 (characterization of plant).

5. WTC annl. repts., 1914, 1917.

6. WTC annl. repts., 1916–1917; FEW Record, 711; Long Papers, Long to F. S. Bell, July 21, 1917.

7. WTC Papers, "Historical Financial Information," 30; WTC Annual Report, 1916; *Amer. Lbrmn.*, Sept. 28, 1918, p. 48; O. D. Fisher, Reminiscences. Both Long and FEW interviewed Warren prior to his appointment.

8. Long Papers, F. S. Bell to Long, Oct. 23, 1914; White to Long, Sept. 21, 1914; Long to FEW, Dec. 29, 1914; Corresp., Warren and Long, Sept., 1915–Jan., 1916. While Long did not offer Onstad's services to Warren until Jan. 13, 1916, Onstad was already at Snoqualmie Falls on Dec. 20, 1915, and Long was writing to him about the prospective plant.

9. WTC Annual Report, 1916; *Amer. Lbrmn.*, May 20, 1917, p. 54; Sept. 1, 1917, p. 56; Dec. 15, 1917, p. 60; and Sept. 28, 1918, p. 48; R. B. Hunt, comments made in Sept., 1918 (Everett Mill B furnishing lumber).

10. *Amer. Lbrmn.*, Sept. 28, 1918, p. 48; Long Papers, Corresp., April–May, 1921 (Titcomb and Ingram).

11. FEW Record, 683–686; WTC annl. repts., 1916; Long Papers, Long to O. H. Ingram, June 20, 1910; U.S.D.A., Forest Service, *Timber Depletion, Lumber Prices, Lumber Exports, and Concentration of Timber Ownership,* 63.

12. FEW Papers, FEW to Long, May 28, 1912; Long to FEW, June 3, 1912, and Sept. 17, 1920; Long Papers, FEW to Long, Sept. 2, 1916 (on purchasing); Long to C. H. Webber, Portland, April 30, 1917; WTC Min. Bk., Oct. 16, 1920.

13. WTC Papers, "Historical Financial Information"; WTC annl. repts; FEW Papers, Boner to FEW, Nov. 3, 1910.

14. Statistics on fir-stumpage prices in Greeley, *Forests and Men,* 19; on cost of living, Dept. of Commerce, Bureau of Census, *Historical Statistics of the United States,* 231; Dept. of Commerce, Bureau of Corporations, *Lumber Industry,* Pt. 2, 14, 1921.

15. WTC annl. repts., 1916 (CCTC cutting green timber); "Historical Financial Information." As previously noted, the Sound Timber Co. had made some of the first Weyerhaeuser timberland purchases on the coast (Sound Tbr. Co. Papers, "In Memory of J. L. Bridge," and Min. Bk., Feb. 5, 1953). See also FEW Record, 546,666, 714–716; JPW Papers, Bridge to JPW, March 31, 1922; Long Papers, Long to Bradstreets, Feb. 8, 1918. By 1922 two-thirds of STC's logs were going to Mill B.

16. Long Papers, Warren to Long, Aug. 21, 1920. The electric system was abandoned in 1932 owing to high costs, breakdowns, and thefts of equipment.

17. Hunt, Reminiscences.

18. *Ibid.; Amer. Lbrmn.,* Dec. 5, 1914, p. 5; WTC Papers, L. N. Reichman to CDW, April 16, 1951; *ibid.,* "Historical Financial Information." For ships docking at Everett Mill A, see *Amer. Lbrmn., passim.*

19. WTC Annual Report, 1914; Long Papers, Long to D. E. Skinner, May 22, 1915; *Amer. Lbrmn.,* June 26, 1915, p. 39.

20. Rates on lumber to Chicago from the Northern Pacific Coast early in 1915 were 55¢ per 100 lbs., and 70¢ on sash and doors. Dealers in Iowa, Illinois, and Wisconsin protested to the Interstate Commerce Commission, which on March 30 ruled that the rates had not been shown to be unreasonable. And apparently fir was selling in the Middle West. See *Amer. Lbrmn.,* April 3, 1915, p. 38.

21. Long Papers, FEW Papers, correspondence, 1915–1916; R. E. Saberson, Reminiscences.

22. Hunt, Reminiscences; Long Papers, Boner to L. S. Case; May 27, 1916; FEW Papers, FEW to Boner, Sept. 8, 1916, and Oct. 26, 1916; Long Papers, Long to Boner, July 21, 1916.

23. FEW Papers, Long to Thompson, Dec. 22, 1915; WTC Papers, "Historical Financial Information."

24. FEW Papers, statement enclosed, letter of Thompson to Long, July 30, 1917 (indebtedness); Long Papers, Long to FEW, Nov. 26, 1917; FEW Papers, memo from Long to FEW, Nov. 23, 1917; LN Papers, F. S. Bell to Allison Laird, Jan. 23, 1918.

25. FEW Papers, Sales Agreement, Dec. 16, 1918, and deed to WTC, Sept. 4, 1919; FEW to JPW, Sept. 4, 1918; Long Papers, Long to CAW, Sept. 7, 1918. Charles Weyerhaeuser negotiated the purchase of the Twin Cities tract from Barrett & Zimmerman, its owners. They had supplied horses to logging camps.

26. JPW Papers, FKW to parents, Aug. 9, 1920; FKW to the authors, July 17, 1959.

27. WTC Papers, Thompson Yards, "Schedule of Certain Significant Operating Figures," Exhibit I; "Historical Financial Information," 31; FKW to authors, Sept., 1958 (general causes of Thompson Yards difficulties).

28. WTC Papers, Thompson Yards; Annual Financial Statements, Yards Securities Co. (Weyerhaeuser vault, St. Paul); "Historical Financial Information," *ibid.,* 31. Thompson had advanced money to underwrite the building of certain apartment house buildings in Sioux City and Minneapolis without the knowledge of the stockholders.

29. WTC Annual Report, 1917 (an additional 6.43 acres at Baltimore was acquired in 1918); Long Papers, Long to G. R. Willis, June 25, 1918.

30. Long Papers, Long to C. R. McCormick, Sept. 19, 1919.

31. FEW Papers, memo by Long to FEW, July 8, 1919, with blueprints; *Salesmen's Log,* July 17, 1922; *Weyerhaeuser Log,* March, 1926; WTC Annual Report, 1921.

32. U.S.D.A., Forest Service, *Timber Depletion,* 61.

XVI

Under Fire

IT WAS INEVITABLE that after the purchase of its huge timberland holding in the Pacific Northwest the Weyerhaeuser group should come under sharp attack from several quarters. One source of hostility was the muckraking movement of the early 1900's, as national magazines, like *McClure's, Cosmopolitan,* and *Everybody's* competed in exposing a wide variety of actual evils and some alleged abuses that did not exist at all. Another source was the deep-rooted and justifiable hatred of the American people for monopoly and their tendency to equate corporate bigness with monopolistic perils. A third was the growing belief that the natural resources of the nation were limited, belonged to all, and should not be allowed to pass carelessly into the hands of corporations bound to deal selfishly, and perhaps disastrously, with them. Finally, the crusade for the conservation of forests, indicting the wasteful malpractices of lumbermen, fixed public attention on the largest timber holders, regardless of their behavior.

All this presented a problem in public relations, and leaders of the Weyerhaeuser group failed to meet it effectively for many years. Though not secretive, they had a habit of silence. The fire opened against them was by no means so heavy as that poured upon Rockefeller, Carnegie, Morgan, the Dukes, the Havemeyers, and various railroad magnates. Knowing the talk of a "lumber trust" and monopoly to be absurd, they simply shrugged it off. As a matter of fact, the few attacks by muckrakers, lurid and slapdash, were in sum total rather silly. Combining a little truth, much inaccuracy, and some mendacity, they impressed few readers. But the assaults by the enemies of big business who shouted "Greed!" and by the conservationists who cried "Waste!" should have been taken more seriously. Members of the Weyerhaeuser group unquestionably realized that, holding huge tracts while they doubled or trebled in value, they incurred the charge of locking up timberland for the unearned increment. They might have tried harder to comprehend the point of view of the conservationists, to expound the economic and political situation of lumbermen, and to create mutual understanding as a basis for cooperative action.

2

The conservation movement indeed offered the one substantial challenge to the public position occupied by the Weyerhaeuser interests. In the Pacific Northwest the two elements that counted most in forest management early in the century were the national government and private holders. The states had a distinctly lesser influence, for they possessed only a small fraction of the regional timber, hardly 16 billion feet out of a total of about 1,132 billion. State politics were often corrupt, and state leaders showed little wisdom.[1] In the end they would have to cooperate by liberalizing their tax laws, helping in fire protection, and taking other cooperative measures, but they waited. Meanwhile, practical conservation could best be fostered by federal agencies and large corporations—and in awakening public opinion the United States Forest Service took the lead. Theoretically the Weyerhaeusers could have marched in the van, but economic conditions limited them, and some company heads did not have the vision required. The associates moved forward but slowly, meanwhile suffering from some sharp criticism.

If anyone believed on Washington's Birthday in 1897, when Grover Cleveland set aside thirteen great Forest Reserves, that conservation would thenceforth have an easy path, he was soon disillusioned. Young Gifford Pinchot, who was to bear the banner of the crusade, was not deceived. He had witnessed McKinley's inauguration on March 4th with a keen realization that "the worst of our troubles were still ahead of us." As an extra session of Congress began, Westerners whetted their knives to cut to pieces the thirteen tracts, totaling 21,280,000 acres. Press dispatches announced that at McKinley's first full Cabinet meeting the sole question of public importance discussed was whether Cleveland's conservation order should be rescinded. An assault on this order was already under way in North Dakota, where the powerful Homestake Mining Company was determined to continue cutting mine timbers in the new Black Hills Forest Reserve. Cornelius N. Bliss, head of the Interior Department, was willing to let the Homestake have its way, without cost and without limit.[2]

Immediately it became evident that friends of the Forest Reserves would have to consent to certain compromises. They had to agree to a suspension of Cleveland's proclamation (except in California) for one year, during which the lands would be open to continued entry. McKinley himself was friendly to the reserves. But as he told Pinchot and Charles D. Walcott, head of the Geological Survey, when they went to the White House to plead for the forests, "Everybody who comes here brings a crisis along." Needing the support of anticonservationist congressmen in dealing with the Spanish troubles, the currency question, and the tariff, the President had to make concessions. Fortunately, during the one-year period little really important timber was lost to the government.

Meanwhile McKinley signed the memorable Pettigrew Amendment to the Sundry Civil Appropriations Act (June 4, 1897), which on the whole greatly aided the cause of sound public forestry. This legislation, important to Weyerhaeuser as well as to other lumber interests, gave the Secretary of the Interior power to administer the reserves for the proper use and preservation of the forests. It authorized him to sell the "dead, mature, or large growth of trees," when properly inspected and marked; to permit free private use of timber and stone for various purposes; to build wagon roads and other improvements; and to allow the use of water for mining, milling, irrigation, and similar purposes. In a word, it put an end to western fears that the reserves (an unfortunate term) would lock up valuable natural wealth, and assured everybody that the formula would be utilization, not hoarding. Although the timber and stone clause was so loosely interpreted that it allowed some unfortunate grabbing by mining, ranching, and lumbering interests, the total effect of the Pettigrew Amendment was to make possible proper forest protection and management by skilled and public-spirited men. It remained the basic law of the National Forests long after its chief sponsors were dead.[3]

The unhappiest feature of the law for the conservationists was the "land lieu" or "forest lieu" section. Its far-reaching potentialities are evident from its text:

> That in cases in which a tract covered by a bona-fide claim or by a patent is included within the limits of a public forest reserve, the settler or owner thereof may, if he desires to do so, relinquish the tract to the government, and in lieu thereof select a tract of vacant land open to settlement, not exceeding in area the tract covered by the claim or patent.[4]

As originally drafted, this clause had applied only to settlers and was intended to relieve homesteaders isolated by Forest Reserve restrictions. The addition of the two words "or owner" gave rise later to some unfounded suspicions. Senator R. F. Pettigrew found it sinister that the conference committee on the bill was headed by William B. Allison for the Senate and Joe Cannon for the House, both friends of big business.[5] An irresponsible Hearst writer went further in inventing a malicious allegation: "It has been charged, and circumstances lend plausibility to the charge, that the scheme was concocted in the land office of the Northern Pacific Railroad Company in St. Paul, and for the benefit of the Weyerhaeuser interests."[6] Circumstances negate this theory: the Northern Pacific land office was not concerned, and the Weyerhaeusers in 1897 had no interest in Northern Pacific lands. Gifford Pinchot himself has punctured the idea of a nefarious plot. He confesses that the first forestry bill that he and Walcott introduced read "settlers or owners" in a similar connection!

Nevertheless, as Pinchot writes, the two words cost the government many millions of acres of its best lands. "What they [the framers] meant was that any lumber company, mining company, railroad company, cattle outfit, or any other large owner could get rid of their cutover land, their worked-out claims, the valueless portion of their land grants, or any other land they had no use for and take in exchange an equal area of the most valuable non-mineral land they could find anywhere in the Public Domain."[7] The Northern Pacific directly and the Weyerhaeuser group indirectly were among the chief beneficiaries. But they profited not only from a single carelessly worded law but from the whole system of carelessness that made it impossible for the government to identify the truly valuable parts of its domain.

For, writes Pinchot: "Many of the then boundary lines of the Forest Reserves were, and could have been, nothing but shots in the dark. Many of them had not even been surveyed. As to how much worthless or unsuitable land was included, one man's guess was almost as good as another's."[8] In dealing with the vast timber resources of the Far West, the government, corporations, and individual settlers alike were working largely in the dark—all groping, all taking risks.

The fate of the Forest Reserves once settled, a revolution in government forestry became possible. Able as Bernhard E. Fernow was, under him the old Forestry Division had got nowhere. He was convinced that the main hope for conservation lay with the states and had insisted that the division should be merely an information bureau, "to preach, not practice." Happily for Pinchot and enlightened government action, in 1898 Fernow accepted the headship of the new forestry school at Cornell University. On May 11th of that year the Secretary of Agriculture, "Tama Jim" Wilson, offered the Forestry Division to Pinchot with a free hand in running it. "I could appoint my own assistants, do what kind of work I chose, and not fear any interference from him," wrote Pinchot later. It was an epochal day for American forest policy when on July 1, 1898, he took charge with the new and appropriate title of Forester.

Yet Pinchot's appointment was only a first step. His Forestry Division had no authority whatever over the Forest Reserves or other government timberlands. They were controlled by a division in the General Land Office, managed by clerks who knew little forestry and who had probably never seen a government tree. Pinchot's chief functions at first were to make scientific surveys of the forests and to promote forestry on private lands. As he had only a tiny office force and scanty funds, his principal assets were his almost fanatical zeal, unflagging energy, and skill in making influential friends.

Determined to drop mere exhortation and put really practical forestry into the woods, Pinchot had to face the fact that the whole country contained only eight or ten expert foresters—all, like himself and Fernow, trained in Europe. It was clearly important to educate young men at home to augment this force. From 1898 to 1913 Carl A. Schenck and others trained many practical foresters in his Biltmore Forestry School at Biltmore, North Carolina. Beginning in 1899 Pinchot started appointing annual batches of student assistants, green college boys whom he put through a rigorous field discipline. Then, with the cooperation of President A. T. Hadley, in the fall of 1900 he launched the Yale School of Forestry with an endowment of $150,000 (soon doubled) from the Pinchot family, and with Henry S. Graves, another skilled and zealous forester, as the first dean.[9]

From the beginning Pinchot, who was essentially a hardheaded, moderate man, laid emphasis upon an offer of government assistance to private interests. This, his public duty, also met his personal views. Since private owners held something like two-thirds of all the forest lands of the nation, a half-billion acres, Pinchot fully understood that the national forester must become their partner. His Circular 21, issued late in 1898 with an offer of practical help on the ground in working out plans for judicious lumbering, brought a quick response. Within less than a year 123 lumbermen asked for aid on 1,500,000 acres in 35 states, thus establishing a pattern of the utmost importance.[10]

It was obvious that the next logical step would be to give the Forestry Division full authority to manage government timberlands. All the foresters were under Pinchot in the Department of Agriculture and were restricted to giving advice. When Theodore Roosevelt became President he called on Pinchot and reclamation expert F. H. Newell to write the parts of his first annual message dealing with forestry and irrigation;[11] and Pinchot at once saw that this was a heaven-sent chance. Not only did the message declare that the preservation of the forests was "an imperative business necessity," and emphasize the value of the Forest Reserves to mining, grazing, irrigation, and other interests; it asserted that all responsibility for the Reserves should be united in a Bureau of Forestry.[12] The new Secretary of the Interior, Ethan Allen Hitchcock, shared these views. In 1901 by law, the desired change was made, and the

Bureau began to make a technical study of the conditions and needs of government woodlands.

For four years, however, Congress failed to effect a proper union of expert forestry and the national forests. While the administration waited, a series of exposés of land frauds shocked the country. Though none of these exposures affected the Weyerhaeusers, they altered the whole atmosphere of the group's public relations.

3

The revelations began late in 1902 when Secretary Hitchcock telephoned Binger Hermann, head of the General Land Office, to bring him a certain report. Hermann, a lame-duck congressman from Oregon when McKinley appointed him, was a fat, long-bearded, vulpine politician who thought solely of his and his friends' profit. As Pinchot put it, he believed that "a public office is a private snap." The document he fetched to Hitchcock was a report that had been prepared on Hitchcock's initiative the previous year by a special agent of the Department of Agriculture in Phoenix, Arizona; it alleged that a group of wealthy men had conspired to rob the government of hundreds of thousands—perhaps millions—of acres of choice land.[13]

"You have sat on this report for six weeks without saying a word about it," Hitchcock sternly told Hermann. "Why?" As Hermann stuttered, he cut the man short: "I dismiss you from office. I have President Roosevelt's authorization to do so." Hermann lingered long enough to destroy important evidence. Enough remained, however, to prove extensive land frauds. Before Hitchcock left office in 1907, the government had found more than a thousand indictments and had convicted 126 public land thieves.[14]

The government disclosures shook the whole West. At first the public centered its attention on the fencing of public lands by horse and cattle companies in Kansas, Nebraska, Colorado, Montana, and other states with large semiarid stretches. Grazing companies, acquiring key tracts of railroad lands, would fence them and the intermingled public lands into one huge enclosure, shutting homesteaders out of the national domain. The Nebraska Land & Feeding Company, for example, had thus fenced 400,000 acres.

The focus of interest soon shifted, however, to the Far Northwest. Young Francis J. Heney had brilliantly prosecuted certain frauds in California. When the work of a special Interior Department investigator showed in 1903 that Oregon was a center of corruption, Roosevelt appointed Heney as Assistant Federal Attorney for Oregon to continue the inquiry and press the prosecutions. Here, even more than in other parts

of the West, a large number of important citizens had engaged in espio-
nage, falsification of the public records, collusion, bribery, and other illegal acts to rob the government.

Though some northwestern leaders of the highest political standing
were affected, Roosevelt, Hitchcock, and Heney carried their purgation
through with iron resolution. Much of the fraud had involved use of the
land-lieu clause. That is, the conspirators had fabricated illegal patents
to railroad lands taken from the government domain and had then exchanged them for the choicest acreage they could find outside. Heney,
with the assistance of William J. Burns, a secret-service agent of great
talents, obtained the indictment of Binger Hermann, of Congressman
J. N. Williamson, of mayors, public attorneys, legislators, and finally, as
a climax, of Senator John H. Mitchell. This seventy-year-old Republican
leader had first entered the upper chamber in 1873! On the edge of his
grave, on January 17, 1905, he delivered to the Senate a ringing denial
of the charges against him. But they were sustained by the confession
of his partner, and he was sentenced to a term in jail, which he never
lived to serve.[15]

These exposés and prosecutions, producing a tremendous impression
on the nation, naturally strengthened the sentiment for a firmer federal
control over the public domain. Roosevelt dealt drastically with the violent opposition of the anticonservationists in Congress, led by Senators
Patterson (Colorado), Heyburn (Idaho), Fulton (Oregon), and Carter
and Clark (Montana). In 1906–1907 he issued broad executive orders
enlarging the Forest Reserves and withdrawing mineral lands from private
exploitation.[16] "I acted on the theory," he writes, "that the President could
at any time in his discretion withdraw from entry any of the public lands
of the United States and reserve the same for forestry, for waterpower
sites, for irrigation, and for other public purposes. Without such action
it would have been impossible to stop the activity of the land thieves."
The Weyerhaeuser group, who acted scrupulously within the law, had
obtained its large Pacific Coast holdings in the nick of time, for some of
the land would soon have been withdrawn from purchase.

The objectionable land-lieu clause was repealed March 3, 1905.[17]
Constant vigilance was maintained in guarding the public lands—and
much it was needed. At the cost of a great deal of friction with vocal
western elements, the East rallied in almost solid support of the conservationist measures of Roosevelt and Pinchot.

Roosevelt accompanied his activities with some utterances that were
sensible and healthy and some others that were irrational. An example
of his judicious statements is offered by his letter to Senator Heyburn on
June 13, 1905, which is of special note because it plainly refers to Weyerhaeuser properties. He was commenting on unidentified clippings from
some Idaho newspapers that Heyburn sent him:

One specially interesting article contains an interview in which the opinion is expressed that the recent temporary withdrawal in the Coeur d'Alene and Lewiston districts was encouraged by certain large corporations, which corporations already hold large bodies of timberland in Idaho and adjacent States. It is argued that if this temporary withdrawal is made permanent these corporations will be the only people who can purchase the timber from the Government; and that they will be able to make purchases at a very low figure and in that way stifle competition. . . . In reality, in such cases as this, the establishment of a forest reserve offers the fairest possible solution of the questions at issue. At present, since by far the greater part of the lands are unsurveyed, the timber cannot be lawfully disposed of. Just as soon as a forest reserve is established the mature [timber] is for sale and for sale to the settler, the miner, and the stockman; to individuals, companies, and corporations. It is for sale in large or small amounts. Moreover, the Government is at liberty to sell as much or as little as conditions may warrant, and at such a price as circumstances may call for. But it is for sale; it is not to be stolen, and this simple fact accounts for much of the hostility to our policy.[18]

This letter suggests a desire for cooperation between the federal forester and the intelligent timberman. Roosevelt expressed the same sentiment and faith in the growing enlightenment of lumbermen, when he told the American Forest Congress in 1905:

Henceforth the movement for the conservative use of the forest is to come mainly from within, and not from without; from the men who are actively interested in the use of the forest one way or another, even more than from those whose interest is philanthropic and general. The difference means, to a large extent, the difference between mere agitation and actual execution; between the hope of accomplishment and the thing done.

This unique Congress, held January 2–6, brought together representatives of all the great interests with a stake in forest preservation. Ambassador Jules Jusserand told what had been done in France, Aubrey White what had been done in Ontario. James J. Hill sent a letter, and Howard Elliott, president of the Northern Pacific, spoke. F. E. Weyerhaeuser, who with other lumbermen had visited Pinchot before the meeting to offer the cooperation of western timberland corporations, made a brief, effective address in which he championed practical forestry. Livestock growers also appeared.

Unfortunately, at this Congress Roosevelt departed from his manuscript and, facing a number of lumbermen in attendance, denounced the men who "skin the country and go somewhere else . . . whose idea of developing the country is to cut every stick of timber off of it, and leave a barren desert for the home-maker who comes in after him. That man is a curse." In the opinion of some careful students of the northwestern industry, this ill-founded accusation of "skinning the land" (for in general second-crop timber sprang up abundantly) retarded the period of mutual cooperation by years. Pinchot made an entirely sound statement to the

Congress: "The forests of the private owners will have to be set in order if the overwhelming calamity of timber famine is to be kept from this nation."[19]

As a result of the exposures, prosecutions, and public preaching, Roosevelt and Pinchot won their administrative goal. Congress by Act of February 1, 1905, transferred the Forest Reserves from the Department of the Interior to the Department of Agriculture, with the Bureau of Forestry (renamed Forest Service) in full control over the Forest Reserves—soon to be renamed the National Forests. The Bureau in January, 1905, governed some 63,000,000 acres. By December it administered nearly 98,000,000 acres, a larger area than any state except Texas and California.

Pinchot forthwith received from Secretary James Wilson a letter that was a virtual charter of powers and activities. The recipient completely approved of its key sentence: "All the resources of forest reserves are for *use*, and this use must be brought about in a thoroughly prompt and business-like manner, under such restrictions only as will insure the permanence of these resources." It was a statement that was to mean much to the Weyerhaeuser interests. In Oregon, Washington, and Idaho they were close neighbors of the National Forests, and in time worked out a set of friendly and mutually beneficial arrangements with the government agents.

Roosevelt's most spectacular coup for the National Forests came in 1907. The anticonservationist members of Congress, led by Senator Charles W. Fulton of Oregon, amended an appropriation bill to divest the President of any right to create new National Forests in Oregon, Washington, Idaho, Colorado, Montana, and Wyoming. Instantly Pinchot put every available man to work drawing up proclamations for forests in these states. Roosevelt signed and issued the proclamations before he assented to the appropriation bill, thus adding 16,000,000 acres to the reserved area. "The opponents of the Forest Service," he wrote later, "turned handsprings in their wrath." Altogether, before he left the White House he had added 148,000,000 acres to the national forests.[20]

4

Meanwhile, the work of making the American people "forest conscious" was ably forwarded by a number of responsible scientists and publicists, as well as by the steady stream of bulletins and reports from the Bureau of Forestry or Forest Service. One of the first important articles, by Henry Gannett of the Geological Survey in the *Forum* in 1900,[21] bore the ominous title, "Is a Timber Famine Imminent?" His answer was "Yes, unless . . ."

Gannett, perhaps the most eminent American geographer of his time, used statistics to support a plea for efficient lumbering methods and reforestation. The country possessed, he believed, about 1,380 billion feet of timber. The cut in 1890 had been about 25 billion feet and had since increased. It would therefore appear that the national stock of timber would meet the present demands of industry and people for less than two generations; but this gloomy conclusion must be modified by the fact that, in spite of fires, the country grew about 30 billion new feet a year. "It seems, therefore, that if we could reduce the sources of waste to a minimum, the prospect of a continuous supply of timber from our woodlands would be good." This, however, would demand a radical change in lumbering practices. Too much immature timber was cut; too little attention paid to establishing conditions that would encourage new crops; too often the harvesting was mere butchery, "from 60 to 75 per cent only of the tree being cut and utilized as lumber." The nation, he said in effect, must awake.

Various writers took a still graver view of the possibility of a national shortage. With fuller knowledge, Forest Inspector R. S. Kellogg sounded an alarming note in his circular on "The Timber Supply of the United States" issued by the Department of Agriculture in 1907. He pointed out that in spite of the rising price of wood and the many respects in which it was being supplanted by steel, concrete, glass, and other materials, the country was using, not only absolutely but relatively, more of it than ever before. While between 1880 and 1900 the population increased 52 percent, the lumber cut rose by 94 percent. Americans used each year about 400 feet of lumber apiece as against only 60 feet used by Europeans. This fact meant that unless lumbermen and consumers radically changed their habits the nation must face a shock.

"It has been shown," wrote Kellogg, "that the present annual cut of forest products requires at least twenty billion cubic feet of wood. To produce this quantity of wood without impairing the capital stock, our 700 million acres of forest must make an annual increment of thirty cubic feet per acre. Under present conditions of mismanagement and neglect, it is safe to say that the average annual increment is less than ten cubic feet per acre for the entire area."[22]

This general indictment of lumbering practices applied to the Weyerhaeusers, of course, as well as to all other private owners. Four-fifths of the woodlands of America remained in private hands. Here it was that reform was most imperative. The nation had treated its forests as if they were a vast mineral deposit, to be exploited without any attention to a renewal. It would have to follow Europe in regarding timber as a slow crop, which must be made to keep pace with consumption. The crop had been garnered three times as fast as it grew; now disaster plainly awaited a failure to achieve some real balance.

Year by year the chorus of protest against waste and improvidence grew. A dozen magazines, notably the *Century, Harper's Weekly, Collier's,* and the *Outlook,* printed frequent articles. Many states appointed forest commissions or hired expert foresters to advise the innumerable woodlot owners. Publishers issued books on German, British, and Scandinavian forest practices, and writers reviewed them with a crusading note. The eminent naturalists John Muir and John Burroughs, too honest and perceptive to indulge in random abuse, nevertheless warmly espoused conservation. When an irresponsible lumber concern near Littleton, New Hampshire, laid waste the lovely wilderness around Glen Ellis Falls and Carter Notch, deep in the White Mountains, a dismayed outcry arose. Such episodes helped effect the passage in 1911 of the Weeks Act, which authorized the government purchase of timberlands east as well as west of the Mississippi and brought about the creation of National Forests in various parts of the Appalachians.

The Weyerhaeuser interests were aware of the rising demand for scientific, balanced, and self-sustaining forestry. About 1902 they authorized a payment of $5,000 to the Bureau of Forestry for an examination of certain timber properties; the Bureau made the study in 1904 and recommended more intensive fire protection, which the company promptly put into effect. In 1903 the Weyerhaeusers requested that a scientifically trained forester, C. S. Chapman, be assigned by the Forest Service to examine their Pacific Coast holdings and to give his opinion on proper management. (Much later—1924—he joined the Timber Company's staff.) In 1907 Clyde S. Martin, also scientifically trained, was employed by George Long for W.T.C. In the same year Frederick E. Weyerhaeuser acted as chairman of a group collecting funds to endow a chair of forestry at Yale, and Weyerhaeuser Timber contributed $10,000 to this fund. Two years later Long aided in hiring E. T. Allen, a distinguished forester, to form the Western Forestry and Conservation Association. In other ways, as noted later, the group showed an interest in modern forestry and conservation policies; if for a time they failed to take the vigorous leadership they were finally to assume, theirs was as progressive an outlook as that of any lumber group in the Pacific Northwest.

5

The attack of the muckrakers on the Weyerhaeusers, meanwhile, had a popgun quality in sharp contrast with the howitzer bombardments that roared against the Harrimans, Rockefellers, Carnegies, and Morgans. The assaults were few in number and puny in argument. Indeed, the entire

lumber industry escaped lightly. Considering how much public indigna-
tion the politico-economic activities of such lumbermen as Isaac Stephenson and Philetus Sawyer of Wisconsin aroused within their own state, it is
remarkable how little national attention they received. They were bosses
and spoils politicians. Robert M. La Follette accused Sawyer of attempting to bribe him, and in his autobiography lashed him with stinging words:
"He regarded Congress as a useful agency for the promotion of business
enterprises in which he and his friends were identified or interested."[23]
Stephenson had to undergo a sensational investigation of his campaign
expenditures for the Senate. Joseph L. Fordney of Michigan, another
lumberman, was co-author of a highly controversial tariff law. But the
lumber industry was wildly competitive, with thousands of small units
scattered over the whole map, and its general business practices after
1890 were so little open to attack that only a few sensational journalists
tried to put it in the pillory.

The Weyerhaeusers and their associates took scant interest in cau-
cuses or elections. "Mr. Weyerhaeuser is very positive in his demands that
our representatives keep out of politics," F. E. Weyerhaeuser wrote in
1906.[24] This closed one possible avenue for attack. Still, the wealth and
power of the Weyerhaeuser co-investors were so great, and after the northwestern purchases of 1900 on so gigantic a scale, that they could not hope
to escape some honest criticism and some malicious misrepresentation.

In 1906, the year in which Upton Sinclair published *The Jungle* in
book form, William Randolph Hearst turned an investigator loose on
Weyerhaeuser firms. Charles P. Norcross, head of Hearst's Washington
bureau, appeared in St. Paul and Tacoma. Business friends, including
James J. Hill, warned the elder Weyerhaeuser of his presence. "So far
as I can see," F. E. Weyerhaeuser wrote George S. Long, "his [Norcross's]
effort is to show that Mr. Weyerhaeuser as a stockholder of the Northern
Pacific Railroad bought its timber at a cheap price and perhaps took
Mr. Hill in as a partner in consideration of his influence in favoring the
deal."[25] Later, Norcross was to gain notoriety as an assailant of the sugar
trust. He now produced, in what seems to have been the first real attack
on the group,[26] an article that had the explosive impact of a penny fire-
cracker.

His article in the *Cosmopolitan* for January, 1907, "Weyerhaeuser—
Richer than John D. Rockefeller," brought the elderly lumberman the
congratulations of acquaintances astonished to learn that somebody
thought him the richest man on the globe. Full of allegations, it was empty
of any substantial facts. The Weyerhaeuser wealth had been amassed
from the ravaging of forests, wrote Norcross; nobody knew what part
of his timberlands had been gained by fraud, but it was certain that the
land-lieu law had given him his chance for a "big steal." Norcross went on

to say that Weyerhaeuser trusted R. L. McCormick, one of his principal lieutenants, implicitly, and McCormick was not only the keenest lumberman of the West but the suavest politician. (Actually, McCormick's experience as manager for the North Wisconsin Lumber Company lay well in the past, and in the Far West he had dealt with business and public-relations matters. He was not a "keen" lumberman compared with men like Boner, Raught, or Minot Davis.) The Weyerhaeuser group, continued the journalist, had acquired an immense tract in Oregon by using the old federal grant for a military road and, with the help of Senator Fulton, had exchanged poor military road lands for a compact body of extremely valuable forest. Weyerhaeuser and his friends, wrote Norcross, practically controlled the Washington and Oregon woods.

This emanation of the "diseased Hearst mind," wrote F. E. Weyerhaeuser, outdid Baron Munchausen. He could not find words to express his astonishment "that such d——d rot is published by any periodical." The group could think of no better protection than a dignified silence. But R. L. McCormick answered some of the charges in the Tacoma *Daily Ledger,* while the *Mississippi Valley Lumberman* lost no time in writing "absolutely false" across the whole article.

It was of course false to assert that the Weyerhaeusers had made any use of the military road grant; they had given up a temporary option on it. It was false to declare, as Norcross did, that for the past thirty years Weyerhaeuser had been practically the timber agent for the Northern Pacific lands; his large interest in these lands was recent, and he had never exercised anything remotely approaching such a function. It was false to imply that his purchase of the railroad tracts was in any way besmirched by fraud or special favor. The *Lumberman* gave the true history of the purchase. The Northern Pacific was paying 8 percent or more on $6,000,000 of bonds to be retired by the sale of the lands; the directors, eager for relief, sought a purchaser; Weyerhaeuser succeeded in getting together a group able to raise the $6,000,000, and made the purchase at a fair market price. Subsequently the Weyerhaeusers bought land from private owners at lower rates. Norcross's estimate of the Weyerhaeuser fortune and of the profits of his companies was grossly magnified.

When Norcross "has endeavored to tell of methods," remarked the *Lumberman,* "he has manufactured much out of whole cloth. In other words, he has willfully lied, or has been equally guilty of publishing, without investigation, the lies others have told him."[27]

Most of the few other muckraking efforts simply echoed this irresponsible article. The most notable was Charles Edward Russell's "The Mysterious Octopus: Story of the Strange and Powerful Organization That Controls the American Lumber Trade," in another Hearst periodical, *The World Today,* in 1912.[28] Russell added some touches of his own. He asserted that "the whole lumber industry of the United States is held together by a matchless and wonderful organization"—not a trust but an octopus. He declared that Weyerhaeuser "might be called the Twentieth Century's Man in the Iron Mask, so curious is the mystery that for some reason has grown up around him." A sketch of Weyerhaeuser's early career presented him as an early pioneer for the business trinity of consolidation, combination, and simplification. Like Norcross, Russell believed that the leader leaned heavily on one lieutenant; but he identified this man not as McCormick but as Edward Hines. The article repeated the suggestion that Weyerhaeuser was the world's richest man but abstained from any charge of dishonesty. On the contrary, wrote Russell:

> The combination that dominates, controls, manipulates, and spies upon the American lumber trade is not composed of bad men, but men of the highest possible standing in their communities, eminent and respected leaders of business, men of character and worth; and the ends for the sake of which they resort to such extraordinary means are ends that they hold to be right. . . .
> This fact elevates their story far above any mere trust story that ever was told. These men are fighting daily and risking imprisonment for what they believe to be a principle, and the thing for which they fight is medieval, reversionary, and so economically unsound that if they knew anything about either economics or the real history of the race they would revolt at it. And yet they are willing to go to jail for it. In the United States of America, Twentieth Century A.D.[29]

This picture of a trade-controlling octopus in the loose, sprawling association of the various Weyerhaeuser interests, holding a very small fraction of the highly competitive lumber business, beguiled few other writers. It was not mentioned by Emerson Hough in his article in *Everybody's* in 1908 entitled "The Slaughter of the Trees."[30] This reputable author went no further than to write: "Perhaps the greatest of the lumber kings is Mr. Frederick Weyerhaeuser, who is said to be as honest, personally, as any man, but whose agents in many cases were not." Hough did not substantiate this accusation against the agents. He stated of the Northern Pacific purchases: "The acquisition of these lands from the railroads seems to have been an ordinary business deal." Nor when the equally reputable Stewart Edward White dealt in the *American Magazine* the same year with "The Fight for the Forests" did he indulge in any unfounded allegations. His article was an able, hard-hitting, fair-minded plea for the National Forests, coupled with sharp criticism of "The Silver Tongues" opposing their creation—Heyburn, Carter, Patterson, and Fulton.

In the early 1900's Weyerhaeuser and his associates became involved in a dispute with a farmer, John F. Dietz, about the driving of logs on the Thornapple River in Sawyer County, Wisconsin. The Chippewa Lum-

ber & Boom Company owned the Cameron Dam on this stream and had
used it for driving logs for twenty-seven years. About 1900 the widow of
H. L. Cameron sold forty acres of land, on which part of the dam was
built, to Mrs. Dietz (Hattie E.), but without any mention of a reservation
dating back to 1877 that had permitted the construction of the dam and
guaranteed its continued use to its builder and owner, with the right to
flood adjacent acres during log drives. The Chippewa Lumber & Boom
had acquired the dam and all rights associated with it.

In 1904 the company undertook to drive 6,500,000 feet of logs past
the dam. Dietz, who claimed to own the dam, not only threatened to shoot
anyone attempting to use the facility but also demanded $8,000 in toll for
logs driven since his wife had acquired the property.

As one commentator remarked, Dietz had no more title to the dam
than to the White House in Washington. The attorney for the Chippewa
Lumber & Boom Company later pointed out that the transfer of the forty
acres by Mrs. Cameron without any reservation "might give Mrs. Dietz a
claim for damages against Mrs. Cameron, but could not possibly give
Mrs. Dietz any claim to the dam or against the Company, as Mrs. Cameron manifestly could not sell something she did not own."

The company applied to the circuit court of Sawyer County for an
injunction restraining Dietz, and it was granted; but Dietz ignored it, and
continued by threats to block the driving of the logs. Eventually the company brought suit in the Circuit Court of the United States and won a decision that any interest the Dietzes possessed in the dam was subject and
subordinate to all rights of the logging company. An attempt by the sheriff
of Sawyer County to arrest Dietz in 1904 (which the Chippewa Lumber
& Boom asserted that it did not request and had not even known about in
advance) resulted in the wounding of a deputy by Val Weisenbach, a
friend of Dietz, and his subsequent capture, conviction, and sentence to
a twelve-year penitentiary term. Dietz was not apprehended, and continued to defy the law and advertise his claim against the boom company.

He won many partisans as a staunch defender of his alleged rights
against a large corporation. The general mood of the time was anti-Big-
Business, and he was particularly applauded by farmers and small landowners who felt that logging companies had damaged their properties or
underpaid them for stumpage or had obtained their timber by "land
grabs" or abuses of the public land laws. Dietz enjoyed being a law in himself. "I am the only man," he once boasted, "that single-handed ever held
up a township, a county, and I was almost going to say a state." Temporarily he *could* say it, for Governor Robert M. La Follette was then refusing to act against him because of the public sympathy he commanded.

The Mississippi River Lumber Company (acting with its boom company) offered to arbitrate the case. Dietz agreed, but soon withdrew his

assent. Finally Frederick Weyerhaeuser, who wanted no violence, persuaded a tactful logger, W. E. Moses, to negotiate with the rancher. On
Moses's recommendation he finally paid a bill of $1,717 that Dietz
claimed for services to the boom company. (According to its officials,
these were mostly fictitious.) Moses had stipulated that, if paid, Dietz
would permit the removal of the logs (except a few on his own land), and
their transportation across country to the Flambeau River, some ten miles
distant. This was done at considerable expense. Chippewa Lumber &
Boom had no further dealings with Dietz, who later shot and killed one
of twenty state deputies who were attempting to arrest him for assaulting
a man in the nearby town of Winter.

In the entire affair between Dietz and the company it was the corporation that suffered, and not the champion of alleged individual rights.
Again, throughout, the corporation was the law-abiding party, although
it never pressed its wholly sound case for fear of precipitating violence,
and Dietz was the transgressor.[31]

The Dietz affair was one that the muckrakers might well have exploited had it offered the slightest basis for an attack on Weyerhaeuser. It
did not. And while savagely and often justly eloquent in indicting wasteful exploitation and promoting government conservation, the writers
against corporate abuses never found any real explosive ammunition for
a campaign against the Rock Islander and his associates. It was left for
the Bureau of Corporations, which Theodore Roosevelt had created, to
aim at the group a long-delayed and final blow.

6

The idea that some pernicious type of combination controlled the
production and marketing of lumber naturally persisted in the era of
"trust-busting." Nearly everybody used lumber. When in the first decade
of the century the prices for it rose more sharply than those for farm
products, many suspected a "trust." Though it was impossible to believe
that so loose a group as the Weyerhaeuser associates, responsible for so
small a part of the national output, constituted a controlling agency, men
asked if some trade association comprising numerous large producers
were not at work.

A Minnesota legislative committee in March, 1907, began an investigation of complaints that the Northwestern Lumbermen's Association was
allocating sections of the market to selected firms, fixing prices, and boy-
cotting wholesalers who sold direct to consumers. The association's secretary, W. G. Hollis, denied the charges under oath.[32] Its purposes, he declared, were simply to gather information on lumber stocks in hand,
examine complaints of railroad discrimination against certain dealers, and

to find broader uses for wood products. As this did not convince critics, the inquiry continued. Already Senator A. B. Kittredge of South Dakota, a Yale graduate and lawyer of distinction who held Progressive ideas, had declared in Washington that a combination existed, that it fixed a scale of lumber prices which it compelled retail dealers to accept, and that it thus enabled the manufacturers to make a profit of 200 percent. Now he made similar assertions. Lumber that cost the sawmills $10 was being sold, he said, at $20—for trade associations held the market in a vise. The Minneapolis *Journal* and other papers printed hot denials by lumbermen.[33] George W. Thompson, treasurer of the Northwestern Lumbermen's Association, made a detailed defense of existing prices. It was obvious, however, that a larger investigation was required.

The upshot was the Senate passage of a resolution introduced by Kittredge directing the Department of Commerce and Labor to ascertain whether the lumber industry was violating the antitrust laws. Although no firms were mentioned, the Minneapolis *Journal* carried a portrait of Weyerhaeuser beside its headlines: "Eyes on Lumber Baron," "Rich Timber Kings Now Face Inquiry," "Weyerhaeuser, Walker, et al. Must Explain Their Deals in West."[34]

At once the Bureau of Corporations began the fieldwork for an intensive survey. In September, 1907, its head, Herbert Knox Smith, appeared with Gifford Pinchot in St. Paul and held conferences with leaders of the industry. Frederick E. Weyerhaeuser had several meetings with them, emphatically denied any participation in a "lumber trust," and offered to throw open the books and papers of the associates in the freest possible manner. Pinchot, he reported to friends, was astonished to learn how small the Weyerhaeuser share of the market really was. In the Northwest the investigators received a friendly reception from the Weyerhaeuser Timber Company. George S. Long frankly expressed his conviction that the lumber business had been handicapped by the federal policy of repressing every effort on the part of manufacturers to combine in reducing output, for overproduction was the chronic evil from which lumbering suffered most. But he made it clear that his company meant to obey the law. The Bureau later complained that some railroads were reluctant to give it needed data, but the Weyerhaeuser group withheld nothing except the lists of its stockholders.

As the investigation continued in 1908–1910, responsible lumbermen became impatient for early publication of the report. The unfounded cry of "lumber trust," they said, was being used against them in their contest for fair tariff rates and in other connections. Frederick E. Weyerhaeuser made a personal appeal to Herbert Knox Smith early in 1909. But the Bureau report on the Lumber Industry, in four parts, did not appear until 1913–1914.[35]

Those who searched the report for indications of a combination in illegal restraint of trade found no substantial evidence for it. The Bureau, to be sure, entered into an extended discussion of price lists, market reports, and price tendencies. But although it implied that the efforts of lumber manufacturers to diffuse information about lumber values looked toward a conspiracy to control prices, it furnished no proof of illegitimate practices. The *American Lumberman* declared that the Bureau had overstrained its interpretation of its material—without result. "Every effort by manufacturers, who saw in continued overproduction nothing but bankruptcy and financial oblivion, to curtail production to a point where the markets of the country would not be glutted with stock is viewed as evidence of an intent of those manufacturers to violate the law," it scornfully remarked.[36]

The real gravity of the report lay elsewhere, in the assertion that the lumber industry, largely because of the government's own unfortunate acts, was marked by an unhealthy concentration of power in a few corporate hands. The Bureau asserted that 250 timber owners held one-half of the privately owned timber resources of the nation and that in the Pacific Northwest 38 owners held one-half. In the five states of Washington, Oregon, California, Idaho, and Montana, which possessed five-elevenths of the country's privately owned standing timber, three great organizations, the Southern Pacific, Northern Pacific, and the Weyerhaeuser group, held nearly a quarter of the timberland. This concentration, according to the Bureau, placed in a few corporations too great a control over the future lumber supply of the United States. But Herbert Knox Smith admitted that this situation was "primarily the result of our public land policy, long continued."[37]

Collectively, according to the report, the Northern Pacific with 32,-664,000 acres, the Southern Pacific with 15,762,000 acres, and the Weyerhaeusers with 2,000,000 controlled about 50,000,000 acres on the Pacific Coast. But as respected timber, these statistics were deceptive. Much of the railroad domain was bare of trees. The significant figures, according to the Bureau, were those of stumpage. It computed that the Southern Pacific held 106 billion board feet of timber; the Weyerhaeusers 90 billion board feet; and the Northern Pacific, a poor third, 36 billion board feet. The report noted that the holdings of the three companies lay in the most valued forests of the Coast, those of Douglas fir, ponderosa, and white pine. This fact, it suggested, gave them a key position.

In sharp language the Bureau attacked the policies of the large holders as adverse to the public interest. The Weyerhaeuser associates, it argued, had made vast speculative purchases and then held the timberland for price advances. Thus they had gained, it alleged, an enormous unearned increment. The Bureau arraigned the railroads for grimly holding on to so much land. "The largest holders are cutting little of their tim-ber," wrote Smith. "They thus reserve to themselves those incalculable profits which are still to accrue with the growth of the country, the di-minishing of timber supply, and the further concentration and control thereof. Many of the very men who are protesting against conservation and the national forest system because of the 'tying up' of natural re-sources are themselves deliberately tying them up far more effectively for private gain."

This statement was the more effective because timberland values were now almost at their highest point. The Bureau intimated that they would continue to rise, and quoted an officer of the National Lumber Manufacturers Association as predicting that timber owners would reap a rich harvest when "the supply in other parts of the country is gone. Then they can ask and get their own prices."[38] Actually, timberland prices later receded and, especially in the 1930's touched some very low points.

The report also argued that economic factors did not demand con-centration. Four-fifths of the lumber output, it noted, came from mills each cutting less than 25,000,000 board feet a year. Indeed, small saw-mills operated efficiently all over the map. In 1909 a total of 46,584 sawmills cut 44,609 million board feet of lumber. So large a part of the ordinary log was waste that it was best, argued Smith, to cut it up near where it was logged. The economic factors that made large manufacturing concentrations important for oil or steel simply did not apply to wood industries. The larger the mill, the greater under ordinary circumstances would be the cost of bringing it enough logs.[39]

The findings of the Bureau were sharply contested by spokesmen for the larger units of the industry, including the Weyerhaeusers. They in-sisted that the degree of timber concentration on the Pacific Coast was exaggerated. In this contention they found support from the government itself when in 1920 the Forest Service published a bulletin entitled *Tim-ber Depletion*. This estimated that small holders held a much larger share of the northwestern timber than previously assumed. It maintained that that Bureau of Corporations had overstated the rate of timber depletion on the West Coast and that its alarmist warnings of an imminent timber famine were unjustified.

Spokesmen for the industry also bluntly contradicted the Bureau on the economic value of large holdings and large manufacturing units. Large companies, large mills, and large capital resources, they asserted, gave stability to the industry. Such companies could introduce conserva-tion measures for forest-protection quite beyond the reach of small con-cerns; they could cooperate with and even surpass the Forest Service in fire prevention, as the major Weyerhaeuser companies cooperating with others, had demonstrated in Washington, Oregon, and Idaho; and they could institute policies for systematic reforestation. Their labor record, moreover, was in general much better than that of small mills struggling to survive.

The Bureau of Corporations report in effect exonerated the lumber trade associations; they were not, it was plain, a menace to the lumber industry or the public welfare. The report resulted in no important government action. Great as was the concern that it expressed over timber concentration, it recommended no measures designed to reduce or split up the large holdings. Herbert Knox Smith's findings were of course laid before the Attorney General, but it was obvious that no basis for any suits existed.

In some peripheral situations the Weyerhaeuser group suffered from sporadic gusts of criticism. It was not involved in a bitter quarrel between the National Park Service and the Forest Service over the beautiful Olympic Peninsula, where Cleveland created a Forest Reserve from which a National Park was later carved; but some people supposed it was. It became a target in some tariff controversies. It was indirectly and remotely involved in the litigation over the old congressional land grant of 1866 to the Oregon & California Railroad, a line subsequently acquired by the Southern Pacific; that is, it was involved through its subsidiary, the Pokegama Sugar Pine Lumber Company, which had a contract for the delivery of lands by the Southern Pacific.[40] In tax and labor controversies, noted elsewhere, the Weyerhaeuser interests occasionally figured.

On the whole, however, the associates escaped lightly in an era when Big Business was under almost constant assault. They would have escaped still more easily had they pressed the development of manufacturing in the Northwest more rapidly (the charge of holding timberland for unearned gains would have been less tenable) and had they been able to forward those large-scale conservation measures that (as well as practical business reasons) amply justified the existence of a great organization and that in due course they fruitfully adopted.

NOTES

1. Johansen and Gates, *Empire of the Columbia*, 603–605.
2. Pinchot, *Breaking New Ground*, 113–114; *New York Times*, April 3, 1897; U.S. Dept. of the Interior, Annual Report, 1897. Bliss was head of the great New York drygoods firm of Bliss, Fabyan.
3. Pinchot, 115–118.
4. 30 Stat. 11, 34.
5. Pettigrew, *Imperial Washington*, 17.
6. Norcross, "Weyerhaeuser—Richer than John D. Rockefeller," *Cosmopolitan*, XLII, Jan., 1907, 252–259.
7. Pinchot, 118.
8. *Ibid.*, 119.

9. Dana, *Forest and Range Policy*, 135. The Weyerhaeuser family presently made a substantial gift to the Yale school and in time employed a number of its graduates.

10. Pinchot, 140–147.

11. Roosevelt covers conservation in his *Autobiography*, 408–436.

12. Richardson, ed., *Messages and Papers*.

13. Pinchot, 193–194; Henry S. Brown, "Punishing the Land Looters," *Outlook*, LXXXV, March, 1907, 427–439.

14. U.S. Dept. of Interior, *Annual Report of the Sec. of Interior*, 1906, 18–30.

15. Morison, ed., *The Letters of Theodore Roosevelt*, IV, 1127–1128, with footnote.

16. Richardson, X, 7682 ff.

17. Pinchot, 249.

18. Morison, IV, 1216.

19. Some 400 men attended, and the speeches of Pinchot, Secretary James Wilson, F. H. Newell, and Charles D. Walcott were especially valuable. Parts of the addresses were printed in Forest Service Circular No. 35, "Forest Preservation and National Prosperity" (1905, p. 31).

20. Pinchot, 300–301; Roosevelt, *Autobiography*, 419; Lillard, *The Great Forest*, 273.

21. *Forum*, XXX, Oct., 1900, 147–156.

22. For the impact of Kellogg's brochure, see "Our Forest Balance Sheet" in *Nation*, LXXXIV, May 9, 1907, pp. 425–426.

23. La Follette, *Autobiography*, 56–60, 138. La Follette draws a caustic portrait of Sawyer, a squat, heavy-set, illiterate politician shrewdly intent on promoting land "steals" (cf. *Current, Pine, Logs and Politics*). Stephenson in his *Recollections* defends himself against similar criticisms.

24. FEW Papers, FEW to A. E. Rickard (Bonners Ferry), March 22, 1906.

25. *Ibid.*, July 25, 1906.

26. The editor of the Minneapolis *Journal*, J. S. McClain, on Dec. 14, 1901, had indulged in an indiscriminate attack on the Lake States lumbermen then moving into the Pacific Northwest. These predatory interests, he declared, were invading the Far West as the swarms of locust had invaded Egypt; they were bent on destroying the Cascade forests as they had destroyed those of Wisconsin and Minnesota. But he gave no names.

27. Norcross, *op. cit.; Miss. Val. Lbrmn.*, XXXVII, Dec. 28, 1906, pp. 1, 24.

28. *The World Today*, XXI, pp. 1735–1750.

29. Russell's article gives the impression of a halfhearted effort written under Hearst orders.

30. *Everybody's*, XVIII, May, 1900, pp. 579–592.

31. *American Magazine*, LXI, Jan., 1908, pp. 252–261 (White); Lillard, *The Great Forest*, 233–236; *St. Paul Pioneer Press*, Aug. 29, 1906; "A Statement of Facts: John F. Dietz and the Chippewa Lumber & Boom Company," etc., Oct. 28, 1910 (pamphlet issued by CL&B Co. and MRLC); "Hero Dietz of Cameron Dam," FEW Record, 286–305. All but the first situation cover the Dietz case. The FEW Record contains a detailed statement by W. E. Moses (March 24, 1933) not unsympathetic to Dietz, whom he thought a misguided but honest and hospitable man, almost insanely suspicious and extremely violent in speech.

32. Minneapolis *Journal*, March 5, 13, 1907.

33. See files of the same publication, a vocal critic of the industry, between March 15 and April 15, 1907.

34. T. B. Walker was accused, with C. A. Smith and the elder Weyerhaeuser, of controlling more than half of the nation's standing timber. In an extended reply in the Minneapolis *Journal*, May 20, 21, 1909, Walker declared that this was absurd; the three together held perhaps one-half of one percent of the standing timber.

35. FEW Papers, H. K. Smith to FEW, Feb. 13, 1911.

36. *Amer. Lbrmn.*, July 25, 1914, p. 24.

37. The introductory material by Herbert Knox Smith, *The Lumber Industry,* I, vii ff., compactly summarized the principal assertions and conclusions respecting the Weyerhaeuser group.

38. *Ibid.,* I, 5. The official had made his statement in Aug., 1910.

39. *Ibid.,* I, 3–5. Even a mill of very moderate size, wrote Smith, could build a logging railroad; no huge establishment was needed.

40. The most comprehensive and balanced synthesis of all the developments sketched in this chapter is contained in Dana, *Forest and Range Policy,* Chaps. 6–8.

XVII

New Leaders, New Goals

L IKE A GREAT PINE that has grown to maturity and yields branch by branch to the slow assault of the years, the group of friends associated with Frederick Weyerhaeuser had begun to dissolve even before the new century. It was inevitable, for by 1895 Weyerhaeuser and Denkmann had already been active in lumbering for thirty-five years, and many of their associates for a longer period.

The first outstanding members to die were W. J. Young in 1896, William Carson, Sr., in 1898, Young's rival Artemus Lamb in April, 1901. Four years later death came to F. C. A. Denkmann at the age of eighty-four. The Laird, Norton leaders, who for decades had presided at Winona, all became less active after 1900, James L. Norton dying in 1904, W. H. Laird in 1910, and Matthew G. Norton in 1917. In September, 1910, came the death of Peter Musser, for decades the close friend and co-worker of Weyerhaeuser, and next year Edward Rutledge and R. L. McCormick followed him. Unexpectedly, in 1912 A. E. Macartney, legal adviser for the Weyerhaeuser group, succumbed to a heart attack. Frederick Weyerhaeuser himself died in April, 1914, the last, except for M. G. Norton, of the older group he had so successfully led through their multiple enterprises.[1]

2

"After father's death," wrote Frederick E. Weyerhaeuser years later, "there was no central control of the many activities of the associated interests. A word from him had been sufficient to bring about any desirable cooperation; with very few exceptions his judgment was not questioned."[2]

Yet the Weyerhaeuser group had already been renewing itself. In

1914 the four Weyerhaeuser sons were all proved executives, active in the companies their father had fostered: Charles at Little Falls and Minneapolis with Pine Tree and Northland; Rudolph at Cloquet with Northern, Cloquet, Johnson-Wentworth, and Northwest Paper; John in the affairs of the Weyerhaeuser Timber Company and other western firms; and Frederick E. in the St. Paul office where he had already shown a high talent for supervision and coordination.

Other families, however, also contributed a large group of able executives. From the Mussers came R. Drew and Clifton R., the son of P. M. Musser. At Winona F. S. Bell, W. H. Laird's son-in-law, had shouldered the chief managerial burden; he was also a director and an important influence in the Weyerhaeuser Timber Company. E. P. Clapp and F. H. Thatcher, sons-in-law of the Nortons, and A. W. Laird (a nephew of William H. Laird) were active in Laird, Norton affairs and in the western companies, while W. L. McCormick at the Weyerhaeuser Timber Company was quietly taking over many of his father's duties and would soon become secretary of the company, bringing a legal training and a wise judiciousness to his work. Other second-generation executives of associated families who had already shown ability were F. C. Denkmann, H. J. Richardson, who had married a granddaughter of F. C. A. Denkmann; John A. Humbird, son of T. J. Humbird; H. H. Irvine, son of Thomas Irvine; and George F. Lindsay.[3] This list could be extended.

Outside the families a large group of officials had attained varying degrees of importance. George S. Long, administering the Pacific Coast empire, undoubtedly stood among the foremost leaders in ability and influence. A number of others held strategic positions—H. C. Hornby at Cloquet, C. A. Barton with Boise Payette, Louis S. Case in sales affairs, William Carson as president of Boise-Payette, and Huntington Taylor of the Edward Rutledge Timber Company. Such managers and superintendents as W. H. Boner, W. H. Peabody, A. L. Raught, R. A. McDonald, E. H. O'Neil, and W. W. Warren had been or were soon to become important to Weyerhaeuser Timber's success, and Minot Davis played an indispensable role in buying, selling, and logging its timber.

With the companies staffed by such executives, the death of Frederick Weyerhaeuser produced no visible confusion. "I don't think there was any noticeable change," said Charles McGough, then in the St. Paul office. "It was known that he hadn't been in good health for some time, and I think things had been pretty well anticipated."[4]

Nevertheless, it was clear that important changes had to be made. Frederick Weyerhaeuser's office in St. Paul had served as a loose but vital agency for financial management. From it had gone out calls and assessments. It had initiated the first work in standardized statistics and accounting. But its pervasive activity and influence had stemmed from

Weyerhaeuser's interest in numerous companies and his acknowledged probity and sagacity. He had deftly pointed the policies of many firms, although of course he could take no part in their day-to-day activities. His was the coordinating force of a strong personality; there was no individual who could replace him; and consequently a different and more formal control was now needed.

Frederick E. Weyerhaeuser, as indicated, was keenly aware of this fact. Of all the able men in the related companies, he had perhaps the longest and broadest vision. "Mr. F. E. was more the executive type," says Leonard Nygaard of the St. Paul office, in comparing him with his brothers. David H. Bartlett believed that "in this organization made up of all these families, all these groups, Mr. F. E. was the focal point about which they all revolved." His broad outlook was partly the result of character; he was the student of the Weyerhaeuser brothers, the Phi Beta Kappa graduate who combined practical knowledge with mental capacity. At the same time, he had no specific managerial responsibilities and was freer to observe and plan in a larger way. It was he who had launched the drive to improve and standardize auditing, and he was interested already in the development of a common sales force and policy.[5]

But while he perceived that the loss of his father called for restorative action of a new type, he with others recognized another important aspect of the situation. They saw that both the Weyerhaeuser companies and the lumber industry as a whole faced a period of changing conditions that would challenge shrewdly any type of leadership they might establish.

By 1918 extremely heavy taxes were being levied on lumber firms and officials, for the federal Corporation Excise Tax of 1909 and the federal Income Tax of 1916 had been augmented to meet war costs. Various state levies were also vexatious. The standardization of auditing was still in process. Again, for the first time in the many years of the associates' activity, labor unrest was sufficiently serious to call for common consultation and action. But the big problem lay in the improvement of manufacturing, the development of by-products, and in marketing; for the entire industry as well as the Weyerhaeuser group faced a challenge from other types of materials that were making sharp inroads on the use of lumber.[6]

Comparatively speaking, Frederick Weyerhaeuser and F. C. A. Denkmann had launched their lumber business of 1860 in a world of wood. Dozens of implements, surfaces, and structures that later came to be made of steel, concrete, asphalt, plastic, glass, and aluminum were then fashioned from products of the forests. Even in 1905, when John P. Weyerhaeuser's son Frederick K. thrilled to the glimpse of his first automobile, it displayed a wooden body and wooden wheels.

But in the new century substitutes for wood were pushing into wide use. The old snake fence was being replaced by one of barbed wire. Cement culverts and stone and cement bridges were ousting wooden units; steel plates, steel beams, iron and steel window units, and iron and steel doors were being employed in city office and industrial buildings; concrete sidewalks and macadamized, asphalt, and finally concrete roads were making plank roads and wooden sidewalks a curiosity. Paper cartons began to replace wooden boxes. The wood-burning or heating stove was giving way to units fueled by coal or oil. The steel railroad car, metal, tile, or composition roofing, and brass and iron beds had appeared. The per capita American consumption of softwoods had dropped from 381 board feet for the United States in 1904 to 311 in 1914, and this shrinkage of nearly one-fifth would continue rapidly as the figure sank to 259 in 1919 and 215 in 1929. In 1917 Midwest retailers testified that between 1907 and 1914 they had lost 42 percent of the fencing trade, 35 percent of the shingle business, 15 percent of the siding, and 14 percent of the flooring trade to substitute materials.[7]

Even early in the century Frederick Weyerhaeuser had recognized this menacing cloud on the lumber horizon. "We have lost the wooden fence and sidewalk business," he remarked to a group of friends one night. "We are losing the packing box business—and this is a large part of our sales—and we are threatened with other substitutes for wood so that our market is being more and more restricted."[8]

F. E. Weyerhaeuser, always inclined to be a prophet of doubt if not of gloom, had shared his father's apprehension. For years he had urged action by lumber associations. But he was particularly startled in October, 1914, by a preposterous demonstration on the Chicago lakefront, where under the auspices of the National Fire Protection Association "a flimsily built [wooden] structure, probably saturated with oil, was burned to the ground in a few minutes, while a cement box shaped building standing close by was not damaged by a little fire started within." Weyerhaeuser and A. W. Laird at once intensified their efforts to win financial support for a nationwide campaign against misrepresentation by makers of nonlumber building materials, to be sponsored by the National Lumber Manufacturers Association. At the same time Frederick E. Weyerhaeuser was planning the White Pine Bureau, established in January, 1915, and to be described later. Unfortunately, this unit was the only one to persist as a medium of intensive action for even a part of the industry (it served sixteen companies, eight non-Weyerhaeuser), and opposition to wood substitutes was to become increasingly an activity for the associates and their firms.[9]

Thus, at the time of Frederick Weyerhaeuser's death the problem of leadership was related to factors larger than personal ones. The associates must not only fill the vacuum left by their leader's passing—they must

also provide coordinated action to meet the problems raised by social, political, and industrial changes. If F. E. Weyerhaeuser saw the need more
clearly than any of the others, they, like him, were determined to meet it.
After the annual meeting of the Weyerhaeuser Timber Company in 1914,
a representative body of stockholders for all Weyerhaeuser enterprises
assembled in Tacoma. A General Advisory Committee was formed, and
it appointed, in F. E. Weyerhaeuser's words, "a group of committees to
study the benefits of cooperative action in the fields of logging, manufacturing, selling, auditing, merchandising, transportation, insurance, by-
products, etc." One of these subcommittees dealt with labor.

It was an act looking toward unified effort in all aspects of the business. The composition of the General Advisory Committee gives some
indication of the chief leaders at this time. The complete list shows
George S. Long, F. C. Denkmann, J. P. Weyerhaeuser, William Carson,
T. J. Humbird, W. L. McCormick, F. S. Bell, C. R. Musser, H. H. Irvine,
F. H. Thatcher, William Irvine, and H. J. Richardson as comprising this
key group.[10] Frederick E. Weyerhaeuser, Charles A. Weyerhaeuser, and
Rudolph M. Weyerhaeuser do not appear in this body but were all as
influential as any of its members. They served on the subcommittees.

The reorganizing action was timely and comprehensive. The tasks
to be faced were formidable. It remained to be seen whether the machinery established would provide the vigorous direction that was unquestionably required.

3

While the committee system was taking its first uncertain steps, F. E.
Weyerhaeuser was promoting another device for unified action. It has
been noted in earlier chapters that the older Frederick Weyerhaeuser had
been shocked to find sales representatives of several associated mills competing in the same markets, that Charles, Rudolph, and their brother
Frederick had shared their father's desire to coordinate selling efforts, and
that experiments had been made in joint sales offices in Chicago and
Minneapolis and finally in 1916 in a section of Iowa.

Behind this latter test had lain some years of preparation which went
back to the days of the senior Weyerhaeuser. Indeed, the younger Frederick E. later remarked that while "these cooperative efforts were largely
developed after Father left us, nevertheless the most important of them
were begun under Father's direction [but, it seems certain, proposed by
the son!]—notably the auditing department and the early efforts to coordinate sales."

To analyze the sales situation Weyerhaeuser had installed in the St.
Paul office J. E. Rhodes, formerly secretary of the Northern Pine Manu-

facturers' Association, and put him to studying sales orders for the various Weyerhaeuser firms. This activity began in 1909. Rhodes and young F. E. Weyerhaeuser developed the ideas of trademarking lumber and of marking it for species and grades. However, for various reasons there was little receptivity toward such proposals, and finally in 1912 Rhodes became discouraged, and left.

An able successor was found in Louis S. Case, the brilliant sales manager of the Chippewa Lumber & Boom Company, which had closed out its activities in 1912. Case and F. E. Weyerhaeuser at length succeeded in getting copies of all sales orders for all the associated companies sent to St. Paul, and spent more than a year in analyzing this material. As they worked on it, the glaring inconsistencies, omissions, and errors became apparent, and they planned a single coordinated service.[11]

F. E. Weyerhaeuser was now ready to present to the chief stockholders the idea of a single sales company that would assume responsibility for marketing the products of all the associates. At a meeting in St. Paul in late 1915 or early 1916 he explained his plan. "It is almost amusing to me now," he wrote some four years later, "to remember the all day session in our office. . . . I argued and pleaded and argued without making the slightest impression. Finally, one after another had to buy tickets, call on relatives and what not, till Mr. Case, Mr. Clapp and I were left alone." Case was in despair. But Weyerhaeuser, if dashed, was not daunted. "They didn't say 'No,' " he remarked. "We'll go ahead with our plans."[12]

Fortunately Frederick E. could command the support of Charles and Rudolph, and of his associate George F. Lindsay. At a meeting on February 15, 1916, he won the approval of the stockholders for the test in Iowa already mentioned. Four salesmen were to sell lumber in northeastern Iowa for the five Minnesota companies and the Weyerhaeuser Timber Company (fir). Each man was given a smaller territory than usual and was to cover it intensively for all mills he represented. Further details were worked out at a sales conference on February 22nd, and selling began on March 1st.[13]

By the end of the first four months of 1916 (two of them under the new system) each participating unit had increased its sales in the selected territory by at least one-half, while Northern doubled and Pine Tree tripled its previous showing. Allowance had to be made for the fact that the entire lumber business had sharply improved; still, the returns were encouraging. In May, therefore, the territory was enlarged to include Iowa and parts of Illinois and Nebraska. More salesmen were transferred from Little Falls and Cloquet, and one of Boner's Iowa representatives was taken on. By October, 1916, all the western mills were ready to come in, and the states of Iowa, Illinois, Missouri, Kansas, Nebraska, and parts of Wyoming, Colorado, and Minnesota were assigned to an enlarged force.[14]

The original plan for a unified sales company had been summarized by F. E. Weyerhaeuser in a memorandum distributed to the associated companies on March 3, 1916. It aimed at greater efficiency in the field and a central control over price-making and general sales policy (never previously established). Other objectives were the provision of larger and more varied stocks of lumber and the creation of a Weyerhaeuser reputation that would permit the transfer of custom from mills going out of business (as in Wisconsin and Minnesota) to new ones established by the associates.[15]

In October, Weyerhaeuser issued a second memorandum setting forth these objectives anew. It was persuasive rather than authoritative, and stressed the advantages that would be realized. Individual mills would have a fuller representation than most of them could afford if each maintained its own sales forces; they could "avoid the necessity of selling through middlemen" (but could still sell to them if they desired); they could share in the demand based on the Weyerhaeuser reputation. But, ran the memorandum, "each mill can and should market its lumber to its own best advantage," and the proposed sales company would not "suppress competition," or "control or affect prices," or interfere "with the individuality or independence of the selling departments of the various mills."[16]

However, Case and "F. E." were in a difficult position. Stockholders like F. H. Thatcher and many of the mill managers opposed the idea of a strong central selling agency, largely on the ground that some good existing sales organizations, like that of Potlatch, would have to be scrapped. Even F. S. Bell, while more moderate, would have shied away from a sales company with real teeth, as, for various practical considerations, would most of the mill managers.

The important thing was to demonstrate the great effectiveness of the Weyerhaeuser Sales Company, still a formative agency. Once established, it could be endowed with increased powers.[17]

The effect of the memorandum, however, was to launch the new unit with a dual character, and at a difficult time. To its proponents it was a beneficent giant in the making; to the mill managers it was a convenient agent they meant to keep in its place. The mills retained the real power to set prices and terms, and even to make policy. "Sometimes it seemed that the woods foremen, the camp cook or section hand set the policy," remarked Case ruefully. Once George S. Long grilled him shrewdly as to his status. "Who is your boss?" he demanded. "F. E. Weyerhaeuser," replied Case. "No," snapped Long, "your boss is the mills who pay you."[18]

Already the First World War had started, and as will soon appear, its effect upon the lumber industry had not been wholly a happy one. The Sales Company did not expand during the conflict. Fortunately, the coming of peace activated a long unsatisfied demand for housing and made the outlook for 1919 a bright one.[19]

The Sales Company had run a difficult course with fair success and now looked forward to a heartening future. At first it made hay in the sunny period of quickening demand. Case could report on November 22, 1919, that it had "gained something like 12 or 13 hundred cars on the mills in the last thirty days." But meanwhile disruptive factors had appeared. Case, as indicated, had no real authority to set policy. With a boom market, the mills were relatively independent and tended to pursue their separate courses. In February, 1919, they had agreed not to sell to wholesalers, who inclined to hold lumber for speculative rises and release it suddenly in competition with the Sales Company. But managers quickly broke this agreement as wholesalers dangled enticing offers before them. An advertising program, to be described later, had been developed to extol Weyerhaeuser lumber; but now the middlemen often controlled that product. They frequently bought for future delivery and might demand their shipments at the very time the Sales Company was putting in orders. Mill managers angrily defended selling to wholesalers, arguing that it was insurance against the future and that the Sales Company was exacting and ineffective in any case. Stockholders like Thatcher supported the millmen who proposed junking both the Sales Company and the advertising campaign.[20]

To F. E. Weyerhaeuser the situation had become intolerable. He had worked for ten years to promote coordinated action. Now he saw it flouted, with the Sales Company in particular apparently headed for disintegration. His wife was in a hospital, and his daughter Virginia became dangerously ill. He suddenly withdrew from activity in company affairs. "I came to feel last summer that I was a first class nuisance," he wrote to his brother John some months later. "I was trying to work out something for the joint interests that very few outside of our family wanted, had any use for or did not [sic] actively oppose. . . . If the manager's voice is louder than those of the members of the committees— what is the use? . . . I would rather raise oranges than try further to force my services on the crowd when they don't believe in what we are doing." He retired to southern California.

Indeed, during the next several years he proposed to dissociate the name Weyerhaeuser from both the advertising campaign and the Sales Company. Fortunately, his three brothers opposed such moves. Later he reproached himself bitterly for a failure in leadership and for abandoning the helm at a time of crisis. But after his daughter's death and the partial vindication of his ideas, he was gradually to return to an active role.[21]

As to the Sales Company, the situation was to grow darker before it became brighter. Hostile managers and stockholders made Louis Case's role a bitter one: in August, 1919, he tendered his resignation. It was not accepted, but in that very month came an action that seemed to justify it. Confident that the sales organization was doomed to failure— a failure they themselves had promoted—a majority of the mill representatives at a meeting in Kansas City actually voted it out of existence!

But immediately some of the abler managers had second thoughts. At a private conference Humbird, Long, and Carson decided that they, representing Humbird Lumber, Weyerhaeuser Timber, and Boise Payette, would form their own joint sales agency. Rudolph for the Cloquet group and the Edward Rutledge Timber Company insisted that they be included, Potlatch and Bonners Ferry made the same demand, and the Sales Company rose from the dead!

More important, the group recognized the need for a stronger and more firmly established unit. In September, A. W. Clapp proposed a plan under which the western managers would act as directors and the Sales Company, formally incorporated, would operate through contracts with the associated companies. On December 2nd an agreement was executed that established the new unit as the exclusive sales agency for the mills over a period of five years. It was to sell all lumber, lath, shingles, boxes, and other materials, but did not obligate itself as to logs, posts, ties, and other by-products. The mills agreed to fill all orders promptly, to meet Sales Company requirements as far as was possible, to advise it on records and inventories, and to accept no other orders except with Sales Company approval. The latter was to operate on a cost basis with a 2 percent profit margin.

T. J. Humbird was chosen president of the new organization, and proved to be an excellent leader. To maintain closer relationships with the mills, now mostly in the Far West, the general office was moved from St. Paul to Spokane.[22]

The period of difficulty was not over. In the runaway boom of early 1920, the Weyerhaeuser Sales Company took the revolutionary step of holding its prices with the belief that this act would check inflationary tendencies in the lumber industry. The move was loudly resented by some of the Weyerhaeuser competitors and by certain of the associates' own mill managers who wanted to profit while they could. Almost immediately the depression of 1920–1921 closed in, and sales abruptly dropped. In September, 1921, the Cloquet companies withdrew from the agency, and while their production was small, the moral effect of the act was unfortunate, though in 1924 Rudolph Weyerhaeuser brought them back. In a period of persisting depression, for the lumber market continued to be demoralized even after the general recovery in 1921, the Sales Company seemed again to be headed for possible dissolution.

To meet this emergency John P. Weyerhaeuser stepped forward with a constructive program. He proposed a searching examination of conditions in the industry with reference to the work of the Sales Company. Arranging a series of meetings with the salesmen and mill managers and stockholders, he tabulated opinions and suggestions and finally helped to organize a meeting of the "allied Weyerhaeuser companies" at Tacoma on May 22–24, 1922, where all differences, complaints, and suggestions were examined in a spirit of fairness. The gathering was a success. Faced with the basic question of whether or not the Sales Company was sound in conception, all conferees—stockholders, managers, and sales officials —agreed that it was. More than fifty of its representatives now covered the country and demonstrated the effectiveness of size and overall control in reaching the retail markets. Complaints, both from the mills and from the salesmen, were thoroughly sifted, and steps were taken to meet those that had substance. For example, in response to the assertion that the salesmen did not sufficiently know the mills, a grand tour was scheduled that would take them to all the chief plants and acquaint them with the resources and difficulties of the mill managers.

The common examination of problems brought a large amount of agreement, and John Weyerhaeuser was congratulated by some of his associates for having in a few months vindicated the work of his brother Frederick, whose ten years of effort now were recognized as an outstanding and persistent task of pioneering. Frederick had not attended the final sessions. "When you consider the amount of friction that developed over my attempt at running the Sales Company," he had written F. S. Bell, "I really feel that it would be better for me not to be at the Tacoma meetings." But he wrote to John on June 13th, warmly expressing his appreciation of what had been accomplished.[23]

The Weyerhaeuser Sales Company was thus firmly established; yet the establishment was a beginning as well as a terminal accomplishment. The organization was still in process of growth and still needed a program embodying processes and standards that would do justice to the Weyerhaeuser products. Certain managers and salesmen who could not adjust to unified action had to go, and a closer relationship both to the mills and to Weyerhaeuser advertising had to be developed. But the course of larger action had been set and was a promise for the future.

4

Meanwhile, the committee system, with the General Advisory Committee governing ten subcommittees, had begun to function as an agency for developing and correlating the activities of the associated companies.

From the beginning the performance of these units was uneven. Some never convened. Of the Insurance Committee, which was "to consider ways and means of reducing the costs of insurance on plants and inventories," F. E. Weyerhaeuser later remarked that its existence had been the happiest of the ten: "Its chairman [William Irvine] has let it sleep from the beginning." Under Huntington Taylor the Labor Committee did effective work in improving the living conditions at camps and mills during World War I, but it never functioned for any extended period. The Logging Committee quickly encountered resistance from the various woods superintendents, each of whom wanted no interference from the "outside" with problems and practices he felt were special to his own region. F. K. Weyerhaeuser later stated that it "broke down," and his uncle Frederick termed it "a bust."

The truth was that the executives of the various firms all had the habit of independence and no experience in a self-government that demanded common participation. Their own problems possessed them completely and often urgently, and a summons to spend half a day discussing larger matters seemed almost frivolous and found them impatient or already otherwise engaged. Typical of what too frequently occurred was John Weyerhaeuser's experience as a committee chairman in March, 1918. "Today we had a Manufacturers' meeting," he wrote his brother Rudolph, "and I was the only one present, so I had all the benefit of the ice cream provided."

With the Legal Committee the case was different. It got off to an excellent start with a first session in October, 1917. Apparently it continued to function vigorously, for in the fall of 1919, when the Sales Company was threatened with a lawsuit, F. E. Weyerhaeuser wrote to his brother that "our legal committee" had gone over the correspondence, telegrams, and orders related to the dispute, and recommended a course to be followed.

The committee doubtless flourished because its members had common interests in the tax problems that affected all the associates. On some matters W. L. McCormick for Weyerhaeuser Timber or Oldenburg for the Cloquet corporations, or F. H. Thatcher, Stiles W. Burr, and A. W. Clapp for the various companies in which they were interested could act independently. But the federal corporation and income taxes forced them all to go to Washington. Even in 1915, before the Legal Committee was organized, F. E. Weyerhaeuser noted that Oldenburg, Clapp, Thatcher, Richardson, "and other attorneys" were in the capital.[24] From the beginning they could thus meet conveniently, and they worked on the numerous difficult points that were important to establish as the basis for federal levies. To explain the processes and arguments by which they dealt with these technical problems would require a small volume; it is enough to record that they were successful in establishing interpretations of the acts involved that were satisfactory both to the government and to the associates. F. E. Weyerhaeuser felt that the committee had done admirable work, particularly with tax problems.[25]

The Auditing Committee satisfied him also. What was true to an extent of the legal unit was wholly true of this one: it carried forward work that had been planned, initiated, and shaped by experience while the older Weyerhaeuser was still alive. Indeed, according to Charles J. McGough, who could observe operations shrewdly from St. Paul or Coeur d'Alene, Idaho, the committee did nothing but approve the capable work of Frank B. Poole. "I don't think they ever changed a figure." Nevertheless, it presided over an area in which important objectives were fully attained in this crucial period.[26]

Members of the By-Products Committee operated in a relatively new field—relatively, because while boxes, shingles, railroad ties, and cedar poles had become well established subsidiary products of operations in the woods, no one had touched the real possibilities of utilizing "waste." These uses now loomed large on the horizon. If wallboards could be made of plaster, gypsum, and glue, why not of discarded wood? What of wood plastics, wood briquettes, chemicals from wood refuse? Such questions brought a recognition that not only might the lumbermen fight successfully against the increasing introduction of substitutes for wood by utilizing wood more fully but that such activity might well become an important item on a plant's balance sheet and even represent the difference between profit and loss.

William Carson, as chairman of the committee, took the initiative in October, 1917, by going with F. E. Weyerhaeuser and two of his committee members to confer at Madison, Wisconsin, with officials of the Burgess Laboratories there. This agency was experimenting with wood products and made a proposal to conduct research on which the By-Products Committee felt "it was worth gambling $25,000." The Wood Conversion Company, a Delaware corporation formed on January 31, 1921, and owned by the manufacturing firms themselves, was the result; and the committee not only followed its work but discussed and promoted other ideas. Wood Conversion's activities were so promising that William L. Hall, a former Assistant Chief Forester in the federal service, wrote Carson in 1921 that "Weyerhaeuser Companies are doing a great service to the country" in promoting the utilization of the waste forest products.

In 1928 Potlatch Lumber Company directed W. D. Humiston, who had been studying wood waste, to investigate by-products, but he originated no activity of a commercial character. The Weyerhaeuser Timber Company helped finance Wood Conversion, and its keen interest in the firm will soon appear. Yet for a number of years the western companies were to make slight contributions in the way of special new products.[27]

If the Manufacturing Committee had on one occasion left John with an embarrassing amount of ice cream, his brother Frederick nevertheless thought that it "had accomplished some good." He must have been more enthusiastic about the Publicity Committee, headed by his old associate in timber purchasing, George F. Lindsay. Like the Legal Committee, it operated in a field where action was imperative.

As previously noted, the lumber industry had recognized as early as 1915 that to check the growing use of substitutes it must bring home to the public the advantages of wood. The Publicity Committee began to function at a time when Weyerhaeuser officials were becoming convinced that they could never meet the situation adequately by contributing to campaigns by the National Lumber Manufacturers Association. Already the promotional program of the industry was becoming feeble, and action by specific manufacturers was indicated. Lindsay had able associates in William Carson, George Long, T. J. Humbird, and H. C. Hornby.

Lindsay himself had the vision and energy the task demanded. From the outset he advocated the trademarking and grade-marking of lumber and proposed a vigorous advertising program. Later he developed special services to encourage and extend the use of lumber.

Despite the fact that Long, together with William Carson, H. H. Irvine, T. J. Humbird, and others had for some years, and for practical reasons, opposed grade-marking, by 1920 Long was supporting Lindsay in the main. His basic conception was that publicity and advertising should open new fields for sales and in general aid in strengthening the activities of the Sales Company. As will be seen, he accomplished these objectives. Had most of the committees done as much as his, the scheme of centralization by committee might have become a living force and the associates might have carried on their businesses more effectively and profitably than they did.[28]

Unfortunately, the final overall record was disappointing. While the auditing, legal, by-products, and publicity areas were well covered, work in the others lapsed. The General Advisory Committee never took action to reinvigorate the functional committees or to pull together and promote the whole program. Stockholders and managers, when brought to the brew of centralization, simply would not drink. They clung to the familiar policy of developing their respective companies separately. Men like F. E. Weyerhaeuser, F. K. Weyerhaeuser, and Charles J. McGough all agreed that committee control as a whole was a failure.[29]

Yet to reverse a grimly humorous comment from the field of medicine, the operation was a failure but the patient throve. In legal and auditing work the constructive new procedures endured, and in that related to by-products and advertising not only were helpful attitudes established, but units were also set up that continued to function capably long after the last committee had ceased to meet. In particular, a common Sales Company and an effective advertising group created a dual device that bound the associates together and in the end compelled a large measure of coordinated action.

These results would in time reflect credit upon the second-generation leaders, but regardless of what they failed to achieve in coordination, a number of them stand out as able and creative. Of the four Weyerhaeuser brothers, John, the oldest, and Frederick, the youngest, made the more important contributions. The gruff, warmhearted Rudolph supported both of them and performed well as head or director of various western firms, and in the Cloquet area his was the dominant influence. Charles also served capably as a director in various corporations; but his best work was done as a company manager, and after 1920 he discontinued such activity. On the other hand, Frederick supplied the vision and force that resulted in such accomplishments as the Sales Company and Weyerhaeuser Forest Products, and as he returned to active participation in the middle 1920's, he continued to act as a judicious and forward-looking leader.

John's nervous breakdown after the death of his first wife and his reluctance to speak in public have obscured his traits, which were notable. As a supporter of Frederick he was quietly persistent and effective. The correspondence shows also that he acted as a kind of liaison agent for the associates, receiving and dispatching information, making timely suggestions, and in general promoting a loose but important teamwork. With common sense and discriminating judgment he presided over the Weyerhaeuser Timber Company and helped in the development and administration of other far-western firms. As noted, when the Sales Company was in danger, it was he who stepped in to preserve, enlarge, and improve it.

In the Far West George S. Long emerged as the giant of the coast enterprises; he with Frederick and John Weyerhaeuser undoubtedly supplied the central leadership for the associated families. Yet the fine energy and judgment of F. S. Bell commands admiration, while in Idaho William Carson and T. J. Humbird performed in their spheres with signal ability. Later Laird Bell, the son of F. S. Bell and grandson of William H. Laird, was to become a creative force in Idaho and in the affairs of the Weyerhaeuser Timber Company. Humbird's firm and statesmanlike administration of the growing Sales Company also did much to ensure the success of that unit.

A. W. Clapp not only ranked high along with Thatcher and Oldenburg in providing legal services (his role as architect of the Sales Company will be recalled), but developed brilliantly as a counselor on general problems. "It goes without saying," F. S. Bell wrote Charles Weyerhaeuser on one occasion, "that we must have A. W. Clapp attend the conference, not only on account of the preferred stock matter but on almost every other subject of the conference." H. H. Irvine and C. R. Musser were also contributing notably to company policy and action. While Long once flared out with the assertion that George F. Lindsay "has a visionary and artistic temperament and is not a practical lumberman," there is no question that the latter's work in advertising and promotion put him likewise among the second-generation leaders. The men who guided the Weyerhaeuser enterprises through this period deserve better than F. E. Weyerhaeuser's sour comment in 1929 that since 1914, with the exception of Long, "we have not had the semblance of leadership."[30]

5

In 1920 John Weyerhaeuser had reached his sixty-second birthday, Charles his fifty-fourth, and even Frederick, the youngest of the brothers, had attained the age of forty-eight. Some men in the related families like F. S. Bell and F. H. Thatcher had reached the peak of their powers: indeed, in another year Thatcher's forebodings as to his heart would be confirmed. What is almost a protest against persisting responsibilities creeps into one of Charles's letters to John in March, 1924. "It is too bad that we boys are obliged to do so much traveling," he observed. Fred, he remarks, should have gone to Hot Springs, Virginia—he had worked too hard all winter and was nervously exhausted. Rudolph had not only scurried repeatedly from Middle West to Far West but had "practically run the entire town" at Cloquet, where all the other managers were away except McNair and Wilson, both ill. John himself had been resting under the eye of a physician.[31]

Charles had realized even earlier that the day would come when the four brothers and their chief associates would have to look to the third generation. "John, I am very glad that you will take Frederick [F. K.] to our annual meetings," he wrote on the last day of 1918. "In only a few years it will be father's *grandsons* looking after the property he left us." He also mentioned Edwin Davis, Fritz Jewett, and Frederick, then a boy of twelve and son of his youngest brother. He added almost wistfully: "For twenty-seven years we have worked hard here at Little Falls [Pine Tree and Northland were still active], and have only sawed 1¼ billion feet of timber. . . . The Weyerhaeuser Timber Company own 60 billion feet now—so see the work we have for all our nephews."[32]

Frederick K. Weyerhaeuser, John's son, was the oldest of the grandsons and the first to enter the business. Born in 1895, he had been familiar with lumbering since as a child at Nebagamon, Wisconsin, he had lived near a mill and known the camps of the northern woods. In the summer of 1916, before graduation from Yale, he and his brother Phil had done surveying and timber estimating for the Weyerhaeuser Timber Company. Next year he had taken the first post of responsibility held by any of his generation when he was elected a trustee of the Edward Rutledge Timber Company, although the war took him away before he became active in this capacity. He went eventually to Italy and a flyer's role as a lieutenant in the La Guardia contingent there. When he returned his father urged him to begin with the retail branch of the business, and his first position was with the Potlatch Lumber Company. Later he went to the Boise Payette retail yards, traveling with an auditor and working at Blackfoot, Idaho, and similar small operations. During the fall, after some experience at the head office of Thompson Yards in Minneapolis, he accompanied George P. Thompson on a trip through Minnesota and South Dakota to visit yard managers. Then in 1920 he became assistant to the sales manager of the Snoqualmie Falls Lumber Company, and by that summer he had joined the sales force in Iowa. It was at the beginning of the 1920–1921 depression, and there was not only a buyer's market but practically no market at all. "Am enjoying work but wish I could sell more," ran his comment.

His father wrote to Frederick E. Weyerhaeuser: "I hope he will turn out to be a strong man and will be able to take my place soon. The facts are that we are getting along in years [John was sixty-four] and some day we will be called to install managers for our interests suddenly and we will not have time to judge whether those that are at hand will be competent or no. Therefore, I believe in the training of young men, particularly of those that have their money invested in our united efforts."[34] Frederick K. was soon progressing rapidly in the Weyerhaeuser Sales Company.

By that time more of the grandsons were taking on active responsibilities. Edwin W. Davis, son of John's sister Apollonia, had finished his course at Yale, gone to war, and in 1921 on Rudolph's invitation had taken over the management of the Wood Conversion Company at Cloquet. George Frederick (Fritz) Jewett, son of Margaret Weyerhaeuser and almost two years younger than his cousin Frederick K., had also seen war service, had been working in the St. Paul office under Poole, had gone to Idaho with the Edward Rutledge Timber Company, and was to become its vice-president and general manager in 1928.

Young John P. Weyerhaeuser, Jr. (Phil), born in 1899, had succeeded his brother Frederick K. as a trustee of the Rutledge Company in 1922. Graduated from the Hill School and Yale, he was a second lieutenant in World War I (he never went overseas) and had become sales manager for Rutledge in 1920. He and his brother F. K. spent some time in 1921 under the tutelage of George Long, who trained them, his own son George, and for a time Edmund Hayes in cruising timber, dealing with log rafts, and in aspects of lumber manufacture. Phil progressed rapidly, took the managership of the Clearwater Timber Company in 1925, and supervised the construction of its mill at Lewiston.[35]

Like Frederick K. Weyerhaeuser, his brother-in-law F. R. Titcomb, born in 1886 and husband of John's daughter Elizabeth Lucy, had served in aviation during the war. On his return he began to learn the business at Everett, became assistant to W. W. Warren, the manager at Snoqualmie Falls, succeeded to this post on Warren's death, then in 1925 became George Long's assistant and four years later his successor as manager of the Weyerhaeuser Timber Company. Although older than any of the Weyerhaeuser grandsons, he was essentially of their generation.

Two men, Charles H. Ingram and Edmund Hayes, both grandsons of O. H. Ingram, became active in the Weyerhaeuser Timber Company at about the same time as young Fred K. Charles Ingram began his lumber career in 1915 with the Edward Hines Lumber Company at Winton, Minnesota, spent some time with the Ingram-Day Lumber Company at Lyman, Mississippi, and after serving with the 10th Engineers in France joined the Company at Everett in June of 1919.

In April of 1921 he went to Snoqualmie Falls as assistant manager, later became manager, and then assistant general manager at Tacoma in 1929. Possessing a flair for operating management, he was to make great contributions to the Company as its general manager, teaming up perfectly with Phil Weyerhaeuser, Jr., who was to become the executive head of the Weyerhaeuser Timber Company.

Edmund Hayes joined the Company at Snoqualmie Falls in 1920 after military service in World War I, beginning a long and active career in the forest industries and W.T.C.'s active management. Contributing particularly to the development of the Oregon operations, he was to become active in the field of forest protection and forest management, supporting strongly the Company's developing leadership in these fields.

Later to come into active work were C. Davis Weyerhaeuser, son of Frederick E., John M. Musser, son of C. R. Musser, and Norton Clapp, son of E. P. Clapp and grandson of M. G. Norton, who were also to take important roles in the Pacific Coast enterprise. Meanwhile, promising executives unrelated to the chief stockholders' families were being developed. In St. Paul, Carl L. Hamilton was to do brilliant work in Weyerhaeuser Forest Products and help shape the mature Weyerhaeuser Sales Company. In the Far West, Long and others had found a gifted group of lieutenants, among them Minot Davis, an outstanding expert in logging and land purchases; W. H. Boner, W. W. Warren, E. H. (Tip) O'Neil (superintendent of Mill B and manager of Snoqualmie Falls), Robert Hunt (sales manager at Snoqualmie Falls), and, as already noted, A. L. Raught. The list could be readily extended, as ensuing pages will reveal.[36]

Thus a new generation of leaders was already in training or sharing authority with those of the second as the 1920's advanced. They were to play some part in the effort to centralize associated activities and to adapt the numerous plants to the changing conditions of the stormy third decade of the century. The full story of the adjustment of the Weyerhaeuser companies to this challenge must be reserved for a succeeding chapter.

NOTES

1. FEW Record, 209, 474, 707–709; Pine Tree Lumber Co., Min. Bk., May 3, 1911; Norton Clapp, Reminiscences.

2. FEW Record, 758.

3. The original Musser group, it will be recalled, comprised the brothers Peter and Richard and their nephew P. M. Musser. R. D. ("Drew") Musser was Peter's son. FEW Record, *passim;* FEW and JPW Papers, memoranda and correspondence.

4. *Ibid.;* McGough, Reminiscences.

5. Nygaard, Bartlett, and F. K. Weyerhaeuser, Reminiscences.

6. FEW and JPW Papers; Hugo Schlenk, Reminiscences; and FEW Record, 515–520.

7. NLMA, *Lumber Industry Facts,* 1953, Table 42, p. 30; Rolf Thelen, "The Substitution of Other Materials for Wood," *U.S.D.A. Report 17.*

8. FEW Papers, Haydn S. Cole to Mrs. (F. E.) Weyerhaeuser, Nov. 14, 1935. Cole thought the occasion of these remarks had been "twenty-five or thirty years ago."

9. FEW Papers, Arthur Bolling Johnson (ed., *Lumber World Review*) to L. S. Case, Oct. 21, 1914; FEW to A. W. Laird and T. J. Humbird, March 9, 1915; FEW to CAW, Feb. 27, 1915; A. W. Laird to FEW, March 22, 1915. For White Pine Bureau, see later chapter. The response of the NLMA was not sustained.

10. FEW Papers, Memorandum with personnel of General Advisory Committee and the 10 subcommittees. These covered Logging, Manufacturing, Trade Extension, Insurance, Auditing, Labor, Finance, Legal, Publicity, and By-Products. R. M. Weyerhaeuser and J. P. Weyerhaeuser served on the Logging and Manufacturing subcommittees, C. A. Weyerhaeuser on Trade Extension, J. P. Weyerhaeuser on Manufacturing and Labor, and F. E. Weyerhaeuser on Auditing and Finance. Others not on the General Advisory Committee who served on subcommittees were: H. C. Hornby (Logging, Labor, and Publicity), Minot Davis (Logging), Huntington Taylor (Logging, By-Products, Labor), W. H. Boner (Manufacturing), C. A. Barton (Manufacturing), A. W. Laird (Manufacturing), James Clapp (Manufacturing), H. Oldenburg and Stiles W. Burr (Legal), George F. Lindsay (Publicity), C. I. McNair (By-Products), W. W. Warren (By-Products), and R. D. Musser (Insurance).

11. FEW Record, 512–516; FEW Papers, FEW to George S. Long, March 10, 1909; JPW Papers, FEW to JPW, June 16, 1920. Rhodes spent a portion of his time on publicity but gave a considerable amount of it to sales.

12. The date of the meeting at which FEW first presented the idea of the sales company is uncertain. Case presumably came to the St. Paul office late in 1912 or early in 1913. The sales orders (copies) were not obtained at once, but were probably available by 1914. FEW states in the Record (Note 11, above) that he and Case worked on them *for more than a year,* and 1915 is the probable date for the meeting of which he speaks. It could not well have been the meeting of Feb. 15, 1916, for concerning the first meeting FEW says that the stockholders did nothing, while at the 1916 meeting of Feb. 15 they named the sales company and approved the Iowa experiment. "Mr. Clapp" was doubtless A. W. Clapp, who later drafted plans for the more mature sales company.

13. LN Papers, H. J. Richardson to F. H. Thatcher, March 3, 1916; RDM Papers, L. S. Case to J. E. Watts, Feb. 16, 1916; FEW Papers, memo on Sales Co. Personnel, Nov., 1919; *The Big "W"* (WSC organ), Sept., 1921. J. E. Watts, R. V. Clute, Harry Barker, and Charles Ainsworth were the four original salesmen in 1916.

14. JPW Papers, L. S. Case to JPW, May 10, 1916; Case to JPW, May 10, May 23, 1916 (these letters give reports on the progress of the experiment and the first enlargement of territory).

15. FEW Papers, Memorandum of FEW to Associated Companies, March 3, 1916. FEW had also outlined his plans to various associates, e.g., FEW Papers, FEW to A. W. Laird, Jan. 27, 1916.

16. FEW Papers, second Memorandum of FEW to Associated Companies, Oct., 1916.

17. FEW Record, 514.

18. FEW Papers, L. S. Case to R. M.

Weyerhaeuser, Sept. 4, 1928; Case to FEW, Aug. 20, 1919.

19. This period was marked by an extension of WSC Territory and the increase in the force of salesmen, who numbered 52 in 1922, with 33 in Illinois and more eastern areas. Richard G. Keizer, with offices in Chicago, directed all activities in Illinois and the East. See JPW Papers and WSC, annl. repts., 1916–1919.

20. FEW Papers, Case to FEW, Feb. 15, March 10, 22, 1919; FEW Papers, correspondence, 1919, especially F. S. Bell to FEW, July 9, 1919; F. H. Thatcher to FEW, Aug. 16, 1919; FEW to CAW, Nov. 5, 1919.

21. JPW Papers, FEW to JPW, July 18, 1920; FEW Papers, numerous letters, and particularly those in CAW folders.

22. FEW Papers, Case to FEW, Aug. 20, 1918, and William Carson to F. H. Thatcher, Aug. 28, 1919; Long Corresp., Long to Thatcher, Sept. 2, 1919; WSC Papers, Copy of Original Sales Contract, dated Dec. 2, 1919; FKW, "History of the Weyerhaeuser Sales Co.," 90.

23. Minneapolis *Morning Tribune,* Feb. 26, 1920; *MVL,* Feb. 27, 1920; Correspondence in JPW, FEW, and LN Papers, 1920–1922.

24. FKW, "History of Weyerhaeuser Sales Co.," 2; JPW Papers, FEW to JPW, June 26, 1920; FKW Reminiscences; JPW Papers, JPW to RMW, March 16, 1918. Stiles W. Burr was active as an attorney for the associates. The Clapp here mentioned is Newell Clapp, a St. Paul attorney, whose son was A. W. Clapp. Neither was related to E. P. or Norton Clapp, his son.

25. JPW Papers, H. J. Richardson to JPW, Oct. 15, 1917, and FEW to JPW, Sept. 4, 1919; FEW Papers, FEW to F. Wyman, Feb. 11, 1915; JPW Papers, 1915–1919, *passim,* and FEW to JPW, June 26, 1920.

26. *Ibid.;* McGough, Reminiscences.

27. JPW Papers, FEW to CAW, Oct. 6, 1917; FEW Papers, W. L. Hall to Wm. Carson, July 27, 1921; WCC

Annual Report, 1921; LN Papers questionnaire, Feb. 5, 1921; FKW Papers, letters of E. W. Davis to Carson and others, 1921; FEW Papers, several reports of W. D. Humiston, 1930 and 1931. See also FEW to CAW, FSB, and the Mussers, Nov. 7, 1928.

28. Memorandum on Committees, cited in Note 10 above; JPW Papers, FEW to JPW, June 26, 1920; Weyerhaeuser Forest Products, St. Paul Collection consisting of Summary of Receipts and Disbursements, some correspondence, and reports by Lindsay, 1917–1924; Long Papers, Long to Lindsay, 1918–1920. Actually, the WFP exhibit contains Lindsay's Report of May 28, 1926, which surveys the work of previous years to an extent, and also the Articles of Association for WFP, dated May 1, 1918. Work had apparently gone forward briskly before this date.

29. JPW Papers, FEW to JPW, June 26, 1920; FKW, Reminiscences; McGough, Reminiscences.

30. FEW Papers, FSB to CAW, May 1, 1929; FEW to H. C. Hornby, Feb. 11, 1929; JPW Papers, FEW to JPW, March 13, 1918. Appraisals of the leaders are based on general correspondence and reports dealing with the period.

31. FEW Papers, CAW to JPW, March 31, 1924.

32. JPW Papers, CAW to JPW, Dec. 31, 1918.

33. JPW Papers, FKW to his parents, Oct. 23, Nov. 22, 1919, and July 15, 1920; JPW to FKW, July 21, 1920.

34. FEW Papers, JPW to FEW, June 21, 1922.

35. FEW Record, 799–805; Long Papers, Long to Bell, May 2, 1921.

36. G. Harrie Thomas in FEW Record, 604; Norton Clapp, Reminiscences; F. K. Weyerhaeuser, Reminiscences; R. R. Macartney, Reminiscences; Bob Hunt, Reminiscences; Otto C. Schoenwerk, Reminiscences. Macartney had begun work at Cloquet, and came west later.

XVIII

An Industry at War

W EEKS BEFORE the declaration of war by Congress on April 6, 1917, the lumbermen of the United States had pledged their support to the nation. R. H. Downman, President of the National Lumber Manufactures Association, had made a formal offer of aid, even volunteering his own services. The *American Lumberman* had warmly approved and on March 31st had declared with respect to professions of service: "The time is near at hand when these resolutions must be put into effect and when every member of the industry must be prepared to do his part." On April 21st, with war an actuality, it renewed its exhortations. "Let everyone take hold and help." Meanwhile, leaders like Charles S. Keith of the Southern Pine Association were promising substantial results, while George S. Long of the Weyerhaeuser Timber Company was busy both in Tacoma, where the fir mills offered complete cooperation with the government, and in Washington, where he joined the Lumber Committee Council for National Defense.[1]

While there can be no question of the complete sincerity of such attitudes and statements, there can also be little question that many lumbermen viewed the American entry into the war with something like relief at the end of uncertainty. For half a dozen years theirs had been a difficult situation. From the early 1900's they had been battling with increasing intensity against wood substitutes. Since August, 1914, the war in Europe had compounded their difficulties. With the United States nominally neutral, with shipping in demand, and with submarine warfare a menace, they had faced a condition of uncertainty that had worked against home building and unsettled the export trade. A January, 1917, report issued by the United States Forest Service had noted that since

1906 "the home consumption of lumber per capita had dropped nearly a fourth." George S. Long termed this document "the most accomplished analysis of the timber and lumber situation that has ever seen print." The *American Lumberman* in March referred to the industry as in "the slough of despond." The mental confusion of the lumbermen was compounded by the fact that the opening of the Panama Canal and a promising price situation had induced them to erect such new mills as Everett B, Snoqualmie Falls, and the Emmett plant of Boise Payette. Now the canal was closed and prices were down. The industry had suffered the disadvantages of war, and American participation promised to balance them with certain advantages.[2]

Some of these were obvious. Lumber would be needed for cantonments, ships, airplanes, new Army posts, crating for military supplies, and for temporary railroad lines. As a matter of fact, the early months of 1917 saw a burst of renewed activity. "Orders were never so plentiful in the history of the American lumber industry," affirmed a news item late in April, and, what was quite as important, prices were good.[3]

The Weyerhaeuser companies worked shoulder to shoulder with their competitor-associates. Food-for-victory plots were provided employees rent-free. Though Frederick Weyerhaeuser had been German-born, his whole active life had been American, and his sons and grandsons were completely American in their associations and attitudes. The second generation joined in Liberty Bond drives and took a prominent part, through the League of Patriotic Americans of German Origin, in promoting widespread support of the war. The grandsons volunteered promptly for the Armed Forces—Frederick K., J. P. Weyerhaeuser, Jr., G. F. Jewett, and Edwin Weyerhaeuser Davis; the sons of other stockholders, or officials like Charles H. Ingram, Edmund Hayes, George S. Long, Jr., James N. Clapp, and John A. Humbird, also volunteered. George S. Long, as noted, was active in government work from the start.[4]

But neither the industry nor the Weyerhaeuser companies were to have a simple role in the war. Government orders were not to materialize in the forms or to the degree anticipated. Problems of transportation and priorities were to paralyze profitable activities again and again. And, more important, the relationship of the lumbermen to labor was to pose a threat the size and character of which no one at the time could possibly have imagined.

2

Soon after America's entry into the war, a lumber committee was formed as a unit of the Raw Materials Division of the Council of National Defense. Organized to advise Washington officials on purchases, it consisted of fourteen members, four representing the Pacific Coast. George S. Long was one of these, along with J. F. Gregory of the Fir Tree Lumber Company of Tacoma and E. T. Allen of Portland, manager of the Western Forestry and Conservation Association. After early discussions, Gregory returned from Washington to Tacoma, somewhat rashly announcing that "the lumber industry of the Pacific Northwest need have no fear of the surety of its market for the next few years, due to the enormous demands being created by war requirements."

The committee of fourteen arranged that government contracts should be handled through nine regional committees. In the West a fir emergency committee, organized by the West Coast Lumberman's Association and led by Long and Gregory, allocated orders. Later it passed through several reorganizations and finally emerged as the Fir Production Board.[5]

The immediate demand was for more than a billion feet of lumber to build cantonments. Soon it became apparent that the bulk of these orders would go to producers of southern yellow pine, for most of the Army camps lay in or near the South. However, the Northwest supplied lumber for cantonments at American Lake, Washington, and at Des Moines, Iowa, and later provided fir and pine for the Rock Island (Illinois) Arsenal. The Weyerhaeuser Timber Company received its share of cantonment orders, and of 7,000,000 feet of pine required by the arsenal, 3,000,000 were delivered by the Weyerhaeuser Sales Company. Nevertheless, the chief advantage of the cantonment program lay in removing yellow pine as a commercial competitor in the northern states.[6]

The Pacific Northwest fared better with government orders for the building of wooden ships. No less a person than Major General George W. Goethals, head of the Emergency Fleet Corporation, had jested skeptically in early war days: "Birds are still nesting in the trees of which wooden ships are to be built." This did not long remain true. A formidable program for the construction of such vessels got under way by May, 1917, and in orders for this work the Northwest went far toward taking the role played by the South in the case of the cantonments.[7]

Meanwhile, a third important activity loomed up in the provision of wood for airplanes. Despite the fact that Americans like the Wright brothers, Glenn Curtiss, and others had pioneered in the first successful flights, aviation in the United States up to 1917 had remained largely experimental. Meanwhile, the European nations, employing airplanes for military purposes, had developed a new industry for their manufacture; with the American entry an extension of this activity had shot up in the United States almost as if flashed across the Atlantic by cable.[8]

Airplanes in 1917 were still made largely of wood, and there was some uncertainty whether spruce, fir, or pine offered the best material for the beams and struts of the frames (mahogany was preferred for propellers). The Everett mills, the two Weyerhaeuser plants among them, in 1917 supplied Italy with 25,000,000 feet of fir for planes used in the campaigns against Austria. However, American engineers regarded spruce as the most desirable wood. It was the lightest, saving about seventy-five pounds on a small training plane as compared with fir, and was both resilient and nonsplintering. It came rapidly into strong demand.

For the lumberman, spruce had disadvantages. Only about 15 percent of it could be utilized for plane manufacture, and since the wood had never won a strong place for itself commercially as against fir and pine, the remainder was useful chiefly for boxes. Thus as the timber was logged and milled, a large amount of unsuitable grades accumulated and glutted the market. Perhaps even more important, spruce seldom appeared in concentrated stands but was scattered, often in remote areas, where for economical operation other timber such as fir, cedar, and hemlock would have to be logged. Current market demand did not justify cutting these species.[9]

In June, 1917, Major Charles R. Sligh, formerly a furniture manufacturer in Grand Rapids, Michigan, but now acting for the Signal Corps with the encouragement of Secretary of War Newton D. Baker, undertook to procure spruce for the numerous American factories that had sprung up to manufacture airplanes for the government. On the advice of E. T. Allen, Sligh appointed George S. Long chairman of an Emergency Spruce Committee.

In September, Sligh sent Allen to the Northwest to take personal charge of spruce procurement. The latter had ample authority as far as the lumbermen were concerned, for on September 6, 1917, the government had commandeered all available supplies of spruce lumber. Yet during a brief stay in the West, for reasons soon to be noted, he could report little progress. But before going further into the spruce-procurement jungle, it will be well to consider the chief obstacles that lumbermen and government officials alike had faced during the first half-year of American participation in the war.[10]

3

One obstacle was the shortage of freight cars for the shipment of lumber from mill to market. This shortage had existed recurrently since 1914 and had become so endemic to the industry that in February, 1917, two months before Congress declared war, the Everett mills could find transportation for less than half their product. The situation was worsened by government embargoes. So congested with freight cars did the chief port areas become that at times all new shipments east of the Mississippi were forbidden until traffic was again flowing smoothly. Such measures naturally affected shipments from the Northwest. As to the short supply of cars, this continued to be chronic throughout the war. Even by April, 1918, the western mills could get a bare 40 percent of their requirements, and shipments for the government took 70 percent of what was available. As a result, the Northwest became an unreliable source of supply for eastern projects, and a number of orders that might otherwise have been placed in Idaho or with Pacific Coast mills were diverted by Washington to the South.[11]

But if the car shortage was a grim deterrent to realization of the industry's hopes for war orders, labor conditions were developing in a way to threaten lumbermen's capacity to fill them. Here too there were shortages and frictions.

With the entire nation springing to arms and engaged in an unparalleled industrial expansion, manpower was at a premium. The youth of the nation were pouring into Army camps and naval stations, first as volunteers and later as drafted recruits. Overnight tens of thousands of young loggers and millworkers disappeared as if swept away by a tidal wave. Two forestry regiments, containing the pick of woodsmen, sawyers, filers, and foremen, and containing many men from various Weyerhaeuser companies, were assembled and quickly trained for service in France. Other lumber workers found more attractive jobs in the new, high-paying war industries. The lumber industry had no priority rating until September 17, 1917, and then was allotted only a Class IV deferment status. Also disastrous was the immediate lapse of immigration from abroad—hitherto an important source of manpower for the logging camps and mills.[12]

Yet the scarcity and inferior quality of workers was a less disturbing factor than the deep restlessness of such labor as the lumbermen could employ. The unusual conditions of the time offered a rare opportunity for forces bent on the organization of the industry and for an attempt to revolutionize working conditions both in the mills and in the camps.

The camps had for some time been the objects of unfavorable criticism by union organizers and writers on labor conditions. Located in remote spots, many offered the workers cramped quarters, infestation by insects, and a lack of lighting and bathing facilities. There were complaints of "rotten grub." Actually, a considerable number of western companies, including Cherry Valley Logging, Snoqualmie Falls Lumber, and Clarke County Timber companies, the primary Weyerhaeuser logging units, had been modernized prior to 1917. The testimony today of many men who knew the camps at the time is that they offered roomy quarters and spring bunks, supplied clean blankets, and served ample food of good quality. However, as reactions to wartime conditions were to demonstrate, further improvement was possible, and the coming of logging railroads and motor trucks made quite feasible the introduction of better buildings, portable electric lights, and modern toilets and wash-rooms.

Several factors had worked against progress. One was the long-stand-ing tradition that woods life and work were rough and that rugged men did not require "pampering"; another was the fact that a majority of the camp workers were foreign-born and used to a minimum of improvements. And while the bulk of the workers were sober and steady, a considerable number were drifting and irresponsible, a "womanless, homeless, voteless" group who carried their verminous blankets from place to place, spent their wages as received, and were both ignorant and contemptuous of sanitary arrangements. However, they were quick to respond to the exhor-tations of "agitators," and even the more responsible employees, conscious of long, hard days, gave ear to the talk of shorter hours and better work-ing conditions. The mills, as noted, did much more for their employees than logging camps, but they still kept the ten-hour day, and their workers had limited power to bargain for wages, hours, or conditions of work.

Had there been effective unionism, drastic changes now long overdue might have been easily achieved. To be sure, the idea of organizing work-ers throughout the industry was not new. In the pulp mills, related in their activity to lumbering, the workers had maintained their unions (one existed in the Northwest Paper Company at Cloquet in 1915), and in the lumbering industry itself there was one successful union, that of the Shingle-Weavers. Founded in January 1903 as an A.F. of L. affiliate, it had maintained an active existence ever since, calling strikes and exact-ing wage increases and other concessions. The A.F. of L. had made spo-radic attempts from 1907 on to organize other workers in both the mills and the camps, and in 1917 granted a charter to the International Union of Timber Workers, with which the Shingle-Weavers were to merge a year later.[13]

A separate and more flamboyant drive for the improvement of the lumber workers' lot had been conducted for some years by the Interna-tional Workers of the World. Founded in 1905 by a group of socialist or socialist-anarchist labor organizations, it had emerged in 1908, after shaking off the conservative and "intellectual" elements, as a body of proselyting radicals with a Marxist philosophy and a practice of direct action. While the union talked boldly of its intention to "take possession of the earth and the machinery of production and abolish the wage system," it had little patience with mere doctrine. It rejected all politi-cians as "sterile chatterers," and relied on bellicose appeals to the mob and on strikes, slowdowns, and the destruction of property. While the I.W.W., as it was soon called, had its national and local headquarters,

its members maintained staunchly that the rank and file ran the organization.

Such a philosophy helped to give the movement a distinctive character. It attracted hundreds of shrewd, ingenious, rebellious, and highly
vocal misfits and idealists. It developed "a vituperative cant of its own,"
similar to later communist jargon, but more picturesque and profane.
It also worked out a variety of practices for action (sometimes tricky,
violent, and hypocritical, but often dramatically effective); and built up
a body of popular songs ("Hallelujah, I'm a Bum!" "Pie in the Sky," the
Joe Hill ballads, and so forth) that appealed strongly to discontented
workers and won an amused popularity with the general public. The
I.W.W.'s lashed out at the "capitalists," courted arrest for "free speech,"
and persistently urged direct action as the only effective weapon of the
downtrodden, among whom they proudly enrolled themselves.[14]

As early as 1907 the I.W.W.'s had seized the leadership of a sawmill
strike in Portland. They set commendable goals: the termination of an
eleven-hour day and the winning of a three-dollar-a-day minimum wage.
They failed as far as the strike was concerned but gained in the esteem
of the workers. In succeeding years they fomented strikes at Seattle, Walla
Walla, and other centers, easily wresting leadership from the less resourceful A.F. of L. As in their first attempt, they lost these strikes but set objectives that won the approval of the men: the reform of camp conditions,
the eight-hour day, and free speech on employer abuses. They concentrated
attention on chosen localities, seeking in each case to establish a nucleus
of loyal supporters for future operations.

In the summer of 1916 a group of I.W.W.'s invaded Everett, seeking
to "muscle in" on a strike of the Shingle-Weavers. The latter kept aloof
from the "Wobblies," and the sheriff and a group of citizens ran them out
of town. Early in November about eighty I.W.W. organizers set sail on
the *Verona* from Seattle, proclaiming that they were going to Everett to
establish free speech there. On November 5, 1916, the incoming vessel
was met at the wharf by the local sheriff and a large group of armed
deputies, including some Weyerhaeuser employees, and amid firing was
prevented from docking. Five men were killed on the ship and two deputies on shore. On its return to Seattle seventy-four men, presumably
I.W.W.'s, were held on a murder charge but because of a lack of specific
evidence were finally acquitted.

The Shingle-Weavers were unsuccessful in their strike, and one led
late in the year by the I.W.W.'s at Virginia, Minnesota, against the Virginia & Rainy Lake Company also ended in defeat. The employers made
some increases in wages, but in a time of rising prices the men were dissatisfied with their pay, hours, and conditions of work, and increasingly
turned to the unions for leadership. The Shingle-Weavers, the A.F. of L.

Timber Workers, and the I.W.W. were all resolved to win important concessions. Theirs was no united front, for the "Wobblies" scoffed at the other unions as unworthy of representing labor, and the A.F. of L. detested the I.W.W. Nevertheless, all three agreed on certain main objectives, and never had they been in a better position to support their demands, for manpower was badly needed and the supply daily diminishing.[15]

The I.W.W. met in Spokane on March 4–6, 1917, making their usual demands and launching Lumber Workers' Union 500, to operate specially in the Inland Empire. The Shingle-Weavers and Timber Workers met later, separately, but coordinated their moves and called a strike for July 16th unless their demands, including the eight-hour day, were met before that date. The employers ignored these activities until July 9th, when they assembled at Seattle, formed the Lumbermen's Protective Association, and condemned the eight-hour day as "impossible in wartime." They promised to preserve the ten-hour work span "for the purpose of maintaining the maximum production in the lumber industry."

The I.W.W.'s in some localities called out their supporters from Idaho mills and camps even before July 1st, and tried to take credit for the strike on the coast by jumping the July 16th deadline set by the Shingle-Weavers and Timber Workers. But the latter held off until the date they had set.[16]

The combined efforts of the three groups were strikingly effective. On the coast, from 40,000 to 50,000 workers had walked out by the night of the 16th, and by August 1st not more than 15 percent of the mills and logging camps were running. Up to 1916 the Weyerhaeuser companies had met with little union opposition, but now they felt the full impact of both A.F. of L. and I.W.W. activity. Their operations were sharply curtailed everywhere and in many places entirely suspended. At Everett, W. H. Boner had raised wages several times. Long wrote to F. E. Weyerhaeuser that there was not a man in either of the two plants receiving less than $3.00 a day, yet on the 16th practically the entire working force had left. "We knew," he remarked, "that what they wanted was eight hours."

It was an impressive demonstration of union power. Long, noting in a letter to F. E. Weyerhaeuser late in July that the Snoqualmie Falls Lumber Company was operating and that the Clarke County Timber Company was limping along with one crew, suggested that the eight-hour day would probably have to be granted in August because of widespread public sentiment. Weyerhaeuser replied: "I hope that we shall not have to concede an eight-hour day, and I particularly hope that we shall not have to recognize unions." His was the feeling of most employers, and of the *American Lumberman*. By August 15th Secretary of War Baker had advocated the adoption of the shorter work period, and Governor

Ernest Lister of Washington in a proclamation on that day urged it, as well as time and a half for overtime.

But the *Lumberman* stood staunchly in opposition. "With a little firmness on the part of the Government," its editors declared on August 18th, "the situation could be relieved and the mills permitted to operate." The western employers, it pointed out, "have declared their willingness to adopt such a working arrangement provided it is made national," but understandably would not accept an eight-hour day while in the South workers were paid less for ten hours of labor.

Two circumstances stiffened employer resistance. The companies could not get rid of inventory accumulated in recent years. This objective was practically stated in the Weyerhaeuser Timber Company's annual report for 1917, which characterized the strike as "not a wholly unfortunate thing," since there might otherwise have been "overproduction" and "lower prices." The shortage of railroad cars also fortified resistance to the strike, for it restricted shipments in any case. Both factors applied in the case of the American Lake cantonment (Camp Lewis), which was being constructed of inventory stock. Long and Gregory told a trade reporter that the supply of lumber on hand to complete the work was almost adequate and that "the chief problem [was] one of loading."[17]

In Idaho, meanwhile, the I.W.W. had been notably successful. Firms in the Inland Empire that had employed 6,842 men in June found themselves on August 18th with only 3,404, a half-force. Of the Weyerhaeuser companies Humbird, Edward Rutledge, and Bonners Ferry were crippled, and A. W. Laird told his Potlatch stockholders that the logging camps in the north of the state were all closed. Of Potlatch itself he reported, "Our labor force is loyal." Actually, he closed the large Potlatch plant on July 21st but kept the smaller mill at Elk River going with the aid of sympathetic residents of that community. Most of the strikers in Idaho were I.W.W.'s or their sympathizers, although the Timber Workers maintained an organization there with 736 dues-paying members.

The brightest spot in Idaho for the Weyerhaeusers was Boise Payette. There C. A. Barton reported on August 9th: "We have had no particular trouble with the I.W.W.'s as yet." He explained to F. E. Weyerhaeuser that local sheriffs were arresting them, thus helping "to clean up and get rid of all these undesirables."[18]

According to Weyerhaeuser officials, the "Wobblies" played very rough. Al Raught at Yacolt later asserted that they drove railroad spikes and files into logs, put emery dust in engine bearings, and threw switches that derailed logging trains. Ralph Boyd at Everett vividly described such activity. "I saw logs come into the mills containing drift bolts, railroad spikes, staples, and pieces of wire rope cunningly and ingeniously concealed. I saw head saws break as the result of such sabotage. I saw a piece of broken headsaw come out on to the carriage and curl around the tail-dogger. It's always been a marvel to me why that fellow wasn't killed." Maxwell told of similar practices at Potlatch in Idaho.

I.W.W. headquarters disclaimed responsibility for such acts, blaming them on the employers; but the evidence is overwhelming that many individual "Wobblies" resorted to violent acts. The effect was to antagonize loyal workers and solidify their support of the management, and to line up the sober citizens of many communities against the union. The Idaho legislature passed a law making sabotage a criminal offense, and popular feeling ran strong against the I.W.W. as a lawless, unpatriotic organization. The Shingle-Weavers and Timber Workers supported the war, but argued that it was the patriotic duty of the lumbermen to grant their demands. In contrast, the I.W.W. categorically opposed "the European war of conquest and exploitation" (they denounced all wars), and their methods were regarded by many as proving their disloyalty. They were tagged not only as "I Won't Work" men but also as "Imperial Wilhelm Warriors" and "I Want Wilhelm" agents. Weyerhaeuser officials like Jackson F. Kimball, company representative at Klamath Falls (Oregon), wanted to run the "agitators" out of the area. "I feel as good," he exploded, "as if I were permitting a rattler to hang around the house and waiting to see if he would try to bite anyone before killing him."

Potlatch, according to Maxwell, was eventually successful in dealing with the problem. The workers, he says, found some of the saboteurs at work and were bitterly resentful. The time came when, if a stranger were seen in the woods, the limb under which he was standing would be snipped off by a bullet. A company man would then come along, gun in hand, and remark, "Oh, I'm awfully sorry, but I thought I saw a deer over here!" As a result, "Those fellows got frightened, finally, and decided it was a good time for them to leave."[19]

Thus the struggle continued bitterly through the summer. The promising outlook of the preceding April had dimmed. "Labor agitators," declared the *American Lumberman* early in September, "have succeeded in striking down a great industry and rendering it helpless." The menacing character of the I.W.W. was recognized by the government to the extent that raids were made on union headquarters by federal agents in Chicago, Pittsburgh, Cleveland, Seattle, and other cities. Haywood was arrested, and papers in the various offices were seized.[20]

Meanwhile, one of the chief objectives of the strike had been met by many of the employers: they had accepted the necessity for a reform of conditions in the logging camps and mills. Undoubtedly one factor in persuading them to this sweeping concession had been the Army cantonments. Many of these were located in places as remote as logging sites, yet provided the soldiers with hygienic and comfortable quarters. When the Army at length came to the forests, its example doubtless set a final seal on the process of reform, but this had been set in motion during the summer.

For the Weyerhaeuser companies a Labor Committee—Huntington Taylor, H. C. Hornby, H. H. Irvine, T. J. Humbird, and J. P. Weyerhaeuser—had drafted recommended standards for living conditions of their employees: social halls for both camps and mills, places for entertainment, books and magazines, special housing for married men, and new bunkhouses with every improvement the I.W.W. had demanded, from clean bedding to porcelain dishes, electric lights, and showers. Already in early September, Louis S. Case was exclaiming over the transformation. "It is simply wonderful," he wrote, "what the loggers and millmen are doing in the West for the comfort of their men. . . . If some of the old time Wisconsin and Minnesota lumberjacks could have spring beds, electric lights, shower baths, etc., I do not believe they would know what to do with them." Nevertheless, the transformation was a significant fact.[21]

The men began drifting back in September. With some, improvements in work conditions were undoubtedly a factor, but in the main they wanted their jobs and pay envelopes again. The prospect of the Army taking over their work may also have been a consideration. The I.W.W. sped the process of return by a decision to shift the fight to "a strike on the job." Its resources were limited, its leaders had been arrested, its offices raided, and it could not operate in the open. The men needed cash; well, let the bosses supply it. The Timber Workers did not call off the strike, refusing such action until the eight-hour day was established; it did, however, permit its members to return to work.

By mid-September the strike was over. The Weyerhaeuser Timber Company reopened the Everett mills on the 17th. Nominally the lumbermen were victorious. They kept the ten-hour day; they recognized no union. To be sure, life in the camps had been improved. But the I.W.W.'s were sternly warned away from the new "paradise" their pressure had helped to create. Every returning worker was required to sign a statement denying membership in the execrated organization. Naturally, this represented no hurdle for its supporters; if a few known organizers were excluded, the rank and file came back, and employers soon became aware of that fact. There were exasperating slowdowns, missing key workers, cessations of work after eight hours.[22]

While the Timber Workers did not join in such tactics, they resented their failure to win the eight-hour day, labored grudgingly, and helped infuse the industry with a sense of uncertainty and unrest. The conditions that were needed to enable the lumbermen to meet their war obligations had still to be established. Most workers were sullen and unresponsive;

the employers everywhere were fearful of new outbreaks of sabotage. Lumber was not being produced in quantity.

4

The efforts of Major Sligh to expedite the production of spruce were initiated at a most disturbed time. The I.W.W.'s were already calling out their men; the full strike came while he was still seeking authority to buy spruce, and he did not really begin effective work until the government commandeered all such lumber on September 6, 1917. He sent Allen to the coast some days later, and about September 17th the latter called a meeting of spruce manufacturers, which George S. Long attended. Allen also conferred with Long and made a statement to the press outlining his objectives. The situation was confused, for while the strike had been broken, the atmosphere in camps and mills was one of uncertainty and suspicion. Allen could hardly make much progress in this period, but on September 24th, impatient for action, Sligh demanded his resignation.[23]

Long was apparently as impatient with Sligh as Sligh was with Allen. Long visited the major in Washington and later stated that while he was "a pleasant gentleman . . . and a very patriotic one," he was quite unfamiliar with the situation on the West Coast. Sligh asserted that Long came "to get my scalp," but Long denied any such intention. However, the major soon found that a Spruce Division had been organized under Colonel Brice P. Disque, a West Pointer who had earlier left the Army and served recently as a prison warden in Michigan, then had reentered the service. Early in October, Disque had made a hurried trip to the Northwest to check on the spruce situation there. On November 8th, now in Washington, he was apparently established in authority, and Sligh soon resigned from his spruce procurement post. Later he attacked his successor as a blowhard and an incompetent, a characterization hotly resented by officers associated with Disque and by numerous lumbermen in the Northwest who had worked with him for more than a year.[24]

What is generally agreed is that, with Sligh out of the way, Disque rapidly took command of the spruce situation and adopted measures that gave direction and drive to the entire lumber activity in the Northwest. His first act looked toward solving the labor difficulties that were halting action everywhere; he founded an employer-employee organization named the Loyal Legion of Loggers and Lumbermen, the 4L. Some evidence exists that this "union," actually an industrial council, grew out of his first survey trip in October, 1917. It was not necessarily Disque's idea; Jensen in his *Lumber and Labor* credits the plan to an employer or a group of employers. It is certain that Disque quickly appropriated and developed the project. His assistant, Lieutenant Colonel Cuthbert P.

Stearns, who arrived in the Northwest early in November, testifies that at that time all the lumbermen were desperately concerned about labor difficulties. "We could not talk with any logger or lumberman for five minutes before he got off on the I.W.W. situation. . . . He was simply eaten up with it; it was so hindering his work."

Disque quickly perceived the possibilities of the Loyal Legion and got both Samuel Gompers of the A.F. of L. and Secretary of War Baker to approve of it. He then began to promote the 4L as a device by which the workers and the operators would merge their efforts for the good of the country. At the same time, participants would consider all aspects of the job—hours, pay, work and camp conditions, and reach an agreement on what was fair in every instance. To expedite local acceptance of the Loyal Legion, Disque and Stearns selected personable and energetic young officers to talk to employers and workers in the various localities. In each case they checked the working conditions, and if these were substandard, exerted every effort to get them improved. Simultaneously they proposed that all 4L members should pledge to "support this country against enemies, both foreign and domestic." And although spruce production was the point of departure for action, the new organization was to cover the mills and camps of the entire industry, thus including office and clerical workers.[25]

The young officers did their work well. From November 30, 1917, when the first local was founded, the project "took like wildfire in the woods." The employers were willing to cooperate: they had had their fill of "a strike on the job." Hating the I.W.W., having the blessing of Gompers, and trusting a friendly government, the nonradical labor leaders were equally receptive. "Practically all our membership in the Northwest," declared the president of the Timber Workers in May, 1918, "are loyal members of the 4L." On January 1, 1918, the new organization already boasted of more than 10,000 members, by March it could count 50,000 in the coast areas alone, and locals were forming in the Inland Empire. Total estimates of enrolled membership by summer ran as high as 125,000. Weyerhaeuser companies both in Idaho and on the Pacific slope established 4L chapters.[26]

The 4L was a powerful weapon that Disque was not slow to use. He was able not only to standardize camp conditions but also to prepare the ground for changes in hours and pay. "After its [the 4L's] organization there were no strikes," said Stearns two years later; "sabotage, which had been rampant, gradually died out; and the I.W.W. element was practically stamped out." The change in atmosphere was dramatic. The big question was the eight-hour day. Disque indicated that he favored this, but did not force the issue. Events soon aided him and the workers, for in December the chief Inland Empire mills, including the Weyerhaeuser companies, announced that on January 1, 1918, they would establish eight hours as the normal day. Boise Payette, however, held tenaciously to ten hours.

Meanwhile, two investigations were airing the controversy on this and other matters in dispute. The Washington State Council of Defense conducted one under the able guidance of Dr. Henry Suzzalo, President of the University of Washington; the other was instituted by President Wilson, who appointed a Federal Mediation Commission headed by M. B. Wilson to canvass the labor difficulties of the lumber industry in the Northwest. The commission's hearing, and a report made in January, 1918, together with the work of Suzzalo's committee, clarified the situation. The federal committee found that many operators had used the excesses of the I.W.W. as a pretext for crushing all unions. It condemned the lumbermen's opposition to the eight-hour day. Lumbering, it pointed out, was "almost the only industry on the coast" in which that work period was not accepted as standard. "In truth," it concluded, "we cannot escape the conviction that with too many opposition . . . has become a matter of pride instead of judgment, a reluctance to yield after having defeated the strike."

As a result of these investigations, public opinion for the eight-hour day was stronger than ever, and the coast employers, including Long and his associates, bowed to it at a Portland meeting on February 27, 1918. Disque issued an "order" on March 1st establishing an eight-hour day for the lumber industry of the entire Northwest, with time and a half for overtime and a forty-eight-hour week. His decisions were now accepted on everything in the field of labor and camp and mill conditions.[27]

The Weyerhaeuser firms took the event ruefully but in stride. The Inland Empire group had already instituted an eight-hour day, and finally Boise Payette grudgingly adopted it. On the coast, Long wrote F. E. Weyerhaeuser that his firm had "eased into" the new schedule, "having it apparently come as a suggestion from the Federal Government, through the activities of Colonel Disque." He saw one "gleam of sunshine," a possibility that labor would now become more dependable and give "a more honest effort."

F. E. Weyerhaeuser viewed the change with mixed feelings. "I am sorry to see it come," he wrote Long, "but on the other hand, I am convinced that the eight-hour day is going to become fairly established all over the United States, as well as greatly improved living conditions for the laboring class." Mindful of the competition of low-paid yellow pine labor, he still hoped to keep a ten-hour day "in the Northern states."[28] Until wage-and-hour scales were the same in the lumber industry throughout the country, southern mills had the advantage over those in the upper Middle West and Far West.

During this entire period Disque had been busy with other matters besides labor. Almost on arrival he had begun to bring soldiers to the coast to assist in getting out spruce lumber. By February he had 5,500 men, and eventually the total number was to reach 30,000. Disque sent his soldiers to camps and mills that were short of workers, and arranged that the employers should pay each soldier enough in addition to his Army allotment to make his total wage equal that of a civilian doing comparable work.

Meanwhile, at Vancouver he built a government remanufacturing plant, which began operations on February 7th, and made contracts with loggers and millowners for both spruce and fir. Even before January 1st he was encouraging the production of fir airplane stock to supplement the insufficient supply of spruce and to serve the Allies, who had always used it. Later he began work on a thirty-eight-mile railroad that would tap certain isolated rich stands of timber.

A number of such activities came into question both during and after the war. Disque was accused of favoritism, ineptitude, and needless prodigality. But he seems to have worked quickly and prodigiously, employing experts for advice, and to have won the support of both employers and workers. Long approved of him, and in August, 1918, a group of lumbermen in Spokane presented John D. Ryan of the Aircraft Production Board with a paean of praise for the colonel and recommended his immediate appointment as a brigadier general! (He received the promotion in January, 1919.) While Disque won the support of labor for reasons noted, on many matters he saw eye-to-eye with the employer. He told the West Coast Lumbermen's Association at its annual meeting in late January, 1918, "When you gentlemen find the price is not right we will make it right."[29]

The drive for aircraft spruce and fir had its epic aspects. The increasing troops of soldiers setting up their camps in remote areas, the civilian workers rallying to the call for patriotic action, the eventual response of the operators to the demands of labor, the saws of the fallers set against giant trees, the roads and railroads pushed into wilder regions—all were stirring and panoramic. Against these positive forces had been ranged the sabotage of the I.W.W.'s, the slowdowns of the workers, the grudging attitude of the lumbermen. These obstacles had now been swept away, and it was a war of the skill and muscle of men against time, distance, and inadequate transportation.

Disque, whatever his faults, gave the members of his immense team a deep sense of their importance. He infused operators, workers, and soldiers with a conviction that their task, six thousand miles from the battle-fronts, was not "inferior soldiering." Production meant victory. "And it is coming," affirmed the *4L Bulletin* for May, 1918, "with the toot of the spruce locomotive and the crash of the falling trees and the shrieks of the saws and the long train of clear, clean spruce that builds the battle fleets of the air, the war eagles that carry the glad tidings of freedom to all the world."[30]

The powers that Disque had assumed were varied and exacting, and as the production of spruce grew, his responsibilities increased. As 1918 advanced he took steps to shift labor problems to the 4L. On August 19th the directors of that organization adopted a constitution that accepted "existing principles" and provided for twelve districts, eight in the fir regions and four in the Inland Empire. Interestingly, in the constitution the employer-employee relationship received a greater emphasis than formerly. However, the Legion was defined as "not a labor union in the common acceptance of the term" but a patriotic unit that would neither organize nor disrupt "any legitimate labor unions."

Nevertheless, when the Timber Workers, increasingly dissatisfied with the 4L as their sole means of representation, attempted to organize the workers separately, uniformed men broke up their meetings, and Disque advised the A.F. of L. union to suspend such activities until after the war.[31]

Major John E. Morley, head of legal work for the Spruce Production Division, and Colonel Stearns, Disque's executive assistant, later vigorously defended his activities. They pointed out that the demand for aircraft lumber was incessant and loud and that Disque was forced to make quick decisions and err on the side of doing and paying too much. According to them, Disque met the demands of the Allies and of domestic aircraft companies. Morley testified before a House committee that "from the time we got organized out there and got under way [presumably from May 1918 on] we . . . were meeting the ever-increasing requests put upon us." In October, 1918, he said, the division shipped 20,000,000 feet of spruce airplane lumber. Stearns gave a figure of 143,000,000 feet as the total shipped during the year following November, 1917, an average of almost 12,000,000 feet a month. When Disque was finally called before the same House Investigating Committee, he admitted errors but justified his record in view of the emergency he had faced.[32]

5

What was the Weyerhaeuser contribution to the solution of the aircraft lumber problem? The answer is somewhat complicated. The Weyerhaeuser Timber Company never made a contract with the Spruce Production Division, yet it was able to further the work of that unit to no small extent. It owned extensive spruce stumpage. Long estimated that of all such timber in the vicinity of the Columbia River, Willapa Harbor, and Grays Harbor in the state of Washington, the chief areas from which the government drew its supply, his firm possessed a third or more. He early offered cooperation in utilizing this supply. "Undoubtedly our company will be called upon quite freely to grant permission to those who want to get out rived spruce," he wrote Disque in December, 1917, "and I assure you in advance that we are willing to do this." He added that he was assigning a man to determine the chief spruce stands.

Finally, the Weyerhaeuser Timber Company, which had no mill of its own near its spruce holdings, let important contracts for the cutting of that timber. The Siems-Carey Company, which had a large Spruce Division contract, the Warren Spruce Company, the Grant Smith-Porter Brothers Company, and the Airplane Spruce & Lumber Company all made agreements for logging Weyerhaeuser timber.[33]

The Timber Company concentrated its own efforts on fir for ships, cantonments, silos, and other farm buildings. In addition, it processed fir airplane materials, roughing these out for the government cutting plant at Vancouver. In August, 1918, it stood second among all the mills supplying such lumber to this unit. At Vancouver the stock was prepared to exact specifications for shipping.

The use of fir for aircraft construction was much greater than commonly recognized. Its manufacture for this purpose was well launched by early 1918; one small Tacoma firm had already dispatched 300,000 feet. J. H. Bloedel was appointed by the Aircraft Production Board late in January to speed the output of this lumber. Later he was replaced by Major Everett G. Griggs, a Tacoma lumberman, who in early September, 1918, reported to a meeting of West Coast lumbermen that fir airplane stock was being shipped in increasing quantities. "Fir is now entering upon its own," he declared, "and is equal to spruce for aircraft material and in some respects superior to it and is being so recognized." By the autumn of 1918, for every 30,000,000 feet of spruce procured, 20,000,-000 feet of fir seem to have been supplied. In November, 1918, the A and B Everett plants were cutting fir airplane stock as one of their chief activities.[34]

Disque's solution of the labor problem had paved the way for greater production in other war lumbering activities. In January 1918, the wooden ship program had actually been halted. Charles A. Piez, general manager of the Emergency Fleet Corporation, admitted at the time to a government committee that he had suspended the letting of further contracts because of a shortage of labor on the West Coast. This was at a time when Tacoma shipyards had 26 ships under construction and Seattle yards 60. With labor difficulties adjusted, new ship orders were forthcoming. By September, according to the *American Lumberman*, 208 wooden ships had been launched, and the government contemplated ordering 244 more. For such vessels the Weyerhaeuser Timber Company had steadily supplied timbers and lumber. All told, the Emergency Fleet used 790,-000,000 feet of lumber, while the Navy, for which the Everett plant also labored, consumed 122,000,000 feet.[35]

The building of cantonments continued steadily throughout the war. New centers were being constructed even as late as the autumn of 1918. More important, as the total of soldiers and sailors exceeded 4,000,000 and the war effort was intensified, the demand for new warehouses, munitions depots, training stations, hospitals, and housing developments for war workers became insistent. The first half-year of the conflict after American entry had seen the purchase of more than 1,000,000,000 feet of lumber for war-construction uses; by the end of the conflict the total used had risen to between 5,000,000,000 and 6,000,000,000.[36]

The Weyerhaeuser mills at Everett received a goodly share of orders for such buildings. News reports in November tell of their producing ships' timbers, airplane fir stock, cantonment materials, and lumber for the Navy at this time. Production for civilian needs was also constant— a new addition to the Everett planing mill was entirely devoted to "silos, grain bins, [and] tanks."[37]

As to Weyerhaeuser activities in other sections of the country, they were of necessity less keyed to the war. In Minnesota there is no clear evidence of substantial work done there for the government either before or after the fire of October, 1918 (which ended all activity), but the Cloquet plants undoubtedly supplied boxes and crating and shared in such orders as the 3,000,000 board feet of "northern pine" for the Rock Island Arsenal.

The Idaho plants were eager to participate in war production but lacked opportunities to do so. "Until recently," ran an article in the *American Lumberman* of August 3, 1918, "the pine manufacturers of the Inland Empire . . . have been called upon by the Government for comparatively little of their production for war needs." Indeed, in March, 1918, when the only government orders at these plants were for boxes and crating, J. P. Weyerhaeuser actually suggested privately that all mills in eastern Washington and Oregon and in Idaho and Montana should close and loyal men be sent to the coast to help get out airplane stock and ship lumber.

But in early August, 1918, came a decision by the Aircraft Production Board to employ selected white pine for building planes. The Idaho companies, after experimentation and demonstration, proposed to start shipments of 125,000 feet a month, then to increase them. Potlatch contracted to furnish 200,000 feet of white and western pine for experimental work with aircraft wings. In late September, however, the government announced that its spruce stocks were now sufficient and that no further white pine orders would be issued after October 1st.

Actually, the collapse of the white pine airplane project was no serious blow to the Idaho firms. The milling of selected stock, which never ran to more than 20 percent of a log, was neither easy nor particularly profitable. Moreover, as the *American Lumberman* remarked, "white pine is white pine," and as the long-favored wood of the central states it was sufficiently in demand throughout the war "to absorb all the stock" that was "ready for sale in the face of a steadily decreasing labor supply." Movement of lumber for farm buildings and farmhouses enjoyed priority on the railroads. White pine shipments from both Idaho and Minnesota were good in 1917 and 1918, although somewhat less than before the American entry into the war. The relative inactivity of the Idaho and Minnesota firms in war work, together with the considerable civilian production of the Weyerhaeuser Timber Company, doubtless explains a statement by Louis S. Case to Humbird in late October, 1918, that as far as the Weyerhaeuser companies were concerned, the government, military, and defense requirements for lumber were insignificant in the total marketing picture.[38]

It should be added that all lumber companies profited to an extent from a steadily rising civilian demand, and would have done a much larger business in this field but for the shortage of railroad cars and the occasional embargoes on rail shipments. Harbors were being improved, farm activities expanded, new office buildings erected, and home building was limited only by the ability of lumber dealers to make deliveries. The voracity of the market in 1918 is well illustrated by the case of Tacoma. There in August permits for dwellings rose to 405 as against 81 for the same month of the preceding year, while the press announced that in the next four months one thousand new homes would be erected![39]

6

The lumber companies in general during the war turned out less lumber than during 1916. Their production in 1917–1918 ran much below capacity and from 3 to 5 percent below normal. Shortages in both labor and railroad cars had led to curtailed output, though sales managers were able to sell at good prices most of the lumber manufactured. Their greatest problem continued to be the accumulation of lumber left over after the choice grades had been supplied. Particularly was this true of spruce and fir. Companies that supplied the government with quality materials—airplane stock, ship's timbers, and so forth—faced a continuing difficulty in marketing the residue. The government, however, made a considerable effort to use such "slow" items for boxing, crating, and temporary buildings.

On the whole, the war years had been prosperous ones for the industry, including Weyerhaeuser companies in Minnesota, Idaho, and on the Pacific. Among all the Weyerhaeuser mills only Boise Payette showed a marked increase in production over that in 1916, but large inventories of lumber, which had faced many firms like threats of bankruptcy, were almost entirely worked off. Prices were good, and a tremendous demand for civilian construction had built up, which promised a good market when peace came.[40]

Meanwhile, under war conditions most American logging camps had greatly improved and the status of labor had been raised in the forests and mills. Labor had fought hard for its right to bargain, and if its only gains survived in the 4L, an agency too close to a company union to satisfy the A.F. of L. or the I.W.W., still the workers had demonstrated an inherent power. The great gains in the camps and in the mills represented a permanent step forward.

As to the war, the industry had done its part. Despite car shortages, embargoes, labor disputes, and a shortage of workers, it had helped house the nation's Armed Forces, build its air fleets, and expand its ocean tonnage, so essential to counter submarine warfare. It had furnished its quota of men to the Army and Navy, including the battalions of logging and lumber experts who operated in France. It had contributed the essentials asked of it. With their associates, the Weyerhaeuser companies had vigorously participated in these operations, vital to the prosecution of the conflict and to final victory.

NOTES

1. *Amer. Lbrmn.*, March 31, 1917, p. 24, and April 21, 1917, pp. 1, 35; Letter of S. P. Johns, Jr. to the authors.

2. Greeley, *Public and Economic Aspects of the Lumber Industry*, 4, 54; Long Papers, G. S. Long to FEW, Aug. 28, 1916; *Amer. Lbrmn.*, March 31, 1917, p. 24.

3. See comments in *Amer. Lbrmn.*, particularly March 24, 1917, p. 30; May 5, 1917, p. 32, and April 28, 1917, p. 24.

4. Long Papers, March–Dec., 1918, *passim;* FEW Papers, FEW to Mrs. J. R. Jewett, Aug. 21, 1918. As to bond sales, Long Papers, Boner to

Long, May 7, 1919, show that up to May 7, 1919, the total for Everett alone was $240,000.

5. Clarkson, *Industrial America in the World War*, 497; *WC Lbrmn.*, May 1, 1917, p. 32; *Amer. Lbrmn.*, June 16, 1917, p. 66; Baruch, *American Industry at War*, 212, n. 3.

6. G. S. Long in *Amer. Lbrmn.*, Oct. 27, 1917, p. 41, and July 28, 1917, p. 56; JPW Papers, L. S. Case to JPW, Sept. 6, 1918; FEW Papers, Case to FEW, March 21, 1917, and FEW to O. O. Axley, June 12, 1917.

7. *Amer. Lbrmn.*, Aug. 11, 1917, p. 28; Clarkson, 423; *Amer. Lbrmn.*, April 28, 1917, p. 24.

8. For list of American aircraft firms see U.S. Congress, *Hearings Before Subcommittee No. 1 (Aviation) of the Select Committee on Expenditures in the War Department,* 66th Cong., 1st Sess., 506 ff. (hereafter cited as *Hearings on Expenditures*).

9. *Amer. Lbrmn.,* Sept. 29, 1917, p. 57; FEW Papers, Long to Howard F. Weiss, Nov. 14, 1917; Sligh testimony—Aug. 11, 1919, *Hearings on Expenditures,* 574 ff.; see also U.S. Congress, Senate, *Hearings Before the Committee on Military Affairs,* 65th Cong., 2nd Sess., 2303–2319 (hereafter cited as *Hearings on Military Affairs*).

10. *Amer. Lbrmn.,* Sept. 22, 1917, p. 49.

11. *Amer. Lbrmn.,* Feb. 24, 1917, p. 72; March 24, 1917, p. 28; and April 20, 1918, p. 37.

12. *Amer. Lbrmn.,* Jan. 18, 1919, p. 42. For competition of other industries, see LN Papers, A. W. Laird, July 25, 1917. FEW Papers, Long to H. F. Weiss, Nov. 14, 1917, shows that the WTC at that time had only 70 percent of the logging crew it had employed the previous year. The effect of the sharp curtailment of immigration is noted in *Amer. Lbrmn.,* Feb. 3, 1917, p. 33.

13. Jensen, *Lumber and Labor,* 3, 122. As to the camps, many Weyerhaeuser officials testify as to their good beds, clean blankets, and excellent food. Transportation was often furnished by the camps to married men who visited their families on weekends.

14. Brissenden, *The I.W.W., passim.;* Jensen, 119–120; Gambs, *Decline of the I.W.W.,* 176–177.

15. Jensen, 119–124; Mittleman, "The Loyal Legion of Loggers and Lumbermen," *J. of Pol. Ec.,* XXXI, June, 1923, pp. 323–327; see also Long Papers, W. W. Warren to Long, July 27, 1917.

16. Mittleman, 326; Jensen, 124–125; *Amer. Lbrmn.,* June 23, 1917, p. 54, and June 30, 1917, p. 30. There was no strike in Minnesota. "I think conditions in Minnesota are somewhat better as to the I.W.W. situation,"

wrote F. E. Weyerhaeuser to A. W. Laird on July 30, "particularly in the lumber plants."

17. Jensen, 126–127; Long Papers, Long to FEW, July 30, 1917, and FEW to Long, Aug. 8, 1917; Portland *Oregonian,* Aug. 15, 1917; *Amer. Lbrmn.,* Aug. 18, 1917, pp. 24, 54, July 28, 1917, p. 32; WTC Annual Report, 1917.

18. *Amer. Lbrmn.,* Aug. 11, 1917, p. 30; LN Papers, A. W. Laird to stockholders, July 25, 1917; FEW Papers, C. A. Barton to FEW, Aug. 9, 1917. The Potlatch mill at this time had a daily capacity of 375,000 feet, the Elk River plant one of 160,000.

19. See the reminiscences of Raught, Boyd, and W. L. Maxwell; Jensen, 128; *Amer. Lbrmn.,* March 17, 1917, p. 61; Haywood, *Bill Haywood's Book,* 294; *Amer. Lbrmn.,* June 23, 1917, p. 26; Long Papers, J. F. Kimball to Long, July 11, 1917.

20. *Amer. Lbrmn.,* Sept. 9, 1917, p. 36.

21. *Amer. Lbrmn.,* Sept. 29, 1917, 30; JPW Papers, L. S. Case to JPW, Sept. 12, 1917, and JPW to Huntington Taylor, Dec. 22, 1917.

22. *Amer. Lbrmn.,* Sept. 22, 1917, p. 44, and Sept. 29, 1917, p. 30; Jensen, 127.

23. *Hearings on Expenditures,* 574–585.

24. Tyler, "The United States Government as Union Organizer: The Loyal Legion of Loggers and Lumbermen," *MVHR,* XLVII, Dec., 1960, pp. 434–441, provides the latest summary of labor conditions in the Pacific Northwest; *Hearings on Expenditures,* 574–626; *Amer. Lbrmn.,* Feb. 9, 1918, p. 35; *Hearing on Expenditures,* 626–667 and 691–819; Jensen, 129.

25. Jensen, 129–131; Tyler, 441–451 (summary of 42 actions); *Hearings on Expenditures,* 591, 771.

26. *Hearings,* 771; C. Todes, *Lumber and Labor,* 143; Howd, "Industrial Relations in the West Coast Lumber Industry," *Bulletin of the U.S. Bureau of Labor Statistics,* No. 349, 73; Mittleman, 338.

27. *Hearings on Expenditures,* 771; Jensen, 128–129, 132; *Amer. Lbrmn.,* Dec. 15, 1917, p. 33.

28. *Amer. Lbrmn.,* March 2, 1918, 37; Boise Payette Papers, C. A. Barton to T. A. McCann, Jan. 11, 1918; FEW Papers, Barton to FEW, March 12, 1918; Long Papers, Long to FEW, March 8, 1918; FEW to Long, March 13, 1918. Barton reduced the pay of his men when he established the 8-hour day, and boasted that he had got rid of some I.W.W.'s.

29. *Amer. Lbrmn.,* Dec. 8, 1917, p. 42; Feb. 2, 1918, p. 87; Feb. 16, 1918, p. 36; Aug. 3, 1918, p. 32; Long Papers, Long to Downman, Jan. 5, 1918; *Hearings on Expenditures,* 643, 695, 771.

30. Quoted in Jensen, *Lumber and Labor,* 130.

31. *Ibid.,* 132–133.

32. *Hearings on Expenditures, passim.*

33. *Ibid.,* 332–336; Long Papers, Long to Disque, Dec. 22, 1917; "Historical Notes" by R. E. Brown, Detroit, Sept. 21, 1954; Long to Reuben Hitchcock, June 12, 1918. The Siems-Carey Co., which subsequent investigations made the object of repeated attacks and charges, never produced any spruce. The other companies delivered 60,368,855 feet of cants and logs.

34. *Amer. Lbrmn.,* Sept. 7, 1918, p. 51; Sept. 21, 1918, p. 65; Oct. 19, 1918, p. 52; Nov. 2, 1918, p. 60; Jan. 12, 1918, p. 62; Feb. 2, 1918, p. 57; June 8, 1918, p. 58. Numerous references in the *Amer. Lbrmn.,* starting in January, mention fir aircraft stock.

35. *Amer. Lbrmn.,* Oct. 12, 1918, p. 51; Jan. 5, 1918, p. 63; Jan. 12, 1918, p. 35; Jan. 26, 1918, p. 35; Baruch, 213.

36. *Amer. Lbrmn.,* Sept. 7, 1918, p. 63; Sept. 14, 1918, p. 37; Oct. 19, 1918, p. 35.

37. Long Papers, corresp. with Thompson Yds.; *Amer. Lbrmn.,* Sept. 14, 1918, p. 60.

38. *Amer. Lbrmn.,* Jan. 5, 1918, p. 63; Feb. 2, 1918, p. 36; Aug. 3, 1918, pp. 25, 32; Sept. 28, 1918, p. 69; JPW Papers, JPW to RMW, March 18, 1918; Case to Humbird, Oct. 22, 1918.

39. The files of the *Amer. Lbrmn.* tell of constant civilian activity; see Sept. 14, 1918, p. 60, for article on Tacoma activities.

40. *Ibid.,* Sept. 28, 1918, p. 32; Adolph Pfund, "What Is the Outlook for the Retail Lumber Business?" and "Depicts Rosy Future for West Coast Trade," *Amer. Lbrmn.,* Dec. 7, 1918, pp. 1, 46B; FEW Papers, "Statement of Production and Shipments" of Weyerhaeuser mills; JPW Papers, corresp., *passim.*

XIX

Processes, Products, Economies

W HILE THE Weyerhaeuser associates were busy with their committee system in 1917, lumbermen were watching the invasion of their field by nonwood materials. The *American Lumberman* had noted the multiplication of skyscrapers. Every city, it remarked bitterly, would prohibit the use of wood in construction if the fire insurance and fireproof-materials interests had their way.[1] The director of the government's Forest Products Laboratory at Madison, Wisconsin, had reported that while in 1907 nearly 80,000 wooden railroad cars had been made, in 1914–1915 conversion to metal had become complete; 65,000 all-steel cars had been built within the year. Within the decade 1905–1914, he noted, the use of nonwood roofing had increased eleven times. Advertisements for plaster wallboard, metal lath, and composition roofing were studding the pages of the *American Lumberman* itself.[2]

Clearly the use of steel, cement, glass, and asphalt in construction would increase, not decline, for skills in fabricating and using them were growing. Wood must also be at an increasing disadvantage as Lake States timber was becoming exhausted; this meant that lumber for the most populous states must bear heavy freight charges from the South or the Far West. The head of the Forestry Service, W. B. Greeley, pointed out in the *Saturday Evening Post* that lumber reaching Chicago had formerly paid $3 a thousand feet for freight and by 1915 cost $13. The freight bill, in fact, was often larger than the original cost of the lumber at the mill.[3]

To meet these challenges lumber manufacturers had to reorganize and revitalize their activities. They must reduce their basic costs in logging and manufacturing; they must seek to utilize wood that had hitherto been wasted. Above all, they must make the consuming public aware of the many uses and special values of wood; why it should be employed, and where, and in what varieties.

2

The beginnings of the Weyerhaeuser Sales Company, already traced, marked an effort to improve the modes of reaching industrial concerns and retail dealers. To develop sales promotion was the function of the Publicity Committee, appointed June 15, 1917, and headed by George F. Lindsay. Actually, its antecedents antedated the committee system. In 1914 the Weyerhaeuser companies manufacturing white pine in Idaho, with other firms, had organized the Idaho White Pine Manufacturers' Agency to sell their product, and had shortly combined with the Northern Pine Manufacturers' Association in the Lake States to form the White Pine Bureau, which acted as a promotional agency for both parties. Lindsay and his brilliant young assistant, Carl L. Hamilton, took charge of this work.

The campaign had been waged on two fronts. To make a general appeal, Lindsay placed advertisements in seventeen magazines, such as *House and Garden, National Geographic,* and *Popular Mechanics,* and in lumber journals. He also carried on contests and distributed promotional materials. To reach builders, he published the White Pine Series of Architectural Monographs, edited by Russell F. Whitehead, a distinguished architect. This presented authoritative illustrated articles on notable American houses built of white pine in the East and South. Lindsay himself spent much time procuring data on memorable houses. The monographs, which the White Pine Bureau published free until it died in 1925, went to as many as 6,500 architects and 23,000 contractors and retail dealers. Later they were issued by Whitehead personally until 1940.[4]

Lindsay and Hamilton tackled their tasks with energy and imagination. Lindsay, a graduate of the University of Iowa, keenly interested in music, painting, and architecture, was regarded as visionary by some hard-fisted lumbermen; but he had a thorough practical knowledge of lumbering in the Far West, Middle West, and South, for he had been president of the Sound Timber Company on the Pacific, a stumpage buyer in northern Minnesota, and secretary-treasurer of the Southern Lumber Company of Warren, Arkansas.[5] He and Hamilton realized that the production of white pine in the Lake States was becoming a trickle and that they should turn their primary attention to fir, ponderosa pine, hemlock, and other western woods. White pine obviously would become increasingly *the* quality wood in the Weyerhaeuser offering.[6]

To serve the new purpose of promoting the whole Weyerhaeuser output east and west, a company entitled Weyerhaeuser Forest Products was incorporated as a nonprofit association on May 1, 1918. It was to serve all twenty mills then comprising the Weyerhaeuser group.[7] The George L. Dyer Company of New York, which had popularized the Gillette razor, became adviser on copy and layout.[8]

The main goals fixed by the stockholders for Lindsay's Publicity Committee had included, first, the development of a Weyerhaeuser trademark; second, the introduction of a trademarked, grade-marked, guaranteed product; and third, the development not only of effective advertising but of promotional aids based on research in the requirements and attitudes of customers.

Accordingly, in the summer of 1918 Hamilton and George Dyer, with two aides, toured the mills to convince the managers that lumber could be more effectively merchandized. Some of the mill executives bristled with doubts. Realizing instinctively the difficulties in advertising their products on the scale suggested, they feared that it would involve a great deal of labor, largely futile, on their part. Trademarking and grade-marking were familiar but had never been utilized in the intensive fashion proposed. And at the outset Lindsay precipitated a storm by levying an assessment, to meet promotion costs, of 45 cents a thousand feet on production during the second half of 1918. Amid a chorus of protest, the entire advertising program was brought up for reconsideration.[9]

The complaints were varied in character. One related to the scale of the entire undertaking. Long regarded the proposed expenditures as excessive. Some of the mill managers objected to trademarking, and yet more vigorously to grade-marking. Even with white pine, they said, the retail yards would object to having the manufacturer set rigid standards. Logically, standards were desirable, permitting the dealer to order with a certainty that he would get just what he specified. Later the dealers in increasing numbers were to demand accurate grading. But in 1918 they usually preferred to do their own. They could reclassify the lumber they received, marking some #2 as #1, or #3 as #2, and thus increasing their profit. The mills were ready to indulge this practice to keep retailers happy. Again, the number #1, #2, and #3 were confusing; lumber of #3 grade might be just as good for a certain purpose as #1 lumber, yet the grade made it appear inferior. Finally, millmen objected that the stamping of lumber would take time, care, and labor.[10]

The status and program of Weyerhaeuser Forest Products were threshed out in a meeting of stockholders, mill managers, and sales officials in St. Paul in mid-January, 1919. Lindsay won a general endorsement of trademarking, and a tentative approval of his advertising program. Before long, Huntington Taylor of Rutledge Timber made a successful demonstration of marking. Early in 1920 the Publicity Committee recommended the advertising campaign, and the Weyerhaeuser

Timber Company then approved trademarking and the levy of 45 cents a thousand feet. The first of a new series of Weyerhaeuser advertisements appeared in the *Saturday Evening Post* on September 11th, while Weyerhaeuser Forest Products announced that month in a full-page display in *American Lumberman* that its trademark would thereafter be plainly stamped on all wares. "You can see it yourself at the lumber yard or on the job after it is delivered."

The advertising issued by Lindsay and Hamilton was varied in character, excellent in quality, and thoroughly honest in content. It appealed to industrial builders, home builders, manufacturers, and shippers. The costs were not excessive. Up to September, 1924, Weyerhaeuser Forest Products spent less than $1,400,000, all but a few thousands drawn from assessments on the mills—a modest total for five years of planning and experimentation and three of intensive advertising.[11]

Yet the mill managers regarded the performance with jaundiced eyes. In Tacoma, George Long brooded over the figures and finally launched a shrewd attack. In a letter to Lindsay on February 18, 1925, he heartily seconded the praise that had been given the brochures and other advertisements. But, he went on, "we are in business to make money," and he thought that the cost had outweighed the financial benefits. The Weyerhaeuser Timber Company had paid $250,000 for publicity that benefited lumber in general rather than its interests in particular. The Weyerhaeuser associates, he went on, owned only a dozen out of some 30,000 mills in the country. Lumber as a general commodity should be publicized by lumber associations. Weyerhaeuser could better spend money on direct appeals to retailers or industrial plants, or on the new product, Balsam-Wool. He recommended more personal solicitation and, except for the White Pine Monographs, the substitution of trade for general advertising.

Lindsay was not the man to take such an assault meekly. He replied on March 6th, asserting that since the beginning of his campaign the sale of lumber in general had increased sharply and that the Weyerhaeuser companies had won new customers. The crating service, through which engineers employed by Lindsay had demonstrated how industrial firms could save money by a more economical use of lumber, had made corporations like Studebaker regular users of Weyerhaeuser lumber for all purposes. The ultimate consumer, not the retailer, Lindsay argued, was the man to be reached. Association advertising had time and again proved to be ineffectual. The Weyerhaeusers could well afford to spend some money popularizing lumber in general, and Weyerhaeuser Forest Products *had* promoted special Weyerhaeuser services and products: crating, lumber for industrial customers, Balsam-Wool. Moreover, many appeals had been placed in trade journals, reaching the retailer.

While Lindsay had a case, and seems definitely to have helped increase Weyerhaeuser sales, Long had one with a more practical appeal. That Weyerhaeuser money should chiefly serve a definite Weyerhaeuser product was difficult to deny. Yet actually, as Long admitted, when the advertising campaign was first approved, such a definite product had been envisaged, namely, guaranteed, trademarked, species-and-grade-marked lumber bearing the Weyerhaeuser name. He admitted also that the blame for the "present fiasco" lay with those who had at first agreed to trade-marking and grade-marking and later had opposed grade-marking (he himself was one of them!).[12]

The remedy was obvious, and Carl Hamilton soon bent his talent to supplying it. When he at length produced a program that incorporated guarantee, trademark, and specie and grade mark along with special packaging, Long promptly approved it. But that accomplishment lay several years in the future.

3

Meanwhile, in 1917 the By-Products Committee under William Carson had begun working on the problem of wood waste. When Carson, F. E. Weyerhaeuser, and others visited the Burgess Laboratories at Madison, Wisconsin, in 1917, they decided to gamble $25,000 on experimentation with wood products. Dr. Howard F. Weiss, formerly head of the federal government's Forest Products Laboratory, was added to the Burgess laboratory staff, and he soon began investigating possibilities for utilizing wood waste. Among these were the fireproofing of wood shingles for West Coast mills, briquettes for logging locomotives in Idaho, derivation of chemicals from wood, cattle food from larch, composition boards and blankets. The manufacture of a wallboard made of sawmill waste was the first objective of the Wood Conversion Company. Another product that had been submitted to the government was a secondary dressing for wounds: a fluffy material that was soon discovered to have merit as an insulating element and to be called Balsam-Wool. In 1921, after more experimentation, conferences, and correspondence, these two items still seemed to be the strongest candidates for manufacture as salable products from wood waste.[13]

The Wood Conversion Company was launched early in 1921, with an authorized capital of $1,000,000. As noted in Chapter XVIII, Burgess Laboratories received 500 shares of the stock of the new firm in exchange for their patents, development work, and agreement to continue research in wood for the associated companies. The remaining 4,500 shares of the original subscription of $500,000 for plant and equipment were purchased by various associated companies, who regarded the organization as a pioneering unit that would break ground for an effort in which all might soon share. Weyerhaeuser Timber took the largest amount of stock, 25 percent, and Snoqualmie Falls, Boise Payette, Potlatch, Rutledge Timber, Humbird, Bonners Ferry, Northern, Cloquet, and Northwest Paper all participated.[14]

Present at the conference preceding incorporation was Edwin Weyerhaeuser Davis, a grandson of the original Frederick. After being graduated from Yale, he had served in the field artillery in World War I and then attended the Harvard Business School. He had put in an apprenticeship of some months in the plant and woods at Snoqualmie Falls and returned to St. Paul.

Young Davis had never felt a wholehearted enthusiasm about lumbering. When after the meeting his uncle Rudolph asked him if he would like to go to Madison and assist Weiss in the laboratory, on the payroll of the new company, he was attracted by the pioneering character of the venture, and promptly accepted, becoming the first employee of the new firm. He showed an interest in and grasp of technological problems. After working with Weiss on the wallboard for three months, he was appointed on April 7, 1921, as the company's general manager, with authority to build and equip a plant.

He arrived at Cloquet in May to begin construction of the wallboard factory and took over direction of work on Balsam-Wool from the Northwest Paper Company. With Weiss, A. H. Onstad of the Weyerhaeuser Timber Company, and Harry Payzant, also sent from the West Coast because of his wizardry in solving problems that frustrated engineers, young Davis proceeded to erect both factories and install machinery. The wallboard was made from sawmill waste. It was composed of ground wood and was formed in a gigantic press into sheets 3/16 of an inch in thickness and measuring 4' x 16'. It emerged from the press in apparently perfect form but when stacked showed a tendency to warp. The fault clearly lay in the drying process, and experimentation was continued. Balsam-Wool gave less difficulty, and by August, 1922, this product was ready for the trade.[15]

The "wool" was made of screenings or waste fiber purchased from the paper mill. It was turned out in a continuous mat enclosed between two waterproof paper liners to which it was glued with asphalt. Earlier products of a comparable nature had been marketed, but Balsam-Wool came in a form easier to apply and of superior insulating value. Eventually the edges were sealed against moisture, and reinforced flanges permitted stapling between joists and studs. In 1923 the Weyerhaeuser Sales Company advertised it as a waterproof, dustproof, and fire-resistant material that would shut out cold or heat, reduce winter fuel bills, and keep the interior of buildings cooler in hot weather. The "wool" could also be used as a sound-deadener in apartment houses and as insulation for iceboxes and refrigerator cars.

George P. Thompson of Thompson Yards, Inc., had shown great enthusiasm for Balsam-Wool and had assured Davis that he could market all the new factory could produce. So positive was Thompson that the young manager married and departed on his honeymoon in the fall of 1922. Thompson's confidence was not justified, for the construction industry was still uneducated to the value of insulation, and soon he confessed that his lumberyards could not sell it at a rate that would absorb the increasing production. The Weyerhaeuser Sales Company promptly took over, advertising the product and pushing it vigorously, but it too was blocked by the retailers, who were inclined to regard the unfamiliar product with indifference or, even when enthusiastic, found that their customers associated the word "insulation" with electric wiring. Architects, contractors, and home builders were still unaccustomed to the idea of insulation, and regarded it as unnecessary or ineffective, or both.[16]

In the end Davis had to organize his own sales department, and started with a force of two early in 1923. Working directly with selected, potential customers, and supported by local newspaper advertising, he met with modest success; other salesmen were added, and production was raised. In July, 1923, six men were selling Balsam-Wool and by 1924 eighteen, operating from nine centers in the Middle West. Sales rose from 2.6 million square feet in 1923 to 11 million in 1925.

Long, whose company was the chief stockholder of Wood Conversion, had backed the project strongly from the first, envisaging branch plants in the Far West that would consume the wood waste of his mills. On June 25, 1926, he proposed a composition-board plant at Longview, and on October 5th, after a report on further progress, wired Davis: "Mail too slow for me to express highest degree of elation over your report of October 1. Hurry up development of Nu-Wood and let us build a plant here!"[17]

What indeed had happened to Nu-Wood, as the wallboard had now been named? Experiments to prevent curling and warping had continued, and finally Weiss, by working with a thicker board—half an inch instead of 3/16—was successful. By the spring of 1927 Nu-Wood was ready to go into production. It entered the insulation-board field, in which it found sturdy competitors, particularly Insulite (dating from 1916) and Celotex (dating from 1921), both still in use, as is Nu-Wood.

The Wood Conversion Company prospered. During its first years it operated at a loss, but in January, 1926, Davis wrote Long: "The 1925 statement will find us still in the red but have hopes of earning our first dollar in 1926." He did; and in 1928 the venture showed a profit of $99,807. By that time the markets for both products were well developed. Davis had seventy salesmen in the field. In 1930 Wood Conversion paid two $3.00 dividends.[18]

Since 1926 Carson had been urging construction of new plants, and Long agreed; he kept pressing invitations on Davis, suggesting as a suitable location the Longview, Washington, development. "That is the place to make it [Nu-Wood] in large quantities, where we have cheap raw material and cheap power and [freight] rates by water which will enable us to put it very cheaply on the Atlantic Coast and distribute it well back into the heart of our legitimate territory." Finally Davis came out to the West Coast and was enthusiastic. The Cloquet lumber companies had now curtailed their operations, and Davis's local source of wood waste for Nu-Wood was diminishing; it would be logical to restrict operations at Cloquet (wood waste was still available from non-Weyerhaeuser sources), and develop a larger unit where raw material existed in practically unlimited quantities. Production of a third product, K-25—a fluffy, fibrous material introduced in 1927 and particularly suited to use in refrigerators—might also be expanded. As late as December 10, 1929, Davis was expecting a decision by his directors to build at Longview, but the depression now deepened, and action was deferred.[19]

Thus the Wood Conversion Company up to the depression had been a local activity, with attractive possibilities for later development by all the Weyerhaeuser group. Parallel activities by some of the Idaho companies were discussed by their directors, but with Longview as a second probable point of manufacture, the launching of a Balsam-Wool/Nu-Wood Idaho factory was never seriously considered. However, from 1927 on, Potlatch Lumber explored other opportunities for utilizing waste.[20]

Meanwhile, in 1929 at Lewiston, Robert T. Bowling of the Clearwater Timber Company had developed Pres-to-Logs, billets for fuel made from shavings and wood fragments, and their manufacture later was taken up by the Idaho and Washington companies. But in the end all the far-western firms were to find an almost complete answer to their wood-waste problems in the establishment of pulp and paper mills.

Except for the Cloquet region, the problem of utilizing waste wood was thus left unsolved during the 1920's. The mills were fully receptive, but, while waiting for experiments to prove commercially sound, still confined themselves to the manufacture of boxes and crating, and deferred other activities. Yet the Wood Conversion Company had made a demonstration that impressed all Weyerhaeuser mills and prepared them for constructive action later.[21]

4

Like components of a complex machine, the committee system, the Sales Company, Weyerhaeuser Forest Products, and the Wood Conversion Company had all driven toward one goal: the more efficient operation of the Weyerhaeuser companies as a group. In a large sense, all moves had been for economies. If duplication of effort were avoided, if a reputation and market for Weyerhaeuser lumber were established, if hitherto waste products were converted into a "cash crop," the total achievement of the group was thereby improved.

But regardless of how these overall measures operated, each Weyerhaeuser company was largely dependent on its own accomplishments. While administration was mostly a matter of developing a good manager, logging and milling were affected by modern methods and equipment. Particularly was this the fact in the period under discussion. Two chief forces were responsible: electricity and the development of automotive devices.

By 1920 the automobile, and with it the gas-driven truck and tractor, were coming of age. World War I had proved and improved both, and steam-operated haulers, loaders, and even the steam-driven locomotive were declining in use. The Fordson tractor had pushed into American markets, where larger tractors already at work had been challenged to improve their performance. Similarly, trucks had become more powerful and dependable. In electricity the telephone and electric light were now commonplace, the electric-driven trolley car a standard unit, while electric-operated equipment of all conceivable types—cranes, turret lathes, milling machines, and other tools of special design—were revolutionizing American factories.[22]

What had been the attitude of the Weyerhaeuser companies toward these innovations? The answer must be that, true to past Weyerhaeuser practice, executives had noted the new machines but had waited to study performance. As early as July, 1905, S. S. Davis, son-in-law of Frederick Weyerhaeuser and father of Edwin W. Davis, had sent F. E. Weyerhaeuser information about electric appliances available for lumber mills and had received the laconic comment, "I would like to let the other fellow do the experimenting." However, by 1914 that experimenting had largely been done, and the Weyerhaeusers were prompt to accept it and even to improve it. On the Pacific Coast George Long and his assistants had utilized, both in logging and in manufacturing, the best practices that others had evolved for handling the enormous fir timber of that region, and added some refinements. In Idaho the rough, unschooled William Deary had been alert to employ any mechanical contrivances that might simplify or quicken his operations.

Well before 1917 most Weyerhaeuser company managers and stockholders held views similar to Deary's; and the Logging and Manufacturing committees were supposed to promote efficiency in the forests and the mills respectively. Though neither persisted long, the Logging Committee established the Logging and Engineering Bureau and made E. J.

Brigham, a man of some engineering experience, its chief, with instructions to work particularly with logging in the Inland Empire. Unfortunately, his role was purely advisory, and he did not get on well with the logging superintendents, who regarded him as an intruder. At length Taylor, Humbird, and McCoy agreed to discontinue the Bureau. John P. Weyerhaeuser deplored this action, and wrote ruefully to Rudolph on August 13, 1920, "It seems our managers are running our business, but if we give them the authority to do it, we can find no fault with them but recognize a weakness in ourselves."[23] It was a repetition of the experience with grade-marking, except that Hamilton and Lindsay even when balked did not give up, whereas the Logging and Engineering Bureau collapsed at the first opposition.

Nevertheless, the Weyerhaeuser companies accepted trucks and tractors in the woods and new machinery in the mills. Here they went with the industry, for in 1920 the Pacific Coast Lumbermen's Annual Congress reported that the track-laying tractor, gasoline-driven, was "now incorporated into the logging industry as a permanent adjunct in transportation." Similarly, gasoline motor trucks and cranes and comparable electric equipment were approved. The *American Lumberman* frequently compared tractors with horses, one of its many articles asserting that a $10,000 job with horses could be done by a tractor for $3,000. Meanwhile, managers of mills and lumberyards were employing electric power, installing more advanced dry kilns, and improving the design of factories.

Some Weyerhaeuser companies followed such practice more quickly and thoroughly than did others, but all followed. Deary's work at Potlatch had been continued after his death; by 1921 all phases of company operations were largely mechanized. In 1915 the new Mill B at Everett was termed "one of the most completely electrified sawmills in the United States," as such being less wasteful, safer, and more efficient than a steam-powered plant. Similarly, as noted, Snoqualmie Falls had electrified practically all its mill operations and was extending electrification to logging. Newer Weyerhaeuser mills, like those at Longview, Washington, and Lewiston, Idaho, incorporated many features that helped the companies to cut costs. The Klamath Falls plant in southern Oregon, designed by A. H. Onstad in consultation with its manager, R. R. Macartney, son of the onetime head of the Weyerhaeuser legal staff, provided a continuous flow of lumber through the establishment. Macartney, visiting a number of outstanding mills, had adapted features from each. Klamath Falls exhibited a new stacker and unstacker system and a box factory shrewdly designed to utilize waste. Since the production records of the various plants were compared frequently, improvements in one were often adopted by others.[24]

It was in vain, after the war, that West Coast manufacturers pleaded for a reduction of the high freight rates paid to the Middle West and the East. They naturally turned to the Panama Canal, which after its opening on August 15, 1914, had been closed by the war. Long and his stockholders had created the Baltimore yard as part of their plans for its use; the first part of that story has been told; more will follow later.[25]

5

Meanwhile, the Weyerhaeuser Sales Company and its promotional ally, Weyerhaeuser Forest Products, had been strengthened and expanded. After the meeting of May, 1922, from which the Sales Company emerged with new prestige, that unit tightened its policies, forbidding sales to wholesalers, and remonstrating sharply with mills that did not cooperate as to the type of lumber produced and its disposal. Certain refractory officials were eventually dismissed by their companies' directors in order to ensure compliance with the common policy. At Potlatch, for example, C. E. McGibbon, the assistant general manager, who had installed manufacturing and grading policies hurtful to the company, was asked to resign. The results were salutary: manufacturing, grading, and shipping at Potlatch all improved under R. E. Irwin, appointed to harmonize its practices with Sales Company needs and policies.[26]

In this period the Sales Company, even with the cooperation of the firms it served, faced a difficult problem. The mills could operate profitably only if a large volume of sales was maintained, and their need for a selling service which would permit them to manufacture close to capacity had been conceded at the May, 1922, meetings. Yet conditions did not favor a volume-sales performance. For while the country in general had recovered from the depression of 1920–1921, the lumber industry had shared little in the ensuing prosperity. Its best customers, the farmers, as a result of adverse conditions, were engaged in a struggle for survival that persisted through the 1920's. Substitute building materials were more active than ever.[27]

Louis Case and his WSC associates recognized these factors. There were also further complications, stemming from the control and management of the companies they served. For example, the owners and directors of these firms really had little conception of the size of the task the Sales Company was attempting. Moreover, a Board of Trustees composed of the chief stockholders, who came from Minnesota, Idaho, and Washington, met each month and set lumber prices. Some directors felt it right to inform competitors of their decisions, so that often, according to F. K. Weyerhaeuser, "competition in the field knew our prices as much as a week before our salesmen got them." Again, mill managers and plant sales managers resented the loss of authority they had suffered, and tended to criticize the Sales Company. Some stockholders still deplored its existence! Nevertheless, Case staunchly bent to his task, planning to enlarge and intensify his efforts. The West Coast mills did fairly well in 1922–1923, but those of the Inland Empire complained that their product was slighted—a reflection of their difficulty in showing profits during this period. Late in 1923, Case announced a quota of 1,250,000,000 board feet for 1924, 420,000,000 higher than the figure for 1923. He added new salesmen, some to push white pine in selected territories.

Meanwhile, Weyerhaeuser fir lumber was establishing itself in the East. While sales for 1924 fell short of hopes (at 812,000,000 feet they were less than for 1923), the work of expanding and tightening the sales force continued. Early in 1925, when a large sales conference was held in St. Paul, Weyerhaeuser Sales was operating in eleven districts, each with its own manager, and had a total of 60 salesmen on the road. Sales rose rapidly, although prices were relatively low; and in August the trustees increased the selling force by 25 percent. In 1926, to provide for more prompt attention to policy, they established an executive committee of five, on which served Long, Humbird, Case, F. E. Weyerhaeuser, and F. K. Weyerhaeuser. Sales reached 955,000,000 board feet in 1925 and rose slightly to 957,000,000 in 1926.[28]

It was a strenuous period, during which Case labored prodigiously. Humbird, as president of the Sales Company, assumed his share of work and faced the responsibilities of a superumpire, noting constantly the selling effort as a whole in its relationship to the individual firms it represented. Most of these recurrently protested that their products had not received sufficient attention from the salesmen. Under the dual strain of managing the Humbird Lumber Company and guiding the great merchandising organization, Humbird's health broke in 1925; he wished to resign but was persuaded to wait until he had taken a rest and appraised the situation anew.

In this year W. H. Boner died, and about then F. E. Weyerhaeuser came back into active participation as vice-president of the Sales Company. This move strengthened the influence of the stockholders and proponents of united action as against the sniping faction of mill managers. Humbird completely recovered his health, but Case had now worked himself into nervous exhaustion, and by 1927 he was so shattered in health that he was forced to resign. Weyerhaeuser Forest Products had been diligently carrying on its promotional work. The Weyerhaeuser products, however, were still not generally identified by trademarking and species- and grade-marking, although certain firms did stamp their lumber with the trademark, and after 1924 all the Idaho companies had labeled their "Genuine White Pine" as such.[29]

A national movement for grade-marking and trademarking had now

gathered considerable headway. The idea was old; Rhodes had proposed
it for the Weyerhaeuser companies even before 1912, and in April, 1915,
the *American Lumberman* had endorsed trademarking, asserting that
"there is no good reason why lumber transactions should not be governed
by the same merchandising principles that obtain in many other fields."
Prominent lumbermen agreed. Though the Weyerhaeuser Forest Products
trademark had been discontinued in 1922, in the early 1920's the drive
for action gathered new life. Some manufacturers like Long-Bell, then
operating in the South, had trademarked their products since 1918, and
Edward Hines, who not only headed the Virginia & Rainy Lake Company
but other firms in the Lakes area and the South, advocated branding all
lumber with grades and the trademark of the appropriate association.
Hines asserted that if measures were not taken by the industry, the government would inevitably step in to end certain nefarious practices of unscrupulous wholesalers.

Color was given to this warning when Secretary of Commerce
Herbert C. Hoover appealed a few days later for grading and inspection
by the lumber associations. "If you think it wiser," he remarked to them,
". . . we could probably secure the enactment of a 'pure food law' in
all building materials. I would much rather see the trades themselves
establish their own standards."

Such a statement was bound to create alarm. An American Lumber
Congress was promptly established that approved the principle of grade-
marking, and this was also endorsed by the directors of the National
Lumber Manufacturers Association in Chicago and by wholesalers' and
retailers' conventions. William A. Durgin of the Department of Commerce
attended a number of lumbermen's gatherings, emphasizing Hoover's
desire to have the trade regulate itself. All persons interested soon noted
that an abyss lay between approval in principle and a code of practice
acceptable to all groups in the industry. Yet the practical advantage of
marking lumber had now been thoroughly advertised.[30]

These events were unquestionably viewed with approval by F. E.
Weyerhaeuser, Lindsay, and Carl Hamilton. But the latter, as noted, had
also been impressed by George Long's insistence that Weyerhaeuser
money ought to advertise a specific Weyerhaeuser product. From the
summer of 1925 on, Hamilton slowly developed a project. As 1926 advanced, he evidently perceived a solution, and assembled at the Weyerhaeuser St. Paul office Huntington Taylor, manager of Rutledge Timber;
Harry Payzant, and David H. Bartlett of the Sales Company. "Mr. Taylor
was a mill operator," recalled Bartlett years later; "Mr. Payzant was an
inventor, Hamilton was merchandising man, and I was more or less a
salesman or millman." The four spent several days in conference, and

there seems to be no doubt that all contributed something, but Hamilton is generally given credit for the "package" that emerged.

It was "4-SQUARE," the common name for high-quality Weyerhaeuser lumber. F. K. Weyerhaeuser later characterized the idea as Hamilton's biggest contribution to the Weyerhaeuser companies. "We talked about all the things we could think of talking about," he said of the company salesmen up to 1928, "but it wasn't a very convincing argument until we did something to the product, dressed it up and put a mark upon it." He felt that while there was much talk about Weyerhaeuser quality and service, "our quality was probably no better than the average of the industry—until the institution of the 4-SQUARE program."

The plan was to trademark and grade-mark selected Weyerhaeuser lumber and to square the ends precisely. In addition, as F. K. Weyerhaeuser put it:

It involved wrapping lumber of certain types in paper, packaging of molding in cartons, the trimming of everything to exact lengths so as to avoid, insofar as possible, the labor of sawing on the job. Along with it [eventually] went the development of plans for farm buildings and other structures that would use exact lengths of lumber. The plan also involved the cleaning up of the cars, better loading of cars, the use of paper coverings to keep cinders from getting into shipments of lumber so they would arrive in better shape, and a whole lot of refinements that really did improve enormously the appearance of lumber when it arrived at the dealer's yard. It was a revolutionary change.[31]

Indeed, while some lumber for special purposes had been packaged, nothing comparable to the overall program had ever been offered. Hamilton had evolved a quality Weyerhaeuser product. It was to embrace all select grades of lumber regardless of species. Possibly the term "4-SQUARE," connoting both integrity and exactitude, owed something to young Frederick K., who at the sales meetings in February, 1925, had stirred his listeners by emphasizing the tradition of square-dealing associated with his grandfather.

The "package" was not immediately accepted by the group of manufacturing companies. There was much talk and letter writing between managers, directors, sales, and advertising officials as 1927 advanced; but Taylor, Hornby, Long, and F. K. and F. E. Weyerhaeuser endorsed the plan, experiments in May, 1927, at Coeur d'Alene produced attractive samples, and on December 14th the Sales Company trustees approved the plan. There were protests from some managers as to the time and expense involved in stamping and packaging, and even Humbird for a time was doubtful. But the enthusiasm with which the salesmen received the plan in February, 1928, swept aside all opposition.

The bold project was launched in the spring of 1928, after the selection by salesmen of a limited group of dealers who would effectively sell the new quality lumber. Advertisements in outstanding newspapers and in the *Saturday Evening Post* were features of the introductory campaign. Promotion was keyed particularly to the trade; the first double-page color advertisement, a novelty for such periodicals, appeared in the *American Lumberman* on April 14th. This advertisement was repeated at intervals until mid-October. It proclaimed the characteristics already described, emphasizing that every consignment was marked as to species and grade, trademarked, and guaranteed.[32]

While there were difficulties in bringing all 4-SQUARE consignments up to exact specifications, these were overcome by such devices at Payzant's Wizard Saw for end-trimming and his sealing fluid for the ends of boards. The reception in the trade was enthusiastic, and sales in 1928 for the first time topped the billion mark (1,068,517,000 board feet), and in 1929 reached a high of 1,164,673,000. Even in 1930, with the Great Depression under way, a sale of 1,035,000,000 was recorded.

Meanwhile came Humbird's final resignation, and on December 11, 1929, F. K. Weyerhaeuser took over the presidency of the Sales Company. He had won a liking and confidence everywhere, for he had shown the happier qualities of both his grandfather and his popular uncle Charles. J. P. Weyerhaeuser, Jr. ("Phil"), F. K.'s younger brother, was soon to step into a dominant role in the Weyerhaeuser Timber Company (executive vice-president in 1933).[33]

The Sales Company and its allied promotional agency, Weyerhaeuser Forest Products, had done more to promote the unity among the companies which F. E. Weyerhaeuser had sought earlier than any of the other measures or organizations born of the desire for greater centralization. They had established a common Weyerhaeuser product, a single sales force to market it, and a single unit to promote it. Although the numerous mills remained separate, they were bound together by the method of selling. Cooperation was a corollary to this common action. It was limited but organic.

6

Yet the dream of a fuller unity persisted. The deaths of Charles A. Weyerhaeuser, George S. Long, and A. W. Laird in 1930 indicated again the desirability of closer union. Hamilton in particular felt that it was essential. At a series of meetings in St. Paul in July, 1930, he proposed the creation of a general service agency, the plans for which he had formulated to fill the need for coordination. As a result, on October 9, 1931, General Timber Service, Inc., was organized by the principal stockholders of the Weyerhaeuser companies. It took over Weyerhaeuser Forest Products, both functions and personnel, and all the auditing activities.

Moreover, by its charter it was empowered "to furnish management services of every kind," or information and advice, for every conceivable type of activity and even "to undertake and assume the supervision and/or management of any portion or all of the business or operations of any business enterprises" in the Weyerhaeuser group or beyond it (though little was ever done for outside firms).

This was power enough to weld the separate firms into a supercompany. The only trouble was that the trustees of General Timber Service were also the stockholders of the respective companies, and they soon showed that they did not propose to exercise the great authority the new unit possessed. It did little more than handle auditing and promotion.

But Hamilton still held to his vision, and in the fall of 1933 he proposed a new instrument—a central company in which all the "associated companies," a phrase he seems to have coined, would be represented. It would own and govern the Sales Company, formulate production programs, supervise accounting, traffic, and other activities. "There is no chart in American industry that was ever so big or impressive," commented Saberson, associated with Hamilton in promotion work. "It was the result of years of study on the part of a perfectionist, who also had a thirst for power. . . . Hamilton was determined, by all that was good and holy, that the Weyerhaeuser companies would become one great big compact organization. . . . I think Carl maybe had the idea that if he could bring this about, it would be so successful that he'd share in the power." This statement may be true, yet it was by no means a project that he developed alone, for both F. K. Weyerhaeuser and H. T. Kendall, by then the Sales Company manager, apparently worked with Hamilton to perfect the scheme.[34]

Again nothing happened. Even F. E. Weyerhaeuser apparently regarded the proposal as too impractical and extreme, and soon Hamilton left General Timber Service, not because of the plan, but because F. K. Weyerhaeuser felt his perfectionism, and the slow and secretive way in which he developed advertising plans, were disruptive to the general sales activities.

With time even F. K. Weyerhaeuser came to accept and approve the autonomous position of the separate companies. As the years passed they grew strong and seemed to have need for few common services. "I think there has been a deliberate policy of decentralization," he said in 1953, "and the placing of authority in an individual to do a particular thing. The theory has been that if the individual cannot do it, somebody else should be employed who can do it." As to Hamilton's great plan, "It was never adopted, and I think it would have been unfortunate if it had been."[35] Thus the degree of centralization attained with respect to the companies was limited, and a group that never achieved it and thus never tested it found the policy of doing without it tolerable and in time desirable.

NOTES

1. *Amer. Lbrmn.,* July 18, 1914, p. 21, and Oct. 17, 1914, p. 1.

2. Weyerhaeuser Library, St. Paul, Report of Proceedings of White Pine Salesmen's Conference, auspices of White Pine Bureau, July, 1915; *Amer. Lbrmn.,* Nov. 6, 1920, p. 6.

3. Rolf Thelen, "The Substitution of Other Materials for Wood," *Amer. Lbrmn.,* May 22, 1923, p. 55, referring to Greeley's *Post* article.

4. FEW Papers, Agreement, Idaho White Pine Mfrs. Agency, Aug., 1914; correspondence involving A. W. Laird, T. J. Humbird, CAW, FEW, and others, 1914–1917; Idaho White Pine Bureau, copy Memo of Agreement, Aug., 1914; correspondence on White Pine Bureau campaign, Jan.–May, 1915; T. L. O'Gara to authors, Sept. 25, 1959, on White Pine Monographs.

5. FEW Record, 444, 458, 546, 547; FEW Papers, J. E. Lindsay Folder; Southern Lbr. Co. Papers; St. Paul *Pioneer Press,* Jan. 15, 1944.

6. Bartlett, Reminiscences; JPW Papers; Idaho White Pine Mfr.'s Sales Agency Papers, 1915–1917.

7. They were Cloquet (2 mills), Northern (2), Johnson-Wentworth, Pine Tree, Northland, Bonners Ferry, Humbird (2), Rutledge, Potlatch, Dover, Boise Payette (2), Weyerhaeuser Timber (2), Snoqualmie Falls, and the Southern Lumber Co.

8. FEW Papers, FEW to Hunt Taylor, Aug. 31, 1916; Articles of Association, WFP, May 1, 1918; Long Papers, Lindsay to Long, June 15, 1917.

9. Saberson, Reminiscences; Long Papers, Long to Lindsay, July 10,

1918; Long to Hamilton, Aug. 22, 1918; Long to Humbird, Jan. 7, 1920; Lindsay to Long, July 8, 22, 1920. F. K. Weyerhaeuser later told the authors that the reason for trade-marking a product is to make it easier to advertise and sell. But he pointed out that no lumber manufacturer can meet all the requirements of his customers, or in general of even one customer; he is likely to have a shortage of some items in his line and a surplus of others.

10. Long Papers, Boner to Long, March 13, 1920; JPW Papers, JPW to Lindsay, March 19, 1918; FEW Papers, FEW to O. O. Axley, May 6, 1918. FEW wrote Axley that fir grades "have not been refined and are not so uniform in appearance" as other grades in the country.

11. JPW Papers, Lindsay to JPW, Dec. 17, 1918; Hamilton to JPW, Feb. 27, 1919; Hornby to JPW, March 26, 1920; Long Papers, Lindsay to mill managers, July 26, 1920; *Amer. Lbrmn.,* Sept. 11, 1920, p. 29; May 6, 1922, pp. 22, 23.

12. FEW Papers, WFP Papers, Summary of Receipts and Disbursements; Long-Lindsay Corresp., Feb.–March, 1925; Long to Lindsay, March 23, 1925.

13. FEW Papers, C. F. Burgess Laboratories, Madison, to Carson, Oct. 6, 1917, and copy of tentative contract drafted by Clapp & Macartney; Howard F. Weiss to FEW, Oct. 6, 1917; Report by H. F. Weiss and C. F. Burgess to By-Products Committee, June 25, 1920; C. W. Gamble to Carson, July 2, 1920.

14. See FEW Papers, Oct., 1919–Jan., 1920, for reports of conference and plans for new company.

15. Interview with E. W. Davis, July 16, 1957; F. K. Weyerhaeuser to authors, July 17, 1959; FEW Papers, CAW to JPW, April 8, 1921; LN Papers, E. W. Davis to Directors and Stockholders, Dec. 17, 1921.

16. Davis, interview; FEW Papers, G. P. Thompson to Wm. Carson, March 5, 1919; FKW Papers, Advertising, Thompson Yards, Inc.; LN Papers, Corresp. of E. W. Davis to GFL, FSB, and others, 1922; *Amer. Lbrmn.*, April 14, 1923, p. 11.

17. Davis, interview; Long Papers, Davis to Long and Long to Davis, July 2, 1923, and Jan.–Oct., 1926.

18. LN Papers, E. W. Davis to Directors and Stockholders, WC Co., Dec. 17, 1921; Weiss to WC Co., Dec. 1, 1921; Long Papers, Davis to Long, Jan. 12, 1926; Long to WTC Trustees, March 27, 1929, and Carson to Long, March 8, 1927.

19. Long Papers, Long to Davis, 1926–1929, particularly Dec. 27, 1926; Davis to Long, June 13, 1928, Dec. 10, 1929.

20. FEW Papers, various letters on Potlatch research experiments; Interview, Davis; FEW Papers, reports by WDH to directors, Potlatch and Potlatch Forests, Inc., May 31, 1930, and Oct. 19, 1931. W. D. Humiston, the assistant manager who had undertaken the direction of research, engaged Skinner, Sherman & Esselen of Boston, a firm of industrial chemists, to engage in it. They recommended chemicals.

21. For Pres-to-Logs, see later chapters.

22. For the development of the automobile in this period, see Allan Nevins and Frank Ernest Hill, *Ford: Expansion and Challenge, 1915–1933,* 4–9, 58–63, and 254. In general, while the tractor had its special development, the truck followed quickly on that of the automobile, at first using the same chassis and motor in many cases. By 1920 both were produced in many dependable models.

23. FEW Papers, FEW to S. S. Davis, July 14, 1905; Maxwell, Reminiscences; FEW Papers and JPW Papers, Correspondence on Logging and Engineering Bureau.

24. *Amer. Lbrmn.*, reports on Eleventh and Twelfth Pacific Coast Logging congresses, Oct. 16, 1920, p. 71, and Nov. 5, 1921, p. 52; Macartney, Reminiscences. Other articles in the *Amer. Lbrmn.* during this period describe technical innovation.

25. *Amer. Lbrmn.*, Jan. 13, 1917, p. 54; Oct. 16, 1920, p. 50; Feb. 4, 1922, p. 37.

26. LN Papers; WSC Papers, Min. Bk., Trustees' Meeting, Feb. 12, 1923; R. E. Irwin, Reminiscences.

27. Folwell, *History of Minnesota,* III, 319–322; JPW Papers, "Why the Mills Need Volume;" FKW Papers, Memoranda on General Meeting of May 22–24, 1922; advertisements, articles, and editorials, *Amer. Lbrmn.,* 1920–1924.

28. FKW Papers, Annual WSC Distribution, 1920–1944, dated May 8, 1945; F. K. Weyerhaeuser to authors, July 17, 1959; C. J. Mulrooney to G. S. Long, Jr., Nov. 9, 1959; WSC Papers, Min. Bk., 1923–1925, *passim;* Williamson, Reminiscences; WSC Papers, Proceedings, Feb. 25–26, 1925; FEW Papers, correspondence, 1926. The showing of the Idaho firms in these years was discouraging.

29. For these events see FEW Papers, 1925–1927, WSC Min. Bk., and Long Letters for the period covered; WSC Papers, Trustees' Meetings, Jan. 6, March 12, May 28, Aug. 13, 1924; JPW Papers, JPW to C. R. Musser, March 31, 1922. For Weyerhaeuser Forest Products activities, see Notes 8, 12, and 13 above.

30. The editorials and articles, some of these being reprints of addresses, of the *Amer. Lbrmn.,* 1915–1923, cover fully the progress of trademarking, including Hoover's role. Advertisements in the same magazine show

the use of trademarking by numerous companies.

31. Bartlett and FKW, Reminiscences.

32. WSC Papers, Proceedings of meetings, Feb. 25–26, 1925; WSC Papers, Trustees' Meetings, May 23, Sept. 14, Dec. 14, 1927; FEW Papers, correspondence of officials, 1927–1928; *Amer. Lbrmn.*, April 14, 1928, pp. 20–21, and successive issues. The advertisement was in red and black, and very effective with some changes of copy and illustration. Successive advertisements appeared sometimes every other week. Apparently not all the Weyerhaeuser companies grade-marked lumber, for on Sept. 22, 1929, the trustees of the WSC resolved that "as much of our lumber as possible should be grade-marked."

However, meanwhile, the advertisements all emphasized the fact that lumber *was* grade-marked and specie-marked, as well as trademarked and guaranteed.

33. FKW Papers, Annual Distribution (see Note 30 above); WSC Papers, Trustees Meeting, Dec., 1929; WTC Papers, Min. Bk., Jan. 19, 1933.

34. FEW Papers, FKW to FEW, Sept. 14, 1931; WSC Papers, Meeting, Min. Bk., Sept. 28, 1931; Saberson, Reminiscences.

35. FKW, Reminiscences. Not until after 1936, when FKW wrote a memo advocating coordination of production, sales, and finance, did he abandon the idea of a strong central authority.

XX

Government, Industry, and Conservation

WHEN Thoreau visited the Maine wilderness, he was struck by the unbroken vastness of the forest, stretching from the Atlantic to the White Mountains; by its damp, grim, intricate savagery; and by its distinctive North American quality. The forest was full of evergreens, silver maples, birches, and smooth beeches; full of moss-grown rocks, rapid streams, and amethyst lakes. By day, it resounded at intervals with the notes of the chickadee, bluejay, and woodpecker, the scream of the fish hawk, the laugh of the loon, and the whistle of ducks; by night, with the hooting of owls and howling of wolves. It was the home of the moose, bear, caribou, beaver, and the Indian. "Who shall describe the inexpressible tenderness and immortal life of the grim forest, where Nature, though it be mid-winter, is always in her spring. . . . What a place to live, what a place to die and be buried in!"

So the naturalist wrote of the Bangor and Katahdin region in 1846; and within a long lifetime, in 1906, men were trembling lest the Northwest forests, like those of southern Maine and Michigan, of Minnesota and Mississippi, should all be swept away. In the history of the nation few chapters are more important than that which records how the clashing interests of aggressive lumbermen, scientific foresters, federal bureaucrats, and jealous state officials were reconciled by practical and fruitful compromises to promote the principles of conservation.

2

By 1910 the public reservation of woodlands had reached impressive dimensions. The national forests totaled 190 million acres, including those in Alaska and Puerto Rico, nearly 164 million acres in the continental United States alone. Inasmuch as the national parks and Indian reservations comprehended some 22 million acres of forest and the states owned fully 3 millions, the country boasted some 215 million acres of publicly owned wilderness,[1] exclusive of Alaskan holdings. This was about a fifth of the whole forest area of the land.

The Chief Forester of the United States was now Henry S. Graves, who had been Gifford Pinchot's principal disciple ever since he dropped schoolteaching to take up forest management and who succeeded his mentor when President Taft on January 7, 1910, dismissed Pinchot because of his quarrel with Ballinger.[2] Graves was a quiet, efficient man, with none of Pinchot's flair for the dramatic, but just as determined to enforce sound principles of conservation. In administering the national forests, he had a corps of about 3,000 persons, of whom three-quarters were in the field as supervisors, rangers, guards, and timber and mining experts.[3]

The years 1910–1911 were critical in the history of conservation. Pinchot's dismissal illumined the fact that President Taft, like his Secretary of the Interior, had a restricted enthusiasm for the movement. Far-western hostility to its extension was strong. Almost nine-tenths of the merchantable timber in the national forests lay in five states—Oregon, Washington, California, Montana, and Idaho. Though policies had been steadily liberalized, many of the electorate as well as self-interested corporations of these states still feared that the natural resources would be "locked up" from proper use, and many politicians felt a state-rights resentment that so much of their wealth lay in federal hands. The alarmist contention of Pinchot that the timber resources of the nation would soon be exhausted irritated practical lumbermen, who saw how rapidly under favorable conditions a forest might reproduce itself; and cattlemen, sheepmen, public-utilities men, and miners shared with these lumbermen an uneasy resentment. In view of the opposition under Speaker Cannon and Senators Aldrich, Spooner, and Platt against T. R.'s progressive policies, the whole conservation crusade seemed in danger of collapse.

Nevertheless, events quickly proved that the movement for preserving national resources was still surging forward irresistibly. In the Ballinger affair, public sentiment declared itself against Taft, whom Roosevelt accused of "a most surprising weakness and indecision" in conservation matters. Chief Forester Graves continued all of Pinchot's main policies. Too hardheaded to have any patience with the sensational journalists and reformers who exploited the conservationist crusade for their own purposes,[4] he never faltered in his determination to do his full duty. At all times he had behind him, despite the Cannons and Spooners, a solid congressional majority, and the elections of 1910 strengthened it. The exposure of corrupt western landgrabbing, and Roosevelt's dramatic discomfiture of such obstructive senators as Fulton of Oregon and Carter of Montana, had completed the popular conversion to a conservationist philosophy.

Action in the states was showing how powerful a public sentiment had been aroused. Oregon and Washington, after passing their first forestry legislation in 1903, supplemented it year after year. Destructive forest fires in 1910 furnished a special stimulus—for fire protection was by far the most important element in forest conservation at this early date. Minnesota in 1911 passed a new forest law, regarded, like the Oregon-Washington laws, as a model statute, which reorganized the state forestry work under a nonpolitical board of nine, who were to appoint a state forester. It gave careful attention to fire protection. Michigan had undertaken a program of forest restoration in 1900, taking possession of cut-over or burned-over lands held by the counties for delinquent taxes. The state had enlarged these by purchase, consolidating the tracts and systematically planting them. New Hampshire and Massachusetts in 1911 made notable improvements in their forestry laws. In both East and West, in fact, the creation of state forest commissions, foresters, forest experiment stations, and sound fire-prevention systems was increasing, and Michigan's policy of land acquisition was arousing emulation.

Indeed, to its pioneers scientific forestry seemed entering on a golden age. Education in scientific methods was spreading. Yale, Cornell, and Michigan had developed well-staffed graduate forestry schools; the universities of Minnesota and Washington offered four-year undergraduate and two-year graduate instruction; and more than a dozen other institutions had four-year courses of professional character. Bernhard Fernow even thought that forestry education was being overdone! Meanwhile, alongside the three great initial forestry associations, the American, the Pennsylvania, and the Massachusetts, had sprung up a score of others. Some published excellent bulletins, which aided *American Forestry* (organ of the American Forestry Association) in enlightening the public.[5]

In short, the movement that had been brought into feeble life by Franklin B. Hough and others, and carried through critical early troubles by C. S. Sargent, Bernhard Fernow, and Pinchot, had grown powerful. It was far too alert and influential for selfish interests and reactionary politicians to cripple and too important to the nation's health to be controlled by narrow-minded fanatics. It would grow and broaden.[6]

Two events of 1910–1911 indicated this expansionist tendency. In the former year the Forest Service entered into a partnership with the University of Wisconsin to establish a Forest Products Laboratory at Madison, with McGarvey Cline as its first director. For years a division of the Forest Service had been doing laboratory work with wood. Now an admirably equipped and staffed laboratory was available to explore a great range of possibilities and problems, and was shortly to become the best center in the world for scientific research into wood uses. Out of it was to come a process for making kraft paper from southern pines and jack pines, a method of employing glued plywood for the walls and floors of prefabricated houses, a fan system for the rapid seasoning of lumber in kilns, and a chemical treatment of boards to make them more fire-resistant. Bringing into alliance a federal agency, a body of university experts, and groups of practical lumbermen, it helped dispel the idea that the Forest Service was standing jealously aloof from the industry.[7]

A still more important occurrence in 1911 also had a significance transcending its immediate impact: the passage of the Weeks Act. For years frequenters of the White Mountains had watched with growing anger the defacement wrought by irresponsible lumbermen. Public-spirited men formed a Society for Protection of the White Mountain Forests. They soon joined hands with southern groups anxious to maintain the tawny grandeur of the Great Smokies and other Appalachian stretches. The rising agitation enabled Representative John W. Weeks of Massachusetts (later Senator and Secretary of War) to carry his measure, properly called the Appalachian Forest Reserve Act, through Congress in February, 1911. It made federal forest policy really *national,* creating important eastern national forests to stand alongside those of the West. It also asserted a novel constitutional principle: the power of the government, under the commerce clause, to buy forest land to protect the navigability of streams.[8]

To save the Appalachian woods, the Weeks Act empowered the government to spend $11,000,000 over five years in buying watershed forests. This led to the establishment of the White Mountain and Pisgah National forests. The Act also gave the Secretary of Agriculture an initial appropriation of $200,000 to use in cooperating with any state or group of states in fire protection of wooded watersheds. Each participating state must have a statutory system of fire prevention and spend annually at least as much as the federal government. Before the close of 1911 eleven states, including three in which the Weyerhaeusers were specially interested—Wisconsin, Minnesota, and Oregon—had made cooperative agreements under the law. In all these states federal money was used to hire a specified number of patrolmen to work under the direction of state authorities.

3

Still, in 1910–1911 the country was far from possessing an effective conservation policy. This could be developed only by a broadly harmonious alliance of the national Forest Service, the states, and private holders, all seeking the same goals. Without this triple partnership, the problem was insoluble. In the most important forest states, the holdings of the government, the state, and individuals or corporations formed an elaborately intermeshed pattern, so that proper utilization of land under any one of the three involved the other two. Plans for reforestation, fire-fighting, combating tree pests and diseases, and building roads and trails all demanded a united effort. Enlightened men in all three quarters by 1910 perceived this, as they increasingly saw that systematic reforestation was a national necessity and that this implied tree-harvesting on a sustained yield basis.

Extremists among both government officials and private owners, however, objected to any such alliance. As the Roosevelt administration advanced, and in the years following, Gifford Pinchot drifted toward the doctrine that only an ironclad government control of the forests—or better still, government ownership—could make conservation feasible. He completely distrusted the private owners. In 1916, in a speech at Cornell University, he made an indictment of an unnamed timberland group in terms as exaggerated as those of the Bureau of Corporations report on the lumber industry in 1913–1914, discussed in Chapter XVI:

Today the essential of conservation is to prevent further destruction, as this makes the article that is destroyed high in price to the average buyer. It [conservation] must also take measures to prevent the monopoly of natural resources. Third . . . it must provide for the handling of the concentrations that have already taken place. There are in the hands of one group of Western lumbermen thousands of acres of public timber, passed into private hands partly because of the bad administration and partly because the laws were bad. For less than a tenth of what that timber was worth it passed into the hands of a small group of men from the people of the United States—a property worth, in round numbers, nine hundred million dollars.

Pinchot concluded by advising far more drastic action than the bureau report and saying that the proper course was clear. The nation must impose "public ownership, or such public control as will amount to giving the people of the country and the State the benefit of public ownership."[9]

A much more moderate attitude was taken by a leader of rising influence in forestry affairs, William B. Greeley, Assistant Forester since early 1911. His special study of the difficulties of selling mature timber from the public domain had given him a comprehension of the lumbermen's problems. While he believed with Pinchot that monopoly must be combated and that the government must use its timber to maintain competitive prices, he also felt that the nation needed a vigorous private industry. In a speech at Cornell University in 1914 he assailed monopoly, but added:

> At the same time we conceive it our duty to promote effective utilization of timber and to prevent serious waste of a resource the supply of which is all too limited. In other words, there is a definite point in competitive conditions below which the government will not go in disposing of the public timber. That point is determined solely by considerations of the public welfare, which require stable conditions in a manufacturing industry, rightly adjusted to the available supply of raw materials.[10]

Henry S. Graves as head of the Forest Service stood alongside Greeley in advocating patience, mutual comprehension, and a reconciliation of public and private points of view. So did many other government men. "A split started within the ranks of the service itself," Greeley records. The more ardent crusaders felt that most lumbermen were unregenerate. After thirty years of John the Baptist agitation, they noted, forest fires still raged voraciously, small mills moved into splendid forests, devastated them, and left the land to erosion. When in 1916 the Forest Service circulated a questionnaire with one line reading, "What provision do you make for reproduction?" most lumbermen left it blank; one Minnesota operator wryly responded, "Nothing of the kind allowed in my camps." But Graves, Greeley, and others perceived that many lumbermen understood the situation and that purblind conservatism would have been dissipated faster but for hard economic factors.[11]

The fact was that by 1911 the lumbermen who were being berated for greed were actually feeling a sharp pinch. Demand for lumber was slackening; the next year prices fell sharply, and until the American entry into World War I the market continued weak and uncertain. As noted, competition of other building materials was now increasing apace. Alaska, with its forests of Sitka spruce and hemlock, was a potential threat to the Northwest. Costs of labor and machinery were rising; above all, taxes in many areas were a grievous burden. Some lumbermen felt that the only road to solvency was to cut the best timber and abandon the cutover acres. Greeley recalls a conversation in these anxious years with one of the most successful timbermen of the Pacific Northwest, perhaps George Long, who had built up a barony for his employers by shrewd purchases. This timberman feared that even the low average cost of his stumpage would not save his investments from heavy loss.

"My friend," wrote Greeley, "felt that his duty to his backers required abandonment of his cherished program of gradual cutting over a long period. He must build another sawmill, cut off the timber as fast as possible, and bail out the enterprise before it was too late. A hard man to sell on forest conservation!"

Those in the Far Northwest who sweated in the rough and tumble of fire-fighting, road building, and tree-felling, those who saw what happened to John Doe of Portland when he spent $12 to get logs sawed and then sold the lumber for $10, thought that some federal officials had all but insulated themselves in ivory towers.[12] Greeley, perceiving that the lumber industry in 1912–1916 was really sick, wrote an objective, factual report on its underlying economic difficulties. Pinchot, thinking of it rather as a wicked industry, denounced this report as a whitewash of destructive lumbering. Chief Forester Graves nevertheless published it. Patiently educating refractory lumbermen and training them and the government foresters in a cooperative outlook, Graves and Greeley little by little won important adherents. Leaders of the larger lumber companies, governors and legislators in the states, and graduates of the best forestry schools working for federal salaries began in Wilsonian days to join hands.[13]

Everyone had much to study. How could they harvest timber and yet keep the forest safe and productive? What *was* the rate of growth of trees? How much public control was essential and how could it be applied without raising a revolt among the more ruggedly independent lumbermen and their political allies? On what terms should private cutting be permitted in national forests? As World War I made a sudden heavy drain on the American forest, the manifest depletion and the rising values of 1917–1920 gave everybody a keener interest in these questions.

When the war ended, three powerful bodies of opinion were discernible. One was the radical school led by Pinchot, who to the end of his life continued to denounce "Concentrated Wealth." This school insisted that public ownership or its equivalent was the only satisfactory guarantee of conservation and fair lumber prices. Increasingly, it coupled its demand for expropriation of private property with hot denunciations of the "weak and pliable" Forest Service.[14] The moderate school, represented by Franklin K. Lane in the Interior Department, by Graves and Greeley, by many reasonable congressmen like Bertrand H. Snell of New York, and by such farsighted lumbermen as Frederick E. Weyerhaeuser and George Long, believed in reasonable government regulation, steady utilization of government timber, and broad cooperation in reforestation.[15] The third party was composed of diehard old-school lumbermen who resented all government activity. These forces were to come into grim collision at the close of the war over two conflicting bills in Congress.

4

Just how far had the Weyerhaeusers gone by 1920, the year in which Greeley succeeded Graves as Chief Forester, toward realizing the government's hopes of a scientific reforestation program?

It is important to recognize that in shifting the center of their activ-

ities from the Lake States to the Pacific Northwest, the Weyerhaeusers
had entered a region more favorable to sound forest management. The
excessively scattered holdings, the confusedly intermingled ownerships,
the mixture of high-yield and low-yield tracts, so characteristic of Wisconsin and Minnesota, no longer troubled the timberman; in most of the Far
Northwest he had the benefit of relatively large and contiguous properties.
The white pine of the Lake States was more vulnerable to insect pests and
disease than most western stands. In the upper Midwest much of the
virgin timber had been overmature, hollow, partially decayed, and blown
down or fire-damaged.[16]

At an early date leaders in the Weyerhaeuser group had shown an
enlightened attitude toward progressive forestry. William H. Laird, in his
presidential address to the Mississippi Valley Lumbermen's Association
in 1898, had declared: "We who are so vitally interested in the timber
supply of the country ought to be foremost in forwarding any practical
measures which may continue the industry in which we are engaged. That
this can be done is abundantly illustrated in other lands. May we not take
timely action before it is too late?"[17] For years Frederick Weyerhaeuser
served on the State Forestry Board of Minnesota created in 1899. He and
his associates welcomed the law of 1902, drafted by Pinchot, creating the
Chippewa National Forest and regulating forestry on Indian lands; they
supported the bill for slash disposal enacted in 1910. As noted earlier,
F. E. Weyerhaeuser participated in the American Forestry Congress in
Washington in 1905 and was chairman of the lumbermen's committee
which collected $100,000 for the chair of applied forestry at Yale. The
Weyerhaeuser group showed enthusiastic interest in the program of the
first state forester in Minnesota and in the founding of the Forest Products Laboratory at Madison.

But what of practical timber growing? F. E. and R. M. Weyerhaeuser
took a notable step in 1903 when they asked Pinchot to send an expert
forester to Cloquet to investigate the possibility of harvesting successive
crops of timber from cutover lands. He delegated an assistant in the
Bureau of Forestry, C. S. Chapman, to examine the timberlands of the
Cloquet and Northern Lumber companies in St. Louis County. Although
Chapman concluded in an objective report that over a fifty-year period
a new crop of white pine might repay management costs and yield a small
profit, a number of unfavorable factors would have to be faced. Selective
logging would have to be practiced under the direction of a trained
forester; logging costs would be high; all slashings would have to be
burned promptly and fire kept under control. Moreover, as the growing
season is short in northern Minnesota, stands of white pine would reach
a diameter of only nine inches in fifty years and could not be expected
to yield the best grades of lumber.[18]

Chapman's report confirmed the feeling of the Weyerhaeuser associates—based on much independent observation—that a profitable plan of reproduction would require state and federal cooperation. The two main impediments were the heavy fire risk and the excessive tax burden involved in carrying unproductive lands until the new timber crop matured. With neither difficulty could private holders cope alone. In the Pacific Northwest the Weyerhaeusers held tracts of such extent that they could move more effectively toward fire control, but there, too, taxes were an obstacle.

Consequently, from 1903 on, members of the Weyerhaeuser group, while evincing an active interest in forest conservation, emphasized in repeated statements the importance of a partnership: the individual lumberman and the government must join hands. When F. E. Weyerhaeuser spoke at the American Forestry Congress in 1905, he dilated on this theme. Effective forest reproduction, he said, was impossible without the stoppage of destructive fires, which meant laws to compel slash burning, to employ paid county fire wardens, and to coordinate the work of public and private interests in road building and fire-fighting. It was impossible without a reform in the tax system, which in his opinion meant substitution of a yield tax on timber harvest for a fixed annual tax on timberlands. It was impossible also, he thought, so long as alarmist talk of an impending timber famine caused speculators to make frenzied purchases of woodlands, then rush to cut the trees and thus glut the market with lumber. Not only was overcutting bad in itself, but destructive competition meant that the lumberman was too poor to undertake a slow and costly program of reforestation.[19]

In 1903 the Cloquet companies gave 2,640 acres of woodland to the University of Minnesota as an experimental forest, and they watched its scientific development with keen interest.[20] That same year F. E. Weyerhaeuser wrote Henry S. Graves, then director of the Yale University School of Forestry, offering to hire a number of his young graduates—and thereafter such young men entered the associates' employ in considerable numbers. By 1912 both the Minnesota and Wisconsin State Foresters (W. T. Cox and E. M. Griffith) could count on support from the Weyerhaeuser interests for their undertakings.[21] But the states were doing all too little. As F. E. Weyerhaeuser always said, fire protection was fully three-quarters of the work of conservation; a few scattered forest rangers, without lookout towers, telephone communication, or modern fire-fighting equipment, could not cope with the task.[22]

A congressional investigation of the pulp and paper industry gave Frederick Weyerhaeuser an opportunity in the fall of 1908 to offer constructive views based on his lifelong experience. Answering questions addressed to him by Representative James R. Mann of Illinois, he deplored hysterical exaggerations of the rate of forest destruction. "I can tell you this, there is much more timber than folks have an idea of and it will last longer," he said. To save the forests, he observed, "The main thing is to make laws to prevent fires." What laws? A slash-disposal statute was essential, for "If one does it and the other does not, it doesn't do much good." Effective laws regulating the practices of loggers were equally important; such enactments should require the preservation of seed trees and safeguards against soil erosion. He reminded the committee that in European countries government ownership of forests meant automatic government control of cutting.

Next to the fire hazard, the elder Weyerhaeuser pointed to unscientific taxation as the chief deterrent to forest reproduction. But for this, he said, he and his associates would have tried to grow trees in the Lake States. "The way they are taxing us, we cannot do it," he stated. "We have to pay taxes every year on our full crop. We pay taxes on the land and then pay for the standing timber, and you cannot pay that more than fifty or sixty times during a lifetime, can you?" In some sparsely settled townships the Weyerhaeuser group had been obliged to help pay taxes to build a school and hire a teacher for only two pupils. "We could have sent them to Chicago and boarded them at the best hotel for the same money." He concluded that the existing situation made it impossible for private owners to reforest cutover lands, especially in chilly Minnesota and upper Wisconsin, where trees mature slowly. But it might have to be done. When Chairman Mann asked, "Supposing the forests of the country to be practically exhausted?" Weyerhaeuser promptly responded, "I would commence to try and raise some."[23]

On the Pacific slope, the thoughtful and farsighted George Long, popular with fellow lumbermen and trusted by public officials, was not only keenly interested in conservation and reforestation, he was an active leader in promoting the one and creating conditions favorable to the other. His fundamental views were summarized by a reporter in 1909:

"Do you agree with the conservation people that a timber famine is threatened at the end of thirty years?"

"No," replied Mr. Long. ". . . They do not discriminate between fuel wood and wood cut for other commercial purposes. . . . An analysis of the figures will show that more than half the timber consumed is used as fuel, and is cut from the farm wood-lot, which is reproducing itself faster than it is consumed."

"That would postpone the famine period to sixty instead of thirty years?"

"Yes, if we went on using it at the present rate, the timber would be used up in sixty years."

"Is that what you expect will happen?"

"I think the rate of use will inevitably decrease. Other building materials like cement and iron will have a tendency to replace wood as it becomes dearer."[24]

Long spoke favorably of Pinchot, and with high approval of the establishment of the National Forests. His colloquy with the reporter continued:

"I presume you are opposed to paying taxes on cutover lands?"

"To be perfectly frank, the only way in which the forests are likely to be replaced is for the State either to buy the lands from the lumber companies at a small price, and replant the forests, or for the State to remit the taxes. It is a simple mathematical demonstration that it will not pay the lumber corporation to pay taxes and wait for a new crop of trees on cutover lands."

"Does your concern follow the custom of many lumber companies in letting the land revert to the State by omitting to pay the taxes?"

"No. Our land is valuable for agricultural purposes as soon as the timber is removed, so it justifies taxes."[25]

Both F. E. Weyerhaeuser and Long, although cordial to federal conservation work, believed that government officers should place less emphasis on reforestation and more emphasis on its economic prerequisites. If lumbermen are to be taught to save timber, Weyerhaeuser insisted, then timber must be made better worth saving. "If some of our foresters who have spent their time in political promotion of their work," he wrote in 1924, "had given thought to the production of what we may call by-products, thus making timber more valuable, this country would now be much further ahead on its program of reforestation." Long admitted the same year that his "larger interest" in forestry problems had been taught him by the Forest Service, but he nevertheless reproached such federal agents as Thornton Munger, the author of *Minimum Silvicultural Requirements,* for neglecting the vital economic topics of taxes, slash clearance, and payment for a strong fire service.[26]

Not until the very end of the 1920's was any notable progress made in reforming the state taxation systems in the Far Northwest. Not only was stumpage subject to an annual levy under the general property tax; the assessments were often highly unfair. A Forest Service inquiry in Washington State in 1912 revealed the fact that farmlands were assessed at one-quarter their true value and forest lands at one-third. D. T. Mason, investigating the situation in the Inland Empire four years later, found that average taxes on all private timberlands there came to about $1.10 for each thousand feet of lumber produced. In all the Pacific Coast states, farmers—who usually dominated the legislatures—insisted that lumber companies should bear a disproportionate share of the tax burden. Many owners of woodland therefore felt that they had to obtain their tax money from lumber manufacture. They cut more lumber than the market readily absorbed, left the forest full of litter, and when they had taken the best timber let the land revert to the state. Mason believed that a yield tax of $1.35 a thousand feet, log-scale, would raise an equivalent revenue and encourage sound procedures in harvesting timber and raising new tree crops.[27]

Long and other officers of the Weyerhaeuser Timber Company, seeing that their advocacy of a fair tax system got nowhere, declared that if the state would not permit conditions favorable to private reforestation, then public reforestation was the only recourse. In 1921 Long urged passage of a bill pending in the Washington legislature to authorize a bond issue for the state purchase of cutover tracts and their systematic replanting. "My idea," he wrote to Mark Reed, a legislative leader and conservation-inclined lumberman, "is that the State of Washington should seriously entertain the plan of growing a forest and unless they do it will not be done right by any individual."[28] The measure failed. Thereupon Long declared: "if either the State of Washington or the United States would take care of the taxes on the land, we would see that the timber was grown and keep fire out, and at the end of fifty years we would divide either with the State or with the Federal government the net returns that were obtained on the basis of fifty-fifty, and [we] are willing to give for that purpose acreage equal to 10,000 acres a year for the next twenty years." In 1922 the Weyerhaeuser Timber Company did make an outright gift to the State of Washington of 5,000 acres of cutover land to begin its public reforestation experiment.[29]

Numerous editors and other leaders sympathized with the view that a readjustment of taxation would enable private owners of woodland to deforest and reforest in a systematic way. Little by little sentiment grew. The farming areas of Washington, strongest east of the Cascades, in general controlled the legislature; the region of mixed industries west of the mountains, including the cities of Seattle, Tacoma, Everett, and Bellingham, usually dominated the executive branch. Various governors supported proposals for tax reform, but conservative legislators opposed any change.

In 1925 a former lumber executive, Roland Hartley, a man of trenchant views and strong personality, became governor. Some of the measures he tried to carry through were highly injudicious; in the name of economy he demanded a partial stoppage of road building and the reduction of appropriations for the state university.[30] But he was on sounder ground when he asked for a restudy of the tax laws to check the enforced liquidation of timber properties and to permit of broad programs of private reforestation.

An angry battle between farming interests and lumber interests enlivened the next few years. At first the advantage lay with agriculture. "Eastern Washington, the home of the Granger, ran true to form and opposed any special thing in which the western part of the State was interested," commented Long in high dudgeon.[31] But, undiscouraged, the lumber interests brought forward a constitutional amendment that permitted the legislature to classify taxable property in four groups, one of which was "reforestable land." Again a spirited struggle was waged from Spokane and the Snake to the Olympic peninsula, and again the forces of tax reform were repulsed.

But while nothing was accomplished in Washington, the Oregon legislature at last took the lead with a constructive measure. Early in 1929, without any special pother, it accepted the main recommendations of a commission that had studied the question, and passed a bill that effectively encouraged reforestation. On cutover lands used to grow a new timber crop, taxes were fixed at only five cents an acre, with a yield tax when the mature trees were felled. This was an example for other states to imitate.[32]

There can be no question that with intelligent state assistance the Weyerhaeuser interests would have gone much further in conservation and reforestation. They had a tremendous problem in their vast holdings of cutover lands, particularly in the Pacific region. They fully realized by 1920, if not earlier, that the best use for most of this land would be a new timber crop—if they could afford the long investment and get adequate protection.

In the mid-twenties George Long employed C. S. Chapman, whose previous service has been noted, as a professional forester. He was to give the company advice, to arrange for cooperative action in protecting the timberlands from fire and insects, and to help educate the public to the advantages of reasonable tax laws. That indefatigable apostle of conservation, David T. Mason, visited Tacoma in the fall of 1927, and records in his diary: "talked with Minot Davis and C. S. Chapman on sustained yield." But all practical foresters and lumbermen knew that continuous production depended on one indispensable prerequisite.

"If we can keep fire out, as I believe we can," wrote Chapman, "there will be a new crop in some fifty years." Long, describing the almost complete ruin of the very soil of the Yacolt country, echoed him: "The problem is to keep fire out. Reforestation will not occur in such a region until the fire stops." But as Frederick Weyerhaeuser had once said, to provide "clean ground" in a cutover forest by slash disposal was useless when the nearest tract remained a littered bed of tinder for any spark to set ablaze. And as Long declared, while shortsighted tax laws kept the return on a reforestation enterprise to a risky 2 percent, no man could afford to invest in it. Federal foresters would have to help.

5

To turn back from the Weyerhaeuser position to the activities of the national government is to revert to an intensified debate over policy. The

First World War had made staggering demands upon the nation's forests. Army cantonments, munitions factories, wooden ships, and a thousand other uses had called for unprecedented amounts of lumber. According to Chief Forester Graves, if the war had come fifteen years later, even the materials for general construction would have been difficult to obtain. Southern yellow pine was steadily being depleted; within seven years after the war more than 3,000 southern mills would cease operations; at the end of fifteen years the bulk of southern saw-timber would be gone.[33] As it was, at the end of the war the Lake States, once the greatest timber producers, were paying a freight bill of about $6,000,000 a year to bring in forest products from outside. Late in 1919 and early in 1920 wholesale and retail lumber prices rose to record levels, awakening new fears of a timber famine.

In the aftermath of the war, all schools of opinion agreed that new federal legislation was essential. Systematic conservation and reforestation were imperative. Should the government promote a friendly partnership of nation, states, and individuals to seek these ends? Chief Forester Graves, and the man who succeeded him in 1920, William B. Greeley, stood for such a partnership. Gifford Pinchot, in contrast, demanded drastic federal controls and even full government ownership of forests.[34] The year in which the debate opened, 1919, witnessed some of the worst forest fires in history. Approximately 2,000,000 acres, about half in national forests and half in private hands, were burned over in Montana, Idaho, California, and Michigan.

While conflagrations raged and experts prepared bills, the two sides marshaled their ranks for uncompromising battle. Pinchot, opening his own headquarters in Washington, summoned friendly editors, lawyers, foresters, and politicians to his support. Many urban builders and middle-western farmers, stung by the high lumber prices, eagerly followed him. Fundamentally, his idea was that the government should lay down an ironclad set of rules for forest management and penalize severely anyone who did not obey them. His congressional friends, led by Senator Arthur Capper of Kansas, introduced appropriate bills. One measure would have excluded from interstate commerce any wood product not produced under the new federal stipulations. The most important proposal, the Pinchot-Capper bill, would have levied a heavy federal tax on lumber from private lands and then remitted practically all of it if the owner could prove that he had complied with federal requirements.[35]

The constitutionality of these proposals was doubtful, while they angered believers in states' rights. Neither the Wilson administration nor the Republican leadership accepted them.[36] "Lumbermen should not get worked up over the Pinchot-Capper bill," remarked the *American Lumberman* of May 29, 1920, "which has a very small chance to be passed.

. . . If the bill is let alone and not fought, it will undoubtedly die a quick and silent death."

Moderate counterproposals were embodied in a broad program that Graves laid before the public in 1919, emphasizing reforestation, satisfactory wage and living standards for forest workers, and stabilization of the lumber industry—all this to be effected by a partnership of public and private agencies. Numerous organizations fell into step behind Graves. They included not only the Forest Service and National Lumber Manufacturers Association, but the American Newspaper Publishers Association and the Chamber of Commerce of the United States. To wage their battle, they created a National Forestry Program Committee, which Greeley called "an excellent example of the ability of widely scattered people and organizations to get together overnight"; and it assisted Representative Bertrand E. Snell to introduce a carefully prepared bill.

Under the Snell bill the government was to fix essential requirements for timber cutting and fire control but was not to enforce this code by financial penalties or ride roughshod over state authority. Instead, it was to ask the states to enact regulations recommended by the Secretary of Agriculture, to promote joint action with the nation, local areas, and private interests, and to appropriate dollar for dollar with the federal government for the fire-fighting and the enforcement of proper logging practices.

Pinchot and Greeley showed asperity in exchanging arguments. "You advise control by the States over a problem which is distinctly the concern of the whole nation," wrote Pinchot. "You propose to distribute control over forest devastation among thirty-five timber-growing States, many of which have heretofore handled their forest affairs with striking inefficiency." He was for federal-state cooperation in fire prevention but for federal action alone to stop forest "devastation." What was needed, he declared, was "the continuous, consistent, enduring, nationwide plan which the United States Forest Service alone can lay down, and which the Federal Government alone has sufficient power to enforce."

Greeley disagreed entirely. Whatever our national policy may be, he declared, "I believe we should encourage every sound development toward better forest practice which originates in local sources and becomes effective through local action." It was neither possible nor desirable to put fire control in state hands and timber-cutting control in federal hands. "Fire prevention and silviculture are so interwoven that one administrative organization must handle both." Either the state or the nation must have sole authority; it was the state's province to deal with fires; this was clearly the paramount problem; and so he was for working through the states and their police powers. Many of the state forestry agencies were doing excellent work. "I fail to see," he asserted, "why the state foresters

and their staffs should not deal effectively with the whole of forest practice and the prevention of devastation, including the creation of State
forests, public education in forestry, and regulation of private lands."[37]

To impartial observers Greeley's position was clearly the sounder. At
no time did the Pinchot-Capper legislation have a chance of passage. By
the end of 1922 it was dead. But meanwhile a hostile coalition had
stopped the Snell bill, and a fresh start was necessary. Greeley and Senator
Charles L. McNary of Salem, Oregon, conferred on the subject. Farmer,
attorney, and onetime law-school dean, McNary knew the Douglas fir
region of the Northwest well and was an astute parliamentarian.[38]

"What's the first thing to be done?" asked the senator. "Stop the
forest fires," replied Greeley. "All right," said McNary, "we'll write a bill
around that. But first we've got to build a fire under Congress." The Senate appointed a Select Committee on Reforestation, which under Chairman McNary held twenty-four hearings in as many forest regions. In the
South and the Lake States numerous witnesses told the committee that the
forests could be regrown if, as Representative Bede of Minnesota put it,
"we can keep the fires out and the taxes down."[39] In the Pacific Northwest, George Long made the same statement, saying that while stumpage
values had risen only "substantially," the taxes paid by the Weyerhaeuser
Timber Company had advanced 2000 percent. He went on:

> The business of the W.T.C. is largely the selling of timber. I have said
> to millmen, "Why don't you buy timber in advance, to take care of your future
> requirements?" and they have answered, "So long as you are willing to pay the
> taxes on timber, we are willing to take our chances with the future." I know of
> fifty individual millowners who are actually afraid to own timber for their
> future supply.
>
> Taxes are growing at the rate of 10 per cent annually. We must take care
> of the property by fire protection. We can't see enough certainty in the future,
> because in the young forests the taxes will continue mounting during the fifty
> or sixty years required for the growth of trees of commercial size. I think that
> a very low annual tax on the land and a yield tax would simplify the matter;
> and, if this were a certainty, the W.T.C. would undertake it.[40]

Greeley, attending the hearings, was impressed by the many lumbermen already growing trees or holding cutover land in the hope of reforesting it. Rising timber values encouraged such action. The government itself was doing little. During 1922 only 7,051 acres of national forest in
eleven states had been planted in trees.[41] At that rate it would take two
hundred years to reforest the denuded areas fit for nothing but tree-
growing. "The conviction became strong in my mind," wrote Greeley,
"that industry itself was the great latent force for reforestation if the government could . . . shake off some of its shackles." And it was high
time that this was done. According to the Select Committee, the primeval

forest had shrunk to 138,000,000 acres of virgin woodland and 331,-
000,000 acres of culled second growth and burned-over timber. The current growth in forests was believed to replace only a quarter of the depletion by ax, fire, and disease.

Responding to the committee's proposals, Congress on June 7, 1924,
passed the Clarke-McNary Act. Its heart, Greeley writes, was protection
from forest fires "with the framework of cooperation which had been presented so forcibly by the testimony and experience of the Pacific Northwest," cooperation also in tree planting and forest management. The nation was to encourage the states in adjusting taxation to permit private
interests to carry on large-scale commercial reforestation; it was to increase nursery stock, for the state nurseries were unable to meet the current demand; and it was to assist state acquisition of forest lands. Provision was made for steady expansion of the national forests, partly by
purchase, partly by taking over suitable areas from military and other
federal reservations, and partly by annexation of unreserved public lands.
The new law included a program for encouraging farm woodlots. Again
the dollar-matching plan was effectively used. Greeley wrote in 1951:

> For twenty-five years the Clarke-McNary Act has led a federal policy of
> cooperation in dealing with state and private forest lands. Its passage cleared
> the air of controversy and launched an era of good will and joint effort. Fed-
> eral and state foresters and private owners of woodland were given a national
> pattern, and cooperation is infectious. Federal men had opportunity to aid and
> advise state foresters on local problems of all kinds, and found themselves
> cooperating with lumber companies on almost every phase of forest manage-
> ment and utilization.[42]

Soon Congress took a further important step. In 1928 it passed the
McSweeney-McNary Act establishing fourteen experiment stations in as
many forest regions and began appropriating $1,000,000 a year to main-
tain them. No lumbermen were more enthusiastically interested in the
two new laws than F. E. Weyerhaeuser and George Long, and no men
were more influential. In the postwar years Long was one of the active
officers of the Western Forestry and Conservation Association, the Pacific
Northwest Committee on National Forestry, and served the N.L.M.A. Forest Management Committee, while in 1920 he had been elected chairman
of the standing committee on forestry of the American Lumber Congress.

6

The two McNary Acts invested Northwestern lumbering with a new
atmosphere. Private and public interests no longer fought and obstructed
each other; they made mutual concessions, each recognizing the rights
and virtues of the other. The federal and state governments were at last
willing to carry part of the burden of reforestation, while the lumberman

no longer planted himself on his inalienable right to make a fast dollar even when contrary to long-term national interests.[43]

The Weyerhaeuser Timber Company in the 1920's held about 200,-000 acres of cutover land. After discarding various proposals for dealing with these large tracts, the directors in 1924—the year of the Clarke-McNary Act—accepted a constructive plan hammered out by Long and McCormick. They created a Weyerhaeuser Logged-Off Land Company which was to take the cutover areas and, in the words of the articles of incorporation, make an "intensive study of such land for the purposes of sale, lease, and reforestation, or any other development." Early in 1925 Weyerhaeuser Timber Company transferred 203,765 acres to the new corporation, capitalized at $1,000,000 and headed by Long's nephew A. L. Firmin.

"Our new plan," Long told the press,[44] "is an attempt on our part to fulfill the moral obligation to the public of ownership of such a natural resource as timber. I can say frankly that under our present [state] laws there is no hope of our making a profit on most of the land in our possession. We do hope, however, that by furnishing an object lesson as to what can be done in reforestation we can obtain the cooperation of the State authorities, and perhaps help formulate a State policy along this line. We expect to show that reforestation can be made profitable under reduced taxation, and having shown this conclusively, we can influence public opinion to adjust the tax laws so that other private holders of cutover land can go in for reforestation and thus give the State an inexhaustible supply."

Then in 1927 a striking figure began to take an active role: David T. Mason, already mentioned as a professional forester who for several years was a professor of forestry at the University of California and the writer of a report on timber resources and lumber operations in the Inland Empire. Beginning in 1919 he was employed by the government to organize the timber valuation section of the Bureau of Internal Revenue; later he established a firm which acted as consultant to many western timber owners. Mason was an earnest believer in sustained yield, and in 1927 he began a continuous effort to acquaint lumbermen with its possibilities. He talked with Long in 1927–1928, reporting that Herbert Hoover had said of the principle, "This is the first plan that I have heard which seems to me a real way out for the lumber industry." He also made a study of reforestation for the Clearwater Timber Company that deeply impressed F. E. and F. K. Weyerhaeuser. Indeed, he rapidly converted the whole St. Paul group to his thesis that forests could be perpetuated indefinitely and profitably.[45]

For a time, George Long insisted upon a realistically cautious approach to Mason's doctrine of selective logging and sustained yield. For one reason, he correctly believed that Mason's ideas, while largely sound, were much more applicable to the Inland Empire than to the coastal forests of the Weyerhaeuser Timber Company. He pointed out that the problem in the Douglas fir districts west of the Cascade Range was very different from that in the pine tracts of the eastern Washington and Idaho country. The average acre contained four or five times as much timber; high-lead logging required clean cutting, so that small trees could not be left to grow; and debris after logging was so great that wholesale burning was impracticable.

For another reason, he argued that Weyerhaeuser Timber had already adopted the best of Mason's ideas. "We have already started, over a year ago, a policy directly in line with the kind of work Mr. Mason suggested for the Inland Empire," he wrote F. E. Weyerhaeuser in 1930.[46] Klamath Falls, for example, was practicing a type of selective logging in that it cut only trees sixteen inches or more in diameter.

But F. K. Weyerhaeuser, determined that the principle of sustained yield should be given the fullest test, continued to press Long on the subject. Finally, in May, 1930, the veteran manager gave way. "I do know that Mr. Mason is probably the best authority on this subject," he wrote, and announced that he would invite him—as F. E. Weyerhaeuser wished —to talk with the executive committee of the Timber Company. Some months later the conference took place. Both Mason and his partner of the firm of Mason & Stevens appeared before a group representing the board. The impression they made was so favorable that the executive committee resolved to hire them to study the feasibility of a sustained yield project on the Toutle River in Washington,[47] beginning a brilliant story that must be left for a subsequent chapter.

In the history of forest conservation, the decade of the 1920's opened in turmoil and discouragement, as two radically opposed schools wrangled angrily and blocked every effort to advance. But in its middle years the unwearied efforts of two men of statesmanlike outlook, William B. Greeley and Charles McNary, carried through Congress an Act that laid a secure basis for cooperative action. Meanwhile, the movement for tax relief was making slow but real progress and was destined as the decade ended to gain a victory in one Pacific Coast state that was to have a far-reaching effect on others. On another front, sustained yield and improved methods of selective logging were being developed in both the Douglas fir and the pine regions by Weyerhaeuser firms and others. When the decade ended, the various forces that were to bring the problem of reforestation to a solution had all been advanced to a point where they could at last be applied. The time was ripe for a great and memorable achievement that would have come quickly had not the depression supervened.

NOTES

1. Rodgers, *Fernow*, 498.
2. Pinchot, *Breaking New Ground*, 459. Pinchot would have preferred the appointment of Overton Price, a veteran in the service, but pays high tribute to Graves.
3. Van Hise, *The Conservation of Natural Resources*, 215.
4. Greeley, in *Forests and Men*, 71–72, describes the avidity with which lurid journalists collected materials for exposing (and wildly exaggerating) the destruction of the forests. They descanted upon the "devastation" and the "ghost towns," using touched-up photographs of normal lumbering work. "Our patience," he says of the Forest Service, "was sorely tried by pen-wielders whose ignorance was appalling and who had no interest in forestry beyond whipping up a lurid tale with some greedy lumberman as arch-criminal."
5. *Amer. Year Book*, 1911, 423 ff.
6. Fernow survived until 1923, his final service being the organization of a department of forestry at the University of Toronto. For his feeling that too many were crowding into the new profession, see Rodgers, 503, 511, 528.
7. For an account of the laboratory, see Curti and Carstenson, *The University of Wisconsin*, II; Pinchot, 311–313.
8. For a detailed account of the congressional battle over the Weeks bill, see Ise, *The United States Forest Policy*, 212–214; for the bill itself see U.S. *Statutes at Large*, XXXVI, 961; for the debates, see Cong. Record, June 24, 1910, 8986 ff., 9017 ff., 9049 ff., and Feb. 15, 1911, 2583 ff.
9. Quoted in Rodgers, 541–542.
10. Text in *Forest Quarterly*, June, 1914, XII, p. 299.
11. Greeley, 101–114, gives an engrossing account of the battle of opinion.
12. *Ibid.*, 117; Mason, *Report on the Lumber Industry of the Inland Empire*.
13. The Western Forestry and Conservation Association was formed by Long and other private lumbermen in 1909 and sought federal and state cooperation.
14. Pinchot, 504–510. This denunciation reached its height in Van Name's book, *Vanishing Forest Reserves*.
15. Snell, an Amherst graduate, was for a time identified with the Racquette Paper Company.
16. See Woodward, *The Valuation of American Timberlands*, 29–39, on the diseases of the Lake Country forests.
17. LN Papers, Winona.
18. LN Papers, Winona, Chapman, "Report on the Timberlands of the Northern and Cloquet Lumber Companies."
19. FEW's able and balanced evaluation of reforestation problems is in American Forestry Congress, *Proceedings*, Jan. 2–6, 1905, 137–141.
20. FEW Papers, FEW to Henry S. Graves, Feb. 12, 1907. In 1908 Frederick Weyerhaeuser, as a veteran member of the State Forestry Board, gave 3,000 acres owned by the Pine Tree Lumber Company to Itasca State Park, selling the virgin timber thereon to the state at current stumpage prices (FEW Papers, Memorandum by FEW, Oct. 19, 1912).
21. The Weyerhaeusers consulted with the Minnesota State Forester on replanting cutovers. See FEW Papers, FEW to Griffith, March 17, 1909. Griffith, trained in Germany and at Biltmore, was long hampered by a feeble state law and feeble appropriations.
22. When State Forester Cox appointed Percy Vibert of Cloquet one of the original forest rangers, the latter's equipment consisted of a shovel, ax,

grub hoe, and packsack (*Pine Knot,* Dec. 6, 1935, p. 5).

23. U.S. Congress, House of Representatives, 60th Cong., 2d Sess., House Doc. 1502, IV, 2492–2496.

24. St. Paul *Daily News,* Nov. 12, 1909.

25. Long at first encouraged farmers to settle on properly classified logged-off land in southwestern Washington; then, seeing their unprofitable struggle to grub and burn stumps, decided that the best use of most of the land would lie in regrowing a forest.

26. FEW Papers, FEW to John Blodgett, Jan. 14, 1924; Long Papers, Long to George H. Cecil, Feb. 7, 1923.

27. Mason, *Timber Ownership and Lumber Production in the Inland Empire,* was written while Mason was professor of forestry at the University of California from 1915 to 1916.

28. Long Papers, Long to Reed, Feb. 15, 1921. Reed was chief executive of Simpson Logging Co.

29. WTC Min. Bk. B, May 29, 1922, 118.

30. Pollard and Spencer, *Hist. of the State of Washington.*

31. Long Papers, Long to Carl Stevens, Nov. 9, 1925.

32. The Oregon Reforestation Commission had made careful studies 1924–1926 and developed a model bill. Gov. Patterson signed the new Act Feb. 29, 1929 (*The Timberman,* March, 1929, p. 49). Louisiana as early as 1922 had a law that forbade any increase in tax assessments during the growing period of a new tree crop; and the *Amer. Lbrmn.,* Nov. 18, 1932, p. 32, states that this had stimulated "a start in tree growing."

33. *Amer. Year Book,* 1919, 501–503.

34. Greeley, 102 ff. Greeley, a graduate of the University of California and the Yale School of Forestry, had been in the Forest Service continuously since 1904 except for two years as the technical head of the forestry section in the American Expeditionary Force in France consisting of 21,000 forestry troops and 95 sawmills scattered from the Somme to the Pyrenees. Graves resigned in March, 1920, as a protest against the wretched lack of support for the Forest Service—his own pay being only $5,000 a year.—*Amer. Lbrmn.,* March 13, 1920, pp. 39, 44.

35. *Ibid.,* May 29, 1920.

36. This Report on Senate Resolution 311, 66th Cong., 2d Sess., was published by the Forest Service June 1, 1920. It emphasized "cumulative forest depletion in regions formerly supplying the big lumber markets of the country," particularly the Great Lakes area.

37. The *Amer. Lbrmn.,* Oct. 22, Nov. 6, and 13, 1920, summarizes the exchange of arguments. Greeley writes (*Forests and Men,* 108): "It seemed to me that the same public agencies which directed how a forest should be cut must also be responsible for its protection and its taxation."

38. Under the Van de Vanter decision of the Supreme Court in the momentous case of the *U.S. v. Utah Power & Light Company,* Congress was held to have the exclusive power to determine in what manner any lands belonging to the United States might be acquired or used. No state could exercise the right of eminent domain on federal lands within its bounds. This decision put an end to the states' rights movement in the West to control national lands. A leasing system thereafter offered the natural compromise between ideas of state control and of federal reservation. Robbins, *Our Landed Heritage,* 393–394; Ise, *The United States Oil Policy,* Chap. 24.

39. On the inquiry of the Select Committee, see the U.S. Forest Service, *Reports,* 1923, 1924.

40. Long's testimony is given in the *Amer. Lbrmn.,* Sept. 22, 1923, p. 40.

41. U.S.D.A. Annual Report, 1923, 317.

42. *Forests and Men,* 110–111.

43. Robbins, *Our Landed Heritage,* 409. See the editorial in the *Amer. Lbrmn.,* March 20, 1920, p. 63, pointing to these attitudes as the

ideal. E. T. Allen, Forest Counsel of
the Western Forestry Conservation
Association, was McNary's forestry
adviser and helped write the Clarke-
McNary Act.

44. This statement is in Tacoma *News
Tribune,* Nov. 12; South Bend
(Wash.) *Journal,* Nov. 14, 1924, and
other local newspapers.

45. A number of letters from FEW and
FKW indicating this are scattered
through the Long Papers, 1928–1930.

46. Long Papers, Long to FKW, April
26, 1930.

47. *Ibid.,* Long to FKW, May 14, 1930;
WTC Papers, Executive Committee
meetings, Dec. 20, 1930. Mason's
diaries, in Loehr, ed., *Forests for the
Future,* 78–80, show that on Feb. 4,
1930, he spent an hour or more with

Minot Davis of WTC "discussing
sustained yield for some of their
units, selective logging for Klamath
and Longview, and cruising." On
Feb. 13 he "talked sustained yield
idea" for four and a half hours in
Tacoma with FK and Phil Weyerhaeuser, Fritz Jewett, Harold McCoy,
and others representing the Clearwater Timber Co., Humbird Lumber
Co., and Potlatch. "Extremely satisfactory talk." On May 26 he presented his ideas again for three hours
to the Board of Directors of the
WTC, eleven in number; and finally
on Dec. 14 three members of the
executive committee called on Carl
Stevens and him for "a fine discussion."

XXI

Problems and Growth

in the Northwest

To SELL LUMBER in 1921 was "like pulling a sled with no snow and lots of stones," complained the once buoyant George Thompson of Thompson Yards. Not only did the depression of that year drag on sales, but as a consequence, mills operated part time, workers were employed sporadically, and logging operations ran by fits and starts. No Weyerhaeuser operation came to a full stop, but officials were deeply concerned. J. P. Weyerhaeuser, president of the Weyerhaeuser Timber Company, thought in July, 1921, that "this is the worst depression that our family has experienced since we were in business."[1]

The twenties began in depression and ended in deeper depression, yet between the two low points, despite fluctuating markets, the development of Weyerhaeuser enterprises proceeded steadily. New logging operations provided raw material, new mills arose, and new marketing channels were opened. In the twenties the Weyerhaeuser Timber Company had to decide how it should provide additional income to pay timberland taxes that had jumped to over $1,000,000 per year, how much it should log its own timber, how it could improve marketing, and how far it should expand its manufacturing. Essentially all these problems centered on the last. If manufacturing were to expand, the company would have to find more logs, more income for taxes, and more markets for its product.

To understand the Timber Company's manufacturing enterprises in the early 1920's, only two spotlights are necessary: one played upon the mills at Everett, the other upon the Snoqualmie Falls Lumber Company. At this time, Mill B and the Snoqualmie plant were in their early stages. Although Mill A at Everett had been operating for more than a dozen years, it was small, and the Everett plant did not become a significant factor in far-western lumber production until Mill B was completed. Moreover, with the war interrupting normal operations, it was not until 1919–1920 that Everett Mill B fulfilled expectations. The two Snoqualmie mills, both opened during World War I, also had to await the twenties before they could prove their value.

In some ways the new ventures of Weyerhaeuser Timber in manufacturing resembled each other; in other ways they diverged. Though one operation took place under the designation of a "branch" and the other under the name of a separate company, the managers of both scrupulously reported their activities to George S. Long. Actually, in the early twenties the Everett branch manager (Boner) exercised far more independence from the Timber Company's central office than did the Snoqualmie Falls manager (Titcomb). Long was president of the Snoqualmie Falls Lumber Company, and though the Weyerhaeuser Timber Company owned only two-thirds of the stock, the parent body treated the Snoqualmie operations as one of its own. Of the two, the Everett operation was the larger. The two Everett mills cut Douglas fir, while at Snoqualmie only one mill sawed fir and the other was designed to handle cedar and hemlock.

At Everett in the twenties significant changes occurred in manufacturing, in marketing, and also in management. At Snoqualmie some changes were made in logging techniques, but more important ones occurred in management: these indeed were basic. It is essential to understand the character and functioning of the two plants, for both were to have an effect upon the decision of whether or not to expand manufacturing.

2

In the early days of Everett Mill A's history, the Weyerhaeuser Timber Company had cut its own logs, but this practice had soon been discontinued, and the company had turned to buying on the open market. Much of the supply was drawn from operations owned by the company or its stockholders—the Cherry Valley Logging Company, the Cherry Valley Timber Company, and the Sound Timber Company, for example. But such sources could not furnish the full amount needed, and in the twenties, as the margin between log prices and lumber prices narrowed, the Everett mills had to find considerable quantities of cheap logs to make a profit. With this in mind, in 1923 the Port Blakely mill company and the WTC formed the jointly owned Siler Logging Company, to cut 10,000 acres of intermingled timber in King and Snohomish counties. The Weyerhaeuser Everett mills received a preference in buying the Siler Company's cut but were not compelled to buy it. However, from 1924 to 1929 this company provided a supplementary source of logs for the Everett branch. In general, the policy was that when the price of logs was up, Everett purchased primarily from the Siler Company, while if the price was low, the branch bought from outsiders.

Log purchasing was itself an art, with the task of predicting prices always difficult. Assistant manager E. B. Wight had charge of this function at Everett, and he discouragingly reported to Long in 1924: "If I buy logs the prices will go down before I get them sawn, and if I don't buy, the prices will go up, so I am proceeding cautiously." His comment could be applied to the rest of the decade.

It was, however, impossible to proceed cautiously in finding more logs, since they were essential if Everett mill operations were to continue, much less expand. The Everett management sought logs from many sources and found them in regions as remote as the lower reaches of Puget Sound. Others came from British Columbia. In the twenties the Timber Company officials also considered growing trees to obtain a perpetual supply, but this was only an idea, for state and local taxes still made reforestation prohibitively expensive. Meanwhile, the Siler Logging Company's stumpage would soon be exhausted. Before the end of the decade, the mills at Everett would have to turn to previously untouched Weyerhaeuser timberlands for a supply.

To cope with this problem, in 1928 the Weyerhaeuser Timber Company opened a new logging operation at Skookumchuck (Vail and Rainier, Washington). In this region the company owned some 4,000,000,000 feet of reserved timber. Minot Davis, Lloyd Crosby, and Walter Ryan made plans for opening up the area. New equipment was purchased and old equipment acquired from logging companies that had now finished operations; some was bought from the Clarke County Timber Company, discontinued in 1923. The aggressive Ronald MacDonald had charge of the operation in the field. Once it was under way, Skookumchuck, also called the Vail operation, provided the Everett plants with about two-thirds of logs required.

Meanwhile, the Snoqualmie Falls Lumber Company did not have a comparable log shortage; it could draw timber from its own 2,000,-000-foot reserve. In 1925 there was talk of Cherry Valley selling its logging operations to Snoqualmie Falls, but the two parties could not agree on terms. In 1926, however, the logging company sold to the lumber company a large area of timberland—the Griffin Creek tract. By 1927 Cherry Valley had cut almost all its remaining stands, and three

years later closed down completely. At this time the Snoqualmie Falls
Lumber Company still had enough timber of its own to serve its needs.[2]

The second decade of the century saw changes in logging technology,
most keyed to the use of new gasoline-driven equipment. Snoqualmie Falls
had at first used electricity in logging, but discontinued this in the late
twenties and began to use the gasoline donkey. Probably the most important innovation was a special gasoline or diesel tractor to haul logs.
The standard four-wheeled farm tractor had been tried, but it lacked the
necessary power and provided poor traction. Now engines were designed
to give extra power. Best Company and Holt Manufacturing Company
experimented with the problem of traction and independently came up with
the caterpillar tread. The device permitted the tractor to travel over rough
terrain. It could reach into the woods and "snake" the logs down to the
loading sites with an ease hitherto unknown. With them, logging became
far more efficient. The Weyerhaeuser companies in general adopted these
tractors toward the end of the decade.

Meanwhile, Everett was also perfecting and expanding its manufacturing plants. The Timber Company used the firm of Hessler, Taylor
& Company of Seattle to study labor and manufacturing costs at its
branch. The consultants, Long wrote to Humbird, "discovered many little
things and some big ones about the costs of manufacturing around his
[Boner's] plants that have been quite enlightening and quite important
and enabled him to make some pronounced economies in manufacture."[3]
It is of significance that the Timber Company was calling in efficiency
experts at this early date.

Moreover, in addition to improving existing facilities, the Everett
branch built a new mill. If the log shortages in the twenties made another
fir mill at Everett undesirable, this did not apply to hemlock. This wood
was relatively easy to obtain, so in November, 1924, a third Everett mill
opened, located near Mill B. This modern, so-called "Mill C," built under
the direction of Boner, sawed only hemlock. But it was highly useful, for
it salvaged a wood that would otherwise have been wasted. Like Mill B, it
adopted the newest technological improvements. In both mill construction
and operation the Timber Company was in the vanguard in using modern
methods.[4]

At Snoqualmie no plant expansion took place. But when in 1930 a
disastrous fire there completely destroyed the cedar-hemlock mill, it was
immediately rebuilt and in six months was once again producing lumber.

3

Notable as was the growth of both logging and manufacturing enterprises in the early twenties, more important still was the fresh opportunity

for western woods to compete in eastern markets. Never before in the history of the lumber industry had it been profitable to cut in the West and market in the East. But with the Panama Canal the situation changed, making the East an area of opportunity. With the end of the depression in 1922, the Weyerhaeuser Timber Company vigorously developed the possibilities for water transportation.

As noted earlier, the Baltimore Yard was opened in 1922 with the particular function of serving as an outlet for lumber shipped at cost from the Everett mills. It was to handle their output exclusively. Prosperous from the start, when Everett earned a gross profit of $900,000 in 1923, the year-old Baltimore yard almost matched it with $700,000. Soon it began to show even greater gains, and by 1924 and 1925 the yard was absorbing 40 percent of the output of the three Everett mills. More notable, while the plants at Everett operated at a loss in 1924 and 1925, the profits earned by the East Coast yard tipped the balance to the credit side of the ledger; during the two years, operations at Everett showed a deficit of $142,016, while those at Baltimore netted a profit of $506,081.[5]

Retail dealers in the East had quickly recognized that a fresh, large lumber supply was available at their doors, and had begun to order regularly. The fir handled by the eastern yard competed successfully with yellow pine, eastern white pine, and Pennsylvania and New England hemlock. It stayed straight even when green; and its high proportion of clear wood pleased customers everywhere. Favorable rail rates enabled Baltimore Yard manager James Long to sell in Pittsburgh, Buffalo, Syracuse, New England, and New Jersey.

The opening of the Panama Canal and the push of Weyerhaeuser products eastward had thus become an important fact in the eastern retail market and a highly strategic development for the Weyerhaeuser Timber Company. It was difficult to realize that but a decade earlier no western wood had competed on the Middle Atlantic slope, for now nearly half of the Everett output was being marketed there.

To maintain the flow of lumber to the "new territories," Boner and Long required adequate shipping facilities. They had the alternatives of renting cargo space or buying vessels. At first, Everett lumber went through the Canal on the ships of other firms. The Timber Company would either buy a limited space on eastbound ships or charter an entire vessel. Long and Boner used the ships of the Isthmian, Admiral, and Norton, Lilly & Company lines, most of which had been acquired from the United States Shipping Board.

But Long and Boner soon realized that to acquire and operate vessels might be more profitable than to rent them. They had had experience in this field, since, from 1905 on, Long had invested modestly in coastal vessels belonging to Charles R. McCormick. But when McCormick offered to haul Weyerhaeuser lumber eastward, Long rejected his proposal, believing that McCormick geared his shipping too much to his own lumber business and that his rates were too high. Furthermore, Long saw that McCormick made substantial profits from his shipping.

Long and Boner soon shrewdly assessed the factors involved and came to similar conclusions. "I . . . have been giving some little thought to this steamship business," wrote Boner to his chief on November 10, 1922, "and the conclusions which I have come to are that we want to go into the steamship business." He proposed the purchase of *ten* vessels. Long knew that the directors would "never endorse a plunge of that kind." He counseled an experiment with one or two ships, writing, "then the subject of enlarging this field to a great capacity is one which I think could be handled more intelligently. . . ." He gave Boner a free hand to proceed along these lines.[6]

In May, 1923, Boner purchased from the federal government the *Pomona* and the *Hanley,* each at a cost of $351,720. Each ship could carry 6,200,000 feet of lumber and complete a round-trip voyage in three months. The ships were under Boner's financial direction, with the expenses handled by the Everett branch. The management, however, was initially put under the New York shipping firm of Houlder, Weir, & Boyd. The ships, which on the eastbound voyage carried Everett lumber exclusively, proved an immediate success, with gross profits in the first year reaching $97,963.[7]

Long therefore began looking eastward for more distribution depots. The good results with both the yard at Baltimore and the shipping ventures inspired him to send his brother James to investigate yard sites at Providence, Newark, and in the Bronx. In 1924 the Timber Company purchased more than one hundred acres at Portsmouth, Rhode Island, and in 1925 leased a thirty-acre tract at Newark, where yards were completed in 1926 and 1927, respectively. At Newark a sales office was opened, designed to coordinate the activities of the eastern yards, and the number of Weyerhaeuser salesmen in Atlantic Coast territories multiplied.

The expansion on the East Coast led to the purchase of additional ships. The Timber Company in 1925 added to its fleet the *Hegira* and the *Heffron,* the trustees approving the purchase the same day as they approved the Newark lease.[8] William Carson remarked that his little nephew used to say that "he liked a bay horse, no matter what color it was. I feel that way about ships."[9] The purchases were a prelude to more. The growth of the Weyerhaeuser Timber fleet and expansion in the East came almost simultaneously.

Throughout the twenties, Everett built up its eastern trade, curtailing in the process its rail trade in the Mississippi Valley. By 1930 Long had ceased to insist that the Everett mill manager should look eastward and

George S. Long, Sr., on a skid road at the Weyerhaeuser Timber Company Camp No. 1, King County, Washington, July 1, 1903.

Sailing schooners loading lumber for eastern markets in Puget Sound waters in the early 1900's.

William Deary

A. W. Laird

William P. Davis

C. L. Billings

Laird Bell

"King of the White Pines," the largest known white pine tree, felled
in 1911 by the Potlatch Lumber Company.

The Bonners Ferry Lumber Company (TOP) and the Edward Rutledge Timber Company mill on Lake Coeur d'Alene, two disappointing Weyerhaeuser enterprises in northern Idaho.

Edward Rutledge Timber Company group in early 1920's.

FIRST ROW — LEFT TO RIGHT:
C. J. McGough, J. Philip Weyerhaeuser, Jr., Huntington Taylor, William J. Merrigan;

SECOND ROW — LEFT TO RIGHT:
Douglas Osborne, Miss Alene Long, Miss Corda Acton, Clarence O. Graue;

THIRD ROW — LEFT TO RIGHT:
G. R. Hudson, G. J. McCoubrey, K. E. Weller

C. W. Gamble

O. D. Fisher

W. W. Warren

S. G. Moon

E. P. Clapp

F. R. Titcomb

C. H. Ingram

John Philip Weyerhaeuser, Jr.

W. H. Boner

C. A. Barton

A. L. Raught

John A. Wahl

L. S. Case   George F. Lindsay   Harry T. Kendall

Frederick King Weyerhaeuser   William Peabody

T. J. Humbird   George P. Thompson   R. S. Douglas

Weyerhaeuser brothers under a portrait of their father.

F. E. Weyerhaeuser, J. P. Weyerhaeuser, C. A. Weyerhaeuser, R. M. Weyerhaeuser.

Weyerhaeuser's "4-Square" program, unveiled in 1928 with national advertising (BOTTOM), went beyond early trade and grade marking (CENTER) and introduced many refinements in manufacturing, shipping, promoting and packaging (TOP) lumber.

The Mark of 4 SQUARE Lumber

4 SQUARE

Packaged and Guaranteed

Introducing a Vigorous National Advertising Campaign on 4-SQUARE Lumber designed to reach:

1st - THE GENERAL PUBLIC

Weyerhaeuser's new 4-Square Lumber is of national importance because it establishes fundamental improvements in a basic American industry.

The public at large will want to know about 4-Square Lumber. They should know about it. They will know about it, soon.

For Weyerhaeuser has planned to broadcast the many advantages of this new development to American property owners through a dramatic advertising campaign in the leading national magazines.

Millions of city, suburban, small town and farm property owners will read about this new *"Wasteless Lumber — trimmed square at both ends — packaged — ready to use."* They will readily recognize what it means to *them.* They will talk about it among their friends and neighbors. They will—beyond a doubt— ask their architects, contractors or lumber dealers for 4-Square Lumber.

The following pages show specimen advertisements such as will appear, from month to month, in the SATURDAY EVENING POST, COUNTRY GENTLEMAN, BETTER HOMES & GARDENS, etc.

2nd - CONTRACTORS

Contractors and Merchant Builders will be especially interested in 4-Square Lumber. They will, we believe, be the first to demand and adopt it. Advertisements similar to those shown in a following section will be used every month in all the important publications reaching this group of lumber buyers.

3rd - ARCHITECTS

4-Square Lumber establishes entirely new standards of lumber quality for architects. Therefore, the 4-Square Campaign will include an impressive series of advertisements in the leading architectural publications. See the following pages for specimen advertisements.

4th - CARPENTERS

4-Square Lumber saves hard work for the carpenter. He will welcome it. And here, also, no stone will be left unturned to make him acquainted with it. Sample advertisements taken from the campaign in THE CARPENTER Magazine are also shown in this portfolio.

5th - YOUR LOCAL MARKET

In order to bring the 4-Square message forcibly to the attention of YOUR prospects a campaign of newspaper advertising will localize the effects of the national campaign. This feature of the 4-Square Campaign and its value to you, is fully explained in a subsequent section of this portfolio.

WEYERHAEUSER SALES COMPANY
SPOKANE, WASHINGTON

Weyerhaeuser Company's Mill B at Everett on the Snohomish River, constructed in 1915.

The Everett kraft pulp mill, completed in 1953, now produces 330 tons of pulp a day.

Weyerhaeuser initiated its own shipping fleet in 1923 to carry lumber to the East Coast.

Twin City distributing yard.

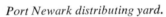
Port Newark distributing yard.

The Clemons Tree Farm tenth anniversary in 1951, with (LEFT TO RIGHT) *Chapin Collins, Mrs. Clemons, J. P. Weyerhaeuser, Jr., and Col. W. B. Greeley.*

Efficient fire-fighting personnel and up-to-date methods and equipment used to protect company tree farms.

was emphasizing that "we have to shape our production in a way that will not overlook the largest consuming territory available to us . . . between the Allegheny and the Rocky Mountains."[10] Whereas Everett, with its steamships and its distribution yards in the East, had turned to Atlantic Coast markets, Snoqualmie Falls took on a large share of the responsibility in the twenties of supplying lumber for the midwestern markets. Snoqualmie Falls owned no steamships and operated no distributing yards.

Both Everett and Snoqualmie Falls used the Weyerhaeuser Sales Company as a marketing agent. Both sold lumber to the Twin Cities Yard, the ownership of which in 1925 had been transferred from Thompson Yards to Weyerhaeuser Timber. Served by the Sales Company, the Twin City Yard and the eastern distributing yards, the Weyerhaeuser companies marketed almost on a national scale. They benefited, too, from the more efficient transportation facilities of the United States after the First World War. Not only was the Panama Canal open, but overland transport had improved: new roads, better trucks, and more efficient railroads all made for faster distribution.

In enlarging their markets outside of Washington and Oregon, Weyerhaeuser mills paralleled actions of competitors, as statistics for regional distribution show. In 1910 four-fifths of the Douglas fir lumber cut was consumed in the Pacific Northwest, but by 1923 only 18 percent was used in Washington and Oregon, most of the remainder going to the East and the Midwest.[11]

The extended markets had one major effect on the thinking of Weyerhaeuser executives. If the East was open to their mills, if the Weyerhaeuser Sales Company could effectively market their product, the time had come for further expansion in manufacturing. Before such action was taken, important changes occurred in the management of the existing manufacturing ventures.

4

Unfortunately, just as production at the third Everett mill began, Boner's health declined, so that he was forced to give up more and more of his work. In December, 1924, he was writing Long: "My physical condition is such that it seems to be impossible for me to do anything like justice to the position of manager here." The general manager in Tacoma found it hard to realize that Boner was no longer fit. "I confess feeling wholly unprepared for this situation," Long wrote, and "cannot get reconciled to the idea." Yet he had to reconcile himself, for in February, 1925, Boner suffered a fatal heart attack.

Long had no successor in mind. Three men who had worked under

Boner's supervision were aspirants for the post. One was E. B. Wight, Boner's son-in-law, who had been assistant manager. His experience, however, had been primarily in log purchasing, and he lacked a general knowledge of other departments. Another, Robert Hunt, had been Everett's excellent sales executive. Long tactfully told him, "Bob, you're too damn good as a sales manager to ever make a [plant] manager out of you." Then there was F. B. Martin, office manager and an able administrator within his domain. Long, after considering these three, informed the directors that nobody at Everett had the precise equipment to take Boner's place.[12]

While the general manager searched for a suitable successor, the triumvirate of Wight, Hunt, and Martin ran the Everett mills under Long's close supervision. Twice a month he went to the branch to inspect operations. Finally he made his choice, selecting the salty-tongued William H. Peabody, who had worked his way up from the post of timekeeper on construction at Everett to become superintendent of Mill B. He had less seniority than any of the triumvirate and at first had not been considered. Yet he possessed more general experience and proved to be a wise choice. E. H. O'Neil became assistant manager under Peabody, for Wight resigned to become vice-president of the competing Walton Lumber Company in Everett.[13]

Meanwhile, at Snoqualmie three changes in management had taken place. With the death of W. W. Warren in 1921, F. Rodman Titcomb, son-in-law of J. P. Weyerhaeuser, took charge of the operation. Young Titcomb worked closely with George S. Long, consulting him frequently and following his advice with meticulous care. Evaluating Titcomb's talents, Long shortly reported to Fisher: "There is no question about his interest and about his willingness to take responsibility and to keep things moving. . . . He is learning very fast and in my judgment making good."[14] By 1925, so pleased was Long that he brought Titcomb to Tacoma as his understudy. The leadership of Snoqualmie Falls then fell to Titcomb's assistant, Charles H. Ingram, a member of the Eau Claire family.

Ingram was to have a long career with the Weyerhaeusers, and this promotion was but the beginning. In 1921 he had been night superintendent at Everett Mill B and had worked his way up to the position of assistant to Titcomb. From 1925 to 1929 he served a managerial apprenticeship at Snoqualmie, and then, like Titcomb, was transferred to Tacoma, there to become an understudy for the position of general manager, Titcomb, having been promoted to that post.[15] It is evident that the Snoqualmie Falls Lumber Company was serving as a training ground for Timber Company executives. Ingram was replaced at Snoqualmie by E. H. O'Neil, who left Everett.[16]

5

Once committed to manufacturing, the directors of the Timber Company seemed eager to build more mills and enlarge the output. All the opposition to large-scale production that had been heard in the early years of the century disappeared.

Experiences at Everett and Snoqualmie seemed to warrant further expansion. It had been plainly demonstrated that lumber from the major species of trees in the Pacific Northwest could find a ready eastern market. Moreover, the Weyerhaeuser Timber Company needed more income to pay its rising taxes. During the boom years of the Harding and Coolidge administrations the value of standing timber rose sharply, and the company could not afford to keep too much capital locked up in the forests.[17] Throughout the twenties the Weyerhaeuser group had considered a marked expansion of sawmill facilities, but they took decisive action only in the last years.

By that time lumber prices had fallen, and leaders in the industry were pressing lumbermen to cut down production. W. B. Greeley and Dr. Wilson Compton, as experts in the lumber field, urged mills to restrict their output. News that the Weyerhaeuser interests were expanding naturally aroused widespread protests. Long received letters of sharp criticism.

But the plans for building had been made before the discussion of curtailment began, and Long would not abandon them.[18] When the decade ended, the Weyerhaeuser Timber Company therefore had two large new manufacturing plants in operation. Both represented a shift of activities southward, for one was at Klamath Falls, Oregon, and the other at Longview in lower Washington.

The Klamath Falls mill of the Weyerhaeuser Timber Company, its first mill in Oregon, was geographically separate from other operations of the firm. In a country of magnificent stands of ponderosa and sugar pine, and red and white fir, the Klamath holdings were set, as indicated earlier, among the beautiful lakes of southern Oregon: Crater, Klamath, Agency, and Aspen. The great Klamath Indian Reservation flanked Klamath Lake on the east and north, and the district remained wild into the twentieth century. Until the Southern Pacific Railroad arrived in 1909, the town of Klamath Falls had been served by stagecoaches, and tales of holdups were well remembered long afterward.

Though George Long had acquired large holdings of timberland for his company before 1920, he had held firmly aloof from manufacturing. He stoically watched competitors make investments in neighboring timber and soon activate sawmills. But he considered existing transportation facilities unsatisfactory, and the market for ponderosa pine as anything

but certain. Furthermore, other projects of Weyerhaeuser Timber and
allied firms had called for heavy application of available funds until the
1920's.

Down to the First World War lawless men cut a good deal of timber
on the public and private domains without payment. "Nobody seemed to
care much about it," one observer recalls. Indeed, this veteran resident
draws a picture of general confusion and irregularity:

> When the larger timber companies came in, every company tried to get
> control of a certain locality by buying as much as it could. Probably if it could
> buy more in a certain area than another company, it would get control and
> buy the other companies out. Later, other people coming in to file on timber
> claims or homesteads, did not know what had been deeded and what had not.
> They began squatting on a lot of this land owned by the different timber com-
> panies. There were the A. C. Hopkins estate, the Pokegama Sugar Pine Com-
> pany, the Western Pacific Land and Timber Company, the Oshkosh Company,
> and others. They all had trouble with squatters. . . .
>
> In the early days, whenever the residents in this country wanted a tree
> they just went and got it. Anyone who wanted to cut a thousand shakes, for
> instance, for his roof, would go out in the Pokegama country and sample maybe
> a dozen great big ponderosa trees that might have from ten to twenty thousand
> feet apiece, till he found one that split well. Then he'd fell it, make part of it
> into shakes, and leave the rest on the ground to rot. It was the custom, and it
> was a hard custom to break.[19]

It was George Long's settled policy as general manager of the
Weyerhaeuser Timber Company never to erect a mill where it would be
dependent on one railway line. So long as the Klamath district was
reached by the Southern Pacific alone, he refused to begin manufacturing.
But by the early 1920's the 215,000 acres of Weyerhaeuser timberland
in Klamath County had many overmature trees, and the costs of holding
so large an investment without return were growing irksome. Long therefore began to negotiate with the Northern Pacific and the Great Northern
for the construction of a line into the district; if they would provide the
rails, he would build a huge mill at once and furnish ample freight.

For a time he hoped both railroads would build, and Paul Shoup of
the Southern Pacific raised a wail of dismay. "I must have some Mormon
blood which hankers for three brides instead of one," Long wired Shoup
in the fall of 1925. Shoup replied: "I guess we are rather a jealous sort of
lady that doesn't want any other girls introduced in what we think to be
our house and home, even by so charming a helpmate as we know you
to be."[20]

After complicated and tedious negotiations, President Ralph Budd
of the Great Northern agreed to build south to Klamath Falls, which was
reached in June, 1928. Long had promised to have his new mill ready by
that time, but it was not completed until the fall of 1929. Manufacturing

actually did not begin until mid-December, after the beginning of the depression.

Standing four miles south of Klamath Falls, the big mill embodied some useful innovations. "I think we were the first mill," commented its first manager, "to have a cross-flow dry kiln, and our stacker and unstacker system was quite new. The mill had four double head-rigs, with a gang-saw in the center. All the lumber passed around the periphery of the mill and then came back to the center. Ample storage space for logs was provided, so that if the mill received a run of timbers adapted to the gang-saw, it could keep some of them in storage; then when a run of logs not suited to the gang-saw came, the storage logs could be mixed with them." George Long once said, "The gang-saw has no brains." In this mill, however, it did not need them. Visitors used to exclaim over the well-arranged flow of lumber, though production was far from impressive in early years—only 87,934,000 feet in 1930, even less in 1931, and a small 61,404,000 in 1932.[21]

Most of the logs had to be brought a considerable distance, from country lying at an elevation of 4,000 to 6,000 feet. Winter snows would have prevented manufacture at times had mills been placed in these uplands, but year-round activity was possible at Klamath Falls. To reach part of the timber the Klamath men built a railway west into Jackson County. Later, to get logs from eastern Klamath County and western Lake County, they constructed a line north from the Oregon, California & Eastern near Beatty. Competition between the Great Northern and Southern Pacific ensured proper car supply and prompt service, and gave entry to markets east, north, and south.

But as the Great Depression deepened, markets became elusive—a mythical Golden Fleece that no Jason could attain. Every lumber company was reaching madly for orders. Klamath marketers taxed their ingenuity to get trade. They followed the well-established plan of mixed shipments to lumberyards, packing in an ordinary boxcar a wide variety of materials—ponderosa boards, finish, moldings and lath, and fir beams and joists. In 1930 they also opened a box factory, planned from the beginning. Utilizing parts of the log that were useless for other purposes, it could meet the keen demand of California and Oregon growers of fruit and vegetables for crates. An earlier box factory in the area had done well, but at first the management of Klamath took the box business casually: "We just took what was no good for anything else," states Macartney, "and used the box factory as a scavenger." But in the stormy depression seas it proved a lifeline, utilizing as much as a quarter of the lumber manufactured. California at one time used a billion feet a year for boxing fruits and vegetables, and the Klamath Falls unit got its share of the orders. Its sales department sent pineapple crates to Cuba, orange boxes to

South Africa, and date boxes to Algeria and Tunis, though gradually paper boxes and cartons began to replace wood, so that the box trade of the Klamath Falls branch by 1953 was only about half what it had been in the 1930's.

It should be added that this happily situated plant has always prided itself on the high standards of its production. "When I have visited our retail customers from Los Angeles to New York and as far south as New Orleans," testifies one of its older executives, "I've been told that because of the fine quality of our Klamath Falls boards, the dealers can get a dollar or two more when they sell them."[22]

In managing the Klamath branch, R. R. Macartney proved quietly effective. A native of Stillwater, Minnesota, and a graduate of Yale, he had received his training at Cloquet. "That was the kindergarten for the Weyerhaeuser outfit at the time," he later recalled. "All the young fellows went to Cloquet." He had won the high regard of F. E. and R. M. Weyerhaeuser before—with William Carson's warm backing—he went to the Pacific Northwest. When he reached Klamath Falls he found nothing but timberland, building materials, and a dispute respecting two possible sites. After deciding which to use, he helped the veteran Weyerhaeuser mill designer, A. H. Onstad, to plan the new plant. "If I were going to build another mill today," he said in 1953, "I wouldn't build it much different from the way it is laid out now." With advice from top executives in Tacoma and the aid of carefully chosen assistants, Macartney successfully guided the Klamath Falls branch through the depressed thirties and prosperous forties.[23]

6

The Klamath Falls operation, while more than satisfactory, was dwarfed by that at Longview, also activated just in time to meet head on the crash of 1929. The town of Longview owed its origin to R. A. Long (no relation to George S.) of the Long-Bell Lumber Company, which bought a mill site on the north side of the Columbia River west of Kelso and after World War I decided to build a town there. In 1923 it was platting Longview, where it erected the largest lumber mill in the world. But the site was too large for one company, and as early as 1920, R. A. Long pointed out to George Long that it offered room for both Long-Bell and Weyerhaeuser. The Long-Bell head suggested that the Timber Company buy part of the site and build a mill there.

In 1923 the Weyerhaeuser directors seriously discussed the idea, but F. E. Weyerhaeuser objected. "I do not think we ought to locate in Long-Bell Lumber Company's back yard," he wrote to George Long in May. On the other hand, the general manager urged that the offer was well worth their attention. The location was good, with excellent railroad connections. Moreover, it was near 30,000,000,000 feet of Weyerhaeuser timber, and the site large enough for a number of mills. The WTC had been planning to expand manufacturing, and this town seemed a most satisfactory place. The trustees hesitated while other sites were reviewed and railway costs were compared and debated. Then in October, 1924, George Long was authorized by the trustees to enter into contract negotiations.

Finally, late the following March, Long as agent for the Weyerhaeuser Timber Company made a preliminary contract with Long-Bell to buy a tract at $323.87 per acre and to select the exact area within sixty days. The company agreed to build and incorporate a common carrier railroad to connect with the Northern Pacific, while Long-Bell on its side engaged to extend part of its railroad and lease it to the Weyerhaeuser Company for ninety-nine years. The matter seemed settled, and R. A. Long wrote to George Long extending him a hearty welcome to Longview.[24]

To the end, C. R. Musser was skeptical about the wisdom of building so close to Long-Bell. "I note," he wrote to George Long on April 8, 1925, "that you decided to locate a new mill at Longview. This may be the right thing to do, but I can't see it. I do predict, however, that whoever sells the product of this mill will have to step fast to keep in line with Long-Bell's selling policy."

Long, who felt certain that the advantages of the site far outweighed the disadvantages, believed his company would be able to "step fast."[25] On June 4, 1925, he selected the exact site, and on May 27, 1926, the trustees approved the purchase. The tract included 544 acres and had two miles of waterfront.[26]

Long chose A. L. Raught to take charge at Longview. Raught had been a Weyerhaeuser employee since 1906, when at the age of eighteen he had gone to work for the Clarke County Timber Company. Long appointed him the Weyerhaeuser "general representative" at Longview. When Raught inquired what his title meant, his superior parried the question, replying, "Darned if I know." Pragmatically, Raught coped with each problem as it occurred. A few months after he went to Longview the two men met again. Long remarked, "I understand you're the boss down there." Raught modestly responded, "Oh, is that so?" This exchange marked the formal appointment of Raught as manager. For two years, he led a force which, as he recalls, "did quite a lot of studying and thinking as to how that tract should be opened up." The main task consisted of getting acquainted with the country and the timber.

A basic problem for the Longview pioneers was where to locate their railroad. Long, Minot Davis, and Raught all insisted that the company

should not use the Long-Bell Lumber Company's line, for they feared that
if it did, the WTC venture would become subordinated to Long-Bell. It
was necessary to have a separate right of way. The decision involved a
multitude of difficulties, for both technical and political problems seemed
immense; but under Raught they soon were solved and a suitable railroad
was built.[27]

Not until 1928, however, did construction begin on the sawmills.
A. H. Onstad, by now a veteran in designing Weyerhaeuser plants, participated in the planning. Harry Morgan, former manager of the Ham-
mond Lumber Company mill in Garibaldi, Oregon, was induced to join
the Longview staff. He was an authority on sawmilling, and Raught later
gave Morgan "substantially all the credit for getting the manufacturing of
the mills at Longview working." It was Morgan, along with Raught, who
carried into practice Onstad's suggestions.[28]

The three men, always in consultation with George Long, worked
in close cooperation, and as their ideas and practices became concrete,
the startling size of the new venture began to set tongues wagging and to
make many in the industry envious. For Longview, Onstad had a double
objective: maximum utilization of each log and of the whole forest
growth. With this in mind, he planned three sawmills and a shingle mill,
each sawmill to cut a different type of log. Mill Number 1, to cut fir only,
was equipped with a giant headrig and two eight-foot pony rigs. The
headrig was unique in that it had two motors, which on the same shift
could run at different speeds, 250 and 300 horsepower, according to the
needed power. Mill Number 2, to cut hemlock and medium-sized fir, had
three nine-foot double-cut band saws, two 20″ x 48″ gang saws, as well
as one vertical resaw. The third mill, for cedar and hemlock, contained
one ten-foot double-cut headrig, one gang, one horizontal resaw, and two
edgers.

In all plants, machinery was furnished to lift logs and lumber, saving much manual labor. To produce power to run the operations, the
Longview branch used a maximum of the sawmill waste. The cardinal
feature of the power plant was fuel economy. With an eye to achieving
this goal, Onstad designed special equipment.

Innovations were also made in planing, with faster feed equipment
and automatic handling. Onstad drew up designs for new machines to
take away the product behind the fast feed planers. For the first time, in
the planing process, automatic systems for raising and lowering the feed
rolls were introduced.

The Timber Company likewise introduced the latest models in dry
kilns. Wherever possible, the lumber was to be kiln dried before shipping.
One original feature of the new operation was the cargo dock, which, by

using two giant Brute ore-bridge gantry cranes, could load four ships at a time.

From the bare tract the impressive structures rose rapidly. Early in June, 1929, Weyerhaeuser Timber Company officials and stockholders arrived at Longview to "look over operations and see the start of actual manufacturing at Mill No. 1." They included Long, Titcomb, W. L. Mc-Cormick, E. P. Clapp, F. E. Weyerhaeuser, C. R. Musser, and George S. Long, Jr. The powerhouse, the planing mill ("the largest in America"), a number of the projected fifty dry kilns, storage sheds, and loading facilities had all been completed for the opening of the first unit. Said Long: "The 160-acre mill site is only a part of the total 600 acres acquired. . . . The extent of property will enable us to expand in any line that appears desirable—the manufacture of pulp or paper, of sash and doors, of boxes and other products—without ever feeling handicapped for want of space." He added that the new manufacturing complex was scheduled to take over from Everett the shipments to the Atlantic Coast distributing centers, while Mill B at that location would chiefly serve the Northwest and Middle West.

Longview was a showpiece from the start. Trade-journal reporters gaped at the spectacle: the miles of riverfront, with log storage capacity of 50,000,000 feet, the storage sheds capable of holding 100,000,000 feet of dry lumber, the three sawmills, the shingle and planing mills, and the impressive power and loading facilities. The development was significant, pronounced the *American Lumberman,* "not only because of its magnitude and a number of unique features in its design, but also because of its effect upon lumber distribution for the Pacific Northwest." Long prophesied a production of 400,000,000 feet a year, which would, however, not be reached "until the indefinite future."[29]

No sooner was the plant in operation than the predicted expansion into pulp production became a definite project. It had been considered by the Timber Company executives for some years. In 1926 they had authorized Onstad to investigate the possibility of erecting a pulp mill at Everett to salvage the waste of Mill C, the hemlock mill. Onstad wrote to the Northwest Paper Company at Cloquet to ask about costs. On the basis of the reply and of additional data, the plant engineer concluded that a pulp mill producing 60 tons per day would require 130 to 140 cords of wood waste daily. A pulp mill of this size could be profitable, but the Everett mill had only 25 tons of waste available. On the other hand, a small pulp mill would not pay, because the labor costs for producing 12 tons of pulp would be the same as for 60 tons. He therefore reported that it would be better to continue selling the waste rather than to build a new plant.[30]

But the hemlock operations at Longview were far larger than those at Everett, and Titcomb suggested to Long in November or December, 1929, that a pulp mill be installed at the new location. Long approved of the idea, and, in a letter to his directors, pointed out that much of the remaining forest in Washington was hemlock and would afford a surplus of this wood that could be consumed by the projected mill.

Titcomb's idea did not get overwhelming approval. In fact, Long's letter encountered skepticism. F. E. Weyerhaeuser replied, citing the experience at Cloquet that in his opinion showed that paper and pulp mills were unsatisfactory; they paid few dividends. But although he wrote that "I should feel inclined to move slowly," and although he thought the paper pulp industry "foreign" to lumbering, he agreed to let an expert study the problem.[31]

William Einzig, an engineer, made the report. After exploring the subject in all its ramifications, he recommended that the Timber Company build a mill to make bleached sulfite pulp. It could take its power from the Longview sawmills and could utilize the waste from the hemlock mill. He suggested the sulfite process rather than sulfate because the product was of higher value and would find a heavier demand. Einzig was convinced that this pulp mill would be profitable, for the site was ideal, and the costs of overhead, water, wood, power, and steam would be low. Other experts, among them O. C. Schoenwerk, likewise recommended that the Timber Company build a pulp mill at Longview. Finally on June 30, 1930, the executive committee authorized its construction, which Schoenwerk undertook and Titcomb expedited. By 1931 the new $2,925,-000 enterprise was ready to start production. R. B. Wolf, former president of the Pulp Bleaching Corporation, was made the new manager. Under his direction the early output of the mill reached 170 tons of pulp daily!

The three sawmills and the shingle mill opened at Longview just before America entered its worst depression. The mills turned out 68,-525,000 feet of lumber in the last seven months of 1929, a total of 213,441,000 feet a year later, then 219,048,000 in 1931, and a "trifling" 136,848,000 in 1932, an unsatisfactory volume for a plant with a capacity of 400,000,000 feet yearly.[32] The pulp mill began production when the Timber Company was operating at a loss. These were unfortunate years for new undertakings, and it was not until World War II that Longview met the expectations of its founders.

The year that saw the opening of its mills found the Weyerhaeuser Timber Company participating in a further extension of manufacturing facilities. The White River Lumber Company had operated for many years at Enumclaw, in King County, near the White River and about twenty-five miles in an air line east and slightly south of Tacoma. Its head, Axel G. Hanson, was an able lumberman who had bought timber from the WTC and knew that it still had large holdings in the area. His own stumpage was rapidly diminishing. As early as 1924 a new, jointly owned company was discussed; Long delayed for several years, but finally, on December 17, 1929, joined in the incorporation of a new White River Lumber Company.[33] Into this, Hanson and his associates put their timberland, mill and inventory, ten acres of tideland property in Tacoma, and six retail yards. The Weyerhaeuser associates canceled a Hanson indebtedness of $134,300 and conveyed about 1,000,000,000 feet of timber and some timberland contracts to the new corporation. Of the total 40,000 shares representing a capitalization of $4,000,000, they held 23,526 and Hanson and his associates 16,474.

With Long as president and Hanson as vice president and general manager, the company enlarged its plant in 1930 and 1931. In the former year it cut 70,000,000 feet of lumber; this output fell in the ensuing depression years, but with better times and an improved mill rose to 104,-367,000 feet in 1936. After the 1938 depression, an average of from 67,000,000 to 94,000,000 was maintained. While not large, the operation enabled the Weyerhaeuser firm to have its timberland in the area cut and milled.

This was its essential purpose in undertaking a second combination with a group of mills located on Willapa Bay, on the coast just north of the mouth of the Columbia. As early as 1907 the WTC had purchased a site at South Bend in the area, for it had extensive timber holdings "tributary" to the harbor. Already in 1927 some of the stockholders favored moving into the district. Although Ralph H. Burnside of the Willapa Lumber Company and C. L. Lewis of the Lewis Mills were both able executives, their firms were not in a flourishing condition. If the WTC built a plant, the local units were bound to suffer; to include them in a new, stronger company seemed the more constructive course. Titcomb, after inspecting the mills at South Bend and Raymond, the chief towns, all but shuddered at that prospect: "I was terribly disappointed in the situation," he wrote F. E. Weyerhaeuser on September 9, 1930. The installations were "built almost entirely on piles"; there were grave deficiencies in equipment. "The advantages of the consolidation are in my mind more or less questionable." However, the joining of interests was agreed upon early in May, 1931, and the Willapa Harbor Lumber Mills was incorporated on the sixth.

It brought in six local units, including a boat and a boom company. The Weyerhaeuser Timber Company put in 31,681 acres of timber, and of the $3,000,000 capitalization, held shares representing $2,105,720. However, the management of the new concern was put in the hands of J. W. Lewis, who, on his death in 1936, was succeeded by W. H. Turner. The mill was rebuilt in 1934, and manufactured from 90,000,000 to

123,766,000 feet of lumber annually, paying dividends after 1936. In May, 1949, it was merged with the Weyerhaeuser Timber Company.[34]

These operations expanded existing facilities for manufacture. With the new Klamath Falls and Longview operations they made clear the decision of the Weyerhaeuser Timber Company to undertake milling on an extensive scale, including pulp and other products as well as lumber. George S. Long, who for sound reasons had moved slowly into the field of manufacturing, had thus before his retirement given the company a major impetus in that direction. Its next task would be to make sure that its forests would supply a perpetual source of raw material for the mills.

NOTES

1. FEW Papers, G. P. Thompson to E. V. Sarles, Dec. 2, 1921; JPW Papers, JPW to O. O. Axley, July 21, 1921.
2. U.S. Dept. of Commerce, Bureau of Census, *Historical Statistics of the United States,* 125; Long Papers, E. B. Wight to Long, May 13, 1924; WTC Papers, "Historical Financial Information." The Cherry Valley Logging Company in 1939 sold the remnants of its holdings to the WTC and in 1947 it was formally disincorporated.
3. Long Papers, Long to Humbird, June 13, 1924.
4. *Amer. Lbrmn.,* Nov. 8, 1924, p. 69.
5. Long Papers, Long Report, Feb. 25, 1924; Long to E. P. Clapp, May 5, 1925; B. L. Orell to R. W. Hidy, March 27, 1961.
6. Long Papers, Boner to Long, Nov. 10, 1922; Long to Boner, Nov. 18, 1922; Long to Boner, Dec. 19, 1922.
7. FEW Papers, Long to FEW, May 11, 1923; Long Papers, Long to E. P. Clapp, May 5, 1925.
8. Long Papers, Long to J. E. Long, Sept. 22, 1925; trustee's approval Nov. 17, 1925.
9. Long Papers, W. Carson to G. S. Long, Sept. 29, 1925.
10. Long Papers, Long to W. H. Peabody, June 18, 1930.

11. Natl. Lbr. Mfrs. Assn., *National Lumber Handbook,* Series II, April, 1925, p. 2.
12. Long Papers, Boner to Long, Dec. 12, 1924; Long to Boner, Dec. 13, 1924; Robert Hunt, Reminiscences.
13. *WC Lbrmn.,* Nov. 15, 1926, p. 26.
14. Long Papers, Long to O. D. Fisher, Dec. 13, 1923.
15. Ingram, Reminiscences.
16. *WC Lbrmn.,* March, 1929, p. 19; L. N. Reichmann was promoted to be assistant manager at Everett.
17. U.S. Census Bureau, *Historical Statistics of the United States,* 125.
18. Issues of *Amer. Lbrmn.* at end of twenties; Long Papers, J. S. Owen to Long, Dec. 6, 1927; Long to Nettleton, June 20, 1929. Greeley was secy.-mgr. of the West Coast Lumbermen's Association, and Compton secy.-mgr. of the National Lumber Manufacturers Association.
19. Harold H. Ogle, of the Klamath Falls Protective Association, Reminiscences.
20. Long Papers, Long to Shoup (telegram), Oct. 3, 1925; Shoup to Long (telegram) same date.
21. R. R. Macartney, Reminiscences; WTC Papers, statistics on "Lumber Production—W.T. Co. vs. Industry."
22. Jack Bishop, Reminiscences.
23. The staff included Harold McCoy as first assistant manager and Hugh

Campbell as his second; Earl Weimar as plant superintendent; Bert Johnson as sawmill superintendent; and Thomas Zinn as planing mill superintendent. See WTC annl. repts., 1929–1930.

24. Long Papers, FEW to Long, May 15, 1923; Long to F. C. Denkmann, June 6, 1923; Long to W. L. McCormick, JPW, and F. S. Bell, Aug. 21, 1923; C. R. Musser to Long, Oct. 22, 1924; FEW to Long, Feb. 12, 1925, and R. A. Long to Long, March 30, 1925. Trustees' Meeting, Oct. 23, 1924, WTC Min. Bk. B, 147; FEW Papers, WTC Contract with Long-Bell, March 28, 1925.

25. Long Papers, C. R. Musser to Long, April 8, 1925; Long to Musser, April 13, 1925.

26. Long Papers, George Long to R. A. Long, May 16, 1925; George Long to Long-Bell, June 4, 1925; Trustees' Meeting, May 27, 1926, Min. Bk. B, 184; *WC Lbrmn.,* June 15, 1926, p. 44, which errs in acreage statistics.

27. Raught, Reminiscences; *4-Square News,* Sept. 1, 1929; *WC Lbrmn.,*

Dec. 1, 1927, p. 22; Long Papers, Raught to Long, Sept. 29, 1927.

28. Raught, Reminiscences.

29. C. H. Ingram, Reminiscences; *Timberman,* May, 1928, p. 40; *WC Lbrmn.,* July, 1929, p. 43; *Amer. Lbrmn.,* July 6, 13, 1929.

30. Long Papers, Onstad to NW Paper Co., April 12, 1926; Onstad to E. B. Wight, April 26, 1926.

31. Long Papers, Long to Bell, FEW, H. H. Irvine, W. L. McCormick, Dec. 2, 1929; FEW to Long, Dec. 17, 1929.

32. WTC Papers, Einzig's "Summary Report of Pulp and Paper Possibilities at Longview," May 1, 1930; interview O. C. Schoenwerk, Aug. 18, 1955; WTC Papers, Annual Report, 1931; Exec. Cmtee. Mins., June 30, 1930; F. R. Titcomb to trustees, Nov. 13, 1931; Statistical Files.

33. The original White River Lumber Co. was changed in name to the Hanson Timber Company so that the "White River" title could be retained.

34. FEW Record, 697, 705; WRLC, WHLM, Articles of Incorporation and Minutes, 1929–1949; Long Papers, Correspondence, 1927–1931.

XXII

A Better Deal for Labor

ITH THE END of World War I, labor in the lumber industry occupied the best position it had ever enjoyed. To be sure, like the position of labor in many industries at the time, by modern standards it left much to be desired. But the workers had made notable gains: improvements in living and working conditions, the eight-hour day, and a step toward collective bargaining in the consultations between employer and employees in the 4L. The question now was, Would these gains endure, and perhaps grow?

Certain factors did not promise an affirmative answer. For instance, shortage of manpower, during the war period had been labor's most effective weapon; but now four million men and women were returning to civilian life and work. Tens of thousands were former mill and camp employees. Just as there had been a shortage of labor for almost two years, there might now be a glut. Again, employers were now free of constraints the war had imposed. Many of them had resented the "coddling" of workers, and looked on the ten-hour-day with all the nostalgia of an unhappily remarried man for a docile first wife. F. E., Rudolph, and Charles Weyerhaeuser, and C. A. Barton of Boise Payette fell into this group. Charles and Rudolph still kept the ten-hour span in their Minnesota plants, arguing that southern competition made it a necessity.

On the other hand, the demand for lumber now promised to be both widespread and sustained. "Peace will bring prosperity to the lumber trade!" announced the *American Lumberman* on November 16, 1918, while jubilant echoes of Armistice Day still hung over the land. Prosperity meant high production, and no one speaking for the industry proposed to antagonize the workers who would be needed to effect it. On November

23rd the National Lumber Manufacturers Association asserted that "the men in our employ are . . . our people," whose welfare "it is not only our duty to watch and guard but also our pleasure," and flatly opposed any wage reductions "that are not in keeping with general adjustments of living costs and economic conditions." Many individual lumbermen echoed such sentiments.

Doubtless the workers placed less reliance on such statements than on their own organizations. There were three in the field. The International Union of Timber Workers, a merger of the Shingle-Weavers and Timber Workers, and now a chartered unit of the American Federation of Labor, proposed in 1919 to renew its drive for membership. Quite as resolute was the Lumber Workers Union 500 of the I.W.W., which surged back into the lumbering scene with renewed vigor. "The I.W.W. are better organized now than they have ever been," wrote E. J. Brigham of Spokane in October, and a parallel vitality was apparent in Minnesota, where three-fourths of all camp laborers either carried I.W.W. cards or were ready to make common cause with those who did.

Finally, there was the 4L. In November, 1918, this organization counted almost 80,000 members, and a movement to adapt it to the peacetime industry was gathering momentum. While less powerful in the camps than in the mills, it had the potentiality of setting a labor pattern for the entire lumber activity in the Pacific Northwest, and its supporters already saw it extending eastward to the Lake States.[1]

2

Employers, remembering the dramatic manner in which Disque and the 4L had delivered them from the I.W.W. and later curbed the Timber Workers, were the first to propose the Legion's continuance. A conference of lumbermen at Portland, Oregon, on November 16th passed resolutions praising the "Loyal Legion" and declaring that "we oppose any reduction in wages even should lumber fall in value *and then not until after a conference with the Loyal Legion*" (italics ours).

This vote of confidence was soon translated into action. After referendums by 4L locals, conventions representing these were held in Portland on December 6th and in Spokane on December 9th. At the Portland gathering, graced by the mayor and presided over by Lieutenant Colonel Cuthbert Powell Stearns, committees were appointed to adapt the 4L to peacetime uses and to begin a drive for membership on a paying basis. Hitherto there had been no dues. Disque was called upon to speak, and as he rose prolonged applause testified to his popularity. "The time has come," he declared, "when the businessmen of this country must think in terms of the laboring man; and the laboring man must think in terms of the businessman, each striving to put himself in the other's place." He specified fields of activity for the new Legion—not only cooperation between employers but also programs for health, safety, better housing, recreation, education, and the maintenance of employment offices.

After Disque concluded he was invited, on his release from the Army, to become the general manager of the postwar 4L. Both the Portland and Spokane conventions endorsed the new organization, so that it began its life with the support of the Pacific Coast and the Inland Empire regions. Disque soon accepted the presidency and took charge of the Legion's activities: the *4L Bulletin,* the membership drive, the organization of twelve districts, the establishment of employment offices, and the formulation of policy on wages and hours.[2]

No Weyerhaeuser official served on the committee that reorganized the 4L for peace, but Idaho firms like Edward Rutledge, Bonners Ferry, Humbird, and Potlatch were loyal supporters, and Boise Payette joined in March, 1919. On the West Coast the Snoqualmie Falls Lumber Company also formed a local chapter.[3]

Unfortunately for the 4L, a number of employers, now that the war was behind them, were indifferent to the Legion. They wished it well but felt they could now return to their former practice of dealing directly with individual employees without any union as intermediary. Such was the attitude of most mill and camp managers of the Weyerhaeuser Timber Company in 1919.

The cause lay in the fundamental character of the 4L. Theoretically, the employees of a camp or mill might join the Legion whether the company did or not. In a few instances they did so, forming locals and persuading their reluctant bosses to come in. But if the employer did not join, there could be no discussion of grievances, no joint decisions on wages and hours. What usually happened, accordingly, was that if an employer joined the Legion, a large body of his men did also, and if he did not join, no employees did either. Disque himself acknowledged this. "The difficulties being experienced," he wrote in the March, 1919, *Bulletin,* "are not in securing employee members, but in securing employer members. . . . Of approximately 800 operators, less than 300 have agreed to join the organization."

The membership nevertheless reached an impressive total of 33,448 at its peak in 1919, with an average for the year of 16,703. The I.W.W. and the Timber Workers together could not match the total, and in many regions the 4L was accepted by both management and labor and able to enforce its decisions. Its recognized status worked for its survival. Nowhere could the I.W.W. command recognition, and rarely could the Timber Workers do so.[4]

Even during war days these two unions had attacked the 4L. The

Timber Workers asserted that it was merely a company union. They argued that the conventions of December 6 and 9, 1918, which brought it into a peacetime existence, did not represent the men, who feared to stand up and vote their real opinions in the presence of their employers. While they erred in this, for the popularity of Disque and the Legion with thousands of workers was real, they had a better point in the fact that, without employer encouragement, few locals had ever been launched.[5]

The I.W.W. were even more sweeping in their hostility to the new union. "The 4L's cannot strike," wrote one of them in the widely read *Survey*. "The sole ability to achieve the . . . aims and ideals of its members lies in the gift of gab. Talk notoriously never gets the goods." The boss, he argued, was all-powerful. "He can fire an employee whenever he so desires for any cause and, because the 4L has no ability to apply force . . . it cannot furnish them with job security and so is doomed to eventual decay even among the small percentage of timid workers that comprise the present membership."

Legion members rejected such characterizations. "The Loyal Legion is a fusion, not a compromise," declared Robert S. Gill, editor of the *4L Bulletin,* also in the *Survey*. He pointed out that the locals and the central organization both voted their decisions, with a final appeal, if desired, to arbitration. He cited cases in which employers had been overruled, one being unable to raise wages without a vote of the local board! R. R. Macartney, head of the Weyerhaeuser Klamath Falls plant, which opened in 1929, made a similar appraisal of the 4L as he knew it in that later period (its character was still the same). "They were independent," he insisted. "They were not dominated by the employers at all."[6] The statement was undoubtedly accurate in many areas.

As the year 1919 advanced, the position of the 4L with respect to both the Timber Workers and the I.W.W. was to become clear. In February a general strike in Seattle, led by the city's Labor Council, was effectively resisted by local businessmen and the authorities. Disque spoke out against it in the March *4L Bulletin,* terming it "a knockout blow" by "foreign anarchists" through "Bolsheviki reign of terror." This was an unjust characterization, for on the whole the strike was orderly. Later, in a magazine article on the 4L, Disque stated that during the war he had been "hampered" by organized labor. "I say this regretfully because I believe in unions."[7]

The Timber Workers, as noted, with the advent of peace had begun to build up their membership and late in July felt strong enough to make a test of strength at the Bloedel-Donovan Mills in Bellingham, Washington, where a 4L local had been organized. Some four to five hundred men walked out in protest against the discharge of three A.F. of L. organizers. The strike quickly spread to several other lumber companies in the area.

At Bloedel-Donovan the strikers were only about a quarter of the full work force, and the firm refused to bargain. "We will not deal with the Timber Workers union," it declared in a public statement, "which is dominated by the I.W.W. [this was untrue], preaches class hatred, and depends on the closed shop, the sympathetic strike, and the boycott as weapons." Some of the other companies went further and refused to employ any but 4L workers. The strike was finally broken and the 4L gained in reputation; its members received raises in pay. The result was a severe blow to A.F. of L. aspirations.[8]

This was in Washington. In Idaho the Timber Workers also made a determined effort to unionize various plants. At Edward Rutledge, after a considerable amount of preparatory work, they finally struck on July 29, 1919, demanding wage increases and union recognition. The 4L employees remained on the job, other employees followed their example, and the strike failed.[9]

During this period—from January to September—the I.W.W. had been diligently at work, particularly in the logging camps, and it was here that the most bitter struggle was to occur. The woods, indeed, made a dramatic backdrop for the entire conflict in lumbering, whether in the lake-broken pinewoods of Minnesota, the steep, treed slopes of the Inland Empire, or the broader areas of the West Coast fir regions. In all these areas the I.W.W. had been busy. At least three abortive strikes had occurred in Washington. Lumbermen everywhere were troubled. However, the union finally selected Idaho as its main battleground.

Here and elsewhere during the final year of the war the logging contractors had adopted in many camps a piecework system that had attracted workers with the prospect of higher earnings and at the same time was calculated to make them indifferent to hours or a daily wage. The I.W.W. detested this practice and coined a contemptuous term for those who accepted it—the "gyppos."[10] Leaders of the Wobblies urged their card-carrying members to deal roughly with such workers—"kick them in the ass and run them out of camp." But this was not always practicable, and the I.W.W. had gradually infiltrated the piecework crews. So successful were they that when their strike call sounded the logging contractors discovered that an astonishing number of men working on a piecework basis were actually Wobblies!

By October the strike was in progress. The demands were for higher wages, an eight-hour day to include all the time spent in travel to and from the job, $1.00 a day for board, and no charge for blankets or bed laundry. The walkout all but paralyzed lumbering in the Inland Empire. Ernest J. Brigham, then working in the Inland Empire for the Logging Committee, wrote H. G. Hornby in Cloquet on October 21 that 90 percent of the "monthly men" and 50 percent of the "jyppos" [sic] had abandoned their jobs. Of the Weyerhaeuser firms, the Rutledge, Humbird, Potlatch, and Bonners Ferry companies were crippled; only Boise Payette was little affected. It was, Brigham asserted, "the most complete walkout here among woods crews that has ever taken place." He complained bitterly of the Spokane banks and merchants who, he alleged, encouraged the strikers. Thirteen I.W.W.'s had just been acquitted in the Spokane courts.[11]

The 4L was weaker in the woods than in the mills, but it proved a valuable ally in the crisis. Its members stayed on the job, and its employment agencies fed workers into the camps. The lumbermen agreed with each other to employ no more I.W.W. men. But the troubled condition persisted and might have worked more favorably for the strikers had it not been for a tragic episode that occurred in November, 1919.

This was the "Centralia Massacre," a violent outburst in a town in the southwestern part of Washington. There the I.W.W. had for some time been organizing workers despite the opposition of businessmen and the American Legion. The I.W.W.'s headquarters had been wrecked, but they established a "hall" in a hotel with the tacit protection of the town police. On Armistice Day, 1919, a parade was held under American Legion auspices, and the marchers came to the hall. A number of Wobblies were there, armed, and prepared to protect their property. What happened at this point is in dispute. Perhaps a shot was fired from the hall or from an adjoining roof. At any rate, there was firing, three Legionnaires were killed in the street, the hall was stormed, and one fleeing member of the I.W.W., Wesley Everest, was pursued. Brought to bay, he shot a Legionnaire. Then he was overpowered, beaten, and jailed, to be lynched that night. Previously, a number of the Legionnaires had been wounded. Eleven I.W.W.'s were then charged with murder. In an atmosphere of bitter feeling they were tried and seven were convicted of second-degree murder. An unofficial A.F. of L. "jury" of six, selected by the unions of the Northwest, sat through the proceedings and reported the defendants not guilty, holding that they had merely defended themselves when their hall was attacked.[12]

The Centralia tragedy provoked bitterly conflicting opinions. Many liberals denounced the attack on the hall and the conviction of the accused men as hysterical and unjust, but business and patriotic groups held the I.W.W. responsible and called for its extirpation. Lumbermen in particular were aroused. They saw the incident as a culminating proof of the violent, anti-American character of the organization. "Scotch the I.W.W. Snake" read a caption in the *American Lumberman* of November 15th. Both in the state of Washington and the Inland Empire a new drive was begun to harry the Wobblies out of the lumber areas. So virulent and widespread did public hostility become that even the American Federation of Labor felt constrained to adopt resolutions repudiating "the policy of Bolshevism and I.W.W.-ism as being destructive of American ideas and impractical of application."[13]

The career of the I.W.W. was by no means ended. It showed activity in Minnesota and Michigan in 1920 and 1921, calling a strike on May Day, 1923, against "class war" imprisonments and for improvement of camp conditions. Though it was revealed that Wobblies had infiltrated a few 4L locals, the effort soon collapsed.

Actually, the organization was crumbling. Since the Russian Revolution many of its members had turned to Communism and persistently sought to lead the entire body into the larger fold. John S. Gambs in *The Decline of the I.W.W.* estimated that during the 1920's at least two thousand members became Communists and that in 1932 from a tenth to a fifth of Communist party members were former Wobblies. Haywood had gone to Moscow and shifted his allegiance; W. Z. Foster had once belonged to the I.W.W.; Harrison George, editor for a time of the *Daily Worker*, and Earl Browder had been Wobblies. Meanwhile, organized employer and governmental hostility had increasingly blocked the union's activity, and the increasingly settled pattern of the American economy discouraged the individualistic migratory worker who had once made up its rank and file. "It was adjusted to a semi-frontier that had ended with the war [World War I] period," remarked one authority. At any rate, in the lumber world it was more and more a boogeyman and a memory.

The 4L had played its significant role in the defeat of this rowdy, tough-talking and tough-acting group, which with its championship of the underdog, acid humor, and picaresque antics had won popular notoriety. (With the I.W.W., color and humor went out of the radical movement; the Communists had neither.) Similarly, the 4L had helped to balk A.F. of L. activity. After the failure of a protracted strike for the eight-hour day at Klamath Falls in 1922 (against the Big Lake Box Company), the Union of Sawmill and Timber Workers became a mere ghost in the lumber world, and on March 23, 1923, surrendered its charter to the American Federation of Labor. The 4L was left as the sole active labor group in the industry.[14]

3

The Loyal Legion had passed through a period of considerable difficulty. The opposition of the Timber Workers and the I.W.W. was a constant factor during its early years, and the struggle to maintain its locals never ended. Disque remained as president only until June, 1919, when he departed for the East and a far better paid position. His successor was Norman F. Coleman, a Canadian-born professor of English at Reed

College, Portland, who directed the organization with a quiet efficiency. By 1920 its average membership had declined to 17,732, sagged further during the depression of 1921 (8,777), recovered by early 1922 (10,372), and held close to this total during the 1920's.

Maintaining membership required constant efforts by the field agents and officers, a total force of eight to ten, excluding employment agency personnel. The major difficulty was the apathy of employers. Said Coleman in his 1922 report: "Employer after employer has said to the field officers and to me, 'I am getting along all right. There are no trouble-makers in my crew. The 4L cannot do me any good.' "

From the beginning the peacetime 4L stood staunchly by the eight-hour day, and its support was effective. It also issued minimum-wage schedules for both the Inland Empire and the Pacific Coast, and these undoubtedly helped to maintain standard rates. If the wages paid were lower than an aggressive A.F. of L. union might have won, they were also probably higher than the employers would have paid voluntarily. Four-L decisions continued to recognize the interests of the worker, down into the depression years of the middle 1930's.

Publications comprised another chief activity of the Legion. The *4L Bulletin* continued in essence the periodical Disque had founded during the war, its articles and editorials seeking to interest both management and workers in sawmill and logging-camp conditions. A second publication, the *4L News Letter,* furnished the same groups with recent news of lumbering throughout the Northwest. The *News Letter* appeared on the 1st and the *Bulletin* on the 15th of each month. The latter had a subscription list of from 5,500 to 6,500. In 1922 Stewart H. Holbrook, later to become known as the author of *Burning an Empire, Holy Old Mackinaw,* and *The Age of the Moguls,* appeared as editor of the *News Letter,* and he continued to be identified with the 4L well into the 1930's.[15]

Locally, the Legion early assumed a social aspect. It promoted the 3L's for women members, influenced employers to build social halls and boardinghouses, and its units, in accordance with the 4L constitution, sponsored lectures, athletic contests, picnics, and dances that lent color and enjoyment to numerous isolated lumber towns.

Meanwhile, it maintained employment offices free to all members, employers or workers. By 1922 five had been established: in Portland, Aberdeen, Tacoma, Seattle, and Spokane. In 1921–1922 these units together placed 7,198 men, and showed a comparable activity in succeeding years.

When Coleman resigned the presidency of the 4L in 1925 to become head of Reed College, W. C. Ruegnitz, executive secretary of the organization since 1921, was elected his successor. Born in Wisconsin, he had followed constructional engineering for some years in the Middle West and Canada, and then served as employment manager and purchasing agent for several lumber companies in Portland. The Legion had thus been served by a general, an educator, and finally by an engineer with experience in the business and human relations fields. Under Ruegnitz in 1928 it celebrated its tenth anniversary at Tacoma. Disque could not attend, but the gathering listened to Governor Roland Hartley of Washington, to Major Everett G. Griggs, who had served under Disque in 1918, and to Huntington Taylor of the Edward Rutledge Timber Company, who spoke of the value of the 4L to an employer.[16]

In general, observers who have studied the Legion have designated it as a quasi-company union. The crucial importance of employer participation gave this characterization some warrant. Yet, on occasion, 4L officials faced employers staunchly. When Boise Payette withdrew in 1922 and established a ten-hour day, Coleman expressed his disapproval of the longer work span. When Barton, who faced financial difficulties and felt that the ten-hour day was essential for his company, protested against 4L support of the eight-hour day, Coleman replied that support was the fixed Legion policy, and it could not single out Boise Payette as a deserving exception. Later Barton remonstrated because some of his best workers had left and Coleman had assisted them to procure positions in eight-hour plants; the 4L president replied that the men were members and had requested his aid.

Ruegnitz followed Coleman's lead in advocating the eight-hour day and seeking to promote a wage level in 4L plants somewhat above that in most firms not affiliated with the Legion. He also worked to make disability insurance available to members, and in early 1927 could report that 3,000 of them had taken out policies. However, a careful student of lumber-labor relationships in the Northwest, Vernon H. Jensen, doubted the usefulness of the organization. His verdict was that "the functioning of the 4L never matched its ideal, formal structure," that it made the workers more passive, and that they "had no power to keep the individual employer in line."

Charlotte Todes, writing in 1931 from a radical point of view, asserted with some truth that "The Four-L is now primarily an organization of small and middle-sized operators and even among these it is of little consequence." She quoted workers to the effect that the management dominated many locals and that the 4L was working for a nine-hour day —which of the central organization at least was untrue.[17] Undoubtedly the relatively small membership of the Legion and its dependence on employer participation severely restricted its usefulness.

Yet its officials and publications, within limits, served the millworkers well, though aside from helping break the grip of the I.W.W. on the camps, it had made little headway among the loggers. That it could and would speak up for labor was shown again in 1928 by Ruegnitz, who announced: "The Industry is heading straight for trouble if something is not done to secure . . . steady annual employment for the greatest number of men." (Lumbering had experienced depressed conditions and irregular employment to an extent since 1926.) He repeated and sharpened his warning in May, 1930.[18]

By this time all lumber companies were feeling the pinch of the great depression, and even Humbird in Idaho was recommending wage cuts. By 1931 the situation was so serious that F. R. Titcomb, general manager of the Weyerhaeuser Timber Company, had cut the workweek to four days and was studying means of finding employment "for men who are walking the streets." At first feeling that the economic crisis was temporary, he soon scrapped this initial appraisal. "The employment situation is becoming more serious every day," he told his directors on November 13th. With their agreement, he cut all salaries 12½ percent in September, and wages in the mills and camps were cut 10 percent on March 15, 1932. The Weyerhaeuser Timber Company had been paying a minimum of $3.00 per day for common labor, with higher rates for the skilled and semiskilled. The new scale brought the company's minimum to $2.70, higher than most firms were paying, and 10 cents above the 4L minimum.

One effect of the depression had been to turn an increasing number of employers toward the 4L, a trend Ruegnitz worked hard to encourage. He approached C. L. Lewis at Willapa Bay and Titcomb at Tacoma. The latter was favorable to establishing a local at Longview: Long-Bell was ready to set one up if the Weyerhaeusers did. C. H. Ingram, now taking over much of Titcomb's work, approved, but Al Raught, in charge at Longview, was cool to the idea, and so was Lewis at Willapa. What was decisive was the unreceptive attitude of the Weyerhaeuser Timber Company's executive committee, which felt as late as December, 1932, that "some other organization might serve the purpose better."[19]

The election of Franklin Delano Roosevelt in 1932 and the first 1933 activities of Congress gave both the industry and the Weyerhaeuser executives occasion to rethink their course. The bill that would soon establish the National Industrial Recovery Administration proposed a bold program for American business, involving codes for each major industry in the land and provisions for the hours and wages of labor. In Section 7A it guaranteed employees "the right to organize and bargain collectively through representatives of their own choosing." Since organized labor was known to wield influence in Washington, the chance had greatly increased that lumbermen would have to deal with unions of some type. The 4L now fairly glowed with attractiveness!

On May 16, 1933, Ingram wrote Ruegnitz that he had attended a meeting of the West Coast Lumbermen's Association which had discussed the proposed NIR bill and passed a resolution "that the Association should get behind the 4L or a similar organization at once." Ten days later the Weyerhaeuser Timber Company's executive committee assembled and reversed its December attitude, advising "that the 4L organization may be made a valuable medium through which to secure cooperation between employers and employees," and authorizing management "to set up 4L locals in whatever plants it might choose."

Action followed promptly at Longview, Enumclaw (White River Lumber Company), and in the Everett plants. Meanwhile, a code for the industry was in process of formulation, as discussed elsewhere, and became effective on August 22, 1933. Milo Perkins for the NRA soon made the 4L an accredited bargaining unit under the new agency. Ruegnitz was all but ecstatic. He saw a bright new day dawning for his organization, and indeed between May and November it trebled its membership.

Unfortunately for their own immediate interests, the lumbermen had been slow in coming to a decision. Encouraged by prospects held out in pending national legislation, the A.F. of L. had already sent its agents to the mills and camps of the Northwest, and by summer the union that had vanished from the scene ten years before rose miraculously as from a refreshing sleep. In July, 1933, the Northwest Council of Sawmill and Timber Workers Unions met at Enumclaw. Plans were made for further activity, and at plants like Longview and Everett the A.F. of L., stimulated by N.I.R.A., began to gain supporters every day. The revived union soon showed its power by leading sympathy strikes with the Longshoremen when they walked out in May, 1934.

Thus, the decision to work through the 4L had come too late. Units were indeed formed at Everett and Longview, but the task of establishing them was wholly different from what it would have been in 1931. At that time there would have been no opposition. Now the operators were like men trying to bring a large contingent into a hall already crowded. In no plant did the 4L win a majority of the workers. Moreover, it was challenged by the A.F. of L. as no true bargaining agent for the men because it included employers in its membership.[20]

4

The year 1935 opened with the executive committee of the Weyerhaeuser Timber Company discussing the situation created in 1933 by the reappearance of the A.F. of L. and the attempt to convert the company plants into 4L centers. The latter attempt had not been very successful, and the A.F. of L. locals at Longview, in both Weyerhaeuser and Long-Bell plants had filed complaints with the Regional Labor Board, denouncing improper company promotion of the 4L and asking for recognition of the

Sawmill and Timber Workers unions as employee representatives. The case had now been referred to the National Labor Relations Board, and arguments would begin before that body on January 22nd. The executive committee decided to wait on events. Like many other employers, the members were perplexed and uneasy.

Similarly, A.F. of L. workers in camps and mills all through the region were restive. While they had struck in sympathy with the Longshoremen in May 1934, demonstrating considerable power, they themselves had won nothing and now were ready for a strike for objectives of their own. To date their movement had shown spontaneity and strength but had not been well directed. Each local was a member of the Northwest Council of Sawmill and Timber Workers, but while this organization had the blessing of the American Federation of Labor, it as yet had no specific place in the national organization.

However, on March 23, 1935, the Council met at Aberdeen, Washington. The national A.F. of L. had recently given jurisdiction over all lumber-industry workers to the United Brotherhood of Carpenters and Joiners of America and had sent A. W. Muir, of that union's executive board, to confer with the Council. If it accepted control by the Carpenters, he was to take charge in the Pacific Northwest. Somewhat surprisingly, for the mill and camp workers were an independent lot, they approved the proposed relationship. Muir, with the president and vice-president of the Council, accordingly drew up plans for a campaign. The status of the local union was now regularized, the workers were impatient for action, and the time seemed ripe to prepare for it.

A list of demands to be presented to the industry was made, and May 6th set as the date for a strike in case they should not be met. The chief stipulations were (1) that the A.F. of L. local unions be recognized as sole bargaining agents for the men at all mills and plants, (2) that the working hours should be six per day and thirty per week (the depression precluded a higher total), (3) that a basic wage of 75 cents per hour be set, and (4) that vacations with pay be granted.

Unpublicized for a few weeks, in mid-April the proposals were trumpeted abroad by the Associated Press, by individual papers, and by Charles Hope, regional director of the National Labor Relations Board. They made colorful news and stiffened the morale of hesitant A.F. of L. groups. The 4L angrily asserted that "part of the Northwest press unwittingly played into the hands of the lumber unionizers." It soon completed a two-week "survey" and announced that 90 percent of the men did not want the strike and that it would bring hatred between employers and employees and suffering for the conflicting parties and the public. The declaration was repeated in the *4L Lumber News* up to the time of the strike. Of course, the 4L never conceded publicly that if a settlement were negotiated with the new unions, as the Sawmill and Timber Workers proposed, industrial conflict could be avoided.[21]

The Weyerhaeuser and Long-Bell officials were prompt to open talks with Muir and his associates. As noted earlier, none of the second generation of the Weyerhaeuser family wanted unions, but John, living in an area of progressive social attitudes, was inclined to be realistic, while his son "Phil" (J. P. Weyerhaeuser, Jr.) was completely so. F. E. Weyerhaeuser also did not oppose negotiations with the A.F. of L. employees. The Weyerhaeuser Timber Company thus took a position that was liberal in comparison with that of many employers. "It was just considered heresy," remarked Al Raught, who assisted in the discussions, "for an operator to give any consideration to talking to a union about wages or working conditions or anything like that. They were wild-eyed about it." Many stubbornly proposed to "wait it out." After all, jobs and not men were in demand. However, recalcitrant executives did not realize that the state relief administration was prepared to classify strikers as jobless men or that the Carpenters and other trades unions had financial resources for helping lumber workers, and meant to use them.

The Weyerhaeuser and Long-Bell officials were conferring regularly with Muir well before the date of the strike, and at Longview and all other WTC mills but Everett, where "radicals" were in control, work went on as usual pending a settlement. But just as many of the employers were stubborn and refractory, so were large groups of workers. Neither side, excluding Muir, had ever had much experience in negotiating. The employer had sometimes met union demands, as in 1917–1918, but did so unilaterally. As a result, the men had come to regard direct action as their only effective weapon, and a continuing, responsible relationship was as strange to them as it was to management. In the months to come, both groups were to pay dearly for their inexperience.

The Everett plants, as far as the workers were concerned, first showed the effect of this inexperience. There a sense of independence and perhaps something of the I.W.W. tradition was strong among the men. Actually, a majority of the Sawmill and Timber Workers resented control by the Carpenters. To them, Muir and his imported assistants were strangers with no real understanding of the Pacific Northwest or the lumber industry. Moreover, the Carpenters was a craft union, and the mill and camp employees anticipated C.I.O. philosophy in regarding themselves as a single industrial group. They were suspicious of concessions that Muir might make. While the negotiations related to the workers at Everett as well as to those at Longview, Willapa, and Snoqualmie, the former would not wait for a settlement beyond May 6, 1935, but walked out. Phil Weyerhaeuser wrote his uncle (F.E.) that the "union officials [at Everett] admit that the strike is out of hand."

At Longview the same impatience characterized the men, but they remained at work and negotiations continued. An agreement was reached May 9th, providing for recognition of the union but no closed shop, a 50-cent per hour wage, a 40-hour week, and time and a half for overtime. Then, the same emotion that had prevailed at Everett surged through the plant, and dramatically, before they even knew what had been achieved for them, the rank and file left their jobs![22]

The Communists, who had now succeeded the I.W.W.'s as extremists, claimed credit for what occurred, but distrust of Muir and a faith in direct action were the real factors. When the terms of the agreement were finally revealed to the men and they voted upon it, their conviction that they had got less than was possible led the loggers to reject it by a 9 to 1 vote, and the mill employees by 8 to 1. A second offer with the base pay raised to 55 cents was also voted down by 2 to 1, and the company broke off negotiations, attempting to operate neither camps nor mills.

Meanwhile, the strike had taken out 10,000 men on May 6th, and when negotiations failed at Aberdeen on May 7th, an additional 4,000 to 5,000 left their posts. There was picketing but no disorder. Both state and federal authorities vainly sought a settlement. Operators were particularly angered when the Relief Administration paid benefits to strikers. "Roosevelt intends to finance the A.F. of L. in its fight to force the lumber industry into a closed shop!" declared a supporter of the more stubborn employers. But with the collapse of the Longview negotiations, 90 percent of the northwestern plants and camps, involving more than 30,000 men, stood idle. There was no prospect of a settlement. Finally E. P. Marsh, United States Labor conciliator, brought about an agreement between Muir and one fairly important group of employers. This offered some hope, but the split in the ranks of labor continued, and the Communists worked busily to widen it.

While the governor of Oregon ordered an investigation and while efforts to promote federal mediation failed to prosper—neither the employers nor the unions wanted it—the sudden invalidation of the N.I.R.A. by the United States Supreme Court brought further confusion. The immediate effect was favorable to the operators, even though the future Wagner Act was already before Congress. Muir was able to assemble the Longview workers and get a practically unanimous vote for the agreement they had spurned three weeks earlier. This was decidedly a step toward a general settlement.

Yet it was less effective than it would have been on May 9th. The extremists on both sides showed unusual stubbornness, the "radicals" advocating direct action as the only remedy and the diehard employers feeling that with the N.I.R.A. and the lumber code dead, they could sit tight and wait for victory. However, with the aid of the A.F. of L. officers in Washington, Muir was able to regain fairly full control of labor, and Governors Charles H. Martin of Oregon and Clarence D. Martin of Washington both promised to protect all men who returned to work. Although there was mass violence, and for a time state troops patrolled the Tacoma plants, additional settlements were made, and the long strike ground to an end. The general basis of settlement was that adopted at Longview. The role of the governors of Washington and Oregon had been decisive. Both, according to R. L. Neuberger, later United States Senator from Oregon, were archconservatives, but they did break an impasse that served the interests of neither capital nor labor.[23]

So far as the Weyerhaeuser companies were concerned, the strike marked the end of an epoch for both employers and workers. As noted, up to 1935 the chief stockholders and company officials had never accepted a bona fide union as a collective bargaining agent and had never made a contract with one. But with 1934 had come a tentative recognition of union status, and by July, 1935, Phil Weyerhaeuser was prepared to go further. "I do not think that the desire of our employees for a union had diminished materially," he wrote his uncle Frederick on the 5th, "and I do not think we can refuse recognition of the union in some way in the future. One thing which seems very definite is that the 4L has done us no good whatsoever, and is completely dead at our plants, with no members at Snoqualmie or Longview." He proposed to negotiate with the "new unions," and refused to join others in requesting military rule at Everett.[24]

With the 1935 settlement this attitude became official and permanent. The Sawmill and Timber Workers were recognized as a bargaining agent, and an agreement was made. The Weyerhaeuser companies in the Pacific Northwest from this time forward were to operate under such pacts. As for the workers, for the first time they found themselves an accepted force in the industry, with rights and responsibilities.

5

Even before the 1935 strike had clarified employer-worker relationships in the Northwest, the Weyerhaeuser Timber Company had adopted a liberal policy for the employees in its first pulp mill. On August 3, 1934, Robert B. Wolf, manager of the Pulp Division, negotiated a contract with the International Brotherhood of Paper Makers that recognized this union as the collective bargaining agent for the workers. Wolf was a firm believer in friendly relations with organized labor, and he made a fair contract which was renewed yearly with changes agreed upon in conference. Speaking of the Pacific Northwest, Howard Morgan, his successor, asserted in 1955 that "there's never been a work stoppage in the industry [that is, the pulp-making industry] since that [the original union] was organized." The construction of a second pulp mill at Everett, 1935–1937, added to the number of unionized workers. Because of the satisfactory relationship between the union and the management, its members never participated in strikes at the mills. In Minnesota a comparable situation did not develop until after Stuart Copeland took over the management of the Northwest Paper Company in 1936.[25]

The relationship of the unions to the Weyerhaeuser companies in the camps and lumber mills showed nothing like this harmony in the period following the 1935 strike. The officials, accepting the principle of collective bargaining with contracts as a corollary, were hopeful of peaceful relationships, but labor was in a period of change marked by internal dissension, and this fact affected its relationships with employers.

The dissension stemmed from the presence of separate and hostile groups among the 30,000 workers of the area. In the first place, the 4L had continued to maintain itself in Idaho, Oregon, and California, although Muir and his aides were pledged to drive it out of every mill and camp in the Pacific Northwest. By a Supreme Court decision upholding the Wagner Act in April, 1937, the Loyal Legion of Loggers and Lumbermen, if it was to act as a bargaining agency for the workers, could not contain employer members or accept employer support. As a result, on May 1, 1937, in Portland, the Industrial Employees' Union was formed. It barred employer membership or contributions. To avoid identification with the 4L, Ruegnitz resigned, and A. D. Chisholm took the presidency of the new organization. Twenty-three locals participated in its founding, and its constitution included a provision sanctioning the strike. Although the A.F. of L. had made steady and often devastating progress against the 4L, the I.E.U. quickly showed a surprising vitality and was to win a number of contests for the role of bargaining agent.

During the period prior to the founding of this new union, resentment among the Sawmill and Timber Workers against Carpenter control had boiled into active revolt. In addition to their detestation of the craft union, the lumber workers had specific grievances: instead of being consulted on general policy, they had been given orders; and many decisions as to their affairs had been made at Carpenters' conventions, which their representatives were permitted to attend as observers only.

It is not important here to trace the seething internal differences that marked union affairs in the lumber industry of the Northwest during the next few years. Some happenings, however, must be noted, for they affected the lumber operators in the region. The mounting tide of dissatisfaction among the S.T.W.U. (Sawmill and Timber Workers Union) found an escape from the arrogant control of the Carpenters in the formation late in 1935 of the Committee for Industrial Organization

(C.I.O.) by John L. Lewis and others. These leaders had assembled a group of industrial as opposed to crafts unions, organizing each unit on the basis acceptable to the lumber employees, who had always counted each worker as a member of the total group engaged in lumber activity. What was quite as important, the C.I.O. welcomed the idea of a single large union comprising mill and camp employees, and promised it independent status, with no control by any other labor group.

Naturally Muir and his supporters were furious at the prospect of losing the S.T.W.U. They were able to command considerable support within it because many of the members disliked and distrusted Harold Pritchett, the chief advocate of affiliation with the C.I.O. Yet the pressure for this step increased rapidly, and on July 19, 1937, a majority of the delegates from S.T.W.U. locals voted for it, and a new union, the International Woodworkers of America, was created. The I.W.A. would have been the I.W.W. of America had not "Woodworkers," originally two words, been made one. This the A.F. of L. adherents were quick to point out. "It *is* the I.W.W. anyhow!" exclaimed Frank Duffy, national secretary for the Carpenters.[26]

Thus by 1937 there were three unions in the field, and actually, in effect, there was soon a fourth, for a growing body of I.W.A.'s opposed the "administration" forces headed by Pritchett and later by O. M. Orton. And although the various feuds in the labor camp have no direct bearing on Weyerhaeuser relationships with employees, the resultant confusion did, since like other operators the Weyerhaeuser companies had to deal with *some* body of workers and were to find difficulty at times in knowing which one.

While the I.E.U. maintained a stiffer fight than might have been expected, it was under suspicion as the lineal descendant of the 4L. Frequently charged with being unduly favored by the employers, it was eventually supplanted by one or the other of the two chief unions. (Despite its internal dissensions, the I.W.A. never ceased to be a single body.) By 1942 the I.E.U. had gone out of existence.[27]

Many employers were at first pleased to find the unions divided, but they miscalculated the effects of division. It did not diminish in the least the workers' desire to organize and bargain collectively. Instead, it promoted a series of intraplant contests between the A.F. of L. and the I.W.A., or between the insurgent and administration groups of the latter, which put the winning unit in fighting trim for a final test with the operators, much as a challenger for a boxing title profits from frequent bouts on his way to the championship test. Furthermore, the unions vied with each other in exacting terms from the operators. If the I.W.A. won a favorable settlement for a group of mills, the A.F. of L. was not satisfied to accept an identical one for its plants but felt that it must do better!

Executives of the Weyerhaeuser Timber Company and other employers were distracted by the difficulty of establishing something like industry-wide standards for wages and other items. Phil Weyerhaeuser once reported to his uncle Frederick a wage increase he had conceded—"the only justification being that we are buying peace—and will probably find that we didn't get it!" One continuing difficulty was the inexperience of both unions and operators in bargaining and in keeping agreements. Only as both became more familiar with these processes was something like stability to be achieved.[28]

Gradually a succession of elections established the unions that held power in certain plants. Moreover, as each local contest ended, the losers often packed up their household effects and sought jobs in plants where their own group held power. When the I.W.A. was completely victorious at the Everett mills and later at Longview, a limited exodus of A.F. of L. men took place. Such practice stabilized local situations and gave the employers something like assured peace in each mill or camp.

Thus a pattern developed, with the I.W.A. winning the greater number of mills and camps, but the A.F. of L. firmly entrenched where it had been successful. The companies, including Weyerhaeuser units, accepted the result and dealt with the winning unions—a condition that persisted up to the merger of A.F. of L. and C.I.O., and after it, for that matter.

The employers enjoyed a brief period during the depression of 1938 when it appeared that they might win wage reductions and other concessions. In some instances they did, but the return of prosperity with the beginning of World War II in Europe ended the movement to pare the past gains of the workers.

In 1938, to promote unity of action and present a solid front to the unions in bargaining conferences, some three hundred employers formed the Lumbermen's Industrial Relations Committee. It was a fact-finding as well as a negotiating body, and the Weyerhaeuser Timber Company contributed regularly to its support. Led by Al Raught, a group of WTC officials for years took a leading part in the Committee's negotiating activities. (However, in the end the company felt that its interests would be better served by negotiating separately, and in 1950 resigned.)

After an extended period of negotiations that brought a settlement with the A.F. of L. unions, failure to agree with the I.W.A. on union status, wages, and other matters led to a strike early in May, 1941. This affected fifty-two plants (W.T.C.'s among them) and became comparable with the walkout of 1935, although it affected fewer workers. Because of the government interest in the defense program, now of growing importance, the dispute was soon brought before the National Defense Mediation Board in Washington. Its recommendations were issued on May 23rd and accepted by the operators. They embodied union maintenance, wage increases, vacations with pay, and a study of piecework by joint employer-employee committees. Differences arose as to the meaning of union maintenance, and on June 13th the Board redefined this to mean that present members would be required to maintain membership and all new employees to join the union within forty days; the second part of this interpretation the operators refused to accept. They would go no further than to insist on maintenance by new workers if and after they joined. Finally the men went back to work while negotiations were resumed, but no agreement had been reached when the American entry into World War II drastically altered the entire labor situation.[29]

Since 1935 the internal differences of the labor unions had not been resolved, but the clear tendency was that already described: both of the two chief unions would continue to exist, and employers, including Weyerhaeuser Timber, would deal with both. As to the general standing of labor, what has previously been won had now been consolidated and even extended. The period of growing pains was not ended, but lumber company managers now faced the fact that workers occupied an acknowledged position from which they could defend the basic rights they had struggled so long to establish. Executives could expect union leaders to open new questions affecting the welfare of their members whenever the time seemed appropriate.

NOTES

1. *Amer. Lbrmn.,* Nov. 16, 1918, p. 27, Nov. 30, 1918, p. 35, and issues of Nov., 1918; Feb., 1919, *passim;* Jensen, *Lumber and Labor,* 135–136; FEW Papers, Brigham to H. C. Hornby, Oct. 21, 1919.

2. *Amer. Lbrmn.,* Nov. 23, 1918, p. 43, Dec. 14, 1919, p. 45, and Jan. 18, 1919, p. 38; Jensen, 133–135; Howd, *Industrial Relations in the West Coast Lumber Industry,* 84–88.

3. *Amer. Lbrmn.,* Jan.–March, 1919, *passim;* JPW Papers, N. F. Coleman to JPW, March 16, 1922.

4. Jensen, 35–36; 4L annl. repts., 1919–1925; Howd, 90, 97–101. In 1919 the I.W.W. could show only 4,500 members and the revived Timber Workers (with the Shingle-Weavers), 8,241.

5. Jensen, 133.

6. *Ibid.;* Winsted, "Enter a Logger," *Survey,* XLIV, July 3, 1920, pp. 474–477 and Gill, "The Four L's in Lumber," *Survey,* XLIV, May 1, 1920, pp. 165–170; Macartney, Reminiscences.

7. Jensen, 136; Disque, "How We Found a Cure for Strikes," *System,* XXXVI, Sept., 1919, p. 384. Jensen says that the strike was orderly.

8. *Amer. Lbrmn.,* Aug. 2, 1919, p. 49, and subsequent issues into September, particularly Aug. 9, p. 53, and Aug. 30, 1919, pp. 40, 60.

9. *Coeur d'Alene Evening News,* Aug. 26, 1919; *Labor World,* Jan. 15, 1921.

10. Naturally, "gyppos" came from the slang word "gip" or "gyp," meaning to cheat or worst someone by sharp practice. As the I.W.W. viewed mat-

ters, a piecework arrangement destroyed the wage-hour pattern and, it asserted, set such low rates that the men got nothing from it.

11. Gambs, *The Decline of the I.W.W.,* 230; *Amer. Lbrmn.,* Oct. 25, 1919, p. 72; FEW Papers, E. J. Brigham to H. C. Hornby, Oct. 21, 1919.

12. *Amer. Lbrmn.,* Nov. 8, 1919, pp. 38, 61; Jensen, 137–145; Gambs, 31; *The Centralia Case,* cited by Gambs. The defendants were granted a change of venue, were dissatisfied and asked a second, which was denied.

13. *Amer. Lbrmn.,* Nov. 15, 1919, p. 45, Nov. 22, pp. 40, 54, and Dec. 20, p. 54; Jensen, 145.

14. Jensen, 145–146; Gambs, 87–91; Lillard, *The Great Forest,* 308–309.

15. Jensen, 135, 137; Howd, 90, 96; FEW Papers, 4L semiannl. repts., May, 1922, 1924, 1925.

16. Howd, 90, 96; Jensen 146–147; E. A. Aitchison, Reminiscences; Potlatch Lbr. Co., Potlatch Annual Report, 1919; Constitution and By-Laws of the Loyal Legion of Loggers and Lumbermen, 19; FEW Papers, 4L Semiannual Report, May 18–19, 1925, and Minutes of Directors' Meeting, May 18. See WTC Papers for copies of various letters to Disque in April 1925; *Amer. Lbrmn.,* May 30, 1925, p. 54, and April 30, 1927, p. 74.

17. Mittleman (see Note 15, Chap. 18), 339–340; Howd, 93–96; JPW Papers, correspondence between Coleman, JPW, and Barton; Jensen, 136–137; Todes, *Labor and Lumber,* 146–148.

18. Jensen, 151; 4L Semiannual Meeting, Portland, May 19, 1930.

19. WTC Papers, Titcomb to FEW, H. H. Irvine and the WTC Executive Committee; Ruegnitz correspondence May–July, 1931; WTC Min. Bks., Dec. 13, 1932; *4L Lumber News,* Jan. 1, 1932, p. 1.

20. WTC Papers, CHI to Ruegnitz, May 16, 1933; JPW to Ex. Cmtee., Feb. 10, 1934, and JPW, Jr., to Ex. Com., same date; FEW Papers, WTC Folder, Ex. Cmtee. Minutes, May 22 and 27, 1933; JPW, Jr., to FEW, June 14, 1934; Potlatch Lumber Co., Papers, 4L file, 1933–1934; *4L Lumber News,* Oct. 1, 1933, pp. 3–6, and June 1, 1934, p. 8.

21. Jensen, 164–165; *4L Lumber News,* April 24, May 1, 1935.

22. Jensen, Chap. 9, *passim,* and 164, 167–169, 185; FEW Papers, FEW to Laird Bell, April 25, 1935; WTC Papers, JPW, Jr. to FEW, May 2 and 6, 1935; Raught, Reminiscences.

23. Jensen, 168–171, 174–185; WTC Papers, JPW, Jr. to FEW, July 5, 1935; Neuberger, *Our Promised Land,* 246–264, 272–274, 313–314. Neuberger handles the two Martins, both conservatives, without gloves.

24. WTC Papers, JPW, Jr. to FEW, July 5, 1935; Jensen, 181–182.

25. Howard Morgan, Reminiscences; JPW Papers; Northwest Paper Co. Papers, 1936–1940. Northwest Paper had a prolonged strike in 1921.

26. Jensen, 203–212, 227–229.

27. *Ibid.,* chaps. 11 and 12.

28. *Ibid.,* 168–274; WTC Papers, JPW, Jr., to FEW, April 4, 1936.

29. Jensen, chaps., 12–13; Interview A. A. Peterson of WTC, April, 1956; WTC annl. repts.; Jensen, 246–247, 250–271.

XXIII

The New Deal and Recovery

I N THE MIDDLE 1920's lumbermen watched industries other than theirs making prodigious profits.[1] Their own were either nominal or nonexistent. Prices for standing timber were declining. Mill capacity had expanded far beyond limits warranted by market demand, and lumbermen were waging continuous war against wood substitutes.

Long before the depression began in 1929, the lumber industry was in the doldrums. In 1926, 27.2 percent of the West Coast mills had stood idle; in 1927, 30.1 percent; and in 1928, 28.8 percent—grim evidence of an unhealthy condition. Lumbermen naturally looked for paths back to prosperity. They considered imposing production and price controls but shrank from such remedies because of the specter of antitrust legislation.

But with the stock-market crash and its paralyzing aftermath the demand for controls—for voluntary organization of the industry—became "insistent."[2] The thirties brought efforts to meet the situation, but many questions were raised. How effective could government control be? How much could industry control itself? Just what was to be the relation of government and the lumber industry as each tried to loosen the coils of depression?

2

Soon after the crash leaders in the lumber industry began to offer remedial suggestions. Colonel W. B. Greeley, for example, recommended in November, 1929, that the "extreme fluctuations" in the market be moderated by the restriction of each company's sales to a percentage of the "adjusted capacity of the industry." But in January, 1930, Attorney

General William D. Mitchell refused to approve or disapprove; indeed he remarked that should such a plan go into operation, "it seems not unlikely that the Department of Justice would find it necesary to test its legality in the courts."[3]

In 1931 some Weyerhaeuser associated mills and other western manufacturers sent copies of orders for lumber to either the Western Pine Association or the Davis Exchange in Portland, both agencies using the data to compile current price information for the guidance of the industry. Lumber salesmen urged that a method be developed to inform the sales force in advance what the mills were going to produce the coming year in order to permit intelligent pricing. Wilson Compton of the National Lumber Manufacturers Association presented a plan to obtain wider markets and a better control of supply. His scheme involved monthly lumber association meetings and the adoption of "production quotas."[4]

Plans were also proposed for mergers, which, it was argued, would result in better financing, more efficiency, and greater control of production. Officials of associated Weyerhaeuser firms discussed several mergers that never reached fruition,[5] though some plans of combination, like those producing the White River Lumber Company and the Willapa Harbor Lumber Mills, both affiliated with WTC by earlier agreements, did succeed. Most important was the union in 1931 of three northern Idaho companies into Potlatch Forests, Inc.

Lumbermen saw that although the combinations and mergers were on too small a scale to violate antitrust laws, effective plans for production and price control might mean such a violation. They therefore vigorously voiced their opposition to existing legal restrictions. The revision of antitrust laws for which they labored would end the threat of prosecution, so that lumbermen could organize production in a manner most advantageous to the industry.

Before the New Deal only one plan for improving the lumber industry had come out of Washington. President Hoover in 1930 had approved the formation of the United States Timber Conservation Board to devise methods for coping with the "consequences of overproduction in the forest industries." The Board issued reports, compiled statistics, and appointed an advisory committee on privately owned timber (which included Laird Bell, W. B. Greeley, and E. T. Allen). It urged a wide range of remedial steps, including "regulation of timber cutting, mergers, state agreements and interstate compacts for control of production, and modification of the antitrust laws."[6] It strongly recommended sustained yield management of timber on both public and private lands. But more than studies and suggestions were needed.

As the depression deepened, all industries suffered, and lumbering as much as any. Of the country's mills, 52 percent in 1930 lay idle.

Weyerhaeuser Timber was in the anomalous position of increasing production with its new plants at Longview and Klamath, but, as the economic quagmire deepened it also began to curtail. Early in 1931 most
of its mills ran on an uneconomical four-day week schedule. F. Rodman
Titcomb, who had succeeded George S. Long as manager in 1929, gave
typical instructions: "Cut all expenses;" "Buy nothing that costs too
much." In 1931 two of the associates' Minnesota mills had closed, two
in Idaho had shut down permanently, and four others would operate
only part time.[7]

With economy and curtailment the policy, Weyerhaeuser Timber
Company production in 1932 fell almost to half that of the previous year.
The president reported to the stockholders that "due to the stringent financial condition of a number of producers, fixed charges and in some cases
even stumpage were given away in an effort to stave off bankruptcy."
Complaints of hard times were universal. E. W. Davis of Wood Conversion Company, for instance, lamented: "Business is terrible, and I have
been making further reductions in salaries and personnel which are harm-
ful to the organization but have no choice in the matter." This year four
out of five of America's lumber mills lay idle. It was the third consecutive
year that the Weyerhaeuser Timber Company and the associated companies had operated at a loss.[8]

Gloomy indeed were the prospects when Americans went to the
polls in November, 1932. F. K. Weyerhaeuser, through Titcomb, sent
circulars to the branch managers suggesting that the Republican administration had been sympathetic to the lumbermen's plight and there was
no need for a change. He hoped that Hoover would be reelected.[9] Thus
most Weyerhaeuser officials were not pleased when by an overwhelming
vote Franklin Delano Roosevelt became America's thirty-second President.

But as 1933 opened, the outlook for the Timber Company was not
wholly dark. One ray of light came with the appointment of a new executive vice-president, J. P. Weyerhaeuser, Jr. Then thirty-four years old,
"Phil" brought the promise of new vigor and efficiency. Titcomb had
brought to the perplexing conditions of the time the talents of an excellent
engineer and a trained administrator. In a period that saw all business
and industry in difficulty, he had labored gallantly but ineffectually. Phil
Weyerhaeuser was able to share responsibilities that the crisis had made
too heavy for any one man; and the two made an effective team in combating the depression. When C. H. Ingram became general manager in
1936, he worked even more closely than had Titcomb with Phil Weyerhaeuser.[10]

Two months later, when Franklin Delano Roosevelt took office, the
Weyerhaeusers thought that "hopes seem to have revived," and their stock-

holders learned that business for the moment, as compared to the previous year, had improved. WTC officials saw America as "on the verge of an era of controlled individualism," of "revolutionary laws."[11] That spring found plans tumbling out of Washington, D.C., and new agencies appearing to wrestle with the ills of the stricken country.

Most comprehensive of early New Deal measures was the National Industrial Recovery Act. Under this law the activities of scores of industries came under close regulation. In lumbering everything from cutting down trees to cutting down wages was included. At first lumbermen looked upon the plans for their industry with qualified approval. "The possibilities of good in this legislation," wrote Wilson Compton, "far outweigh its probabilities of evil."[12] The industry perceived that it could control production and prices, objectives it had sought since the mid-twenties—without fear of violating the antitrust laws. The Weyerhaeusers joined others in helping formulate the rules for "industry self-government" under the new act. Little did they anticipate the many difficulties that would be encountered.

3

When President Roosevelt signed the Recovery Act on June 16, 1933, he heralded it as "the most important and far-reaching legislation ever enacted by the American Congress." The new law provided for a code to govern each industry, written by the members. Lumbermen responded through the National Lumber Manufacturers Association, which on July 3rd selected a twenty-man Emergency National Committee —soon to be incorporated as the Lumber Code Authority. John D. Tennant of the Long-Bell Lumber Sales Corporation chaired the committee, which had among its members S. L. Coy of Northwest Paper, Ralph Macartney of Klamath Falls, and F. E. Weyerhaeuser, soon to be president of the Weyerhaeuser Timber Company. Laird Bell and A. W. Clapp were particularly helpful in putting the Code in action.[13]

Not all of those active in the committee work were confident of success. F. E. Weyerhaeuser had the strongest reservations. Steeped in the principles of economics taught him by Arthur T. Hadley at Yale, he could not understand the methods of the New Deal or the policies of the N.R.A. Indeed, he wanted as few restrictions as possible: no production control, no minimum prices, and no limits on new mill construction. A. W. Clapp, however, had a more flexible outlook, and cherished hopes of developing a workable lumber code.[14]

The committee submitted a tentative code to General Hugh S. Johnson, the National Recovery Administrator, on July 10th. When public hearings began ten days later, Laird Bell (a classmate of F. D. Roosevelt and a Democrat) was one of the five who conducted them, and Ralph Macartney and Harry T. Kendall, manager of the Sales Company, were among those who gave testimony. The Code was rewritten and approved on August 19, 1933.

The completed instrument comprised ten articles dealing with labor, production control, price levels, and conservation. When it was accepted, many in government and industry applauded. David Mason, soon to head the Lumber Code Authority, recorded in his diary on August 20, 1933, that it was "generally recognized in N.R.A. as the best code worked out so far—best in general but especially in administrative setup."[15]

This optimism was unwarranted, for like an untried, complicated machine the new agency at once developed frictions. Some companies clamored for higher production allotments; in contrast, Weyerhaeuser officials thought all allotments too high! At the same time it became apparent that the code, like a policeman without a club, carried no serious penalty for exceeding the prescribed quota! A. W. Clapp, whose legal acumen was widely admired, noted as early as September, 1933, that the lack of enforcement power literally eviscerated the control system.[16]

To devise formulas for production and price controls proved a complex undertaking that moved from dispute to dispute. John Tennant resigned from the Code authority in protest. Phil Weyerhaeuser wrote in August, 1934, that he doubted if the lumbermen could ever get satisfactory formulas. The Weyerhaeuser Timber Company, White River Lumber Company, Willapa Harbor Lumber Mills, and Snoqualmie Falls Lumber Company proclaimed their opposition to the allotment formula adopted in December, 1934. They asserted that it did not consider overhead, taxes, depreciation, insurance, or timber expenses; that it fettered the energies of selling organizations; and that it took business from one operation to give it to another. It discriminated against mills built for continuous operation in favor of those erected for "partial operations." It encouraged high-cost mills at the expense of low-cost mills, and thus penalized efficiency. The Weyerhaeuser companies insisted that the formula favored the small millowner to the disadvantage of the large concerns.[17]

Nor were certain parts of the administrative procedure as successful as Mason had anticipated. Ralph Macartney knew much about western pine but was hardly an authority on "mop handles and broom handles." He later complained that members of the Lumber Code Authority were expected to rule on "things you knew nothing about. . . . And anyway, when you tried to do something, why you ran against this government wall."[18]

The code's minimum price provision, designed to cover the costs of production, soon resulted in an almost fantastic situation. "Vast numbers of rumors floating around and our industry practically hysterical over the price situation," commented David Mason as he worked over the price provisions in June, 1934. It may have reassured some to hear General Johnson repeat that he'd "iron things out," but it did not reassure the majority. District court decisions in the fall of 1934 resulted in greater confusion, for minimum prices were ruled legal on the west bank of the Mississippi, but not on the east bank,·and on one bank of the Columbia River but not the other![19]

In the areas where minimum prices were held valid, violations became common. Trustees of the West Coast Lumbermen's Association held a meeting in Portland on September 25th to review the matter, which at one time became so riotous that J. H. Bloedel, president of Bloedel-Donovan Lumber Mills, arose and declared the gathering resembled a longshoremen's convention rather than a meeting of businessmen. This rebuke calmed the turbulent session, and eight days later the trustees voted 14 to 7 to do their utmost to obtain the abandonment of "cost protection." Weyerhaeuser officials were in accord with this decision. A. W. Clapp prepared a statement for the Weyerhaeuser and Shevlin interests explaining that minimum prices were "impracticable and economically unsound," "an economic mistake," "a subversion of justice," and "a canker sore of dishonesty in our industry." He declared that their inflexibility ran counter to the law of supply and demand. Clapp was ready, however, to salvage the other features of the Code.[20]

But as the year 1935 opened, the din against the entire Code became louder. Lumbermen everywhere regarded it as totally unenforceable. Titcomb estimated in March 1935, that of the pine (southern particularly) manufactured, from 50 to 60 percent was produced without the slightest effort to observe Code requirements. A questionnaire sent out jointly by the West Coast Lumbermen's Association and the government revealed the emphatic dislike of West Coast lumbermen for the regulations. When in May 1935, the Supreme Court in the Schechter case declared unanimously that the N.R.A. was unconstitutional, few lumbermen mourned its passing.[21]

When they looked back on the N.R.A., many lumbermen totally forgot that the industry had played a major role in formulating the Code. Many later agreed with the statement, "I don't suppose anybody much in the industry liked the Recovery Act."[22] Phil Weyerhaeuser recalled in 1953: "It was a great day when the N.R.A. was voted out, as far as I was concerned. Industrial self-government is just not possible."[23] Yet as A. W. Clapp declared in October, 1934: "No organizations were more active [than the Weyerhaeusers and Shevlins] in the formative stages of the Lumber Code; none have been more anxious that its administration should be free from criticism; none have contributed any more in manpower from their respective organizations in its administration, up to date."

Some contemporaries realized they had learned a lesson: "We have always said," Clapp wrote, "that if our industry could be freed from the restrictions of antitrust laws and permitted to make fair voluntary agreements, we could rescue it from the depths to which it had sunk. I think it has been fairly well proven that this is not true. I do not believe that there would have been or would be any more compliance with voluntary agreement than there has been with the code provisions."[24]

From the Lumber Code a few items were retained. Lumbermen would not have price controls again until O.P.A. in World War II, and these would be ceiling rather than floor prices. However, the policy of giving an 8 percent discount to wholesale dealers, established under the Code, continued until World War II, and numerous labor provisions similar to those in the Lumber Code were incorporated in the Wagner Act. Finally, Article X, the conservation article, which will be discussed in detail later, had a lasting effect.

4

If the N.R.A. was largely a fiasco for the lumberman, other New Deal measures worked to better effect. The accomplishments of the Civilian Conservation Corps will be described later. The Agricultural Adjustment Act, passed in May, 1933, attempted to increase agricultural purchasing power. As in early lumber history, so in the thirties the farmer was an important customer of the lumberman, and the improvement in his ability to buy meant a better market for lumber products. The Farm Credit Act of 1933, by aiding the farmer, also indirectly benefited the lumberman. Among the New Deal Schemes designed to encourage building were the Federal Emergency Relief Act of June 16, 1933, which had a slum-clearance provision, and the Public Works Administration (set up in 1933), which had a housing division.

For the Weyerhaeuser companies the most significant of New Deal measures affecting lumber was the National Housing Act of 1934. This sponsored a type of activity that Weyerhaeuser officials had been discussing when the 4-SQUARE campaign was launched. The Lumbermen's Finance Corporation, which included a number of non-Weyerhaeuser firms, was created in May, 1929, and its activities are traced in detail in Chapter XXV. Engaged in making mortgage loans as a stimulus to the sale of lumber, the company was notably successful.[25] When the Act was still a project in the spring of 1934, it contemplated under Title I of the proposed law the issuance of government loans on notes for the repair and modernization of buildings. Under Title II it also authorized mortgage loans on new buildings, and this portion of the Act was written largely on information supplied by L. J. Luhman, general manager of the LFC. Unfortunately, when the Act was passed on June 27, 1934, the wording of this title was ambiguous. However, the Lumbermen's Finance Corporation utilized Title I for the issuance of notes on repair projects involving lumber, and after the renewal and clarification of the legislation in April, 1936, it also made mortgage loans under a revised Title II. How the Act as a whole stimulated the creation of a larger Weyerhaeuser agency, Allied Building Credits, Inc., and was of valuable assistance to it, will also be described in Chapter XXV.[26]

5

While the New Deal and Weyerhaeuser stockholders were developing these new instrumentalities, the country was gradually emerging from the depression. The Weyerhaeuser Timber Company in 1933 and 1934 operated at a very small profit. In 1935 it did better; in 1936 and 1937 better still; and the temporary recession of 1938 failed to put the Timber Company back in the red, though the profit level fell from $9,000,000 to $2,000,000.[27] The years after 1938 saw a steady revival of business. They also witnessed an important change in the Weyerhaeuser policy— an increasing diversification of business in which the manufacture of pulp, plywood, and other nonlumber products steadily gathered volume and importance.

Indeed, as they pulled out of the slough of deep depression, the firms began to expand in several directions. The Weyerhaeuser Steamship Company purchased two new ships in 1935 to supplement its four-ship fleet, and in 1937 purchased two additional vessels. This was one evidence of improving markets and also of rising rail costs. Simultaneously, in view of the larger quantities of lumber being produced, the marketing facilities were improved and expanded.

In the mid-thirties the Weyerhaeuser Timber Company owned three plants in its own name which produced lumber: one at Everett (three mills);[28] a plant at Longview (three mills); and another at Klamath Falls, Oregon (one sawmill and a box factory). There were three subsidiary operations, the Snoqualmie Falls Lumber Company, White River Lumber Company, and Willapa Harbor Lumber Mills. The three mills at Longview that had opened in 1929 had been held back by the depression, and in 1936, for the first time, full production began. The other mills made adjustments in production to handle the quickening markets.

As for wood by-products, the company was now to give them an attention that in time would result in impressive consequences. To understand what was about to happen, a brief glance must be given to the first depression years. In 1931, as a result of F. R. Titcomb's persistent efforts, a pulp mill had been opened at Longview. For the Timber Company it was an experiment. Its manager, Robert Bensen Wolf, who had about fifteen years of experience in paper and pulp manufacturing before coming to the Timber Company, was perceptive, active, and imaginative. Though the Weyerhaeusers were aware that "in a sense we made a mistake in building the pulp plant when we did," for a depression seemed no time to expand, still even in 1932 it was only a slight financial burden—the losses of the new pulp mill amounted only to 3 percent of the company's total loss. In fact, the pulp mill had such good prospects that Clapp had to remind himself and Titcomb: "We are lumbermen, and must remain lumbermen. We cannot allow the tail, even a healthy tail, to wag the dog, even a mangy one."[29]

The pulp mill throve, and in 1934 its earnings actually turned the total Weyerhaeuser Timber Company balance from a loss to a profit. During that year it netted $590,698, while the parent body exclusive of the pulp mill lost about $110,000.[30] The "tail" indeed had wagged the dog, and he was fortunate that it had.

With the new Longview mill performing a depression miracle, the Timber Company soon considered expanding in the pulp line. Titcomb suggested in March, 1934, that the company should build a mill on Puget Sound that would use the Vail, Snoqualmie Falls Lumber Company, and White River Lumber Company's hemlock. But F. E. Weyerhaeuser held back: "I should warn you that we are all feeling conservative as to any capital investments in plants at the present time." He left open, however, the possibility of a study.[31]

Then Phil Weyerhaeuser endorsed the project, approaching the directors with a drive and force that indicated his confidence in victory. He pointed out that the company had a surplus of hemlock it would be wise to utilize in a new Weyerhaeuser mill. He used a carefully prepared report by Wolf to illustrate his case and supported it persuasively in other ways. Laird Bell was among the first to become convinced. "I have been over the papers in regard to the pulp mill, starting with my ears laid back and a slight feeling that Wolf was a mesmerist. I seem to have succumbed and agree to Phil's recommendation," he wrote in July 1934. Others followed, and in October the Executive Committee authorized the new pulp mill at Everett. O. C. Schoenwerk, who had built the Longview mill, was engaged to design and construct the new plant, which began operations in June, 1936.[32] And as the Weyerhaeusers moved to turn their hemlock into pulp, they also acted to transform shavings and chips into the new product, Pres-to-Logs, which is described elsewhere.[33]

Meanwhile, the Wood Conversion Company had found the depression so hard to weather that in February, 1934, it seemed possible that it would go into receivership; its accumulated floating debt that year totaled $900,000. "In our entire business history we have never been placed in a position like this," complained F. E. Weyerhaeuser to nephew Phil Weyerhaeuser. To aid their affiliate, associated companies accepted convertible debentures in 1934 to the amount of $900,000 owed them by Wood Conversion. These were called for redemption in 1937 and 1938 and were mostly converted into common stock, holders of only $50,000 electing to receive cash. Weyerhaeuser timber thus enlarged its holdings of Wood Conversion's stock to 40 percent, to be increased in 1945 to 43 percent and in 1948 to 51 percent.

Among the new products that Wood Conversion Company brought forth at Cloquet was a beveled plank for side walls, furnished in various widths and variegated colors. It also increased its production of ceiling tile in a wide variety of sizes, shapes, and colors, to be used for the interior finish of theaters, restaurants, churches, hospitals, and business offices. A new commercial product, known as Tufflex, made from sulfite pulp and used for industrial cushioning or insulation, was developed in the late thirties. After the depression a fresh emphasis was put on experiments with nonbuilding products, for the years of reduced construction in the nation had taught Wood Conversion officials to diversify their output. The research work of the company was invaluable to all Weyerhaeuser firms, and the Timber Company began to make extensive use in its own plants of men trained by the Cloquet Company.[34] The pooling of development facilities, personnel, and results served to benefit both corporations.

The Timber Company also moved into the plywood field, for during the 1920's improvements in glues, lathes, driers, presses, and other manufacturing machinery had made plywood a desirable product. The depression, lack of the requisite managerial talent, and allocation of funds elsewhere, had delayed the entrance of Weyerhaeuser companies into this area. F. K. Weyerhaeuser had proposed such action as early as 1936. Three years later the Weyerhaeuser Timber Company's executive committee decided to buy into a plywood venture, the Washington Veneer Company. For $613,000 the Timber Company got not only 51 percent of the stock in the Veneer Company but also a connection with its subsidiary, the Springfield Plywood Corporation, of which Washington Veneer owned 60 percent of the shares. In January 1940, the acquisition was completed.[35]

Thus, in the thirties Weyerhaeuser firms entered into pulp, Pres-to-Log, and plywood production. And as recovery from the depression proceeded, they were shaping plans for venturing into other areas of wood utilization.

6

Yet recovery brought no lessening of government interference in the activities of lumbermen. If the New Deal legislation to expedite credit, build up construction indices, and increase purchasing power had aided the lumbermen, the recipients were only partly grateful. As for the Weyerhaeusers, Republican in politics and generally laissez faire in economics, much of the New Deal antagonized them. They had sampled the N.R.A. and found it unpalatable, and other aspects of the New Deal were equally repugnant.

The Secretary of Interior, Harold Ickes, was the special *bête noire* of lumbermen. His plans for increasing the national park area aroused the resentment of the industry, which suspected him of a desire to lock up trees while lumbermen grew old and wasted away. They opposed vigorously the increasing New Deal practice of transferring large areas of publicly owned stumpage from the Forest Service to Ickes's National Park Service. The Forest Service had granted cutting rights on a businesslike basis. In contrast, the National Park Service, following its policy of preserving its properties in natural state, warned loggers from its lands almost as sternly as the angel with the flaming sword before Eden. Miller Freeman could have spoken for most lumbermen when he wrote:

> Mr. Ickes, we wonder if since becoming Secretary of the Interior you have read the parable of the Talents and have considered Christ's view of hoarding, compared with utilization, expressed in this Parable? You may remember that the "wicked and slothful servant" only saved the talent with which he had been entrusted; but the "good and Faithful servant" employed his talents and increased them—put them to "multiple use," if you will.
>
> It seems to us that this parable applies to public servants and the public domain with singular directness.[36]

Two concepts of conservation were at issue: Should it save or serve? The Forest Service would permit the logging of mature timber on a sustained yield basis, prospecting and mining, the grazing of animals on specified pastures, and the utilization of water for power and irrigation. On the unreserved public domain the Department of Interior likewise allowed prospecting and mining, water-conservation projects, and grazing under state and federal laws, but it forbade logging; and in National Parks no logging railroads, donkey engines, or stumps were to mar the beauty of scenic areas.[37]

Moreover, the policy of the New Deal, to the regret of lumbermen, came to emphasize increasing public ownership of land. In 1935 Franklin D. Roosevelt had written the governor of Oregon: "It will be necessary . . . to restore to public ownership a great deal of forest land that unwisely was allowed to pass into private control." The Forest Service revived its early policy of lambasting lumbermen: "For three hundred years our forests have been chopped, burned, and depleted. Yet with care and forethought there seems no excuse for a timber famine of national proportions." It, too, recommended increased public ownership. And this policy was supported by the Joint Committee on Forestry, a committee that Congress created in 1938 and that presented its report in 1941.[38]

In the 1920's and early thirties many a lumberman, including Weyerhaeuser officials, had advocated increased state ownership of cutover land.[39] Then taxes were so high as to make private ownership prohibitive; private ownership meant high fire-protection expense, with the risk that a fire or insect blight might in a single swoop obliterate the entire investment. Lumbermen expected the government to let them log reforested lands when the timber on such areas was "ripe," and they wanted neither the risks nor the taxes.

In the mid-thirties, however, the idea of expanded public ownership became repellent to lumbermen. Some basic changes, including a revision of taxation, new methods of fire protection, and rising prices of stumpage, were making private reforestation feasible. Lumbermen's talk of increasing public ownership of cutover lands ceased, while the growth of public landownership continued steadily. In the decade 1937–1947 federal ownership increased throughout the United States: in the state of Washington from 32 to 35 percent; in Oregon from 46 to 53 percent; in Idaho from 58 to 64 percent; and in Nevada from 82 to 87 percent. The Weyerhaeusers regarded the trend with alarm.[40] F. K. Weyerhaeuser soon wrote: "One hundred years ago the policy of our government was to get land into the hands of the people, today it apparently is to get private lands into the hands of government."[41]

7

Not only did the federal policy of controlling production (under the N.R.A. Code) and of tightly controlling and increasing public lands (under the National Park Service and the Forest Service) turn lumbermen against the New Deal; antitrust policy under Thurman Arnold also gave offense. The relations of the industry with government entered a new and less happy stage.

In 1936 Congress passed the Robinson-Patman Act, amending the Clayton Antitrust Act. It made illegal any discriminations in prices where the effect might be substantially to lessen or destroy competition.

While the Act was aimed mainly at chain stores, the *West Coast Lumberman* predicted that it would affect lumbermen's activities, and the prophecy proved sound. In December, 1937, an attorney of the Federal Trade Commission called on the manager of the Weyerhaeuser Sales Company, H. T. Kendall, to investigate a complaint against the Weyerhaeuser Sales Company for violation of the Robinson-Patman Act. The allegation, he told the manager, was that it had made prices more favorable to one customer than to another. The lawyer requested copies of sixty invoices, which the Sales Company had photostated. He spent a day and a half questioning Sales Company employees. It soon appeared that the F.T.C. would make a wide investigation of the firm's activities; and Kendall instructed the salesmen that if Commission representatives called, they should decline to answer questions and refer the investigators to the St. Paul office.[42]

In February, 1938, Kendall, after giving full information to F.T.C. representatives, discerned that the investigation would center on the allowance of wholesale discounts. "Thank goodness," he wrote, for the Sales Company had been scrupulous in restricting wholesale discounts to bona fide wholesalers. In fact, Kendall believed that many outside companies had been loose in giving discounts and that an F.T.C. investigation would perform a useful work in making the rest of the industry conform to the rules.[43]

No complaint was filed against Weyerhaeuser companies at this time, but the investigations did not cease. In May, 1939, the Department of Justice issued a news release that applauded the antitrust laws and told of "the blighting encroachment of monopoly." Thurman Arnold two months later stated his desire to "de-N.R.A.-ise" the building industry and to restore free competition. The spotlight of antitrust investigation now turned on the lumber industry, as it had on many others, and the Weyerhaeuser companies came under attack in the process.[44] And Department of Justice policy changed sharply from the sanctioned production and price control of N.R.A. days.

Though lumbermen had disliked the controls of the N.R.A., they still had no taste for unrestrained, destructive competition in their depressed industry. After the demise of the Blue Eagle, Weyerhaeuser executives and other lumbermen naturally continued to be concerned about prices. Some men carelessly opened themselves to suspicion by loose statements, and the fact that lumbermen sometimes posted identical prices on identical products strongly suggested collusion, though proving it was another matter.

The Department of Justice found in the Weyerhaeuser Sales Company's letter files statements from salesmen declaring, "We know what our competition is doing." According to A. W. Clapp, the Department of Justice took this literally, following the dictionary definition of the word "know," when frequently a salesman only *thought* he knew and the next morning was surprised to find what his competitor had really done. The Department of Justice, Clapp asserted, also found letters calling a man a "chiseler," and took this to imply that he sold under some agreed price.[45]

After a careful accumulation of such suggestive evidence, in September, 1940, the Justice Department indicted five lumbermen's associations, 69 individual corporations, and 25 individuals under the Sherman Act. Among the 69 corporations were the Washington Veneer Company, the Weyerhaeuser Timber Company, the White River Lumber Company, and the Willapa Harbor Lumber Mills. Another indictment covered the Western Pine Association, 98 individual corporations and 28 individuals. Among the corporations included under this charge, which applied to the pine industry exclusively, were Boise Payette Lumber Company, Potlatch Forests, Inc., the Weyerhaeuser Timber Company, and the Weyerhaeuser Sales Company.

The charge in these cases was almost exactly the same, that from about October, 1935, the associations, companies, and individuals had combined and conspired unduly, unreasonably, directly, and oppressively to restrain trade. The indictments charged that the organizations and individuals in concert had violated the antitrust laws by curtailing production, fixing prices, and adopting arbitrary rules.[46]

When a consent decree was offered, the Weyerhaeuser Timber Company, like many other corporations in similar circumstances, signed it, though many executives, like F. K. Weyerhaeuser, then and later had the same doubts as Laird Bell. That outstanding lawyer wrote: "I dread this business of the consent decree. It is cheap and painless at the moment but I can't but think that it is dangerous in the long run."[47] The Company also paid a fine.

The West Coast Lumbermen's Association explained the industry's position: the signing of the consent decree was no admission of wrongdoing. It showed, the association claimed, only that the rules had been changed; since the passing of the N.R.A. uncertainty about the legality of business behavior had reigned supreme. The Western Pine Association similarly pointed out: "Only a few years ago during the N.R.A. of which the Lumber Code was part, lumber manufacturers were subject to compulsory regulation of production and establishment of fixed minimum prices. They were taught that in the public interest they must curtail production and sell their lumber at or above cost."[48]

Unquestionably, a government *volte-face* had taken place since the early days of the New Deal. Some lumbermen, and men in other industries too, undoubtedly had difficulty in adjusting their thinking after the Schechter decision; to them the government's position seemed ambiguous. And the lumbermen's files contained correspondence suggestive of business practices condemned by the F.T.C. before and after the N.R.A., especially with reference to collusive pricing.

The consent decree embarrassed Weyerhaeuser officials in minor ways. As Don Lawrence explained, the decree made "it inconvenient for us because we couldn't talk to our competitors about things of general character which might have been helpful to everyone." However, it had little effect on the fundamental operations of any of the companies.[49] Nevertheless, the shadow of the original indictment hangs over them, and more than one executive now believes the case could have been won had it been fought.

With the New Deal had come recovery from the depression, but also a revolution in the relations of industry and government. The federal authorities had invaded every branch of business to advise and regulate. In banking, in transportation, in public utilities, in the basic industries— coal, steel, and oil—in social welfare, in labor relations, and in farming the government played a more active role than ever before. The self-help view of Samuel Smiles, typical of early America, had by the thirties been put on a back shelf. Government regulation in the public interest had been generally accepted. It carried with it both penalties and advantages for everyone. While in general lumbermen disapproved of the new interventions, later many will be seen taking more favorable views of cooperation with "big" government.

NOTES

1. The phrase is used by W. E. Leuchtenburg, in *Perils of Prosperity*.
2. Peter A. Stone, *et al.*, "Economic Problems in the Lumber and Timber Industry," 164; A. C. Dixon, Appendix to Stone, 238; *WC Lbrmn.*, "West Coast Lumber Facts," 10; FEW Papers, Timber Conservation Board, "Memo for the Press, 1932."
3. Dixon, 247. Greeley's plan is to be compared with his views in 1917: see his *Some Public and Economic Aspects of the Lumber Industry*, 79– 80, wherein he also complains of fluctuation and instability, but states: "Joint control of the lumber cut by manufacturers would threaten the competitive character of the industry but offers little promise of overcoming its weakness."
4. WTC Papers, F. R. Titcomb to FKW, Oct. 2, 1931; FEW Papers, J. E. Long to I. N. Tate, Jan. 12, 1931; Dixon, 250.
5. FEW Papers, letters on mergers; Interview, Laird Bell, Sept. 10, 1954.
6. Dixon, 248; FEW Papers, Timber Conservation Board, "Memo for the Press, 1932." Dixon, 240–260, has splendid discussion of the many plans for production control.
7. *WC Lbrmn.*, "West Coast Lumber Facts," 10; WTC Statistical Files, "Net Lumber Production"; WTC Papers, F. S. Bell to F. R. Titcomb, Jan. 16, 1931; Titcomb to Wolf and Larabee, Nov. 5, 1931; FEW to Charles S. Keith, Sept. 10, 1931.
8. WTC Annual Report, 1932, pp. 1, 10; WTC Papers, E. W. Davis to Titcomb, Aug. 29, 1932; *WC Lbrmn.*, "West Coast Lumber Facts," 10.
9. WTC Papers, Titcomb to managers, Oct. 10, 1932; FKW to Mark Reed, Oct. 5, 1932.
10. Interviews; WTC Min. Bk. C, Jan. 19, 1933, 26.
11. WTC, Annual Report, 1932, 74 ff.
12. *Amer. Lbrmn.*, July 8, 1933, p. 1.
13. *Amer. Yrbk.*, 1933, p. 6; *Amer. Lbrmn.*, July 8, 1933, p. 38; Mason,

117; WSC-Potlatch Forest, Inc. Papers, Statement of A. W. Clapp on behalf of Weyerhaeuser and Shevlin Interests, Oct. 3, 1934.

14. FEW Papers, FEW to John Blodgett, June 14, 1933; FEW to John Blodgett, Aug. 2, 1933.

15. Mason, 119.

16. Mason, 122; WTC Papers, JPW, Jr., to F. S. Bell, Dec. 20, 1933; G. S. Long, Jr., Reminiscences; WTC Papers, A. W. Clapp to Davis T. Mason, Sept. 6, 1933; A. W. Clapp to John D. Tennant, Sept. 6, 1933.

17. WTC Papers, JPW, Jr., to FEW, Aug. 1, 1934; copy of protest in WTC Papers, JPW, Jr., file, 1934.

18. Ralph Macartney, Reminiscences.

19. Mason, 136–137, 145, 152.

20. *WC Lbrmn.*, Oct. 1934, 20; Nov. 1934, 5; Mason, 146; WSC-PFI Papers, Statement of A. W. Clapp on behalf of Weyerhaeuser and Shevlin Interests, Oct. 3, 1934, 2–3.

21. WTC, Annual Report, 1934; WTC Papers, Titcomb to FEW, March 27, 1935; *A. L. A. Schechter Corp.* v. *U.S.A.*, 295 U.S. 495 (1935).

22. Except Article X; see Macartney, Reminiscences, for example.

23. Phil Weyerhaeuser, Reminiscences.

24. WSC-PFI Papers, statement of A. W. Clapp on behalf of Weyerhaeuser and Shevlin interests, Oct. 3, 1934, 1, 4.

25. Correspondence, 1928, FEW Papers; WSC Papers, 40, D. A. Eitsert, "Lumbermen's Finance Corporation," etc.

26. WSC Papers, General Timber Service, annual reports, 1934, 1937.

27. WTC Papers.

28. Mill A was torn down in 1935 to provide a site for a sulfite plant.

29. WTC Papers, Clapp to Titcomb, July 5, 1932.

30. WTC Annual Report, 1934; WSC Papers, General Timber Service Audit, 1934.

31. FEW Papers, Titcomb to FEW, March 23, 1934, and FEW to Titcomb, March 29, 1934.

32. FEW Papers, Bell to FEW, July 3, 1934; WTC Papers, Exec. Com.

Mins., Oct. 31, 1934, 83; WTC Papers, JPW, Jr., to F. R. Titcomb, Nov. 7, 1934.

33. *Family Tree*, Jan. 1940, 1, 4.

34. FEW Papers, FEW to JPW, Jr., Feb. 6, 1934, and Feb. 12, 1934; interview with Edwin W. Davis: *Duluth Herald*, July 9, 1936; FEW Papers, FEW to F. S. Bell, H. H. Irvine, Laird Bell, A. W. Clapp, JPW, Jr., June 16, 1936; Wood Conversion Co., "Historical Information," 46; *Weyerhaeuser News*, Feb. 1951, pp. 8, 9.

35. WTC Papers, Exec. Com. Mins., Nov. 17, 1938; Dec. 26, 1939; JPW Papers, JPW, Jr., to H. H. Irvine, Nov. 22, 1939; *WC Lbrmn.*, Feb. 1940, p. 37.

36. Miller Freeman to Harold L. Ickes, Aug. 20, 1940, in *Franklin D. Roosevelt and Conservation*, II, 466.

37. Ickes to *The Mining World*, Aug. 7, 1940, in *ibid.*, II, 464.

38. FDR to Gov. Charles H. Martin, Aug. 12, 1935, *ibid.*, I, 410–411; *Report of Chief of Forest Service, 1938*; Greeley, *Forests and Men*, 214; *Forest Lands of the United States. Report of the Joint Committee on Forestry*, 77th Cong., 1st Sess. Washington, 1941.

39. For example, address of G. S. Long, *Amer. Lbrmn.*, July 29, 1922, pp. 1, 36–37.

40. F. K. Weyerhaeuser, "Of Trees and Men," *Weyerhaeuser News*, June, 1952, p. 21.

41. *Ibid.* As letters at the time indicate, F. K. Weyerhaeuser's sentiment could easily have been expressed in the late thirties.

42. HTK Papers, Harry T. Kendall to FKW, Dec. 22, 1937; Kendall to Morris, Mulrooney, Peabody, Lawrence, Dec. 27, 1937.

43. HTK Papers, Kendall to the Nicola, Stone & Myers Co., Cleveland, Feb. 11, 1938.

44. HTK Papers, copy of release, May 19, 1939; Compton to James McNary, July 27, 1939; see also U.S. Dept. of Justice, *Report of Asst.*

Atty.-General Thurman Arnold, 1939.

45. Lawrence, Reminiscences; HTK Papers, A. W. Clapp to E. J. Fountain, Jan. 3, 1941.

46. WTC Papers, Indictments of West Coast Lbrmn.'s Association and Western Pine Association in the District Court of the United States for the Southern District of California, Central Division, Sept., 1940, term.

47. WTC Papers, Laird Bell to JPW, Jr., Oct. 9, 1940; FKW to the authors, Sept. 19, 1958.

48. WTC Annual Report, 1940, 5; *WC Lbrmn.*, May, 1941, p. 50; Nov. 1940, p. 21.

49. Lawrence, Reminiscences.

XXIV

Lumbermen in World War II

WHEN German tanks smashed into Poland on September 1, 1939, the period of agonizing appeasement which had preceded that event came to an end. England, France, Australia, Canada, New Zealand, and South Africa quickly followed one another in declaring war. Professing a firm adherence to peace, President Roosevelt began to expand the long-neglected military capacities of the nation. On both sides of the Atlantic many people, including some in the forest-products industry, thought that inevitably the United States would be involved.

Most leading lumbermen accepted this possibility and forecast a discouraging period for their camps and mills. "Today," wrote A. Fletcher Marsh of the Marsh & Truman Lumber Company on September 6, 1939, "the lumber industry does not produce a 'critical' commodity and is not generally regarded as manufacturing a 'vital' commodity." He explained that "the airplane demand of 1917–1918 for wood is gone, and there will be no wooden shipbuilding program for the next war." He doubted if even a call for boxes and crates was certain, as these might be replaced by substitutes. He was joined in this appraisal by Wilson Compton, Secretary-Manager of the National Lumber Manufacturers' Association, who agreed that "lumber is not a war industry."[1]

These pessimistic predictions were not to prove valid. The industry's share in the mobilization of American resources, the demands to be made upon it, and the unexpected course of its price curve during hostilities would all present a very different picture to that painted by the experts in 1939.

The first indication of the true war role of the lumber industry came when the British government early in 1940 placed with the Weyerhaeuser Timber Company a large order for aircraft lumber. Forty-one types of British planes called for wooden parts; Britain could not fill the requirements, and the mills of Longview hummed as parts for Hurricane fighters and Mosquito bombers were fashioned there.

But with its large natural resources, the American government was not inclined to concern itself about lumber. Theoretically this industry would be dealt with by the Advisory Commission of the Council of National Defense, formed during World War I and revived in May, 1940. Although its Industrial Materials Division included a lumber group, the Council foresaw no shortage of wood products, nor did the pulp and paper group in the same division. The Army and Navy Munitions Board prescribed for the country's needs, listing fourteen *strategic* and fifteen *critical* materials in two categories—the first embracing products that must be procured wholly or in part outside of the United States. Wood appeared on neither list. "Forest products," later remarked a forester, "somehow were regarded as a great reservoir of material which could be drawn upon almost at will."[2]

Nonetheless it was clearly evident that there would be government orders for wood. To report from Washington on plans for the use of lumber, the Weyerhaeuser Sales Company in June, 1940, selected John Philip Boyd, until then in charge of industrial and retail sales in the Chicago area. He was also to assist government departments with their specifications in order that Washington would get the most for its money and at the same time have the largest available sources of supply.

The capable Boyd found his task onerous. By September the federal government had become the largest buyer of lumber in the United States. That month it placed an order for two billion feet to be used in the construction of cantonments. While southern producers furnished most of this wood—as they had for cantonments in the First World War—the Weyerhaeuser Sales Company received a contract for more than fifty million feet. Additional orders followed rapidly.

Even in September, Harry T. Kendall, Manager of the Weyerhaeuser Sales Company, wired a prospective customer, "Our mills are now hopelessly oversold for long period." When the customer persisted, Kendall responded laconically, "Have orders for all we can ship balance of year."[3]

The size of the demands startled Sales Company officials, but it was the disorganized federal purchasing program that truly complicated the task of the Washington representative. Each civilian agency and each branch of the armed services bought separately. When Wilson Compton, Secretary-Manager of the National Lumber Manufacturers Association, proposed a complete revision of the federal purchasing program, his suggestions were heartily endorsed by Weyerhaeuser executives. Compton advocated a government purchasing agency, federal stockpiles of lumber to be drawn upon in emergencies, and the elimination of strict specifications on the wartime lumber purchases. Not one of these proposals was immediately adopted. Government units could stockpile only materials defined as critical and strategic; since lumber was neither, buying continued to be haphazard. Relaxation of specifications was also a matter for the future.[4]

If the government was not ready to coordinate the purchase of lumber, that fact did not hinder Weyerhaeuser officials from organizing their own sales routines. In September, 1940, they opened a sales office in Washington, with Boyd in charge. Thence all inquiries from federal agencies on stocks and prices could be teletyped simultaneously to Sales Company offices in Tacoma, Spokane, and St. Paul—the last-named city controlling activities throughout the country.

Similarly, while the government showed no interest in accumulating inventories for emergencies, Weyerhaeuser agents, whenever a slackening of demand permitted it, made the building of special reserves a part of their policy. In every important area their mills increased supplies of lumber in anticipation of military demands. Partly through foresight and partly through the need to maintain the volume of shipments from the mills, the Timber Company also stocked the Eastern Yards during 1940 and 1941. Its eight-ship fleet was soon busy carrying lumber by way of the Panama Canal to depots at Baltimore, Newark, and Portsmouth.

Thus the Pacific Coast and Idaho companies prepared for government needs. But since it was uncertain that orders would continue at the September volume, the companies likewise acted to encourage the purchasing of wood rather than wood substitutes. With this in mind, and to remove, if possible, the threat of federal pegging of prices, in 1940 the Sales Company announced that it would "freeze" its current quotations on fir and hemlock for cantonment construction; and held them until March, 1941. At the same time, the Sales Company kept its prices well under the top market figure, advancing them only when they were so far below the market level as to have no effect upon it. Boyd followed this policy in his dealing with federal agencies, selling at figures definitely lower than those commonly quoted in the trade. The volume of business showed a steady increase.[5]

As a result of the expanded activity, the year 1940 set a record, the net value of Sales Company's shipments for both government and nongovernment uses totaling $49,059,014. Thus, despite labor troubles at Snoqualmie and Everett and despite the indictment of the Weyerhaeuser Timber Company, Potlatch Forests, Boise Payette Lumber Company, and the Weyerhaeuser Sales Company for violation of the antitrust laws, noted earlier, the year had been profitable for all these companies.

How long would the scarcity of wood continue? Weyerhaeuser officials wondered, for they retained their earlier beliefs that this war of oil,
steel, and aluminum would have little need for wood. "Our best judgment," wrote Harry T. Kendall in December, 1940, "is that we should
consider each week as it comes as the last week of good business. Inasmuch
as we have had a sharp advance we shall have a sharp decline which may
carry us below the 1938 lows."[6]

2

During 1941 the uncertainty about the future continued; and as
Kendall wrote at its close, it was "one of the most exciting and at times
the most puzzling years of a business lifetime." It was marked by alternating elation and gloom, by unprecedented war orders and early government restrictions, by labor difficulties and the reconciliation of labor and
management, by good prices and sudden decline.

The year began with a spate of business activity. In January alone
Weyerhaeuser lumber went on government orders to Portland Airport,
Puget Sound Navy Yard, Camp Grant, Wright Air Field, Fort Lewis,
Camp Murray, and at least a half-dozen other military installations.[7] Still
acting without coordination, government representatives made their purchases with astonishing inefficiency. When Senator Harry S. Truman in a
1942 Senate investigation of the defense program questioned Clarence L.
Forsling, assistant chief of the Forest Service, he emphasized the unhappy
effects of this haphazard buying. "There was plenty of waste," he insisted.[8]
Because lumber was urgently needed for the cantonments, the government had bought in a frenzy and without any overall program.

Lumber continued to be purchased in uncoordinated fashion, not
only for camps but for so many other projects that the total demand was
unexpectedly heavy. To no small extent the shortages stemmed from the
fact that wood had been labeled neither critical nor strategic. Thus, in
Washington, when construction engineers of the Office of Production
Management (successor to the National Defense Advisory Commission)
prepared their designs for various installations, they made free use of
wood.[9] Overnight, on the Mare Island Navy Yard site near San Francisco,
a new city of 20,000 residents sprang up in 1941. Here, an architectural
highlight of the year was to be seen in the Federal Works Agency's wood-
frame prefabricated buildings, a glowing achievement of the designer,
W. W. Wurster. For these prefabricated structures, as well as for others,
Weyerhaeuser firms provided wood.

In prefabricated buildings and elsewhere, wooden beams began to
replace steel. Wood was found satisfactory for hangar construction as well
as for factories, warehouses, and all types of housing for defense workers.

Boxes and crates to ship supplies now began to absorb the cheaper grades of wood, while pontoon lumber came into new demand. As metals became scarcer, veneers and plywood were substituted in American as well as English aircraft; the Timber Company, which had just entered the plywood field, was ready to supply this need. Its officials were rapidly discovering almost unlimited opportunities for product development in wood. Thus, when the government's large cantonment orders were filled in March, 1941, the market remained active, with the government continuing as "*the* customer for West Coast *woods*."[10]

In the spring of 1941 federal officials acted to liberalize the lumber specifications. Permitting the use of a wider range of species, lower grades, and a higher moisture content, Washington showed its need for larger quantities of wood. The relaxation in specifications was the first step in the federal implementation of Compton's suggestions.[11] When the government placed its orders, the Weyerhaeuser Timber Company had stocks to fill them at once, since normally its mills carried sufficient logs for sixty days' operations. Many independent mills carried no inventory, and asked the Timber Company to sell them lumber. It reaped the benefit of its large accumulations.[12]

Meanwhile, the Weyerhaeuser companies were encountering problems in labor relations. In the spring of 1941, costly strikes swept the steel, chemical, and aircraft plants, and the general unrest spread to the lumber industry. Although labor difficulties in the camps and mills never assumed the proportions they had reached during World War I, they sprang from the same source; when the companies prospered, the unions felt that the men too should profit. The unions demanded higher wages and more benefits. A strike at Snoqualmie, which had an A.F. of L. union, was settled in April. In May, an industry-wide lumber strike sponsored by the C.I.O. union in the Pacific Northwest stopped work in 52 plants, among them the Weyerhaeuser mills at Everett and the White River Lumber Company. Elsewhere—at Longview and Klamath, for example—no stoppage occurred, but labor problems existed, chiefly in the form of jurisdictional disputes. One of these at Willapa Harbor resulted in a brief shutdown. In Idaho, as in Washington, management found that labor relations involved a large expenditure of time and effort, though no strikes occurred in the former state.

Events soon stabilized the labor situation. When Germany attacked Russia in June, the C.I.O. woodworkers' union, which had heretofore opposed the war, reversed its position. World War II saw no I.W.W., and all organized labor supported the Allies' cause. While the industry experienced a few spontaneous walkouts, many demands for higher wages, and a number of jurisdictional disputes, the halting of production by strikes, fairly common in World War I, became a rarity.[13]

When in July and August, 1941, government orders soared to new peaks and British and Russian Lend-Lease requirements were urgent, Phil Weyerhaeuser reported to his uncle that Willapa Harbor Lumber Mills, Longview, and Everett were already, and Snoqualmie Falls very shortly would be, running on Saturday, while the White River Lumber Company was organizing a second shift. Frederick E. Weyerhaeuser approved the extension of operating time, giving his endorsement not only because it was needed to fill government requirements but also because it might discourage new and perhaps opportunistic and temporary lumber enterprises.[14]

Yet just as overtime production gathered momentum and the output of lumber reached new heights, suddenly the market reversed itself. The end of September found it headed for shipwreck, with prices declining precipitously. The cause was evident. To conserve vital metals, the Supply, Priorities, and Allocations Board in that month drastically curtailed building construction and in October prohibited any nonessential public or private construction under Order L-41. These measures were intended to save metals, not lumber, but they contributed to a drop of 24 percent in building in the eastern states between September and December, 1941, with consequent impact on lumber sales.

The industry now received its first taste of price controls. In the fall of 1941 the Office of Price Administration fixed the ceiling prices on Douglas fir lumber, peeler logs, plywood, and doors. The Weyerhaeusers believed that the fir price ceilings averaged about $3 per thousand feet under the existing price levels but approximately $3 per thousand over Weyerhaeuser prices. On the other hand, the *West Coast Lumberman* thought that most of the ceilings were near market prices. In any case, by fall the lumber industry was already under limited but specific wartime regulations.

With the market declining in September and government restrictions in effect, lumbermen found the outlook discouraging. In October log prices stiffened, but, though there were still orders, November was a bad month. The seller's market that had existed from January to October disappeared as government demands became fewer. The business activity of the summer months seemed a thing of the past.[15]

Then, on December 7th came the Japanese bombing of Pearl Harbor, and America was in the war. Overnight the government plunged into a frenzy of buying. Lumber was needed as never before, and prices rallied quickly and strongly. A Weyerhaeuser official on the West Coast replied to an army officer's phone call about an urgent order:

"Yes? Lumber for dispersal revetments? You need lots of 3x12x18's? Hold the wire until I see what we have on hand. . . . We've got 118,000 feet in the yard. . . . We'll have it ready for you. No, you can't back your trucks right up to the piles. We'll have to bring it out to loading points on our narrow gauge railroad. But you can start your trucks. We'll have it ready for you."

And they did—in ninety minutes.

This was but one of the innumerable long-distance emergency telephone calls. After Pearl Harbor lumber orders came in torrents. Even the Weyerhaeuser steamships were recruited when the War Shipping Board commandeered the entire fleet. As the year ended, the industry had supplied Washington with 24,000,000,000 feet of wood, about 73 percent of the total national consumption. So numerous were the war orders that the Weyerhaeuser Timber Company could unreservedly report, "War dominated our activities in 1941."[16]

3

For a time Weyerhaeuser marketers refrained from furnishing a variety of grades when only a specific grade was required. "But as the offers by Government agencies to purchase wide ranges of grades, and frequently wide ranges of sizes . . . became more and more common at the auctions and in private negotiations, we [the Weyerhaeuser Sales Company] began to take some business of this character."[17]

Orders for airplane lumber, ship timber, prefabricated wood products, wood for construction purposes, and wood for boxing and crating poured into company offices. Drawing on the experience of World War I, the government at first requested Sitka spruce for airplanes, but the supply soon proved utterly inadequate. W. B. Greeley described both the futile pursuit and the solution: "We have searched our timber for the right type of log; we have worked out the problem of specification with the Forest Products Laboratory; we have been able to get additional species of timber included in the airplane specifications." Douglas fir, West Coast hemlock, and a new species, Noble fir, were approved. With the government's acceptance of these woods the Weyerhaeuser Timber Company took the industry leadership in producing aircraft materials.

Three stands of Noble fir were found on the Longview holding, none accessible to existing railroad facilities. But by extending railroads and utilizing skyline skidder systems and caterpillar tractors, the loggers reached out into the forests and obtained the wood. At Longview, a fourth Weyerhaeuser mill was opened, especially designed for the processing of aircraft lumber. Logs were cut into cants at the other three Longview mills; then selected stock went to the new mill to be sawed into the material needed by the factories fabricating airplanes and parts. The new so-called "Tiffany" mill handled only specialty items.

Wartime shortages in building materials created a continued interest in prefabricated structures. In response, the Timber Company built five prefabrication plants; two on the West Coast, at Everett and Longview, and the other three at the Distributing Yards in Newark, Baltimore, and Portsmouth. These five filled the wartime demand for roof trusses, airplane hangars, gun towers, bridges, drydocks, and a hundred other vital prefabricated timber items—at the rate of a million feet of prefabricated timber weekly. Meanwhile, the Navy called for large timbers for ships, and all the military services required boxing and crating. Potlatch Forests, Inc., near the site of Camp Farragut, shipped more lumber to it than any other company. All the buildings in this naval training station were of wood. In fact, every Weyerhaeuser mill was in 1942 cutting large war orders.[18]

The activities of the Sales Company office in St. Paul were greater than ever before. With business already booming, the company received a telephone call from the War Department on Sunday, April 9th. Could the Sales Company secure 15,000,000 feet of lumber for *immediate delivery?* The proposed order was for cantonment needs in the West. That same Sunday afternoon the company agreed to undertake the task. To fill the mammoth order, its salesmen turned buyers. Explaining the government need and emphasizing the emergency, it held auctions in crucial areas at which retailers bid on such amounts of lumber as they could furnish. (These were really auctions in reverse, in that the retailers were bidding to sell and not to buy materials.)

This special government demand was soon filled, some deliveries being completed in May, the rest in June. Eventually the government purchased 35,849,000 feet for $2,009,501. The records show that the Sales Company's net profit was $9,038. It was with a sigh of relief that D. H. Bartlett would write to Kendall in June, "Personally, I have a very strong feeling of satisfaction and feel that it has been a job worth doing and that it has been fairly well done." The War Department agreed: "We want you to know that the spirit of cooperation and, at times, of sacrifice in attending to our needs at fair and equitable prices is thoroughly recognized and appreciated."[19]

As the government demands for lumber continued heavy, many began to ask if the lumber would last. Was the supply really unlimited?

4

In the spring of 1942, Washington officials, for the first time, became officially aware that lumber might become scarce. From the logging to the milling, from the purchasing to the pricing, from the transporting to the using, lumber and lumber products now came to be subjected to a maze of governmental regulations. The first major restriction came when War

Production Board Ruling L-121, May 13, 1942, put under tight proscription the distribution of softwood construction lumber for nonmilitary use —timbers, framing, dimension, drop siding, and flooring. Amended on July 10th and superseded on August 27th, order L-121 was a forecast of regulations to follow. Detailed priority ratings on lumber and controls on specific grades were introduced with Conservation Order M-208, which replaced L-121. Under this ruling, the Weyerhaeusers had to renegotiate all their orders, screening out those that did not have preference ratings and giving top priorities to military necessities.

Further price ceilings were imposed in 1942, and those in existence were adjusted, amended, and supplemented. An example appears in Regulation MPR-26 on Douglas fir lumber, which was not only rewritten to conform with the Emergency Price Control Act of 1942 but was also amended eleven times during 1942 to advance the prices on boards and dimension. The price listings on wood products filled a book which O.P.A. administrator Paul Porter once compared in bulk to a Sears, Roebuck catalog.

One federal directive was destined to have long-range value. To cope with the car shortage, the Office of Defense Transportation in 1942 issued a "Maximum Loading Order." Lumbermen kept extremely accurate accounts of the weights of lumber loaded, and the industry learned precisely how much of what kind of lumber could be loaded in various types of railroad cars—a point of controversy for decades. Records show that the Weyerhaeusers loaded more lumber per car than the average of the industry.

With the rapid crescendo of administrative restrictions on priorities, grades, prices, and loading, lumbermen's correspondence turned into a coded set of hieroglyphics, a "seemingly endless parade of rules and regulations."[20] But all the headaches were not confined to lumbermen. Ferdinand Eberstadt, chairman of the Army and Navy Munitions Board, asked F. K. Weyerhaeuser for advice on the government's dilemmas in coping with the nation's lumber needs and requested him to head for the Board a program to promote the cooperation of the lumber industry. Weyerhaeuser refused, feeling that his competitors might resent his assuming this role, but finally recommended J. P. Boyd, whom Eberstadt in the late summer of 1942 appointed chairman of the lumber committee of the Army and Navy Munitions Board. Boyd, leaving the Sales Company, became director of the Lumber and Lumber Products Division of the War Production Board in January, 1943. Weyerhaeuser also recommended that purchasing for the Army, Navy, and other branches of the services should be centralized. It will be recalled that Wilson Compton had proposed centralization nearly two years earlier; now that lumber was in high demand, the suggestion no longer fell on deaf ears.[21]

Under the auspices of the United States Engineers, a Central Procurement Agency promptly took charge of straightening out the tangled situation. Colonel F. G. Sherrill headed it, working in close cooperation with the Lumber and Lumber Products Division of the War Production Board. A Washington official later in 1942 remarked that the new agency "did more to bring about good feeling between the Army and Navy and other armed services than any other one thing that has happened since the outset of the war," a statement which F. K. Weyerhaeuser fully endorsed. Coordination in lumber procurement for the armed services had finally been achieved.[22] However, the unification of purchasing for civilian agencies was still two years distant.

The Central Procurement Agency found that the large number of detailed orders poured in upon sawmills forced them to slow down production. It would be far more efficient for the mills to accumulate all sizes and stockpile them. Specific needs could then be drawn from the stockpiles, and lumber could be remanufactured according to government requirements. This, of course, was what lumbermen had said for a long time. So effective was the reform that by October, 1942, some mills began to complain that the government was stockpiling too much![23]

To accelerate production, the Forest Service suggested that federal money be spent to construct new mills, build access roads, assist in the cutting of small farm woodlots, and support a "procurement-production-sale" program to help small mills find markets, credit, and transportation. Weyerhaeuser officials opposed aid to the small mills: the program, they argued, would take supplies and equipment away from existing mills, which already found themselves unable to obtain the materials required for maximum production, and the small mills would be wasteful of manpower and timber resources. Weyerhaeuser officials insisted that the need was not for new subsidized mills but for higher priorities to alleviate the shortage of tires and machinery that retarded capacity output and for measures to prevent the dispersion of manpower from the woods and existing mills. The Committee on Forest Conservation of the National Lumber Manufacturers Association, under George F. Jewett, lobbied against the Forest Service proposal to aid small mills, and the bill was defeated. Later, however, when production difficulties became really serious, Congress voted such aid.

In 1942 Congress did adopt legislation enabling existing mills to obtain logs more easily. In June it passed the Access Roads Act, and by February 1943, projects for 554 miles of access roads had been approved under the government's lumber program.[24] Federal agencies also gave some attention to the shortage of facilities in the logging camps and sawmills and took remedial measures.[25]

But even more crucial were the difficulties arising from the drift of men away from the lumber industry. The complaint of Boise Payette was typical. "We have lost about 175 men of our Emmett crew alone and proportionately about the same from our woods crew and the Council mill; some of them through the draft, but most of them have left without warning to secure jobs in defense construction work and defense industries where much higher wages are paid," wrote S. G. Moon in September, 1942. The high wage scales in the shipyards and aircraft factories attracted lumber workers, and the draft took men skilled in operating heavy and hazardous logging and sawmill equipment. Before 1942 ended, more than 3,100 employees of the Weyerhaeuser operating units and subsidiaries were in uniform. More were still to go.

Obviously the manpower problem demanded prompt attention. Abe Fortas, Harold Ickes's undersecretary, reported to the Secretary of the Interior: "The timber supply and mill capacity are adequate to meet the present unprecedented demand for lumber. However, the skilled labor, and in some areas the unskilled labor, available to convert standing timber into logs and lumber is inadequate." In September, 1942, the War Manpower Commission classified the major forest industries as essential, and designated lumber as the "number one manpower problem" in the western states. To keep workers in the industry, Paul V. McNutt, the chairman of this commission, issued the so-called "freeze order," requiring workers who quit and who wanted to be rehired to show a separation certificate from the United States Employment Service. This move had a mixed effect: when it was announced nearly every operation lost at once some men who did not want to be tied by red tape; it also discouraged some new men from coming into the industry; but for the men who remained the order substantially reduced the turnover.

The War Manpower Commission also publicized the need for loggers. Donald Nelson, chairman of the War Production Board, instructed the lumber industry to adopt a 48-hour week, wherever possible: by November, about 60 percent of the logging operations and 40 percent of the sawmills were on that basis. From the Selective Service Board came Occupation Bulletin No. 19, which likewise attempted to improve the situation by providing draft deferment eligibility to workers in forestry, logging, and lumbering. Meanwhile, the War Labor Board endorsed substantial wage increases.

As these government agencies acted to ease the shortage, the lumber industry took steps on its own behalf. As early as May, 1942, Potlatch asked for draft exemptions for key employees, for it had lost 500 men to the Armed Forces and was running short. The draft board complied with its request, deferring such skilled men as log sawyers, machine operators, and maintenance men. Other Weyerhaeuser companies made similar requests of local boards.

Lumbermen objected to running their operations overtime. Wilson Compton explained that "the ceiling prices fixed on lumber are not geared to overtime work and overtime pay; and there is, therefore, a gap between prices predicated on straight time and the increased cost of overtime production." Nonetheless, longer hours became increasingly common in Weyerhaeuser operations. Snoqualmie Falls started a 48-hour week in April, 1942; Potlatch in November, 1942, initiated overtime pay for Saturdays and holidays; and the Weyerhaeuser Timber Company mills soon adopted the longer week. So in 1943 did Boise Payette, at the order of the War Manpower Commission.[26]

The Weyerhaeuser logging operations and sawmills recruited as labor women, old men, teen-agers, interned Italian seamen, physically disabled men, malaria convalescents, and even two college professors. Women made the greatest contribution. "If the mill had not been able to use women in many jobs hitherto thought impossible for women to hold, it is difficult to see how they could have operated at all," wrote Harry Kendall in the Weyerhaeuser Sales Company Annual Report for 1942. Clad in slacks, low-heeled shoes, and short-sleeved blouses, "lumberettes" controlled the bull chain that brought the logs up into the mill, worked in planing mills, tallied the green lumber before it went to further manufacturing processes, and tested aircraft stock to determine fiber length and strength. These represented only a few of their jobs.

But even with the influx of women, labor remained short.[27] Women, while useful in the mills, could not do most outdoor work in the logging camps, which required men. Frequent absenteeism both in the camps and mills presented problems, and high wage demands added to the difficulties of management. Average wages in Weyerhaeuser operations rose from 81.5 cents per hour in 1940 to 91.5 cents in 1941 to $1.089 in 1943; they would continue to spiral upward. Labor was in a good bargaining position, since the call for lumber was great and the labor supply limited.

5

In the later stages of the war lumber was most in demand for packaging. In 1941 the country used 5½ billion feet of lumber for boxing and crating; by 1943 the figure had risen to 15½ billion. Powder, TNT, ammunition shells, and food needed careful protection. In fact, "everything that goes overseas which is in any way made of metal," as John Philip Boyd reported, had to "be tightly boxed, not boxed like it is for domestic shipment but completely boxed to protect it from the salt air. . . . Lumbermen found that in boxing and crating . . . wood has not even a close competitor."

For packaging, poor logs that had previously been wasted could be salvaged. At Longview "1943 was the first year," wrote manager Harry Morgan later, "that we began to clean up our forests of low-grade logs." Similarly at Potlatch, mixed species—red fir, larch, white fir, and cedar—were cut and used for war purposes, while the high-grade white pine stands were logged unselectively to fill the heavy demand.[28]

The call for airplane lumber was heavy in 1943, declined slightly in 1944, then rose strongly because of needs in the Pacific Theater. Islands bared of human habitations had to rehouse not only their own inhabitants but also the occupying Americans. At many overseas bases construction was chiefly or even entirely of wood. Because of their large capacity, Weyerhaeuser firms could fill orders that smaller companies found impossible. Special commendation went to Longview, which had the honor to be the first lumber plant to receive an Army-Navy "E" for patriotic contributions. Willapa also received an Army-Navy award.[29]

Already in 1942 the nation showed a small decrease in estimated softwood production from the 1941 level: 29.51 as against 29.87 billion feet. The figure sank still further in 1943, when softwood production fell to about 26.9 billion feet. Although in 1942 the output of Weyerhaeuser mills did not reflect the national decline—on the contrary, the total production of Weyerhaeuser Timber Company mills rose from 1.21 billion feet in 1941 to 1.34 billion feet in 1942—in 1943 the Timber Company's production fell to 1.24 billion feet. For the rest of the war nothing could prevent a continuing decline in both national and Weyerhaeuser figures. By 1944 national softwood production had slumped to 25.16 billion feet, and the Timber Company production was down to about 1.15 billion.[30]

The reasons for the fall were listed in 1944 by the Chief Forester as shortages of standing timber, labor, and equipment. The O.P.A. price levels were not a factor, for when the demand for boards and dimension increased, the O.P.A. raised its prices. The Secretary of Agriculture and the Chief of the Forest Service might twit lumbermen on the "destructive cutting practices in the past that had depleted forest resources," but, in the main, manpower and equipment shortages were responsible for the declining output.

The drift away from the mills and woods continued. By the end of 1944, the loss of manpower in the industry since 1942 stood at 23 percent. The Selective Service Boards had quotas to fill. The United States Employment Service recruited men from the industry for the shipyards and other war work. Not until near the end of the war did the War Manpower Commission give sawmills and logging operations a priority rating that would permit them to hire men.[31]

The Weyerhaeuser companies at the end of 1943 had 4,477 men in uniform, and in 1944 they lost 486 more to military service.[32] Moreover, the government aggravated the situation in the logging camps when it tried to impose short rations on lumberjacks. In July, 1943, a work stoppage occurred at Potlatch Forests, Inc.; 64 of the 115 men employed at Camp No. 40 signed a petition complaining of the food. They wanted less attention to fish, strawberries, and raspberries, and more to beefsteak. E. C. Rettig, assistant manager, went to Spokane to discuss the matter with the O.P.A. administrator. He took some A.F. of L. men with him. But he got nowhere. The O.P.A. allocated the same ration points for logging camps as for city mills and factories. Finally, in response to repeated complaints, the government agency sent a nutrition expert to a Puget Sound camp. He went into the woods, worked "his own shifts with a double-bitted ax and cross-cut saw," and after ten days reported that the life of a logger was totally different from that of a factory worker: the O.P.A. rations were then revised.

If labor ranked as the major cause of reduced production, inadequate equipment did not lag far behind. As the war progressed, new machines became ever harder to obtain. To replace worn-out parts became impossible. An acute shortage existed in equipment to clear trails and haul logs. The heavy trucks and tractors required for logging operations were the very type urgently needed by the Armed Forces. Rubber tires were at a premium, the demand far exceeding the supply. R. V. Clute, in the W.S.C. Washington, D.C., office during the war, recalls that since the associated companies gave full cooperation in the war effort, the governmental agencies were eager to reciprocate, and there were "very few" problems in getting equipment and supplies. Correspondence in company files does not bear out this recollection; the mounting complaints of threadbare tires and rundown equipment indicate that serious problems existed. But there is also indication that in some cases Weyerhaeuser companies received preferences in new equipment, although as Clute himself reports, "it required constant contact and battle to get all the evidence up on the table so that somebody could make a decision as to whether Weyerhaeuser was going to get it [a piece of equipment] or who was going to get whatever was available at the moment."[33]

Laird Bell, a director of the Weyerhaeuser Timber Company, was summoned to Washington early in 1944 by the Navy Price Adjustment Board for six months' service. He watched the cases on war contracts pass before the committee; then he wrote Phil Weyerhaeuser: "I found that we were allowing around eleven and twelve percent profit on adjusted sales to good performers pretty regularly, [and] I began to feel that you had been harshly treated with your 10%." Bell, however, concluded of the Timber Company: "I take it therefore that probably once more you paid some penalty for being big and prosperous."

The O.P.A. was another government agency that turned to lumbermen for advice. Weyerhaeuser officials were members of the committee on Inland Empire woods, but not on coast woods. In coastal lumbering the company policy was to keep prices down, while the industry as a whole wanted to raise them. The W.T.C. felt that because its policy differed from that of other lumbermen, its officials should not serve on this advisory committee.[34]

The growth of government controls was correlated with the decline of lumber supplies. By 1944, when controls were both numerous and complex, Kendall circulated a War Production Board bulletin that stated: lumber has "become one of our most critical materials." In this year it was "chief of the tight materials"—more critical than steel. Reversing the previous pattern, steel now was used *instead* of wood in Army cars, truck bodies, railroad cars, and furniture! Both logging and lumber went on the Production Urgency List.

For the first time, on March 22, 1944, the War Production Board initiated comprehensive lumber control with Order L-335, the new plan going into operation in the third quarter of 1944. The purchasing for the Army, Navy, Air Force, and Coastal Services had been coordinated since mid-1942, but not until now had the War Production Board itself become alerted to distribution problems and a similar reorganization occurred in the procurement procedures of the civilian agencies. Thus, all the Wilson Compton suggestions made four years earlier had been put into practice: for two years the government had been stockpiling and granting lenient specifications on lumber; now it finally centralized all its purchasing.

From the last quarter of 1944, through the spring of 1945, lumber controls remained very rigid. Early in 1945, when V-E Day seemed close, the War Production Board's Committee on Demobilization of Controls After Victory in Europe recommended "the retention of orders on many nonmetal products, such as textiles, lumber, containers, and certain chemicals, until a more satisfactory supply-demand position prevailed" and also "the retention of general controls over construction and equipment, because of the shortage of lumber." This was a far cry from the earlier War Production Board view that lumber was an inexhaustible product. By the time victory came in 1945, lumber had attained recognition as a commodity more precious than steel and almost as vital to victory as oil.[35]

6

The government controls on lumber were removed slowly. Although the War Production Board voided a large number of limitations in the weeks after V-E Day, May 5th, the orders affecting lumber were all retained. But by the end of June, the situation looked more promising.

Because the Army had sent no wood to Europe since April, controls were relaxed. The sharp decline in the demand for lumber for military purposes continued; and immediately after V-J Day August 14th, the War Production Board drastically revised lumber control Order L-335. Now any lumber supplier could "sell any kind of lumber to any person on unrated orders provided that the sale did not interfere with the filling of rated orders." This meant a virtual revocation of the order; and its actual demise followed on September 30th. With the annulment of Order L-41 on October 15th, the government removed all limits on new construction; except for price controls, lumbermen were now free.

Directly after V-J Day, the government canceled more than 100,000 contracts. Overnight orders for over $23,000,000,000 in war goods became null and void. However, lumbermen still had markets, for civilians flooded the Sales Company offices with innumerable requests.[36]

With war over, mills returned to the 40-hour week. Peace brought an end to the quasi-peaceful labor relations of wartime. Potlatch began to have labor difficulties, with a major and prolonged strike tying up everything except the sawmill. The employees at Klamath struck in August. Like the other Weyerhaeuser Timber Company mills, with the exception of Snoqualmie Falls, Klamath had a C.I.O. union. After a seven-week stoppage, the strike terminated with a compromise. Meanwhile, the A.F. of L. unions everywhere in the pine and fir region of the West (omitting California) struck for wage increases. Snoqualmie Falls was the only Weyerhaeuser mill directly affected, and it was shut down fully ten weeks. By October, strikes had interrupted production in the Douglas fir area, bringing that region's production to about 34 percent of the October, 1944, level.

The A.F. of L. won part of its demands, securing a 15-cent-per-hour increase in the operations it had organized. The Timber Company management then lifted wages of C.I.O. workers. "The 15 cent wage increase has become a fact throughout the fir industry, including both C.I.O. and A.F. of L.; it has been extended to the pulp workers as well," Phil Weyerhaeuser wrote the directors in December. But labor had made many gains during the war and was determined to have them introduced into the new contracts. By 1947 the Timber Company's average wage stood at $1.60 per hour, whereas in 1940, as noted earlier, it had reached only 81.5 cents per hour.[37]

Price controls were the last wartime restrictions to be removed. During 1945 and a large part of 1946, government officials were reluctant to eliminate them, fearing an immediate rise in prices. The Weyhaeuser Sales Company in 1945 asked the O.P.A. to revise the ceilings, giving preferential prices to housing items and reducing prices on export lumber, heavy clears, and other wartime specialties. This was the first request for a price rise that the company had made, and the company did not favor the abolition of price controls, believing the extension of ceilings for one postwar year would be wise. The Weyerhaeusers had up to now consistently held to a low-price policy.

But the O.P.A. did not revise its prices on house-building items, which were advantageous to the consumer, with the result that some lumbermen turned to markets with higher prices, some to black-market dealings, and all to vigorous complaint. Finally, in March, 1946, the O.P.A. was forced to modify the ceilings. By this time, black-market activity flourished. When in November, 1946, the O.P.A. removed price controls, lumber prices soared. The former black-market prices became the openly quoted prices of most shippers.

If lumbermen looked back on the price curve during the war, they could see a steady rise. Not only was the slope upward steeper than the average for all commodities; it was even steeper than the rise for other building materials. The contrast with the price curve of World War I is startling, for in 1917–1918 lumber prices had lagged behind the average price rise.

The war, however, was but a harbinger of postwar prosperity, and Weyerhaeuser's early fear of heavy competition from other building materials proved totally unwarranted. Civilians, deprived of lumber during the war, and earning more than ever before, clamored for lumber. Moreover, during the war years uses for wood never previously imagined had been discovered, including many applicable to peacetime needs. General Timber Service engaged in various experiments during the war, but nothing of a permanent nature came out of them. Most important, in this half-decade lumbermen had learned that woods they had thought unmerchantable were in fact salable. The postwar markets absorbed these less popular woods. The vistas opened by the wartime experiences were many and profitable.

NOTES

1. A. Fletcher Marsh in *Chicago Journal of Commerce*, Sept. 6, 1939. Marsh was a graduate of Yale Forestry School, Captain in the Construction Division at Washington, D.C., in 1917, and in the employ of various wartime bureaus until the end of World War I. He had been in contact with Army specialists since that time. HTK Papers, Report of Secretary-Manager to the Directors of the National Lumber Manufacturers Association, Nov. 10, 1939; Horn, *This Fascinating Lumber Business*, 235.

2. U.S. Civilian Production Adminis-

tration, *Industrial Mobilization for War, History of the War Production Board and Predecessor Agencies, 1940–1945*, I, 30, 68, 71 (Henceforth this work will be referred to as *Industrial Mobilization*).

3. HTK Papers, H. T. Kendall to J. P. Boyd, June 24, 1940; Kendall, "Memo on Activities of J. P. Boyd at Washington, D.C.," June 22, 1940; WSC Annual Report, 1940; GTS, Annual Report, 1940, 35; Horn, 223; HTK Papers, Telegram, Kendall to Ernest W. Pavey, Nov. 6, 1940.

4. HTK Papers, suggestions by Wilson Compton, endorsed by FKW in FKW to John W. Watzek, Jr., Sept. 30, 1940. Watzek was head of the Lumber Division of the Advisory Commission to the Council of National Defense.

5. GTS, Annual Report, 1940; WSC Annual Report, 1940; HTK Papers, Kendall to mill managers, etc., Dec. 5, 1940; GTS, Annual Report, 1941.

6. Harry T. Kendall, Foreword to WSC, Annual Report, 1941.

7. HTK Papers, "Reports-Record of National Defense Orders 1941."

8. *Hearings Special Committee Investigating National Defense Program*, 77th Cong., 2nd Session, Pt 15, Testimony Clarence Forsling, 6197.

9. *Industrial Mobilization*, 160; "History of the Product Development Department" in GTS Annual Report 1945, 5.

10. *The New International Yearbook—1942*, 30; HTK Papers, "Reports-Record of National Defense Orders 1941;" Clute, Reminiscences; Horn, 223; GTS Annual Report, 1941; *WC Lbrmn.*, March, 1941, p. 72.

11. *Family Tree*, May, 1941, 1.

12. WTC Papers, *Manager's Report*, 1941, 6.

13. WTC Papers, "File on Labor"; Jensen, *Lumber and Labor*, 261, 267; PFI Papers, Min. Bk., Directors' Meeting, May 22, 1941.

14. FEW Papers, JPW, Jr., to FEW, Aug. 5, 1941; FEW to JPW, Jr., Aug. 14, 1941.

15. WSC, Annual Report, 1941; Forsling testimony, *op. cit.*, 6192; *Industrial Mobilization*, 161; *New International Year Book—1942*, 533; WSC Papers, "Weyerhaeuser Price Policy" memo, undated; *WC Lbrmn.*, Oct. 1941, p. 84.

16. *Weyerhaeuser News*, 1942, p. 6; Horn, 223; WTC Annual Report, 1941, 6.

17. Forsling testimony, *op. cit.*, 6194; WSC Annual Report 1942.

18. Testimony of W. B. Greeley at Senate Hearings, 6159; *Weyerhaeuser News*, 5, 1942, pp. 2, 11; Horn, 234; *Family Tree*, Feb., 1943, 1, 4.

19. HTK Papers, "Government Procurement—1942" folder; D. H. Bartlett to Kendall, June 11, 1942; WSC Annual Report, 1942; WSC Papers, Major General E. Reybold to J. P. Boyd, May 25, 1942. Major General Reybold, Chief Engineer of the War Department, stated that he had found transactions with the WTC "remarkable for the absence of misunderstandings, errors, and failure to make delivery at the specified time."

20. *March of Pine*, 1945; HTK Papers, general correspondence; copy of statement by Paul A. Porter, March 23, 1946; G. H. Shafer, Memo, Oct. 12, 1945; A. J. Russell to J. E. Morris, Sept. 21, 1942.

21. *Industrial Mobilization*, 219; GTS Annual Report, 1942, 24; FKW to the authors, Sept., 1958.

22. F. G. Sherrill, "Lumber Procurement for the Army," *Journal of Forestry*, XL, Dec. 1942, p. 917; WSC Annual Report, 1942; F. K. Weyerhaeuser to authors, July 17, 1959.

23. *WC Lbrmn.*, Oct. 1942, p. 72.

24. HTK Papers, Kendall to FKW, Nov. 12, 1942; GTS Annual Report, 1942; HTK Papers, statement by Col. W. B. Greeley, Dec. 1942, "Government Control of Local Forest Enterprise;" *Industrial Mobilization*, 645.

25. Testimony of W. B. Greeley before the Senate hearing, 6158; H. J. Cox, *Random Lengths*, 215–216; R. V. Clute, Reminiscences.

26. B-P Papers, S. G. Moon to Dr. E. P. Clapp, Sept. 30, 1942; *Industrial Mobilization*, 645–646; *Weyerhaeuser News*, #5, 1942, p. 24; Arthur Upson, "Our Forest Resources Are Contributing to Victory-Lumber and the War Production Board," *Journal of Forestry*, XL, Dec. 1942, pp. 911–912; Charles E. Wilson to Marvin Jones, July 12, 1942, cited in *Industrial Mobilization*, 646 n; Abe Fortas memo to Harold L. Ickes, Sept. 24, 1942, in *Franklin D. Roosevelt and Conservation*, II, 559; testimony of Greeley, Senate hearing, 6158, 6162–6163, 6173; *WC Lbrmn.*, April 1943, p. 66; Nov., 1942, p. 16; Jensen, 278; Wilson Compton, "Our Forest Resources Are Contributing to Victory-Discussion," *Journal of Forestry*, XL, Dec. 1942; p. 918; SFL Co., Annual Report, 1942; C. L. Billings, *Daybook*, Nov. 24, 1942; WTC Papers, R. B. Wolf to Exec. Com., March 1, 1943; B-C Papers, S. G. Moon to Dr. E. P. Clapp, March 17, 1943.

27. WSC Annual Report, 1942. Potlatch was exceptional when in January, 1943, it could declare that "Generally speaking Potlatch Forests, Inc., has had, and still has, plenty of manpower," *St. Maries Gazette-Record*, Jan. 14, 1943. Later it too would have manpower problems.

28. W. B. Greeley, *Forests and Men*, 169; HTK Papers, Kendall to FKW, April 25, 1947; U.S. Forest Service, *Report of the Forester 1945*, 10; copy of John Philip Boyd speech, March 14, 1944; *Weyerhaeuser News*, #6, n.d., 16; Longview, *Manager's Report*, 1950, 6; *Family Tree*, March 1944, p. 4.

29. *Industrial Mobilization*, 833; *WC Lbrmn.*, Oct., 1943, p. 12; WTC Annual Report, 1943.

30. *Report of the Forester, 1945*, p. 10; WTC, Annual Report, 1944; Henry B. Steer, *Lumber Production in the United States, 1799–1946*, p. 10; WTC Papers, Statistical Records: "Lumber Production-W. T. Co. *v.* Industry."

31. *Report of the Forester, 1944*, 5; WSC, Annual Report, 1943; Claude Wickard to Franklin D. Roosevelt, Oct. 12, 1942, in *Franklin D. Roosevelt and Conservation*, II, 562; *Monthly Labor Review*, Nov., 1947, Table A-5; Dept. of Commerce, *Construction and Construction Materials Industry Report*, Nov., 1947, p. 22; Fred H. Brundage, "Northwest Woods Have Gone to War," *Journal of Forestry*, XLI, Sept. 1943, p. 657; HTK Papers, Harry G. Uhl, "Appraisal of Wartime Situation," June 27, 1945.

32. *Weyerhaeuser News*, #6, n.d. 1943, p. 24; *Weyerhaeuser News*, 1944, p. 24.

33. Clute, Reminiscences; PFI Papers, Minutes of Woods Foremen's Meeting, March 11, 1944.

34. U.S. War Production Board, *Directory of Industry Advisory Committees* (Washington, 1943), 77, 79; WTC Papers, Laird Bell to FEW, Jan. 10, 1944; *ibid.*, Laird Bell to JPW, Jr., Jan. 12, 1944; HTK Papers, Statement by Paul A. Porter, March 23, 1946; WSC Papers, "Weyerhaeuser Price Policy," n.d.; WTC, Exec. Com. Mins., Feb. 27, 1943, II, 333.

35. HTK Papers; *American Year Book, 1944*, 364; Quarterly Report of the National Lumber Survey Committee of the Secretary of Commerce, March 16, 1944; *Industrial Mobilization*, 834, 911.

36. WTC Papers, JPW, Jr., to directors, Aug. 17, 1945; *Industrial Mobilization*, 649, 920, 930, 954.

37. WTC Papers, J. P. Weyerhaeuser, Jr., to trustees, Nov. 7, 1945; JPW, Jr., to directors, Nov. 30, Dec. 31, 1945; Billings, *Daybook*, May 25, Sept. 24, 1945; Klamath Falls, Manager's Report, 1945; National Lumber Survey Committee, *Quarterly Report*, Nov. 23, 1945.

XXV

Toward Modern Marketing

EVENTS inside and outside the Weyerhaeuser Sales Company dictated greater attention to lumber marketing problems by 1932. Despite the loss of its manager, Louis Case, in September, 1927, the firm had done well in the ensuing two years. With I. N. Tate at the helm, it had expanded 4-SQUARE shipments and maintained sales at an encouraging figure through 1930. Declines in volume even then caused F. E. Weyerhaeuser to observe, "This is a badly weakened and discouraged industry." And the downward pull of the worldwide depression showed clearly by 1932; the volume of sales fell from the 1929 high of 1,164,673,000 feet to 611,195,000.

The situation was even worse than the figures indicated. With the opening of the Longview, Klamath Falls, and Lewiston plants, the manufacturing potential of the associated firms had notably increased. The new mills cried for a proportionate rise in sales when the downward spiral of the entire American economy had abruptly reduced residential and farm building, and industrial construction had all but ceased. By 1932 lumber consumption in the United States was less than half of normal, and prices stood at their lowest in seventeen years.[1]

Obviously the path to a better future had to lead through better sales. Could Tate and his associates deliver improved performance in the teeth of their great difficulties? The wrong answer could blast the hopes of the 1920's, the correct one make the Weyerhaeuser Sales Company a symbol of high achievement in the forest products industry.

Fortunately, the way had been prepared for a favorable change. As early as 1927 T. J. Humbird, the Sales Company president, had planned to retire. At that time F. E. Weyerhaeuser had protested strongly. He pointed out to Humbird that he had looked forward to seeing his nephew, Frederick K. Weyerhaeuser, eventually take over the direction of sales. In charge of the Minneapolis district in 1925, and assistant manager of the company in 1926, the young man, argued his uncle, needed a period of work with Humbird himself before assuming greater responsibilities. In deference to this and other pleas, Humbird had stayed on for two more years, then late in 1929 insisted on bowing out. To succeed him on December 11th of that year the Sales Company trustees unanimously elected F. K. Weyerhaeuser.[2] This proved to be a first step in a vital strengthening of that organization. The new president had the vision to see what the times required of his organization and the resourcefulness, confidence, and drive to provide it.

One of his first acts was to propose the removal of sales headquarters from Spokane to St. Paul. He had suggested this as early as 1927; both Humbird and the mills at that time preferred to keep it in the Far West. On December 10, 1930, Weyerhaeuser gave the trustees a memorandum that outlined the advantages of a middle-western location: a better vantage point for controlling sales activity, nearness to banks and railroad traffic departments, and proximity to actual markets and the largest customers for lumber. He pointed out that numerous western lumber manufacturers had their sales headquarters in central United States and recounted how, when Case had informed Edward Hines that the Sales Company would operate from Spokane, the latter had asked, "Why didn't you put it in Alaska?" Weyerhaeuser won his point: by September, 1931, the central sales offices had been established in St. Paul.[3]

But other and more basic changes were required. Despite its success up to 1930 in raising the volume of sales, despite the introduction of the '4-SQUARE program and a steady increase in personnel (thirty were added in 1929), the agency required reorganization and a new status among the associated companies. For many years regarded as an experiment, the Sales Company had been given few important powers, and F. K. Weyerhaeuser believed that its relatively humble status had curtailed its effectiveness. "The stockholders and the directors had never given the management of the Weyerhaeuser Sales Company any real authority," he stated later. Reorganization and greater powers both seemed to him essential. Tate, he felt, was not the man to effect such changes; his talents ran in other directions. He had dealt staunchly with a difficult situation and later was to show high gifts in the handling of public relations. Nevertheless, his was the great disadvantage of being associated with the development period of the Sales Company and its recent difficult past. A dynamic outsider, the new president believed, could deal more effectively with the situation.

Such a man was available. At industry conferences F. K. Weyerhaeuser had become acquainted with Harry T. Kendall, a Kansan by birth who since 1926 had been sales manager and assistant general manager of the Central Coal and Coke Company of Kansas City. Kendall was respected throughout the industry for his knowledge, integrity, warmth, and capacity for work. The financial difficulties of the Central Coal and Coke at this time permitted him to accept an invitation to join the Weyerhaeuser Sales Company. He did so in July, 1932, and at once began to study its problems and confer with its personnel. He was appointed manager the following year.[4]

With the support of F. K. Weyerhaeuser, Kendall soon improved the morale of the Sales Company. He promulgated a distribution policy for his firm and preached a gospel of confidence. He also moved to improve the structure of the organization. Hitherto this had consisted of the central staff and district offices scattered about the country. As the company had expanded, the number of districts had increased. At the same time, each had been handling a large amount of routine, including the maintenance of stock and price lists. One of Kendall's first acts was to take this administrative work from them and center it in three zone offices. These were located at Newark, St. Paul, and Tacoma.

The purpose was to relieve the district managers of office detail and permit them to concentrate their energies on selling. "The chief duty of the District Manager," ran a memorandum of February 1, 1933, "will be to check the functioning of the salesman, assist in improving his technique, and assist in special sales situations that may arise." A few of the district offices were closed. Under Kendall, William H. Peabody (who was replaced at Everett by Lyndon Reichmann) took charge of the Eastern Zone, C. J. Mulrooney of the Central, and J. E. Morris of the Western. By July, 1933, the reorganization had been completed, and in January, 1934, the revitalized company was functioning, directed by Kendall from St. Paul. Weyerhaeuser, while working closely with him, was left more freedom to operate in the larger area of policy.[5]

Meanwhile Weyerhaeuser and Kendall had won a position of greater strength for the Sales Company among the associated firms. As Weyerhaeuser remarked in 1959, "the crisis of the depression" worked for them. The stockholders and the mills were losing money. The Sales Company was the logical instrument to pull them out of the red. They were now desperate enough to give it the powers they had hitherto denied it. A contract of December 1, 1933, between the Sales Company and the mills put the marketing organization on a wholly new footing.

By this pact for the first time in its history the Weyerhaeuser Sales Company acquired new powers permitting it to plan and act with a confidence it had never previously known. It took over responsibility for invoicing lumber and for the carrying and collecting of accounts. It also took over the management of the Eastern Yards.

But the contract offered more than increased authority. It provided for a schedule of consultation and planning to be followed jointly by sales officials and the various manufacturing units whose lumber they marketed. Quarterly, the heads of each individual mill would confer with Kendall and Weyerhaeuser or their representatives. The parties would consider "all known factors having a bearing upon the planning of an operating program" and agree upon a course likely to provide the greatest possible profit for the mill. For such conferences each mill was to supply all possible information as to its inventories and future stocks. The Sales Company would offer a record of costs and expenses during the preceding quarter. Of course, consultations had been held in previous years but never on the basis of such full information. The arrangement tightened and intensified teamwork between the mills and the selling firm and soon promoted a new mutual confidence. F. K. Weyerhaeuser later stated that as a result of the powers provided by the contract, and the new cooperative planning also initiated by it, the Sales Company "was first put in a position to do business in 1933." This overstates the case, since the company had "done business" for fifteen years; yet now it possessed an independence and an authority that fully matched its responsibilities.[6]

2

The Sales Company still faced its basic task—to move the lumber of the mills. All of these had drastically reduced production and were losing money: Longview alone showed a deficit of $500,000 for 1932. The new contract provided for a budgeting policy that would avoid undue expansion, yet utilize the resources of each company. Kendall and Weyerhaeuser were realistic about production possibilities in a depression period, but they firmly rejected a policy of curtailment. They planned rather on volume selling, with emphasis on 4-SQUARE, so that production could be steadily increased. While the NRA Code imposed quotas, it left room for expansion and would be subject to modification as business improved.

Acting to implement this policy, Kendall in March of 1933 launched a drive to enlist new dealers in a modified 4-SQUARE program. He also solicited wholesalers, jobbers, industrial plants, government agencies, railroads, shipyards, and other potential customers. Important in such activity was his chief merchandising lieutenant, T. L. O'Gara. By the end of the year, 1,339 new dealers had signed contracts, bringing the total to 2,100. The Sales Company took immediate steps to provide these dealers with better products and a host of marketing services.

To implement the program described above, a Wholesale Lumber

Purchasing Division was established in Tacoma in 1934 to supplement supplies of plywood, shingles, and lumber, and in particular to furnish the distributing yards of the Weyerhaeuser Timber Company with a fuller assortment of stock. A Railroad & Car Materials Division was also created in 1935. Peabody, in charge of the Eastern Zone, in March, 1934, also assumed direction of the Weyerhaeuser Steamship Company and the Eastern Yards. Peabody soon established yards in Philadelphia, Brooklyn, and Boston. These agencies and establishments all expanded Weyerhaeuser selling potential.

At the same time, Weyerhaeuser and Kendall established a liberal credit policy for dealers that markedly facilitated the sale of their lumber. They placed reliance on the judgment of the credit managers in three zone offices, and the results fully justified their confidence. Net losses on credit from 1934 to 1943 on shipment of $479,089,436 value amounted to $181,141, or less than .004 of 1 percent. It was amazingly low for a period of economic uncertainty.

The Sales Company had always been aware of the importance of the farmer as a potential customer. However, from the early 1920's up to 1933 his economic plight had been desperate. But the Agricultural Adjustment Act of that year promised to restore some of his purchasing power, and in 1934 the Sales Company launched a 4-SQUARE building service, providing a variety of designs that offered "the best value in farm buildings from the standpoint of structural soundness, economy of erection, and fundamental efficiency." A manual, *Farm Buildings for Less Money,* was also made available through retail dealers. These measures were soon to be implemented by a company to promote building on time-payment plans.[7]

This unit had a relationship to an earlier effort in which several firms of the associates had participated: The Lumbermen's Finance Corporation, established on May 3, 1929, with central offices in Winona, Minnesota. Jointly owned by ten retail lineyard companies, most of them located in the northern Middle West,[8] the company had the purpose of stimulating the sale of lumber by making first-mortgage loans. Among those active in the organization were F. K. Weyerhaeuser (the F. Weyerhaeuser Company), and George R. Little (Laird, Norton), but a number of non-Weyerhaeuser firms were members of the group. Little became its director and Ludwig J. Luhman its secretary and manager.

The Lumbermen's Finance Corporation prospered despite the quickly descending depression. By 1934 it had made 764 loans and increased its capitalization. Early in that year the Federal Housing Administration was being created, and offered great possibilities for the stimulation of lumber sales. Luhman spent four months in Washington in connection with it. The act as passed on June 27, 1934, empowered the FHA to make loans under Title I for the repair and modernization of dwellings and other structures. Title II, based on information supplied by Luhman, permitted mortgage loans. Unfortunately the phrasing of Title II was ambiguous, and no use of it could be made until the renewal of the act and its revision in April, 1936. The LFC accepted notes under Title I.[9]

The success of the Lumbermen's Finance Corporation was of course well known to Sales Company officials. At any other time than that of mid-depression the company would doubtless have launched a program on a wider scale before 1934, based on LFC experience. No lumber producers or distributors of national scope had provided a financing service up to that time for the building of homes, although both mail-order firms and automobile companies had won marked success in the time-payment field. With the improvement in the lot of farmers generally, and the FHA legislation, the time now seemed ripe for a nationwide program of installment financing in the lumber industry. This would fortify the general promotion efforts of the Sales Company and its services to farmers.

John M. Musser had already proposed taking advantage of Title I of the National Housing Act providing for guarantee of loans for repairing and remodeling buildings, as a service for customers of W.S.C. Early in 1934 F. K. Weyerhaeuser deputed W. A. King of General Timber Service to make this effective. As a result, on October 4, 1934, General Timber Service signed a contract with the First Bancredit Corporation, which agreed to purchase notes meeting FHA requirements under Title I. At first limited to $750, in August, 1935, loans as high as $2,000 were accepted. General Timber Service guaranteed 25 percent of loan value, FHA 20 percent. "So far as we know," stated the GTS Annual Report for 1934, "we are the only lumber manufacturer, or wholesaler, with a financial plan for its customers."[10]

In July, 1935, in order to take advantage of the mortgage provisions under the amended Title II of the FHA Act, General Timber Service helped organize the General Home Financing Corporation. Its stock was owned by the Weyerhaeuser Timber, Snoqualmie Falls, Potlatch, and Boise Payette companies. Credit was supplied principally by New York, St. Paul, and Chicago banks. For reasons of public relations, the name was soon changed to Allied Building Credits, Inc. (ABC), and capitalization was increased from the original $250,000 to $1,250,000. With F. K. Weyerhaeuser as president, W. A. King as vice president, John M. Musser as treasurer, and J. L. Hall as general manager, this agency through the Sales Company pushed the purchase of both Title I notes and Title II mortgages, and during 1936 made agreements with 1,526 lumber dealers.

By 1937 ABC began to purchase notes and accept mortgages directly, and soon terminated its arrangement with Bancredit. In addition to the Title I loan provision under FHA, it devised its own supplementary

installment note plan and began making Title II mortgage loans for sale
to banks and insurance companies. By the end of that year it was serving
5,685 dealers and had greatly increased its personnel. Overcoming some
early difficulties, ABC continued to grow; by 1940 it had acquired and
was servicing $13,523,728 in installment notes and $10,859,563 in mortgage loans, had 288 employees and 15 branch offices.[11]

Along with the services to farmers previously described, Kendall and
O'Gara had offered in 1937, through the Weyerhaeuser Home Building
Service, designs and specifications for twelve different houses and an illustrated Plan Book explaining principles of construction. These materials
had been popular with dealers, trade associations, and even with public
housing bureaus. Allied Building Credits, Inc., had undoubtedly increased
Weyerhaeuser lumber sales; later the salesmen themselves felt that it
might have added 10 percent to the total volume of business. This estimate represents an impression only, but the agency had a marked value,
both psychological and financial. "It contributed materially to the rapid
buildup of the volume of our lumber business from 1935 to 1939," said
F. K. Weyerhaeuser later, "and helped to introduce and expand installment financing of repairing, remodeling, and new house construction in
many parts of the United States."

A word may be said here about its later life among the associated
companies. As early as 1939 the program had been challenged but had
survived. It grew with a flourishing vigor, and by 1944 was servicing $30,-
044,444 in mortgages and $7,618,152 in installment notes. By that date
many stockholders felt that it had been needed in the depression but no
longer served the Weyerhaeuser interests sufficiently to justify being retained as a promotional unit. Lumber provided only about 15 percent
of the cost of a building. During the war lumber was so much in demand
that no devices to aid in its sale were necessary. Some stockholders were
concerned about the enormous sums of money involved in ABC operations, and financing houses was much more complex than financing sales
of household appliances and automobiles.

Kendall and F. K. Weyerhaeuser at first favored continuing the organization but ultimately changed their minds. "It is not the fear of impending operating losses that brings us our greatest problem," said the
latter in 1945 to his directors, "but the fear of too much prosperity. We
are approaching a situation where instead of operating a finance company as an adjunct to a lumber sales program, we may be running a business (lumber sales operation) as an adjunct to a finance company."
Finally, in June a decision to sell the prosperous subsidiary was reached.
John M. Musser conducted the negotiations, and on October 19, 1945,
F. K. Weyerhaeuser announced it had been bought by the Transamerica
Corporation of San Francisco. It remained an available resource for
Weyerhaeuser salesmen and dealers. Actually, Allied Building Credits

had done its work so well that agencies for home financing were now numerous, dependable, and moderate in their charges.[12]

During the 1930's the 4-SQUARE program had been an important part of Weyerhaeuser activities. It may justly be called, in the words of a company executive, "one of the most significant developments that has ever taken place in the marketing of lumber." No lumber manufacturer had ever offered a "package" approaching it in quality of product, completeness of identification, and range of merchandising services. In addition, great care was taken in shipping the product, and orders from 4-SQUARE dealers received expeditious handling. Soon further improvements were made, such as a liquid seal to prevent end-checking, "easing" the edges of dimension, and guideline framing.

By 1931 the program had inspired numerous imitations—clear testimonials to its success. But as it made headway, it was to alter somewhat in character.

The original plan was to establish 4-SQUARE dealers to whom a wide assortment of quality lumber could be shipped. There was never a precise franchise for members of this group, but they could depend on service, and comprised a valuable special outlet, particularly desirable in the depression.

It should be emphasized that 4-SQUARE lumber represented only a percentage, and at first a small one, of the output of the Weyerhaeuser mills. By 1933 its proportion was growing rapidly and in the middle 'thirties ran from 17 to 18 percent of the total. The remainder comprised unbranded lumber which received no special attention for shipment.

Various influences were now to show the difficulty, and even at times the undesirability, of making 4-SQUARE as exclusive a category as had at first been contemplated. For example, in 1934 the Inland Empire mills developed a number of specialty white pine products: carpenter kits, trellises, garden furniture, and sandboxes. The Sales Company proposed to market such items entirely through 4-SQUARE dealers, but the mills insisted on their being sold to any qualified retailer. Meanwhile the coast mills began to produce fir specialties that were also sold to any dealer willing to stock them. The effect of both these developments was to break down somewhat the exclusive position of the 4-SQUARE dealers. This was altered further when the installment financing program, which the Sales Company wanted to offer only to its 4-SQUARE group, was made available to all retail customers. Finally, New Deal legislation worked against the maintenance of a special group of dealers, for the NRA Code prohibited all selling premiums, and the legality of making FHA loans available to selected persons was doubtful. The Robinson-Patman Act of May, 1936, ended all doubt by prohibiting price or service discrimination between customers.[13]

To follow the original policy thus became impracticable and in the intensive drive to push Weyerhaeuser products would probably not have been expedient. In a broadening market the trend was toward a larger variety of outlets. Competition also induced some changes in practice. In 1938, when sales to non-4-SQUARE dealers showed a lag, the sales agency discovered that many of these were selling competitors' branded lumber at the expense of unbranded Weyerhaeuser products. It was decided to "bring out some new [pine] brands that could be sold to these dealers and to wholesalers." As a result three new brands, Potlatch (white pine), Rex (ponderosa), and King Tree (for wholesalers) appeared. They marked the adoption of a more flexible practice pointing to a greater volume of sales, but it was abandoned after war was declared.

But 4-SQUARE continued to be a central feature of Sales Company merchandising. It held up a standard that competitors tried to match. If when general advertising, which had been to a large extent suspended in 1932, was resumed in 1937, the chief emphasis was perhaps on home and farm building, 4-SQUARE shipments had established a firm reputation and were steadily growing. In 1940 they amounted to 20.8 percent of the total W.S.C. sales.

Throughout this period Weyerhaeuser lumber sales had risen. While in 1933 the total had increased but little (661,438,389 feet), after the reorganization and the introduction of a budget system it mounted steadily, reaching 982,051,000 board feet in 1935, 1,306,928,000 in 1936, and almost 1,500,000,000 in 1939. In succeeding years this figure was to be steadily surpassed.[14]

It had been a Sales Company policy to sell lumber directly to the retail dealer and not through the wholesaler. As noted in earlier chapters, the mills had often been reluctant to follow this practice. But with the onset of the depression Weyerhaeuser Sales had taken a more kindly view of wholesale distributors. Kendall in particular valued them as an emergency outlet, and during the 1930's he opened accounts with hundreds of such agents. As early as 1933 he had established a special division managed by Louis M. Rick, with headquarters in Pittsburgh, solely to handle such traffic. However, emphasis upon retail selling remained; as late as June, 1938, Kendall informed zone managers that sales should be made to wholesalers only when an order could not otherwise be obtained.[15]

Nevertheless, wholesale business, negligible in 1934, when Rick's division disposed of but 14,780,000 feet of lumber, steadily increased. It brought with it some of the problems encountered in the 1920's, for in 1935 wholesalers were quoting prices on Weyerhaeuser lumber lower than those of the Sales Company itself. Kendall was outraged. "We will be better off not doing any wholesale business at all," he wrote in January, 1936, "than doing it on a basis under our own asking price."

Nevertheless, the volume of such sales steadily increased, until in

1939 they represented 22.76 percent of all orders and in 1940 a flat 23 percent. "Probably the most serious problem in our distribution policy," warned assistant general manager Don Lawrence in the latter year, "is our growing use of wholesalers. If this trend continues, we may have to revise our sales policy."

Other officials were disturbed, and a committee headed by Luther Atkinson, the company's research marketing authority and later one of its vice presidents, was appointed to study the problem. But by mid-May of 1941, when Atkinson was ready to report, World War II had been raging for almost two years, America was deeply involved in aiding the Allies, and wholesaling had ceased to be a factor in Sales Company business! As the nation improved its defenses, and soon afterward entered the conflict, the Weyerhaeuser problem was one of supplying enough lumber to retail dealers to keep them alive as future elements in its marketing program.[16]

3

As noted in Chapter XXIV, the conflict had quickly reversed the early expectations of a decline in the demand for lumber and had produced the boom the industry had eagerly expected in the 1930's. The accomplishments of the Weyerhaeuser companies during the five years of warfare have already been described. For the Sales Company, a serious development was the increasing tendency of government agencies to buy directly from the mills. Its own operations were unexpectedly simplified, and at the same time its dealers found their normal activity sharply reduced. "Our business is dreadfully dull," wrote manager A. S. Russell of the Weyerhaeuser Timber Company's own Stockton yard in the summer of 1942, "because the government takes all the lumber directly from the mills as fast as it can be manufactured."

The question of how to meet the situation precipitated a heated debate among Weyerhaeuser officials. Some of them favored selling as much as possible to the government—even nonrestricted items that could have been diverted to retailers. Kendall disagreed. Once the war was over, he pointed out, the retailer would again "be the backbone of the entire marketing process." He should if possible be kept alive until that time.

The answer finally determined upon was a system of allocation. Every effort would be made to distribute fairly among the company's established customers whatever lumber was available for civilian use. A list of such customers was compiled, with their prewar purchases, and a percentage of lumber allotted to each. "It was the job of each salesman," Kendall stated later, "to see to it that each of our customers got some lumber from us during the war."

Actually, the reduction in what the Sales Company distributed to retailers was not so great as might be imagined. Their share fell from 55 percent in 1939 to an average of 37 percent for the years 1942–1944. But for the retailer his situation was relatively worse than these figures indicate because he did not get so much lumber from other wholesalers.[17]

The allotment of supplies to the dealers was a difficult operation. To the retailer lumber was life, and while he had got enough of it up to the fall of 1942, and even in some cases to the end of the year, for the remainder of the war he often waited for it as vainly as a dustbowl farmer for rain in a time of drought. R. E. Saberson, who made an informal survey of dealers midway in the conflict, reported that "we didn't have a single satisfied customer left in the United States. . . . We couldn't give them enough lumber to meet local demand." This of course was true for only a brief period; furthermore, Saberson himself reported that the dealers understood the company's difficulties and did not blame it for the scarcity. One Minnesota dealer said that "his allotment was very fair and they [the Sales Company] lived up to it to a 'T'," and he had decided "to throw Weyerhaeuser the balance of his business after the war." Otto H. Leuschel of the Potlatch organization felt that "our customers had a full realization of the problems confronting the mills." He believed that the salesman had "distributed such lumber as had been allocated to each of them among their customers in a way that will retain the finest customer relations." The Sales Company showed courage in making retail calls on never-satisfied dealers; most lumber companies had simply abandoned their retailers "for the duration." However, many of these half or wholly forgotten men managed to survive only by expanding into other than their normal activities and by stocking substitute building materials.[18]

Although the Sales Company officials had been able to do much to prevent the retail dealer from becoming a war casualty, they could not do so well by 4-SQUARE. With the government commandeering much of the mills' output, quality selection became difficult, and what was more important, labor required for the exacting preparations of 4-SQUARE materials soon ceased to be available. By the end of 1942 4-SQUARE shipments, like civilian cars in the automotive field, had disappeared. Nevertheless, Weyerhaeuser advertising from 1943 onward kept both the industry and the public conscious of the program as something that would be revived with the coming of peace.

4

When the Sales Company directors gathered at Tacoma for their annual meeting on May 28, 1945, the end of the war was in sight. Had they taken at face value the prophecies of many writers on the postwar period, the meeting would have been a gloomy one. The war had demonstrated new possibilities in applied science—fabrics, electronics, plastics, factory processes. A much-advertised luxury of the future was a "dream house" built entirely of steel, glass, and concrete, with composition walls and floors. In this dwelling wood was to be no more than decorative. Fortunately, Weyerhaeuser Sales had made its own study of the future in which the place of lumber was more realistically appraised.

Postwar planning had been launced as a vigorous W.S.C. activity in 1943, and on December 20th of that year a steering committee composed of D. H. Bartlett, R. S. Douglas, C. J. Mulrooney, J. M. Musser, and T. L. O'Gara had reviewed investigations and recommendations made by ninety-eight members of the organization. Their report offered a tentative plan for future operations. Estimating with approximate correctness the duration of the war, they prophesied a five-year period of brisk prosperity after it, with "a good overall demand for lumber." They saw only normal competition from other lumber producers but the probability of "increasing competition from other competitive materials." These included steel, aluminum, plastic, and glass products. They proposed to meet such threats by developing new wood products, by training their salesmen, and by cooperating with lumber associations to promote the use of wood.

Company expectations remained much the same in 1945. As late as June of that year F. K. Weyerhaeuser expected the industry to "pass into a highly competitive stage, at least insofar as other building materials are concerned."[19]

But in reporting to his directors at about this time, on May 28, 1945, he did not propose any retrenchment on the part of the Sales Company. It was true that there might be severe competition. It was quite as evident that the war had decreased the output of lumber and that the volume might be expected to diminish further with peace. Some of the associated companies were now operating on a sustained yield basis, and their product would be less by perhaps 20 percent than during the war. These factors might suggest a reduction in Sales Company personnel, but such a reduction, Weyerhaeuser felt, would be bound to hurt morale. He proposed to avoid it by adopting an expansive program. "A drifting or diminishing organization does not attract the best personnel or stimulate the best efforts." His solution was to aim at volume selling. He pointed out that a sale of 2,000,000,000 feet in normal times was essential to ensure the sale of 1,250,000,000 in slack years. He set this as a goal. Part of the lumber would be purchased from other companies. "The Weyerhaeuser Sales Company," concluded its president, "must assume a position of LEADER in the lumber market after the war."[20]

It is worth pausing at this point to note the growth and existing resources of the Weyerhaeuser Sales. It was now as different from the company of the 1920's as a mature man is from a child. It had won a position of strength among the associated firms. The 1933 contract had been revised in 1941 to permit the Sales Company to operate on a profit-and-loss basis, its surplus account was rapidly growing, and in 1942 it had finally paid a dividend to its stockholders. It operated after May, 1942, under directors from the stockholding companies, who replaced the former trustees, and delegated authority to an executive committee of five. They in turn were advised by an operations committee of plant and Sales Company officials. There were three zone managers, operating under two divisions, Eastern and Western.

The Sales Company sold all the lumber of the associates' mills. As already noted, it had established various special divisions and since 1940 had supervising distribution at the Twin City as well as at the Eastern Yards. It rendered sales accounting services to numerous related companies, such as Wood Conversion, W.T.C. (pulp, log sales, and Pres-to-Log sales), and Rilco Laminated Products. In 1940 it had taken over from General Timber Service responsibility for traffic, public relations, and market research and had its own engineering section. Its operating costs were remarkably low.[21]

The company's resources permitted a coverage of the market that few if any lumber firms could match. They enabled Weyerhaeuser Sales to dispose not only of the stock of its associated mills but also of much additional lumber and lumber products its Wholesale Purchasing Division fed into the distributing yards. While it did some business with wholesalers, and a considerable amount with industrial firms and railroads, its chief outlet was its trade with retailers, for in 1945 three-fourths of all the lumber the Sales Company shipped went to the retail dealer.

Kendall and Weyerhaeuser continued measures they had previously used to increase their business with this large body of customers. In his report of May 28, 1945, Weyerhaeuser proposed to "strengthen the retail lumber dealer, an operation requiring long and continuous effort." He would continue services already in existence—the furnishing of a wide variety of staple items "of a quality and manufacture unsurpassed by any one in the industry," use the distributing yards, maintain liberal credit and sales policies, and set fair prices. He would improve customer relations by such items as the *Weyerhaeuser News,* which not only gave information about the associated companies but also about reforestation, merchandising, and so forth. He would provide building aids, plans, and new ways of using lumber. He would educate the retailer in the use of new products, including prefabricated panels, plywood, and veneer. The dealer would be offered displays and motion pictures, and through ABC, Inc., a mortgage and note-buying service. As particular postwar measures,

Weyerhaeuser proposed the more intensive utilization of waste, the treating of lumber for its preservation, the buying of additional retail lumberyards, the improvement of services to industrial customers, and the development of exporting.[22]

The general program was approved, and at an executives' meeting, June 10–12, 1945, further action was taken to implement certain phases of it. The gradual centralizing of all outside purchasing was approved, and individual mills were meanwhile urged to buy such available lumber as they could. It was voted to sell, and not give away, most dealers' helps and to start a training program for salesmen. The Merchandising Syndicate, an activity being developed by R. E. Saberson to train dealers, was approved. Financing services, treated lumber, and experimentation with prefabricated structures were endorsed. The postwar program of the company was under way.

With only 76 salesmen on company rolls (the normal complement in 1940 had been 105), the training program for new men became an important activity. Shipments of 4-SQUARE lumber were resumed. In 1945, as a part of the already existent Farm Building Service, an encyclopedic *Farm Book* was issued for dealers (which they bought), and a smaller edition for farmers was published that contained drawings and illustrations of 120 farm buildings and items of equipment. The service, closely keyed to 4-SQUARE lumber, was advertised in farm publications and by tabloids mailed to individual farmers. During the first postwar years the results came in slowly but by 1949 were gathering pace and volume.

Success in the nonfarm residential field came faster. In 1946, according to housing expeditor Wilson Wyatt, 1,250,000 homes were needed in America, and 1,500,000 the following year. Americans had the savings with which to buy them—an awesome reservoir of $140,000,-000,000. The Weyerhaeuser Home Building Service produced in 1946 the *Book of Homes,* comprising 62 designs (50 previously published in 1941), and instituted a "House of the Month" program, featuring a new design each month. Dealers were also supplied with a 250-page portfolio of designs, with illustrations, plans, descriptions, and helpful sections on Principles of Construction and Principles of Planning. An additional publication, "The High Cost of Cheap Construction," defined the reasons for using good lumber and helped to fortify a growing recognition of the value of the 4-SQUARE service. It is significant that in 1947 a $130,195 profit was realized from the sale of such promotional materials.[23]

During the war General Timber Service, which in the 1930's had carefully considered prefabricated housing and reluctantly abandoned it then as impracticable, had carried on experiments with two types of houses in this field. Five of one type were built and offered for inspection.

With the advent of peace, various producers of prefabricated houses began promoting the sale of their products direct to consumers. In order to help the retail customers of Weyerhaeuser Sales Company meet their new competition, G.T.S. purchased a factory in Dubuque, Iowa, and began the manufacturing and marketing of several house models through retail lumber dealers. More than a thousand of the Dubuque houses were sold.

The steel, glass, and plastic dwelling never appeared except in a few experiments involving faulty construction and long-delayed deliveries. As an idea this house was attractive; as a reality it required careful engineering, special designs, special fabrication, and workmen familiar with it. Wood was already on the ground and could be adapted to new demands. Its flexibility and popularity were proved by the special farmhouses designed by WSC engineers in 1949. These contained central heating, modern kitchens, the fullest plumbing and refrigeration, utility rooms, and in general satisfied the growing number of rural home builders.

The hopes of the Sales Company to achieve volume selling were at first only modestly realized. For some years total sales were not to reach the two billion mark. In 1946 they stood at 1,183,679,000 feet, rose in 1948 to 1,419,958,000, and increased yearly as the peacetime organization manifested a growing efficiency. The goal was eventually to be reached, but two important events were to precede its achievement.[24]

5

The first occurred in 1948, when the Sales Company became a wholly owned subsidiary of the Weyerhaeuser Timber Company. The chief cause for this change in status was the continuing growth of the great West Coast company, with its mounting production of lumber, plywood, and other products. Already the Timber Company furnished 70 percent of the dollar value of the products sold by W.S.C., and received only one-third of the profits, while Boise Payette, supplying 6 percent of the lumber, took an 18 percent share. There was also a feeling on the part of Boise Payette, which expected soon to terminate its activities, that the firm could sell its own lumber without the Sales Company. This belief was based partially on its diminishing output and partly on the existing good market for lumber, which seemed to make selling an easy process.

J. P. Weyerhaeuser, Jr., for Weyerhaeuser Timber, pushed the proposal for complete ownership by his company. F. K. Weyerhaeuser, who had previously made considerable exertions to keep the Inland Empire firms in the Sales Company, was at first opposed. However, when an informal agreement was reached that the selling agency would continue to market the products of the companies it had been serving to the extent that they desired, he then urged Boise Payette, Potlatch, and Northwest Paper to sell their stock, which they did. The new ownership became effective during 1948.[25] As will appear later, the expected demise of Boise Payette did not take place.

The second step was a further reorganization of the Sales Company. As already noted, the administrative structure of the firm had become quite complex by 1944. On December 30th of that year F. K. Weyerhaeuser in a general letter to executive personnel had recommended a simplified structure: "The prompt handling of management problems with a minimum of lost motion and confusion makes a more cohesive organization essential." The beginning of postwar work and the change in ownership had delayed action, but in 1948 the management consultant firm of Booz, Allen & Hamilton was asked to study the activities of both the Sales Company and the Weyerhaeuser Timber Company and to recommend organizational changes.

In general, their report confirmed what Weyerhaeuser, Kendall, and their chief aides knew, and a streamlining of the selling agency's activities was promptly undertaken. The objectives were a simplified general structure and clarified lines of authority. Three completely integrated divisions were set up which were responsible for direct and out-of-yard shipments and for all credit, traffic, and accounting. Each head—A. N. Frederickson in the East, A. D. Franklin in the Midwest, and R. S. Douglas in the West—reported directly to the vice-president in charge of sales, C. J. Mulrooney (a new position), who in turn reported to the general manager (Kendall) and the president (F. K. Weyerhaeuser). A clear distinction was drawn between staff and operating departments, the former handling merchandising, traffic, credit, accounting, and public relations, and the latter sales, price, and stock. The cumbersome operations committee was abolished. Special divisions reported either to Mulrooney or to Kendall.[26]

The ensuing years were prosperous. The volume of business increased, shipments reaching 1,572,641,000 board feet in 1950, 1,812,-090,000 in 1953, and in 1955, with 2,030,000,000, passing the two billion mark for the first time since 1942.

The proportion of 4-SQUARE stock to the total has risen sharply in recent years: in 1959 for all the Pacific Coast mills it stood at 69.90 percent. The rise has shown the influence of several factors. One was the abolition in the 1930's of the extra charge of from $3.00 to $3.50 per thousand formerly levied on 4-SQUARE shipments; another, the handling of that type of lumber recently by numerous distributing yards that formerly did not stock it. Finally, the end-capping of upper grades of lumber has been simplified.

The company in recent years has also augmented its merchandising of specialty products, such as industrial wood parts, special joists and panelling, and modular, laminated, and timber-connector items that require unusually creative selling. The merchandising program has continued to be extensive, with plan books and other materials on modern construction. These include items for dealer use in home, farm, repair, and remodeling activities.[27]

For some time the Weyerhaeuser Timber Company (name changed to Weyerhaeuser Company in 1959) has assumed a growing responsibility with respect to the public. This is set forth at some length in a statement approved by its board in 1957 and issued as "Company Objective" on January 1, 1958. "The basic objective of the Weyerhaeuser Timber Company," reads an early paragraph in this statement, "shall be the continual building of a vigorous, sound, and profitable enterprise, designed for furthering the long range interests *of shareholders, employees and the public.*" (Italics ours.) The meaning of this assertion is further explained in ten rules for the guidance of company stockholders and officials. These cover among other matters the maintenance of forest lands on a sustained-yield basis and the education of the public in company purpose and policies. As the reader who has come this far will understand, the attitudes and activities described in these rules had now become common Weyerhaeuser practice, most of them for a dozen years or more.[28]

In addition to publicizing products, the sales organization has cooperated with Weyerhaeuser Timber in a broader national program. That company, in national advertising and in a series of special motion pictures, has tried not only to familiarize Americans with the Weyerhaeuser name and products but also to carry information about the forests of the nation and their use. Its advertising, under the general direction of Walter De Long, has made it clear that a permanent supply can be maintained for the future and that Weyerhaeuser activities are conducted so as to conserve and utilize this supply. In emphasizing that timber is a crop and that Weyerhaeuser operates on a sustained-yield basis, Weyerhaeuser Sales advertising echoed that of WTC.

This message was carried effectively in colored magazine advertisements of the Timber Company but was most vividly presented in its films on the forests and their utilization. These began to appear in 1937; "Trees and Homes" (1938), "Green Harvest" (1948), "New Paul Bunyan" (1950), "The Promise of the Trees" (1955), and "Tomorrow's Trees" (1959) have been issued. After the first film, all have been made by professional motion-picture organizations, and the Sales Company handled the showing to clubs, theaters, church groups, and similar organizations.

Altogether, more than 260,000,000 people have seen these pictures. "Green Harvest" and "New Paul Bunyan" have both had total audiences of 80,000,000. These documentaries bring to all who see them a sense of the richness and the value both in use and beauty of the American forest domain. They also show its enemies at work: fire, destructive insects, blights, and demonstrate the measure taken by both private and government personnel to prevent or check the damage they can do. The wild life of the woodland, the role of trees in water conservation and in recreation are shown together with the methods used in growing new stands and in harvesting the timber when ripe.[29]

A terminal point in the history of the Weyerhaeuser Sales Company was reached on September 30, 1959. On that day it ceased to function as a separate organization and became a part of the Lumber and Plywood Division of the Weyerhaeuser Company.[30]

The event marked the conclusion of forty-two years of activity. With F. E. Weyerhaeuser, the originator of the Sales Company idea, and T. J. Humbird, Louis S. Case, and I. N. Tate guiding it through its early years, the company had come in 1929 under the leadership of F. K. Weyerhaeuser. Assisted by H. T. Kendall and, after his retirement, by R. S. Douglas, F. K. Weyerhaeuser gave Weyerhaeuser Sales his care and inspiration for thirty years. This period saw the development of 4-SQUARE, the fostering of a mature and vigorous merchandising program, the creation of a financing agency that was perhaps the largest influence in making home financing both widespread and dependable, the preservation of the selling organization during the war, and its adaptation to peace afterward.

The original purpose of the Sales Company, as earlier chapters bring out, was to provide a selling organization for a group of mills. If the aim was difficult, its realization enabled the organization to command a wide range of lumber products, to offer more varied products than its competitors and to serve its numerous patrons with a success that would have been impossible had it served but one or even several of them.

At the same time, the breadth and volume of Sales Company activity built up certain special advantages its officers have cherished. They believe that the pricing policy of the company has been exceptionally sound, that their training programs have given their salesmen special advantages, that the company has been able to maintain a valuable statistical service, establish a strong credit policy, and carry on as part of the cost of selling, activities in advertising and public relations that rivals have usually charged as additional expense.

As a Sales Company for a number of firms the organization has ceased to exist. It now functions in one division of the Weyerhaeuser Company. Yet because of the volume and variety of Pacific Coast lumbering, much of the essential work of past years will be carried forward, and the great advantages realized under the older organization will be active in the new.

NOTES

1. Bureau of the Census, *Historical Statistics of the United States, 1789–1945*, 125; WSC annual reports, 1931–1932; FEW Papers, FEW to C. A. Barton, July 28, 1930.

2. *Ibid.*, TJH to FEW, July 18, 1927 and FEW to TJH, Aug. 1, 1927; *Weyerhaeuser Log*, May 1926 (FKW's advancement).

3. FEW Papers, FKW to FEW, Aug. 17, 1927; WSC Min. Bk., 1930–1931; Memo of FKW to trustees, Dec. 10, 1930; *Miss. Valley Lbrmn.*, Sept. 4, 1931.

4. FKW Papers, material on HTK by Leo V. Bodine, May 5, 1952.

5. HTK Papers, WSC Files, St. Paul, Chart of Organization, Feb. 1, 1933, and memoranda to salesmen, Jan.–July, 1933; HTK to Clapp, Elmquist, Briggs, Gilbert, and Macartney, Feb. 21, 1933; WSC Min. Bk., Sept. 6, 1933.

6. WSC Min. Bk., Dec. 13, 1935; FKW to authors, Sept. 9, 1958.

7. WSC Files, T. L. O'Gara, "History of Product Improvements and Other Related Efforts," undated release (after 1950); WSC annl. repts., 1933–1935; WSC Files, Statistics on Losses from Bad Debts. Prior to 1933 efforts had been made to promote prefabricated silos and milk houses, and it was considered an evidence of the farmer's low purchasing power that neither could be marketed successfully.

8. The firms were: Botsford Lumber Co., Hayes-Lucas Lumber Co., C. M. Youmans Lumber Co., Standard Lumber Co. (all in Winona, Minn.); J. F. Anderson Lumber Co., Central Lumber Co., L. E. Streator Lumber Co. (Minneapolis); Thompson Yards and F. Weyerhaeuser Co. (St. Paul); O.&N. Lumber Co., Menomonie, Wis., and Boise Payette and Potlatch Lumber Cos. (in 1930).

9. FEW Papers, Memo from R. E. Saberson to C. L. Hamilton, Sept. 8, 1928; H. H. Irvine to F. S. Bell, G. S. Long, and FEW, Nov. 23, 1928; Report to Stockholders by L. J. Luhman, April 30, 1930; WSC Files, St. Paul, Doren A. Eitsart, "Lumberman's Finance Corporation," etc., Sept., 1954.

10. GTS annl. repts., 1934, 1935.

11. *Ibid.*, 1937–1940.

12. HTK Papers, WSC Post-War Planning Project, "Non-Farm Residential Market for Lumber," July 28, 1943; "Conclusions on ABC, Inc.: Questionnaire Submitted to WSC Salesmen," J. M. Musser to FKW, Dec. 20, 1944; FKW to authors, July 17, 1959; HTK Papers, FKW to HTK, Dec. 22, 1944, and FKW to FEW, April 18, 1945; WSC annl. repts., 1939, 1940; WSC Min. Bk., Jan. 1, May 18, Oct. 19, 1945; Statement by FKW same date.

13. WSC annl. repts., 1931–1938; WSC statistics on shipments, 1928–1943. In 1933 4-SQUARE shipments were 17.1 percent of the total; in 1935, 16.4; in 1936, 18.2; in 1937, 17.2; and in 1940, 20.8 percent.

14. WSC annl. repts., 1938; WSC statistics on shipments, *op. cit.;* WSC annual reports, 1933–1940.

15. WSC Annual Report 1934; HTK Files, HTK to zone managers, June 9, 1938.

16. WSC annl. repts., 1934–1943; HTK Papers, HTK to zone managers, Jan. 13, 1936; WSC Statistics, Percentage of Wholesale to Total Shipments, 1939, 1940; D. Lawrence to HTK, April 17, 1940; Report of Atkinson to HTK, May 20, 1941. Atkinson and his associates advised the selective use of wholesalers. By 1943 shipments to wholesalers had declined to 4.6 percent of the total.

17. HTK Papers, A. S. Russell to Capt. Edgar B. de Mont, Aug. 25, 1942;

HTK to FKW, July 2, 1943; WSC annual reports, 1943, 1945; T. L. O'Gara to the authors, Jan. 11, 1960.

18. FKW Papers, HTK to FKW, July 2, 1943; R. E. Saberson, Reminiscences; HTK Papers, Comments of O. H. Leuschel at Eastern Zone meeting, 1944; WSC Annual Report, 1945.

19. WTC Files, Postwar Planning Program, Final Report of the Steering Committee, Dec. 20, 1943; HTK Papers, FKW to HTK, June 7, 1945.

20. Statement to Directors, WSC Annual Meeting, May 28, 1945.

21. WSC Files, Revision of Contract, signed Dec. 20, 1941, effective Jan. 1, 1942; WSC annl. repts., 1938–1942; National American Wholesale Lumber Assn., N.Y., Bull. 15–48, June 24, 1948.

22. Statement to the Directors, op. cit. Lumber was treated with creosote, with Wolman salts, zinc chloride, or pentachlorophenal. Railroad ties when treated lasted 30 years. Creosote provides a "dirty" treatment, since it rubs off. The other preservatives are "clean" and permit painting afterward.

23. WSC Min. Bk. Executives' Meeting, June 10–12, 1945; WSC annl. repts., 1940–1947; HTK Papers, WSC Postwar Planning Project, "Non-Farm Residential Market for Lumber," July, 1943. The Book of Homes sold to dealers for $15, the House of the Month for $5. These prices indicate the quality of the materials, while the profits from their sales show their popularity.

24. WSC annual reports, 1946–1950; WSC Statistics, Shipments by Sources of Supply, 1916–1953.

25. HTK Papers, Memo by FKW, Dec. 16, 1947; Statement by FKW, Sept. 19, 1958; WSC Min. Bk., Jan. 2, 1948.

26. Annl. repts., 1949–1953; HTK Files, FKW to all mills, WSC Offices, etc., Dec. 30, 1944.

27. WSC Statistics on Shipments; annual reports, 1950–1959. All 4-SQUARE lumber is kiln dried. Green lumber, of which a considerable amount went to the East Coast, carries the trade name WEYCO.

28. WSC Annual Report, 1957.

29. FKW to the Authors, Dec. 23, 1959; Statement by Bernard J. Orell, v.-p. Weyerhaeuser Co., Feb. 23, 1960.

30. Weyerhaeuser Company, Annual Report, 1959.

XXVI

Timber Is a Crop

Oh, the shanty man has a brand-new song.
He makes it up as he goes along.
There's a new Paul Bunyan—
A new Paul Bunyan—
—A new Paul Bunyan in the woods.
        —*Theme song of Weyerhaeuser movie.*[1]

WEYERHAEUSER MYTHOLOGY, rivaling the folklore of early logging days, became a product of the post–World War II years. Never in the time of the tall tales about Paul Bunyan had the dream been so expansive. The giant had never been credited with such grand operations as the Weyerhaeusers came to sponsor: the Weyerhaeusers were growing trees.

In these years the now familiar slogan, "Timber is a Crop," became the Weyerhaeuser trademark. It signified far more than most trade labels, for it symbolized a dramatic change in the operations of the lumber industry.

For years American foresters had studied in Europe, where they saw what care was taken to reproduce the forests and to log selectively. At the close of the Middle Ages, except for such districts as southwestern France, the forests in Europe had already become more and more places for "rationalized timber production." In France, Jean-Baptiste Colbert in the great Ordinance of Waters and Forests (1669) had severely limited the right of owners to cut their wood.[2] Many of the large private forests in Europe had been maintained by the landed aristocracy. Often these forests were entailed and kept for generations in the same family, which used them both as a source of raw materials and as hunting preserves. Other private forests in Europe owed their origin to industries dependent on wood, and as the woodlands were limited, early attention was given to reforestation.

490

But as earlier noted when our foreign-trained foresters like Bernhard Eduard Fernow, Gifford Pinchot, C. A. Schenck, and Henry S. Graves urged the people of the United States to preserve American forests carefully, theirs were literally voices in the wilderness. Standing timber was so plentiful and cheap that few lumbermen could afford to practice scientific forestry. Paradoxically, it was not until our foresters were no longer trained overseas but educated at American schools that they began to find a receptive audience for their ideas. And it must be said that our first professional government foresters themselves needed education. The four men named above were primarily interested in establishing a system of preserves, not in creating economic units growing timber for the future.

2

As indicated earlier, in the late twenties the Weyerhaeusers began to consider seriously both selective logging and sustained yield. "It's unprofitable and it costs you money to cut small logs," C. L. Billings, the new assistant manager of the Clearwater Timber Company at Lewiston had argued early in 1927.[3] Billings, with both Forest Service and industry experience, presented impressive data. He urged upon executives in the associated northern Idaho companies the economic value of selective logging. This practice would mean that only mature trees (and diseased and insect-plagued ones) would be cut; trained foresters would select the timber most suitable for logging, and healthy young trees would be left to reseed the land and grow to suitable size. The goal would be to keep the forest forever productive. For reasons already explained, clear cutting is the only practicable method in Douglas fir; selective cutting appertains to pine and mixed species.

Confirmation of Billings's opinions came that same year when Mason & Stevens reported on Weyerhaeuser operations in the Inland Empire. The firm's consultants worked out detailed selective logging designs for the Clearwater, Potlatch, and Edward Rutledge companies.[4]

Clearwater took the lead in initiating its plan. On October 24, 1929, David T. Mason and Billings informally applied to the local representative of the Forest Service for enough national timber to round out a cooperative sustained yield unit for the Clearwater Company, enough to produce a perpetual cut of about 200,000,000 feet yearly. At last a demonstration of the new method of forest management was under way, the first major program of selective logging on privately owned land in the West. "It's the most progressive attempt at real forest conservation ever made in this country," boasted the Weyerhaeuser publicity man in St. Paul. "What it amounts to is that Clearwater Timber Company is staking its future operation on an act of Providence. If the idea works out right, it'll show the rest of the industry—and the public—what real conservation combined with sensible utilization is."

Phil Weyerhaeuser explained to a reporter that the lumber business had always been rather hit-or-miss. "Well, we thought we ought to prove out our methods, at least as far as we could, while our operation was still fairly new;" the Clearwater Timber Company, though incorporated in 1904, had not begun logging until the summer of 1927.[5]

Under the direction of Ed Rettig as chief forester, Clearwater men, working in the old-growth timber, cut all merchantable white pine, ponderosa, and spruce but left the white fir and cedar standing. In second-growth stands they dealt with the trees according to four types of growth. In general, where more than 70 percent of the forest was white pine, the loggers left about 40 percent of all trees standing; where 40 to 70 percent was white pine, they left half the stand; where 10 to 40 percent was white pine, they left 60 percent; and where white pine averaged less than one-tenth the stand, they cut nothing. They took no white pine less than 13 inches in diameter, no spruce or ponderosa under 17 inches, and no fir of less than 23 inches. In certain specified belts they cut no white pine less than 17 inches thick or spruce or ponderosa below 23 inches.

Rettig strictly enforced the rules for selective logging. "We actually mark the timber to be cut," he informed J. P. Weyerhaeuser in 1929, "and have a saw boss . . . see that only marked timber is cut and that there is not excessive breakage of the timber left standing. So far our experience has been very good, and even the saw gangs are getting into the spirit of it and hate to cut the small timber. If anything, we are actually saving a little in our sawing by this method." The camp foremen were taking a new attitude, Rettig wrote. "At first they were very skeptical and opposed the step, fearing their logging costs would be increased, but their attitude is much different now."

The new rules left a fairly uniform growth everywhere. Such stands were perhaps safer from fire than forests of uneven density, where open spots gave the wind opportunity to fan blazes, and they were less likely to be infected by blister rust and other diseases that start more readily in sunlight than under heavy shade.[6]

The result of selective logging at Clearwater was immediately and strikingly apparent. For two years the company had logged off land by the old clear-cutting method. That land provided an example of "forest devastation"—the term United States Forest Service officials had used for many years to describe the operations of "wicked lumber barons." The Service described areas bald but for unsightly stubble of charred and whitened stumps, broken-off snags, and raggedly tufted shafts seared with sunscald. In sharp contrast appeared the land logged under the new method, where but for the "few broken tops [which] showed, you'd never imagine that the loggers had been in there." Yet Rettig told a visitor with well-warranted pride: "That face has yielded us a paying cut. What you see left there will be merchantable timber for another generation."[7]

Clearwater's emphatically successful experience with selective logging led the associated companies to expand their forest management projects. This was an important factor lying behind the 1931 merger of Clearwater, Potlatch, and Edward Rutledge companies into Potlatch Forests, Inc. In the combined operation, Phil Weyerhaeuser and C. L. Billings could develop the forestry methods started by Clearwater Timber— with the result that Potlatch Forests soon offered one of the best examples of forestry in the West. The Mason & Stevens plan was used to guide the new undertakings.

While these forestry engineers were active in Idaho, Stevens's partner, David T. Mason, was trying to persuade other Weyerhaeuser officials that they should attempt a selective logging and sustained-yield program. He converted both F. K. Weyerhaeuser and his brother Phil, and they helped him work on Titcomb, Minot Davis, and others. Through talks with Mason and his own study of the facts, F. E. Weyerhaeuser came to believe that planned forestry on a sustained-yield basis was the "only real way out" of the lumbermen's difficulties. The Timber Company, then headed by F. S. Bell, began a trial study at Longview in 1931.

But as to selective logging, F. E. Weyerhaeuser did not get broad support. He wrote his nephew that selective logging "seems not to have appealed to the management at Tacoma" and that T. J. Humbird thought the whole program "a lot of bunk." Phil Weyerhaeuser, a leader in forestry activity, assured his uncle that he personally had full confidence in selective logging in proper areas—which of course did not include Douglas fir stands.[8]

Not long after this exchange between the two Weyerhaeusers, a new President of the United States was elected, one who was fascinated with forestry. In his first week in office Franklin Delano Roosevelt took time to write letters about tree planting on his Hyde Park estate. He had grown trees for some years, was a member of the American Forestry Society, and, like his distant cousin T.R., would have a significant influence on the activities of timberland owners.[9]

While private industry was debating the forestry problem, the President entered the discussion. George Frederick Jewett, grandson of the first Frederick Weyerhaeuser, wrote the Weyerhaeuser tax committee of his pleasure that America had found a leader "so deeply interested in conservation measures."[10] Such New Deal ventures as the Tennessee Valley Authority, the Agricultural Adjustment Administration, and the Works Project Administration all had an impact on forestry practices. Even the Shelter Belt project, itself a failure, helped arouse public interest in trees and conservation. However, the Roosevelt innovations that most deeply affected the Weyerhaeusers' thinking on forest management were two depression measures, the Civilian Conservation Corps and the National Recovery Administration.

The C.C.C. aimed primarily to provide work and training for unemployed youths and secondarily to carry out projects for the public good. Its spotlight shone on forestry problems. For this, numerous critics attacked the government agency as catering to a "presidential hobby."[11] Yet occasionally hobbies are constructive, and this one was. Lumbermen, whose criticisms of the New Deal were intense and often bitter, found nothing but praise for this particular measure.

Young men in C.C.C. crews throughout the Northwest, on public and private lands, made parks, fought soil erosion, cut roads through inaccessible forests, strung telephone lines, constructed bridges, and planted trees. One estimate credited half of all forest planting in the entire United States during the depression to the C.C.C. crews: "a billion young trees" was the total given by Chief Forester F. A. Silcox—a glowing achievement.[12]

Equipped with fire-fighting devices to supplement the equipment of state and private agencies, C.C.C. men roamed the woods to reduce the damage from conflagrations. Since expert direction was essential, every C.C.C. camp employed one or more officials from the state or federal forest services, most of whom would otherwise have been temporarily retired or used only during the summer fire season. Moreover, the C.C.C. aided private fire-fighting organizations. By 1935 in the state of Washington, for instance, the camps supplied much of the hand tools, pumps, hoses, and trucks for projects in fire control. The Weyerhaeusers, a prime force in this fire association, appreciated the contribution. In Idaho, also, C.C.C. men were prompt and efficient in suppressing fires, among them blazes in the timber of Potlatch Forests, Inc. Incidentally, the state and federal forest services used C.C.C. boys to control about two hundred fires that were set to permit research in visibility, rates of fire spread, and methods of fire prevention. From the results, state and national agencies prepared basic studies in forest management.[13]

While lumbermen, as noted earlier, had many reservations about the N.R.A., they had reluctantly agreed to the inclusion of Article X on conservation. Having accepted it, they grew more and more to appreciate its importance to themselves and the public. Article X is said to have been the only Lumber Code provision in which Roosevelt showed any interest. At the President's request it was amplified to provide for conferences of public and private representatives to initiate and administer measures "necessary for the conservation and sustained production of forest resources."[14]

Weyerhaeuser representatives zealously participated in the conferences held in October, 1933, and January, 1934. David T. Mason writes, for example, "Jan. 28 (C. S.) Chapman and I spent part of day discussing nature (of) code amendment and in about 4 hours in evening I wrote the first draft." This, with minor revisions, became Schedule C of the Forest Conservation Code.[15] From the conferences came a well-organized program for sustained production in the forest, one stressing fire, insect and disease prevention, reforestation, adequate slash disposal, selective logging, and sustained yield.

The Weyerhaeusers were prompt to submit a sustained-yield plan under Article X. Phil Weyerhaeuser, who left Potlatch to become executive vice-president of the Weyerhaeuser Timber Company in 1933, inaugurated this program the year after his arrival in Tacoma. Its operations covered the Longview unit, spanning 481,455 acres in five counties, of which 72 percent was owned by the Weyerhaeusers and the rest by the state of Washington, the Northern Pacific, and the Western Timber Company. The cut was to be limited to 325 million feet annually, the equivalent of the growth.

Longview was the only sustained-yield operation that the Weyerhaeuser Timber Company presented to the Lumber Code authorities, but at the time it had under consideration three other units that offered possibilities. The firm also assisted in sponsoring other conservation activities. For instance, C. D. ("Dave") Weyerhaeuser, the son of F. E. Weyerhaeuser, became an assistant to C. S. Chapman in his work of securing general company compliance under Article X; and Clyde Martin, a professional forester who some years later entered Weyerhaeuser employ, administered Article X through the Western Pine Association. Weyerhaeuser executives agreed that the Article was what one called "the life buoy of the industry" and that it served to educate the industry in forestry methods.[16]

Article X has justly been described as the only part of the Lumber Code that "finished stronger than it began." When the Supreme Court ruled the N.R.A. unconstitutional in the Schecter case of 1935, few lumbermen were dismayed; however, they did deplore the loss of this vital section. It had become, as Colonel W. B. Greeley pointed out, "a striking sort of internal combustion engine, creating its own power from forces within the industry itself." Such organizations as the National Lumber Manufacturers Association, the West Coast Lumbermen's Association, the Pacific Northwest Loggers Association, and the Western Pine Association all urged that the article be maintained on a voluntary basis. The Weyerhaeuser companies wholeheartedly agreed.[17]

But the path to planned forestry projects was still strewn with obstacles. Weyerhaeuser officials, despite their attempts at sustained yield under the code, were in the mid-thirties not totally convinced of the practicability of such operations. F. E. Weyerhaeuser, though their champion in principle, insisted as the depression continued that lumbermen must first get their investment out of their timberlands; conservation, he wrote his nephew in October, 1935, was a second consideration. Similarly, his son, C. D. Weyerhaeuser, warned that sustained yield must not be thought a panacea for timber management problems. He believed it had "become a fetish, almost worshipped for its own sake," and that it was practicable only when favoring circumstances could be established. "Too much," he asserted, "cannot be sacrificed today in the way of curtailed income, purely for the sake of assuring a complete continuity of operations." Both Weyerhaeusers based their reluctance on economic conditions, for the depression continued severe, and the stockholders, who had all suffered, tended toward conservatism.[18]

3

Even more than hard times, another factor was blocking sustained-yield operations and conservation in general—the inequitable taxation on both state and county levels. The case of an unnamed Mississippi timberman illustrates the fact that the power to tax is the power to destroy. This timberman cut pine from his large tract. He carefully saved the hardwood timber; it *might* be profitable to harvest these trees at a future time. County assessors, seeing the standing timber, taxed the land as a full timber tract. In vain the owner protested that he was trying to save a currently unproductive source of possible future wealth. The law gave the tax assessor no choice but to levy the tax. The result was that the timberman cut down his hardwood trees, left them on the ground, and, for his destruction, was rewarded with the lower tax rate applying to stripped land.

This example indicates the basis for the nationwide protests made by lumbermen against unjust taxation. In some counties there was "quite literally a race between the tax collector and the private timber owners to see whether the tax collector can collect all the money they [*sic*] want in the county before the timber is gone, or whether the timber owner should hurry up and get his timber cut before it is taxed to death," as David Mason explained at a later government hearing.

Starting in the 1920's Professor Fred Roger Fairchild of Yale directed a comprehensive study of forest taxation, sponsored by the United States Forest Service. He concluded, like others before him, that the current tax laws were badly framed. His inquiry into the experiments and proposals in forest taxation—the yield tax, adjusted property tax, deferred timber tax, and differential timber tax, for example—convinced him of the importance of revising tax practices along consistent and constructive lines. G. F. Jewett, W. D. Humiston, and C. S. Chapman, among Weyerhaeuser officials, wrote letters, speeches, articles, and bills to suggest means of coping with this problem. Their solution was not identical with Fairchild's, but the pressure the men put on state authorities was influential.[19]

Moreover, when taxes became prohibitive, the Weyerhaeuser companies, like others, stopped paying them. In Oregon, Washington, Idaho, and Minnesota they simply abandoned some cutover land for tax delinquencies.

In Oregon the Weyerhaeuser Timber Company decided not to pay part of its taxes on cutover lands because the money could be better used elsewhere and because C. S. Chapman thought that the "tax strike" might awaken local bodies to the difficulties of the lumber industry. It did in fact result in greater tax flexibility. The next year the Weyerhaeuser Timber Company executive committee instructed its officials to pay some Oregon taxes in person. The manager was to inform the county officials that it was a sacrifice on the part of the company to make this payment but that it did so as a reward for reductions made and as an incentive to the granting of further concessions and that if nothing was done prior to the time when the next half-year's taxes were due, they would not be paid at that time.

In Idaho, Potlatch Forests paid only a little more than 40 percent of its taxes in 1932. Cutover lands in Washington were likewise left delinquent in tax payments.

Meanwhile, the Weyerhaeuser companies in Minnesota had an even worse tax situation than their affiliates farther west. When in 1927 Minnesota passed a Forest Auxiliary Law, and lumbermen's hopes rose, the Northern and Cloquet Lumber companies offered 170,000 acres to be classified under the provisions of the Act. But the commissioners procrastinated, and in the end the two companies withdrew the offer. "We finally gave up any hope of tax relief and did not pay the 1928 taxes on a large portion of our cutover land," H. C. Hornby announced. As a consequence of tax problems and the depression, the companies refused to pay taxes on cutover lands in subsequent years, and much of their land reverted to the state.[20]

Yet despite all obstacles, by the mid-thirties the prospects of good forestry were by no means hopeless. The states slowly applied new tax laws favorable to reforestation, signs of recovery from the long depression multiplied, and the federal government began to promote legislation for the encouragement of sustained-yield plans. The fact that the government also increased its threats to police the lumber industry if it did not take independent action looking toward better forestry also gave private timber holders an incentive to reform their practices.

In the late twenties and early thirties several western states had passed reforestation acts. C. S. Chapman had assisted in the writing and passing of these acts in Washington and Oregon, and G. F. Jewett and W. D. Humiston had lobbied for the new laws in Idaho. In all three states a basic tax was now put on the land, and the timber tax was deferred until the trees were actually harvested. The premium on rapid cutting was thus removed, and planned logging practices could be introduced.

However, the acts immediately provoked extensive litigation, for county tax assessors ignored them and attempted to collect under the old illiberal statutes. Test cases in Idaho courts in 1933 resulted in decisions favorable to the Potlatch company. In Washington, the Mason County Logging Company obtained a writ of mandamus to compel county tax officials to assess property according to the new law. Losing its case in the lower court, where the judge ruled that the reforestation Act was unconstitutional because the legislature was without power to fix valuation for purposes of taxation, it won a victory in 1934 when the Washington Supreme Court reversed the decision and upheld the constitutionality of the new Act. Under this ruling, as the cautious C. D. Weyerhaeuser observed, it was "barely possible for the first time in the history of timber liquidation to hold onto cutover lands for purposes of reforestation."[21]

The year 1936 found the Weyerhaeuser Timber Company facing its first foreclosure suit on land where taxes had been left unpaid. About 70,000 acres were involved, and an additional 265,000 acres had tax delinquencies. Faced with the choice of giving up the land or paying about $175,000 in tax arrears, plus 10 percent interest penalty, the company decided to pay $106,000 and to reclaim 204,000 acres. It selected the acreage to be redeemed on the basis of a study on growth potential it had conducted from 1925 to 1936. County and state authorities, glad to have the taxes to fill their depleted coffers, waived the 10 percent interest penalty. From this time forward, Weyerhaeuser Timber Company policy was to hold all cutover lands and to purchase additional acreage.[22]

While the Pacific Northwest received the benefit of tax adjustments, in Minnesota lumbermen did not obtain comparable relief. During 1937 the Cloquet companies felt obliged to forfeit 63,656 acres of their land rather than pay the confiscatory taxes. Additional forfeitures followed, for the state levies remained prohibitive.[23] But Minnesota was an exception, and in general the Weyerhaeuser interests by the second half of the thirties gained the advantage of revised laws.

Moreover, by that time the ledgers once more showed profits; and though these were sometimes modest, the Timber Company could spend more freely in carrying out good forestry practices. It should be noted that the proper management of forests is expensive, and only over a long period of time can it be expected to bring satisfactory returns. It in-

volves, for example, the employment of specialists, the building and up-
keep of roads for fire protection, and the steady employment of a staff
to supervise the areas under reforestation.[24] Consequently, good forestry
plans are difficult to initiate in depression periods. It was not until recovery was well under way that Weyerhaeuser companies began once
more to turn with vigor to scientific forestry measures on an extensive
scale.

As the new tax situation made sustained yield prospects more feasible, so the passage by Congress in 1937 of Public Law 405 likewise gave
fresh encouragement to planned forestry. Under this Act the federal
government put the revested Oregon and California Railroad Lands on
a cooperative sustained-yield basis. This meant that not only would the
O.&C. timber be cut on a perpetual-yield plan but also that the government would manage the timber in cooperation with other owners. The
Act, which lumbermen supported, dealt with a limited territory, but it
laid the foundation for more extensive applications of the principle.[25]

Yet lumber interests at the same time expressed great apprehension
over the inexorable extension of governmental activity, fearing an excessive degree of state and federal regulation. The Weyerhaeuser companies
had always taken a more liberal attitude. For many years they had desired and received state and federal cooperation in fire protection. They
had also supported extensive *cooperation* in insect control, in planning
for timberland management, and in sustained yield projects, and they had
openly stated their approval of government aid. Frederick K. Weyerhaeuser urged conferences between the company and the Forest Service
on operations at Klamath Falls and Longview, believing they would be
"very productive of good results."[26]

But as for forest *regulation,* all lumbermen held rigidly to the creed of
private business. Free enterprise, they insisted, could better manage forest
and industry than could the government. Chapman expressed the con-
sensus of opinion in the industry when he urged a strict limitation of the
power of the Forest Service "to police the industry."[27]

Nevertheless, the threat of government interference challenged the
industry to vindicate itself. Chief Forester F. A. Silcox of the national
service had declared on numerous occasions, "Forest devastation must
stop, and sound forest practices must begin now, not in the nebulous
future," and again, "Practices on private lands must be supervised by
public agencies and not left to the industry." He was but echoing the Pinchot
refrain: "Devastation and depletion of our timberlands has not been
stopped. Voluntary forestry has failed the world over." Only an effective
program could answer such accusations and avert drastic federal action.
Thus Jewett insisted, "I feel strongly that unless the industry has a definite

workable plan or course of action, we are going to be told what to do whether we like it or not."[28]

Happily, in the more favorable economic situation of the late 1930's, creative experimentation was both possible and practicable. Less than two years after C. D. Weyerhaeuser had expressed his objections to the "panacea" of sustained yield, his cousin J. P. Weyerhaeuser, Jr., told the stockholders of the Timber Company: "We are . . . committed to the business of growing trees as part of a sustained yield program."[29] It must be emphasized that basic economic conditions had been largely responsible for the old outlooks and policies. So long as the annual production capacity of the industry was half again as great as the annual demand for lumber, as had been the fact early in the 1900's, the low prices put lumbermen under pressure to get what return they could out of the capital tied up in standing timber, that is, to practice hasty low-cost logging. And the lumbermen's policies impelled the Forest Service to continue its emphasis on mere preservation.

Meanwhile, the Timber Company implemented its new policy with new administrative procedures. The Weyerhaeuser Logged-Off Land Company was liquidated in 1936, as all company lands became producing properties, and its assets were transferred to the Timber Company. The latter in turn formed a Reforestation and Land Department to supervise these holdings. A. F. Firmin, who became the new manager, had authority to lease and option lands, and he was also to conduct thorough studies on reforestation.[30]

To implement the new program, Weyerhaeuser Timber began acquiring large tracts of cutover land. Clemons Logging Company was dissolved in December, 1936, and its cutover reverted to the parent firm, which, the next year, purchased an additional 5,793 acres from the Thomas Irvine Lumber Company and from the O'Neal Land Company. In 1939 it acquired the Cherry Valley cutover land. The Timber Company obtained such tracts not only from subsidiaries and affiliates but also from other companies. The prices were low, for there was little demand as yet for areas already logged.[31]

The plan was to accelerate the reforesting of cutover land. Wherever possible the reforestation would be by natural means. Only land badly burned by fire had to be replanted by hand; most tracts reseeded themselves naturally and would do so rapidly if properly cleared and protected from fire. In new logging operations, "Before cutting is started," wrote C. S. Chapman in 1939, "seed areas are designated to be left to insure that restocking will take place. These areas are in turn carefully safeguarded when burning the debris resulting from logging. . . . Natural seeding is usually accomplished without difficulty."

Although the reforestation program had been launched with reservations, enthusiasm quickly replaced all uncertainties. Frederick E. Weyer-haeuser observed with exhilaration the first visible results: "I shall never forget," he wrote a friend in 1939, "Ed Baker's taking George Crosby, Sumner McKnight and a few others with myself down a short trail through some fairly recently logged-over lands to show us the great number of fir and hemlock seedlings that were shooting up through the grass and brush." Weyerhaeuser's guide, the head of woods operations at Longview, stopped, leaned against a stump, and pointed to thirty or forty seedlings at the roots. Weyerhaeuser "couldn't help feeling that a great many years must pass before those little shoots will seem to bear any relation to the big tree which had stood on this little plot of ground." But he was convinced "that our policy is entirely sound in seeing to it that cutover lands are restocking naturally."

Other Weyerhaeuser properties revealed an equally heartening situation. By the end of the 1930's, sections of Potlatch Forests, Inc., had been under selective logging for about a dozen years. Men in the industry pointed to these forests as an example of what could be accomplished. At Boise Payette Lumber Company in southern Idaho, the directors in 1938 unanimously passed a resolution to study the possibilities for reforestation; this was a start in the very slow process of converting that company to a sustained-yield program.

The one Weyerhaeuser company in the South had initiated in 1937 a comprehensive plan of reforestation, for M. N. Richardson of the Southern Lumber Company in Warren, Arkansas, had become convinced that if the company acreage were increased, future cutting on a sustained-yield basis was feasible. The stockholders agreed, and after new acreage was purchased the program went into operation.

In Minnesota, however, the prospects were not so favorable. The tax laws, as noted, made logging that looked to a sustained yield out of the question. Aside from some selective logging to save "advanced young growth and immature trees," and cooperation in fire protection, The Northwest Paper Company, now the major Weyerhaeuser unit in Minnesota, did not practice scientific forestry: "Under present conditions advanced forest practices are not economically possible and would not bring a return on the investment necessary to put them in effect," wrote a company official.[32]

During 1939–1940 a committee of ten members of Congress investigated the ownership and management of forest lands of the United States. Hearings of this Joint Committee on Forestry were held throughout the country and served to stimulate public interest in the forests. The Weyerhaeuser group had come to agree with the Forest Service on certain general principles. J. P. Weyerhaeuser, Jr., wrote the chief forester in 1939 that the Forest Service and private industry held common views on forestry: each looked to the future, each understood the necessity of cutting old growths and raising new crops, and each believed in forest management.[33]

But despite the similarity in viewpoint, at the end of the thirties Weyerhaeuser forestry practices were still in their infancy, and power to speed their development was lacking. A Weyerhaeuser Timber forester, E. F. Heacox, would visit all the companies' branches and the logging sites, attempting to promote good forestry practices, but he had "no authority to tell anybody what should be done." And he does not today. Heacox recalled later that "it was just simply trying to wheedle a logging superintendent into not burning a piece of slash or doing something which I thought would be better practice or would leave a seed source. . . ." From the Tacoma office a few other foresters also traveled to the WTC branches "to try to sell, promote, and develop forestry." They visited the logging operators and the major contractors buying Weyerhaeuser stumpage, yet in each instance the center of their activities was Tacoma. Years had to pass before modern forestry concepts had permeated the entire organization.

Thus, though the Timber Company directors were all in favor of forestry, when their suggestions filtered down through the various departments in Tacoma to the branch managers and the logging superintendents, there was little result. Top managers of the company were dissatisfied; they had made a start on the road to planned forestry but no more than a start.[34]

In the 1940's Weyerhaeuser forestry methods took more definite form and were imposed with firmer authority. The depression was now well in the past. These were the years in which sound forestry practices were worked out on privately owned timberland and in which extensive forestry research was undertaken by the experts of the Weyerhaeuser Timber Company and Potlatch Forests, Inc. In this decade the former would initiate the "tree farm" movement, and others in the industry, including Potlatch, would follow its lead. This pioneering project was filled with glamor and excitement, for the tree farms caught public interest and demonstrated that lumbermen were no longer derelict in their duty toward the forests.

Phil Weyerhaeuser and Charles Ingram led the Timber Company in formulating and implementing a farsighted program. They realized that for the success of its forestry program it needed far more than a "cluster" of foresters in Tacoma. Instead, trained men must be assigned to the branches. This started in 1940. Heacox left Tacoma to go to Longview, and Tom Orr joined the staff at Klamath Falls. Other experts went to Vail and to Snoqualmie Falls.

Phil and Dave Weyerhaeuser, Minot Davis, and Charles Ingram

journeyed to Klamath in 1942 to persuade Ralph Macartney and Hugh Campbell to adopt forest-management techniques in the Klamath area, where from the beginning no tree of diameter smaller than eighteen inches had been logged. The two Klamath men thought the branch would be economically "better off to keep on the way we were." Top management disagreed. Three days later, Campbell recalls, "direct orders" came down: Klamath should undertake selective logging according to the most advanced forestry practices, which it did.[35]

The resistance to change at Klamath was not atypical. Everywhere the foresters and top management found that the experiments they wanted to perform were difficult to initiate since each area had its established patterns of practice. What "we needed [was] to demonstrate forestry off somewhere apart from any logging operation," recounts Dave Weyerhaeuser.[36] And from this realization sprang the greatest of Weyerhaeuser successes.

Weyerhaeuser Timber owned an extensive tract of land in the Clemons area in Washington. Two bad fires had scorched much of the region, which was one of the best timber-growing areas in the United States. On this ruined land, "Operation Rehab" was projected. The company's forestry experts were to be granted free rein to put into practice theories that their contemporaries considered visionary. In trying out their "wild ideas" they would interfere with no logging operations and upset no programs sanctified through time. The foresters were to give this area the most effective possible plan of protection and reforestation commensurate with sound economics. Thus was planned America's first tree farm. Before an overflow crowd in Montesano, Washington, Governor Arthur B. Langlie in June, 1941, dedicated the project. Here the company committed 130,000 acres to the enterprise, while other owners, state, county, and private, added about 65,000 acres intermingled with or adjacent to the Weyerhaeuser timber. Naturally, the Weyerhaeuser interests took a large part of the responsibility and tended to think of the Clemons Tree Farm as their own accomplishment. The company, cooperating with the Forest Service, worked out the basic forest-management techniques and set up logging schedules, and was mainly responsible for the basic design.

As ideas on Clemons materialized they assumed extensive proportions. The first goal was to make the forest safe from fire. Provision was made for detection, communication, transportation, equipment, and water; and the plan was broader than any ever before initiated.

At appropriate points in the forests, men erected fire-detection stations from which foresters could scan the cutover and wooded areas for smoke. Of six such lookout towers, five were built and staffed by Weyerhaeuser employees. Throughout the forest, men strung miles of telephone line. Old-timers briefly scoffed when Weyerhaeuser employees began putting radio into the woods; but shortly the radio completely replaced the telephone.

Bulldozers, developed for the first time in the thirties, made cheap roads possible, and they aided immeasurably in the colossal task of cutting a pattern of roads through the forests. Three hundred miles of trails and road soon spidered the Clemons Farm. The plan was to approximate a city fire-department type of protection. "If a fire started you just would go immediately with water and put it out," explained a forester. Much had been done elsewhere in preventing and extinguishing fires, but too often immediate suppression had not been feasible. Now with the road pattern, motorized units could travel within a half-mile of any spot, a totally new accomplishment in 1941. While the Clemons operation was not unique, it could be termed an outstanding example of successful enterprise.

To round out the fire-control project, Weyerhaeuser Timber brought in the best modern equipment. Forester Ed Heacox recalls that when the company introduced pumper-tank trucks at Clemons, a few wise old men in the district laughed; but as elsewhere, the fire trucks scored a brilliant success. By fully using waterholes, streams, and earthen dams, it became possible to bring water to any place on the tree farm within an hour's notice. Alert for twenty-four hours a day, an emergency fire crew, hired by the Timber Company, was ready for immediate action at any hint of smoke. The foresters' goal had been 99.75 percent fire prevention and control; the achievement was 99.90 percent.[37]

The Tree Farm also experimented with methods of tree growing. "Scratching, salvaging, seeding, and spraying" kept the region in a hum of activity. "Scratching" involved preparing the land for the crop by scarifying the surface soil. This was mainly done by company employees, partly by contract workers, who cut into the ground, breaking the entanglement of salal, salmonberry, vine maple, and alder; much of the material cleared away was salvaged.

Because of its burned land, the Clemons tree farm would not restock naturally, and the seeding had to be done by man. Attempts at hand-seeding and the transplanting of seedlings proved both slow and expensive. Experiments in aerial seeding were thwarted by rodents that delightedly ate the seeds. A solution to the rodent problem was not found until the fifties. Spraying was used extensively on the farm to kill brush but of course had no effect on small animals.[38]

As a forestry method was found successful at Clemons, it was in turn adopted by the Weyerhaeuser Timber Company branches. Thus the new techniques in design planning, fire control, seeding, and spraying quickly made their contribution to the modernization of company practices.

Moreover, the idea of "Tree Farms," exemplified by the Weyerhaeuser experience, spread throughout the industry. When forester Ed

Heacox had first suggested them to the pulp and paper people and to the American Forestry Association, both groups had been amused. Yet as success followed in Clemons operations, the forest-products industries rapidly prepared to follow Weyerhaeuser precedent.

In 1941 the lumber, pulp, paper, and plywood industries formed the American Forest Products Industries, an organization designed, among other objects, to stimulate tree growing, encourage better forestry practices, and promote public understanding and cooperation in the general field of its activities. Two specific functions may be noted: one to certify "tree farms" for its members and the other to sponsor "keep green" programs. The "keep green" campaign attempted to make the public more alert to the dangers of fire. F. K. Weyerhaeuser was a member of the Executive Committee when the work was launched, and the Timber Company contributed financially, offering to match the combined contributions of other members up to $30,000. Under AFPI's guidance, many states posted "Keep Green" signs along highways bordered by woods. But the AFPI's tree-farm program was by far the more important of its two ventures.

"Tree Farms mean," explained one writer in the *Journal of Forestry,* "adequate forest protection, efficient cutting practices, necessary artificial reforestation and good wood utilization." Large or small private owners of forest property who practiced basic forest management could apply to the AFPI for inspection and certification as a tree farm. The phrase "tree farm," suggested by a Weyerhaeuser public-relations man, Rod Olzendam, was chosen as having a wider, more general appeal than "a property on sustained yield," for, as C. D. Weyerhaeuser put it, "anybody can do tree farming." Timber owners who did not aim at perpetual forest crops could still meet the minimum requirements and make their lands into tree farms.[39]

In the tree-farm movement lumbermen found a golden opportunity to destroy the unhappy prejudices that had arisen in some quarters against their industry. Readers will recall that in 1940–1941 the Weyerhaeusers, along with others, had been indicted by the Department of Justice and signed a consent decree; they will also recollect that for years the public had read of the lumbermen's "ruthless exploitation" of the forests. According to a Princeton public-opinion poll, taken in 1942, four-fifths of the American people believed that measures for perpetuating forest industries were largely the work of public authorities.[40]

By forming lands into tree farms, lumbermen could show the public that they were devoting themselves to the nation's welfare. They could encourage a public attitude of friendliness instead of disdain. The plan to turn privately owned forest land into tree farms would be not only sound business but also excellent public relations. As timberland owners recognized this fact, the practice of tree farming spread rapidly.

Another industry-wide project at the beginning of the forties was the Nisqually Tree Nursery, established by the West Coast Lumbermen's Association. To become part of this larger cooperative effort, the Weyerhaeuser Timber Company abandoned its own nursery. Obviously, the cooperative principle was sounder than individual company effort, and united enterprise was also more economical. "We let an industry nursery raise trees for the whole group," explained Clyde Martin, a Weyerhaeuser forester. Charles Reynolds, formerly of the company nursery at Snoqualmie Falls, went to Nisqually to head the new project. The nursery, which is now named for Colonel Greeley, provided enough seedlings to plant thousands of acres annually. The first crop was lifted from its carefully tilled acres in 1942, and these baby seedlings were then hand-planted on private lands.[41] They were particularly needed for restocking areas that had been scarred by fire or were not adjacent to forest areas that would reseed them naturally.

While the tree-farm movement grew, America entered World War II. The widespread demand for wood and the development of new wood-using industries gave the movement a special impetus. Heavy wartime cutting made lumbermen aware of the need to replenish the supply, a need underscored by the rising price of standing timber. Moreover, the war ushered in a period of great economic prosperity, and a new financial security enabled many firms to experiment with long-term methods.

In 1942 Weyerhaeuser Timber established a forestry research department and employed its first full-time *research* forester. By this time the company had 1,155,131 acres in tree farms. Klamath, Mount St. Helens, Snoqualmie Falls, and Vail had received tree-farm certificates in September, 1942; Klamath Falls became America's first Western Pine tree farm, for the earlier units had all been in the fir region. Next the associates turned to Potlatch Forests, Inc., and in 1943 this property, already under forest management for many years, was properly certified by the AFPI as Idaho's first tree farm. Other undertakings followed in rapid succession—McDonald, White River, Calapooya, Willapa, Cooper Creek (Mollala), Millicoma—until practically all of the Timber Company's woodlands had been certified.[42]

Meanwhile, the federal government had by no means abandoned the promotion of better forest protection and better forestry practices. The year 1944 gave birth to four important forestry acts, all of which benefited lumbermen everywhere. The first amended the Clarke-McNary law of 1924 by increasing the annual appropriation for cooperative fire protection, from $2,500,000 to $6,300,000 for 1945, a sum to be increased before long to $9,000,000.

The second Act provided funds for completing a national survey of forest resources. Under authority granted in 1927, the Forest Service had been surveying the "extent and condition of forest land, the quantity, character, and location of timber, its rate of growth and depletion, and trends in requirements for forest products." The information thus gathered was invaluable to the lumberman.

A third Act revised the tax laws. Previously the tax procedure had given an advantage to the owner who sold his standing timber because the excess of market value over its historical cost was taxed at capital gain rates. In contrast, the owner who cut his own timber was required to treat the excess of market value as ordinary income, subject not only to tax rates much higher than those on capital gains, but, in the case of corporations, also subject to excess-profits tax rates. The discrimination was now eliminated.

The fourth and most important Act instituted a federally sponsored sustained yield program. It was introduced in the Senate by Senator Charles L. McNary of Oregon, who called it a "milestone in the history of federal forest legislation." Its goal was "to stabilize communities, forest industries, employment, and taxable forest wealth." Under the Act the government was authorized to establish sustained-yield units entirely on federal land and also in cooperation with private industry and state and local authorities. The government was permitted to sell national timber in the cooperative units at appraised value without competitive bidding. In federal sustained-yield units competitive bidding was mandatory.[43]

With characteristic initiative, the directors of Potlatch Forests, less than two months after this new McNary Act passed, decided to utilize some of the cooperative sustained-yield provisions. The forestry program of Potlatch Forests received new encouragement at this same meeting when the board agreed to purchase additional cutover lands "as a long term investment to safeguard the Company's permanent forest management." Likewise, directors of the company made plans for a research program as soon as qualified laboratory personnel became available.[44]

In southern Idaho the program of organized forestry was slower in getting under way. Boise Payette in 1944 considered a sustained-yield program, rejected the idea in 1945, and made plans for ceasing operations by 1948. Yet 1948, 1949, and 1950 came and went, and the company seemed destined to continue operations. In 1950 John Aram, soon to become president of Boise Payette, persuaded the board of directors to organize the company's timberland into a tree farm. His idea met with reluctance: "I had quite a time selling that to the board. They [the members] were afraid of committing themselves to something they couldn't live up to." But Aram persisted, and the proposal was approved unanimously.[45]

Later in 1950 Skykomish became a tree farm—the last of the Timber Company's properties to be so organized; and thus by the opening of the second half of the century it had twelve farms of its own and two others in which it shared ownership. Potlatch and Boise Payette were now also operating on a similar basis. In Minnesota a large part of The Northwest Paper Company's land would be very shortly so managed.[46] Tree-farm acreage of Weyerhaeuser associated firms thus had become practically synonymous with Weyerhaeuser ownership.

Among the associated families, credit for the remarkable achievement of Weyerhaeuser Timber in forest management is assigned largely to the planning, foresight, and courage of Phil Weyerhaeuser, aided by C. H. Ingram, the man who made sure that high policy was effectively carried out on lower echelons. Of those men who implemented policy, John Wahl was undoubtedly outstanding. He came to Snoqualmie Falls in 1930 and ultimately became manager of WTC's logging department. He vigorously supported the transition of logging from railroad to truck and the creation of tree farms. As much as any one man, he was responsible for inculcating loggers with advanced ideas on sustained yield, accident prevention, safety programs, and scientific forestry in general.

The action of government both as a threat to private property and as an initiator of forestry schemes, the government-industry cooperation in better fire-control methods, the introduction of skillfully constructed forest-managment plans, the contribution of advanced forestry techniques, the revision of tax laws, and the recognition of the absence of cheap stumpage have all contributed to the change from the old destructive to the new constructive policy. To a Weyerhaeuser firm "the whole company's investment is dependent upon its raw material existing in the forests." The new idea is that the basic asset of the company "is not so much the stumpage standing, but the land that will produce stumpage continuously."[47] Once an ideal that seemed all but attainable, timber as a crop has become the basic practice and the promise of the industry.

NOTES

1. *Weyerhaeuser News*, June, 1952, p. 14.
2. Parain, "The Evolution of Agricultural Technique," *Cambridge Economic History of Europe*, I, 163; Clough and Cole, *Economic History of Europe*, 341.
3. Quoted in Jenkins, "Permanent Production on Potlatch Forests," reprinted from *American Forests*, Aug., 1938.
4. Mason, in Loehr, ed., *Forests for the Future*, 68; plans in PFI Papers.
5. Mason, 76; *Family Tree*, June, 1948,

2; Simons, "Forests for the Future," 4-*SQUARE News,* March 15, 1930, 1; Clearwater Timber Co. Papers.

6. CTC Papers, E. C. Rettig to JPW, Aug. 12, 1929.

7. Simons, 7.

8. Mason, 89; FEW Papers, FEW to JPW, Jr., June 15, 1932, and JPW, Jr., to FEW, June 24, 1932; F. K. Weyerhaeuser to the authors, Sept. 19, 1958.

9. Nixon, ed., *Franklin D. Roosevelt and Conservation, 1911–1945, passim.*

10. Jewett Papers, Jewett to members of Weyerhaeuser committee on taxation, Nov. 10, 1933.

11. Cited in Brogan, *Roosevelt and the New Deal,* 35.

12. Gulick, *American Forest Policy,* 111; Silcox, "Our Adventure in Conservation," *Atlantic Monthly,* CLX, Dec., 1937, p. 721.

13. *Annual Report of Washington Forest Fire Association, 1935;* in *ibid.,* 1938, 15, Chief Fire Warden C. S. Cowan writes of the C.C.C. "Most willingly, I give my meed of praise for a job well-done"; U.S. Forest Service, *Report of Chief Forester,* 1935, p. 41.

14. Ward Shepard to Roosevelt, July 4, 1933, in *Franklin D. Roosevelt and Conservation,* I, 187; Greeley, *Forests and Men,* 137; Mason, 119, 265.

15. Mason, 129–130. Weyerhaeuser representatives at conferences were C. S. Chapman and G. F. Jewett.

16. WTC Papers, CDW memo, 1934; *ibid.,* C. S. Chapman, W. H. Price, and Walter Ryan, "An Analysis of Sustained Yield Possibilities—Longview Unit," Oct. 1934; C. D. Weyerhaeuser, "Sustained Yield: Forest Management," *Forestry News Digest,* Sept. 1936, p. 3; C. D. Weyerhaeuser, Reminiscences; *WC Lbrmn.,* May 1934, p. 11; Shepard, "Analysis of Private Forestry and Public Acquisition Program," March 14, 1940, in *Franklin D. Roosevelt and Conservation,* II, 434; R. R. Macartney, Reminiscences.

17. Loehr in Mason, 7; *WC Lbrmn.,* June, 1935, p. 41; *A.L.A. Schecter Corp.* v. *U.S.A.,* 295 U.S. 495 (1935); Greeley, *Forests and Men,* 135; *WC Lbrmn.,* July 1935, p. 38; WTC Papers, Statement of Pacific Northwest Loggers Association and WC Lbrmn.'s Assn., Nov. 15, 1935; Mason, 182.

18. FEW Papers, FEW to Jewett, Oct. 29, 1935; C. D. Weyerhaeuser, "Sustained Yield," 3 (internal evidence indicates that this 1936 article was written in 1935).

19. PFI Papers, address by Wilson Compton, mgr. Natl. Lbr. Mfgers. Assoc., Oct. 15, 1931; testimony of David Mason: U.S. Congress, *Hearings of Senate Committee on Interior and Insular Affairs, Sustained Timber Yield,* 80th Cong., 2nd Sess., II, 207; Fairchild, *Forest Taxation in the United States.* Fairchild's researches in forest taxation go back to 1908. His major study began in 1926.

20. WTC Papers, C. S. Chapman to G. F. Jewett, Dec. 31, 1931; instructions to manager, WTC Exec. Cmtee. minutes, May 23, 1932; PFI Papers, C. O. Graue to Jewett, Dec. 20, 1932; WTC Annual Report 1932, 35; H. C. Hornby report, Cloquet Lbr. Co., Min. Bk., Feb. 1, 1939; *ibid.,* annl. repts.

21. Oregon's yield-tax law, Feb. 20, 1929 (S.L. Chap. 138, p. 107); Idaho, March 14, 1929 (S.L., Chap. 185, p. 329) and March 2, 1931 (S.L. Chap. 71, p. 124) wherein procedure of classification is amended; Washington, March 12, 1931 (S.L., Chap. 40, p. 124), description in Fairchild, *Forest Taxation,* 372; C. D. Weyerhaeuser, Reminiscences; CTC Papers, for example, Humiston to State Senator John D. Robertson, April 9, 1928; Potlatch Forests, Inc., Min. Bk., Directors' meeting, Jan. 19, 1933; *Washington Reports,* CLXXVII, 65–82; *Pacific Reporter,* 2nd ser., XXXI, pp. 539–546; C. D. Weyerhaeuser, "Sustained Yield," 3.

22. WTC Papers, C. D. Weyerhaeuser, "Report on Logged-Off Land Owner-

ship of the Weyerhaeuser Timber Company," May, 1936, and C. D. Weyerhaeuser, memorandum, undated; C. D. Weyerhaeuser, Reminiscences; JPW, Jr., Papers, FEW to JPW, Jr., Dec. 21, 1939.

23. Cloquet Lbr. Co., annl. repts.

24. Chapman estimated in 1939 that the cost of the extra protection was approximately $150,000 per year: Statement by CSC before Joint Committee on Forestry, 1947.

25. It was much later that *small owners* came to oppose the sustained-yield plan for the O.&C., insisting that it (1) gave monopolies to the big companies, (2) was too regulatory, and (3) interfered with "free enterprise" and was therefore un-American. See statement of Warren Smith, U.S. Congress, *Hearings of Senate Committee on Interior and Insular Affairs, Sustained Timber Yield,* 80th Cong., 2nd Sess., II, 361. The larger owners retained their approval.

26. JPW, Jr., Papers, JPW, Jr., to F. A. Silcox, April 3, 1939; FEW Papers, Jewett to Silcox, Jan. 15, 1938.

27. WTC Papers, Memo by JPW, Jr., and FKW, Sept. 19, 1940; C. S. Chapman to Austin Cary, July 5, 1935.

28. WTC Papers, Silcox to Society of American Foresters, Jan. 28, 1935; Pinchot to Franklin D. Roosevelt, Jan. 20, 1933, *Franklin D. Roosevelt and Conservation,* I, 130; PFI Papers, Jewett to Laird Bell, Jan. 4, 1934.

29. Address to shareholders, May 1, 1937, in WTC Annual Report, 1936. The committal came at the end of 1936. Though Phil Weyerhaeuser reported this to the stockholders, the matter was still not settled. Clyde Martin, WTC forester, recalled in 1956 that "it wasn't until 1944 that the company, in an annual report, officially agreed to back us."—Martin, in C. D. Weyerhaeuser, Reminiscences. The record proves Martin wrong in believing that this was the first such official endorsement; however, Martin's *belief* that it was in-

dicates company hesitancy for the first eight years.

30. C. D. Weyerhaeuser, Reminiscences; WTC Exec. Com. Mins., Sept. 28, 1936; FEW Papers, W. E. Heidinger to FEW, July 28, 1936.

31. WTC Annual Report, 1939.

32. Statement of C. S. Chapman in U.S. Congress, *Hearings of Joint Committee of Forestry,* 76th Cong., 1st Sess., 1246; FEW Papers, FEW to Harry Morgan, June 15, 1939; *WC Lbrmn.,* March 1938, p. 9; Ward Shepard's testimony, *Hearings of Joint Committee of Forestry,* 1848–1849; *The Eagle Democrat* (Warren, Ark.), April 5, 1951; NW Paper Co. Papers, cutting regulations; *ibid.,* Forest Survey Report," 1938; see also FEW Papers, Stuart B. Copeland to FKW and others, July 7, 1937.

33. JPW, Jr., Papers, JPW, Jr., to Silcox, April 3, 1939.

34. Heacox in C. D. Weyerhaeuser, Reminiscences.

35. Campbell, Reminiscences. Campbell misdates the Klamath incident as 1942 instead of 1940. For 1940 date see WTC Papers, "Historical Financial Information," 9. J. P. Weyerhaeuser, Jr., thought he "worked indirectly" on the Klamath men to convince them of the merits of selective logging. Interview, Feb. 24, 1956. Neither Macartney's Reminiscences nor C. D. Weyerhaeuser's clears up this point.

36. C. D. Weyerhaeuser, Reminiscences.

37. The CCC, writes one officer of the WTC, had been the forerunner of the standby fire-suppression crew of later days. Ever since the middle of the 1920's some men in Oregon and Washington had urged plans to reduce the time of arrival at a fire to one hour or less.

38. *Weyerhaeuser News,* 1941, pp. 2–3, and Feb. 1957, pp. 8–9; *WC Lbrmn.,* July, 1941, p. 12; Heacox, Martin, and C. D. Weyerhaeuser in C. D. Weyerhaeuser, Reminiscences.

39. Clyde Martin's address to the NAM, *Weyerhaeuser News,* Feb., 1951, p. 12; W. D. Hagenstein, "Trees and

Taxes," *Journal of Forestry*, LII, Dec., 1954, p. 902; J. P. Weyerhaeuser, Jr., Reminiscences; C. D. Weyerhaeuser, Reminiscences.

40. WTC Papers, Roderic Olzendam to WTC forestry meeting, March 26, 1942.

41. *WC Lbrmn.*, Oct., 1941, p. 58; Martin in C. D. Weyerhaeuser, Reminiscences; *Weyerhaeuser News* (n.d.), p. 14, and Oct. 1955, p. 6.

42. WTC Annual Report 1942, p. 42; WTC Papers, "Tree Farms Certified"; *WC Lbrmn.*, Sept. 1943, p. 20; *March of Pine*, Dec., 1943. S. G. Moon deserves credit for the initiation of selective logging by Boise Payette.

43. U.S. Forest Service, *Report of Chief Forester, 1944,* 10, 21; Loehr in Mason, 232–233.

44. PFI Papers, Min. Bk. of Directors' Meeting, May 20, 1944.

45. BPLC Executive Committee Minutes; Norton Clapp, Reminiscences; John Aram, Reminiscences.

46. WTC Papers, "Tree Farms Certified." The two jointly owned tree farms were Schafer and South Olympic; by the end of 1955, Northwest Paper Co. owned 112,046 acres, of which 99,450 had been placed in 17 tree farms scattered throughout northern Minnesota: See NW Paper Co., annl. repts.

47. WTC annl. repts.; Martin and Heacox in C. D. Weyerhaeuser, Reminiscences.

=

XXVII

Revival in Northern Idaho

Y THE MID-TWENTIES the Weyerhaeusers and their co-investors in the various northern Idaho companies realized that drastic new measures would have to be adopted if they were not to lose large sums of money. The Humbird Lumber Company alone was having consistently satisfactory earnings. Accounts of enterprises at Bonners Ferry, Coeur d'Alene, and Potlatch were showing far more red ink than black. The Clearwater Timber Company was absorbing funds in excess of $200,000 annually in carrying charges, and no move had yet been made to cut its timber.[1]

The poor record of the Idaho undertakings down to 1920 was not difficult to explain. It was part and parcel of the poor record of the entire lumber industry of the Inland Empire. Throughout Idaho and eastern Washington, from 1900 until the World War, profit margins were small and precarious. David Mason, after studying all the major undertakings, reached in 1916 a gloomy conclusion. "A very few companies have paid moderate dividends consistently," he wrote; "some have paid one or two dividends; but most of the companies have not paid any dividends at all."[2]

The difficulties which had made Idaho a Valley of Despond included not only the burdensome state and local taxes but heavy transportation charges to market as compared with the Pacific Coast and the South. To these factors must be added the high percentage of woods other than pine, low percentage of clear lumber, special exposure to fire and insect pests, and the high logging costs imposed by the relatively small amount of timber per acre and by the rugged terrain. In the 1930's many of its timber resources were pronounced "perhaps permanently inaccessible."[3]

It was a land of rugged mountains, precipitous chasms, dashing torrents, and smothering winter snows, as well as of lovely valleys, fertile plains, and harsh arid stretches. Loggers in the high country had to cope with appallingly steep slopes, stretches where road building was practically impossible, and streams too rocky for driving logs.

In fact, Idaho lumbermen had to meet every variety of obstacle and adventure. Mountain camps in midwinter reported snows six to eight feet deep, with the thermometer sometimes twenty below zero. Near one camp, loggers had to dig down to find the tops of telephone poles, while bulldozers had hard work to clear a narrow road through precipices of white. Lumberjacks here took up skiing. "Anybody taking the trouble to look may see them on a nearby hillside, with their stagshirts flying out behind and their tin pants flapping in the breeze."[4] Spring naturally brought floods, muddy terrain, and slippery paths and roads. With summer droughts came the peril of forest fires. In the wilder spots bears were sometimes a nuisance. One spring the Potlatch management grumbled that they were making the vicinity of the cookhouses in the logging camps dangerous; a luckless land agent stumbled on a black bear taking a bath in a pool, while a logger who walked between a mother and her cub had to sprint for his life, Ma Bruin getting the seat of his trousers.

Until the autumn of 1923 little had been done to develop the lordly domain of the Clearwater Timber Company in north central Idaho: more than 200,000 acres, comprising perhaps the finest body of western white pine then in existence.[5] Ten years earlier F. E. Weyerhaeuser had written his brother John: "Now is the time to market white pine," for he believed that the differential between it and other woods would soon disappear.[6] But the European war and the relative inaccessibility of the timber, with other considerations, had delayed action. For the quarter-century since its founding in 1900 the company had substantially confined itself to the purchase of standing timber, selling only a few parcels here and there.

In May, 1923, however, J. P. Weyerhaeuser submitted an all-important memorandum to the officers and directors of the Clearwater Timber Company. He recommended that they ratify a tacit understanding with the Union Pacific for making railroad connections with the Clearwater Company's timber and its projected mill; that they secure options for purchasing property for a dam site and a mill site at Lewiston; that a large mill be located on such property; and that "the officers be authorized to take all necessary steps to finance the new operation, construct mills, logging railroads, camps, mill ponds and purchase all necessary material and equipment."[7] This was the recommendation that was to activate the impressive plant at Lewiston and the utilization of the magnificent holdings of Clearwater Timber.

Not until November, 1924, did the chief stockholders, including John, Charles, and F. E. Weyerhaeuser, meet in St. Paul to make the final key decisions. They had to choose a manager who could obtain a revenue from the proposed investment, for interest charges were high and state taxes seemed all but confiscatory. Until recently men had thought that a railroad into the timber holdings was impossible, but in 1922 an engineer named J. A. Chamberlain had made a report that had afforded some encouragement. Understandings with the Northern Pacific and Union Pacific railroads had then followed. What was much more important, studies of logging possibilities made by E. C. Rettig for the company in the winter of 1923–1924 had promised a sound basis for operations. The estimate of holdings ran to 5,000,000,000 board feet, half of it white pine of high quality. If an able manager could be found, a bright future for the enterprise seemed assured.[8]

At the St. Paul meeting the stockholders canvassed the potentialities of several candidates. The name of Frederick K. Weyerhaeuser was suggested, but his main interest was in selling, not manufacturing. Huntington Taylor, the manager of the Rutledge Timber, came under consideration but was rejected.[9] Finally, the choice fell upon J. P. (Phil) Weyerhaeuser, Jr. He was indeed younger than his brother but had more experience in manufacturing, and satisfied the group. For assistant manager C. L. Billings, then with Rutledge Timber, was chosen.

Phil Weyerhaeuser has been discussed in detail elsewhere, but Billings, only mentioned before, demands notice here. While J. P. Weyerhaeuser, Jr., was soon to become identified with the Weyerhaeuser Timber Company in Washington, Billings would become the guiding executive of the northern Idaho enterprises. A Minnesotan by birth, he had come to the Pacific Northwest in 1910, working first as a timber cruiser in the Lolo area with the United States Forest Service. After studying forestry at the University of Montana, he had taken charge of the United States Forest Service office in Missoula. Then he had joined the Edward Rutledge Timber Company at Coeur d'Alene in 1920 at the age of thirty-two. He was responsible for the forest properties that fed its sawmill, those on Marble Creek, a tributary of the St. Joe River; he looked after contract logging, the sale and exchange of timberland, forest taxes, cruising, and fire protection.

Billings was a man of exceptional force, breadth, and versatility. He was fond of reading, and collected a substantial library on the history of the Pacific Northwest, on which he became an authority. A fluent and witty public speaker, he improved the public relations of the company. A lover of the woods and a stout believer in conservation, he kept abreast of the newest scientific developments in forestry and maintained friendly touch with the Forest Service. Calm and quiet in manner, though blunt of speech, he understood human nature and handled his subordinates astutely. Just as Long had become an important figure in Washington and Oregon, so Billings was to become one of the dominant personalities of the Inland Empire, influential from Spokane to Boise.

2

Both Phil Weyerhaeuser and Billings were determined to use the Clearwater Company to write a new record for Idaho. They made a bold start before the Great Depression struck the West in 1930.

They had not only 200,000 acres of untouched timberland but also a district of remarkable natural attractions. No American river is more picturesque than the Clearwater, with its North, Middle, and South Forks. These streams flow down from mountains covered with white pine, Douglas fir, red cedar, Engelmann spruce, alpine fir, and lodgepole pine. In places they pour through high canyons or past slopes rich in spring with dogwood, syringa, mountain laurel, and wild currant; and their tributaries sometimes enclose attractive meadows or pleasant little lakes. Color can be seen everywhere: the color in spring of millions of blossoms and flowering shrubs, in fall of vivid maple, aspen, and mountain ash. The rivers themselves have color, for the South Fork is bright yellow in summer, the Middle Fork is a lucent silver, and the Clearwater is blue. Much of the forested country remains full of game animals and birds. Everywhere the trees delight the eye—the lodgepole sometimes a solid wall, the spruce lifting their bright plumes aloft, and the white pines towering high and clean into the air.

The railroad built from Lewiston to Headquarters, the main logging camp, was the joint property of the Union Pacific and Northern Pacific, and required a minimum of investment by the Clearwater Company. Nevertheless, the new management, making heavy demands on stockholders for capital, had to undertake a many-sided and formidable construction program. This included a sawmill of the latest design at Lewiston, feeder railways into the timber to bring out logs, numerous roads, minor logging camps, and the improvement of the channel of the Clearwater for log drives.

In April, 1925, Phil Weyerhaeuser opened an office in Lewiston, taking Billings, G. F. ("Fritz") Jewett, and Rettig with him. For almost a year they worked to obtain title to an adequate tract for the sawmill at what had been the county fairgrounds. Part of the ground was intensively cultivated in fruits and vegetables by more than forty families. It took much persuasion as well as money to buy the land; but leading people of Lewiston aided the company in acquiring titles and paying for land, the monetary gifts being later returned. The building of the sawmill finally began in February, 1926, and the first logs were sawed with much rejoicing on August 8, 1927.

A tremendous dam was required here across the Clearwater, its length 1,100 feet, its height varying from 35 to 55 feet, and its thickness at the base 50 feet. By agreement the Inland Light and Power Company constructed it, with an efficient hydroelectric plant. The water filled a 320-acre pond, nearly a mile and a half long, and in places 35 feet deep. Logs came down to it both by river and rail. The plant enjoyed a great advantage in such ample water facilities and in the electric power to drive its machinery; and it owed both in great measure to the foresight of J. P. Weyerhaeuser. With a companion, he had traveled in a bateau down the Clearwater, the Snake, and part of the Columbia looking for a place where logs might be held; and from this trip, in part, had sprung the decision to place the Clearwater operation at Lewiston.

The sawmill itself, built by F. W. Horstkotte of Portland, was designed to so utilize five band headrigs that all could be kept continuously supplied with logs, and the flow of lumber to the sorting works would be uninterrupted. The best saws and trimmers were installed.[10] Special attention was paid to lumber storage. At the beginning the mill had thirty-seven dry kilns, all of reinforced concrete and more than a hundred feet long. They were soon increased to nearly twice that number, capable of drying at least nine-tenths of the lumber cut. The plant also included a planing mill, a large remanufacturing plant, and a box factory to utilize trimmed remnants and spoiled lumber.

Meanwhile, the necessary railroad construction had been rapidly carried out. The Union Pacific and Northern Pacific undertook jointly to complete the 41-mile line from Orofino (which lies on the Clearwater due east of Lewiston and is county seat of Clearwater County) to Headquarters. The difficulties may be gathered from the fact that as originally plotted the line crossed Orofino Creek fifty-one times in a dozen miles. After leaving the Clearwater the railway climbs 2,600 feet with maximum curves of twelve degrees. It crosses the divide to the North Fork in deep cuts with abrupt slopes and then gradually drops 500 feet to its terminus. At Headquarters was erected a machine shop capable of repairing locomotives.

At Headquarters the line also made connections with the logging railway the Clearwater Company built into the forest. Before the sawmill cut its first log, ten miles of this logging spur were ready. Its standard-gauge tracks intersected a series of wooded ridges stretching up from the Clearwater like the fingers of a hand; the managers planned to run feeder railways along these ridges, some for twenty miles. The company bought four Heisler locomotives and brought in 400 Union Pacific and Northern Pacific flatcars. It also acquired a number of power loaders.[11]

The first logging was naturally done close to the river and the railroad. Seven camps were fitted out with bunks, cook sheds, stables, and blacksmith shops. Primeval solitudes suddenly awakened to life, as the whistle of locomotives, the whine of saws, the thud of axes, the neighing of teams, and the shouts of men that summer of 1927 echoed through them. From some camps on perilous slopes horses dragged logs along greased chutes to railway loading platforms; from others, loggers, using caterpillar tractors, pulled timber down to the foaming Clearwater.

All along the lower course of that stream the company had blasted out ledges and boulders that might have obstructed logs, and had built wing dams to shut off side pools and sloughs that would have caught floating timber. A little paddle-wheel steamer, the *Clara,* was used chiefly in the log pond for picking up deadheads and pile driving. Five miles above the entrance to the Lewiston log pond a 600-foot fin boom threw logs to the east side of the river, and nearer the entrance two smaller booms completed the diversion. Massive rock-filled cribs held the booms in place.[12]

The Clearwater managers counted on sawing 200,000,000 board feet of lumber a year, anticipating that 150,000,000 feet of logs would be brought out of the woods by rail and the remainder by water.[13] They would be floated down the river for 80 miles at first, and longer distances later, by trained log drivers under Captain J. L. Webb, who had a long experience with the Upper Mississippi drives. One striking feature of the company's transportation system was the construction of large flumes to carry logs from inaccessible forest areas. Along Evans Creek ran a four-and-a-half-mile stretch of "V" flume, made of heavy timbers and practically watertight. Along Big Creek ran another eight-mile stretch, with sides three feet high. Logs were piled at convenient points; a heavy head of water was dammed back at the top of the flume and then suddenly released; and the logs, tipped into the crest of the flood, went bobbing down the swift current as fast as a man could run.

For a time before the sawmill opened, its managers hoped that lumber might be carried by steamboat down the Snake from Lewiston to the Columbia and then to salt-water ports. The Snake covers 151 miles from Lewiston to its junction with the Columbia at Pasco, Washington. An expert employed in the early 1920's reported that its channel was from 10 to 20 feet deep, with 1 percent of its course broken by small rapids having 5 to 7 feet of water.[14] He thought that wing dams could be built at moderate cost to eliminate the rapids and that steamers drawing four feet could run over any of them anyway. The Columbia from Pasco to Celilo Locks at the Dalles covered a water distance of 152 miles. The channel nearly all the way was from 10 to 30 feet deep and a half-mile or more wide. The Columbia, too, had its rapids, apart from those by-passed by canal at the Dalles gorge. However, the agent wrote that they could be traversed upstream or down by light-draft steamers "without any trouble whatever." Unfortunately, a later and more careful study proved that the impediments on the Snake in particular were too grave to be overcome. The dream of steamboats rolling down to Portland vanished.

3

The Clearwater Company, at huge expense, had made a bold start; and boldness characterized all its operations. Phil Weyerhaeuser and Billings, young and determined, had surrounded themselves with youthful executives. It encouraged them to see the bright, clean Lewiston mill rumbling busily to meet its capacity mark of 350,000 feet of lumber every eight-hour day. It cheered them to see a chunky Heisler locomotive rattle a line of timber-loaded flatcars down the valley of Alder Creek. They delighted in watching a hundred horses steaming at twilight in the Headquarters stables as they munched their oats; in observing a knot of lumberjacks with peaveys topple log after log into the Evans Creek flume; in following an old-fashioned wanigan, built of cedar logs held together by twisted chokecherry vines or other materials, as it carried its crew along the North Fork; and in witnessing the spectacular spring drive on the Clearwater.[15]

Boldness characterized timber-management activities of the company. Theodore Fohl knew the timber intimately. E. C. Rettig, now in 1960 executive vice-president, became the company's land agent and chief forester. A graduate of the University of Idaho School of Forestry, he had begun work with the Weyerhaeuser interests in 1920 as a timber cruiser, working out of Orofino. Like Billings, he took a passionate interest in the woods and in scientific conservation. While cruising, he had been an assistant fire warden for the Clearwater Timber Protective Association. Nobody knew the white pine stands of the Clearwater region better.[16]

Rettig's study on behalf of Weyerhaeuser interests, conducted during the winter of 1923–1924, had acquainted him with the different methods of logging, types of camps, modes of handling labor, and transportation problems of a number of Washington and Oregon companies that cut timber in steep, rough country. His report threw light on the marked postwar progress in mechanization, and provided a guide for Clearwater's own logging plans. Rettig learned that gasoline skidders (laymen would say log haulers) had come into widespread use in the Pacific Northwest. A small skidder made by Ford—a Fordson tractor with drums in place of rear wheels—struck Rettig as specially useful in some difficult areas. It handled timber for distances up to 2,000 feet, cleared logs, stumps, and small trees from the right-of-way of logging roads, and did all manner of odd jobs. Light, cheap, easily operated, using a minimum of fuel and water, it could be very helpful. But Rettig found ground-skidding open to serious objections. It did not work well in "small, short, and sharp cross ravines"; it was subject to sudden stops; and it "destroys all reproduction and standing timber." He therefore closely scrutinized the several modes of high-lead and skyline skidding.

These types of logging had reached a fairly high development. The Ledgerwood system of skyline timber handling at this time employed steel spars a hundred feet in height as alternatives to tree spars. Heavy cables were attached by block and pulley. A main skidding engine, a four-drum utility engine, and a small engine for tightening guy lines operated the steel spar gear. In addition, a three-drum engine operated a swinging boom loader that placed logs aboard trucks. "Of all the different methods of power logging I have seen," wrote Rettig, "I believe this method to be the best for our country. It seems to be more flexible and can be more easily adapted to logging either large or small logs, in rough or level country, than other rigs." However, the Ledgerwood system had its disadvantages. The steel tower, engines, and other equipment were heavy, up to 150 tons or more; and even if divided between two trucks of sixteen wheels each, required strong bridges and fills. They also demanded highly skilled labor. Finally, the equipment cost so much that overhead charges were prohibitive unless it could be kept in almost continuous operation. Rettig, therefore, felt it necessary to describe various alternative types of power logging.[17]

He still thought horse logging the cheapest method in small timber. "My belief is that power and horse logging can be combined." This was a wise conclusion, which the management approved. Combined they were for many years, and while still using, in part, the simple older logging methods the Clearwater Company moved cautiously in the purchase of power-logging machinery.

A notable feature of Rettig's report was his attention to labor problems and his emphasis on the fact that the Pacific Coast was ahead of Idaho. The logging camps of Washington and Oregon would soon be as modern as a good hotel, and already offered recreations not found in small towns:

Moving pictures, card and pool tables, reading rooms and even a dance hall are getting to be quite common.

The bunk houses and camp cars are being subdivided so that fewer men are living in the same room. Sheets and pillow cases are supplied and some camps have a bedmaker. Such camps always have a neat and orderly appearance and should instil a higher morale among the men. It is claimed that segregating the men into smaller bunches makes it harder for men with Wobbly principles to get together and organize strikes and labor disturbances in the camps.

Another striking thing about the camps on the Coast is the fact that there is a growing tendency to equip them for married labor. This is a strong point in averting labor troubles.

In applying the principles enunciated in the report, Rettig was cordially supported by Billings, Jewett, and J. P. Weyerhaeuser, Jr. The previous chapter has told how Clearwater led in initiating the sustained-yield ideas of David T. Mason and how it rapidly adopted the best forestry practices.

Under the direction of chief engineer Robert T. Bowling, the Clearwater group also experimented boldly in making wood-fuel briquettes from the mass of sawdust, splinters, and chips formerly fed constantly into the tall burner. Many inventors had tried to utilize such refuse, and failed. They had attempted direct pressure, to which the material would not permanently yield, for the cellular structure of wood is too resilient. Bowling soon found that a combination of pressure, moisture, heat, and cooling, each component applied according to careful formulas, was necessary. The heat of hot flue gases was first used to dry the wood. Pressure— gradual, continuous, intense—then melted the hemacellulose in the wood and broke down the cell wall, rendering the material semiplastic; and as the lignin cooled in a tight mold, it set the composition in a very dense form. The result was an excellent fuel that burned slowly with great heat. But once these principles were determined, they must be applied through an effective machine. Bowling brought much ingenuity and persistence to its design and use in making the resultant briquettes, called Pres-to-Logs.[18]

It was found that the logs could be made from practically all varieties of wood and indeed any fibrous material. They were ideal for city fireplaces, for dining cars on trains, and other places where concentrated, almost smokeless fuel was needed. Before long the company was making machines which it installed on a rental basis with a number of firms; by the Second World War, thirty-five were in use in the far-western states and one in South Africa. Bowling in 1939 improved the pressure heads so that the briquettes became structurally stronger and had greater durability in burning. At that time the 35 installed machines, 27 of which were operated by the Weyerhaeuser interests, could make about 120,000 tons of Pres-to-Logs a year.

4

Economic depression had struck the lumber industry of the West as early as 1926 and took a tighter grip in 1929. Overproduction, long a crippling factor, now became disastrous. As industrial and home construction came to a stop after the stock-market panic of 1929, demand for lumber dropped sharply. For three years of the Great Depression, domestic building averaged only 15 percent of that in the prosperous mid-twenties. Small business collapsed, and the bigger companies staggered.[19]

For some time the Inland Empire had been especially hard hit. Logging costs were high because of the exceptionally rough country, and the relatively light stands per acre. The Panama Canal permitted Coast lumber to reach the Atlantic Coast for $10 to $15 per thousand less in transportation costs than the all-rail charge of shipment from Idaho. At the same time, state and local taxes were increasing, for as Idaho developed, roads, schools, public health services, power lines, and governmental agencies required planning and building. The tax burden placed a specially heavy strain on owners of large forests. Capital costs were also painfully high for the Weyerhaeuser ventures in Idaho, for the bulldozed roads, the laboriously-graded logging railroads, the flumes, and the camps had involved heavy outlays. Lumbering which depended largely on driving logs down creeks and river, as in the Clearwater region, bore a peculiar burden. An entire season's cut of logs had to be financed before any could be sawed and sold as lumber.[20]

All the Idaho companies but the Humbird became fearful of bankruptcy. The Bonners Ferry operation was terminated in 1926. Edward Rutledge Timber Company never really recovered from two terrible conflagrations of the 1920's, which not only devastated the trees, but burned out camps, flume chutes, and other installations. The fire of 1922 gutted the wonderfully fine stand on Marble Creek. An injudicious effort was made to salvage the injured timber by bringing it over the ridge and dropping it down an inclined railway to a branch of the Milwaukee Railroad near Clarkia; a grimy, choking, dangerous task, whose frustrations were remembered for decades. The managers, Huntington Taylor and E. J. Gaffney, had to meet some dismaying impediments. They had to build expensive dams; the timber driven down Marble Creek was "broomed" at both ends; supplies had to be hauled in by mule teams over poor roads and up steep grades. In the spring mud season both men and animals suffered great hardships. An odor of misfortune and discouragement clung to the Rutledge Company.[21]

The Potlatch Lumber Company, with rich forests and a large mill, stood in a better position. But neither of its first two managers really mastered lumber manufacturing. William Deary, with his thunderous brogue, swift decisions, and driving energy, was primarily a logger, as the quiet, sympathetic A. W. Laird, keenly interested in the town of Potlatch and the welfare of its people, was primarily a financier. Much of the lumber produced in the early 1920's, because of the mistaken policies of a sawmill manager brought from Northland Pine, was poorly cut.

When R. E. Irwin went to Potlatch in 1923 to take charge of logging and lumber manufacture, he found that salesmen had become reluctant to handle Potlatch material, because many boards had to be remanufactured before they were usable. He and Frederick K. Weyerhaeuser, who went to work for Potlatch at the same time, succeeded in altering the situation, but only at great expense. Changes had to be made in the sawmill, a remanufacturing plant built and better drying sheds erected. "It cost about a million dollars to develop this," recalled Irwin later, "but we got it to a point where it was a good operation."[22] Among other improvements, he erected a box factory. A sandy-haired, soft-spoken Scot with a genial twinkle in his eye, he became immensely popular with everyone. When Laird died, Irwin was appointed manager. "No one," men said, "knew pine better." Potlatch Lumber, however, had not got a really sound start before the depression came.

Bankruptcy for Rutledge, for Potlatch, for Clearwater—this lay ahead unless drastic measures were undertaken. The prospect was too dreadful to be regarded calmly. In Tacoma, Lewiston, and St. Paul men searched for a remedy. Most of them concluded that the three companies must be merged.

Much of the Clearwater timber could best be taken to the Potlatch mill and some even to the Rutledge mill; some of the Rutledge timber properly belonged to Potlatch. Above all, a great deal of the Rutledge and Potlatch work could well be transferred to Lewiston. A unified management could divide the timber efficiently, assigning to each of the three operations its proper type of produce. Some machinery could be pooled and labor interchanged.

As early as 1927 Fritz Jewett had advocated a consolidation, and won the support of the engineer E. J. Brigham, who prepared a plan. One by one the executives fell into line. By the summer of 1929 F. E. Weyerhaeuser was suggesting a merger that should take in not only Clearwater, Rutledge, and Potlatch, but Humbird, the Boise Payette Company, and Klamath. The gigantic company which resulted should devote itself, he thought, to white and ponderosa pine. One officer liked a broad consolidation but would omit Boise Payette. C. R. Musser suggested two unifications, one in northern Idaho, the other adjoining Boise Payette with Klamath.[23]

Finally, when in 1930 Laird Bell became head of a committee to study the problem, the proposal really began to move. Bell, who had thus far devoted himself principally to his law practice in Chicago, explained that he had no definite ideas but did not wish to be chairman of a body which reported progress year by year without actually progressing! One day he, Jewett, Charles J. McGough, and C. R. Musser sat down in St. Paul under the delusion that they might "put together the merger that afternoon." They spent two hours wrangling over the first item, the disposition to be made of the cash in each company's coffers. Questionnaires were then sent to the five companies asking for information. By the time the answers were digested, more modest ideas concerning the scope of the merger had prevailed.[24] For geographic reasons, Boise Payette and Klamath were dropped from the list. Because the Humbird Lumber Company had a body of timber ripe for harvest, was nearing the end of its cutting, and wished to enjoy alone the profits that it was expected to bring, it also was omitted. This left Clearwater, Potlatch, and Rutledge.

The three companies made a natural geographical unit. As Charles J. McGough writes, one who himself did accounting work of the greatest value, their union was so logical that in the end it was unopposed:

The merger was put together on the basis adopted by the committee. The relative values of assets of timber and of lumber were discussed prior to the stockholders' meetings of the various companies with the managers of the interested companies, who in turn discussed it with their principal stockholders and directors. So when it came time actually to put this to a vote of the stockholders, it was a mere formality. Mr. Laird Bell did a tremendous amount of work and really put it over. He had great influence with all the associates. His first real assignment in the lumber business constituted his grand entry into it, because he did a swell job. It was a lot of work; it was also a lot of fun. I think the merger saved a tremendous amount of money because it resulted in more efficient operations.[25]

The heaviest single task in consummating the merger was the appraisal of the timber holdings of the three companies in a way that would satisfy all stockholders. To assist in this the associates retained the firm of Mason & Stevens, which had made such valuations all over the West. H. L. Torsen, the treasurer, did most of the accounting work and computed income taxes.[26] One Potlatch Lumber stockholder named Fred K. Wright, an early associate of Deary, fought the consolidation tooth and nail on the ground that it did an injustice to his particular interests, but he died before the litigation he started was completed.

The new corporation came into existence April 29, 1931, under the name of Potlatch Forests, Inc. (P.F.I. for short), with a capital stock of 300,000 shares (no par value). The retail yards of the old Potlatch Lumber Company were transferred to a new concern called Potlatch Yards, Inc. All the properties of the Clearwater Timber Company were made over to Potlatch Forests, Inc., for approximately 160,700 shares of its stock and $700,000 in debentures; and all the properties of the Edward Rutledge Timber Company for approximately 18,300 shares and $2,015,000 in debentures. Final legal action was taken by two lawyers in an attorney's office in Augusta, Maine.

The great step had been taken just in time. Half the industries of the nation were almost prostrate, none worse stricken than the lumber industry. "Had Potlatch Lumber been in danger of shutting down?" an interviewer later asked Charles J. McGough. "I think all the companies were," he replied, "because there wasn't really enough white pine business to go around."[27]

5

From this time forward the history of the associates in Idaho was the record of just two large companies, Potlatch Forests, Inc., in the north and Boise Payette in the south. The Humbird Lumber Company in the panhandle soon ceased to count; it stopped logging and sawing in 1931, sold its remaining timberlands and mills, ran its planing mills till 1934, and liquidated its inventory of lumber. Dividends from 1900 to 1937, totaled 430 percent, with some residual payments still to come.

For several years the economic storm beat disastrously on P.F.I.; Phil Weyerhaeuser, Billings, Jewett, and Rettig were harassed by one problem after another. In 1931–1932 the lumbermen of the Pacific and Mountain states did only a quarter to a third of their normal business. Blind competition, price slashing, and wage cuts, with part-time operation where mills kept going at all, were the general story. The Loyal Legion of Loggers and Lumbermen in March, 1932, tried, as noted, to hold the wage line at $2.60 a day, but many desperate companies had reduced their scale to $2. In Seattle alone that spring 50,000 to 60,000 men stood in the breadlines.[28] Potlatch Forests, Inc., did its best to care for its employees, but it also had to cut wages. By the end of 1932 it was unable to pay its tax bills or to meet the interest on its railroad obligations.

In this crisis the ability of Potlatch to close down unprofitable activities with a rapidity and decision that the separate companies could never have shown was of vital importance. The Elk River unit, which had stopped in 1930, was kept closed. It furnished machines and parts for repairs and replacements in the other mills, then was totally dismantled in 1936.[29] The Potlatch plant did not run in 1932 except to ship lumber in storage, and on November 1st of that year its accounting department was taken to Lewiston. At the same time the Edward Rutledge unit at Coeur d'Alene was closed. Fritz Jewett, announcing the fact with the deepest regret, declared that the company could no longer afford to run at a loss. "I wish to call your attention," he told the Coeur d'Alene townspeople, "to the fact that excessive taxation is an important factor in this economic situation. Last year Potlatch Forests, Inc., paid in taxes and fire-protection charges, a form of taxation, almost exactly a half-million dollars. Although these taxes have been somewhat reduced this year, we are forced to meet this expense in December, or suffer confiscation of our property." In another letter he asserted that the average tree in Idaho had already been taxed greater sums than it could be sold for in normal times.[30]

The start of 1933 saw a change in P.F.I. management. When Phil Weyerhaeuser became vice-president of the Weyerhaeuser Timber Company, Billings by general consent was promoted to fill his place as chief executive of Potlatch Forests. Facing his new responsibilities, Billings showed an unusual power of continued growth. He had strong outdoor tastes, strengthened during his long experience in the Forest Service, and refused to stick closely to his Lewiston desk. Men working in the old Potlatch and Rutledge woods saw him on frequent tours of inspection. He liked to take parties of state officials, federal foresters, and business visitors into the field, carrying on hot discussions with them—for he enjoyed a clash of ideas. He made systematic efforts to hire able young men who would staff the company for years to come. "I'm proud that we're a company of young executives," he would tell callers.

Happily, the year 1934 brought some improvement in economic conditions, and further gains were slowly made. In 1937 P.F.I. showed net income carried to surplus of $500,945, actually a consolidation of earnings for 1936 *and* 1937. All other years from 1931 through 1939 produced losses, and stockholders received a total of only $280,899 in dividends, all in 1937. "We started 1937," the general manager reported, "with all mills shipping at near capacity and with the Clearwater sawmill running two shifts." Then came a renewal of the depression, but this proved fairly brief. The manager was glad to report that pay increases in 1936–1937 brought wages to the highest figure ever paid by the company.[31]

Late in the 1930's the company began to reap the full benefits of the merger. The principal fruits may be summarized under a half-dozen heads.

First, Billings and his co-workers carried through an integration that resulted in much more effective management of resources, manpower, and equipment. For physiographic reasons, which any relief map of Idaho would make obvious, the activities of P.F.I. gravitated toward Lewiston as head and center. A great part of the combined timber holdings could be better handled there. For a time residents of Coeur d'Alene and Potlatch feared decline and decay. "It looked," writes a Potlatch resident of those days, "as if most of their timber would be headed toward Lewiston, and that eventually the two towns would dry up." These fears proved exaggerated. After all, the Potlatch unit, with its great mill and large forest holdings, were certain of permanence. Though Rutledge was weaker, its new management under Jewett, with Clarence Graue as assistant, was enterprising and efficient. Both were terribly depressed by the prospect that the plant might be closed down permanently. When Frederick K. Weyerhaeuser suggested that they might buy lumber from little mills scattered through the hills and fetch it down to Coeur d'Alene to be planed and seasoned, they eagerly adopted his proposal. They also bought standing timber to supplement the original holdings. Thus the Rutledge unit was sustained, after being closed down in the depth of the depression, with a production of perhaps 40,000,000 feet a year, "a beautiful little operation."[32]

All three units—Coeur d'Alene, Lewiston, and Potlatch—were kept well coordinated. The managers exchanged tractors, trucks, power saws, and other apparatus; they shifted men and horses as needed; they ended a costly amount of duplication. By employing only one set of accountants and one sales force, where three had formerly operated, they reduced overhead. Rettig, applying his ideas of conservation, saw that cutting was much more carefully managed. As had been the case earlier, the strong central direction unhesitatingly expunged any unprofitable undertaking. Thus early in 1940 Billings sold the bank the associates had long maintained in Potlatch to some Boise financiers who engaged to maintain it for at least some years.[33]

As a second gain, the consolidated company now had larger capital resources with which to pursue a policy of mechanizing all possible activities in the woods and mills alike. Because much of the ground was too steep for tractors, horses continued to play an important role in logging. But by 1937 one large camp in the Clearwater Forest used tractors alone, and so did one of the contract loggers. The company owned more than fifty tractors, large and small. By that date road construction had been revolutionized by the advent of bulldozers, of which every logging camp had one or two in constant use. Trucks were seen everywhere transporting logs and were able to climb even thirty-degree slopes. All along the railroads logs were placed on flatcars by heavy gasoline or oil-burning hoisting machines, able to load daily 125,000 feet of timber apiece. Most of the railroad logging camps had been pleasantly improved. Only fourteen men were put in a bunk car, which was lighted by electricity and heated by Pres-to-Logs, while meals were served at small tables in dining cars, and the cooks prided themselves on the variety of the fare and the attractiveness of the service.[34]

Moreover, the consolidated company could efficiently utilize materials that had once been wasted. It took great pride in the Pres-to-Log machine. It developed also a sizable cedar-pole business for supplying telegraph, telephone, and power companies.[35] In forest practice P.F.I. cut the large white pines selectively, felling them to avoid damaging smaller trees and groves of seedlings. These careful logging methods saved the standing cedars. Logging finished, special crews went into the best stands to take the merchantable cedar poles. These were floated down the Clearwater—12,000 in one June drive in 1939—to Ahsahka, where a special treating plant and yard had been provided; here they were hauled from the water and piled by caterpillars. "Cedar makers," as the loggers were called, were expert craftsmen, who felled, trimmed, and peeled about a dozen poles each per day.[36]

One innovation deserves special mention. In 1940 the company successfully launched an edge-gluing process by which narrow stock was converted into lumber of any width. The ingenious R. T. Bowling, author of Pres-to-Logs, constructed a machine that, by the use of heat, pressure, and glue, fastened boards at the edges all but indissolubly. The product was so tough that if stress was applied, the board would split in the grain and not in the glued seam. It could be surfaced so evenly that the glued boards remained even flatter than the solid wide lumber. Nor was the cost excessive.[37]

A progressive temper animated the company. In 1940 it employed an expert from the University of Michigan Forestry School to carry out time and cost analyses of the woods operations.[38] Throughout all these years it conducted an award system under which employees were paid for constructive suggestions. It fought steadily to reduce the accident rate, posting such signs as "It's Hell to Be a Cripple" everywhere and setting new national records for safety in sawmills and planing mills.

Perhaps the largest of all the fruits of the P.F.I. merger was the ability of the consolidated company to work out with the national and state governments a conservation program of greater efficiency than the three separate corporations could have achieved. The striking success of the company's forestry program has been noted.

In some parts of Idaho the P.F.I. holdings, the federal and state forests, and small homesteaded tracts were intermingled in the most confused fashion. "In our territory," Fritz Jewett wrote just as the merger was completed, "we find the government a serious competitor in the matter of timber holdings. The government is selling some of its stumpage at a price less than the taxes that we have paid over a period of years."[39]

The basic need facing the large owners was to block up their timber in such a way that cutting for the various mills could be supported on a perpetual-yield basis. To effect the needed arrangements, the Potlatch management had to carry on protracted negotiations, use great tact, and make compromises that were sometimes painful.

But despite the pressure for heavy indiscriminate cutting to reduce the losses of the depression period, Potlatch under Billings kept the permanent stability of the industry steadily in mind. Indeed, everyone concerned with Potlatch—the Weyerhaeusers, the Mussers, Laird Bell, and the Lewiston executives—was concerned to make the sustained-yield program a success.

Year after year P.F.I. gave much time, largely through Fritz Jewett ("Mr. Private Forestry"), Billings, and Rettig, to the education of the public.[40] The company persuaded state officers to help arrange public exhibits illustrating Idaho's timber resources and products, some of them in the state capital itself. It assisted such speakers as State Senator John D. Robertson of Weiser to lecture widely. These spokesmen and various editors were encouraged to emphasize the importance of forest industries, to describe the best means of fire protection, to popularize ideas of re- forestation and conservation, and to explain how the antiquated tax sys- tem of the state compelled hard-pressed timber owners to resort to reckless cutting. Meanwhile, Billings, Rettig, and their associates were making steady progress in putting conservation practices into effect.

6

If the 1930's, from the standpoint of company management, had been a decade of gloom, the war years brought—along with many prob- lems—a more cheerful financial outlook. A report of P.F.I. for the decade ending December 31, 1940, abounded in depressing items. The net loss for the period had been $8,740,000. A number of investments, including the Elk River plant and railroad, had been written off completely. Average lumber prices had fallen as low as $23.80 per thousand in 1932, then risen to $36.71 in 1937, only to decline again in the recession of 1937– 1938. Subsequent rises in price were still not enough. But a five-year re- port at the end of the war (December 31, 1945) showed profits for the period after income-tax deductions of $5,144,000. The company had distributed dividends aggregating $26.50 per share during the preceding five years. The liquidation of surplus facilities had ceased. During these five years P.F.I.'s federal and state income taxes had come to $3,785,000.

Best of all, the prospects for the future were bright. The Clearwater, Potlatch, and Rutledge units were all thriving. For the first time the finances of the firm permitted consideration of large investments for ex- pansion and fuller utilization of available timber and wood products; stockholders could anticipate plowing a substantial portion of earnings back into timberland, improving existing plants, and erecting new plants for full-scale integrated operations.

Before the war ended, in fact, directors and officers of P.F.I. had begun to plan for future developments. In 1943 the sum of $50,000 per month was set aside as a contingency reserve fund; it totaled $1,200,000 by May, 1945, and stood ready for use in fostering new products and bettering plant facilities. In 1944 Billings constructed an engineering re- search laboratory at Lewiston, with Bowling in charge. "Fifteen separate projects," boasted the company, "divided into four general classifications, are now under way or soon to be undertaken in the workshop built for P.F.I.'s engineering department." Early the next year Billings reported

to the executive committee on the application of new machines for manufacturing white fir slots, shooks for boxes, and sawed and tapered fenceposts. Possible installation of log-barking machines were also discussed.[41]

Between 1945 and 1948 P.F.I. under Billings initiated further adjustments to the changed situation inside and outside the firm. In response
to the implications of their first tree farm, started in 1943, and the need
to use all species of trees available within the company's cutting area, the
Potlatch mill was modernized, the volume of production reduced but the
plant enlarged to provide more varied fabrication of lumber. New, specialized machinery was also installed at Coeur d'Alene and Lewiston. Late in
1946 Rettig announced that the company planned to produce logs according to a set schedule of 42 percent white pine, 20 percent ponderosa pine,
16 percent red fir and larch, 19 percent white fir, and 3 percent cedar and
spruce. The plan had to be modified from time to time, but the significant
aspect of the report was the wide use of mixed woods and the diminishing
reliance on white pine. During the next year directors and officers discussed all the problems involved in manufacturing veneer and plywood
as well as pulp, finally deciding to build a veneer plant and to continue
study of the possibilities of a pulp operation.[42]

Unfortunately, Billings died (June 1948) before he could see the
two new ideas become realities. Since coming to the Clearwater Timber
Company as assistant general manager in 1925, he had helped write a
dramatic chapter in the history of northern Idaho. The story was in large
part his own after he became general manager of P.F.I. in 1933, though
he worked closely with Presidents Phil Weyerhaeuser, R. M. Weyerhaeuser, and G. F. Jewett. Three companies, important not only to the
Weyerhaeusers and their co-investors but to the prosperity of half a state,
had for a time been threatened with catastrophe. A timely unification,
and the efforts of a remarkably able group of men, had saved them.

Under Billings the new firm had weathered a violent depression,
adopted new techniques of lasting value, provided leadership in selective
cutting of timber and in establishing tree farms, increased output of wood
products for the nation, and furnished employment to thousands of wage
earners. He had drawn foremen into his counsels, and had experienced
only two serious brushes with unions—in 1936 and 1947. He had brought
to P.F.I. "the good will of his former associates in the United States Forest
Service,"[43] a factor of major importance in his efforts to work collabo-
ratively with federal and state officials on conservation and wise use of
forest resources.

Urged on by Frederick K. Weyerhaeuser, directors of P.F.I. had
found time, even during the heat and hurry of World War II, to plan
a plant at Lewiston to peel large white pine logs into rolls of veneer. Roy

Huffman, charged with developing new products, gave three years of study to the undertaking. The peeling of successive layers or strata from Douglas fir to make plywood was now familiar to the whole nation, and a large market for such materials was being created. Preliminary studies, which seemed encouraging, were carried out. The hope was that P.F.I could make a white pine veneer which would be practically a new product in the United States and would satisfy a special demand. The decision to manufacture the product was reached in 1947, and on August 5, 1948, initial output of the veneer began. Men dreamed of the time when rooms from New York to San Diego would be paneled—living rooms, bedrooms, playrooms, libraries—in knotty white pine veneer from the forests of northern Idaho. Unfortunately, this undertaking proved expensive and impractical, but the veneer establishment was later converted into a fully equipped plywood plant, which did achieve success.[44]

Not until a year after Billings's death did discussion of pulp manufacturing at Lewiston lead to action. Already the directors had read masses of data and heard recommendations made by Grellet N. Collins, a consultant on pulp manufacture, and numerous officers of the company. As early as May, 1948 the minutes of P.F.I. had carried the succinct statement: "It is determined that this corporation build up its own organization to sell its own pulp." On May 2, 1949, Fritz Jewett, Norton Clapp, and E. W. Davis were named as a committee to employ "an executive competent to plan, build and operate a pulp or paper mill and to manage the other operations of the company." They chose William P. Davis, a man who had already distinguished himself in the pulp and paper industry.

A graduate of Mississippi State College in electrical engineering in 1918, Davis was first employed by the Southern Paper Company at Moss Point a year later. By 1922 he was chief engineer of the plant, a title he continued to hold after the International Paper Company purchased the Moss Point mill in 1929. In 1934 he was promoted to officer in charge of engineering and development of International Paper's Kraft Division. Later, through "rebuilding and revamping" many of International's largest plants, Davis attained a national reputation for himself and a high position in the company. A man of great ambition and driving energy, he coolly set goals and worked quickly toward them. Some men found his leadership inspiring; others felt that he set a killing pace for all employees.[45]

Without doubt Davis possessed outstanding abilities as a planner, organizer, and administrator. He set his course with Potlatch Forests even before he accepted the leadership of the corporation. In July, 1949, he expressed the opinion that in addition to building a pulp mill the company should construct at least three converting plants to make such products as paper milk bottles and other containers. When he arrived in Lewiston he announced that the "utilization of waste woods and the co-ordination of a lumber mill and a paper and pulp mill are the most important tasks in the woods industry today." By the time he was elected a director, general manager, and president (succeeding G. F. Jewett) on October 3, 1949, Davis thought the "ultimate goal of the company was white paper," but cautioned the directors that time would be needed to "find customers for new products," and suggested that after the pulp mill was completed other units should be added only as favorable markets developed.[46]

Annual reports[47] show that the executive committee's authorization of Davis to construct a 150-ton pulp and 130-ton paper mill on November 17, 1949, set off an almost explosive chain reaction in expansion of P.F.I. The mill was built and the first pulp was produced on December 23, 1950. Since then the rated capacity of that Lewiston mill has been quadrupled. In 1952, to ensure the most remunerative utilization of logs, the plywood operation began using ponderosa pine, knotty white pine, fir, and larch. Year after year the directors of the company authorized large expenditures for timber purchases, for more efficient equipment, such as log barkers and riderless carriages at head saws, and for additions to and improvements of old and new plants.

Beginning in 1952, Davis made certain that there would be new plants to improve and additional timberland to manage under a program of long-range full utilization. Through purchase and mergers he added a paper mill in California, sawmills in Idaho and Washington, and enough timberland to raise P.F.I. holdings to 425,000 acres in the Far West. Then by other mergers, beginning with the Southern Lumber Company of Warren, Arkansas, in 1956, and large capital investments, Davis and his successor acquired more sawmill capacity, 350,000 more acres of timberland, and facilities for manufacturing such items as milk carton blanks, folding cartons, paper cups, and paper plates. By 1960, P.F.I. had plants located in twelve states of the Union and was catering to markets ranging from the Atlantic to the Pacific.

During the decade of the 1950's the executives of P.F.I. had charted a completely independent course. P.F.I. directors and officers were devoting their entire attention to affairs arising in Lewiston offices, and the company's books were audited by its own outside auditor. Funds for expansion, beyond those from reinvested earnings, now came from outside sources, not from stockholders as in the first five decades of the century. Robert E. Bundy, who became chief executive after the death of W. P. Davis in 1958, now has the problem of applying to P.F.I. the most recent ideas for achieving sustained growth in the forest-products industry.

NOTES

1. Clearwater Timber Company (hereinafter cited CTC) Papers, data from 1927 questionnaire for federal income tax; Potlatch Lumber and Rutledge Timber companies, annl. repts., 1920–1924.

2. Mason, "The Lumber Industry in the Inland Empire." Mason's conclusion was founded on a careful analysis of the financial reports of all the companies active.

3. WPA, *Idaho: A Guide*, 170. See also corroborative statements in *Idaho Forest and Timber Handbook*, passim.

4. *Family Tree*, Jan.–March, 1936.

5. More than three-fourths of Idaho's timber lay between the Salmon River and the Canadian line. Western white pine, the most valuable tree commercially, was found only in the northern part of the state. More than ten million of the thirteen million acres in northern Idaho were wooded. *Idaho: A Guide*, 169–170.

6. FEW Papers, FEW to JPW, Nov. 11, 1914; CTC Papers.

7. FKW Papers, JPW to Officers and Directors of the Clearwater Timber Company, May 9, 1923.

8. Mason, "The Lumber Industry in the Inland Empire"; CTC Papers; *Timberman*, July, 1927, pp. 2 ff.

9. FEW Papers, Nov., 1924, correspondence.

10. Machinery for the mill was supplied by Filer & Stowell of Milwaukee. Two parallel bull chains or log hauls brought the logs into the mill; the longest logs coming up at one side, where they were cut to proper length by an overhead circular cutoff saw. The logs were pushed through five nine-foot roller-bearing double-cut band saws, of Atkins make. The five twenty-foot carriages which carried the logs forward were equipped with pneumatic dogs and setworks, while one had a pneumatic receder. The headrigs and in fact all the principal machines of the mill were operated by 2,200-volt Westinghouse motors of sleeve-bearing type; the smaller machines were driven by 440-volt motors. Back of the headrig was a 52-inch Diamond gang saw mounted on a heavy concrete base. The mill had a refuse burner 110 feet high. *Timberman, loc. cit.*

11. This multiplicity of activities may be followed in the JPW Papers.

12. *Timberman*, July, 1927.

13. CTC Papers, JPW to FEW, Nov. 12, 1924. Actually early drives ran only from 40,000,000 to 45,000,000 feet of logs.

14. JPW Papers, Report of J. L. Webb.

15. See the *Family Tree*, April, 1939, for a vivid account of the wanigan.

16. The author of this chapter in 1953 talked at length with E. C. Rettig.

17. PFI Papers. Rettig's interesting report, based on inspection of a full score of logging concerns, fills eighteen typed pages. Minot Davis disagreed with some of its conclusions.

18. See "Mechanical Development of a Wood-Briquetting Machine," *Mechanical Engineering*, Feb., 1941. Bowling received many honors from the engineering profession.

19. *Forests of the Future*, 77.

20. *Family Tree*, 1937.

21. John W. Titcomb, J. J. O'Connell, and E. C. Rettig to the author of this chapter, July, 1953. One minor casualty of the depression was the Bonner's Ferry Company, operating near the Canadian line and in fact owning some timber in Canada, which has hardly seemed worth listing among Idaho undertakings. J. P. Weyerhaeuser on Oct. 19, 1932, wrote F. E. Weyerhaeuser suggesting that the timber across the line be relinquished to the Canadian government, for it had little or no value. "The Bonner's Ferry Lumber Com-

pany plant at no time," he added, "that I can remember made a profit" (FEW Papers). Earlier that year he had written, "We find that we could not give the Bonner's Ferry Lumber Company away." An offer of all its properties for $25,000 had gone without a taker. In 1937, however, the Montana holdings of the company were sold for $185,000, while Jewett and others salvaged a little more (FEW Papers, Jewett to R. M. Weyerhaeuser, May 28, 1937).

22. Irwin, Reminiscences.

23. PFI Papers, Jewett letters.

24. McGough, Reminiscences.

25. Actually, Laird Bell shared credit for this achievement with three other men in particular: John P. Weyerhaeuser, C. L. Billings, and G. F. Jewett (E. C. Rettig and others to author, July, 1953).

26. Torsen had gone to the Lewiston mill in the spring of 1926 as assistant to Jewett; and the following year took over Jewett's position as treasurer.

27. McGough, Reminiscences.

28. John A. Humbird, "History of Humbird Lumber Co.," manuscript; PFI Papers. See the letters of W. C. Ruegnitz, president of the Loyal Legion, Portland, 1932–33: "Creditors and even bankers," he wrote the locals in March 1932, "have forced some companies to low wage levels."

29. In retrospect it appeared doubtful to many whether the Elk River mill, set in a difficult terrain subject to heavy snows and deep spring mud, should ever have been built (*Family Tree,* Nov. 1936).

30. PFI Papers, Letters Oct. 7, Dec. 22, 1932.

31. *Ibid.,* Annual Report of PFI for 1937 to informal stockholders meeting in St. Paul, Feb. 4, 1938; Min. Bk. Lewiston, historical "Statement of Income and Earned Surplus" of Potlatch Lumber Co. and PFI, 1908–1952.

32. "In purchasing these small mill stocks," said C. A. Graue in a public address in 1936, "we started out in a very small way, being careful to see that the lumber was thick enough to be remanufactured to our standard size and that the stock was dry. First they bought only white pine, but later ponderosa as well."

33. FKW Papers, Billings to the director, May 13, 1940.

34. *Family Tree,* Jan., 1937.

35. *Ibid.,* June, 1939. Western red cedar poles at this time were in keen demand, outstripping all competitors except the Southern pines. Cedar trees often attain an age of 1,000 years but can best be harvested at 120 to 150 years. *U.S. Forest Service Survey,* 1939.

36. *Family Tree,* June 1939.

37. PFI Papers, Reports of General Manager, 1932–1935; "Glued Boards," *Family Tree,* Oct., 1940.

38. This was Professor B. M. Mathews (*Family Tree,* June, 1940).

39. PFI Papers, Cd'A Letters, Jewett to Judge William S. Bennett, May 15, 1931.

40. W. D. Humiston of PFI was secretary-treasurer of the North Idaho Forestry Assn. and chairman of the Forest Taxation Committee of the Western States Taxpayers' Conference. The PFI Papers contain much correspondence with him from 1928 on.

41. PFI Papers, Min. Bk., Feb. 3, May 24, 1945: *Family Tree,* Sept., 1944. The four categories were Research, Product Development, New Products, and Plant Improvements.

42. PFI Papers, Min. Bk., 1946–1947.

43. *Ibid.,* quoted from a memorial approved May 3, 1949.

44. PFI Papers, Lewiston; interviews with Roy Huffman, J. J. O'Connell, C. Rettig, and Robert Bowling; Frederick K. Weyerhaeuser to the authors, Sept. 10, 1958.

45. *Lewiston* (Ida.) *Morning Tribune,* March 19, 1958, obituary write-up; interviews with officers and workers of PFI.

46. PFI Papers, Min. Bk., July 29, Oct. 3, 1949; *Lewiston* (Ida.) *Morning Tribune,* March 19, 1958.

47. The ensuing evaluation of activities of PFI is all drawn from the minute books of the company and from its annual reports, 1949–1958.

XXVIII

Southern Idaho: Reverses

and Triumph

A SORT OF ORPHAN down in South Idaho," one of the Weyerhaeusers once remarked of the Boise Payette Lumber Company. A struggling, discouraged Boise Payette indeed was for years after World War I a bantling that many men thought should be abandoned. Actually, of the two formerly associated firms now in Idaho—Potlatch Forest, Inc., and Boise Cascade Lumber Company, successor to Boise Payette—the last-named has had the more striking history. It is the record of an enterprise that, after long being considered temporary and expendable, was converted with brilliant success into a permanent industry of marked social and economic value to half of the state.

The very name of "Boysey" Valley, as the explorer Bonneville had called it, means "wooded." The trees his party saw as they emerged from the sagebrush planes upon the margin of the Boise Basin were only cottonwood, wild cherry, aspen, and willow along the river; but on the hills that swept back to the Owyhee and Blue ranges stood dense forests of ponderosa pine and white fir.

Boise Payette's operations depended largely on ponderosa, the most plentiful western pine—a stately tree, distinctive in the division of its bark into large, flat, yellow-brown or blackish plates. No tree was more at home in the Rockies, the Sierra Nevada, or on the eastern slope of the Cascades. In total stand in the United States it ranked second only to Douglas fir. Once an unfounded prejudice against its yellow wood was overcome, its lumber was recognized as valuable for a wide range of uses, from building construction to furniture. It offered the basis of a profitable operation, but numerous difficulties barred the road to achievement. Among them was the fact that the company's own timberlands, walled in by state and national forests, seemed to be inadequate.

As for transportation, in the spring of 1926 Boise welcomed the first through passenger train of the Union Pacific with pretty girls, bands, and cheering crowds. Long before that memorable date the Intermountain Railway assured the flow of logs from forest to the Barber mill, and connections with the Oregon Short Line provided means of carrying lumber to many markets.

The manager of Boise Payette, the resourceful C. A. Barton, running his two sawmills at Barber and Emmett, did well with them during World War I and its early postwar boom, as noted in Chapter 16. The Barber mill stood a half-dozen miles from Boise on the river of that name, occupying the first practicable site after the waters finished their dash through a high-walled canyon. Barton had reorganized and modernized it with much new equipment. The Intermountain Railway rumbled its carloads of fresh-cut logs down steep slopes and around sharp curves a distance of forty miles from Centerville to the plant. The brand-new Emmett Mill, a dozen miles northwest of Boise on the Payette River, in the heart of great cherry orchards, brought its timber from the hills by a branch of the Union Pacific and later also by truck. Logs were shipped along the Payette trough as much as a hundred miles. By 1920 Boise Payette's 72 retail yards gave a controlled outlet for a substantial proportion of the lumber produced by the mills.[1]

The satisfactory profits of Boise Payette from World War I to 1923, with the single exception of the depression year 1921, made everybody optimistic. Then the picture changed to gloom.

Why the sudden slump? The reasons were obviously deep-seated, for from 1924 to 1929, inclusive, the company's annual net profit after taxes averaged less than 1 percent on invested capital, and the firm ran deficits for the next five years. In the three worst years, 1930–1932, the losses averaged $600,000 annually. Barton as manager and William Carson as president made a determined but futile fight. Barton resigned in 1931, discouraged and broken in health, and in July of the following year Carson, equally dejected, died. What were the difficulties?[2]

Like other Inland Empire companies, Boise Payette suffered in competing with coastal timber, which was cut more cheaply and was now shipped East by sea at lower freight rates. The prejudice against ponderosa or "yellow pine" lumber counted, while for years almost no market at all could be found for white fir, an important fraction of Boise Payette's cut. Both the Barber and Emmett mills were subject to winter stoppages.

The company had been fortunate in buying its timberlands at bargain rates, but it was distinctly unfortunate in owning only limited quantities. To be sure, at the time of the 1913 merger the holdings slightly exceeded 200,000 acres, with about 2,400 million feet of timber; but a good deal of the acreage was sparsely forested, while much of the mountain timber could be got out only by uphill hauls which defied the trucks and caterpillars of the mid-twenties.[3]

Moreover, Boise Payette had been forced to invest large sums in installations, such as the grading, bridges, and rolling stock of the Intermountain Railway, which deep winter snows and roaring spring floods made hard to operate. The lumber market the company could reach by truck and rail in Idaho, Utah, southern Wyoming, and western Colorado, not very rich at best, became especially weak as the late 1920's edged into the nationwide depression, the basic cause of the heavy losses.

After Barton and Carson departed, two new leaders of capacity and energy appeared. S. G. (Jack) Moon came in from Wisconsin as manager, to remain until after the Second World War—seventeen years, a remarkable stretch. He was an experienced lumberman who, as originator of the old Barber Lumber Company before the merger, knew the region well. He showed grasp and initiative and was liked by everybody. A prominent layman in the Episcopal Church, he threw himself into civic and philanthropic enterprises and soon became a leading citizen of Boise. He was as keenly interested in logging as in manufacturing, and even in his seventies carried a pair of rubber boots in his car so that he could go into the woods at a moment's notice. He also concerned himself with finance, becoming a director of the Idaho First National Bank in Boise.[4]

A still more remarkable man was the new president, Dr. E. P. Clapp, who succeeded Carson to serve for the next thirteen years. He was an Illinoisan by birth and a physician by profession, who had made a connection with the Laird-Norton interests by marrying Mary Elizabeth Norton. As city physician of Evanston, Illinois, and author of one of the earliest local health codes in the nation, he had attained some prominence. On the death of his wife and his brother-in-law, Frank Thatcher, he had turned to the lumber business in the 1920's. It was fortunate for Boise Payette that a man of such breadth and initiative was available for its presidency. "Father," states Norton Clapp, "worked very closely with Mr. Moon for many years, Mr. Moon on the ground and father doing everything he could around the fringes to help save the situation." He served through the Second World War, retiring in May, 1946, when the redoubtable Moon—one of the most devoted managers the Weyerhaeuser interests ever had—took the presidency.

The period 1931–1934 was one of acute crisis in which these officers had to exert themselves to the utmost. Many of the retail yards closed down never to reopen. Bank failures affected Boise Payette. When a bank at Burlington, Iowa, failed, $100,000 of Boise Payette funds were on deposit. The First National Bank of Boise also closed. The company had considered taking out its money earlier but had not for fear that it would create a run on the bank and that Boise Payette would be blamed for the failure.[5] For part of 1931 and all of 1932 and 1933 the Emmett mill was shut because of overhauls and repairs, combined with the depression. Meanwhile, the Barber mill, also intermittently closed, cut its last readily available timber and in 1934 was dismantled. As this removed all excuse for the Intermountain Railway, in 1935 it was liquidated.[6] The scrapping of the Barber plant was in time recognized as a mistake, for when new policies were adopted timber had to be carried on long hauls right past the site; but the depression nightmare was riding the West hard.

Dr. Clapp's son recalls how sternly the heads of Boise Payette had economized to keep the company alive:

> I know that everybody in the organization took pay cuts. They retrenched everywhere they could. They sharpened their logging practices; that is, they left a lot of trees in the woods that had been brought in before, and harvested only the trees that they could afford to bring in. They went through some rather expensive trades with the Forest Service, trading good but inaccessible timber and land on the Crooked River for timber only in a more accessible area.

But for the abilities of Moon and Clapp and the devotion of their subordinates, the company might not have survived. It emerged from these disastrous years to face a new recession in 1937–1938. Annual reports showed that earnings were either small or nonexistent. Inevitably, the conviction grew both among the Idaho officers and some stockholders that the orphan had better be disowned: Boise Payette should harvest the profitable stands within reach, and cease operations.

2

During Roosevelt's second term and World War II years Moon and Clapp retained this conviction. Their administration was in many ways enlightened and progressive. In 1936–1937 the company recruised all its holdings and mapped out the remaining timber for selective logging. The United States Forest Service assisted in this, providing a senior economist who made a "stand structure study" to determine the probable realization from logs of the different grades. All trees were thereafter given marks ordering "cut" or "leave." By the end of 1946 the company had 484,000,-000 feet of "leave" timber but only 292,000,000 feet marked "cut."[7]

At the same time the management tried systematically to persuade middle-western buyers that yellow pine was as good as white pine, finding that use of the name "ponderosa" assisted them in their sales. They also pushed their white fir. "We had to work hard," later recalled the principal sales executive. "We had to market everything we could through our own retail yards. We had to force them to take it. They wanted to handle Douglas fir." And another innovation that Moon presently originated was the replacement of company logging by contract logging—a definite economy.

When Clapp and Moon took over, E. C. MacGregor superintended the Emmett logging, while James A. Long supervised that for the Barber mill. Both were efficient men, but Moon was convinced that independent firms could do the work more cheaply. Beginning early in the 1940's, Boise Payette gave contracts to the MacGregor Logging Company, headed by Gordon MacGregor, a son of the old superintendent, and to J. I. Morgan, Inc., managed by Jack Morgan. The independent logging companies proved more effective for two principal reasons: they could use their equipment all year long, shifting from woods work to other types of construction in the depth of winter, and in some way, nobody knew how, they got more work out of the men. Moreover, they took better care of the machinery. The two contracting firms, although competing keenly, got on well both with each other and with Boise Payette. "It is a real example of mutual confidence and cooperation," remarked Norton Clapp.

To reduce timber haulage a single-band portable sawmill was erected in 1936 in Garden Valley on the middle fork of the Payette River, about forty-five miles from Emmett. The lumber sawed there was shipped to the Emmett mill to be refinished. After three years the mill was discontinued (November, 1939); but about that time the company opened a small mill at the village of Council about a hundred miles north of Emmett in the Weiser River Valley.

During the Second World War, the company suffered heavily despite an apparent prosperity. The War Production Board urged that output be increased. The working force was kept high: 748 employees in 1945 and 800 in 1946. The company had to cut a great part of its timber reserves. Having little opportunity to negotiate timber purchases from the national Forest Reserve, it had to take the best of its own timber within easy reach, emerging from the war with badly depleted resources. Competitive companies that owned larger reserves were less harmed. In thus skimming the cream from its holdings, Boise Payette seemed to make large net profits—$472,000 in 1945 and $1,276,000 in 1946; but these profits were taxed at specially high rates under the excess-profits schedules. The management summed up what had occurred in a bitter paragraph:

The company has known since the country's needs for lumber became insistent under wartime conditions in 1941 that it was sacrificing at least one-half of its annual output of logs at a tremendous loss in order to be able to say that it put forth a hundred percent effort. Others did likewise, no doubt, but with this difference—they will be in business long enough to make good their losses with future production, sales, and profits. The Boise Payette Company will not have that opportunity. It disposed of an irreplaceable wasting asset and will go out of the lumber manufacturing business earlier than it otherwise would had the war not occurred. . . . It could not go out and buy the greater portion of its timber and log requirements to produce its full quota but was compelled to use up its reserves of low-cost lumber and pay the highest taxes in the history of the United States to boot.

At the conclusion of the war a fresh survey of the timber resources left to the company seemed to point to the wisdom of an early liquidation. Harold J. McCoy was borrowed from other activities of the Weyerhaeuser associates to make a study of the possibility of permanent operation, and he obtained the cooperation of Forest Service men in his fieldwork. It was recognized that only systematic purchases of federal and state timber would enable Boise Payette to continue indefinitely. McCoy, beginning his work in 1944, continued it into 1945. His decision was negative. "By this extension of the study," he wrote on April 25, 1945, "additional information has been obtained in view of which it becomes apparent that it would be neither feasible nor economical for the Boise Payette Lumber Company to operate its remaining stands of virgin timber on a sustained yield basis."[8]

One element in the determination to "cut out and get out" was the age of some of the controlling officers. Dr. Clapp's health failed after the end of the war, and he retired to Pasadena, California. Soon afterward Moon's vigor declined. Other executives were growing elderly and tired.

This helps explain why almost nobody questioned the policy of early termination and why for some years company methods were slack and shortsighted. The testimony of impartial observers indicates that the liquidation policy made for improper treatment of labor. It fostered internal bickering, for employees felt no loyalty to an institution about to die, grew irritable over their lack of prospects, and so quarreled. Methods of cutting timber became wasteful; the object was to take the best trees and discard the others. An anonymous officer states that tired men in the top management instructed Harry Shellworth, the land and timber supervisor, to make a quick, rough job of realizing company assets:

His instructions were to get rid of this land as fast as he could, and he did. Some good bargains were put on the block. We begged people to buy. It was cutover land, but it sure had a lot of virgin timber left up in the corners. The loggers did what they pleased. They were just getting their operation over with. They were trying to clear it up and forget about it.

The beginning of 1947 found the company operating its large saw-mill at Emmett and the newer and much smaller one at Council, far north on the Weiser River, the two having a combined annual production of more than 101,500,000 feet. This was drawn from a company domain of 172,000 acres, containing 776,000,000 feet of timber. About one-third of the timber then belonged to the "cut" and two-thirds to the "leave" category. Net profits that year came to $2,381,000, which made possible the distribution of a $6 dividend.

As the year 1947 closed, the company took an important step in the field of marketing. It paid $5,000,000 for the capital stock of the Merrill Company of Salt Lake City, making it a wholly owned subsidiary. The properties consisted of Morrison-Merrill Company, which operated a wholesale lumber business and a millwork factory in Salt Lake City, and three lumber companies—Tri State, Sugarhouse, and Badger—which held 39 retail yards in Idaho, Utah, and Wyoming. This greatly strengthened the selling division of the parent company. Clement W. Gamble, the guiding executive in the Boise Payette retail division, was made president of Morrison-Merrill.[9]

But except for retail marketing, Boise Payette still looked to an early termination of activities. "At the current rate of production," wrote the manager of manufacturing, Willard W. Burns, in 1947, "the remaining estimates of 'cut' and available timber will only provide logs for a little better than three years of continued operations." He added that as the retail yard division had shown profits for twenty-eight out of its thirty-one years, it might be expected to do well after the liquidation of logging and manufacturing.

3

But the word "liquidation" was soon to disappear from the Boise Payette vocabulary. The turning point in the history of the company was reached in 1949–1950. A new and younger board of directors had been elected, including John Musser and Norton Clapp. Youthful and enterprising personnel took charge. The annual report submitted in May, 1949, was signed by Moon as president and Willard W. Burns as manager and vice-president, but they soon gave way to Norton Clapp and John Aram. Other changes took place at the same general time. Clement W. Gamble took the post of executive vice-president. The veteran secretary resigned, and Gilbert H. Osgood took his place. E. A. Aitchison, of large experience and progressive outlook, was made comptroller, veteran A. O. Sheldon and young J. L. Jeremiassen became vice-presidents, and a young man took charge of public relations. Correspondence shows that G. F. Jewett, a director, wished to dispense with practically all the old officers and turn a new page. This almost happened; new blood, and a new constructive attitude became dominant.[10] These changes in 1949 led up to the decision by stockholding families in 1952 to give Boise Payette management full freedom to operate as it thought best.

In the tall, stocky Aram, a man of marked simplicity, one of the noteworthy figures in the history of Weyerhaeuser enterprises made his advent. He had been born in the Salmon River county on a cattle ranch "back in the hills," as he said, the oldest boy in a family who "always had to carry responsibility." Finishing high school, he studied business administration at the University of Idaho. In 1936 he set to work for Potlatch Forests, Inc., as a laborer and student of selling. Billings perceived his abilities and made increasing use of them. "He often called me in to ask what I thought about problems," states Aram. "I had no reservations about telling him, and telling him when I thought he was wrong. He said he was always afraid of being 'yessed.' " Partly under Billings's influence, Aram left sales to take up managerial work. In September, 1940, he was made head of the manufacturing division of Potlatch. He liked the place, did well at it, and in Billings's last years took on increasing responsibilities.

After Billings's death "I just started running the company," he has recalled. Then "John [Musser] and Norton [Clapp] came by for a little look at what was going on, and they decided to appoint me manager" at Boise Payette. He saw in the place an exciting challenge.[11]

From the beginning of their administration Norton Clapp and John Aram hoped and planned to rescue Boise Payette from imminent destruction and to place it on a permanent basis. But how to do it? The company's timber supply would not support it long, little private timber could be bought, and state forests in the area were negligible. The United States Forest Service, which could sell timber from its forests in southern Idaho, seemed unfriendly and had announced that it preferred to assist small mills, which it thought offered more manhour production for each thousand feet. The outlook seemed gloomy.

In the fall of 1948, however, J. E. Bishop, in presenting the management with a modestly encouraging "Survey of Future Operating Possibilities," made two suggestions. The first was that an arrangement *might* be worked out with the Forest Service for the purchase of timber to feed the Boise Payette mills or even for mutually profitable trades of woodland. The second was that the company could afford to hold on to large acreages of cutover forest while waiting for the new growth to mature, because grazing revenues rendered such lands self-supporting.[12]

This was a rift of light in the gloom. On July 1, 1949, Aram set to work to reorganize the land and forestry management and the public-relations policy. His fundamental position was that Boise Payette timber, reorganized and conserved, could be combined with timber purchased from other sources to make the company an efficient, profitable, and permanent unit.

Before August ended he could report that he had done a great deal. He had inspected most of the timber holdings and the adjacent areas. He had appointed a new superintendent of logging, Bert Cochran. He had hired a forestry expert, Vern Guernsey, formerly with Potlatch, to give him expert advice for three months, and had employed a forestry engineer from the Western Pine Association. He had bought nearly 5,000,-000 feet of national Forest Service stumpage and was looking for more. He had spread the welcome word throughout south Idaho that Boise Payette was definitely going to continue manufacturing. He had discovered that the company needed a coordination of the land management, sawmill work, and sales.

Most important of all, he had begun to cultivate good relations with the Forest Service. He wrote to Vice-President Clement W. Gamble:

I have met with the Forest Service of the Payette National Forest and the Boise National Forest. Meetings have been held with the Forest timber sales official and with the Regional Forester, Mr. Rice. In these conversations the following points have been expressed:

1. Boise Payette Lumber Company is in production to stay.
2. The Board of Directors understand and recognize their conservation and social obligations as well as their economic responsibility to the communities in which we operate.
3. Boise Payette Lumber Company management can cooperate and will demonstrate cooperation with the United States Forest Service.
4. As head of the land and logging department, I am in a new field. My intention is to give good effective service, but I need their advice and their help. Their criticisms and suggestions regarding our practices are always welcome.
5. We have responsibilities to employees, communities, stockholders, and customers that demand continued operation.
6. Our plans are to buy a certain volume of green or rough dry lumber from small operators and to give them technical help that make their operations efficient.
7. We hope to work toward high utilization of our timber lands and resources.[13]

Norton Clapp shared these ideas and ambitions. A few days later Clapp wrote a memorandum on "Objectives" that followed parallel lines. They must plan, he declared, to continue the Boise Payette operation, and to this end they must "assure permanent or at least a long time supply of forest products to be available for our yards."[14]

Finding that the company still had parcels of land advertised for sale, Aram and Clapp at once canceled all pending disposals. The expert

forest engineer whom Aram brought in from the Western Pine Association made a rapid survey of the company holdings. He concluded that if
Boise Payette reduced its overhead charges, made its mills more efficient,
and proceeded by a careful plan, it could continue indefinitely. This of
course meant retaining all company lands, buying timber from all available sources, and starting a continuous yield operation on a broad scale.

Without losing a month, Aram began to lay down a long-range program of selective cutting and tree farming. It must be remembered that
ponderosa pine matures more slowly than other species. In developing
forest management, he constantly appealed for advice to the University
of Idaho, Western Pine Association, and Forest Service. "We are just
starting our program," he would say. "We don't know much about it.
Now you are technically trained; what can you tell us?" Early in the
undertaking Aram employed George Hjort, a graduate of the University
of Idaho's forestry school, as a timber cruiser. He rose rapidly, soon taking charge of land management, contributing ideas of his own on conservation, and in time becoming vice-president.

As one argument to his board, Aram pointed out that the policy of
the national office of the Forest Service at this time was to oppose or limit
private forestry. To bolster their case, some officials were constantly on
the watch for horrible examples of woodland butchery. They would be
quick to pounce on Boise Payette failures and abuses, and even exag-
gerate them. The company's prewar and wartime record showed a definite
disregard for conservation. "We have an obligation to clean this thing
up," said Aram. The great Boise and Payette National Forests lying adjacent to company holdings would offer a sharp contrast to defective logging practices.

In the spring of 1950 the Boise Payette lands, with special ceremony,
were officially certified as a Western Pine Tree Farm. Sound logging instructions were issued and enforced. As in other areas, dubious lumbermen soon saw that the new practices meant a dollar-and-cents profit. By
1952 Boise Payette had pledged itself to keep its "lands in continuous
production . . . to harvest a crop of timber every fifty years."[15]

4

But its own tree farms were not enough. Permanent operation was
impossible unless Boise Payette could get steady deliveries of timber from
the National Forests that hemmed it in on three sides. The story of government relations has special interest.

For a time Boise Payette found the government reluctant to assist it.
This was partly because company policy in the "tired" days had really
justified suspicion. The shortsighted treatment of some company timber

has been noted. When this irresponsibility touched government interests, it gave the Weyerhaeuser undertakings a bad name. Once more we can quote an anonymous observer on unfortunate practices in the late 1940's:

There was no purpose to get along with the government. When they got down to where they didn't really need government cooperation, and couldn't make any more exchanges, the attitude was, "Why, the hell with it. Treat 'em as rough as you can." So they treated the government people like a bunch of crooks. This was done, I suppose, by one or two foresters who weren't big enough to look over the hill.[16]

Aram had not only to break down a lingering resentment, but to induce the Forest Service, controlled in this area from offices in Ogden, Utah, to make large sales against which the small mills were sure to protest. Federal officers, favoring these mills, had broken the administration of the National Forests into what Aram calls "small working circles." Boise Payette had no hostility for small sawmills and in fact wished to keep them alive. But Aram and Clapp knew that some were inefficient. They also knew that wherever government timber was scattered over wide distances, small mills could not harvest it as efficiently as large concerns with better equipment.

Little by little the company succeeded in winning the respect of Forest Service officials in southern Idaho. Its logging work was now manifestly based on sound principles of conservation. Moreover, it gave government men a helping hand whenever possible. In the summer of 1950 a terrible fire broke out in the hills of the Payette National Forest. Aram insisted that MacGregor and Morgan halt their logging at once and send every able-bodied hand to fight the flames. Closing the Council and Emmett mills, he dispatched their crews to the scene. In all, about 350 Boise Payette men rallied to help stop the fire. "I just took the stand that all the people of this district must learn that their obligation is to fight fire," said Aram later. That fall another conflagration raged near Council, and MacGregor's men dropped everything to deal with it. This made an impression.[17]

Both Boise Payette and the government had mistakes of policy for which to apologize. It is clear that when Norton Clapp and Aram came in, Forest Service officials in southern Idaho were unprogressive, short-sighted, and unreasonably hostile to large interests. It was holding great masses of overripe timber, much of it decaying and diseased. Now and then it did advertise lots of timber for sale, but partly for political reasons it sold them mainly to the small mills. These mills, generally using circular saws instead of band saws, were wasteful of timber; they sweated their logging contractors, and the roads they built into the hills were poor and impermanent. It was an important gain for both sides when Aram was able to write in August, 1949: "The National Forests personnel are very human and want to get along with us; they seem to recognize that operations like ours are necessary here." He noted a still greater gain in the spring of 1950: "Wholehearted cooperation with Forest Service officials in fire fighting has won their good will."

Meanwhile, significant changes took place in marketing and manufacturing. To satisfy the customer's needs the company adopted the policy of manufacturing lumber to the specific size demanded. In 1954 it established its own trademark for distribution in the intermountain territory, Tru-Grade. So far as possible, it carefully dried, graded, and sorted all lumber. New products, such as manufactured chips (shipped to the paper mill at Lewiston) and packaged paneling, were produced. It successfully undertook the mechanical loading of freight and boxcars to serve customer needs. Moreover, manufacturing facilities at the Emmett mill were improved, and the planing mill there was reorganized with new machinery. With J. I. Morgan, Boise Payette participated for two and one-half years in the manufacturing of lodgepole pine lumber. The company also purchased the sawmill of Halleck & Howard of Cascade, Idaho, which it largely rebuilt.

During this period an infestation of pine butterfly and spruce budworm, unfortunately ignored at first by the higher officials of the United States Forest Service, necessitated forceful action by the private lumber interests of southern Idaho. Aram tells the story graphically. "The butterfly," he writes, "appeared to be spreading so fast that, along with needle cast infestations and the pine beetles, it would kill practically all of the ponderosa pine in southwestern Idaho. It had reached the point where the pine forests of a large area were about to succumb. As a result, the local lumber companies formed what we called the Southwestern Idaho Forest Pest Action Council. We invited the Western Pine Association foresters to give us their leadership and guidance, and we pressed the Forest Service to spray the area as quickly as possible. Unallocated funds in the Forest Service budget were found, and an intense aerial spraying of the area of butterfly infestation was organized in the spring of 1955. Forest Service contractors successfully carried out the work at the lowest cost per acre thus far known. The Forest Service officials took great pride in the accomplishment, for the epidemic was stopped and the timber was saved." As part of this campaign against pests that menaced the welfare of a great part of Idaho, a specially obstructive Forest Service officer in Ogden, Utah, who in Aram's words "had been a road block for many years," was forced out of his place.

Even yet, however, some obstacles remained. From the Emergency Pest Action Council was born a permanent organization called the Southern Idaho Forestry Association. Its leaders urged the Washington authorities to expedite the sales of public timber, for much of it badly needed cutting and was heavily diseased. When the Washington authorities objected to the cost of building access roads, the association replied, in effect: "You can easily construct them. We shall show you the best routes. Part of the construction funds can come from land sales, and we shall help you get the rest from Congress." It had facts to sustain this view, for such men as Vern Guernsey of Boise Payette had inspected the region again and again on foot and by air. "Guernsey showed them where they could sell a hundred million feet on the Boise," states Aram. Indeed, it was being discovered that southern Idaho had forest resources of unsuspected extent. A new survey of the Boise and Payette National Forests in these years revealed that they contained three times as much timber as had been supposed![18]

In promising to help get money for access roads from Congress, the association meant that it would lobby energetically, and it now hurried two agents to Washington to ask for an appropriation. It also induced the Assistant Chief of the United States Forest Service, Ed Croft, to visit Idaho, where he was impressed by the careful logging that MacGregor was doing for Boise Payette, and disgusted by the ragged, improvident character of the cutting done by some small outfits. The result was that sufficient federal money was obtained to enable the Forest Service to build roads up many canyons. Systematic explorations from these new roads verified the suspicion that much of the timber had become badly diseased. All this activity furthered the general cause of cooperation between private forest owners and government agencies.

As access roads were pushed out into the large areas of diseased timber, the Forest Service realized that it had something to learn from private lumber interests. "We had known for years that the country was full of spruce budworm," said Aram later, "and some bureaucrats had declared that nobody could do anything about it." The Southern Idaho Forestry Association continued to assist the Forest Service in obtaining adequate funds for spraying the infested districts by airplane.

Meanwhile, a larger issue between private interests and public authorities became acute. Not only all the substantial private forest owners and most private business in southern Idaho, but the state officers as well, had been irritated by the ceaseless efforts of the National Forest Administration to enlarge the federal domain.[19] The government maintained a steady pressure on farmers whose lands lay within or near the National Forests to let their holdings be incorporated. By the early 1950's the nineteen National Forests in the state comprised more than 20,500,-000 acres. How large would they become? Beyond question majority sentiment in Idaho was growing resentful. The principal groups concerned held a series of meetings in the office of the state forester and stated their opinions bluntly. One vigorous individual in the federal service according to Aram, curtly told his superiors, "You'd better forget about extending the boundaries." In the end the Forest Service men consented to modify their policy. This relaxation of pressure obviously gave private lumbering a better chance.[20]

All the while, Aram steadily improved Boise Payette relations with the State Land Board and State Forester. The years of hard labor that Harry Shellworth had given to the Western Forestry and Conservation Association assisted Aram in this. Boise Payette officials urged members of the State Land Board to attend all the association meetings, and the association paid their expenses. In other ways the company showed its desire for harmony. "Not long after I came here," recalls Aram, "and probably because we were trying to work closely with them, the state forester and state Land Commission recommended that diameter limits and timber-marking controls be written into the state contracts for sales. I told them that we would permit them to mark any timber that we had under contract, and if they didn't have manpower for the work, and would tell us how they wanted it done we'd have our own foresters mark it." Boise Payette was always glad to accept contract provisions that preserved the young trees for future growth.

5

Thus by achieving friendly relations with national and state authorities, gaining the right to purchase a fair share of ripe public timber, buying more timberland when possible, and developing a continuous-yield program on its own domain, Boise Payette became a permanent operation. All southern Idaho rejoiced in the fact. To no small degree, the prosperity of dozens of communities depended on the company's logging operations, its sawmills, and its large wholesale and retail business. Boise Payette had reduced the number of its employees. Annual state and county taxes paid by the company had fallen from a peak of $153,600 in 1928 to less than one-third that amount twenty years later.[21] Now, after the change in policy, employment rose toward the 2,500 mark, property valuations increased, and taxes paid went up year by year. Consolidated sales for the year 1949 were $26,295,000, and consolidated earnings for all departments of the company were $2,535,000. Figures for both items, with some fluctuations, now followed an ascending curve.

The one group that at first viewed the revival of the company grudgingly were the small millowners. As the Boise Payette interests had historically furnished about half the southern Idaho lumber production, the managers believed they should continue to do so. The annual cut feasible on all available lands was 250,000,000 feet, of which 100,000,000 could be taken in the Boise Valley. Some small millowners whose livelihood depended on purchasing state and federal timber could hardly reconcile themselves to seeing Boise Payette get any large amount of logs from public lands. Aram and Norton Clapp slowly overcame this hostility by a program of purchasing rough lumber from many of the small mills to be finished at the Emmett plant. "The problem has been met squarely and honestly," Aram reported to the directors in 1950. Through individual chats, group meetings, and newspaper stories, the Boise Payette officers made it clear that they wished to foster small-mill enterprise.

Small enterprises continued to bid in a good proportion of the public offerings of timber, and Boise Payette then paid fair prices for rough lumber. Payments for such lumber were made promptly at frequent intervals, a point of importance to undercapitalized mills. By furnishing a steady, reliable market Boise Payette managers not only kept small operations healthy but served the public interest by providing for the harvest of many small isolated tracts, and benefited themselves by an increased volume through the Emmett mill, reducing its unit costs. Boise Payette also made it clear to small contractors that they were to reserve the immature timber for a later crop.[22] The latest National Forest survey had proved that there was much more merchantable timber than previously estimated.

When John Aram left Idaho for a post with Weyerhaeuser Timber Company in 1956, he could feel with some pride that he had started Boise Payette on a distinctive path of development. His successor as chief executive, Robert V. Hansberger, a graduate of the University of Minnesota and former executive vice-president of Western Kraft Company, soon embarked on a program of planned, integrated expansion for Boise Cascade Corporation, the new name given the firm in 1957. Through mergers and investment of a substantial portion of earnings as well as borrowed funds, by 1960 Boise Cascade had acquired additional timberlands and stumpage, built a pulp and paper mill, begun fabricating paper bags and containers, added concrete products to its line of building materials, expanded and improved its marketing facilities, and modernized all existing plants.

It was more than obvious that the change in policy in 1948, initiated by key directors representing the Laird, Norton and Musser interests, had started a train of decisions that had all but erased the memory of policies pursued prior to that time. The families that had originally launched and nurtured the enterprise were now decidedly minority stockholders. The former Boise Payette Lumber Company had been completely submerged and its identity lost. Entirely new names and faces among the directors and officers emphasized the fact that Boise Cascade had embarked on a highly independent course of action and had opened a new chapter in the history of southern Idaho. It was producing a wide range of building materials and paper products and was marketing them from the Pacific Coast to the High Plains. Emphasizing tree farms, continuous yield, full utilization of timber, and integrated operations, modern management was paying off for stockholders to the benefit of people in eleven western states.

NOTES

1. The Barber mill, opened 1906, was a three-band mill with resaw equipment, capable of turning out at least 200,000 feet of lumber daily and, when operated on double shift, twice that much. It had a good pond, and it was built on roomy, convenient lines. The Emmett mill was opened May 10, 1917.

2. In 1918 net profits of Boise Payette were $865,000 on a capital investment of $12,674,000. In 1919 and 1920 they exceeded a million. Then, after losses in 1921, they recovered sharply in 1922 and in 1923 reached $875,000. See BPLC Papers, application for income-tax adjustment, 1947.

3. BPLC Papers. In the merger the Barber Company had contributed 68,823 acres, the Payette Company 131,303.

4. Moon had been in the lumber business since 1903.

5. FEW Papers, FEW to JPW, Aug. 30, 1932, and FEW to S. G. Moon, Sept. 8, 1932.

6. BPLC Papers. In 1932 the company reached its lowest point, producing only 28.5 million feet of lumber, receiving an average of only $14.14 f.o.b., and paying common labor only 25 cents an hour. "In this area [Boise] I operated the Intermountain Railway from 1914 to 1935 when I tore it up. It was a common carrier handling as many as 450 carloads of sheep and 17,000 passengers a year, 80,000 passengers in all. About 7,000 carloads of logs were brought in each year, 80% at night, and in the operation of 6,750 trains during 20 years the injuries to the employees amounted to a broken leg for one sectionman, two broken ribs for another and a cut wrist for a conductor." (Excerpted from Charles Mather, 3rd, to Kramer A. Adams, May 3, 1961, by courtesy of Elwood R. Maunder.)

7. BPLC, Annual Report, 1947. In 1937 the company holdings came to 271,415 acres (Report Southern Idaho Protective Association, 1937), but a good deal of this was brush or grazing land of small commercial value. Revenue from grazing fees, $715,000 in the years 1914–1947, helped tide the company over.

8. BPLC Papers, McCoy Correspondence. The Executive Committee of Boise Payette gave McCoy his instructions Aug. 19, 1944. He gained the assistance of Regional Forester W. B. Rive of the national Forest Service, whose office was at Ogden, Utah. Aerial photographs were used to eliminate some areas of brush and grassland.

9. *Ibid.*, Annual Report, 1947.

10. Annual reports of BPLC trace these changes.

11. John Aram, Reminiscences.

12. BPLC Papers. Bishop's report to the Boise Payette executive committee was dated Sept. 20, 1948. He specially considered turning the Emmett mill into a plan for remanufacturing lumber to be purchased from the

numerous small mills scattered through the forests.

13. BPLC Papers. Aram's letter to Gamble was dated Boise, Aug. 19, 1949.

14. Norton Clapp's brief memorandum (BPLC Papers), dated Aug. 25, 1949, was meant for general company circulation.

15. John Aram, Norton Clapp, A. O. Sheldon, Reminiscences; Boise Payette annl. repts., 1948–1952; BPLC Papers, "Proposal Land Timber Management Program for Boise Payette Lumber Co.," Dec. 3, 1952, 1, approved by the Board of Directors.

16. The reporter means lumbermen; at this time the company did not employ foresters.

17. The Forest Service had once needed prodding as well as help in fire control. The initial effort in cooperative fire-fighting in southern Idaho was made by the Boise, Barber, Payette, and A. W. Cooke Companies, 1905–1907. Then, after the state and national forests in the district joined the effort, 1908–1910, the Southern Idaho Cooperative Fire Protection Association was organized in 1911, later changing its name to the Southern Idaho Timber Protective Association. Detailed records for twenty-five years beginning 1914 show a total of 1,520 fires in the area, an average of sixty-three a year, lightning being the principal cause. Annual Report, S.I.T.P.A., 1937.

18. The reminiscences of Aram and Norton Clapp on this period are supplemented by extensive correspondence with federal authorities in the BPLC Papers.

19. The best statistics obtainable indicate that Boise Payette conducted about half the business done by the southern Idaho lumber interests; the rest was largely in the hands of small mills.

20. Aram, Reminiscences.

21. This figure represents general property taxes alone, and does not include state income taxes. In 1949 the state income taxes came to more than $130,000 and the federal income taxes to $1,465,000; BPLC Papers, Annual Report, May, 1950.

22. Aram, Reminiscences. In his annual report of May, 1950, Aram includes a liberal-spirited paragraph on relations with the small mills.

XXIX

Weyerhaeuser Company and

Scientific Management

ALTHOUGH the operations of various companies that grew out of the Weyerhaeuser and Denkmann, Ingram, Laird and Norton, and Musser family groups are now national in scope, the Far Northwest might fairly be regarded in 1960 as their primary base. Here in the states of Washington and Oregon, the Weyerhaeuser Company, the former Weyerhaeuser Timber Company, has its principal holdings of timber for turning out forest products, its most complex manufacturing facilities, and its best-known programs of forest conservation. Here the name Weyerhaeuser has its most immediate meaning to the people, and here lie its closest relations with government.

A large contour map of the Pacific Northwest, such as can be found in texts of physical geography, shows a great oblong terrain with its central spine, the Cascade Range, defined by a line of high snowy peaks. The western side is bounded by the Pacific, and the eastern belted by the northern Rockies. Along the northwestern corner of the map sprawls Puget Sound, indented by peninsulas and dotted by islands; the southeastern corner shows the Snake River running as far west as the Oregon boundary, with some considerable lakes between it and the Pacific— Malheur, Harney, Summer, Klamath, Crater. Midway in the huge oblong the Columbia River sweeps down to the sea, giving Oregon and Washington most of their common boundary. This region of a quarter of a million square miles offers sharp physical contrasts, for it comprehends a number of mountain chains from the Bitter Root to the Olympics, a rough coastal slope, sagebrush desert in one area and the rainiest district of America in another, placid bays, and torrential rivers. But its most prominent features are its vast stretches of forest, broken by the Cascades into two halves; the vivid green of the Douglas fir region lying to the moist west, and the brownish carpet of the ponderosa pines reaching out to the semiarid east.

If the principal Weyerhaeuser Company establishments in Washington and Oregon were picked out in red on the contour map, a reader would count ten. Farthest to the north he would see the mills at Everett on Puget Sound, and the Snoqualmie Falls plants not far away. Four others lie north of the Columbia: the White River mill at Enumclaw within sight of Mount Rainier's majestic cone, Willapa Harbor at Raymond on a pocket of the Pacific Coast, the Aberdeen mill not far away, and the big Longview plants where the Columbia widens to the sea. South of that river the map would show the Coos Bay (North Bend) mill, completed in 1951; the Springfield and Cottage Grove establishments near the university town of Eugene, and the Klamath Falls mill, near enough the California line to be within view of Mount Shasta.[1]

Any students of forest products who visited these ten plant centers would quickly discover wide differences in their positions and character. The Everett plants, with their high smokestacks, massive mills, and cluster of smaller structures belting Puget Sound and the Snohomish River, would appear especially large; so would Longview, with its sawmills, dry kilns, planing mill, plywood, and bark-product plants, Pres-to-Log installation, prefabrication shop, pulp mills, paperboard manufactory, and central research and development laboratory. The compact buildings at Snoqualmie, deep in the forest under the mist rising from Snoqualmie Falls, would seem as landbound as the White River mill in its little valley near Enumclaw, also surrounded by woods. But at Willapa Harbor he would be struck by the fact that the mill lies where logs can be floated down a small river and where oceangoing steamers can tie up at the wharves. At Longview, where two rivers meet, he would similarly see some use made of the Cowlitz, and lumber ships lying at the Columbia piers. Differences in the size of plants would indicate that the range of operations was limited at Aberdeen, but larger at Klamath Falls and very broad indeed at Longview.

The full utilization principle is applied as economic conditions permit. All centers have sawmills, Everett and Snoqualmie Falls having two each, Longview three. All have planing mills, and Aberdeen alone lacks dry kilns. Four have plywood plants—Cottage Grove, Springfield, Longview, and Snoqualmie Falls—and five manufacture Silvatek products—Klamath Falls, Springfield, and North Bend in Oregon, Longview and

Snoqualmie Falls in Washington. Pulp and paperboard mills are located at Everett, Longview, and Springfield as well as at Cosmopolis near the Willapa Harbor and Aberdeen units.

Most striking of all, in a comprehensive view of these operations, is the fact that each large establishment has its own tree farm or forest conserved so that its growth furnishes a perpetual supply of timber. All of them are now owned by the Weyerhaeuser Company alone, though a few have been managed in cooperation with public and private groups. Some mills are served by two sustained yield tracts; the Everett mills, for example, by the McDonald and Vail tree farms and the Willapa mill by the Clemons and Willapa tree farms. The Weyerhaeuser Company possesses twelve perpetual-growth forests, covering more than 2,300,000 acres of woodland, while it maintains another 75,000 acres under cooperative arrangements. Raw material from its tree farms in 1959 furnished 3.7 percent of the lumber, 3 percent of the plywood, and 5.7 percent of the pulp tonnage produced by American forest industries.

As a result of a merger to be described later, the Weyerhaeuser Company now had a remarkably comprehensive coverage of the market for forest products. In addition to the pulp and paperboard facilities already mentioned, in 1959 three other plants in Michigan, New Jersey, and North Carolina manufactured boxboard or paperboard that supplied 21 plants producing shipping containers, 11 turning out milk cartons, and 6 fabricating folding cartons located in 22 states, including Hawaii. (Five other similar plants were nearing operational status.) These new products of the Weyerhaeuser Company catered to the needs of the nation, as had its lumber line for more than forty years. And as of September 1959, the far-flung facilities of the Weyerhaeuser Sales Company became an operating part of its former parent. Now as never before the Weyerhaeuser Company was a truly national institution.

In this history the name Weyerhaeuser has been used to represent a remarkable array of properties and in recent times an equally remarkable range of undertakings. The fact must be borne in mind, however, that the holdings and enterprises embraced under this convenient rubric are now separate and independent entities, each doing a highly individual type of business, some of them competing with each other energetically in certain lines of production. They are not owned by a common body of stockholders, though Denkmanns, Lairds, Nortons, Mussers, and Weyerhaeusers hold shares in most of them. They possess separate boards of directors, have separate managements and separate planning, and exercise complete independence in establishing policy and conducting operations.

Such a state of affairs, so different from the close control of a wide range of firms by family stockholders in Frederick Weyerhaeuser's day, has been developing for a generation and has been accelerated in the last

decade. The election of Stuart Copeland as president of The Northwest
Paper Company in 1936, of W. P. Davis as president of P.F.I., and John
Aram as executive vice-president of Boise Payette in the late 1940's were
steps in the general direction. After the Timber Company became a competitor of Wood Conversion in producing waste-wood and bark-derivative products, completely separate boards of directors and officers seemed
the only logical way to assure the fullest development of the line by both
companies. Motivated by the conviction that achievement is maximized
by having directors concentrate on the affairs of one company and by
giving able officers plentiful authority to plan and to act, since 1952 the
independent boards have steered each of the companies on separate and
distinct courses. The directors have also been influenced by the desire to
have their firms maintain a reputation as respected corporate citizens in
every sense of the word. And through mergers, exchanges of stock, and
sales of stock most of the firms have become publicly held corporations
and have brought numerous former outsiders to their directorates. Not
for many years have the formerly associated firms been the exclusive preserves of the families that gave them their start and nurtured them
through a veritable Slough of Despond.

    As this volume shows, the forest-products industry has been inher-
ently unfavorable to concentration. More than most others, it has given
birth to a wide array of separate corporations organized on a moderate
scale. The ease of access to raw materials, the difficulties of obtaining
capital except on a local basis, the local character of labor problems, and
the advantages of separate local managements have all impeded large-
scale organization. The wonder is that so large an institution as the
Weyerhaeuser Company finally developed and survived.

2

    By the 1950's the three major policies of the Weyerhaeuser Timber
Company had been so fully established that nobody thought of questioning them. They were, first, the fullest possible utilization of timber,
which meant not merely the avoidance of obvious waste in manufacture
but also the scientific selection of the best product that a given log could
make; and second, the integration of each large mill so that it would
combine in one plant a number of the best technologies and thus offer advantageous uses for every log. The other major policy, hardly new though
it had received new applications, was geographical expansion, with the
South as a fresh theater. These policies had been evolved slowly by trial
and error; they were identified in the company as the operating principles of Phil Weyerhaeuser, chief executive and long-range planner, and
Charles Ingram, the decisive and dynamic second in command. Other

men contributed significant ideas, notably Laird Bell and F. K. Weyerhaeuser, but the executive officers were the key men.

In the development of these policies, the scope of the Weyerhaeuser undertakings was a manifest advantage. The company has never owned as much as 5 percent of the commercial forests of the Pacific Northwest, but this suffices the assertion: "It is our policy to manage this land to supply our mills forever." The management of a forest—necessarily a large forest—for sustained yield implies locking the invested capital up for a half-century or more. The owner of a tree farm must thus for two generations pay taxes, combat fires, destroy insect pests, and encourage growth, while he remains uncertain of the final return from his forest. He must feel the type of faith that Frederick Weyerhaeuser expressed when he said, "The only mistake I have made is not buying timber when it was offered to me"; a statement which good lumbermen now amend to read, "My only mistake was in not growing timber when I could."

But the tree-farm owner must possess courage as well as faith. Entrepreneurial risks in America are often large and tend to grow larger; and the risks in tree farming, since modern construction has learned to substitute steel, concrete, plastics, and glass for lumber, are large indeed. In meeting the capital costs of regrowing wood and avoiding the rapid cutting of mature and semimature timber to realize immediate returns, the resources of a large company give it a better position than a small owner can hold.

The integration of manufacture in each establishment—that is, the grouping together of a variety of mills making plywood, pulp, paperboard, hardboard, containerboard, and other commodities, so that every log can be used for the purpose to which it is best adapted and in its entirety—similarly requires the capital, specialized skills, and managerial ability that appertain to a large company. Science and invention have shown since 1900 that full utilization of the forest is impossible unless dozens of products are made and marketed, and this demands no small outlay for plant and equipment. By 1957 Oregon and Washington had nearly a hundred plywood plants—Oregon 54, Washington 37—each depending on a somewhat precarious market. The pulp, paper, and paperboard industries likewise demanded a heavy capital investment and were briskly competitive, for by 1957 more than 70 mills were engaged in this branch of the industry, and they included such companies as Scott, Fibreboard, International Paper, Crown-Zellerbach, and St. Regis. It is not strange that a marked trend toward economic concentration was evident.

Full utilization of logs means specialized and imaginative utilization. That is, it means the use of highly trained research staffs to find new methods and the installation of complicated equipment. Scientists discovered that much unused material could be sent to a pulp mill; that other materials could be defibrated and made into Silvacel; that planing mill shavings could be compressed into Pres-to-Logs; and that bark could be ground, refined, and sold as Silvacon to meet a list of industrial uses from glue-making to additives for oil-well muds. The Research and Development Department of the Weyerhaeuser Company, the largest non-governmental agency of research in the industry, is small in comparison with the research work of the largest chemical, petroleum, and electrical corporations, but it commands a personnel and laboratory facilities above the reach of smaller wood-industry companies.

A glance at the basic internal policies of the Weyerhaeuser Company will reveal a number of interesting features in each.

3

First place in company planning is given to sustained yield, for the careful management and indefinite continuance of the forests is fundamental to the life of the organization. By 1951 the holdings of the Weyerhaeuser Timber Company in the Pacific Northwest had grown from the original 900,000 acres purchased at the beginning of the century to more than 2,750,000 acres. By the end of 1959 southern acquisitions had brought the total to 3,400,000. The largest of the recent northwestern acquisitions was the purchase of about 55,000 acres at Cottage Grove, Oregon, including a sawmill and plywood plant. This was bought to give the Springfield mill more young timber to balance its large stands of overmature trees, and thus enable it to increase its annual cut without endangering the sustained-yield principle;[2] for the great aim now is to keep the almost 3,500,000 acres continuously productive.

Just how much timber do the forest holdings represent? The approximate amount standing on Weyerhaeuser Timber Company lands in the Pacific Northwest was long necessarily a subject of mere conjecture. Even yet it is difficult to find dependable standards of measurement for large forests. Trees grow, cruising standards have been raised, new species have become merchantable. At rare intervals the company lets guarded statements appear, suggesting first that it might own 33,000,000,000 feet and later 40,000,000,000—estimates generally regarded as low. As timber prices increased during and after the Second World War, various financiers suggested to the Tacoma management that it might be well to recapitalize the company on a higher timber valuation, proposals that partly amused and partly irritated J. P. Weyerhaeuser, Jr. At the time of the merger with the Kieckhefer Container Company in 1957, however, the company stated that it had about 60,000,000,000 feet of standing merchantable timber in the Pacific Northwest.[3]

"Continuing calculations," the Weyerhaeuser Timber Company declared in 1957, "are made to determine the quantity of timber which can be cut annually and still assure the sustained production of raw material." The object is not merely the protection of the company's future; more importantly, it is the protection, by full employment, of the communities in which the company operates. These communities must have a stable economic support, and the value of the resources of a large cooperative enterprise or a strong company in giving such assurance was emphasized by David Mason in his statement to a Senate committee holding public hearings at Eugene, Oregon, in 1948:

> The establishment of a cooperative unit prepared the way suitably for frequent investment of more and more capital over a long period of years in order more and more intensively to utilize and refine the forest and its product. The greater the plant investment in a given project, the greater the assurance to the community that the private cooperator will afford stable long-continued support to the community. The greater the investment by the cooperator, the greater the economic pressure upon the cooperator to place additional forest land on the sustained yield management basis. . . .
>
> The maximum contribution to the security and stability of the community is to be secured as indicated above. The minimum of reliable community support is furnished by a relatively large number of small, inefficient operators, lacking assured timber supply, lacking drying and refining facilities, financially unstable, vulnerable to the first chill economic breeze.[4]

To tree protection Weyerhaeuser Company managers give assiduous attention, their foresters and timbermen guarding the woods as strenuously as possible from fire, insects, blights, and windstorms. In every forest, fleets of water-tank trucks are ready to move into action over well-built gravel roads. Portable fire pumps and boxes of axes and other fire-fighting tools are scattered about. The company maintains watchtowers and patrols, builds firebreaks, and uses airplanes. In dry seasons they halt logging operations the moment humidity drops below a certain point, for even a bootnail striking a stone might start a blaze. When the humidity is at marginal level, logging may be done on the "hoot-owl shift," with breakfast at 3:15 A.M., and work continued only from daybreak until the midmorning sun has dried the dew. Sometimes no precautions avail. In 1951 fire struck the Weyerhaeuser forests a stunning blow, roaring through 8,000 acres. The next few years saw little loss, but in 1955 lightning in the Klamath area set off blazes in which 4,000 acres of young growth was so badly burned that the land had to be artificially reforested. Nevertheless, the general showing is satisfactory.

In terms of actual loss, the insect pests that attack various parts of the trees—the flowers, cones, seeds, inner bark, foliage, and stems—nowadays cause more destruction than fire. In the Douglas fir region the bark beetles, which make long tunnels to reach the sugar and starch of the inner bark and cambium, introducing fungi while committing damage of their own, have been especially troublesome. Thriving best in dry weather, they were highly destructive in the Springfield and Coos Bay areas in 1952, but became less menacing in the wet season of 1953. Areas of infestation, discovered by airplanes, were given special logging to remove diseased trees until the epidemic was halted. The spruce budworm and other ailments have to be combated year after year. Foresters maintain a keen outlook for any incipient epidemic. A recent innovation, aerial color photography, has been found helpful in detecting the pests. Forest managers constantly use the airplane for spraying DDT or more effective insecticides, while in stricken areas they give special attention to removal of weak trees and the rapid salvaging of killed trees. The importance of the work is suggested by the estimate of the Department of Agriculture that recent western epidemics of bark beetles have killed 45,000,000,000 board feet of timber.[5]

The story of one skirmish in the general war was told in 1949 in a company magazine:

> Last summer, in the hills near Springfield, Oregon, a trapper was checking his lines when he stumbled upon some new settlers. Swarming over the Douglas fir branches were thousands of inch-long worms, looking somewhat like caterpillars without hair. They were devouring the fir needles.
>
> The trapper reported the invaders, which were soon identified as spruce budworms, ordinarily natives of eastern forests. Oregon's legislature appropriated $125,000 and declared war on the budworm. An equal amount was made available by the federal government. A committee comprised of lumber and forestry associations, Oregon's state forestry board, the U.S. Forest Service and several timber companies, including Weyerhaeuser, joined the battle.
>
> The result: within a year between 95 and 99 percent of the budworms have been killed. The job was done by thirteen airplanes and several helicopters spraying 166,000 acres with DDT and fuel oil.[6]

If the coastal forests have often found rains from the ocean a safeguard against fires or a check on conflagrations, they have also suffered from heavy windstorms, which seldom cross the Cascades. During four years in succession, 1949–1952, gales blew down countless Douglas firs and other tall trees in Washington and Oregon. One forester, traveling by foot through an exposed area in Pacific County, Washington, saw a hundred large trees lying across a short stretch of logging road. Such fallen timber offers a rich harborage to beetles, and has to be salvaged as rapidly as possible.

Altogether, sustained-yield units or tree farms need a large staff of trained foresters. The Weyerhaeuser Timber Company employed 55 such experts in 1950, and seven years later the number had grown to about 170. A forestry headquarters was established at Centralia in 1954 to prosecute research into the culture and conservation of woodlands. Every branch has its head forester. Under their supervision, analysts, timber specialists, map makers, and experts in methods of cutting are scattered over the company domains, while entomologists and soil specialists are in constant demand. All these activities were supervised in 1959 by the Timber and Timberland Division under the direction of E. F. Heacox. The cruiser, still needed, is now likely to be a man with a broad range of scientific and practical knowledge. Any visitor to the Weyerhaeuser branches will be struck by the number of graduates of forestry schools, both eastern and western.

If foresters wage ceaseless war against the enemies of timber, they also labor constantly to help the woods reproduce themselves. Natural reforestation, achieved by the reservation of blocks of timber in each logged area to scatter their seeds on the breeze, is by far the principal reliance of the industry. But nature will not always do the work unaided. The Forestry Department of the Weyerhaeuser Timber Company in the ten years 1941–1951 planted seedlings on 25,000 acres and scattered seeds over much larger tracts; costly as the processes are, they must be used widely. (For the Weyerhaeuser Company aerial seeding is now more important than natural reseeding.) The staff has conducted systematic studies since 1938 in the types of stock best suited to different environments, the improvement of planting tools, and the betterment of planting practices. Helicopters, especially valuable over difficult terrain, are used to sow seeds broadcast—seeds now poisoned or flavored to repel hungry rodents. In 1959, Weyerhaeuser Company seeded by helicopter 19,000 acres of logged-off land and hand-planted another 9,000 acres.

4

The two other fundamental policies of full wood utilization and the integration of manufacturing processes may be considered together, for they are complementary. When in 1949 the White River Lumber Company and the Willapa Harbor Lumber Mills were merged into the Timber Company, J. P. Weyerhaeuser, Jr., explained the reason. No change was contemplated in policy or personnel; the object was solely to gain greater operating efficiency "through the integration of forest management, research, logging, sawmilling, and pulp operation."

Integration and full utilization in the last analysis become synonymous. Integration means having the plants to use all the forest crop to create products having maximum value to the public. That is, it means that on each plant site there should be facilities to get the maximum value out of each log. The managers should be able to decide that a given fir, cedar, or hemlock will go to making pulp, plywood, lumber, or some special product, as science and experience dictate.

In achieving integration certain basic conditions had to be met. One was the development of research, for novel wood derivatives are found only by a many-sided scientific inquiry. One was adequate size, for small forests and limited mill facilities cannot support pulp, paper, or plywood manufacture. Another was careful preparatory instruction of employees, for veteran millhands found each innovation a shock. The pulp industry in particular, had always held itself aloof from lumbering. It had bargained separately with unions, had acquiesced in a union shop, had distributed its products through its own expert sales force, and had maintained standards of cleanliness and quality which sawmills could hardly meet. Old-fashioned lumbermen found it hard to admit pulp workers to their fold. The final requirement for integration, of course, was ceaseless managerial ingenuity to provide a steady stream of innovations, large and small.

Pulp and paper made an especially significant, indeed a cardinal, contribution to the broadening of the lumber industry. Emphasis on pulp and pulp products is basic to the economics of full utilization of trees. When the Weyerhaeuser group entered the pulp field in 1931 with the Longview sulfite plant, Washington and Oregon had only eight mills all told, with a yearly output short of 400,000 tons.[7] Yet it was already clear that the pulp business would soon play almost as powerful a role on the Pacific Coast as that taken in older states. By 1949 the government was able to report that pulp and paper companies held a dominant position in the northern woodlands east of the Rockies: "They control the largest area of land, employ the most foresters, and have the greatest financial stake in sustained-yield forestry."[8] The Pacific slope might continue to give first place to lumber, but it was inevitable that the paper and pulp industry would do much to variegate and balance the wood products picture.

For the Weyerhaeuser Timber Company, this development came principally after the Second World War, though special war demands helped lay its foundations. The Longview pulp mill, which began operating when the depression was heaviest, obtained an adequate supply of western hemlock from the St. Helens tree farms and neighboring forests. While the depression still continued, the second pulp mill was built at Everett in 1936 to make unbleached sulfite pulp, ordinarily imported from abroad.[9] During the next few years improvements in equipment made it possible to manufacture semibleached sulfite; and later still the Longview mill, at the request of the War Production Board, turned to fully bleached sulfite pulp for explosives. The W.P.B. thus had the benefit of some years of Weyerhaeuser research in the production of pulp

Clearwater Timber Company's headquarters camp which became the camp of Potlatch Forests, Inc., after the merger of the two firms in 1931.

Potlatch Lumber Company mill at Potlatch, Idaho, which began operations on September 11, 1906.

Snoqualmie Falls sawmill, built in 1917 by Snoqualmie Falls Lumber Company, a Weyerhaeuser Timber Company subsidiary.

White River Lumber Company, incorporated in 1896 and merged with Weyerhaeuser in 1948.

Weyerhaeuser Company's Longview mills, the world's largest integrated forest-products plant site.

C. Davis Weyerhaeuser

Edwin F. Heacox

C. S. Chapman

Clyde S. Martin

Douglas fir forest, showing clear-cut patches which will be reseeded from mature timber left nearby.

*A high climber topping a spar tree
which will be rigged for high-lead
logging.*

*Hard-hatted, safety-conscious log-
gers felling a huge Douglas fir with
modern power saws.*

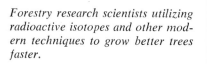

Seeding by helicopter to keep company forest lands continually productive.

Forestry research scientists utilizing radioactive isotopes and other modern techniques to grow better trees faster.

E. H. O'Neil

L. N. Reichmann

Harry E. Morgan

Ralph R. Macartney

Log on carriage in first stage of sawing operation.

Veneer lathes unwind logs, much like a roll of paper, producing plywood — one of the modern building materials.

chemical cellulose, in the form of pulp, paper, and other specialty
ducts, wood is the miracle material for a thousand uses.

w uses for wood, such as versatile particle board panels and other
el products, are being developed for residential construction, com-
rce, and industry.

Hardwood doors, one of many specialty products used for homes and commercial and industrial buildings.

Paperboard made from wood pulp is manufactured into containers, cartons, and folding boxes.

Exposed laminated beams, increasingly used in homes, commercial buildings, and industrial plants.

Board of Directors — 1955

Bark-free logs are cut into eight-foot "peeler blocks" for processing at Weyerhaeuser Company's Snoqualmie Falls, Wash., plywood plant.

Board of Directors, Senior Councilors and Officers — May, 1961

*F. K. Weyerhaeuser,
president in 1957 and chairman of
the board in 1960.*

Norton Clapp, president in 1960.

John L. Aram,
vice president

B. L. Orell,
vice president

John M. Musser,
vice president

Joseph E. Nolan,
executive vice president,
Administration

George H. Weyerhaeuser,
executive vice president,
Wood Products and Timberlands

Howard W. Morgan,
executive vice president,
Pulp and Paper Products

F. Lowry Wyatt,
vice president

useful for nitration. The war was hardly six months old when in May, 1942, the Longview mill shipped its first car of prepared pulp east to be turned into smokeless powder, and before the conflict ended it had supplied the seven government powder plants with many thousands of tons of such material.

Since the war, Howard W. Morgan has been the salient figure leading Weyerhaeuser Timber, as part of its integration program, to devote a much greater effort to pulp and paperboard manufacture. In a report of 1949 to the executive committee he discussed various modes of expansion and diversification. He pointed out that the market for pulp products was large and expanding. At the same time the company had a tremendous mass of low-grade logs and sawmill scraps crying out for utilization: at Raymond 105,000 tons a year of such materials, at Everett 80,000 tons of sawmill waste and cull logs, and at Snoqualmie, Coos Bay, and White River 45,000 additional tons. With these materials and its available capital the company could make any type of pulp it pleased. Containerboard was a logical succeeding step, for the machines it required were similar to those for making pulp, and the product would not need a large special selling staff. It could be delivered to various firms that would convert it to shipping containers, print any required label, and sell them to users. The new Springfield mill in Oregon began turning out containerboard in 1949. The logical ensuing step would be the manufacture of bleached kraft paperboard, for which there was a clear and rising demand.

In 1950 Morgan laid before the executive committee a proposal for a paperboard mill at Longview, to use bleached pulp made with the existing facilities, which would be enlarged. An expenditure of about $10,-950,000 was at once approved by the directors. The 1950 annual report announced that this "major expansion" would by 1952 approximately double the output of existing bleached kraft pulp mills and offer means for converting the increased output into paperboard.[10]

Thereafter continuous progress was made on the basis of Morgan's general program. The Springfield containerboard plant was greatly expanded at the beginning of the 1950's. Additional chippers were installed at Coos Bay, from which the chips were sent by rail to Springfield. In 1953 a bleached kraft pulp mill opened at Everett, for abundant raw material—much of it previously thrown away—was at hand. By September Longview was making its first shipments of bleached paperboard, and the company report the following year noted that the product had an expanding market, particularly in sanitary containers for dairy and other food products. Late in 1953 the directors approved Morgan's proposal for an addition to the paperboard mill at Longview, to cost $7,500,000.[11]

The pulp mill that had been suggested for the Raymond area was meanwhile delayed because of public apprehension that the pulp liquors, poured into the harbor, would kill the oysters abounding there, or the diatoms and other food particles on which they supposedly existed. Morgan had a laboratory built at South Bend and hired a biologist, who made a prolonged study of conditions favorable to the nourishment, reproduction, and general comfort of oysters. His object was not to prove that they could live in dilute pulp effluent but to learn every fact possible about how they did live. One authority had boasted of growing fat oysters in distilled water! Visitors to the laboratory found rows of oysters immersed in varying proportions of sea and fresh water, in different varieties of water combined in varying degrees with pulp liquor, in plastic bags registering the amount of water that passed through the bivalves, and in waters of different temperatures. In time the Weyerhaeuser biologists perhaps knew more about oysters than any other living men. Though they proved that the toxic effects of pulp liquor on oysters could be eliminated, they concluded that the mill would nevertheless be blamed for occasional damage caused by other sources. Moreover, the management found that it would cost too much to develop an adequate water supply at Raymond.

The final decision of the directors was to build the new pulp mill at a place called Cosmopolis near Aberdeen.[12] In the summer of 1955 the company announced that this bleached sulfite pulp plant, one of the few erected on the Pacific Coast in these years, would have a productive capacity of 400 tons daily and would use a magnesium oxide process for treating its hemlock material.[13] It went into operation on March 12, 1957.

This addition of pulp, containerboard, paperboard, and allied commodities to the roster of Timber Company products was the greatest single step in broadening and integrating manufacture. Year after year the president could have repeated the statement in the annual report for 1952: "Major emphasis in the company's recent construction program has been on expansion of . . . pulp facilities designed to use wood leftovers from sawmill operations and low grade logs."[14] The middle and later 1950's found the division still short of materials to supply a hungry market. Manufacturers of plastics, rayon, and similar commodities were eager for sulfite pulp, while sulfate pulp went into an ever-widening range of containers.

To most people the name Weyerhaeuser still meant lumber; yet the organization had become one of the principal pulp and paperboard manufacturers in the land, supplying material for shipping containers and milk cartons, and pulp for a great variety of products. By 1957 one-third of the net sales of the Weyerhaeuser Timber Company came from pulp and paperboard, and in the following year, when output reached 1,300,000 tons, it became clear that this proportion would rapidly be increased. In

1959, net sales of pulp, paperboard, cartons, and containers accounted for almost half the company's total.

The fact that these innovations utilized a vast amount of material once unused especially pleased the management. For decades no honest lumberman had looked at the discarded litter and waste in forest and mill without twinges of conscience. In the woods, a variety of trees—hemlock, spruce, alder, white fir, larch, and poor grades of pine—had been left to mature and die. Meanwhile, the mills had thrown a variety of odds and ends—slabs, edgings, chips, missawed boards—into a burner that turned potential wealth into black pillars of smoke. But the wood residues could not be employed until science showed the way and changing social habits made brisk sales possible.

The contributions of science had been continuous and indispensable. Pulp mills required clean wood to turn into fiber, and for years barkless and knotless lumber had been prohibitively expensive. Knots, for example, once had to be bored out of the wood. Science now found a means of cleaning them from the pulp. The hydraulic barker, developed by the Weyerhaeuser Timber Company and first installed at Longview, stripped the logs until they were shining and white; and at about the same time log chippers—huge wheels fitted with powerful knives—were improved until they could turn the biggest log into bits of fingernail size in a few seconds. Nor was the role of innovation in other industries and social change in furnishing new markets less important. With the rise of the new industries, highly refined pulp went into making cellophane, rayon, photographic papers, and similar products. As the nation's shopping habits altered, stores and supermarkets required paperboard containers of every shape and size, pulp magazines multiplied, and rayon garments became common.

5

Another powerful impetus was given to the full utilization of the forest when plywood became popular. The use of hardwood veneers can be traced far back into the history of cabinetmaking, but softwood veneers are recent. Douglas fir plywood, intended for panels in doors, was unknown till exhibited at the Lewis and Clark exposition in Portland in 1905, and for years thereafter its use was slight. Not until 1920, when the first factory built for the commercial supply of plywood opened its doors, did the public begin to think of the product in larger terms, and even in 1925 only about 150,000,000 square feet of plywood were made from soft timber.

In 1935 the executive committee of the Timber Company, at the insistence of Fred K. Weyerhaeuser, had authorized the building of a plywood plant, but no immediate use was made of the authority. Five

years later the corporation acquired a controlling interest in the Washington Veneer Company at Olympia. Not until after the war, in 1947, did
the company make its real entrance into the industry with the completion
of the large plywood establishment at Longview. This, with an initial
capacity of about 40,000,000 square feet annually, was soon yielding
from 2½ to 3 percent of all the Douglas fir plywood in the country. The
demand proved so keen, in fact, that in 1948 the capacity was raised to
60,000,000, and though the business later had very lean years in profits,
this did not affect volume, which by 1958 stood at 75,000,000. In 1959
all Weyerhaeuser Company plants produced over 200,000,000 square
feet of plywood. This added greatly to the strength of integrated manufacture. Experts could pick out logs suitable for plywood before they
entered the sawmills. The best would be peeled for high-quality veneer
and the next best peeled for inner-core stock. Some of the bark removed
would be ground into the various Silvacon products.[15]

Among other special products that contribute to integration in the
sense of a variegated use of wood within a single plant are ply-veneer,
and the various bark products. Ply-veneer, a minor triumph of ingenuity,
is a sheet of wood faced on both sides with kraft paperboard. It is employed chiefly for packaging articles too heavy for a paper carton and
too light for a wooden box—though it possesses many other uses. Managers of the plywood plant in Springfield found early in its history that
they had a surplus of core layers—that is, of sheets from the inner log,
poorer in quality than the layers that surface the core; they turned to ply-
veneer as a way out of their difficulty; and the engineering department at
Tacoma designed a factory. Problems arising from the dryness of the
veneer and the need for special gluing were conquered, and before the
end of 1953 the plant was successfully placing the new commodity on the
market.[16]

The Silvacon materials likewise sprang from a problem of raw material unusable except for fuel, one that the research and development staff
had to solve—a surplus of Douglas fir bark at various mills. With the
three sawmills of the Longview plant contributing the largest volume, unused bark ran to tens of thousands of tons a year. Money had been invested to haul it to the mills and strip it from the logs: where could a
return be found? Everyone knew how much research on use of waste
products had been done by the Wood Conversion Company. The development staff of the Timber Company finally determined that by scientific
processing much bark could be made usable for molding compounds,
asphalt roofing, magnesite flooring, fertilizer, vinyl tile, chemicals, and
even as an extender for glues and resins.[17] But, alas, most bark taken
from the American forests is still simply thrown away or burned.

Acting on scientific advice, the company built a pilot plant at Long-view, ascertained the existence of a market, and by 1947 was selling more than a thousand tons of bark products a year, initially at levels that yielded no profit. Both demand and price so improved that in 1951 almost 7,500 tons of this material was being sold at an average of $50 a ton. This was the highest mark reached for some years, but, as manufacturing costs fell, the new product continued to be profitable. Although many thousands of tons of bark were still used to fuel the boilers for want of a better market, a beginning had been made in what might eventually prove the complete utilization of a material long wasted.

Much might be said of sundry other products by which scientific re-search and managerial resourcefulness have made the policy of full wood utilization effective. Learning from his early success at Wood Conversion with Balsam Wool, Nu-Wood, and other wares, Clark C. Heritage went to the Timber Company and developed additional wood derivatives—Silvacel, Silvaloy, Silvawool, and others. Each had its special uses—Silvawool as an economical insulating material, odorless and verminless; Silvaloy as a fiber for plastics, roofing felts, and oil filters; and Silvacel for any number of wants. "Volume and variety are increasing rapidly," Clark C. Heritage wrote in 1951 of this last-named product, "for markets such as thermal insulation, paper manufacture, oil well drilling, cold and hot molded plastics, floors, coatings, battery parts, and other applications."

Many additional products have been under study; experiments have even been made, not without promise, in the conversion of wood wastes into molasses for feeding cattle. Science works constantly on two fronts: improved management of the forests to yield more raw material and a wider range of processes and commodities to make all this material useful to the public. It seemed a far cry from old-time lumbering when in 1954 the directors of Weyerhaeuser Timber authorized the erection of its own chemical plant, for the various activities demanded great quantities of chlorine and caustic soda which the company could make economically for itself. The Weyerhaeuser Company also now has a similar but smaller plant at Plymouth, North Carolina.

6

One of the most important postwar policies of the company, its ex-pansion in the South, was undertaken partly as a means of plowing back profits into new facilities, partly to promote integration, and partly to keep abreast of the rapid development of the pulp and containerboard business. The South after the First World War offered virtually a new frontier in forestry, for scientific study proved that fast-growing species of trees lent themselves to a wide variety of the changing demands of industry. The desirability of geographical diversification and balance in all operations stimulated investment by eastern firms in the inviting field.

As opportunity offered, executives of Weyerhaeuser Timber studied a number of possible mergers and purchases. In 1956 the Timber Company bought options on 90,000 acres in Mississippi and Alabama, including a millsite at Columbus, Mississippi. This was an investment for the future, comparable in a minor way to the great original purchase in the Northwest. Though the timberland had been heavily logged and in part burned over, intensive forestry improvement could quickly reclothe it with a mantle of woods. As the first crop of trees grew toward profitable size, the company would erect a modern pulp mill. When feasible, it would also make new purchases of land suitable for timber.

By far the greatest step in the geographical expansion of the Timber Company, and in its advance into the conversion of paperboard and related products, was the merger in 1957 with the Kieckhefer Container Company and its affiliate, the Eddy Paper Corporation. This union recognized a complementary relationship that for some years had steadily grown stronger. Kieckhefer, with its subsidiary, the North Carolina Pulp Company, was engaged principally in producing and selling corrugated containers and milk cartons, while another subsidiary made folding boxes; the Eddy Corporation was similarly occupied in the manufacture and distribution of corrugated containers, with a subsidiary in the folding box business. No merger could have been more logical.

Most of the business of the Kieckhefer and Eddy companies lay in the East, South, and northern Midwest. However, Kieckhefer had valuable manufacturing establishments in the Far West—at Vancouver and Yakima, Washington, at Salt Lake City, and in California. By the summer of 1955 the Weyerhaeuser Timber Company was supplying the Kieckhefer plants on the Pacific Coast with all the bleached kraft board they required and a great part of the unbleached kraft material, these sales reaching nearly $9,000,000 a year. In the following year the Kieckhefer plants bought 46 percent of WTC's bleached paperboard and 21 percent of its unbleached containerboard.

It was so logical for the two corporations to merge that the step encountered little opposition on either side. When Kieckhefer entered the larger company, it brought along not only its Eddy affiliate and its pulp company but the Rochester Folding Box Company of Rochester, New York, the Gereke-Allen Carton Company of St. Louis, and a half-interest in the Ace Folding Box Corporation of Middlebury, Indiana. Though the Kieckhefer-Eddy group seemed to outward view a rather complex structure, its activities were actually well unified, being confined to containerboard, boxboard, and bleached paperboard products.

The move was truly epochal. Geographically, the merger placed the Weyerhaeuser name in scores of communities where it had previously been little known. Eddy and its subsidiaries had an array of plants stretching from Rochester, New York, to Cedar Rapids, Iowa; the Kieckhefer establishments were scattered all the way from Westbrook, Maine, and Tampa, Florida, to Alameda, California. Some 460,000 acres of timberland in North Carolina, Virginia, and Maryland were included in the transaction. In recommending that stockholders vote for the merger, President F. K. Weyerhaeuser, the most influential advocate of the union, declared: "Kieckhefer and Eddy, after many years of work and large expenditures, have developed facilities, experience, know-how, and customer good will which it would require your Company many years to establish. They meet especially the requirements of your company for carrying out its policy of efficient crop utilization." By this single step the WTC pulp division gained an enhancement of vigor that would otherwise have cost years of planning and toil. In no other feasible way could the Weyerhaeuser interests have acquired some forty plants, with such an array of facilities and so valuable a body of land.

The agreement provided that the Weyerhaeuser Timber Company, which increased its authorized stock from 25,000,000 shares to 31,000,-000, should be the surviving corporation. For the 29,889 shares of Kieckhefer stock the Timber Company gave 4,423,572 shares of its common stock; for the 181,415 shares of Eddy stock it gave 1,814,150 shares. Absorption of the new properties into the Weyerhaeuser operations began as soon as the merger was approved in April, 1957, and in June, Howard Morgan was made head of the Kieckhefer-Eddy division. The board of directors of the Timber Company was enlarged to include H. M. and R. H. Kieckhefer.

Thus was accomplished one of the most important enlargements of Weyerhaeuser properties and activities. In 1956 the gross sales of Kieckhefer, Eddy, and their subsidiaries were $132,470,000, and the net profits after taxes $13,553,000. Even though the gross sales of Weyerhaeuser and its subsidiaries amounted to about $325,000,000 and its net income nearly $51,500,000, this was no mean accretion.[18] And thus, also, the balance of the various Weyerhaeuser activities were further shifted; a lesser emphasis fell on what Frederick Weyerhaeuser would have regarded as the "basic" forest products—lumber, lath, shingles, and the like—and a greater emphasis on those new products among which stood pulp and its derivative commodities.

The philosophy behind the steady expansion of plants and activities is of course complex. Healthy growth is essential to the maintenance of profits, to the morale of the organization, to the constant development of new leaders, to the symmetry of the enterprises, and to a fulfillment of the social objectives of the Weyerhaeuser industries. This last consideration is by no means the least important. The nation has been growing in the last generation at an astonishing rate, and a business that supplies so many primary needs in the building of homes and factories has to grow with it. The modern forest-products industry, which may better be called the lumber-plywood-pulp-fiberboard-paper-paperboard industries, must be responsive to the rise of population. It builds the home in which the young couple rear their children, the barn where the farmer houses his tools and cattle, the factory where the worker gains a living; it furnishes the packages in which goods are shipped; it gives the publishers of newspapers, books, and magazines their paper stock; it panels the village library and the city council chamber.

The company policies that most directly interest the public are concerned with the selling of products, with labor, and, since stock ownership has become more widely diffused, with finance. All three functions have witnessed a marked change of emphasis. In the early Weyerhaeuser days manufacturing and transportation were dominant, salesmanship was secondary; now it may fairly be said that salesmanship is dominant and production a less prominent if equal partner. During most of Weyerhaeuser history labor got what it could without benefit of unions; today Weyerhaeuser feels the responsibility of giving the industry leadership in an enlightened policy toward organized labor. Once the Weyerhaeuser finances concerned only a restricted body of families; since 1950 they concern thousands of stockholders, whose ranks any investor may join.

When *The Saturday Review* gave the Weyerhaeuser Timber Company its award in 1956 for the most distinguished advertising in the public interest, its committee was impressed by the emphasis on conservation. The advertisement was part of the Company's campaign on behalf of tree farming as the best mode of ensuring America a permanent wood supply. "This campaign," remarked the group of thirty-eight judges from education, industry, and the arts, "has not only aided conservation and the efficient use of our timberlands, but has dramatized the importance of regarding trees as crops to be scientifically planted and harvested, thus protecting this country against any future exhaustion of its invaluable timber resources."[19] As a matter of fact, when the advertisement was published the country had at last begun growing timber faster, according to some experts, than it was being used.[20] The spread of well-managed tree farms large and small would maintain for the nation an abundant supply of lumber, plywood, paper, rayon, and as the W.T.C. advertisement put it, "about five thousand other products."

Labor relations have presented a brighter picture since the Second World War than ever before. Officers of the Weyerhaeuser Company have learned hard lessons in this field since the New Deal began, and their outlook has broadened. Latterly they have realized that they have an opportunity to set new patterns for the industry in dealing with employees, and a committee of directors is engaged in a continuing study of personnel problems.

The development of the plywood, pulp, paperboard, and bark-derivative activities, and the purchase or acquisition by merger of new facilities, meant a great increase in the labor force. In 1950 the Weyerhaeuser Timber Company had about 13,600 workers; by 1956 the payrolls listed 14,500, of whom more than 10 percent were in the activities just named; and the Kieckhefer-Eddy merger, plus expansion along other lines, brought the aggregate at the end of 1959 to 22,819.

The great majority of the employees were organized in four principal unions. The Lumber and Sawmill Workers were part of the American Federation of Labor; the International Woodworkers of America was a branch of the Congress of Industrial Organizations (C.I.O.); and the two unions of pulp and paper workers were members again of the A.F. of L. The merger of the A.F. of L. and C.I.O. in 1957 partially but by no means completely erased the lines of union division and the jurisdictional frictions that had caused so much difficulty. The International Woodworkers Association constituted the largest single labor group, and was a vigorous spokesman for the workers.

The history of labor relations in the years after the Second World War was in the main one of friendly cooperation between unions and management, punctuated by short periods of sharp conflict as new agreements were negotiated. As noted, Weyerhaeuser Timber, after a temporary association with other lumber companies in bargaining with labor, chose to take its own individual path. In 1950, confronted with demands for a union-managed health and welfare plan, a 7.5-cents-per-hour wage increase, and a union shop, the Timber Company held out after most of the industry surrendered and submitted to a strike. In the end the unions accepted a 5-cent wage increase, three paid holidays, health and welfare concessions, and the agreement of the company to institute a checkoff system, which would maintain union membership. But the union shop was not granted, and the company continued to administer its health and welfare plan. An almost industry-wide strike occurred in the summer of 1954 and led to the appointment of a fact-finding board by the governors of Oregon and California; but Weyerhaeuser Timber was not concerned in this difficulty, for it had already agreed to a labor contract.

The three subsequent years were years of labor peace, in which the heads of the Weyerhaeuser Timber Company seemed to comprehend fully the obligations of a leader in the industry. It granted wage increases and fringe benefits that set an example to other large firms. To enumerate them in detail would be wearisome. But it can be said that in 1955 the company agreed with the I.W.A., representing 7,600 lumber, logging, and plywood employees, for a sliding-scale increase in pay averaging 8.75 cents an hour, with improved vacation benefits, and a pension plan to become effective June 1, 1957. Employees of the pulp division also received a wage increase and other benefits in 1955 and 1956, while in 1957, under an industry-wide settlement on the Pacific Coast, they won a wage advance of 3.5 percent on a sliding scale, new fringe benefits, and a more liberal vacation policy.[21]

Scientific management had its application to labor policy. During 1956–1957 an analysis and evaluation of hourly rated jobs for the determination of more equitable wage rates was carried through at all branches of the lumber division, but it was never completed and accepted because of opposition within the unions. Altogether, the employee-relations policy of the Weyerhaeuser Company management deserves to be called progressive; it involves a firm adherence to what is believed the best interests of all parties concerned (stockholders, suppliers, customers, the general public, *and* employees), a friendly interest in the welfare of every employee, and the maintenance of mutual respect among all personnel throughout the organization.

Since the felling, transporting, and sawing of heavy trees are risky occupations, the Timber Company earnestly strove to reduce the number of accidents by a positive prevention program. It was able to assert in 1957 that its safety record, in each major operating division in the Pacific Northwest, was "materially better than that of the industry, whether considered on a regional or national basis." During that year the company received thirty safety awards, including twenty-two from the National Safety Council. In 1959 the Safety Director could point out that frequency of accidents in the firm's woods operations, lumber mills, and pulp mills ranged from 32 percent to 63 percent lower than averages reported to the National Safety Council and the United States Department of Labor, and that since 1947 the Weyerhaeuser Company had reduced lost-time injuries by 79 percent.[22]

Officials of the Weyerhaeuser Company are quietly proud of the fact that the Timber Company was the first lumber firm in the Pacific Northwest, possibly the first in the United States, to set up programs for group life, accident, and health insurance as well as retirement plans for its employees. Coverage and benefits under the group-life and accident and health-insurance plans have been increased from time to time since first instituted in 1929. Retirement plans were applied to salaried employees in 1945, to hourly employees other than those of the lumber division in 1950 (who chose higher wages instead), and to that last group in 1957.[23]

As a means of making a long-range contribution to labor-management relations and to education generally in the United States, the Weyerhaeuser Timber Foundation was organized in 1948 and made its first contribution a year later. Besides assisting hospital construction and community and youth activities, the foundation currently offers 15 four-year college undergraduate scholarships annually (that is, there are 60 holders in any given year) to children of Weyerhaeuser Company employees and has established graduate fellowships at six leading universities, chiefly for study in forestry, chemistry, and industrial relations. The foundation has also agreed to pay the cost of an unlimited number of scholarships granted by the National Merit Scholarship program to children of Weyerhaeuser Company employees.[24] Not the least significant institution supported by the foundation is the Forest History Society, Inc., which is devoted to collecting documents and stimulating the writing of forest-products history.

One remaining major policy of the Weyerhaeuser Company is of direct concern to the public. As noted elsewhere, managers of the associated companies worked for decades with almost no publicity and with no outside scrutiny of their balance sheets. It is improbable that even inside the groups knowledge of their fiscal operations was widely diffused. The various companies, even when they grew numerous, had short lists of owners, the same names, with variations, appearing for corporation after corporation; most of the stockholders were descendants of the founders and so intimately in touch with the companies that the regular publication of results seemed of minor importance. In 1935 the Weyerhaeuser Timber Company had fewer than 300 shareholders. To many of them dividends were less important than capital growth.

By 1950, however, the number of owners in the Weyerhaeuser Timber Company had risen above 3,000 and was fast increasing, reaching 10,880 in 1959. Growth meant pressure for publicity. The issuance of annual reports by the company had begun in 1934–1935; for a time they were not very revealing, but they have improved every year. No longer could members meet in one small room with a box of cherries on the table; no longer would they be content with a curt circular on results. They cast a careful eye on both operations and returns, and insisted on as full information as that given by managers of other corporations.

Weyerhaeuser Timber policy in the postwar years was to reinvest, on the average, half of the net earnings. This kept the rate of dividend payments at a lower rate than in many companies, but of course the increment of capital was proportionately increased. For various reasons, the chief of which was that shares were selling at a high figure, the W.T.C. directors in 1950 voted to split the stock, giving two new shares for each old one. In 1955 this stock was again split, each existing share this time being exchanged for four new shares.[25] The dividend rate in 1954 was 75 cents a share and in each of the three next years a dollar a share. The

annual reports, with consolidated balance sheets, published by the Weyerhaeuser Company would now satisfy the most captious. That for 1959
showed that the Weyerhaeuser Company enjoyed a net income of
$60,407,000, of which $33,367,000 was paid in dividends and $27,040,-
000 was retained in the business.

In keeping with the tendency toward a more scientific approach
to management, the Timber Company is manned with specialists from the
bottom rung to the top. Although a member of the leading ownership
family, F. K. Weyerhaeuser, who became president after his brother Phil's
death in 1956, until his retirement in 1960, had proved himself a masterly
planner and organizer, with an aptitude for selecting able subordinates.
His successor, Norton Clapp, is demonstrating that he, too, is an outstanding leader. Every vice-president is an expert in his own line, from the specialist in lumber manufacturing to the specialist in financial matters. The
men entrusted with the responsibility for planning, deciding, and carrying
into effect the future policies of the Weyerhaeuser Company, and for
coordinating the multitudinous activities of foresters and loggers, mill
managers and millworkers, lawyers and marketers in this impressive enterprise, are among the most capable corporate executives in the nation.

NOTES

1. Any standard atlas will show these locations.
2. See WTC Annual Reports. Of the 2,695,000 acres owned in March, 1957 by WTC, approximately 2,111,-000 acres were in the Douglas fir region of western Washington and Oregon; 556,000 acres were in the ponderosa pine region of south-western Oregon east of the Cascades; and 28,000 acres were in northern California. See prospectus issued at the time of the merger with Kieck-hefer, p. 11. This chapter is based on annual reports of the companies, their recent correspondence, and conversa-tion with their officers.
3. This figure is by the Scribner log scale, and represents "calculations based on the most recent data avail-able." Proxy statement, p. 11.
4. Rodney C. Loehr, *Forests for the Future,* 251, 252.
5. *Trees,* Yearbook, 1949, p. 409.
6. *Weyerhaeuser Magazine,* I, No. 1, July, 1949, p. 6.
7. Sulfite pulp is made by an acid proc-ess, while sulfate pulp is made by an alkaline process. Sulfite pulp is limited to a few species, notably hemlock, white fir, some spruce and some hardwoods, and is used in mak-ing papers with smooth printing sur-faces. Sulfate pulp is used in making papers and paperboards where strength is important. Unbleached kraft paper goes into paper bags and containerboard.
8. At this time the hundreds of mills the paper and pulp industry operated in New England, New York, and the Lake States owned more than two million acres, maintained their tim-berlands largely on a sustained-yield basis, employed hundreds of for-esters, and were busy trying to restore

cutover areas by large planting programs. They used the best equipment —portable camps, power saws, pulpwood loaders, mechanical skidders, and roadbuilding equipment; they utilized types of trees neglected by lumbermen. And it should be noted that they had commenced their conservation work with commendable promptness. As early as 1920 the Oxford Paper Company had begun to plant fast-growing aspen hybrids in the East to make book paper. Even before the First World War the Finch-Pruyn Company, using spruce and balsam fir, had placed large tracts in the Adirondacks on a sustained-yield program. They thus blazed a path the Weyerhaeuser and other northwestern groups followed. Agricultural Yearbook for 1949, *Trees,* 262–264.

9. Both mills had an initial capacity of 200 tons of pulp a day.

10. WTC *Management Bulletin,* April 4, 1951; Annual Report WTC, 1951, 9. Pulp prices at this time were about $135 a ton. Because of the Korean War a certificate of necessity could be obtained, allowing accelerated depreciation on about two-thirds of the $19,000,000 costs. See Morgan's statement to the directors, approved May 22, 1951, WTC Files, Tacoma.

11. WTC, annl. repts.

12. The story of the oysters is told in various reports by Howard Morgan to the executive committee or full board; see particularly his statement to the board March 4, 1955. The subject is also treated in Tacoma *News Tribune,* April 5, 1955; *Management Bulletin,* April 14, 1955.

13. WTC Files, JPW, Jr., to directors, June 1, 1955. The magnesium oxide process had been worked out partly at Longview and partly by the Howard Smith Paper Co. of Canada in cooperation with the Babcock Wilcox Co. of New York.

14. *Management Bulletin,* June 10, 1955.

15. "It has always seemed to me," writes Mr. Laird Bell, "that a conservation point could be made from the fact that in ordinary lumber manufacture we are trying to make square boards out of round logs with its inevitable waste, while this is not true with respect to plywood."

16. WTC annl. repts., 1953–1955; WTC Statistical Files.

17. Clark C. Heritage, after a career with the Wood Conversion Company, became head of research activities of the WTC by 1942 and reached retirement age in 1955. The Wood Conversion stock owned by Weyerhaeuser Timber was "spun off" in 1953 and distributed to shareholders of the WTC. At Longview, Drs. Heritage, Patnode, and Gregory, in succession, assisted by a large body of chemists, biologists, and other scientific researchers, have had well-equipped laboratories and nearly every facility they could desire. WTC was of course acutely aware that, as metals, cement, plastics, and other materials gained ground, the per capita use of lumber in its old forms was declining in the United States. Research had to point the way for progress in restoring wood to its former position.

18. Weyerhaeuser letter to shareholders, March 22, 1957.

19. *Saturday Review,* April 20, 1957. The advertisement showed a ponderosa pine tree farm of WTC, with a forester selecting mature trees to be harvested.

20. This fact was stated in the Timber Resource Review of the U.S. Forest Service at the beginning of 1956; see *Forestry Digest,* quoted in *Weyerhaeuser News,* No. 31, Feb. 1956, pp. 8, 9.

21. It is impossible in this brief summary of policy to enter into the mass of detailed negotiations year after year on wages, hours, and fringe benefits.

22. WTC Annual Report, 1957, 8; L. B. Hoelscher to R. W. Hidy, May 20, 1960, citing data from Weyerhaeuser Company statistical files in comparison with those from the National Safety Council, Pacific Northwest Loggers' Association, and the U.S. Department of Labor. In 1947

Weyerhaeuser Company employees in the woods had lost-time injuries of 117 per million man hours; the comparable figure for 1959 was 25 lost-time injuries per million man hours. In 1959 lumber mills of the Weyerhaeuser Co. had a lost-time injury frequency 32 percent lower than the average frequency of those mills reporting to the National Safety Council and 63 percent lower than those reporting to the U.S. Department of Labor.

23. George S. Long, Jr., to Allan Nevins, Oct. 21, 1959, and WTC Papers.

24. WTC Papers, Scholarship Program, Weyerhaeuser Timber Foundation; summary of work of Weyerhaeuser Timber Foundation by W. P. Gullander, Aug. 17, 1959.

Non-tax-supported colleges selected by Weyerhaeuser under-graduate scholars are given grants-in-aid of $1,000 per year for each Weyerhaeuser scholar enrolled. Children of parents earning $925 base pay per month are not eligible for Weyerhaeuser scholarships, though children of employees of the various subsidiaries are eligible. A maximum of three scholarships has been awarded in one year under the National Merit Scholarship program. Graduate fellowships have been established at Yale (3), University of Washington (2), Oregon State (2), University of Wisconsin, University of Chicago, and North Carolina State. Fellows have no obligations to the Weyerhaeuser Company. The foundation has also made annual contributions to non-tax-supported colleges in Washington, Oregon, and Minnesota.

25. Detailed reports were written (WTC Files) discussing the reasons for and against the stock split.

XXX

Retrospect and Prospect

I N RETROSPECT, the record of the various companies that grew from the activities of the original Frederick Weyerhaeuser and his associates stands as an impressive one. Singly and jointly, the Denkmanns, Humbirds, Ingrams, Lairds and Nortons, Moons, Mussers, and Weyerhaeusers have made innumerable decisions affecting events in their chosen field of endeavor. Acting in the traditional American way of enlightened self-interest, they have taken an active part in converting a natural resource, the trees of the forest, into products for the American market, and in growing a new forest crop for succeeding generations.

Increasingly in the twentieth century, the firms of the Weyerhaeusers and their co-investors have extended the number of their products and the geographical range of their sales. For more than one hundred years they have turned out lumber for homes, offices, churches, and a host of other structures. Since 1898, and particularly since 1930, their pulp-and-paper output has gone into marketable products ranging from cellophane, rayon, and writing paper to shipping containers and milk cartons. For decades the sales of the firms were regional. Now all the major enterprises cater to a national market, and the names of Boise-Cascade, Northwest Paper, Potlatch Forests, and Wood Conversion are widely known. In addition, the Weyerhaeuser Company has become almost a national symbol of quality products and of long-range planning in the forest-products industry.

Next to their contribution to the growth of the economy, the various families cherish their own close association for more than three generations. Pooling their resources to buy a sawmill, Frederick Weyerhaeuser and F. C. A. Denkmann unwittingly set a pattern of cooperation for years to come, one that has been traced in preceding chapters through various enterprises in the northern Middle West to the larger projects in the Pacific Northwest.

As the decades rolled by, the number of participating families declined. Termination of ventures, deaths, shifts of capital into other industries, and financial pressures narrowed the list of associated groups year after year. Among those once prominent in joint enterprises, but long since off the list, are the Joyces, Lambs, and Youngs of the Middle Mississippi, the Rusts of the Chippewa, Sauntry and Atwood of Northern Wisconsin, and Shaw of Cloquet. Of all the major family groups among the former "partners" of the Weyerhaeusers and Denkmanns in the Upper Mississippi Valley, only a few transferred their accumulated capital and managerial skills to the Far West. Among those of Wisconsin days were the Carsons, Humbirds, Ingrams, Irvines, McCormicks, Moons, and Rutledges, some of whom have since dropped from the roll of participants.

Most significant in the long run was the fact that the Lairds and Nortons and the Mussers joined the trek westward to the forests of the Pacific Northwest. With these two groups the Weyerhaeusers and Denkmanns have engaged in more ventures than with any others. For ninety years the four families have been bound together not only by cooperation in business but also by ties of close personal friendship and mutual respect for one another's integrity and judgment.

Fortunately for all the families concerned, each generation has included men interested in the forest-products industry and capable of directing and expanding the enterprises at hand. Notable among them are William, Clifton R., R. Drew, and John M. Musser, the latter now a director of the Weyerhaeuser Company. The Laird-Norton group has been represented by sons-in-law of founders and their descendants; F. S. Bell and Laird Bell, F. H. Thatcher, George R. Little, E. P. Clapp and his son, Norton, now president of the Weyerhaeuser Company, have made marked contributions to the growth of the joint western enterprises. That some of them have made records of national importance in other fields, Laird Bell in the law field, for example, adds to rather than detracts from their activities in the business world.

Most fortunate have been the Weyerhaeusers in having able men in the direct line each generation. Frederick Weyerhaeuser's four sons—John Philip, Charles A., Rudolph M., and Frederick E.—all possessed marked capacities for business leadership, and complemented each other in temperaments and skills. In the third generation, two brothers, Frederick K. and John Philip, Jr., have done more than any other two family representatives to build the business enterprises with which they have been connected into profitable institutions of national importance. In addition, a cousin, Edwin Weyerhaeuser Davis, has made the Wood Conversion Company his prime interest and major accomplishment. G. F. Jewett played a leading role in conservation and forestry matters and held major responsibilities in the Idaho companies. And were he living today, Phil Weyerhaeuser would undoubtedly be the first to insist that, in guiding the Weyerhaeuser Company to its eminence, he had been aided by many men, the most important by far being Charles H. Ingram, with whom he worked intimately for twenty-three years.

With only one deviation, leaders of the family-associated enterprises have followed the principle of delegating authority for administration wherever possible. Such procedure was a matter of necessity among the early firms cooperating on the Chippewa and other streams. Only ownership of timber and transportation of logs to the mills were under centralized control; no participating firm would tolerate anything but complete independence in manufacturing and marketing until after 1900. Meanwhile, Frederick Weyerhaeuser was delegating a large measure of his responsibilities in the joint efforts on the Chippewa and other streams to such men as Thomas Irvine, William Irvine, and similarly able individuals.

Even after 1900, the attempts of Frederick E. Weyerhaeuser to develop some centralized administration of the widely disparate businesses of the associated families ended in marked success only for the Weyerhaeuser Sales Company. Now its organization functions as the Marketing Department of the Lumber and Plywood Division of the Weyerhaeuser Company. Consistent with the historic practice of decentralization of authority and responsibility, each of the companies today operates under its separate board of directors with policies and programs determined in its best interests. As a result, there is now active competition between the companies.

To name all the nonfamily managers of the associated enterprises would be dull and tedious, but the contributions of some men have been so central to the success of the various firms that they cannot be omitted here. Harry C. Hornby certainly played a prominent role in the growth and perpetuation of the Cloquet area as a continuing field of business endeavor. The modern Northwest Paper Company is really a monument to Stuart B. Copeland, and S. G. Moon carried the Boise Payette Lumber Company through a most difficult period in its history. More than any other single individual, C. L. Billings set the modern pattern of action for Potlatch Forests, Inc., and the forest-products industry of northern Idaho. Harry T. Kendall helped F. K. Weyerhaeuser formulate policies for the Weyerhaeuser Sales Company, then applied them in so masterly a fashion as to make that company an outstanding example of marketing lumber products in the United States.

Ranking above all the managers of the associated companies was George S. Long. Adept at reconciling conflicting interests of men and firms, he was the farsighted leader of the Weyerhaeuser Timber Company and a nationally recognized figure in the forest-products industry. The present Weyerhaeuser Company probably owes more to him, with the exception of Frederick Weyerhaeuser, than to any other person. To single out George Long for special praise surely means no depreciation of many others who have contributed to the numerous enterprises discussed in earlier chapters.

In the twentieth century, family and nonfamily executives, working together, have preserved some policies of their antecedents and greatly changed others. Delegation of administrative responsibility, already discussed, is a policy now tested by long experience. A conservative financial policy has also characterized the history of the associated enterprises from their beginnings. As in the past, the responsible leaders now believe that growth is best attained by limiting long-term debt, by paying modest dividends, and by plowing a substantial portion of earnings back into the businesses.

Modern executives still prefer to acquire timberland in large blocks, as in the past, but they no longer "cut out and get out." Instead, in cooperation with federal, state, and private agencies they seek to manage their timber as a crop, a renewable resource. Through crews of foresters and workers they apply the most advanced knowledge to the protection, utilization, growth, and perpetuation of the forest. Experts decide when, where, what, and how much to cut, then supervise the regeneration of the cutover area. Significantly, in the creation and management of tree farms, modern leaders of the Weyerhaeuser Company have been ready and willing to play the role of industry leader in the Pacific Northwest.

Similarly, the firms have kept pace with changing technology for cutting and transporting logs to the mills. They seem to have adapted the power saw, the caterpillar tractor, and the truck to their needs as effectively as any competitor. For decades men in all the companies have been alert to the most advanced machines for every general or special situation in the woods. Equally important, for twenty-five years they have had the funds to put into new machinery and roads providing access to stands of timber hitherto economically impossible to harvest.

Following a policy initiated by J. P. Weyerhaeuser, Jr., the Weyerhaeuser Company and its emulators now address themselves to growing trees on a sustained-yield basis and to producing a crop that will have a maximum yield annually. The intent is to grow more trees per acre and more trees of higher market value than Nature, without human aid, has been able to produce on a given area. In itself, the program is a comprehensive projection of Phil Weyerhaeuser's faith in trees as a resource and in the abilities of men for generations to come.

Full utilization of the timber crop is a modern goal that nineteenth century family leaders would have difficulty in comprehending. In those early days white and Norway pine lumber was practically the only salable product, and the character of market demand largely determined the kind and size of trees cut. During the past sixty years, officials of the Weyerhaeuser Company and other firms have gradually found explicit uses for formerly unmarketable trees and a variety of products that can be made from former waste. Research has produced new commodities not only for manufacture by plants in the Pacific Northwest but also in the Midwest and the South. If a market has not existed for a new product, the companies have tried to create one, often with success. Now even bark, chips, and sawdust go into marketable commodities. In such fashion full utilization of trees has contributed to the diversification of the product line of the Weyerhaeuser Company and its emulators.

Recognizing that full utilization of the trees called for a battery of specialized plants, J. P. Weyerhaeuser, Jr., and Charles Ingram led the Weyerhaeuser Company in a path-breaking program for integration of plants, first at Longview and later at other sites. Through exhaustive analysis they arrived at the size and number of mills desired at each location, for the manufacture of lumber, plywood, pulp, paperboard, container-board, or bark products. If suppliers could not provide desired machinery, such as a giant chipper, the company made it. The plant-integration program is always in process of study with a view to improvement and further application.

In their forest and mill operations, managers of the associated firms have long since departed from the benevolent paternalism toward workers so characteristic of the companies in their early history. Motivation of this change has been a composite of a sense of fair play, legislative and union pressures, public opinion, the emergence of more literate workers, and the need to compete with other businesses for employees of the desired quality. Evolved over a period of years, present wages, hours, working conditions, and employee benefits of the Weyerhaeuser Company compare favorably with those of any other corporation in the forest-products industry. In this area, too, executives of the company have tended to lead rather than to follow the custom of the industry.

In spite of impressive records in many functions, some observers think that one of the outstanding achievements of the associated families has been in marketing. After many difficult years, the Weyerhaeuser Sales Company became by all odds the leading lumber wholesaling organization in the United States. Through its widespread yards and services, retailers and their customers learned how to use specific lumber products for specific purposes. By a variety of architectural and promotional aides, builders all over the nation were induced to buy Weyerhaeuser 4-SQUARE lumber, a product of guaranteed quality. Now that symbol refers only to the output of the Weyerhaeuser Company, as the Idaho firms have developed their own marks of distinction.

Closely correlated with the national marketing program has been the new departure in public relations during the past thirty years. In this phase of activity the leaders of the Weyerhaeuser Company and other firms have been trying to catch up with advanced practices of some American businesses. Family firms, by their closed nature, have traditionally lagged behind publicly owned corporations in their relations with the public, and the companies here discussed were no exception. First through publication of annual reports, then through advertisements, publicity releases, a wide variety of pamphlets, and moving pictures, leaders of the firms have sought and continue to seek to explain themselves and their industry to business generally, to the public, and to state and federal governmental agencies.

As noted in many pages throughout this book, these changes in policies in the twentieth century have been brought about through trial and error, and enough error to indicate that the Weyerhaeusers and associated families have had their share of fallibility in judgment. Bargains have been missed, mistakes made in transferring techniques of the Midwest to different conditions in the Pacific Northwest. Painful experiences in northern and southern Idaho have been recorded. With the advantages of hindsight, it has been suggested that leaders of the associated firms could have been wiser at early dates in their relations with employees and with the public. But in a record of achievement over a hundred years the number of mistakes seems to have been considerably lower than in the history of many similar firms.

That there will be a market in the future for products of the forest seems assured. The Stanford Research Institute's report on "America's Demand for Wood, 1929–1975," financed by Weyerhaeuser Timber Company, and the recent publication by the United States Forest Service of *Timber Resources for America's Future*[1] both indicate that, in spite of a growing list of substitute commodities, the long-range prospect of demand for all forest products is good, especially for pulp and paper items and softwood plywood.

Nevertheless, one writer has pointed out that "just because the prospect for future demand is good," forest-products firms cannot neglect promotion of wood and wood products. "Markets can be lost, and once lost, they are never easily regained or replaced," he notes. Moreover, the report of the Stanford Research Institute emphasized that the relatively high concentration of forest-product sales in a few markets meant that a "slippage in consumption" in the construction or container industries could have "serious repercussions on the economic health of the forest products industry as a whole," a fact well shown in the 1958 recession.[2]

Actually, the vagaries of the market, both as to price and shifts in type of demand, present only a few of the problems executives of forest-products firms must live with in the future. Maintaining balance between supplies of raw material and the demands of the market constitutes a major issue for the leaders of each company; coordination of functions becomes more harassing as full utilization and integration occur. Fire, insects, diseases, pests, and taxes are almost routine phases of forest management in the 1960's, but other problems plague executives now and will in the future.

Many issues will recur continually. How can the competition of substitutes for wood be met? How can product quality be improved, a preoccupation of Weyerhaeuser management for more than forty years? What new products can be derived from a tree? How much can research accomplish and how much money should be allocated to that function? How can costs be reduced through further mechanization and integration of operations? What market should receive special attention? How can transport costs be kept down when the tendency is toward rising freight charges? What shall be the future role of such firms as Weyerhaeuser Company, Boise-Cascade, Potlatch Forests, Northwest Paper, and Wood Conversion in the forest-products industry, and what will be their responsibilities to society?

The directors and officers of the Weyerhaeuser Company clearly recognize that they have a major problem in managing a large work force. Though they take pride in accomplishments to date in this area of human relations, they know that relatively sophisticated and self-conscious workers, acting through large unions, pose questions of leadership requiring continual study and new habits of thought and action. They desire to work out fair solutions of labor-management issues in an atmosphere of mutual respect, while giving due weight to the interests of stockholders, customers, suppliers, consumers, and governmental agencies. Such a broad statement must be given significant meaning; it must be clothed with specific indications of the executives' real concern for every employee, effectively communicated to all. The task is most difficult, as thousands of American businessmen can testify.

Public relations can also be expected to be a major issue in future management. To be sure, scholars, publicists, and the general public have a better comprehension of the forest-products industry than ever before. Nevertheless, occasional articles of the muckraking types, replete with the old stories of the lumbermen's wastage of forest resources and with an appalling ignorance of economic considerations, appear in leading periodicals. Recently shareholders of Weyerhaeuser Company were grouped with those of several other large firms as "stepchildren" of the Securities Exchange Commission because the shares of the companies were not listed on a stock exchange.[3] That private firms, by following enlightened self-interest and concepts of broad responsibility for the long pull, can pursue as socially beneficial policies as a governmental agency remains to be proved to millions of voters.

In truth, tree farming is still experimental in many respects. What should a firm like the Weyerhaeuser Company do to compete with companies that buy up timber and then "cut out and get out" within ten years or less. The tree farmer operating on a 50-to-100-year cycle has higher costs than his competitor. Another problem connected with the long-growth cycle is how to show in annual accounts a fair evaluation of timber, taking cognizance of fluctuations in the weather, differences in soils, price changes, and other variables. Only time will tell if tree farms are economically practicable for private enterprise in the long run.

Businessmen in the forest-products industry have met and resolved similar issues for generations, the companies in this history more effectively than many. Today, more than ever before, long-range study and planning, rather than letting "the chips fall where they may," characterize the approach to every problem in all major enterprises. If past performance is indicative of the future, then no one will be surprised if leaders of the firms long associated with the name of Weyerhaeuser, now following highly individual paths, make a distinguished record in the years to come.

N O T E S

1. Forest Service, United States Department of Agriculture, *Timber Resources for America's Future* (Forest Resource Report No. 14, Jan., 1958, Washington, D.C.).

2. *Weyerhaeuser News,* March, 1959, pp. 2–3.

3. A. A. Livingston, *The American Stockholders,* Philadelphia and New York, 1958, p. 212.

Appendixes

1. The name was changed to Weyerhaeuser Company in 1959.
2. The name was changed to Boise Cascade Corporation in 1957.
3. For lack of comparable data, only figures for sales and net income are given for 1900–1940, then a summary of operations, 1941–1960.

4. The list of officers and directors of Weyerhaeuser Timber Company is carried through the annual meeting of 1961, and in the case of all other companies through December 31, 1952.

Volume of Logs Rafted at Beef Slough and West Newton, 1870–1906

M bd. ft., Boom Scale, S & S

YEAR	VOLUME	YEAR	VOLUME	YEAR	VOLUME
1870	10,000	1882	417,510	1894	250,046
1871	12,000	1883	445,109	1895	292,640
1872	54,873	1884	518,704	1896	297,391
1873	90,416	1885	535,220	1898	174,965
1874	129,079	1886	463,947	1899	223,694
1875	129,204	1887	405,380	1900	202,698
1876	154,141	1888	542,437	1901	86,535
1877	82,658	1889	400,524[a]	1902	140,000[b]
1878	91,873	1890	610,698	1903	90,000[b]
1879	249,194	1891	281,870	1904	80,000[b]
1880	254,130	1892	632,154	1905	35,000[b]
1881	411,823	1893	488,926	1906	5,000[b]
Total	1,669,391	*Total*	5,742,479	*Total*	1,877,969

[a] Beef Slough and West Newton; West Newton only after 1890.
[b] Estimated from records of logs delivered by the M.R.L. Co. and C.L. Co. to lumbering firms on the Mississippi below Beef Slough in those years.

SOURCES: Blair, *A Raft Pilot's Log,* 53; Laird, Norton & Co., Papers, reports of Beef Slough Manufacturing, Booming, Log Driving and Transportation Company; United States Army, "Report of Major Jones," *Annual Report of the Chief of Engineers, 1894,* Appendix z, 1721, cited by Captain Fred A. Bill, *Burlington Post,* Feb. 7, 1931; *Northwestern Lumberman* and *Mississippi Valley Lumberman & Manufacturer,* 1875–1893.

Directors of Beef Slough Manufacturing, Booming, Log Driving and Transportation Company, 1867–1902

M. M. Davis, 1867–1873, 1876–
1887

T. E. Crane, 1867–1868, 1870–
1871

E. Swift, 1867–1871, 1876–1902

F. Palms, 1867–1881

J. H. Bacon, 1867–1869

F. Lane, 1867–1871

J. Hunner, Jr., 1867

C. Schaettle, 1868–1870

James Jenkins, 1868–1883

F. Morrell, 1871

Hill, Lemmon & Co., 1873

W. J. Young & Co., 1873

Weyerhaeuser & Denkmann, 1873

C. Lamb & Sons, 1873

Dimock, Gould & Co., 1873

Youmans Bros. & Hodgins, 1873

Laird, Norton & Co., 1873

Keator & Wilson, 1873

Hershey & Irvine, 1873

Hemmenway, Wood & Co., 1873

Clinton Lumber Co., 1873

R. Musser & Co., 1873

Pelan & Randall, 1873

James Hill, 1874–1876

F. A. Schulenberg, 1874–1876

Fr. Weyerhaeuser, 1873–1902

W. J. Young, 1874–1893

Artemus Lamb, 1874–1894

L. S. Davis, 1874–1878

W. H. Laird, 1874–1902

E. S. Youmans, 1874–1894

J. S. Keator, 1874–1880

Thomas Irvine, 1874–1902

P. Musser, 1874–1894

A. P. Hosford, 1874–1877

David Joyce, 1874–1894

J. M. Gould, 1875

J. S. Randall, 1874–1882

C. R. Ainsworth, 1877–1894

A. Boeckeler, 1877

E. L. Hospes, 1878–1891

F. C. A. Denkmann, 1881–1892

L. Lamb, 1882–1902

William Hayes, 1883–1902

Charles Barber, 1885–1902

H. C. Davis, 1888–1891

W. J. Young, Jr., 1892–1893

M. G. Norton, 1892–1902

A. F. Hodgins, 1892–1894

C. Lamb, 1893–1894

F. C. Denkmann, 1894–1902

P. M. Musser, 1902

W. T. Joyce, 1902

G. E. Lamb, 1902

F. S. Bell, 1902

T. H. Thatcher, 1902

J. D. Lamb, 1902

SOURCE: Minute Books of the Company. In 1873 the names of the member firms, as well as certain individuals, were included in the list of directors. Representatives of the various companies served individually.

Directors of Mississippi River Logging Company, and the Stockholding Firms They Represented, 1871–1909

DIRECTORS	FIRM
Chancy Lamb, 1871–1873, 1876–1896	C. Lamb & Sons
Artemus Lamb, 1874–1899	
W. J. Young, 1871–1896	W. J. Young & Co.
F. Weyerhaeuser, 1871–1909	Weyerhaeuser & Denkmann
C. R. Ainsworth, 1871, 1875–1898	Dimock, Gould & Co.
J. M. Gould, 1872–1874	
B. Hershey, 1871–1892	Hershey Lumber Company
J. H. Berkshire, 1893–1894	
M. G. Norton, 1871, 1877–1905	Laird, Norton & Co.
W. H. Laird, 1872–1909	
E. S. Youmans, 1871–1897	Youmans Bros. & Hodgins
E. P. Welles, 1872–1873	David Joyce
D. Joyce, 1874–1894	
Peter Musser, 1872–1909	Musser & Co.
J. Randall, 1873–1890	Pelan & Randall
F. A. Schulenburg, 1871–1875	A. Boeckeler & Co.
A. Boeckeler, 1876	
J. B. Paul, 1871–1872	Taber & Co.
J. L. Davies, 1871–1876	John L. Davies
L. Schricker, 1871	Schricker & Mueller
J. Fleming, 1871	W. & J. Fleming & Co.
H. H. Hemmenway, 1871–1872	Hemmenway, Wood & Co.
W. G. Clark, 1871–1874	Hill, Lemmon & Co.
R. B. Clark, 1875	
James B. Hill, 1874–1876	
J. S. Keator, 1871–1881	Keator & Wilson
A. P. Hosford, 1874–1876	Clinton Lumber Co.

SOURCE: Minute Books of the Company. Authors were unable to identify the firm connection of E. L. Hospes, 1877–?

Forest Products Companies in Which Members of the Weyerhaeuser Family Owned an Interest, 1900–1914[1]

Middle Mississippi River

Weyerhaeuser & Denkmann Company
F. Weyerhaeuser Co.
Rock Island Lumber & Coal Company
Rock Island Lumber & Manufacturing Company
Rock Island Sash & Door Works
St. Louis Sash & Door Works
Minnesota Boom Company

Chippewa River

Beef Slough Manufacturing, Booming, Log Driving & Transportation Company
Chippewa Logging Company
Chippewa Lumber & Boom Company
Chippewa River Improvement & Log Driving Company
Chippewa River & Menomonie Railway Company
Mississippi River Logging Company

St. Croix River and Northern Wisconsin

Ann River Logging Company
Atwood Lumber Company
Atwood Lumber & Manufacturing Company
Musser-Sauntry Land, Logging & Manufacturing Company
St. Croix Boom Company
St. Croix Lumbermen's Dam & Boom Company
Nebagamon Lumber Company
Edward Rutledge Lumber & Manufacturing Company
North Wisconsin Lumber Company
Shell Lake Lumber Company
White River Lumber Company

Upper Mississippi River

Mississippi River Lumber Company
Northland Pine Company
Pine Tree Lumber Company—Pine Tree Manufacturing Company

1. Many of these companies had numerous subsidiaries; Weyerhaeuser Timber Company held shares in twenty-seven corporations in 1914.

St. Louis River and Northern Minnesota

Cloquet Lumber Company
Johnson-Wentworth Lumber Company
Northern Lumber Company
Northwest Paper Company (W. Va.)—The Northwest Paper Company
(Minn.)
Virginia & Rainy Lake Lumber Company

South

Calcasieu Pine Company—Calcasieu Timber Company
Southland Lumber Company
Southern Lumber Company (Ark.)
Southern Lumber Company (La.)

Idaho

Barber Lumber Company
Boise Payette Lumber Company
Payette Lumber & Manufacturing Company
Bonners Ferry Lumber Company
Clearwater Timber Company
Dover Lumber Company
Edward Rutledge Timber Company
Humbird Lumber Company
Potlatch Lumber Company

Pacific Northwest

Coast Lumber Company
Sound Timber Company
Weyerhaeuser Timber Company

Lumber Shipments of Major Companies Associated with Weyerhaeuser Investment 1900–1950

(*millions of board feet*)

Year	Chippewa Lumber & Boom Co.	Pine Tree Lumber Co.ª	Northland Pine Co.	Cloquet Lumber Co.	Northern Lumber Co.	Johnson-Wentworth Lumber Co.	Humbird Lumber Co.
1900	58	57		55	58		
1901	71	96		79	92		
1902	56	89		88	93	47	17
1903	65	71		86	107	66	21
1904	62	64		75	110	56	29
1905	66	74		105	112	58	45
1906	47	51	55	104	105	68	43
1907	42	63	79	96	93	53	33
1908	36	24	45	63	64	46	32
1909	49	40	68	94	97	50	51
1910	40	47	66	94	101	60	60
1911	32	53	65	79	88	54	47
1912		71	91	101	105	57	73
1913		58	93	99	105	61	49
1914		35	75	75	77	52	63
1915		42	103	72	67	49	60
1916		70	127	103	96	59	83
1917		63	96	101	96	59	56
1918		28	36	66	60	44	38
1919		39	35	33	27	49	57
1920		16	29	36		46	58
1921			1	26		34	33
1922				54		53	88
1923				44		48	95
1924				49		52	99
1925				54		53	99

ª Pine Tree Manufacturing Co. in 1909 and later.

Bonners Ferry Lumber Co.	Potlatch Lumber Co.[b]	Clearwater Timber Co.	Edward Rutledge Timber Co.	Boise Payette Lumber Co.	Southern Lumber Co.
					4
					21
4	9				25
12	14				28
16					25
14					28
28	75				24
19	127				21
31	141				27
39	123				23
52	196				30
46	135				27
47	167				26
55	144			8	29
33	154		21	40	27
18	142		22	81	27
14	105		34	114	33
31	110		42	125	33
29	129		57	137	25
21	57		34	69	49
41	107		60	143	45
42	128		55	138	52
39	142		75	123	49
41	153		68	77	49

[b] Name changed to Potlatch Forests, Inc., as of 1931, at which time Clearwater Timber Co. and Edward Rutledge Timber Co. were merged with it. Consolidation of shipments was carried back to 1928.

Lumber Shipments of Major Companies Associated with Weyerhaeuser Investment 1900–1950

(millions of board feet)

Year	Chippewa Lumber & Boom Co.	Pine Tree Lumber Co.	Northland Pine Co.	Cloquet Lumber Co.	Northern Lumber Co.	Johnson-Wentworth Lumber Co.	Humbird Lumber Co.
1926				58		56	112
1927				48		47	118
1928							123
1929							108
1930							73
1931							49
1932							30
1933							31
1934							
1935							
1936							
1937							
1938							
1939							
1940							
1941							
1942							
1943							
1944							
1945							
1946							
1947							
1948							
1949							
1950							

Bonners Ferry Lumber Co.	Potlatch Lumber Co.	Clearwater Timber Co.	Edward Rutledge Timber Co.	Boise Payette Lumber Co.		Southern Lumber Co.
38	150		64		132	55
24	132	13	56		121	51
	298				95	50
	354				85	39
	282				67	28
	175				46	18
	98				40	12
	141				44	14
	140				36	15
	202				77	22
	244				82	27
	258				93	32
	188				100	29
	243				117	27
	307			121	118 (7 mo.)	15
	364			139	137	36
	463			134	133	34
	421			133		29
	362			131		24
	335			92		25
	282			95		23
	258			102		28
	313			102		26
	315			95		30
	400			96		33

SOURCES: Annual Reports and Statistical Files of the Various Companies.

Lumber Shipments by Weyerhaeuser Timber Company and Affiliates, 1900–1959[a]

(*millions of board feet*)

Year	Weyerhaeuser Timber Co.	Snoqualmie Falls Lumber Co.	Year	Weyerhaeuser Timber Co.	Snoqualmie Falls Lumber Co.
1900			1930	464	95
1901			1931	536	90
1902	27		1932	372	52
1903	19		1933	408	64
1904	37		1934	368	74
1905	39		1935	560	82
1906	40		1936	766	121
1907	40		1937	774	107
1908	29		1938	710	120
1909	48		1939	854	126
1910	50		1940	938	112
1911	61		1941	926	86
1912	70		1942	1014	129
1913	76		1943	928	115
1914	72		1944	836	95
1915	111		1945	641	65
1916	175		1946	652	82
1917	179	0.4	1947	682	79
1918	188	29	1948	584	58[b]
1919	160	95	1949	880	
1920	187	87	1950	857	
1921	134	77	1951	1019	
1922	229	108	1952	1086	
1923	281	133	1953	1138	
1924	210	105	1954	997	
1925	272	118	1955	1208	
1926	312	120	1956	1236	
1927	314	119	1957	1223	
1928	338	135	1958	1268	
1929	364	120	1959	1347	

[a] Data on the White River Lumber Co. and the Willapa Harbor Lumber mills should be a part of this tabulation and will be found on page 684.

[b] Nine months only.

SOURCE: Annual Reports and Statistical Files of Weyerhaeuser Company, 1900–1959.

The Northwest Paper Company, 1900–1950

(OOO OMITTED)

As of:	1–31–1900	12–31–00	12–31–01	3–31–02	3–31–03
CURRENT ASSETS:					
Cash	$ 4	$ 1	$ 1	$ 1	$ 6
Securities					
Accounts and notes receivable—					
Net					
Inventories					
Unclassified current assets	65	151	125	134	155
Total current assets	69	152	126	135	161
FIXED ASSETS:					
Paper plant properties	395	391	372	375	336
Less reserve for depreciation					
Paper plant properties—Net	395	391	372	375	336
Other fixed assets—Net	6	1	30	30	75
Total fixed assets	401	392	402	405	411
OTHER ASSETS:					1
TOTAL	$470	$544	$528	$540	$573
CURRENT LIABILITIES:					
Notes payable					
Accounts payable					
Accrued taxes and expenses					
Unclassified current liabilities	$212	$293	$278	$295	$275
Total current liabilities	212	293	278	295	275
SLOW LIABILITIES:					
CAPITAL AND SURPLUS:					
Capital	250	250	250	250	265
Surplus	8	1		(5)[a]	33
Total capital and surplus	258	251	250	245	298
TOTAL	$470	$544	$528	$540	$573

[a] Figures in parentheses indicate losses.

SOURCE: Annual Reports of The Northwest Paper Company, 1900–1950.

THE NORTHWEST PAPER COMPANY

(OOO OMITTED)

	3–31–04	3–31–05	3–31–06	3–31–07	3–31–08
CURRENT ASSETS:					
Cash	$ 15	$ 23	$ 2	$ 12	$ 6
Securities					
Accounts and notes receivable—					
Net					
Inventories					
Unclassified current assets	199	185	202	222	246
Total current assets	214	208	204	234	252
FIXED ASSETS:					
Paper plant properties	366	289	198	155	141
Less reserve for depreciation					
Paper plant properties—Net	366	289	198	155	141
Other fixed assets—Net	31	32	27	23	19
Total fixed assets	397	321	225	178	160
OTHER ASSETS:	2	3	2	2	2
TOTAL	$613	$532	$431	$414	$414
CURRENT LIABILITIES:					
Notes payable					
Accounts payable					
Accrued taxes and expenses					
Unclassified current liabilities	$238	$145	$ 91	$ 94	$ 89
Total current liabilities	238	145	91	94	89
SLOW LIABILITIES:					
CAPITAL AND SURPLUS:					
Capital	300	300	300	300	300
Surplus	75	87	40	20	25
Total capital and surplus	375	387	340	320	325
TOTAL	$613	$532	$431	$414	$414

(OOO OMITTED)

3–31–09	3–31–10	3–31–11	3–31–12	3–31–13	3–31–14	3–31–15
$ 39	$ 49	$ 50	$ 42	$ 62	$ 64	$ 25
197	208	217	282	253	269	256
236	257	267	324	315	333	281
143	162	554	567	583	592	631
143	162	554	567	583	592	631
18	17	16	14	9	9	152
161	179	570	581	592	601	783
		325	327	326	328	327
$397	$436	$1162	$1232	$1233	$1262	$1391
$ 48	$ 66	$ 52	$ 45	$ 29	$ 26	$ 121
48	66	52	45	29	26	121
300	300	990	995	995	995	995
49	70	120	192	209	241	275
349	370	1110	1187	1204	1236	1270
$397	$436	$1162	$1232	$1233	$1262	$1391

THE NORTHWEST PAPER COMPANY

(OOO OMITTED)

	3–31–16	3–31–17	3–31–18	3–31–19	12–31–19
CURRENT ASSETS:					
Cash	$ 97	$ 19	$ 33	$ 79	$ 332
Securities					
Accounts and notes receivable—					
Net					
Inventories					
Unclassified current assets	261	762	1096	1532	1440
Total current assets	358	781	1129	1611	1772
FIXED ASSETS:					
Paper plant properties	994	1011	1021	1921	1952
Less reserve for depreciation	83	111	203	297	472
Paper plant properties—Net	911	900	818	1624	1480
Other fixed assets—Net	165	977	1232	406	410
Total fixed assets	1076	1877	2050	2030	1890
OTHER ASSETS:	330	376	386	386	397
TOTAL	$1764	$3034	$3565	$4027	$4059
CURRENT LIABILITIES:					
Notes payable					
Accounts payable					
Accrued taxes and expenses					
Unclassified current liabilities	$ 330	973	1298	1331	1355
Total current liabilities	330	973	1298	1331	1355
SLOW LIABILITIES:					
CAPITAL AND SURPLUS:					
Capital	1201	1496	1496	1496	1496
Surplus	233	565	771	1200	1208
Total capital and surplus	1434	2061	2267	2696	2704
TOTAL	$1764	$3034	$3565	$4027	$4059

(OOO OMITTED)

12–31–20	12–31–21	12–31–22	12–31–23	12–31–24	12–31–25	12–31–26
$ 765	$ 123	$ 203	$ 120	$ 133	$ 97	$ 172
1843	2328	1759	1774	2232	1454	1629
2608	2451	1962	1894	2365	1551	1801
2073	2164	2193	2201	4722	5202	5568
637	808	990	1153	1368	1448	1628
1436	1356	1203	1048	3354	3754	3940
451	409	1916	4537	2441	2452	2375
1887	1765	3119	5585	5795	6206	6315
543	576	579	584	586	576	586
$5038	$4792	$5660	$8063	$8746	$8333	$8702
$1328	$1531	$2151	$3694	$3793	$4334	$4471
1328	1531	2151	3694	3793	4334	4471
1496	1496	1667	2496	4000	4000	4364
2214	1765	1842	1873	953	(1)	(133)
3710	3261	3509	4369	4953	3999	4231
$5038	$4792	$5660	$8063	$8746	$8333	$8702

THE NORTHWEST PAPER COMPANY

(000 OMITTED)

	12–31–27	12–31–28	12–31–29	12–31–30	12–31–31
CURRENT ASSETS:					
Cash	$ 105	$ 132	$ 72	$ 43	$ 47
Securities					
Accounts and notes receivable—					
Net					
Inventories					
Unclassified current assets	1849	4360	5028	5742	4199
Total current assets	1954	4492	5100	5785	4246
FIXED ASSETS:					
Paper plant properties	5823	6127	6669	6931	8486
Less reserve for depreciation	1822	1986	2232	2466	2779
Paper plant properties—Net	4001	4141	4437	4465	5707
Other fixed assets—Net	2349	7561	7268	7295	6598
Total fixed assets	6350	11702	11705	11760	12305
OTHER ASSETS:	664	1649	1631	1638	1392
TOTAL	$8968	$17843	$18436	$19183	$17943
CURRENT LIABILITIES:					
Notes payable					
Accounts payable					
Accrued taxes and expenses					
Unclassified current liabilities	$4159	$ 3762	$ 4628	$ 7046	$ 2560
Total current liabilities	4159	3762	4628	7046	2560
SLOW LIABILITIES:					6060
CAPITAL AND SURPLUS:					
Capital	4861	14220	14263	14261	14261
Surplus	(52)	(139)	(455)	(2124)	(4938)
Total capital and surplus	4809	14081	13808	12137	9323
TOTAL	$8968	$17843	$18436	$19183	$17943

(OOO OMITTED)

12–31–32	12–31–33	12–31–34	12–31–35	12–31–36	12–31–37	12–31–38
$ 56	$ 26	$ 44	$ 72	$ 239	$ 102	$ 133
				807	546	672
				1639	2694	2278
2754	2854	2562	2521			
2810	2880	2606	2593	2685	3342	3083
8529	8583	8667	8709	8706	8809	8867
3056	3397	3740	4088	4203	4473	4745
5473	5186	4927	4621	4503	4336	4122
6399	6309	6143	5284	4999	4827	4762
11872	11495	11070	9905	9502	9163	8884
1605	1626	1467	1451	1832	1732	1742
$16287	$16001	$15143	$13949	$14019	$14237	$13709
			$ 1129	$ 1084	$ 1047	$ 1061
			179	184	267	239
			317	368	362	422
$ 2131	$ 1883	$ 1746				
2131	1883	1746	1625	1636	1676	1722
1085	1115	1144	1195	1268	1442	1465
8774	8774	8774	8774	8773	8772	8772
4297	4229	3479	2355	2342	2347	1750
13071	13003	12253	11129	11115	11119	10522
$16287	$16001	$15143	$13949	$14019	$14237	$13709

THE NORTHWEST PAPER COMPANY

(000 OMITTED)

	12–31–39	*12–31–40*	*12–31–41*	*12–31–42*	*12–31–43*
CURRENT ASSETS:					
Cash	$ 415	$ 352	$ 103	$ 546	$ 1657
Securities				200	400
Accounts and notes receivable—					
Net	828	689	1060	950	954
Inventories	1474	1524	1543	2839	2751
Unclassified current assets					
Total current assets	2717	2565	3656	4535	5762
FIXED ASSETS:					
Paper plant properties	8953	9134	9754	10007	10063
Less reserve for depreciation	4974	5231	5552	5639	5924
Paper plant properties—Net	3979	3903	4202	4368	4139
Other fixed assets—Net	2487	2723	1945	1545	1369
Total fixed assets	6466	6626	6147	5913	5508
OTHER ASSETS:	2377	1358	1352	1069	951
TOTAL	$11560	$10549	$11155	$11517	$12221
CURRENT LIABILITIES:					
Notes payable	$ 1105	$ 146			
Accounts payable	252	276	$ 447	$ 312	$ 357
Accrued taxes and expenses	384	370	452	440	433
Unclassified current liabilities					
Total current liabilities	1741	792	899	752	790
SLOW LIABILITIES:	1296	2194	2017	1745	1665
CAPITAL AND SURPLUS:					
Capital	8772	2957	2958	2958	2958
Surplus	(249)	4606	5281	6062	6808
Total capital and surplus	8523	7563	8239	9020	9766
TOTAL	$11560	$10549	$11155	$11517	$12221

(OOO OMITTED)

12–31–44	12–31–45	12–31–46	12–31–47	12–31–48	12–31–49	12–31–50
$ 1699	$ 1556	$ 410	$ 1028	$ 1342	$ 2154	$ 2067
1100	1760	1600	1199	1299	1199	899
1057	949	1329	1686	1193	1296	1716
2688	2411	3519	3471	4378	3017	2815
6544	6676	6858	7384	8212	7666	7497
10167	10318	10565	11344	13066	14448	15519
6204	6309	6453	6579	6790	7008	7381
3963	4009	4112	4765	6276	7440	8138
1320	1257	2005	2304	1687	1706	2279
5283	5266	6117	7069	7963	9146	10417
934	1006	906	1097	1000	953	1058
$12761	$12948	$13881	$15550	$17175	$17765	$18972
$ 130	$ 58	$ 58	$ 64	$ 54		
228	323	430	456	533	$ 504	$ 708
391	406	461	563	675	689	712
749	787	949	1083	1262	1193	1420
1325	1003	960	204	159		
2943	2943	2943	2943	2927	2905	2905
7744	8215	9029	11320	12827	13667	14647
10687	11158	11972	14263	15754	16572	17552
$12761	$12948	$13881	$15550	$17175	$17765	$18972

Potlatch Forests, Inc., 1908–1950

Years Ending December 31

(OOO OMITTED)

	1908	1909	1910	1911	1912
CURRENT ASSETS:					
Cash	$ 7	$ 8	$ 17	$ 11	$ 108
U.S. Government securities					
Accounts and notes receivable	173	306	381	373	569
Inventories	958	1292	1701	2151	2058
Total current assets	1138	1606	2099	2535	2735
PREPAID EXPENSES	27	51	87	113	137
DEFERRED RECEIVABLES	35	70	112	168	163
INVESTMENTS AND ADVANCES	2919	2701	2720	2290	2073
TIMBER AND TIMBERLANDS	2575	1975	1046	244	(490)[a]
REAL ESTATE, PLANTS & EQUIPMENT:					
Gross book value	1770	2067	2696	3254	3453
Less—Reserves for depreciation		138	294	407	531
Net Book Value	1770	1929	2402	2847	2922
DEFERRED CHARGES		13	11	14	22
	$8464	$8345	$8477	$8211	$7562
CURRENT LIABILITIES:					
Notes payable	$ 53	$ 37	$ 38	$ 33	
Accounts payable	25	70	40	21	$ 62
Federal & State Income Tax					
Other accrued expenses		2	16		35
Total current liabilities	78	109	94	54	97
LONG-TERM DEBT:	350				
DEFERRED INCOME					
CAPITAL STOCK & SURPLUS					
Capital stock	8000	8000	8000	8000	8000
Capital surplus	36	261	383	157	(535)
Earned surplus					
Total capital stock & surplus	8036	8261	8383	8157	7465
Less—Treasury Stock (at cost)		25			
Net capital stock & surplus	8036	8236	8383	8157	7465
	$8464	$8345	$8477	$8211	$7562

[a] Parentheses indicate red.

SOURCE: Balance Sheets of Potlatch Forests, Inc. (known as Potlatch Lumber Company prior to 1931), 1908–1950.

APPENDIX VII, CONTINUED

(OOO OMITTED)

1913	1914	1915	1916	1917	1918	1919	1920
$ 18	$ 195	$ 287	$ 185	$ 124	$ 9	$ 98	$ 281
				35	81	29	91
411	328	460	390	499	699	1146	1727
2264	1683	1465	1664	1571	1922	2966	3620
2693	2206	2212	2239	2229	2711	4239	5719
319	261	254	253	355	453	510	597
166	147	143	145	146	131	133	146
2028	1945	1901	1932	3072	3142	3052	3557
(1003)	(1501)	(1886)	(2414)	13486[b]	13263	12753	12127
3513	3476	3415	3470	3456	3495	3943	4240
633	687	803	941	1077	1218	1697	1441
2880	2789	2612	2529	2379	2277	2246	2799
16	17	21	17	26	31	25	23
$7099	$5864	$5257	$4701	$21693	$22008	$22976	$24968
$ 98	$ 6	$ 12	$ 10	$ 165	$ 10	$ 209	$ 23
49		106	42	50	62	231	850
147	6	118	52	215	72	440	873
8000	8000	8000	8000	8000	8000	8000	8000
(1048)	(2142)	(2861)	(3351)	13478	13936	14536	16095
6952	5858	5139	4649	21478	21936	22536	24095
6952	5858	5139	4649	21478	21936	22536	24095
$7099	$5864	$5257	$4701	$21693	$22008	$22976	$24968

[b] The great increase over 1916 was caused by revaluation of timberlands as of March 1, 1913.

POTLATCH FORESTS, INC., 1908–1950

(OOO OMITTED)

	1921	1922	1923	1924	1925
CURRENT ASSETS:					
Cash	$ 361	$ 262	$ 734	$ 454	$ 184
U.S. Government securities	98	98	297	247	147
Accounts and notes receivable	999	908	815	740	655
Inventories	2801	2386	3232	2706	3025
Total current assets	4259	3654	5078	4147	4011
PREPAID EXPENSES	561	588	280	389	472
DEFERRED RECEIVABLES	123	106	79	98	98
INVESTMENTS AND ADVANCES	3811	3902	3638	2900	2868
TIMBER AND TIMBERLANDS	12046	11781	11519	11262	10921
REAL ESTATE, PLANTS & EQUIPMENT:					
Gross book value	4367	4414	4676	5616	6127
Less—Reserves for depreciation ..	1588	1763	1939	2125	2371
Net Book Value	2779	2651	2737	3491	3756
DEFERRED CHARGES	31	39	24	44	75
	$23610	$22721	$23355	$22331	$22201
CURRENT LIABILITIES:					
Notes payable					
Accounts payable	$ 22	$ 77	$ 33	$ 51	$ 93
Federal & State Income Tax					
Other accrued expenses	345	247	156	107	166
Total current liabilities	367	324	189	158	259
LONG-TERM DEBT:					
DEFERRED INCOME					
CAPITAL STOCK & SURPLUS					
Capital stock	8000	8000	8000	8000	8000
Capital surplus	15243	14397	15166	14173	13942
Earned surplus					
Total capital stock & surplus ..	23243	22397	23166	22173	21942
Less—Treasury Stock (at cost) ..					
Net capital stock & surplus	23243	22397	23166	22173	21942
	$23610	$22721	$23355	$22331	$22201

(OOO OMITTED)

1926	1927	1928	1929	1930	1931ᶜ	1932	1933
$ 365	$ 386	$ 124	$ 33	$ 9	$ 351	$ 288	$ 977
453	453	555	555	308			202
443	459	455	443	313	923	823	574
2437	2001	1933	1716	1978	4229	3248	2543
3698	3299	3067	2747	2608	5503	4359	4296
410	329	451	410	343	888	547	464
102	107	78	68	74	91	70	72
2853	2895	2757	2685	2638	1486	2957	3523
10728	10457	10403	10097	9775	25479	23629	23391
6318	6767	6919	7719	8031	15527	15179	17925
2656	2932	3222	3500	3812	4145	4609	8064
3662	3835	3697	4219	4219	11382	10570	9861
152	97	38			44	42	1
$21605	$21019	$20491	$20226	$19657	$44873	$42174	$41608
	$ 12		$ 5		$ 26	$ 16	$ 6
$ 64	31	$ 24	33	$ 44	150	256	492
102	127	130	135	132	350	359	193
166	170	154	173	176	526	631	691
					3947	3930	3791
8000	8000	8000	8000	8000	26595	26595	26595
7688	7492	7298	7106	6937	16377	16377	16377
5751	5357	5039	4947	4544	(2572)	(5359)	(5846)
21439	20849	20337	20053	19481	40400	37613	37126
21439	20849	20337	20053	19481	40400	37613	37126
$21605	$21019	$20491	$20226	$19657	$44873	$42174	$41608

ᶜ The figures for 1931 reflect the merger of Edward Rutledge Timber Company and Clearwater Timber Company with Potlatch Forests, Inc.

POTLATCH FORESTS, INC., 1908–1950

(OOO OMITTED)

	1934	1935	1936	1937	1938
CURRENT ASSETS:					
Cash	$ 444	$ 462	$ 559	$ 477	$ 392
U.S. Government securities	202	8	8	8	8
Accounts and notes receivable	688	844	1173	1009	1321
Inventories	2793	3322	3941	6259	4945
Total current assets	4127	4636	5681	7753	6666
PREPAID EXPENSES	796	767	1005	952	820
DEFERRED RECEIVABLES	67	48	41	64	58
INVESTMENTS AND ADVANCES	3860	4328	4135	4421	4462
TIMBER AND TIMBERLANDS	22547	21613	20423	20098	19628
REAL ESTATE, PLANTS & EQUIPMENT:					
Gross book value	17742	16385	15016	14433	14259
Less—Reserves for depreciation	8621	8027	7521	8110	8689
Net Book Value	9121	8358	7495	6323	5570
DEFERRED CHARGES	1	84	108	7	8
	$40519	$39834	$38888	$39618	$37212
CURRENT LIABILITIES:					
Notes payable	$ 6			$ 1098	
Accounts payable	570	$ 130	$ 202	604	$ 103
Federal & State Income Tax				50	
Other accrued expenses	239	510	620	486	421
Total current liabilities	815	640	822	2238	524
LONG-TERM DEBT:					
DEFERRED INCOME	3444	3245	2507	2169	2091
CAPITAL STOCK & SURPLUS					
Capital stock	26595	26595	26595	26595	26595
Capital surplus	16377	16407	16141	15574	15571
Earned surplus	(6712)	(7053)	(7177)	(6958)	(7569)
Total capital stock & surplus	36260	35949	35559	35211	34597
Less—Treasury Stock (at cost)					
Net capital stock & surplus	36260	35949	35559	35211	34597
	$40519	$39834	$38888	$39618	$37212

(OOO OMITTED)

1939	1940	1941	1942	1943	1944	1945	1946
$ 983	$ 1536	$ 1416	$ 660	$ 1203	$ 807	$ 797	$ 1076
8	9	409	715	1119	1625	1841	1863
1425	1856	1636	2530	1663	1361	1078	1261
4680	3656	3733	3188	2542	2113	1737	1927
7096	7057	7194	7093	6527	5906	5453	6127
741	835	1374	1676	1818	2120	2225	2460
55	43	42	98	63	65	46	37
4677	4464	4172	4000	4009	3884	1582	1627
19097	18739	17013	16702	16167	15819	16095	15678
14091	14806	15472	16485	17330	18082	18554	18860
9221	9878	9011	9657	10405	11153	11906	12250
4870	4928	6461	6828	6925	6929	6648	6610
14	25	25	22	30	15	25	40
$36550	$36091	$36281	$36419	$35539	$34738	$32074	$32579
$ 265	$ 225	$ 279	$ 356	$ 551	$ 457	$ 448	$ 370
	69	822	982	777	723	375	392
525	491	664	806	697	587	528	584
790	785	1765	2144	2025	1767	1351	1346
1694	1524	789	153	111	95	74	279
1	2	2	2	1	1	2	2
26595	26595	26595	26595	26595	26595	26595	26595
15298	15278	15183	15183	14571	14226	13324	13324
(7823)	(8088)	(8048)	(7653)	(7759)	(7942)	(9267)	(8962)
34070	33785	33730	34125	33407	32879	30652	30957
5	5	5	5	5	4	5	5
34065	33780	33725	34120	33402	32875	30647	30952
$36550	$36091	$36281	$36419	$35539	$34738	$32074	$32579

POTLATCH FORESTS, INC., 1908–1950

(OOO OMITTED)

	1947	1948	1949	1950
CURRENT ASSETS:				
Cash	$ 1981	$ 4461	$ 3454	$ 2459
U.S. Government securities	3605	5270	3890	4230
Accounts and notes receivable	1952	2060	2485	3035
Inventories	2223	2433	5117	2649
Total current assets	9761	14224	14946	12373
PREPAID EXPENSES	2502	3044	2998	4698
DEFERRED RECEIVABLES	25	358	552	943
INVESTMENTS AND ADVANCES	1580	1452	1527	1556
TIMBER AND TIMBERLANDS	15289	15211	14506	14268
REAL ESTATE, PLANTS & EQUIPMENT:				
Gross book value	19568	21397	23856	34806
Less—Reserves for depreciation ..	12552	12811	13394	13787
Net Book Value	7016	8586	10462	21019
DEFERRED CHARGES	87	126	18	58
	$36260	$43001	$45009	$54915
CURRENT LIABILITIES:				
Notes payable				
Accounts payable	$ 553	$ 692	$ 835	$ 2149
Federal & State Income Tax	1850	3605	2538	5520
Other accrued expenses	611	639	773	727
Total current liabilities	3014	4936	4146	8396
LONG-TERM DEBT:				
DEFERRED INCOME	198	23	3	
CAPITAL STOCK & SURPLUS	2	5	4	5
Capital stock	26595	26595	26595	26595
Capital surplus	4057	4201	4201	4201
Earned surplus	2398	7246	10064	15723
Total capital stock & surplus ..	33050	38042	40860	46519
Less—Treasury Stock (at cost) ..	4	5	4	5
Net capital stock & surplus	33046	38037	40856	46514
	$36260	$43001	$45009	$54915

Weyerhaeuser Timber Company

Financial Condition, 1900–1959 Years Ending December 31

(OOO OMITTED)

	1900	1901	1902	1903
CURRENT ASSETS:				
Cash	$ 40	$ 9	$ 45	$ 20
U.S. Government and other marketable securities				
Receivables, less reserves	49	33	9	11
Inventories				
Total current assets	89	42	54	31
CURRENT LIABILITIES:				
Bank loans of partially-owned subsidiaries				
Accounts payable	x	486	754	152
Accrued liabilities				
Provision for Federal taxes on income				
Less—U.S. Government securities				
Total current liabilities	x	486	754	152
WORKING CAPITAL	89	(444)	(700)	(121)
SUPPLY INVENTORIES, PREPAID EXPENSES, ETC.	x	x	9	25
TAX REFUND CLAIMS AND OTHER RECEIVABLES	9	12	232	213
FUND FOR PLANT AND VESSEL REPLACEMENT AND ADDITIONS				
INVESTMENTS			209	572
TIMBER AND TIMBERLANDS	5832	6319	8340	9398
REAL ESTATE, PLANTS AND EQUIPMENT	16	17	23	32
Less—Depreciation and amortization				
	16	17	23	32
Total net assets before deducting debt and minority interest ...	5946	5904	8113	10119
DEDUCT:				
Long term debt of partially-owned subsidiaries				
Equity of minority shareholders in partially-owned subsidiaries				
Total net assets	$5946	$5904	$8113	$10119
SHAREHOLDERS' INTEREST REPRESENTED BY:				
Capital stock	$6000	$6000	$8000	$10000
Increase in value of timber and timberlands				
Earned surplus (unappropriated) .	(54)[a]	(96)	113	119
Earned surplus (appropriated) ...				
Treasury stock				
Total	$5946	$5904	$8113	$10119

x = Less than $500.   [a] Parentheses indicate figures in red.

SOURCE: Annual Accounts of Weyerhaeuser Timber Company, 1900–1959.

WEYERHAEUSER TIMBER COMPANY
(OOO OMITTED)

	1904	1905	1906	1907	1908
CURRENT ASSETS:					
Cash	$ 8	$ 49	$ 161	$ 656	$ 967
U.S. Government and other marketable securities					
Receivables, less reserves	18	33	82	357	369
Inventories				155	135
Total current assets	26	82	243	1168	1471
CURRENT LIABILITIES:					
Bank loans of partially-owned subsidiaries					
Accounts payable	382	1407	1732	51	31
Accrued liabilities					9
Provision for Federal taxes on income					
Less—U.S. Government securities					
Total current liabilities	382	1407	1732	51	40
WORKING CAPITAL	(356)	(1325)	(1489)	1117	1431
SUPPLY INVENTORIES, PREPAID EXPENSES, ETC.	72	81	23	29	8
TAX REFUND CLAIMS AND OTHER RECEIVABLES	227	1290	2304	2346	2201
FUND FOR PLANT AND VESSEL REPLACEMENT AND ADDITIONS					
INVESTMENTS	874	839	840	312	339
TIMBER AND TIMBERLANDS	9458	10579	12330	13461	13767
REAL ESTATE, PLANTS AND EQUIPMENT	50	358	370	689	740
Less—Depreciation and amortization					26
	50	358	370	689	714
Total net assets before deducting debt and minority interest ...	10325	11822	14378	17954	18460
DEDUCT:					
Long term debt of partially-owned subsidiaries					
Equity of minority shareholders in partially-owned subsidiaries		(91)	(91)	(91)	(90)
Total net assets	$10325	$11731	$14287	$17863	$18370
SHAREHOLDERS' INTEREST REPRESENTED BY:					
Capital stock	$10000	$10000	$10000	$12500	$12500
Increase in value of timber and timberlands					
Earned surplus (unappropriated) .	325	1731	4287	5363	5870
Earned surplus (appropriated) ...					
Treasury stock					
Total	$10325	$11731	$14287	$17863	$18370

(000 OMITTED)

1909	1910	1911	1912	1913	1914	1915	1916
$ 945	$ 718	$ 497	$ 2098	$ 1910	$ 1845	$ 758	$ 1360
421	192	890	212	162	181	458	905
216	235	266	279	273	291	1121	1951
1582	1145	1653	2589	2345	2317	2337	4216
12	12	15	21	35	35	97	669
1	x		7	12	17	78	3
						8	14
13	12	15	28	47	52	183	686
1569	1133	1638	2561	2298	2265	2154	3530
14	9	15	13	18	43	67	15
2544	2973	2739	3562	3585	3110	2602	3106
357	551	660	946	1775	1774	1996	3289
14495	15760	15790	15500	140894	140555	139868	136728
809	859	1057	1115	995	1558	2610	2815
53	84	118	169	207	257	332	463
756	775	939	946	788	1301	2278	2352
19735	21201	21781	23528	149358	149048	148965	149020
						(271)	(298)
$19735	$21201	$21781	$23528	$149358	$149048	$148694	$148722
$12500	$12500	$12500	$12500	$ 12500	$ 12500	$ 12500	$ 12500
				125227[b]	121164	120345	116875
7235	8701	9381	11128	11731	15384	15849	19347
		(100)	(100)	(100)			
$19735	$21201	$21781	$23528	$149358	$149048	$148694	$148722

[b] Increase in timberland values as result of re-evaluation (as of 1913) for Federal income tax.

WEYERHAEUSER TIMBER COMPANY

(OOO OMITTED)

	1917	1918	1919	1920	1921
CURRENT ASSETS:					
Cash	$ 1585	$ 1570	$ 1061	$ 1378	$ 1115
U.S. Government and other marketable securities	158	851	2417	3722	2428
Receivables, less reserves	1425	1985	4951	5037	4093
Inventories	2852	5411	6966	11353	8212
Total current assets	6020	9817	15395	21490	15848
CURRENT LIABILITIES:					
Bank loans of partially-owned subsidiaries					
Accounts payable	646	1118	3979	8238	4995
Accrued liabilities	145	229	306	2380	2469
Provision for Federal taxes on income	21	212	461	966	33
Less—U.S. Government securities					
Total current liabilities	812	1559	4746	11584	7497
WORKING CAPITAL	5208	8258	10649	9906	8351
SUPPLY INVENTORIES, PREPAID EXPENSES, ETC.	182	351	582	542	522
TAX REFUND CLAIMS AND OTHER RECEIVABLES	3031	2695	3490	17070	17104
FUND FOR PLANT AND VESSEL REPLACEMENT AND ADDITIONS					
INVESTMENTS	3145	3109	3547	3680	3646
TIMBER AND TIMBERLANDS	136841	134470	130864	118090	116423
REAL ESTATE, PLANTS AND EQUIPMENT	5418	6780	7971	10378	11765
Less—Depreciation and amortization	562	795	1130	1187	1717
	4856	5985	6841	9191	10048
Total net assets before deducting debt and minority interest ...	153263	154868	155973	158479	156094
DEDUCT:					
Long term debt of partially-owned subsidiaries					
Equity of minority shareholders in partially-owned subsidiaries	(3692)	(3860)	(4334)	(4585)	(4670)
Total net assets	$149571	$151008	$151639	$153894	$151424
SHAREHOLDERS' INTEREST REPRESENTED BY:					
Capital stock	$ 12500	$ 12500	$ 12500	$ 12500	$ 12500
Increase in value of timber and timberlands	115126	113032	109857	106003	104244
Earned surplus (unappropriated) .	21945	25476	29282	35391	34680
Earned surplus (appropriated) ...					
Treasury stock					
Total	$149571	$151008	$151639	$153894	$151424

(OOO OMITTED)

1922	1923	1924	1925	1926	1927	1928	1929
$ 1269	$ 1795	$ 1752	$ 4322	$ 6963	$ 4227	$ 5012	$ 2918
4630	8513	8779	12163	16701	17530	14855	11206
4771	3788	1584	3647	4053	2651	2223	3037
8328	8838	5517	7139	7409	8064	7010	7959
18998	22934	17632	27271	35126	32472	29100	25120
3672	3710	164	12	2262	2114	904	1416
2440	2506	2358	2168	1242	5054	5502	5756
359	893	207	580	784	330	488	610
6471	7109	2729	2760	4288	7498	6894	7782
12527	15825	14903	24511	30838	24974	22206	17338
509	423	372	490	699	526	552	1092
17913	18725	23257	16640	8425	14203	14390	14816
3591	4797	5305	4769	4557	3740	3189	3557
111610	106603	102655	99743	99890	96986	94192	92121
12636	14411	12374	17074	19054	23087	30837	44118
2423	2931	2805	4243	4876	6046	7510	10311
10213	11480	9569	12831	14178	17041	23327	33807
156363	157853	156061	158984	158587	157470	157856	162731
(4647)	(4399)	(3801)	(5565)	(5439)	(5182)	(5131)	(7773)
$151716	$153454	$152260	$153419	$153148	$152288	$152725	$154958
$ 12500	$ 12500	$ 12500	$ 12500	$ 12500	$ 12500	$ 12500	$ 12500
99305	93313	88248	83808	76154	73005	70012	64850
39911	47641	51512	57111	64494	66783	70213	77608
$151716	$153454	$152260	$153419	$153148	$152288	$152725	$154958

WEYERHAEUSER TIMBER COMPANY

(000 OMITTED)

	1930	1931	1932	1933	1934
CURRENT ASSETS:					
Cash	$ 1212	$ 1142	$ 3482	$ 2364	$ 2966
U.S. Government and other					
marketable securities	6516	3057	2404	3103	2114
Receivables, less reserves	2270	2245	2232	3337	3013
Inventories	10176	8636	6063	7697	8714
Total current assets	20174	15080	14181	16501	16807
CURRENT LIABILITIES:					
Bank loans of partially-owned					
subsidiaries					
Accounts payable	970	1642	637	998	725
Accrued liabilities	8919	6678	7001	2751	2421
Provision for Federal taxes on					
income	66	19		25	57
Less—U.S. Government					
securities					
Total current liabilities	9955	8339	7638	3774	3202
WORKING CAPITAL	10219	6741	6543	12727	13605
SUPPLY INVENTORIES, PREPAID					
EXPENSES, ETC.	1301	1130	1008	1144	1231
TAX REFUND CLAIMS AND OTHER					
RECEIVABLES	13944	13440	13067	2391	1853
FUND FOR PLANT AND VESSEL					
REPLACEMENT AND ADDITIONS					
INVESTMENTS	4436	3537	3598	3565	3671
TIMBER AND TIMBERLANDS	92192	92768	92125	96723	93701
REAL ESTATE, PLANTS AND EQUIPMENT	47396	52842	52965	53994	51969
Less—Depreciation and					
amortization	12706	14577	16709	19287	18828
	34690	38265	36256	34707	33141
Total net assets before deducting					
debt and minority interest ...	156782	155881	152597	151257	147202
DEDUCT:					
Long term debt of partially-owned					
subsidiaries					
Equity of minority shareholders in					
partially-owned subsidiaries	(8067)	(9043)	(8662)	(8476)	(7691)
Total net assets	$148715	$146838	$143935	$142781	$139511
SHAREHOLDERS' INTEREST					
REPRESENTED BY:					
Capital stock	$ 12500	$ 12500	$ 12500	$ 12500	$ 12500
Increase in value of timber and					
timberlands	63013	59708	59041	57839	56598
Earned surplus (unappropriated) .	73202	74630	72394	72442	70413
Earned surplus (appropriated) ...					
Treasury stock					
Total	$148715	$146838	$143935	$142781	$139511

(OOO OMITTED)

1935	1936	1937	1938	1939	1940	1941	1942
$ 3727	$ 3679	$ 2267	$ 5068	$ 10464	$ 12128	$ 8538	$ 10091
1838	1088	788	1258	133	33	2537	3260
3805	5021	4041	4945	5420	6144	8439	11698
8595	8601	12031	10550	10097	9876	11689	7947
17965	18389	19127	21821	26114	28181	31203	32996
1411	2040	1593	1387	1572	2041	2823	2846
2529	2539	2390	2435	2751	2405	3883	3630
278	909	1279	456				
				1101	3261	10001	19006
(200)	(900)	(1200)	(400)	(1100)	(1200)	(10000)	(19000)
4018	4588	4062	3878	4324	6507	6707	6482
13947	13801	15065	17943	21790	21674	24496	26514
1329	1764	2216	2255	2202	2489	3188	3292
2135	1197	651	549	544	729	917	2776
3727	3703	3643	3620	4350	5149	4910	4661
90718	87885	86225	84258	80300	79497	79421	81791
54428	57156	59936	61948	63555	64966	69971	70474
20428	21655	24125	26495	29075	30315	36003	39128
34000	35501	35811	35453	34480	34651	33968	31346
145856	143851	143611	144078	143666	144189	146900	150380
(7465)	(6508)	(6473)	(6436)	(6377)	(6541)	(6645)	(6783)
$138391	$137343	$137138	$137642	$137289	$137648	$140255	$143597
$ 12500	$ 12500	$ 12500	$ 12500	$ 12500	$ 12500	$ 12500	$ 12500
54954	52593	50179	48320	46340	39212	29329	34188
70937	72250	74459	76822	78449	85936	98426	96909
$138391	$137343	$137138	$137642	$137289	$137648	$140255	$143597

WEYERHAEUSER TIMBER COMPANY

(000 OMITTED)

	1943	1944	1945	1946	1947
CURRENT ASSETS:					
Cash	$ 12861	$ 11382	$ 9990	$ 13080	$ 12873
U.S. Government and other					
marketable securities	1671	4417	13026	2954	1371
Receivables, less reserves	9441	7723	6112	7255	10869
Inventories	7034	6728	5522	6542	10480
Total current assets	31007	30250	34650	29831	35593
CURRENT LIABILITIES:					
Bank loans of partially-owned					
subsidiaries					
Accounts payable	3500	2879	2805	3585	4509
Accrued liabilities	3826	3143	3350	5355	7251
Provision for Federal taxes on					
income	17637	15216	7721	8029	18049
Less—U.S. Government					
securities	(17600)	(15200)	(7700)	(8000)	(18000)
Total current liabilities	7363	6038	6176	8969	11809
WORKING CAPITAL	23644	24212	28474	20862	23784
SUPPLY INVENTORIES, PREPAID					
EXPENSES, ETC.	3235	2848	3357	2796	3606
TAX REFUND CLAIMS AND OTHER					
RECEIVABLES	4251	4895	1941	1960	3693
FUND FOR PLANT AND VESSEL					
REPLACEMENT AND ADDITIONS	8294	11386	13860	22011	21289
INVESTMENTS	4609	4552	2557	2641	2726
TIMBER AND TIMBERLANDS	80629	82588	82310	82409	82704
REAL ESTATE, PLANTS AND EQUIPMENT	70786	71168	73177	75877	92385
Less—Depreciation and					
amortization	42092	44048	45287	44044	45811
	28694	27120	27890	31833	46574
Total net assets before deducting					
debt and minority interest ...	153356	157601	160389	164512	184376
DEDUCT:					
Long term debt of partially-owned					
subsidiaries					
Equity of minority shareholders in					
partially-owned subsidiaries	(6914)	(7242)	(7502)	(7599)	(8144)
Total net assets	$146442	$150359	$152887	$156913	$176232
SHAREHOLDERS' INTEREST					
REPRESENTED BY:					
Capital stock	$ 12500	$ 12500	$ 90000	$ 90000	$ 90000
Increase in value of timber and					
timberlands	32647	31069	30292	36201	35623
Earned surplus (unappropriated) .	93757	96170	19560	9712	21109
Earned surplus (appropriated) ...	7538	10620	13035	21000	29500
Treasury stock					
Total	$146442	$150359	$152887	$156913	$176232

(OOO OMITTED)

1948	1949	1950	1951	1952	1953	1954	1955
$ 16026	$ 18214	$ 18776	$ 24431	$ 17392	$ 15523	$ 15243	$ 14911
5595	17280	22144	26139	26950	35374	52033	60163
13771	15867	21339	17088	22902	21109	22336	28788
15467	12869	15253	15526	15009	14257	16024	16543
50859	64230	77512	83184	82253	86263	105636	120405
810	300						
8926	6969	11927	12676	13421	8572	9630	14230
7393	9115	8840	10108	10801	12017	11938	14569
20766	15980	22304	35078	32977	33813	35756	43348
(20750)	(15900)	(22000)	(34400)	(32800)	(33600)	(34800)	(42500)
17145	16464	21071	23462	24399	20802	22524	29647
33714	47766	56441	59722	57854	65461	83112	90758
6217	4901	4770	6625	5942	5117	5542	5363
7616	3230	5021	5292	5722	4936	4646	4384
601	805	788	712	496	648	645	1746
83177	79693	80136	78658	76706	73848	71951	82541
133167	150317	166795	195752	229246	237149	252368	274944
50075	54915	61636	70025	79420	85060	99038	115628
83092	95402	105159	125727	149826	152089	153330	159316
214417	231797	252315	276736	296546	302099	319226	344108
(1200)	(2700)	(2400)	(2100)	(1800)			
(9016)	(4249)	(5106)	(5506)	(6003)			
$204201	$224848	$244809	$269130	$288743	$302099	$319226	$344108
$ 93999	$108026	$156250	$156250	$156250	156250	$156250	$187500
36813	32112	30654	29595	28607	27693	26826	25771
73389	93449	57905	83285	105377	120784	138528	132678
	(8739)			(1491)	(2628)	(2378)	(1841)
$204201	$224848	$244809	$269130	$288743	$302099	$319226	$344108

WEYERHAEUSER TIMBER COMPANY

(000 OMITTED)

	1956	1957	1958	1959
CURRENT ASSETS:				
Cash	$ 17286	$ 23534	$ 24503	$ 26221
U.S. Government and other				
marketable securities	40071	37978	56209	79055
Receivables, less reserves	23129	30777	32966	40343
Inventories	23477	38130	38246	44152
Total current assets	103963	130419	151924	189771
CURRENT LIABILITIES:				
Bank loans of partially-owned				
subsidiaries				
Accounts payable	17838	14827	13112	14483
Accrued liabilities	15554	19134	20782	22919
Provision for Federal taxes on				
income	37207	36519	40454	43628
Less—U.S. Government				
securities	(36700)	(33900)	(40000)	(42400)
Total current liabilities	33899	36580	34348	38630
WORKING CAPITAL	70064	93839	117576	151141
SUPPLY INVENTORIES, PREPAID				
EXPENSES, ETC.	7065	10731	10257	10322
TAX REFUND CLAIMS AND OTHER				
RECEIVABLES	4670	6128	5955	5543
FUND FOR PLANT AND VESSEL				
REPLACEMENT AND ADDITIONS				
INVESTMENTS	2363	3201	2305	1894
TIMBER AND TIMBERLANDS	86352	107379	114588	109469
REAL ESTATE, PLANTS AND EQUIPMENT	329919	459478	478090	504920
Less—Depreciation and				
amortization	130350	196106	225519	253588
	199569	263372	252571	251332
Total net assets before deducting				
debt and minority interest ...	370083	484650	503252	529701
DEDUCT:				
Long term debt of partially-owned				
subsidiaries				
Equity of minority shareholders in				
partially-owned subsidiaries				
Total net assets	$370083	$484650	$503252	$529701
SHAREHOLDERS' INTEREST				
REPRESENTED BY:				
Capital stock	$187500	$227985	$227985	$229090
Increase in value of timber and				
timberlands	24983	24375	23680	22863
Earned surplus (unappropriated) .	159988	236421	256470	284327
Earned surplus (appropriated) ...				4195c
Treasury stock	(2388)	(4131)	(4883)	(10774)
Total	$370083	$484650	$503252	$529701

c Paid-in surplus.

Wood Conversion Company, 1922–1950

Years Ending December 31

(ooo OMITTED)

	1922	*1923*	*1924*	*1925*	*1926*
CURRENT ASSETS:					
Cash	$ 36	$ 35	$ 2	$ 62	$ 56
United States Government securities					
Receivables (Less reserves)	1	6	19	28	44
Inventories	28	98	89	85	88
Income tax refund claim					
Prepaid insurance, etc.	3	4	7	10	11
Total current assets	68	143	117	185	199
MISCELLANEOUS ASSETS—EMPLOYEES' HOMESITES, INCOME TAX REFUND CLAIMS, ETC.					
FIXED ASSETS:					
Plant property	300	522	556	605	662
Less reserves for depreciation ..	6	22	41	61	86
Plant property—Net	294	500	515	544	576
Patents and applications	151	226	310	358	432
Total fixed assets	445	726	825	902	1008
TOTAL	$513	$869	$942	$1087	$1207
CURRENT LIABILITIES:					
Notes payable—Portion due within one year					
Accounts payable					
Accrued accounts:					
Income taxes	1				
Other					
Total current liabilities	1				
NOTES PAYABLE AFTER ONE YEAR					
DEBENTURES[b]					
CAPITAL STOCK AND SURPLUS:					
Common Capital stock	500	900	1000	1150	1250
Capital surplus					
Earned surplus	12	(31)[a]	(58)	(63)	(43)
Total capital stock and surplus .	512	869	942	1087	1207
TOTAL	$513	$869	$942	$1087	$1207

[a] Parentheses indicate entry in red ink.
[b] 5% convertible debentures, dated April 20, 1934, due Nov. 30, 1941.

SOURCE: Annual Reports of Wood Conversion Company, 1922–1950.

WOOD CONVERSION COMPANY, 1922–1950

(000 OMITTED)

	1927	1928	1929	1930	1931
CURRENT ASSETS:					
Cash	$ 41	$ 108	$ 40	$ 6	$ 7
United States Government securities					
Receivables (Less reserves)	106	121	173	203	147
Inventories	123	207	205	228	203
Income tax refund claim					
Prepaid insurance, etc.	29	5	18	17	24
Total current assets	299	441	436	454	381
MISCELLANEOUS ASSETS—EMPLOYEES' HOMESITES, INCOME TAX REFUND CLAIMS, ETC.					
FIXED ASSETS:					
Plant property	1013	1166	1498	1551	1577
Less reserves for depreciation ..	155	256	448	578	713
Plant property—Net	858	910	1050	973	864
Patents and applications	442	444	446	452	454
Total fixed assets	1300	1354	1496	1425	1318
TOTAL	$1599	$1795	$1932	$1879	$1699
CURRENT LIABILITIES:					
Notes payable—Portion due within one year	$ 100	$ 200	$ 300	$ 450	$ 450
Accounts payable		2	2	1	8
Accrued accounts:					
Income taxes					
Other	1	1	3		
Total current liabilities	101	203	305	451	458
NOTES PAYABLE AFTER ONE YEAR					
DEBENTURES[b]					
CAPITAL STOCK AND SURPLUS:					
Common Capital stock	1500	1500	1500	1500	1500
Capital surplus					
Earned surplus	(2)	92	127	(72)	(259)
Total capital stock and surplus .	1498	1592	1627	1428	1241
TOTAL	$1599	$1795	$1932	$1879	$1699

[b] 5% convertible debentures, dated April 20, 1934, due Nov. 30, 1941.

(000 OMITTED)

1932	1933	1934	1935	1936	1937	1938
$ 8	$ 83	$ 88	$ 235	$ 388	$ 481	$ 490
88	161	175	217	282	314	362
176	156	204	205	184	451	295
17	6	5	5	11	7	24
289	406	472	662	865	1253	1171
2	3	1		3	3	3
1478	1554	1642	1948	2115	2221	2409
784	644	744	827	953	1103	1260
694	910	898	1121	1162	1118	1149
453	199	170	134	104	75	55
1147	1109	1068	1255	1266	1193	1204
$1438	$1518	$1541	$1917	$2134	$2449	$2378

LIABILITIES

1932	1933	1934	1935	1936	1937	1938
$ 555	$ 732	$ 21	$ 116	$ 83		
15	107	98	77	84	$ 82	$ 120
			29	52	114	37
11	19	51	121	94	78	84
581	858	170	343	313	274	241
		38	115	72		
		900	900	900	648	
1500	1500	600	600	600	852	1450
		900	900	900	900	900
(643)	(840)	(1067)	(941)	(651)	(225)	(213)
857	660	433	559	849	1527	2137
$1438	$1518	$1541	$1917	$2134	$2449	$2378

WOOD CONVERSION COMPANY, 1922–1950

(ooo OMITTED)

	1939	1940	1941	1942	1943
CURRENT ASSETS:					
Cash	$ 669	$ 848	$ 632	$ 661	$1010
United States Government securities		15	146	586	537
Receivables (Less reserves)	423	395	532	453	273
Inventories	363	346	587	622	779
Income tax refund claim					
Prepaid insurance, etc.	24	20	28	32	31
Total current assets	1479	1624	1925	2354	2630
MISCELLANEOUS ASSETS—EMPLOYEES' HOMESITES, INCOME TAX REFUND CLAIMS, ETC.	28	23	23	25	39
FIXED ASSETS:					
Plant property	2623	2836	3063	3264	3335
Less reserves for depreciation	1404	1557	1575	1712	1837
Plant property—Net	1219	1279	1488	1552	1498
Patents and applications	42	33	27	31	40
Total fixed assets	1261	1312	1515	1583	1538
TOTAL	$2768	$2959	$3463	$3962	$4207
CURRENT LIABILITIES:					
Notes payable—Portion due within one year					
Accounts payable	$ 109	$ 84	$ 153	$ 124	$ 159
Accrued accounts:					
Income taxes	127	97	177	425	388
Other	102	113	159	167	196
Total current liabilities	338	294	489	716	743
NOTES PAYABLE AFTER ONE YEAR					
DEBENTURES[b]					
CAPITAL STOCK AND SURPLUS:					
Common Capital stock	1450	1450	1450	2350	2350
Capital surplus	900	900	900		
Earned surplus	80	315	624	896	1114
Total capital stock and surplus	2430	2665	2974	3246	3464
TOTAL	$2768	$2959	$3463	$3962	$4207

[b] 5% convertible debentures, dated April 20, 1934, due Nov. 30, 1941.

(OOO OMITTED)

1944	1945	1946	1947	1948	1949	1950
$ 955	$1201	$ 554	$ 512	$ 1016	$ 887	$ 984
419	522	1009	607	201	1205	2114
286	436	726	830	1178	982	1754
791	691	1163	1146	1890	1108	1404
26	24	34	42	86	104	125
2477	2874	3486	3137	4371	4286	6381
111	108	118	115	125	51	48
3363	3474	4013	6480	9866	10916	11530
1978	2110	2209	2248	2348	2679	2855
1385	1364	1804	4232	7518	8237	8675
47	49	55	56	63	57	43
1432	1413	1859	4288	7581	8294	8718
$4020	$4395	$5463	$7540	$12077	$12631	$15147

LIABILITIES

1944	1945	1946	1947	1948	1949	1950
				$ 300	$ 300	
$ 107	$ 145	$ 310	$ 580	749	284	$ 525
158	286	580	958	1145	695	1706
165	194	195	267	412	394	538
430	625	1085	1805	2606	1673	2769
				2200	2700	2400
2350	2350	2350	2350	2350	2350	2350
1240	1420	2028	3385	4921	5908	7628
3590	3770	4378	5735	7271	8258	9978
$4020	$4395	$5463	$7540	$12077	$12631	$15147

Boise Payette Lumber Company

Statement of Income and Earned Surplus, 1914–1950

(OOO OMITTED)

	1914	1915	1916	1917	1918
Net Sales[a]		110	663	1718	2883
Cost of sales		82	458	963	1595
Gross Profit		28	205	755	1288
Other Operating Income[b]		6	64	355	584
		34	269	1110	1872
Selling-General & Admn.		57	171	314	636
Profit from Operations	(43)[c]	(23)	98	796	1236
Non-operative income, less charge ..		39	72	(101)	(364)
Profit before Taxes on Income ...	(43)	16	170	695	872
Provision for Taxes on Income					65
Net Income for Year	(43)	16	170	695	807
Prior Years Adjustments					
Net Income to Surplus	(43)	16	170	695	807
Earned Surplus, Beginning of Year ..	–0–	(43)	(27)	143	838
Transferred to/from capital stock ...					
Distribution					
Other					
Prior years income taxes					
Earned surplus at end of year	(43)	(27)	143	838	1645

[a] Wholesale lumber sales only.

[b] Includes retail earnings except years:

1914	–0–
1915	–0–
1932	(152)
1933	(151)
1934	(71)
1935	(36)

[c] Parentheses indicate figures in red.

SOURCE: Annual Reports of Boise Payette Lumber Company, 1914–1950.

(ooo OMITTED)

1919	1920	1921	1922	1923	1924	1925
3532	5086	1506	3080	4010	3203	3487
1969	3238	1103	2018	2547	2237	2555
1563	1848	403	1062	1463	966	932
692	632	37	365	252	146	273
2255	2480	440	1427	1715	1112	1205
752	970	586	803	836	886	923
1503	1510	(146)	624	879	226	282
(183)	(62)	(54)	20	22	(136)	(171)
1320	1448	(200)	644	901	90	111
152	204					
1168	1244	(200)	644	901	90	111
1168	1244	(200)	644	901	90	111
1645	2813	4196	3755	3318	3694	3207
			(1080)	(450)	(450)	(450)
	139		(1)	(36)		
		(241)		(39)	(127)	(8)
2813	4196	3755	3318	3694	3207	2860

BOISE PAYETTE LUMBER COMPANY

(OOO OMITTED)

	1926	1927	1928	1929	1930
Net Sales[a]	3051	2884	3023	2726	1775
Cost of sales	2337	2163	2242	2014	1614
Gross Profit	714	721	781	712	161
Other Operating Income[b]	254	297	354	331	148
	968	1018	1135	1043	309
Selling-General & Admn.	902	776	766	808	814
Profit from Operations	66	242	369	235	(505)
Non-operative income, less charge ..	(80)	(127)	(186)	(186)	(21)
Profit before Taxes on Income ...	(14)	115	183	49	(526)
Provision for Taxes on Income					
Net Income for Year	(14)	115	183	49	(526)
Prior Years Adjustments					
Net Income to Surplus	(14)	115	183	49	(526)
Earned Surplus, Beginning of Year ..	2860	2561	2408	2306	2330
Transferred to/from capital stock ...					
Distribution	(270)	(270)	(270)		(180)
Other				(3)	(17)
Prior years income taxes	(15)	2	(15)	(22)	(5)
Earned surplus at end of year	2561	2408	2306	2330	1602

[a] Wholesale lumber sales only.

[b] Includes retail earnings except years:

1914	–0–
1915	–0–
1932	(152)
1933	(151)
1934	(71)
1935	(36)

(OOO OMITTED)

1931	1932	1933	1934	1935	1936	1937
1089	695	860	1092	2141	2206	2729
1210	559	529	1026	1630	1623	1903
(121)	136	331	66	511	583	826
130	60	49	–	158	–	267
9	196	380	66	669	583	1093
503	379	358	179	521	434	415
(494)	(183)	22	(113)	148	149	678
(176)	(199)	(97)	(160)	34	73	(172)
(670)	(382)	(75)	(273)	182	222	506
(670)	(382)	(75)	(273)	182	222	506
(670)	(382)	(75)	(273)	182	222	506
1602	725	300	(3)	(290)	(803)	(816)
						816
					(222)	(506)
(207)	(43)	(228)	(14)	(695)	(9)	
					(4)	
725	300	(3)	(290)	(803)	(816)	–

BOISE PAYETTE LUMBER COMPANY

(000 OMITTED)

	1938	1939	1940	1941	1942
Net Sales[a]	2701	2914	3167	4338	4519
Cost of sales	1966	2015	2051	2576	2756
Gross Profit	735	899	1116	1762	1763
Other Operating Income[b]	155	200	185	219	187
	890	1099	1301	1981	1950
Selling-General & Admn.	594	630	620	731	694
Profit from Operations	296	469	681	1250	1256
Non-operative income, less charge	15	(54)	(126)	(592)	(739)
Profit before Taxes on Income	311	415	555	658	517
Provision for Taxes on Income					
Net Income for Year	311	415	555	658	517
Prior Years Adjustments					
Net Income to Surplus	311	415	555	658	517
Earned Surplus, Beginning of Year	–	8	8	38	(2)
Transferred to/from capital stock				(170)	183
Distribution	(311)	(415)	(525)	(658)	(700)
Other				130	2
Prior years income taxes	8				
Earned surplus at end of year	8	8	38	(2)	–

[a] Wholesale lumber sales only.
[b] Includes retail earnings except years:

1914	–0–
1915	–0–
1932	(152)
1933	(151)
1934	(71)
1935	(36)

(000 OMITTED)

1943	1944	1945	1946	1947	1948ᶜ	1949	1950
4681	4925	3409	3969	6032	9548	7268	8160
2902	2907	2248	2366	2890	4227	3838	5729
1779	2018	1161	1603	3142	5321	3430	2431
219	179	245	646	823	916	954	1939
1998	2197	1406	2249	3965	6237	4384	4370
682	642	633	660	715	1499	782	904
1316	1555	773	1589	3250	4738	3602	3466
(58)	34	(44)	108	137	728	33	(13)
1258	1589	729	1697	3387	5466	3635	3453
548	933	257	422	1006	1715	1100	885
710	656	472	1275	2381	3751	2535	2568
710	656	472	1275	2381	3751	2535	2568
–	–		–	–	1797	4972	6982
							(2969)
165	657	578	37				
(875)	(1313)	(1050)	(1312)	(525)	(525)	(525)	(525)
				(59)	(51)		
–	–	–	–	1797	4972	6982	6056

ᶜ Reconstructed from tax return, as a result, classification of accounts is not the same as in other years.

The Northwest Paper Company

Statements of Current Operations and Operating Statistics, 1900–1950

(OOO OMITTED EXCEPT ON * ITEMS)

For year ended unless otherwise noted:	10 months ended 1–31–1900	11 months ended 12–31–00	12–31–01	3 months ended 3–31–02	3–31–03
STATEMENT OF CURRENT OPERATIONS					
PAPER DIVISION:					
Net sales	$123	$296	$439	$105	$488
Cost of paper sold	109	285	429	106	437
Operating profit or (loss)	14	11	10	(1)[a]	51
Other income and (other charges)	(6)	(18)	(11)	(4)	(13)
Profit or (loss) before income taxes	8	(7)	(1)	(5)	38
LUMBER DIVISION:					
Profit or (loss) before income taxes					
COMBINED:					
Profit or (loss) before income taxes	8	(7)	(1)	(5)	38
Provision for income taxes					
Net profit or (loss) to surplus	$ 8	$ (7)	$ (1)	$ (5)	$ 38
DIVIDENDS PAID:					
STATEMENT OF OPERATING STATISTICS					
Tons paper sold*	3846	7768	11537	2839	11652
Tons pulp sold*					256
Net paper sales	$123	$296	$439	$105	$474
Paper sales price—average net per ton*	31.89	38.07	38.04	36.88	40.70
Total net sales—Paper division	$123	$296	$439	$105	$488
Total net sales—Lumber division					
Total net sales—Combined	$123	$296	$439	$105	$488

[a] Parentheses indicate figures in red.

SOURCE: Annual Reports of The Northwest Paper Company, 1900–1950.

(000 OMITTED EXCEPT ON * ITEMS)

3–31–04	3–31–05	3–31–06	3–31–07	3–31–08	3–31–09	3–31–10
$548	$744	$729	$751	$607	$609	$640
477	605	657	729	590	548	569
71	139	72	22	17	61	71
(13)	(11)	(6)	(2)		(1)	1
58	128	66	20	17	60	72
58	128	66	20	17	60	72
$ 58	$128	$ 66	$ 20	$ 17	$ 60	$ 72
$ 15	$ 18	$ 15	$ 15	$ 15	$ 57	$ 75
11864	12032	13019	14704	13151	14379	15443
2396	4332	2803	1744	3173	775	1453
$501	$517	$511	$544	$535	$596	$613
42.25	42.93	39.28	36.99	40.66	41.43	39.69
$548	$744	$729	$751	$607	$609	$640
$548	$744	$729	$751	$607	$609	$640

THE NORTHWEST PAPER COMPANY

(OOO OMITTED EXCEPT ON * ITEMS)

For year ended unless otherwise noted:	3–31–11	3–31–12	3–31–13	3–31–14	3–31–15
STATEMENT OF CURRENT OPERATIONS					
PAPER DIVISION:					
Net sales	$713	$800	$733	$731	$724
Cost of paper sold	650	687	686	640	654
Operating profit or (loss)	63	113	47	91	70
Other income and (other charges)	3	3	6	7	5
Profit or (loss) before income taxes	66	116	53	98	75
LUMBER DIVISION:					
Profit or (loss) before income taxes					
COMBINED:					
Profit or (loss) before income taxes	66	116	53	98	75
Provision for income taxes					
Net profit or (loss) to surplus	$ 66	$116	$ 53	$ 98	$ 75
DIVIDENDS PAID:	$ 46[1]	$ 60	$ 60	$ 75	$ 60
STATEMENT OF OPERATING STATISTICS					
Tons paper sold*	16512	18768	17915	18707	19130
Tons pulp sold*	2158	1989	687		
Net paper sales	$677	$762	$719	$731	$724
Paper sales price—average net per ton*	40.97	40.60	40.16	39.10	37.82
Total net sales—Paper division	$713	$800	$733	$731	$724
Total net sales—Lumber division					
Total net sales—Combined	$713	$800	$733	$731	$724

1. Plus $660,000 in stock dividend.

(000 OMITTED EXCEPT ON * ITEMS)

3–31–16	3–31–17	3–31–18	3–31–19	9 months ended 12–31–19	12–31–20	12–31–21
$837	$1334	$2079	$2704	$2241	$4739	$2044
767	995	1778	2120	1810	2940	2445
70	339	301	584	431	1799	(401)
(3)	(7)	(64)	(93)	(66)	(103)	(60)
67	332	237	491	365	1696	(461)
67	332	237	491	365	1696	(461)
		7	39	111	789	
$ 67	$ 332	$ 230	$ 452	$ 254	$ 907	$(461)
$ 15		$ 22	$ 22	$ 22	$ 135	$ 22
19766	19033	28447	29454	23472	33233	17525
3252	9980	8844	8347	6884	10934	4169
$723	$ 845	$1578	$2181	$1822	$3725	$1730
36.56	44.40	55.46	74.04	77.60	112.08	98.74
$837	$1334	$2079	$2704	$2241	$4739	$2044
$837	$1334	$2079	$2704	$2241	$4739	$2044

THE NORTHWEST PAPER COMPANY

(OOO OMITTED EXCEPT ON * ITEMS)

For year ended unless otherwise noted:	12–31–22	12–31–23	12–31–24	12–31–25	12–31–26
STATEMENT OF CURRENT OPERATIONS					
PAPER DIVISION:					
Net sales	$2775	$2722	$2307	$3186	$3790
Cost of paper sold	2567	2556	2968	3960	3650
Operating profit or (loss)	208	166	(661)	(774)	140
Other income and (other charges)	(109)	(135)	(256)	(205)	(223)
Profit or (loss) before income taxes	99	31	(917)	(979)	(83)
LUMBER DIVISION:					
Profit or (loss) before income taxes					
COMBINED:					
Profit or (loss) before income taxes	99	31	(917)	(979)	(83)
Provision for income taxes					
Net profit or (loss) to surplus ..	$ 99	$ 31	$(917)	$(979)	$ (83)
DIVIDENDS PAID:					
STATEMENT OF OPERATING STATISTICS					
Tons paper sold*	33346	28354	21119	28173	34057
Tons pulp sold*	8530	9705	11669	12725	10715
Net paper sales	$2364	$2175	$1693	$2500	$3140
Paper sales price—average net per ton*	70.89	76.72	80.19	88.74	92.19
Total net sales—Paper division ...	$2775	$2722	$2307	$3186	$3790
Total net sales—Lumber division .					
Total net sales—Combined	$2775	$2722	$2307	$3186	$3790

(OOO OMITTED EXCEPT ON * ITEMS)

12–31–27	12–31–28	12–31–29	12–31–30	12–31–31	12–31–32	12–31–33
$4255	$4132	$4417	$ 4237	$ 3667	$ 2889	$ 3588
3907	3809	4211	4354	4083	3535	3931
348	323	206	(117)	(416)	(646)	(343)
(228)	(300)	(365)	(444)	(811)	(371)	(228)
120	23	(159)	(561)	(1227)	(1017)	(571)
		60	(1106)	(1580)	(475)	482
120	23	(99)	(1667)	(2807)	(1492)	(89)
$ 120	$ 23	$ (99)	$(1667)	$(2807)	$(1492)	$ (89)
40235	39606	41823	39832	43730	42194	56091
10019	9827	12414	16876	4633	3335	6043
$3704	$3612	$3796	$ 3392	$ 3410	$ 2742	$ 3342
92.06	91.19	90.76	85.15	77.98	64.99	59.58
$4255	$4132	$4417	$ 4237	$ 3667	$ 2889	$ 3588
		2890	2175	1179	955	1250
$4255	$4132	$7307	$ 6412	$ 4846	$ 3844	$ 4838

THE NORTHWEST PAPER COMPANY

(OOO OMITTED EXCEPT ON * ITEMS)

For year ended unless otherwise noted:	12–31–34	12–31–35	12–31–36	12–31–37	12–31–38
STATEMENT OF CURRENT OPERATIONS					
PAPER DIVISION:					
Net sales	$3784	$4415	$4924	$5670	$4886
Cost of paper sold	4167	4776	5007	5433	5182
Operating profit or (loss)	(383)	(361)	(83)	237	(296)
Other income and (other charges)	(197)	(175)	(141)	(140)	(163)
Profit or (loss) before income taxes	(580)	(536)	(224)	97	(459)
LUMBER DIVISION:					
Profit or (loss) before income taxes	(170)	96	59	(2)	(117)
COMBINED:					
Profit or (loss) before income taxes	(750)	(440)	(165)	95	(576)
Provision for income taxes					
Net profit or (loss) to surplus ..	$(750)	$(440)	$(165)	$ 95	$(576)
DIVIDENDS PAID:					
STATEMENT OF OPERATING STATISTICS					
Tons paper sold*	47067	52507	56959	59711	53995
Tons pulp sold*	4512	4779	4145	2052	1790
Net paper sales	$3535	$4143	$4662	$5454	$4750
Paper sales price—average net per ton*	75.11	78.90	81.85	91.33	87.98
Total net sales—Paper division ...	$3784	$4415	$4924	$5670	$4886
Total net sales—Lumber division .	1092	867	596	562	389
Total net sales—Combined	$4876	$5282	$5520	$6232	$5275

(OOO OMITTED EXCEPT ON * ITEMS)

12–31–39	12–31–40	12–31–41	12–31–42	12–31–43	12–31–44	12–31–45
$5232	$5645	$8196	$8880	$9881	$11138	$11348
5284	5518	6712	7124	8566	9326	9956
(52)	127	1484	1756	1315	1812	1392
(139)	(94)	(66)	(135)	(68)	(66)	(48)
(191)	33	1418	1621	1247	1746	1344
(66)			(2)			
(257)	33	1418	1619	1247	1746	1344
		42	743	450	740	487
$(257)	$ 33	$1376	$ 876	$ 797	$ 1006	$ 857
						$ 225
62236	63129	81489	76571	77630	80952	81658
1351	756	526	2427	7219	11676	8403
$5138	$5565	$8112	$8684	$9368	$10341	$10754
82.55	88.15	99.55	113.41	120.67	127.75	131.69
$5232	$5645	$8196	$8880	$9881	$11138	$11348
633	37	43	21			
$5865	$5682	$8239	$8901	$9881	$11138	$11348

THE NORTHWEST PAPER COMPANY

(OOO OMITTED EXCEPT ON * ITEMS)

For year ended unless otherwise noted:	12–31–46	12–31–47	12–31–48	12–31–49	12–31–50
STATEMENT OF CURRENT OPERATIONS					
PAPER DIVISION:					
Net sales	$12999	$16982	$19165	$17653	$19686
Cost of paper sold	11074	12636	15452	15427	16814
Operating profit or (loss)	1925	4346	3713	2226	2872
Other income and (other charges)	(41)	1	(41)	(72)	(57)
Profit or (loss) before income taxes	1884	4347	3672	2154	2815
LUMBER DIVISION:					
Profit or (loss) before income taxes					
COMBINED:					
Profit or (loss) before income taxes	1884	4347	3672	2154	2815
Provision for income taxes	742	1765	1435	827	1239
Net profit or (loss) to surplus	$ 1142	$ 2582	$ 2237	$ 1327	$ 1576
DIVIDENDS PAID:	$ 294	$ 294	$ 583	$ 439	$ 437
STATEMENT OF OPERATING STATISTICS					
Tons paper sold*	89986	96546	99353	93684	100433
Tons pulp sold*	3046	1188	716	778	2024
Net paper sales	$12676	$16855	$19081	$17570	$19476
Paper sales price—average net per ton*	140.87	174.58	192.05	187.55	193.92
Total net sales—Paper division	$12999	$16982	$19165	$17653	$19686
Total net sales—Lumber division					
Total net sales—Combined	$12999	$16982	$19165	$17653	$19686

Potlatch Forests, Inc.

Statement of Income and Earned Surplus, 1908–1950

(OOO OMITTED)

	1908	1909	1910	1911	1912
Net sales	$1058	$1988	$2208	$1991	$2865
Cost of sales	1179	1747	1980	1895	2660
Gross Profit	(121)a	241	228	96	205
Other operating income	130	143	163	216	181
	9	384	391	312	386
Selling, general and administrative expenses, etc.	250	321	343	377	427
Profit from operations	(241)	63	48	(65)	(41)
Non-operative income, less changes .	34	82	72	81	67
Profit before taxes on income	(207)	145	120	16	26
Provision for taxes on income					
Net income for year	(207)	145	120	16	26
Prior years adjustments			2	(1)	1
Net income to surplus	(207)	145	122	15	27
Earned surplus, beginning of year ...	243	36	261	383	158
Appreciation—from capital surplus .					
Distribution				(240)	(720)
Other		80			
Earned surplus at end of year	$ 36	$ 261	$ 383	$ 158	($ 535)

a Parentheses indicate figures in red.

SOURCE: Account Books of Potlatch Forests, Inc., 1908–1950 (known as Potlatch Lumber Company, 1908–1928).

POTLATCH FORESTS, INC.

(OOO OMITTED)

	1913	1914	1915	1916	1917
Net sales	$2097	$2571	$2161	$2486	$ 2776
Cost of sales	1938	2987	2041	2149	1797
Gross Profit	159	(416)	120	337	979
Other operating income	183	221	208	194	221
	342	(195)	328	531	1200
Selling, general and administrative expenses, etc.	332	384	373	304	353
Profit from operations	10	(579)	(45)	227	847
Non-operative income, less changes .	89	191	119	146	101
Profit before taxes on income	99	(388)	74	373	948
Provision for taxes on income					
Net income for year	99	(388)	74	373	948
Prior years adjustments	(212)	(66)	(73)	(63)	575
Net income to surplus	(113)	(454)	1	310	1523
Earned surplus, beginning of year ...	(535)	(1048)	(2142)	(2861)	(3351)
Appreciation—from capital surplus .					
Distribution	(400)	(640)	(720)	(800)	(800)
Other					16106
Earned surplus at end of year	($1048)	($2142)	($2861)	($3351)	$13478

(000 OMITTED)

1918	1919	1920	1921	1922	1923	1924	1925
$ 2872	$ 3170	$ 5349	$ 1698	$ 2758	$ 4427	$ 4472	$ 4360
2007	2283	3146	1489	2663	2616	3525	3500
865	887	2203	209	95	1811	947	860
144	365	312	189	236	223	244	254
1009	1252	2515	398	331	2034	1191	1114
375	443	633	518	552	542	603	702
634	809	1882	(120)	(221)	1492	588	412
68	125	178	83	16	77	(531)	59
702	934	2060	(37)	(205)	1569	57	471
	94	457	12			169	63
702	840	1603	(49)	(205)	1569	(112)	408
(4)		32					
698	840	1635	(49)	(205)	1569	(112)	408
				15242	14397	15166	14174
13478	13936	14536	15611				
(240)	(240)	(560)	(320)	(640)	(800)	(880)	(640)
$13936	$14536	$15611	$15242	$14397	$15166	$14174	$13942

POTLATCH FORESTS, INC.

(OOO OMITTED)

	1926	1927	1928	1929	1930
Net sales	$ 3717	$ 3077	$ 3518	$ 3820	$ 3037
Cost of sales	3402	3079	3365	3842	3188
Gross Profit	315	(2)	153	(22)	(151)
Other operating income	259	263	367	293	219
	574	261	520	271	68
Selling, general and administrative expenses, etc.	652	598	621	626	709
Profit from operations	(78)	(337)	(101)	(355)	(641)
Non-operative income, less changes .	58	61	69	72	69
Profit before taxes on income	(20)	(276)	(32)	(283)	(572)
Provision for taxes on income	3				
Net income for year	(23)	(276)	(32)	(283)	(572)
Prior years adjustments		5			
Net income to surplus	(23)	(271)	(32)	(283)	(572)
Earned surplus, beginning of year ...	13942	13439	12848	12336	12053
Appreciation—from capital surplus .					
Distribution	(480)	(320)	(480)		
Other					
Earned surplus at end of year	$13439	$12848	$12336	$12053	$11481

(000 OMITTED)

1931	1932	1933	1934	1935	1936	1937	1938
$5454	$2520	$3565	$4030	$6034	$8051	$9686	$6834
6927	3993	2625	3675	5363	6888	7733	6279
(1473)	(1473)	940	355	671	1163	1953	555
191	64	155	41	108	100	80	155
(1282)	(1409)	1095	396	779	1263	2033	710
1166	785	805	791	807	861	968	794
(2448)	(2194)	290	(395)	(28)	402	1065	(84)
(124)	(607)	(696)	(469)	(329)	(481)	(826)	(508)
(2572)	(2801)	(406)	(864)	(357)	(79)	239	(592)
						50	
(2572)	(2801)	(406)	(864)	(357)	(79)	189	(592)
13		(81)	(1)	15	(44)	312	(20)
(2559)	(2801)	(487)	(865)	(342)	(123)	501	(612)
11481	(2559)	(5360)	(5847)	(6712)	(7054)	(7177)	(6676)
(11481)							
($2559)	($5360)	($5847)	($6712)	($7054)	($7177)	($6676)	($7288)

POTLATCH FORESTS, INC.

(000 OMITTED)

	1939	1940	1941	1942	1943
Net sales	$8036	$10285	$13453	$16768	$16487
Cost of sales	7393	8685	10249	13443	13633
Gross Profit	643	1600	3204	3325	2854
Other operating income	157	144	144	354	289
	800	1744	3348	3679	3143
Selling, general and administrative expenses, etc.	807	991	1169	1552	1400
Profit from operations	(7)	753	2179	2127	1743
Non-operative income, less changes .	(249)	(173)	(100)	97	(24)
Profit before taxes on income	(256)	580	2079	2224	1719
Provision for taxes on income		68	822	983	737
Net income for year	(256)	512	1257	1241	982
Prior years adjustments	1	(265)	28	84	(105)
Net income to surplus	(255)	247	1285	1325	877
Earned surplus, beginning of year ...	(7288)	(7543)	(7296)	(6011)	(4686)
Appreciation—from capital surplus .					
Distribution					
Other					
Earned surplus at end of year	($7543)	($ 7296)	($ 6011)	($ 4686)	($ 3809)

(000 OMITTED)

1944	1945	1946	1947	1948	1949	1950
$15273	$14149	$13654	$17299	$25765	$25929	$36898
12383	11935	11485	11479	15456	17199	22538
2890	2214	2169	5820	10309	8730	14360
181	173	334	569	447	225	290
3071	2387	2503	6389	10756	8955	14650
1261	1391	1491	1888	1900	2264	2894
1810	996	1012	4501	8856	6691	11756
84	72	151	311	413	140	201
1894	1068	1163	4812	9269	6831	11957
723	375	392	1850	3605	2537	5520
1171	693	771	2962	5664	4294	6437
(104)	(33)	(200)	(337)	(241)	(944)	(90)
1067	660	571	2625	5423	3350	6347
(3809)	(2742)		305	2399	7246	10064
	3375	(266)	(531)	(532)	(332)	(1063)
	(1293)			(44)		375
($ 2742)	—	$ 305	$ 2399	$ 7246	$10064	$15723

Weyerhaeuser Timber Company

Sales and Net Income, 1900–1940

(ooo OMITTED)

Year	Sales	Net Income	Year	Sales	Net Income
1900		($54)[a]	1921	13877	(1719)
1901		(42)	1922	19792	3042
1902	$ 308	209	1923	24775	5395
1903	286	6	1924	19936	4431
1904	403	206	1925	21471	4908
1905	488	1406	1926	20963	4729
1906	691	2556	1927	21463	2890
1907	744	1076	1928	24156	4112
1908	406	507	1929	25118	5319
1909	724	1366	1930	22800	(314)
1910	803	1465	1931	19399	(2389)
1911	814	930	1932	12597	(2911)
1912	1007	2247	1933	16919	347
1913	1150	1261	1934	21779	480
1914	997	90	1935	28221	1879
1915	2622	(354)	1936	43062	4368
1916	5508	28	1937	46373	6801
1917	7256	472	1938	36503	2098
1918	11293	1937	1939	45767	4432
1919	18445	2632	1940	56016	8393
1920	24317	3754			

[a] Parentheses indicate figures in red.

SOURCE: Accounts of Weyerhaeuser Timber Company, 1900–1940.

Weyerhaeuser Timber Company[1] and Subsidiaries

Summary of Operations, 1941–1960

(OOO OMITTED)

	1941	1942	1943	1944	1945
Sales	$75202	$ 96654	$93591	$92807	$76265
Other Income	5338	6618	6165	5064	3643
Total	$80540	$103272	$99756	$97871	$79908
Cost of Goods Sold and Expenses	$49365	$ 64457	$62332	$61881	$54688
Depletion and Depreciation	8985	8746	8999	7947	5772
Taxes (Other Than Federal Income Taxes)	2772	3017	2854	3161	2924
Other	438	493	513	670	428
Net Income Before Federal Income Taxes	$18980	$ 26559	$25058	$24212	$16096
Federal Income Taxes	9946	17385	16281	14041	7541
Net Income	$ 9034	$ 9174	$ 8777	$10171	$ 8555

1. The name was changed to Weyerhaeuser Company in 1959.

SOURCE: Accounts of Weyerhaeuser Timber Company, 1941–1960.

WEYERHAEUSER TIMBER COMPANY AND SUBSIDIARIES

(OOO OMITTED)

	1946	1947	1948	1949
Sales	$83243	$128024	$136766	$155663
Other Income	3764	4105	4890	4745
Total	$87007	$132129	$141656	$160408
Cost of Goods Sold and Expenses ...	$55907	$ 75028	$ 81129	$104711
Depletion and Depreciation	5966	6192	7531	10599
Taxes (Other Than Federal Income Taxes)	3256	4295	5072	5981
Other	608	1827	2000	884
Net Income Before Federal Income Taxes	$21270	$ 44787	$ 45924	$ 38233
Federal Income Taxes	7753	16968	16946	13600
Net Income	$13517	$ 27819	$ 28978	$ 24633

(OOO OMITTED)

1950	1951	1952	1953	1954	1955	1956
$176587	$213175	$260001	$276796	$262497	$316733	$324129
5952	6672	4579	6585	6571	7702	7405
$182539	$219847	$264580	$283381	$269068	$324435	$331534
$112292	$127644	$179138	$193035	$183008	$210817	$217697
10623	12704	14288	17964	18099	22491	24310
6025	7314	8410	9005	8751	10786	12480
991	639	638	526			
$ 52608	$ 71546	$ 62106	$ 62851	$ 59210	$ 80341	$ 77047
19700	31600	25400	26100	23700	31100	25600
$ 32908	$ 39946	$ 36706	$ 36751	$ 35510	$ 49241	$ 51447

WEYERHAEUSER TIMBER COMPANY AND SUBSIDIARIES

(OOO OMITTED)

	1957	1958	1959	1960
Sales	$420601	$410360	$458339	$457916
Other Income	6379	7144	9196	8823
Total	$426980	$417504	$467535	$466739
Cost of Goods Sold and Expenses ...	$290641	$282682	$312247	$335531
Depletion and Depreciation	37578	39468	40119	39550
Taxes (Other Than Federal Income Taxes)	15636	15739	17362	20207
Other				
Net Income Before Federal Income Taxes	$ 83125	$ 79615	$ 97807	$ 71451
Federal Income Taxes	29700	30000	37400	23700
Net Income	$ 53425	$ 49615	$ 60407	$ 47751

Wood Conversion Company

Income and Earned Surplus, 1922–1950

(000 OMITTED)

	1922	1923	1924	1925	1926
NET SALES	$ 38	$ 92	$225	$351	$524
COST OF GOODS SOLD	24	43	107	134	171
GROSS PROFIT	14	49	118	217	353
SELLING, SHIPPING, AND GENERAL EXPENSES	1	91	142	219	329
PROFIT FROM OPERATIONS	13	(42)a	(24)	(2)	24
OTHER INCOME	1			3	4
GROSS INCOME	14	(42)	(24)	1	28
INCOME CHARGES:					
Cash discounts on sales	1	1	3	6	8
Experimental, machine written off					
Other—Retirement plan costs, etc.					
Total	1	1	3	6	8
INCOME BEFORE INCOME TAXES	13	(43)	(27)	(5)	20
FEDERAL AND STATE INCOME TAXES	1				
NET INCOME FOR THE YEAR	12	(43)	(27)	(5)	20
EARNED SURPLUS AT BEGINNING OF THE YEAR		12	(31)	(58)	(63)
SURPLUS CREDIT—EXCESS OF INSURANCE PROCEEDS OVER BOOK VALUE OF PROPERTY LOST BY FIRE					
GROSS SURPLUS	12	(31)	(58)	(63)	(43)
SURPLUS CHARGES:					
Dividends paid					
Surplus transferred to capital stock account (Other)					
Total					
EARNED SURPLUS AT END OF THE YEAR	$ 12	($ 31)	($ 58)	($ 63)	($ 43)
STATISTICS—BASED ON SHARES OUTSTANDING Nov. 30, 1952:					
Earned per share	$0.04	($0.15)	($0.09)	($0.02)	$0.07
Dividend per share					
Book value per share at end of year	$1.76	$3.00	$3.25	$3.75	$4.16

a Parentheses denote red ink.

SOURCE: Accounts of Wood Conversion Company, 1922–1950.

WOOD CONVERSION COMPANY

(000 OMITTED)

	1927	1928	1929	1930	1931
NET SALES	$944	$1445	$1973	$1855	$1401
COST OF GOODS SOLD	400	603	847	861	706
GROSS PROFIT	544	842	1126	994	695
SELLING, SHIPPING, AND GENERAL EXPENSES	495	726	978	1052	842
PROFIT FROM OPERATIONS	49	116	148	(58)	(147)
OTHER INCOME	5	7	11	11	8
GROSS INCOME	54	123	159	(47)	(139)
INCOME CHARGES:					
Cash discounts on sales	13	23	29	27	24
Experimental, machine written off Other—Retirement plan costs, etc.	b	b	4	21	24
Total	13	23	33	48	48
INCOME BEFORE INCOME TAXES	41	100	126	(95)	(187)
FEDERAL AND STATE INCOME TAXES ..		5	13	14	
NET INCOME FOR THE YEAR	41	95	113	(109)	(187)
EARNED SURPLUS AT BEGINNING OF THE YEAR	(43)	(2)	93	127	(72)
SURPLUS CREDIT—EXCESS OF INSURANCE PROCEEDS OVER BOOK VALUE OF PROPERTY LOST BY FIRE .			1	b	
GROSS SURPLUS	(2)	93	207	18	(259)
SURPLUS CHARGES:					
Dividends paid				90	
Surplus transferred to capital stock account (Other)			80		(1)
Total			80	90	(1)
EARNED SURPLUS AT END OF THE YEAR	(2)	$ 93	$ 127	($ 72)	($ 260)
STATISTICS—BASED ON SHARES OUTSTANDING Nov. 30, 1952:					
Earned per share	$0.14	$ 0.33	$ 0.39	($ 0.38)	($ 0.64)
Dividend per share				0.31	
Book value per share at end of year	$5.16	$ 5.49	$ 5.61	$ 4.92	$ 4.28

b Less than $500.

(OOO OMITTED)

1932	1933[c]	1934	1935	1936	1937	1938
$ 701	$ 829	$1400	$2190	$3079	$3815	$3297
459	590	991	1339	1877	2290	2107
242	239	409	851	1202	1525	1190
494	394	551	588	736	875	913
(252)	(155)	(142)	263	466	650	277
5	6	5	13	19	21	16
(247)	(149)	(137)	276	485	671	293
11	11	21	37	53	63	55
69	37	68	94	92	70	47
80	48	89	131	145	133	102
(327)	(197)	(226)	145	340	538	191
			29	50	113	34
(327)	(197)	(226)	116	290	425	157
(260)	(643)	(840)	(1067)	(941)	(651)	(226)
b	1	1	16			
(587)	(839)	(1065)	(935)	(651)	(226)	(69)
						145
56	1	2	6			
56	1	2	6			145
($ 643)	($ 840)	($1067)	($ 941)	($ 651)	($ 226)	($ 214)
($ 1.13)	($ 0.68)	($ 0.78)	$ 0.40	$ 1.00	$ 1.47	$ 0.54
						$ 0.50
$ 2.96	$ 2.27	$ 1.49	$ 1.93	$ 2.93	$ 5.26	$ 7.37

b Less than $500.
c Eleven months ending Nov. 30, 1933.

WOOD CONVERSION COMPANY

(OOO OMITTED)

	1939	1940	1941	1942	1943
NET SALES	$3832	$4129	$4649	$5193	$5343
COST OF GOODS SOLD	2245	2593	2885	3282	3500
GROSS PROFIT	1587	1536	1764	1911	1843
SELLING, SHIPPING, AND GENERAL EXPENSES	951	982	1055	1006	1055
PROFIT FROM OPERATIONS	636	554	709	905	788
OTHER INCOME	17	23	26	33	55
GROSS INCOME	653	577	735	938	843
INCOME CHARGES:					
Cash discounts on sales	64	73	81	96	103
Experimental, machine written off Other—Retirement plan costs, etc.	24	35	23	10	5
Total	88	108	104	106	108
INCOME BEFORE INCOME TAXES	565	469	631	832	735
FEDERAL AND STATE INCOME TAXES ..	126	89	177	415	372
NET INCOME FOR THE YEAR	439	380	454	417	363
EARNED SURPLUS AT BEGINNING OF THE YEAR	(214)	80	315	624	896
SURPLUS CREDIT—EXCESS OF INSURANCE PROCEEDS OVER BOOK VALUE OF PROPERTY LOST BY FIRE .					
GROSS SURPLUS	225	460	769	1041	1259
SURPLUS CHARGES:					
Dividends paid	145	145	145	145	145
Surplus transferred to capital stock account (Other)					
Total	145	145	145	145	145
EARNED SURPLUS AT END OF THE YEAR	$ 80	$ 315	$ 624	$ 896	$ 1114
STATISTICS—BASED ON SHARES OUTSTANDING Nov. 30, 1952:					
Earned per share	$ 1.51	$ 1.31	$ 1.57	$ 1.44	$ 1.25
Dividend per share	$ 0.50	$ 0.50	$ 0.50	$ 0.50	$ 0.50
Book value per share at end of year	$ 8.38	$ 9.19	$10.26	$11.20	$11.95

(OOO OMITTED)

1944	1945	1946	1947	1948	1949	1950
$5072	$5985	$8084	$11307	$15561	$14130	$18494
3586	4140	5462	7407	10526	9721	11761
1486	1845	2622	3900	5035	4409	6733
1063	1169	1165	1380	1817	2205	2712
423	676	1457	2520	3218	2204	4021
107	48	95	90	95	110	91
530	724	1552	2610	3313	2314	4112
98	115	157	114	281	256	313
16	b	72	84	214	190	175
114	115	229	198	495	446	488
416	609	1323	2412	2818	1868	3624
145	285	569	957	1136	737	1687
271	324	754	1454	1682	1131	1937
1114	1240	1419	2028	3385	4922	5908
			47			
1385	1564	2173	3530	5067	6053	7845
145	145	145	145	145	145	217
145	145	145	145	145	145	217
$ 1240	$ 1419	$ 2028	$ 3385	$ 4922	$ 5908	$ 7628
$ 0.93	$ 1.12	$ 2.60	$ 5.02	$ 5.80	$ 3.90	$ 6.68
$ 0.50	$ 0.50	$ 0.50	$ 0.50	$ 0.50	$ 0.50	$ 0.75
$12.38	$13.00	$15.10	$ 19.77	$ 25.07	$ 28.48	$ 34.41

Officers and Directors of Five Companies

Boise Payette Lumber Company (Idaho, 1914–1931)—
Boise Payette Lumber Company[1] (Del., 1931–1952)

PRESIDENT

Name	Term
William Carson	1914–1932[2]
E. P. Clapp	1933–1946
S. G. Moon	1946–1949
Norton Clapp	1949–

VICE PRESIDENT

Name	Term	Name	Term
C. A. Barton	1914–1931	W. W. Burns	1945–1950
S. G. Moon	1932–1945	A. O. Sheldon	1948–
C. W. Gamble	1945–1952	J. L. Jeremiassen	1949–
Norton Clapp	1946–1949	J. L. Aram	1950–

SECRETARY

F. S. Bell	1914–1919	G. R. Little	1929–1950
F. H. Thatcher	1919–1929	G. H. Osgood	1950–

TREASURER

F. E. Weyerhaeuser	1914–1941	W. W. Burns	1949–1950
C. D. Weyerhaeuser	1941–1947	Arden E. Dresser	1950–
G. F. Jewett	1947–1949		

COMPTROLLER

E. A. Aitchison	1950–

1. The name was changed to Boise Cascade Corporation in 1957.
2. At the first meeting of the Board of Directors of Boise Payette Lumber Company of Delaware on April 30, 1931, A. A. Fraser was elected president, W. L. Johnson vice president, and C. W. Gamble secretary, and all resigned Jan. 1, 1932.

GENERAL MANAGER

S. G. Moon	1932–1945

DIRECTORS[1]

Name	Term	Name	Term
William Carson	1914–1932	E. P. Clapp	1924–1946
S. G. Moon	1914–	C. A. Weyerhaeuser	1927–1930
William Musser	1914–1919,	G. R. Little	1932–1950
	1920–1923,	R. E. Slaughter	1933–1948
	1925–1933	G. F. Jewett	1933–
F. E. Weyerhaeuser	1914–1933	C. D. Weyerhaeuser	1941–
F. H. Thatcher	1914–1919	C. W. Gamble	1941–1952
Henry Turrish	1914–1924	R. D. Musser	1941–1952
C. A. Barton	1914–1931	Carleton Blunt	1944–1952
Lyon Cobb	1914–1921	W. S. Rosenberry, Jr.	1944–1950
E. M. Hoover	1914–1916	Norton Clapp	1946–
J. P. Weyerhaeuser	1916–1927,	J. M. Musser	1943–
	1930–1935	F. D. McCulloch	1950–
F. S. Bell	1919–1934	F. R. Titcomb	1951–
R. D. Musser	1919–1920,	A. C. Helmholz	1952–
	1941–	G. H. Osgood	1952–
W. W. Burns	1921–1951	W. D. Eberle	1952–
C. R. Musser	1923–1925,		
	1933–1950		

Northwest Paper Company (W. Va.)—
The Northwest Paper Company (Minn.), 1898–1952

PRESIDENT

Name	*Term*
R. M. Weyerhaeuser	1898–1928
H. C. Hornby	1928–1936
H. H. Irvine	1936
Stuart B. Copeland	1936–

VICE PRESIDENT

Name	*Term*	*Name*	*Term*
N. H. Brokaw	1898–1901	W. H. Kenety	1928–1939
R. D. Musser	1901–1925	W. B. Driscoll	1928–1938
C. I. McNair	1910–1924	S. L. Coy	1928–1940
H. C. Hornby	1925–1928	C. W. Boyce	1940

1. The interim (1931–1932) Board of Directors of Boise Payette Lumber Company of Delaware was made up of A. A. Fraser, W. A. Barton, E. H. Barton, C. W. Gamble, G. H. Batcheller, J. S. Hansen, H. C. Shellworth, E. C. MacGregor, and W. L. Johnson.

Name	Term	Name	Term
L. F. Porter	1940–1948	H. T. Kendall, Jr.	1948–
C. I. McNair, Jr.	1940–	B. W. McEachern	1948–
F. A. Kelly	1941–		

SECRETARY

Name	Term	Name	Term
Edgar M. Hoover	1898–1905	H. J. Hamann	1917–1919
Huntington Taylor	1905–1916	Hugo Schlenk	1928–1938
C. I. McNair, Jr.	1916–1917, 1919–1928	E. P. Dupont	1938–1948
		E. W. Spoor	1948–

TREASURER

Name	Term	Name	Term
R. D. Musser	1898–1904, 1916–1934	Hugo Schlenk	1934–1938
		E. P. Dupont	1938–1948
Huntington Taylor	1904–1916	E. W. Spoor	1948–

GENERAL MANAGER

Name	Term	Name	Term
C. I. McNair	1898–1924	W. H. Kenety	1926–1928
R. M. Weyerhaeuser	1924–1926		

CHAIRMAN OF THE BOARD OF DIRECTORS

Name	Term	Name	Term
R. M. Weyerhaeuser	1928–1936, 1940–1946	F. K. Weyerhaeuser	1936–1940, 1947–

DIRECTORS

Name	Term	Name	Term
R. M. Weyerhaeuser	1898–1946	R. E. Peck	1928–1936, 1937–
C. I. McNair	1898–1924		
C. A. Weyerhaeuser	1898–1930	Hugo Schlenk	1928–1936
E. M. Hoover	1898–1908	F. C. Denkmann	1928–1929
R. D. Musser	1898–1934	L. F. Shaw	1928–1936
N. H. Brokaw	1898–1901	C. I. McNair, Jr.	1928–1936
C. R. Musser	1898–1936	Fred Reimers	1929–1936
E. P. Denkmann	1898–1901, 1928–1931	W. B. Driscoll	1930–1938
		T. B. Davis	1931–1936
F. E. Weyerhaeuser	1898–1928	J. M. Musser	1936–
L. B. Grant	1901–1915	F. K. Weyerhaeuser	1936–
Huntington Taylor	1901–1917	S. B. Copeland	1936–
William Musser	1904–1905	B. F. Dow	1936–
W. K. McNair	1908–1936	Frederick Weyerhaeuser	1938–
H. Oldenburg	1915–1926	W. S. Rosenberry, Jr.	1947–1949
M. D. McAlpine	1918–1926	C. C. Cook	1947–
H. C. Hornby	1925–1951	Norton Clapp	1950–
W. H. Kenety	1926–1936	R. S. Schmitt	1951–
G. R. Little	1927–	L. F. Shaw	1951–
E. W. Davis	1928–	J. P. Weyerhaeuser, III	1952–

EXECUTIVE COMMITTEE

R. M. Weyerhaeuser	1928–1936, 1938–1946	G. R. Little	1936–1951
H. C. Hornby	1928–1936	J. M. Musser	1936–
W. H. Kenety	1928–1936	F. K. Weyerhaeuser	1936–
E. W. Davis	1936–	Frederick Weyerhaeuser	1947–
W. B. Driscoll	1936–1938	C. C. Cook	1951–

Potlatch Lumber Company, 1903–1931—
Potlatch Forests, Inc., 1931–1952

PRESIDENT

Name	Term
F. H. Thatcher	1903
C. A. Weyerhaeuser	1903–1930
J. P. Weyerhaeuser, Jr.	1930–1935
R. M. Weyerhaeuser	1935–1946
G. F. Jewett	1946–1949
W. P. Davis	1949–

CHAIRMAN OF THE BOARD OF DIRECTORS

G. F. Jewett	1949–

CHAIRMAN OF THE EXECUTIVE COMMITTEE

J. P. Weyerhaeuser, Jr.	1931–1933	G. F. Jewett	1946–1950
R. M. Weyerhaeuser	1933–1936	F. K. Weyerhaeuser	1950–1952
Laird Bell	1936–1938	G. F. Jewett	1952–

VICE PRESIDENT

Henry Turrish	1903–1926	C. L. Billings	1935–1949
H. J. Richardson	1927–1931	E. W. Davis	1949–
Laird Bell	1931–1949	F. K. Weyerhaeuser	1949–1952
G. F. Jewett	1935–1946		

SECRETARY

F. S. Bell	1903–1929	H. L. Torsen	1950–
George R. Little	1929–1950		

TREASURER

C. L. Andrews	1903	A. W. Laird	1911–1931
R. D. Musser	1903–1911	G. F. Jewett	1931–1949
F. S. Bell	1911	H. L. Torsen	1949–

GENERAL MANAGER

William Deary	1903–1913	J. P. Weyerhaeuser, Jr.	1931–1933
A. W. Laird	1913–1931	C. L. Billings	1933–1949

DIRECTORS

C. A. Weyerhaeuser	1903–1930	Laird Bell	1931–1950
Henry Turrish	1903–1927	F. K. Weyerhaeuser	1931–1947,
F. H. Thatcher	1903–1921		1949–1952
J. B. Kehl	1903–1909	E. W. Davis	1931–
R. D. Musser	1903, 1927-	George R. Little	1931–1952
C. R. Musser	1903–	W. S. Rosenberry	1931–1932
J. P. Weyerhaeuser	1909–1936	R. M. Weyerhaeuser	1932–1947
E. P. Clapp	1921–1947	C. L. Billings	1936–1949
H. J. Richardson	1921–1936	Frederick Weyerhaeuser	1947–
F. S. Bell	1921–1936	Norton Clapp	1947–
J. P. Weyerhaeuser, Jr.	1930–1935,	C. Davis Weyerhaeuser	1947–1949,
	1936–1952		1950–
F. W. Reimers	1931–1935,	W. P. Davis	1949–
	1936–	Thomas C. Taylor	1952–
T. J. Humbird	1931–1935	John W. Titcomb	1952–
G. F. Jewett	1931–	John A. Humbird	1952–

Weyerhaeuser Timber Company[1]
January 18, 1900–May 22, 1962

PRESIDENT

Name	*Term*
F. Weyerhaeuser	1900–1914
J. P. Weyerhaeuser	1914–1928
F. S. Bell	1928–1934
F. E. Weyerhaeuser	1934–1945
H. H. Irvine	1946–1947
J. P. Weyerhaeuser, Jr.	1947–1956
F. K. Weyerhaeuser	1956–1960
Norton Clapp	1960–

CHAIRMAN OF THE BOARD OF DIRECTORS

Name	*Term*	*Name*	*Term*
F. S. Bell	1934–1938	Norton Clapp	1957–1960
Laird Bell	1947–1955	F. K. Weyerhaeuser	1960–
F. K. Weyerhaeuser	1955–1957		

1. The name was changed to Weyerhaeuser
   Company in 1959.

CHAIRMAN OF THE EXECUTIVE COMMITTEE

Geo. S. Long	1929–1930	Laird Bell	1947–1955
F. S. Bell	1931–1934	F. K. Weyerhaeuser	1955–1957
F. E. Weyerhaeuser	1934–1945	Edmund Hayes	1957–
H. H. Irvine	1946–1947		

EXECUTIVE VICE PRESIDENT

Name	Term	Name	Term
J. P. Weyerhaeuser, Jr.	1933–1947	G. H. Weyerhaeuser	1961–
Chas. H. Ingram	1956–1958	J. E. Nolan	1961–
Howard W. Morgan	1961–		

VICE PRESIDENT

W. H. Laird	1900–1910	Edmond M. Cook	1948–1949
F. S. Bell	1910–1928	F. K. Weyerhaeuser	1950–1955
Geo. S. Long	1918–1930	W. P. Gullander	1952–1960
F. E. Weyerhaeuser	1928–1934	J. E. Nolan	1952–1961
W. L. McCormick	1929–1933	Howard W. Morgan	1953–1961
A. W. Clapp	1931–1946	Norton Clapp	1955–1957
J. P. Weyerhaeuser, Jr.	1933–1933	John M. Musser	1957–
Laird Bell	1934–1947	John L. Aram	1957–
W. L. McCormick	1937–1953	C. D. Weyerhaeuser	1958–1958
Edmund Hayes	1946–1957	G. H. Weyerhaeuser	1958–1961
Chas. H. Ingram	1947–1956	Bernard L. Orell	1958–
David Graham	1948–1951	F. Lowry Wyatt	1960–

RESIDENT AGENT—GENERAL MANAGER

Name	Term	Name	Term
Geo. S. Long	1900–1929	Chas. H. Ingram	1936–1956
F. R. Titcomb	1929–1936		

SECRETARY

R. L. McCormick	1900–1911	Norton Clapp	1938–1943
Geo. S. Long	1911–1918	W. L. McCormick	1943–1945
W. L. McCormick	1918–1938	George S. Long, Jr.	1945–1960
		Robert W. Boyd	1961–

TREASURER

F. Weyerhaeuser	1900–1906	F. K. Weyerhaeuser	1946–1948
F. E. Weyerhaeuser	1906–1928	A. D. Orr	1948–1952
H. H. Irvine	1928–1946	H. E. Nelson	1952–

COMPTROLLER

A. D. Orr	1945–1948	Robert W. Boyd	1948–

GENERAL COUNSEL

A. W. Clapp	1930–1946	J. E. Nolan	1948–1961
Laird Bell	1947–1948	Daniel C. Smith	1961–
Edmond M. Cook	1948		

DIRECTORS

Name	Term	Name	Term
	Jan.–	A. W. Clapp	1931–1946
Arthur F. Albertson	June 1900	J. P. Weyerhaeuser, Jr.	1933–1956
William Carson	1900–1932	Laird Bell	1934–1961
F. C. Denkmann	1900–1929	R. M. Weyerhaeuser	1935–1946
C. H. Ingram	1900–1906	George R. Little	1938–1953
Thos. Irvine	1900–1902	Edmund Hayes	1938–
William H. Laird	1900–1910	Norton Clapp	1946–
A. Lamb	1900–1901	F. K. Weyerhaeuser	1946–
Geo. S. Long	1900–1930	E. W. Davis	1947–1953
Robert L. McCormick	1900–1911	Chas. H. Ingram	1947–
S. T. McKnight	1900–1908	Edmond M. Cook	1949–
P. M. Musser	1900–1919	O. D. Fisher	1949–1961
F. Weyerhaeuser	1900–1914	John M. Musser	1950–
L. Lamb	1901–1914	Carleton Blunt	1953–
H. H. Irvine	1902–1947	Henry T. McKnight	1953–1957
F. E. Weyerhaeuser	1906–1913, 1914–1945	C. D. Weyerhaeuser	1953–
		J. P. Weyerhaeuser III	1957–1960
F. H. Thatcher	1909–1921	Herbert M. Kieckhefer	1957–
F. S. Bell	1910–1938	Robert H. Kieckhefer	1957–
William L. McCormick	1911–1953	George C. Crosby	1957–
J. P. Weyerhaeuser	1913–1928, 1930–1935	John H. Hauberg, Jr.	1958–
		Howard W. Morgan	1960–
H. J. Richardson	1914–1947	G. H. Weyerhaeuser	1960–
C. R. Musser	1919–1950	Thomas C. Taylor	1961–
E. P. Clapp	1921–1946	Joseph W. Auchter	1962–
C. A. Weyerhaeuser	1928–1930	Joseph E. Nolan	1962–
Fred W. Reimers	1929–1934, 1938–1958		

Wood Conversion Company 1921–1952

PRESIDENT

Name	Term
W. Carson	1921–1932
R. M. Weyerhaeuser	1933–1946
E. W. Davis	1947–

FIRST VICE PRESIDENT

J. P. Weyerhaeuser	1921–1924	E. W. Davis	1939–1944
F. S. Bell	1924–1938		

SECOND VICE PRESIDENT

R. M. Weyerhaeuser	1921–1933	E. W. Davis	1937–1939
H. H. Irvine	1933–1947	G. R. Little	1939–1944

VICE PRESIDENT—SALES

P. A. Ward	1940–1944

EXECUTIVE VICE PRESIDENT

E. W. Davis	1944–1947

VICE PRESIDENT AND GENERAL MANAGER

P. A. Ward	1944–1944	D. M. Pattie	1947–

VICE PRESIDENT

G. R. Little	1944–

SECRETARY

H. J. Richardson	1921–1932	C. M. Rowe	1945–
F. Weyerhaeuser	1932–1945		

TREASURER

C. R. Musser	1921–1921	R. D. Musser	1921–

DIRECTORS

F. S. Bell	1921–1938	E. W. Davis	1927–
Geo. S. Long	1921–1930	George R. Little	1931–
W. Carson	1921–1932	H. H. Irvine	1933–1947
C. R. Musser	1921–	Walter B. Driscoll	1933–1938
T. J. Humbird	1921–1933	Norton Clapp	1939–1942
R. M. Weyerhaeuser	1921–1946	F. Weyerhaeuser	1939–
F. E. Weyerhaeuser	1921–1945	J. Burgess	1941–1942
H. J. Richardson	1921–1948	J. P. Weyerhaeuser, Jr.	1946–
H. C. Hornby	1921–1948	F. K. Weyerhaeuser	1947–
C. I. McNair	1921–1925	Laird Bell	1948–
H. F. Weiss	1921–1940	C. C. Cook	1948–
H. Oldenburg	1925–1926	John M. Musser	1948–

List of Sources Cited

I. *Primary Sources*

MANUSCRIPTS AND COMPANY PAPERS

Allied Building Credits
Annual reports, auditor's reports, correspondence, company papers in Weyerhaeuser Sales Company offices, St. Paul, now a division of Weyerhaeuser Company.

Bartlett, W. W.
Personal papers in the Eau Claire Public Library, Eau Claire, Wisconsin.

Beef Slough Manufacturing, Booming, Log Driving and Transportation Company. Record books, rafting accounts (1875–1876), and annual statements. Minnesota Historical Society, St. Paul.

Blackwood, Garfield. "History of Lumbering at Fleetwood, Minnesota." Manuscript in the St. Louis County Historical Society, St. Louis.

Boise Payette Lumber Company
Annual reports, company papers, minutes of the meetings of the Board of Directors, and the McCoy correspondence in archives of Boise Cascade Corporation, Boise, Idaho.

Brayer, H. O. "Survey of the Weyerhaeuser Records."
Weyerhaeuser Sales Company Office, St. Paul.

Chapman, C. S. "Report on the Timberlands of the Northern and Cloquet Lumber Companies." Sixty-five-page typescript in the Laird, Norton Company Papers, Winona, Minnesota.

Chippewa Lumber & Boom Company
Company papers and minute books. Minnesota Historical Society, St. Paul.

Chippewa River Improvement & Log Driving Company
Articles of Association, patents, stock book. Minnesota Historical Society, St. Paul.

Chippewa River & Menomonie Railway Company
Miscellaneous company papers. Minnesota Historical Society, St. Paul.

Clearwater Timber Company
Miscellaneous papers and accounts in files of Potlatch Forests, Inc., Lewiston, Idaho, and in F. Weyerhaeuser Company vaults, St. Paul.

Cloquet Lumber Company
Minute books, annual reports, and logging inventories, 1896–1918, in vaults of The Northwest Paper Company, Cloquet, Minnesota.

Coast Lumber Company
Minute books and company papers in F. Weyerhaeuser Company vaults, St. Paul.

Cochrane, C. M. "History of Southern Investments"
Manuscript in Frederick E. Weyerhaeuser Papers, St. Paul.

Crowe, Isaac
Papers in Minnesota Historical Society, St. Paul.

Donner, W. E., and Musser, C. R. "The Musser Lumber Interest"
Manuscript in possession of John M. Musser, St. Paul, Minnesota.

Duluth Logging & Contracting Company
Annual reports in vaults of The Northwest Paper Company, Cloquet.

Duluth & Northeastern Railroad Company
Annual reports, minute books, and company correspondence in vaults of The
Northwest Paper Company, Cloquet.

Dunham, Harold H. "Government Handout: A Study in the Administration of
the Public Lands, 1875–1891" (lithographed, Columbia University, Ph.D. dissertation, 1941).

Engberg, George D. "Labor in the Lake States Lumber Industry, 1830–1920"
(unpublished Ph.D. dissertation, University of Minnesota, 1949).

Fells, K.
Private papers and correspondence.

General Land Office Records. Timber Division
Infractions and papers. National Archives, Washington, D.C.

General Timber Service
Annual reports, auditor's reports, and correspondence in F. Weyerhaeuser Company vaults and in files of Weyerhaeuser Sales Company, St. Paul.

Gillman, Frank H.
Personal papers and correspondence. Minnesota Historical Society, St. Paul.

Henry, Captain Charles Harmon
"Notebooks, 1868–1911" in the Frederick E. Weyerhaeuser Record File, St.
Paul.

Hornby, H. C. "Review of the History of the Cloquet Lumber Company"
Manuscript in the Cloquet Lumber Company Papers.

Humbird, John A. "White River Lumber Company"
Manuscript in possession of the author, Vancouver, British Columbia.

Idaho White Pine Bureau
Memoranda and agreements in F. E. Weyerhaeuser Papers.

Idaho White Pine Manufacturer's Sales Agency
Miscellaneous papers in Laird Norton Company Papers, Winona.

Immigration Land Company
Miscellaneous papers and annual reports in possession of John M. Musser, St.
Paul.

Ingram, Orrin H.
Personal Papers, Wisconsin State Historical Society, Madison.

Irvine, William
Personal papers and correspondence. In possession of Ruth Irvine Richter,
Manitowoc, Wisconsin.

Jewett Papers
Correspondence, in possession of Potlatch Forests, Inc., Coeur d'Alene, Idaho.

Johnson, Robert C. and Reynolds, A. R. "Distribution and Marketing."
Manuscript in possession of the Forest History Society, Inc., St. Paul.

Johnson-Wentworth Company
Annual reports, auditor's reports, and company papers in vaults of The Northwest Paper Company, Cloquet, and F. Weyerhaeuser Company, St. Paul.

Kendall, Harry T.
Correspondence in files of Weyerhaeuser Sales Company, St. Paul, Minnesota.

Kleven, B. J. "Wisconsin Lumber Industry" (unpublished MS thesis, University of Minnesota).

Knife Falls Boom Corporation
Minute books and articles of association in vaults of The Northwest Paper Company, Cloquet, Minnesota.

Laird, Norton Co. Papers
Letterbooks, incoming correspondence, ledgers, journals, account books, company reports. Minnesota Historical Society, St. Paul.

Laird, Norton Co. Papers
Miscellaneous papers in possession of families, Winona, Minnesota.

Little Falls Improvement & Navigation Company
Minute books, articles of incorporation, and miscellaneous papers in possession of John M. Musser, St. Paul.

Long, George S.
Papers and correspondence, including letterbooks. Weyerhaeuser Company, Tacoma.

Mason, David T. "The Lumber Industry in the Inland Empire" (unpublished Ph.D. dissertation, University of California, 1916).

Meany, Edmond S., Jr. "History of the Lumber Industry in the Pacific Northwest to 1917" (unpublished M.A. thesis, Harvard University, 1935).

Mesabe Southern Railway Company
Annual reports in vaults of The Northwest Paper Company, Cloquet.

Mississippi Land Company
Company papers and correspondence in First National Bank Building, St. Paul.

Mississippi Lumber Company
Minute books, annual reports, correspondence, and miscellaneous papers in files of Mississippi Land Company, St. Paul.

Mississippi River Logging Company
Minute books, Minnesota Historical Society, St. Paul.

Mississippi River Lumber Company
Minute books, company papers, minutes of stockholder and director meetings, annual reports, and journals in files of Mississippi Land Company, St. Paul.

Musser, R. D.
Personal papers and correspondence, letterbooks, office files, time books in possession of E. F. Johnson in Little Falls, Minnesota.

Musser-Sauntry Land, Logging & Manufacturing Company
Company papers, correspondence and account books in Minnesota Historical Society, St. Paul.

Nebagamon Lumber Company
Papers and account books in Minnesota Historical Society, St. Paul.

Northern Lumber Company
Minute books, articles of incorporation annual reports, logging inventories (1896–1918), and correspondence, in vaults of The Northwest Paper Company, Cloquet.

Northland Pine Company Papers
Annual reports, minute books, and the Deary-Kehl correspondence on land purchases in possession of John M. Musser, St. Paul, and in Laird, Norton Co. Papers, Winona.

Northwest Paper Company, The "Forest Survey Report of 1938," company papers, annual reports, and minute books of the Knife Falls Boom Corporation, in the company's vaults, Cloquet.

Norton, Matthew G.
Personal papers, correspondence, and letterbooks. In possession of family, Winona, Minnesota.

Payette Lumber & Manufacturing Company
Minute books and papers in possession of Boise Cascade Corporation, Boise, Idaho.

Pine Tree Lumber Company
Minute books, company papers, annual reports (1891–1920), treasurer's reports, and payroll accounts (1891–1911) in possession of John M. Musser, St. Paul.

Potlatch Forests, Inc.
Company papers, letter pressbooks, minute books, company reports, annual reports, and the Jewett Correspondence, in Lewiston, Potlatch, and Coeur d'Alene, Idaho.

Potlatch Lumber Company
Annual reports, company papers and correspondence, "4-L file," and a manuscript on "Potlatch, Idaho" in possession of Potlatch Forests, Inc., Lewiston, Idaho.

Renwick, Shaw & Crossett Company
Minute books in vaults of The Northwest Paper Company, Cloquet.

Rock Island Lumber & Manufacturing Company
Company papers, minute books, and some accounts in F. Weyerhaeuser Company vaults, St. Paul.

Rutledge Lumber & Manufacturing Company
Annual reports in F. Weyerhaeuser Company vaults, St. Paul.

St. Croix Lumberman's Dam & Boom Company
Miscellaneous papers in Laird, Norton Co., Winona.

St. Louis River Dam & Improvement Company
Minute books and company papers in vaults of The Northwest Paper Company, Cloquet.

St. Paul Boom Company
Annual reports in F. Weyerhaeuser Company vaults and in office of Mississippi Land Company, St. Paul.

Salo, Sarah Jenkins. "Timber Concentration in the Pacific Northwest, with special reference to the timber holdings of the Southern Pacific Railroad, the Northern Pacific Railroad, and the Weyerhaeuser Timber Company" (unpublished Ph.D. Dissertation, Columbia University, 1945).

Shell Lake Lumber Company
Annual reports and miscellaneous company records in F. Weyerhaeuser Company vaults, St. Paul.

Sieber, George Wesley
"Sawmilling on the Mississippi: The W. J. Young Lumber Company, 1858–1900" (unpublished dissertation, State University of Iowa, 1960).

Snoqualmie Falls Lumber Company
Company papers and reports, including account books, in Weyerhaeuser Company files, Tacoma, Washington.

Southern Idaho Timber Protective Association
Annual reports and correspondence.

Spoor, Eldon W.
Personal papers and correspondence, including clippings, memoranda, and scrapbooks, in possession of the author, Cloquet, Minnesota.

Union Lumber Company
Minute books and some account books in Minnesota Historical Society, St. Paul.

Virginia & Rainy Lake Company
Annual reports, account books, and other business papers, F. Weyerhaeuser Company, St. Paul.

Walton, J. P. "A Few Facts Selected from the Life Work of Mr. Peter Musser." Manuscript dated February, 1906, in possession of John M. Musser, St. Paul.

Weyerhaeuser, Charles D.
Business papers and reports in Weyerhaeuser Company office, Tacoma.

Weyerhaeuser, Charles D. "Report on Logged-Off Land Ownership of the Weyerhaeuser Timber Company." Manuscript dated May, 1936, in C. D. Weyerhaeuser files, Weyerhaeuser Company, Tacoma.

Weyerhaeuser Forest Products, Inc.
Papers, reports, and industry statistics in Weyerhaeuser Sales Company offices, St. Paul.

Weyerhaeuser, Frederick
Letterbooks, correspondence, notebooks (1875–1877 and 1879–1881), time books (1858–1865), and expense book (1877–1878) in F. E. Weyerhaeuser Record File and in F. Weyerhaeuser Company vaults, St. Paul.

Weyerhaeuser, Frederick E. Papers
Miscellaneous business papers in F. Weyerhaeuser Company office, St. Paul.

Weyerhaeuser, Frederick E. "Record File"
Letters, papers, company reports, and other business papers in the offices of F. Weyerhaeuser Company, St. Paul, used in compiling FEW Record.

Weyerhaeuser, Frederick E. "A Record of the Life and Business Activities of Frederick Weyerhaeuser, 1834–1914." A five-volume manuscript in possession of his nephew, F. K. Weyerhaeuser. This work is cited in the footnotes as FEW Record.

Weyerhaeuser, Frederick K.
Personal papers in his possession, St. Paul.

Weyerhaeuser, John P.
Business papers and correspondence in vaults of F. Weyerhaeuser Company, St. Paul.

Weyerhaeuser Library, St. Paul
Contains miscellaneous papers on the Weyerhaeuser interests, among them the reports of the *Proceedings of the White Pine Salesmen's Conference.*

Weyerhaeuser Sales Company
Business papers, annual reports, minute books, St. Paul. These records, since the merger of Weyerhaeuser Sales Company with the Weyerhaeuser Company, are now the property of the latter.

Weyerhaeuser Timber Company
Annual reports, minute books, miscellaneous contracts, executive correspondence, miscellaneous business letters, minutes of the executive committee, and statistical files in Weyerhaeuser Company offices, Tacoma.

Weyerhaeuser Timber Company. "Historical Financial Information." Manuscript in possession of Weyerhaeuser Company, Tacoma.

White River Lumber Company
Company papers and some account books in files of Weyerhaeuser Company, Tacoma.

Winans, George. "Rafting on the Mississippi"
Manuscript in the Winona County Historical Society. The society has a few other Winans "Scrapbooks" also.

Wood Conversion Company. "Historical Information." Manuscript submitted to authors by E. W. Davis.

Wood Conversion Company
Miscellaneous papers and business records, office of the company, St. Paul.

RECORDED REMINISCENCES IN THE ORAL HISTORY OFFICE
OF COLUMBIA UNIVERSITY, NEW YORK

Aitchison, E. A.
Aram, John
Bartlett, David H.
Bishop, Jack

Boyd, Ralph
Clapp, Norton
Clute, R. V.
Frederickson, A. N.

Henricksen, Carl
Henry, Charles H.
Hewitt, F. W.
Hunt, Robert W.
Ingram, C. H.
Irwin, R. E.
Lawrence, Don
Macartney, R. R.
McGough, Charles J.
McNair, W. K.
Maxwell, William L.
Morgan, Howard
Nygaard, Leonard

Ogle, Harold M.
Raught, Al
Saberson, R. E.
Schlenk, Hugo
Schoenwerk, Otto C.
Sheldon, A. O.
Stevens, James
Turrish, Henry
Weyerhaeuser, Charles D.
Weyerhaeuser, Frederick K.
Weyerhaeuser, John P., Jr.
Weyerhaeuser, Philip
Williamson, Maxwell

RECORDED REMINISCENCES IN FOREST HISTORY
SOCIETY, INC., ST. PAUL

Cowan, Charles S.
Dulany, G. W., Jr.

Author Interviews

Bell, Laird (September 10, 1954)
Bowling, Robert (July, 1953)
Campbell, John C., Jr. (May, 1956)
Chadwick, Albert (June 3, 1954)
Davis, E. W. (July 16, 1957)
Huffman, Roy (July, 1953)
Humbird, Thomas J. (September, 1953)
McGough, Charles J. (June, 1953)
Miller, E. A. (August 17, 1953)
O'Connell, J. J. (July, 1953)
Patience, J. C. (July, 1953)
Peterson, A. A. (April, 1956)
Rettig, E. C. (June, 1953)
Schlenk, Hugo (June, 1953)
Spoor, Eldon W. (June, 1953)
Titcomb, John W. (July, 1953)
Weyerhaeuser, John P., Jr. (February, 1956)
Woodworth, N. D. (July, 1953)

MEMOIRS, DIARIES, LETTERS, AND CONTEMPORARY ACCOUNTS

Bade, William F. *Life and Letters of John Muir* (Boston, 1924).

Baruch, Bernard. *American Industry in the War* (New York, 1941).

Baruch, Bernard. *A Report of the War Industries Board* (Washington, D.C., 1921).

Bill, Fred A. "Navigation on the Chippewa River in Wisconsin," *Burlington* [Iowa] *Post*, November 8, 1930. Author's reminiscences.

Billings, C. L. *Daybook*.

Carman, Harry J., ed. *American Husbandry* (New York, 1939).

Cox, H. J. *Random Lengths: Forty Years with "Timber Beasts" and "Sawdust Savages"* (Eugene, Ore., 1949).

Greeley, Horace. *What I Know of Farming* (New York, 1871).

Greeley, William B. *Forests and Men* (New York, 1951).

Ingram, J. G. "Reminiscences," *The Eau Claire* [Wis.] *Leader.*

Ingram, Orrin H. *Autobiography* (Eau Claire, Wis., 1912).

Keller, Herbert A., ed. *Selected Writings of Solon Robinson* (Indianapolis, 1936).

Loehr, Rodney C., ed. *Forests of the Future as told in the Diaries and Papers of David T. Mason, 1907–1950* (St. Paul, 1952).

La Follette, Robert M. *Autobiography* (Madison, Wis., 1913).

Loyal Legion of Loggers and Lumbermen. *Constitution and By-Laws of the Loyal Legion of Loggers and Lumbermen.*

McClung, J. W. *Minnesota As It Is in 1870* (St. Paul, 1870).

Marshall, Roujet D. *Autobiography* (2 vols., Madison, Wis., 1923–1931).

Morison, Elting E., and Blum, John, eds. *The Letters of Theodore Roosevelt* (8 vols., Cambridge, 1951–   ).

Nevins, Allan, ed. *Frémont's Narrative* (New York, 1928).

Nixon, Edgar B., ed. *Franklin D. Roosevelt and Conservation, 1911–1945* (2 vols., Hyde Park, N.Y., 1957).

Past and Present of Rock Island County, Illinois (Chicago, 1877).

Pinchot, Gifford. *Breaking New Ground* (New York, 1947).

Puter, S. A. D., and Stevens, Horace. *Looters of the Public Domain* (Portland, Ore., 1908).

Quaife, Milo M., ed. *The Early Days of Rock Island and Davenport: The Narratives of J. W. Spencer and J. M. D. Burrows* (Chicago, 1942).

Randall, Thomas E. *History of Chippewa Valley* (Eau Claire, Wis., 1875).

Richardson, James D., ed. *A Compilation of the Messages and Papers of the Presidents of the United States* (Washington, D.C., 1896–1899).

Roosevelt, Theodore. *An Autobiography* (New York, 1913).

Russell, Charles E. *A-rafting on the Mississipp'* (New York, 1928).

Schenck, Carl Alvin [Ovid Butler, ed.]. *The Biltmore Story: Recollections of the Beginnings of Forestry in the United States* (St. Paul, 1955).

Shaw, Noah. "Early Reminiscences of Saw Mill History," *Mississippi Valley Lumberman,* XXVI (February 1, 1895).

Stephenson, Isaac. *Recollections of a Long Life, 1829–1915* (Chicago, 1915).

GOVERNMENT DOCUMENTS: FEDERAL, STATE, AND LOCAL

Chicago Board of Trade. *Annual Reports* (Chicago, 1859–   ).

Heerman *v.* Beef Slough Manufacturing, Booming, Log Driving and Transportation Company, *et al., Federal Reporter,* 145–146 (1880).

Oregon. State Forestry Department. *Annual Reports* (Salem, Ore., 1908–   ).

United States Department of Agriculture

Annual Reports (Washington, D.C., 1894–   ).

Fairchild, Fred R. and Associates. *Forest Taxation in the United States* (Washington, D.C., 1935). U.S.D.A. Miscellaneous Publication No. 218.

Measuring and Marketing Farm Timber (Washington, D.C., 1930). *U.S.D.A. Farmer Bulletin* No. 1210.

Steer, Henry B., comp. *Lumber Production in the United States, 1799–1946* (Washington, D.C. 1948). U.S.D.A. Miscellaneous Publication No. 669.

Thelen, Rolf. "The Substitution of Other Materials for Wood," *U.S.D.A., Report No. 17* (Washington, D.C., 1917).

Trees: The Yearbook of Agriculture, 1949 (Washington, D.C., 1949).

United States Department of Agriculture. Forest Service

Annual Reports of the Forest Service (Washington, D.C., 1883–1962).

Butler, O. M. "Distribution of Softwood Lumber in the Middle West: Wholesale Distribution," *U.S. Forest Service Report No. 116* (Washington, D.C., 1917).

Forest Survey, 1939 (Washington, D.C., 1940).

Greeley, William B. *Some Public and Economic Aspects of the Lumber Industry* (Washington, D.C., 1917). Issued as U.S. Forest Service, Studies of the Lumber Industry.

Gross, L. S. *Timber Management Plans of the National Forests* (Washington, D.C., 1950). A U.S. Forest Service publication.

Report of the Chief of the Forest Service (Washington, D.C., 1930–1947).

Timber Depletion, Lumber Prices, Lumber Exports, and Concentration of Timber Ownership (Washington, D.C., 1920).

United States Department of Commerce. *Construction and Construction Materials Industry Report* (Washington, D.C., 1947).

United States Department of Commerce. Bureau of the Census. *Historical Statistics of the United States* (Washington, D.C., 1949).

Sargent, Charles S. *Report on the Forests of North America* (Washington, D.C., 1884). A statistical summary on forests based from data of the tenth census.

Statistical Abstract of the United States (Washington, D.C., 1879–1962).

United States Department of Commerce. Bureau of Labor Statistics. Howd, Cloice R. *Industrial Relations in the West Coast Lumber Industry* (Washington, D.C., 1924). U.S.B.L.S. Miscellaneous Publication No. 349.

United States Department of Commerce and Labor. Bureau of the Census. Census of Manufactures, 1905. *Lumber and Timber Products* (Washington, D.C., 1907).

United States Department of Commerce and Labor. Bureau of Corporations. *The Lumber Industry* (3 vols., Washington, D.C., 1913–1914).

United States Civilian Production Administration. Bureau of Demobilization. *Industrial Mobilization for War: History of the War Production Board and Predecessor Agencies, 1940–1945* (Washington, D.C., 1947).

United States Department of the Interior. *Annual Reports* (Washington, D.C., 1849–1919). Title varies.

United States General Land Office. *Annual Reports of the General Land Office* (Washington, D.C., 1859–).

United States Department of Justice. Antitrust Division. *Annual Report of the Antitrust Division* (Washington, D.C., 1939).

United States Department of Justice. Antitrust Division. *Report of Assistant Attorney General Thurman Arnold, 1939* (Washington, D.C., 1939). A similar report for 1940 was also issued.

United States Congress. House of Representatives
Congressional Record

Fernow, B. E. "Forestry Investigations of the Department of Agriculture 1877–1898," 55th Cong., 3d sess., House Doc. 181 (Washington, D.C., 1899).

Forest Lands of the United States. Report of the Joint Committee, 77th Cong., 1st sess., House Doc. (Washington, D.C., 1941).

Hearings, Pulp and Paper Investigation, 1908–1909, 60th Cong., 2d sess., House Doc. 1502 (Washington, D.C., 1910). These *Hearings* are in six volumes.

Hearings Before the Joint Committee on Forestry, 76th Cong., 1st sess. (Washington, D.C., 1939).

Hearings Before Subcommittee No. 1 (Aviation) of the Select Committee on Expenditures in the War Department, 66th Cong., 1st sess., Ser. 2 (Washington, D.C., 1919).

United States Congress. Senate
Hearings Before the Committee on Military Affairs, 5th, 2d sess., part iv, (Washington, D.C., 1928).
Hearings of the Senate Committee on Interior and Insular Affairs, Sustained Timber Yield, 80th Cong., 2d sess. (Washington, D.C., 1949).

United States. National Recovery Administration
Stone, Peter A. "Economic Problems of the Lumber and Timber Products Industry." (mimeographed, Washington, D.C., 1936).

United States War Production Board. *Directory of Industry Advisory Committees as of January 23, 1943* (Washington, D.C., 1943).

United States War Production Board. Report of the Chairman. *War Production in 1944* (Washington, D.C., 1945).

United States Works Projects Administration
Von Tassel, Alfred J., *et al. Mechanization in the Lumber Industry* (Philadelphia, 1940). A WPA National Research Project Report, No. M-5.

United States *v.* Beef Slough Manufacturing, Booming, Log Driving and Transportation Co., *et al.*, 24 *Federal Cases*, 1064 (1879).

Washington. Department of Conservation and Development. *Biennial Reports* (Olympia, 1924).

Wisconsin. *General Laws* (Madison, 1866–1875).

Wisconsin. *Private and Local Laws of Wisconsin* (Madison, 1866–1875).

Wisconsin. *Synoptical Index of the . . . Laws of Wisconsin to 1873* (Madison, 1875).

II. *Secondary Works*

American Forestry Congress. *Annual Proceedings* (Washington, D.C., 1947).

American Yearbook: A Record of Events and Progress (New York, 1912–1962).

Bird, Annie Laurie. *Boise, The Peace Valley* (Caldwell, Idaho, 1934).

Blair, Walter A. *A Raft Pilot's Log: A History of the Great Rafting Industry on the Upper Mississippi, 1840–1915* (Cleveland, 1930).

Blegen, Theodore C. *Building Minnesota* (New York, 1938).

Brissenden, Paul F. *The I.W.W: A Study of American Syndicalism* (New York, 1919).

Brogan, D. W. *Roosevelt and the New Deal* (London, 1952).

Brosnan, Cornelius J. *History of the State of Idaho* (New York, 1948).

Brown, Nelson C. *The American Lumber Industry* (New York, 1923).

———. *Lumber, Manufacturing, Conditioning, Grading, Distribution, and Use* (New York, 1947).

Burke, Fred C. *Logs on the Menominee: The History of the Menominee River Boom Company* (Marinette, Wis., 1946).

Carey, Charles H. *A General History of Oregon Prior to 1861* (2 vols., Portland, Ore., 1935–1936).

Carhart, Arthur H. *Timber in Your Life* (Philadelphia and New York, 1955).

Clarkson, Grosvenor B. *Industrial America in the World War: The Strategy Behind the Lines, 1917–1918* (Boston and New York, 1923).

Clough, Shepard B. and Cole, Charles W. *Economic History of Europe* (Boston, 1941).

Compton, Wilson. *The Organization of the Lumber Industry* (Chicago, 1916).

Current, Richard N. *Pine Logs and Politics: A Life of Philetus Sawyer, 1816–1900* (Madison, Wis., 1950).

Curti, Merle E., and Carstenson, Vernon. *The University of Wisconsin* (2 vols., Madison, Wis., 1949).

Dana, S. T. *Forest and Range Policy: Its Development in the United States* (New York, 1956).

Davis, David C., and Davis, Madeline. *Timber Roots* (Winona, Minn., 1954).

Davis, Kenneth P. *American Forest Management* (New York, 1954).

Defebaugh, James Elliott. *History of the Lumber Industry of America* (2d. ed., 2 vols., Chicago, 1906–1907).

Dick, Everett. *Vanguards of the Frontier* (New York, 1941).

Disston, Henry, & Sons. *The Saw in History* (Philadelphia, c. 1921).

Donaldson, Thomas C. *The Public Domain: Its History* (Washington, D.C., 1881).

Donnelly, Charles. *The Facts About the Northern Pacific Land Grant* (n.p., 1930).

Federal Council of the Churches of Christ in America. *The Centralia Case* (n.p., 1930).

Folwell, William Watts. *A History of Minnesota* (4 vols., St. Paul, 1921–1930).

Fries, Robert F. *Empire in Pine: The Story of Lumbering in Wisconsin, 1830–1930* (Madison, Wis., 1951).

Fugina, Frank J. *Lore and Lure of the Upper Mississippi River: A Book About the River by a River Man* (Winona, Minn., c. 1945).

Gambs, John S. *The Decline of the I.W.W.* (New York, 1932).

Gates, Paul W. *The Wisconsin Pine Lands of Cornell University: A Study in Land Policy and Absentee Ownership* (Ithaca, N.Y., 1943).

Glesinger, Egon. *The Coming of Age of Wood* (New York, 1949).

Gregory, John G., ed. *West Central Wisconsin History* (4 vols., Indianapolis, 1933).

Gulick, Luther H. *American Forest Policy: A Study of Government Administration and Economic Control* (New York, 1951).

Hauberg, John H. *Weyerhaeuser & Denkmann: Ninety-five Years of Manufacturing and Distribution of Lumber* (Rock Island, Ill., 1957).

Hayes, W. E. *Iron Road to Empire: The History of 100 Years of the Progress and Achievements of the Rock Island Lines* (New York, 1953).

Haywood, William. *Bill Haywood's Book* (New York, 1929).

Holbrook, Stewart H. *Burning an Empire: The Story of American Forest Fires* (New York, 1943).

––––––. *Green Commonwealth . . . Simpson Logging Co., 1895–1945* (Seattle, 1945).

Horn, Stanley F. *This Fascinating Lumber Business* (Indianapolis, 1943).

Hotchkiss, George W. *History of the Lumber and Forest Industry of the Northwest* (Chicago, 1898).

Idaho Forest and Timber Handbook, as issued.

Ise, John. *The United States Forest Policy* (New Haven, 1920).

––––––. *The United States Oil Policy* (New Haven, 1926).

Jenks, Cameron. *The Development of Governmental Forest Control in the United States* (Baltimore, 1928).

Jensen, Vernon H. *Lumber and Labor* (New York, 1945).

Johansen, Dorothy O., and Gates, Charles M. *Empire of the Columbia: A History of the Pacific Northwest* (New York, 1957).

Johnson, Allen, ed. *Dictionary of American Biography* (22 vols., New York, 1928–1944). Supplementary volume published (New York, 1959).

Johnson, Emory R. *Panama Canal Traffic and Tolls* (Washington, D.C., 1912).

Larson, Agnes M. *History of the White Pine Industry in Minnesota* (Minneapolis, 1949).

Leuchtenburg, William E. *The Perils of Prosperity* (Chicago, 1958).

Lillard, Richard G. *The Great Forest* (New York, 1948).

Longstreth, T. Morris. *The Adirondacks* (New York, 1917).

————. *The Catskills* (New York, 1918).

Moravets, F. L. *Lumber Production in Oregon and Washington, 1869–1948* (Portland, Ore., 1949).

McKenna, Marian C. *Borah* (Ann Arbor, Mich., 1961).

Mason, David T. *Timber Ownership and Lumber Production in the Inland Empire* (Portland, Ore., 1920).

Meany, Edmond S. *History of the State of Washington* (New York, 1909).

Merk, Frederick. *Economic History of Wisconsin During the Civil War Decade* (Madison, Wis., 1916).

Morgan, Murray. *The Last Wilderness* (New York, 1955).

National Lumber Manufacturers Association, *National Lumber Handbooks.*

National Lumbermen's Association. *Lumber Industry Facts* (Chicago, 1953).

Nelligan, John Emmett. *The Life of a Lumberman* (1929).

Nelson, Donald M. *Arsenal of Democracy: The Story of American War Production* (New York, 1946).

Neuberger, Richard L. *Our Promised Land* (New York, 1938).

Nevins, Allan. *Abram S. Hewitt, with Some Account of Peter Cooper* (New York, 1935).

————. *Grover Cleveland: A Study in Courage* (New York, 1932).

————. *Study in Power: John D. Rockefeller, Industrialist and Philanthropist* (2 vols., New York, 1953).

Nevins, Allan, and Hill, Frank Ernest. *Ford: Expansion and Challenge, 1915–1933* (New York, 1957).

Norton, Matthew G. *The Mississippi River Logging Company* (n.p., 1912).

O'Meara, Walter. *The Trees Went Forth* (New York, 1947).

Parker, Cornelia S. *American Idyll* (Boston, 1919).

Peattie, Roderick, ed. *The Cascades* (New York, 1949).

Pettigrew, Richard F. *Imperial Washington* (Chicago, 1922).

Pierce, Bessie. *History of Chicago* (3 vols., New York, 1940–   ).

Pollard, Lancaster, and Spencer, Lloyd. *History of the State of Washington* (4 vols., New York, 1937).

Pyle, Joseph G. *The Life of James J. Hill* (2 vols., Garden City, N.Y., 1917).

Quaife, Milo M. *Wisconsin: Its History and Its People, 1634–1924* (2 vols., Chicago, 1924).

Railway and Locomotive Historical Society. *The Railroads of Wisconsin, 1827–1937* (Boston, 1937).

Rector, William G. *Log Transportation in the Lake States Lumber Industry, 1840–1918* (Glendale, Calif., 1953).

Reynolds, A. R. *The Daniel Shaw Lumber Company: A Case Study of the Wisconsin Lumbering Frontier* (New York, 1957).

Richman, Irving B. *History of Muscatine County, Iowa, from the Earliest Settlement to the Present Time* (Chicago, 1911).

Riegel, Robert E. *The Story of the Western Railroads* (New York, 1926).

Robbins, Roy M. *Our Landed Heritage: The Public Domain, 1776–1936* (Princeton, N.J., 1942).

Roth, Filibert. *On the Forestry Conditions of Northern Wisconsin* (Madison, Wis., 1898).

Rodgers, Andrew D., III. *Bernhard Eduard Fernow: A Study of North American Forestry* (Princeton, N.J., 1951).

Smith, Darrell H. *The Forest Service, Its History, Activities, and Organization* (Washington, D.C., 1930).

Smith, Herbert Knox. *The Lumber Industry.* See U.S. Department of Commerce and Labor. Bureau of Corporations. *The Lumber Industry.*

Smith, J. Russell. *North America: Its People and the Resources* (New York, 1925).

Snowden, C. A., ed. *History of Washington: The Rise and Progress of an American State* (5 vols., New York, 1909–1911).

Sorden, L. G., and Ebert, Isabel J. *Loggers' Words of Yesteryears* (Madison, Wis., c. 1956).

Todes, Charlotte. *Labor and Lumber* (New York, 1931).

Tyler, Robert L. "The United States Government as Union Organizer: The Loyal Legion of Loggers and Lumbermen," *The Mississippi Valley Historical Review,* Vol. XLVII, No. 3 (December, 1960), pp. 434–451.

Usher, Ellis B. *Wisconsin: Its History and Biography, 1848–1913* (8 vols., Chicago and New York, 1914).

Van Hise, Charles R. *The Conservation of Natural Resources in the United States* (New York, 1924).

Van Name, Willard G. *Vanishing Forest Reserves: Problems of the National Forests and National Parks* (Boston, 1929).

West Coast Lumberman. *West Coast Lumber Facts* (Seattle, 1941).

Weyerhaeuser, Frederick K. *Men and Trees* (New York, 1951).

White, Stewart Edward. *The Blazed Trail* (New York, 1902).

Wickstrom, George W., and Ainsworth, Charles P. *Always Lumber: The Story of Dimock, Gould & Co., 1852–1952* (Rock Island, Ill., 1953).

Woodward, Karl W. *The Valuation of American Timberlands* (New York, 1921).

Works Projects Administration. *Idaho: A Guide in Word and Picture* (Caldwell, Idaho, 1937).

Works Projects Administration. *Washington: A Guide to the Evergreen State* (Olympia, 1937).

III. *Trade Periodicals*

American Lumberman

Family Tree
   This is the journal of Potlatch Forests

Forest Quarterly

Four-L Annual Reports

Four-L Lumber News

Labor World

March of Pine

Mississippi Valley Lumberman

Mississippi Valley Lumberman & Manufacturer

Monthly Labor Review

National Lumber Survey Committee. *Quarterly Report*

Northwest Lumberman

Pacific Lumber Trade Journal

Pine Knot

Society of American Foresters. *Journal of Forestry*

Timberman

West Coast Lumberman

Weyerhaeuser News

IV. *General Periodical Articles*

[Anonymous] "Our Forest Balance Sheet," *The Nation*, LXXXIV (May 9, 1907), 425–426.

Bowling, Robert T. "Mechanical Development of a Wood-Briquetting Machine," *Mechanical Engineering* (February, 1941).

Boyd, R. K. "Up and Down the Chippewa River," *Wisconsin Magazine of History,* XIV (March, 1931), 243–261.

Brown, Henry S. "Punishing the Land Looters," *Outlook,* LXXXV (February, 1907), 427–439.

Brundage, Fred H. "Northwest Woods Have Gone to War," *Journal of Forestry,* XLI (September, 1943).

Disque, Brice P. "How We Found a Cure for Strikes," *System,* XXXVI (September, 1919).

Durant, Edward W. "Lumbering and Steamboating on the St. Croix River," Minnesota Historical Society *Collections,* X (1900–1904), 664–675.

Fries, Robert F. "The Mississippi River Logging Company and the Struggle for Free Navigation of Logs, 1865–1900," *Mississippi Valley Historical Review,* XXXV (December, 1948), 429–448.

Gannett, Henry. "Is a Timber Famine Imminent?" *Forum,* XXX (October, 1900), 147–156.

Gill, Robert S. "The Four L's in Lumber," *Survey,* XLIV (May, 1920), 165–170.

Gilman, F. H. "History of the Development of Sawmilling and Woodworking Machinery," *Mississippi Valley Lumberman,* XXVI (February 1, 1895), 59–69.

Guthrie, John D. "The History of Great Forest Fires of America," *Crow's Pacific Coast Lumber Digest* (October 31, 1936).

Hagenstein, W. D. "Trees and Taxes," *Journal of Forestry,* LII (December, 1954).

Heald, W. F. "Cascade Holiday," in Roderick Peattie, ed. *The Cascades.*

Hough, Emerson. "The Slaughter of the Trees," *Everybody's,* XVIII (May 1908), 579–592.

Jenkins, Sidney C. "Permanent Production on Potlatch Forests," *American Forests* (August, 1938).

Joy, George C. "The Fight With Fire," *West Coast Lumberman,* LIV (May 1, 1928), 648.

Kane, Lucille. "Selling Cutover Lands in Wisconsin," *Business History Review,* XXVIII, No. 3 (September, 1954), 236–247.

Kasparek, Val E. "Logging and Lumbering," *Little Falls Herald,* May 6, 1938.

Kohlmeyer, Frederick W. "Northern Pine Lumbermen: A Study in Origins and Migrations," *The Journal of Economic History,* XVI (Dec. 1956), 529–538.

Lillard, Richard G. "Timber King," *Pacific Spectator,* I (Winter 1947), 14–26.

McCulloch, W. F. "The Cascade Forest," in Roderick Peattie, ed. *The Cascades.*

Mittleman, E. "The Loyal Legion of Loggers and Lumbermen," *Journal of Political Economy,* XXXI (June, 1923), 323–327.

Norcross, C. P. "Richer than Rockefeller—Weyerhaeuser," *Cosmopolitan,* XLII (January, 1907), 252–259.

Parain, Charles. "The Evolution of Agricultural Technique," J. H. Clapham, ed. *The Cambridge Economic History of Europe* (2 vols., Cambridge, England, 1941–1952).

Pfund, Adolph. "[Pfund] Depicts Rosy Future for the West Coast Trade," *American Lumberman* (December 7, 1918).

———. "What Is the Outlook for the Retail Lumber Business?" *American Lumberman* (December 7, 1918).

Russell, Charles Edward. "The Mysterious Octopus: Story of the Strange and Powerful Organization That Controls the American Lumber Trade," *The World Today,* XXI, 1735–1750.

Ryan, J. C. "Minnesota Logging Railroads," *Minnesota History,* XXVII (December, 1946), 300–308.

Shepard, Ward. "Analysis of Private Forestry and Public Acquisition Program," in Edgard B. Nixon, ed., *Franklin D. Roosevelt and Conservation, 1911–1945* (2 vols., Hyde Park, N.Y., 1957), II, 434.

Sherrill, F. G. "Lumber Procurement for the Army," *Journal of Forestry,* XL (December, 1942), 917.

Silcox, F. A. "Our Adventure in Conservation," *Atlantic Monthly,* CLX (December, 1937), 714–722.

Simons, H. A. "Forests for the Future," *4-Square News* (March 15, 1900).

Towle, Charles. "The Winona and St. Peter Railroad," *Weekly Philatelic Gossip,* LXIII (January 12, 1957), 606–607.

Upson, Arthur. "Our Forest Resources are Contributing to Victory—Lumber and the War Production Board," *Journal of Forestry,* XL (December, 1942), 917.

Weyerhaeuser, Charles D. "Sustained Yield: Forest Management," *Forestry News Digest* (September, 1936).

Weyerhaeuser, Frederick K. "Of Trees and Men," *Weyerhaeuser News* (June, 1952).

Weymouth, George. "Frederick Weyerhaeuser Made a Millionaire by Luck," [Chicago] *Saturday Tribune,* October 20, 1907.

White, Stewart Edward. "The Fight for the Forests," *American Magazine,* LXV (January, 1908), 252–261.

Winsted, Ralph. "Enter a Logger," *Survey,* XLIV (July 3, 1920), 474–477.

V. *Newspapers*

Burlington [Iowa] *Post*

Chippewa Herald

Coeur d'Alene [Idaho] *Evening News*

Duluth Herald

Duluth [Minn.] *News Tribune*

Dunn County News

Eagle Democrat [Warren, Ark.]

Eau Claire [Wisconsin] *Daily Telegram*

Eau Claire News

Minneapolis Journal

Minneapolis Tribune

Muscatine [Iowa] *Saturday Mail*

Palouse [Washington] *Republic*

Philadelphia *Press*

Portland *Oregonian*

Rock Island *Daily Argus*

Rock Island *Daily Union*

St. Paul *Daily News*

St. Paul *Pioneer Press*

Seattle *Daily Times*

South Bend [Ore.] *Journal*

Tacoma *News Tribune*

Wabasha [Minn.] *Herald*

Winona [Minn.] *Daily Republican*

SUPPLEMENT TO APPENDIX VI, PAGE 594

Lumber Shipments of Weyerhaeuser Timber Company and Affiliates, 1900–1959[a]

(*millions of board feet*)

	White River Lumber Co.	Willapa Harbor Lumber Mills
1930	62	
1931	53	49
1932	35	67
1933	43	102
1934	51	88
1935	67	96
1936	101	137
1937	110	115
1938	74	52
1939	87	108
1940	100	123
1941	89	118
1942	126	147
1943	137	108
1944	132	92
1945	108	69
1946	69	65
1947	65	73
1948	69	62
1949	*6 months* 38[a]	*6 months* 34[a]

[a] Production figures of these mills after the middle of 1949 were included with those of others reported on p. 594 under Weyerhaeuser Timber Company.

SOURCE: Statistical Files of Weyerhaeuser Company.

Index